# ONE WEEK LOAN

# INTERNATIONAL ADVISORY BOARD

**3** EDITION

# Collecting *and* Interpreting Qualitative Materials

## Norman K. Denzin
*University of Illinois at Urbana-Champaign*

## Yvonna S. Lincoln
*Texas A&M University*

### Editors

**SAGE Publications**
Los Angeles • London • New Delhi • Singapore

*For information:*

Sage Publications, Inc.
2455 Teller Road
Thousand Oaks, California 91320
E-mail: order@sagepub.com

Sage Publications India Pvt. Ltd.
B 1/I 1 Mohan Cooperative Industrial Area
Mathura Road, New Delhi 110 044
India

Sage Publications Ltd.
1 Oliver's Yard
55 City Road
London EC1Y 1SP
United Kingdom

Sage Publications Asia-Pacific Pte. Ltd.
33 Pekin Street #02-01
Far East Square
Singapore 048763

Printed in the United States of America

*Library of Congress Cataloging-in-Publication Data*

Collecting and interpreting qualitative materials/Norman K. Denzin, Yvonna S. Lincoln [editors].—3rd ed.
 p. cm.
Includes bibliographical references and index.
ISBN 978-1-4129-5757-1 (pbk.)
 1. Social sciences—Research—Methodology. 2. Qualitative reasoning. I. Denzin, Norman K. II. Lincoln, Yvonna S.

H62.C566 2008
300.72'3—dc22                                    2007031743

This book is printed on acid-free paper.

07  08  09  10  11  10  9  8  7  6  5  4  3  2  1

| | |
|---|---|
| *Acquisitions Editor:* | Vicki Knight |
| *Associate Editor:* | Sean Connelly |
| *Editorial Assistant:* | Lauren Habib |
| *Production Editor:* | Astrid Virding |
| *Copy Editor:* | Gillian Dickens |
| *Typesetter:* | C&M Digitals (P) Ltd. |
| *Proofreader:* | Tracy Marcynzsyn |
| *Indexer:* | Juniee Oneida |
| *Cover Designer:* | Candice Harman |
| *Marketing Manager:* | Stephanie Adams |
| *Cover Photograph:* | C.A. Hoffman |

# CONTENTS

# PREFACE

For nearly four decades, a quiet methodological revolution has been taking place in the social sciences. A blurring of disciplinary boundaries has occurred. The social sciences and humanities have drawn closer together in a mutual focus on an interpretive, qualitative approach to inquiry, research, and theory. Although these trends are not new, the extent to which the "qualitative revolution" has overtaken the social sciences and related professional fields continues to be nothing short of amazing.

Reflecting this revolution, a host of textbooks, journals, research monographs, and readers have been published in recent years. In 1994, we published the first edition of the *Handbook of Qualitative Research* in an attempt to represent the field in its entirety, to take stock of how far it had come and how far it might yet go. The immediate success of the first edition suggested the need to offer the *Handbook* in terms of three separate volumes. So in 1998, we published a three-volume set, *The Landscape of Qualitative Research: Theories and Issues; Strategies of Inquiry;* and *Collecting and Interpreting Qualitative Materials.* In 2003, we offered a new three-volume set, based on the second edition of the handbook.

By 2005, when we published the third edition of the *Handbook*, it was abundantly clear, as had been in 2000, when we published the second edition of the *Handbook*, that the "field" of qualitative research was still defined primarily by tensions, contradictions, and hesitations. These tensions exist in a less-than-unified arena. We have always believed that the handbook, in its first, second, and third editions, could and would be valuable for solidifying, interpreting, and organizing the field despite the essential differences that characterize it.

The first edition attempted to define the field of qualitative research. The second edition went one step further. Building on themes in the first edition, we asked how the practices of qualitative inquiry could be used to address the issues of equity and social justice. The third edition continues where the second edition ended. The transformations that were taking place in the 1990s continue to gain momentum in the first decade of this new century.

Not surprisingly, this quiet revolution has been met with resistance. In many quarters, a resurgent, scientifically based research paradigm has gained the upper hand. Borrowing from the field of biomedical research, the National Research Council (NRC) has appropriated neopositivist, evidence-based epistemologies. Calls for mixed-method designs are now common. Interpretive methods are read as being unscientific and unsuitable for use by those who legislate social policy.

Still, the days of a value-free inquiry based on a God's-eye view of reality are judged by many to be over. Today, many agree that all inquiry is moral and political. Experimental, reflexive ways of writing first-person ethnographic texts are now commonplace. There continues to be a pressing need to show how the practices of qualitative research can help change the world in positive ways. So at the beginning of the 21st century, it is necessary to reengage the promise of qualitative research as a form of radical democratic practice.

We have been enormously gratified and heartened by the response to the *Handbook* since its publication. Especially gratifying has been that it has been used and adapted by such a wide variety of scholars and graduate students in precisely the way we had hoped: as a starting point, a springboard for new thought and new work.

## ▣ THE PAPERBACK PROJECT

The third edition of the *Collecting and Interpreting Qualitative Materials* series of the *Handbook of Qualitative Research* is virtually a new volume. Indeed, in the third edition of the *Handbook,* there are 42 new chapters, authors, and/or coauthors. There are 16 totally new chapter topics, including contributions on indigenous inquiry, decolonizing methodologies, critical ethnography, critical humanism and queer theory, performance ethnography, narrative inquiry, arts-based inquiry, online ethnography, analytic methodologies, Foucault's methodologies, talk and text, focus groups and critical pedagogy, relativism, criteria and politics, the poetics of place, cultural and investigative poetics, qualitative evaluation and social policy, social science inquiry in the new millennium, and anthropology of the contemporary. All returning authors have substantially revised their original contributions, in many cases producing totally new and different chapters.

The third edition of the *Handbook of Qualitative Research* continues where the second edition ended. It takes as its theme the necessity to reengage the promise of qualitative research as a generative form of radical democratic practice. This is the agenda of the third edition of the *Landscape* series, as it is for the third edition of the *Handbook*—namely, to show how the discourses of qualitative research can be used to help create and imagine a free democratic society. Each of the chapters in the three-volume set takes up this project, in one way or another.

A handbook, we were told by our publisher, should ideally represent the distillation of knowledge of a field, a benchmark volume that synthesizes an existing literature, helping to define and shape the present and future of that discipline. This mandate organized the third edition. In metaphoric terms, if you were to take one book on qualitative research with you to a desert island or a mountaintop (or for a comprehensive graduate examination), a handbook would be the book.

It was again decided that the part structure of the *Handbook* could serve as useful point of departure for the organization of the paperbacks. Thus, Volume 1, titled *The Landscape of Qualitative Research: Theories and Issues,* takes a look at the field from a broadly theoretical perspective and is composed of the *Handbook*'s Parts I ("Locating the Field"), II ("Paradigms and Perspectives in Contention"), and VI ("The Future of Qualitative Research"). Volume 2, titled *Strategies of Qualitative Inquiry,* focuses on just that and consists of Part III of the *Handbook*. Volume 3, titled *Collecting and Interpreting Qualitative Materials,* considers the tasks of collecting, analyzing, and interpreting empirical materials and comprises the *Handbook*'s Parts IV ("Methods of Collecting and Analyzing Empirical Materials") and V ("The Art and Practices of Interpretation, Evaluation, and Presentation").

As with the first and second editions of the *Landscape* series, we decided that nothing should be cut from the original *Handbook.* Nearly everyone we spoke to who used the *Handbook* had his or her own way of using it, leaning heavily on certain chapters and skipping others altogether. But there was consensus that this reorganization made a great deal of sense both pedagogically and economically. We and Sage are committed to making this iteration of the *Handbook* accessible for classroom use. This commitment is reflected in the size, organization, and price of the paperbacks, as well as in the addition of end-of-book bibliographies.

It also became clear in our conversations with colleagues who used the *Handbook* that the single-volume, hardcover version has a distinct place and value, and Sage will keep the original version available until a revised edition is published.

## 🔳 ORGANIZATION OF THIS VOLUME

*Collecting and Interpreting Qualitative Materials* introduces the researcher to basic methods of gathering, analyzing, and interpreting qualitative empirical materials. Part I moves from narrative and arts-based inquiry and the performance of revolutionary pedagogy to interviewing, observing, visual and autoethnographic methods, as well as the ethics and politics of online ethnography, analytic perspectives, Foucault's methodologies, strategies for analyzing talk and text, and the critical use of focus groups.

## Acknowledgments

Of course, this book would not exist without its authors or the editorial board members for the *Handbook* on which it is based. These individuals were able to offer both long-term, sustained commitments to the project and short-term emergency assistance.

In addition, we would like to thank the following individuals and institutions for their assistance, support, insights, and patience: our respective universities and departments, as well as Aisha Durham, Grant Kien, Li Xiong, James Salvo, David Monje, and our respective graduate students. Without them, we could never have kept this project on course. There are also several people to thank at Sage Publications. We thank Lisa Cuevas Shaw, our editor. This three-volume version of the *Handbook* would not have been possible without Lisa's wisdom, support, humor, and grasp of the field in all its current diversity.

As always, we appreciate the efforts of Chris Klein, vice president of Books Acquisitions and Books Marketing at Sage, along with his staff, for their indefatigable efforts in getting the word out about the *Handbook* to teachers, researchers, and methodologists around the world. We thank Christina Ceisel for her excellent work in the production phase of all three volumes of this project. Astrid Virding was essential in moving this project through production; we are also grateful to the copy editor, Judy Selhorst, and to those whose proofreading and indexing skills were so central to the publication of the *Handbook* on which these volumes are based. Finally, as ever, we thank our spouses, Katherine Ryan and Egon Guba, for their forbearance and constant support.

The idea for this three-volume paperback version of the *Handbook* did not arise in a vacuum, and we are grateful for the feedback we received from countless teachers and students, both informally and in response to our formal survey. We wish especially to thank the following individuals: Bryant Alexander, Tom Barone, Jack Z. Bratich, Susan Chase, Shing-Ling Sarina Chen, Nadine Dolby, Susan Finley, Andrea Fontana, Jaber Gubrium, Stephen Hartnett, Stacy Holman Jones, Steve Jones, Ruthellen Josselson, Luis Miron, Ronald J. Pelias, John Prosser, Johnny Saldaña, Paula Saukko, Thomas Schwandt, Patrick Slattery, and Linda Tuhiwai Smith.

Norman K. Denzin

*University of Illinois at Urbana-Champaign*

Yvonna S. Lincoln

*Texas A&M University*

# 1

# INTRODUCTION

## The Discipline and Practice of Qualitative Research

### Norman K. Denzin and Yvonna S. Lincoln

W riting about scientific research, including qualitative research, from the vantage point of the colonized, a position that she chooses to privilege, Linda Tuhiwai Smith (1999) states that "the term 'research' is inextricably linked to European imperialism and colonialism." She continues, "The word itself is probably one of the dirtiest words in the indigenous world's vocabulary. . . . It is implicated in the worst excesses of colonialism," with the ways in which "knowledge about indigenous peoples was collected, classified, and then represented back to the West" (p. 1). This dirty word stirs up anger, silence, distrust. "It is so powerful that indigenous people even write poetry about research" (p. 1). It is one of colonialism's most sordid legacies.

Sadly, qualitative research, in many if not all of its forms (observation, participation, interviewing, ethnography), serves as a metaphor for colonial knowledge, for power, and for truth. The metaphor works this way. Research, quantitative and qualitative, is scientific. Research provides the foundation for reports about and representations of "the Other." In the colonial context, research becomes an objective way of representing the dark-skinned Other to the white world.

Colonizing nations relied on the human disciplines, especially sociology and anthropology, to produce knowledge about strange and foreign worlds. This close

**Authors' Note.** We are grateful to many who have helped with this chapter, including Egon Guba, Mitch Allen, David Monje, and Katherine E. Ryan.

involvement with the colonial project contributed, in significant ways, to qualitative research's long and anguished history and to its becoming a dirty word (for reviews, see Foley & Valenzuela, Volume 1, Chapter 9; Tedlock, Volume 2, Chapter 5). In sociology, the work of the "Chicago school" in the 1920s and 1930s established the importance of qualitative inquiry for the study of human group life. In anthropology during the same period, the discipline-defining studies of Boas, Mead, Benedict, Bateson, Evans-Pritchard, Radcliffe-Brown, and Malinowski charted the outlines of the fieldwork method (see Gupta & Ferguson, 1997; Stocking, 1986, 1989).

The agenda was clear-cut: The observer went to a foreign setting to study the culture, customs, and habits of another human group. Often this was a group that stood in the way of white settlers. Ethnographic reports of these groups where incorporated into colonizing strategies, ways of controlling the foreign, deviant, or troublesome Other. Soon qualitative research would be employed in other social and behavioral science disciplines, including education (especially the work of Dewey), history, political science, business, medicine, nursing, social work, and communications (for criticisms of this tradition, see Smith, 1999; Vidich & Lyman, 2000; see also Rosaldo, 1989, pp. 25–45; Tedlock, Volume 2, Chapter 5).

By the 1960s, battle lines were drawn within the quantitative and qualitative camps. Quantitative scholars relegated qualitative research to a subordinate status in the scientific arena. In response, qualitative researchers extolled the humanistic virtues of their subjective, interpretive approach to the study of human group life. In the meantime, indigenous peoples found themselves subjected to the indignities of both approaches, as each methodology was used in the name of colonizing powers (see Battiste, 2000; Semali & Kincheloe, 1999).

Vidich and Lyman (1994, 2000) have charted many key features of this painful history. In their now-classic analysis they note, with some irony, that qualitative research in sociology and anthropology was "born out of concern to understand the 'other'" (Vidich & Lyman, 2000, p. 38). Furthermore, this "other" was the exotic Other, a primitive, nonwhite person from a foreign culture judged to be less civilized than ours. Of course, there were colonialists long before there were anthropologists and ethnographers. Nonetheless, there would be no colonial, and now no neocolonial, history were it not for this investigative mentality that turned the dark-skinned Other into the object of the ethnographer's gaze. From the very beginning, qualitative research was implicated in a racist project.[1]

In this introductory chapter, we define the field of qualitative research, then navigate, chart, and review the history of qualitative research in the human disciplines. This will allow us to locate this volume and its contents within their historical moments. (These historical moments are somewhat artificial; they are socially constructed, quasi-historical, and overlapping conventions. Nevertheless, they permit a "performance" of developing ideas. They also facilitate an increasing sensitivity to and sophistication about the pitfalls and promises of ethnography and qualitative research.) We also present a conceptual framework for reading the qualitative research act as a multicultural, gendered process and then provide a brief introduction to the chapters that follow. Returning to the observations of Vidich and Lyman as well as those of hooks, we conclude with a brief discussion of qualitative research and critical race theory (see also Ladson-Billings & Donnor, Volume 1, Chapter 11). We also discuss the threats to qualitative, human subject research from the methodological conservatism movement mentioned briefly in our preface. As we note in the preface, we use the metaphor of the bridge to structure what follows. This volume is intended to serve as a bridge connecting historical moments, politics, the decolonization project, research methods, paradigms, and communities of interpretive scholars.

## ▣ DEFINITIONAL ISSUES

Qualitative research is a field of inquiry in its own right. It crosscuts disciplines, fields, and subject matters.[2] A complex, interconnected family of terms, concepts, and assumptions surround the term *qualitative research*. These include the traditions associated with foundationalism, positivism, postfoundationalism, postpositivism, poststructuralism, and the many qualitative research perspectives, and/or methods connected to cultural and interpretive studies (the chapters in Volume 1, Part II, take up these paradigms).[3] There are separate and detailed literatures on the many methods and approaches that fall under the category of qualitative research, such as case study, politics and ethics, participatory inquiry, interviewing, participant observation, visual methods, and interpretive analysis.

In North America, qualitative research operates in a complex historical field that crosscuts at least eight historical moments. (We discuss these moments in detail below.) These moments overlap and simultaneously operate in the present.[4] We define them as the *traditional* (1900–1950); the *modernist*, or golden age (1950–1970); *blurred genres* (1970–1986); the *crisis of representation* (1986–1990); the *postmodern*, a period of experimental and new ethnographies (1990–1995); *postexperimental inquiry* (1995–2000); the *methodologically contested present* (2000–2004); and the *fractured future*, which is now (2005– ). The future, the eighth moment, confronts the methodological backlash associated with the evidence-based social movement. It is concerned with moral discourse, with the development of sacred textualities. The eighth moment asks that the social sciences and the humanities become sites for critical conversations about democracy, race, gender, class, nation-states, globalization, freedom, and community.[5]

The postmodern and postexperimental moments were defined in part by a concern for literary and rhetorical tropes and the narrative turn, a concern for storytelling, for composing ethnographies in new ways (Bochner & Ellis, 2002; Ellis, 2004; Goodall, 2000; Pelias, 2004; Richardson & Lockridge, 2004; Trujillo, 2004). Laurel

Richardson (1997) observes that this moment was shaped by a new sensibility, by doubt, by a refusal to privilege any method or theory (p. 173). But now at the dawn of this new century we struggle to connect qualitative research to the hopes, needs, goals, and promises of a free democratic society.

Successive waves of epistemological theorizing move across these eight moments. The traditional period is associated with the positivist, foundational paradigm. The modernist or golden age and blurred genres moments are connected to the appearance of postpositivist arguments. At the same time, a variety of new interpretive, qualitative perspectives were taken up, including hermeneutics, structuralism, semiotics, phenomenology, cultural studies, and feminism.[6] In the blurred genres phase, the humanities became central resources for critical, interpretive theory, and the qualitative research project broadly conceived. The researcher became a *bricoleur* (see below), learning how to borrow from many different disciplines.

The blurred genres phase produced the next stage, the crisis of representation. Here researchers struggled with how to locate themselves and their subjects in reflexive texts. A kind of methodological diaspora took place, a two-way exodus. Humanists migrated to the social sciences, searching for new social theory, new ways to study popular culture and its local, ethnographic contexts. Social scientists turned to the humanities, hoping to learn how to do complex structural and poststructural readings of social texts. From the humanities, social scientists also learned how to produce texts that refused to be read in simplistic, linear, incontrovertible terms. The line between text and context blurred. In the postmodern, experimental moment, researchers continued to move away from foundational and quasi-foundational criteria (see in this volume Smith & Hodkinson, Chapter 13; Richardson & St. Pierre, Chapter 15). Alternative evaluative criteria were sought, criteria that might prove evocative, moral, critical, and rooted in local understandings.

Any definition of qualitative research must work within this complex historical field. *Qualitative research* means different things in each of these moments. Nonetheless, an initial, generic definition can be offered: Qualitative research is a situated activity that locates the observer in the world. It consists of a set of interpretive, material practices that make the world visible. These practices transform the world. They turn the world into a series of representations, including field notes, interviews, conversations, photographs, recordings, and memos to the self. At this level, qualitative research involves an interpretive, naturalistic approach to the world. This means that qualitative researchers study things in their natural settings, attempting to make sense of, or interpret, phenomena in terms of the meanings people bring to them.[7]

Qualitative research involves the studied use and collection of a variety of empirical materials—case study; personal experience; introspection; life story; interview; artifacts; cultural texts and productions; observational, historical, interactional, and visual texts—that describe routine and problematic moments and meanings in individuals' lives. Accordingly, qualitative researchers deploy a wide range of interconnected interpretive practices, hoping always to get a better understanding of the subject matter at hand. It is understood, however, that each practice makes the world visible in a different way. Hence there is frequently a commitment to using more than one interpretive practice in any study.

## The Qualitative Researcher as *Bricoleur* and Quilt Maker

The qualitative researcher may be described using multiple and gendered images: scientist, naturalist, field-worker, journalist, social critic, artist, performer, jazz musician, filmmaker, quilt maker, essayist. The many methodological practices of qualitative research may be viewed as soft science, journalism, ethnography, bricolage, quilt making, or montage. The researcher, in turn, may be seen as a *bricoleur*, as a maker of quilts, or, as in filmmaking, a person who assembles images into montages. (On montage, see Cook, 1981, pp. 171–177; Monaco, 1981, pp. 322–328; and the discussion below. On quilting, see hooks, 1990, pp. 115–122; Wolcott, 1995, pp. 31–33.)

Harper (1987, pp. 9, 74–75, 92), de Certeau (1984, p. xv), Nelson, Treichler, and Grossberg (1992, p. 2), Lévi-Strauss (1966, p. 17), Weinstein and Weinstein (1991, p. 161), and Kincheloe (2001) clarify the meanings of *bricolage* and *bricoleur*.[8] A *bricoleur* makes do by "adapting the *bricoles* of the world. *Bricolage* is 'the poetic making do'" (de Certeau, 1984, p. xv) with "such bricoles—the odds and ends, the bits left over" (Harper, 1987, p. 74). The *bricoleur* is a "Jack of all trades, a kind of professional do-it-yourself" (Lévi-Strauss, 1966, p. 17). In their work, *bricoleurs* define and extend themselves (Harper, 1987, p. 75). Indeed, the *bricoleur*'s life story, or biography, "may be thought of as bricolage" (Harper, 1987, p. 92).

There are many kinds of *bricoleurs*—interpretive, narrative, theoretical, political, methodological (see below). The interpretive *bricoleur* produces a bricolage—that is, a pieced-together set of representations that is fitted to the specifics of a complex situation. "The solution (bricolage) which is the result of the *bricoleur*'s method is an [emergent] construction" (Weinstein & Weinstein, 1991, p. 161) that changes and takes new forms as the *bricoleur* adds different tools, methods, and techniques of representation and interpretation to the puzzle. Nelson et al. (1992) describe the methodology of cultural studies as "a bricolage. Its choice of practice, that is, is pragmatic, strategic and self-reflexive" (p. 2). This understanding can be applied, with qualifications, to qualitative research.

The qualitative researcher as *bricoleur*, or maker of quilts, uses the aesthetic and material tools of his or her craft, deploying whatever strategies, methods, and empirical materials are at hand (Becker, 1998, p. 2). If the researcher needs to invent, or piece together, new tools or techniques, he or she will do so. Choices regarding which interpretive practices to employ are not necessarily made in advance. As Nelson et al. (1992) note, the "choice of research practices depends upon the questions that are asked, and the questions depend on their context" (p. 2), what is available in the context, and what the researcher can do in that setting.

These interpretive practices involve aesthetic issues, an aesthetics of representation that goes beyond the pragmatic or the practical. Here the concept of *montage* is useful (see Cook, 1981, p. 323; Monaco, 1981, pp. 171–172). Montage is a method of editing cinematic images. In the history of cinematography, montage is most closely associated with the work of Sergei Eisenstein, especially his film *The Battleship Potemkin* (1925). In montage, several different images are juxtaposed to or superimposed on one another to create a picture. In a sense, montage is like *pentimento*, in which something that has been painted out of a picture (an image the painter "repented," or denied) becomes visible again, creating something new. What is new is what had been obscured by a previous image.

Montage and pentimento, like jazz, which is improvisation, create the sense that images, sounds, and understandings are blending together, overlapping, forming a composite, a new creation. The images seem to shape and define one another, and an emotional, gestalt effect is produced. In film montage, images are often combined in a swiftly run sequence that produces a dizzily revolving collection of several images around a central or focused picture or sequence; directors often use such effects to signify the passage of time.

Perhaps the most famous instance of montage in film is the Odessa Steps sequence in *The Battleship Potemkin*. In the climax of the film, the citizens of Odessa are being massacred by czarist troops on the stone steps leading down to the harbor. Eisenstein cuts to a young mother as she pushes her baby in a carriage across the landing in front of the firing troops.[9] Citizens rush past her, jolting the carriage, which she is afraid to push down to the next flight of stairs. The troops are above her, firing at the citizens. She is trapped between the troops and the steps. She screams. A line of rifles points to the sky, the rifle barrels erupting in smoke. The mother's head sways back. The wheels of the carriage teeter on the edge of the steps. The mother's hand clutches the silver buckle of her belt. Below her, people are being beaten by soldiers. Blood drips over the mother's white gloves. The baby's hand reaches out of the carriage. The mother sways back and forth. The troops advance. The mother falls back against the carriage. A woman watches in horror as the rear wheels of the carriage roll off the edge of the landing. With accelerating speed, the carriage bounces down the steps, past dead citizens. The baby is jostled from side to side inside the carriage. The soldiers fire their rifles into a group of wounded citizens. A student screams as the carriage leaps across the steps, tilts, and overturns (Cook, 1981, p. 167).[10]

Montage uses brief images to create a clearly defined sense of urgency and complexity. It invites viewers to construct interpretations that build on one another as a scene unfolds. These interpretations are based on associations among the contrasting images that blend into one another. The underlying assumption of montage is that viewers perceive and interpret the shots in a "montage sequence not *sequentially*, or one at a time, but rather *simultaneously*" (Cook, 1981, p. 172). The viewer puts the sequences together into a meaningful emotional whole, as if at a glance, all at once.

The qualitative researcher who uses montage is like a quilt maker or a jazz improviser. The quilter stitches, edits, and puts slices of reality together. This process creates and brings psychological and emotional unity—a pattern—to an interpretive experience. There are many examples of montage in current qualitative research (see Diversi, 1998; Holman Jones, 1999; Lather & Smithies, 1997; Ronai, 1998; see also Holman Jones, Chapter 7, this volume). Using multiple voices, different textual formats, and various typefaces, Lather and Smithies (1997) weave a complex text about AIDS and women who are HIV-positive. Holman Jones (1999) creates a performance text using lyrics from the blues songs sung by Billie Holiday.

In texts based on the metaphors of montage, quilt making, and jazz improvisation, many different things are going on at the same time—different voices, different perspectives, points of views, angles of vision. Like autoethnographic performance texts, works that use montage simultaneously create and enact moral meaning. They move from the personal to the political, from the local to the historical and the cultural. These are dialogical texts. They presume an active audience. They create spaces for give-and-take between reader and writer. They do more than turn the Other into the object of the social science gaze (see Alexander, Volume 2, Chapter 3; Holman Jones, Chapter 7, this volume).

Qualitative research is inherently multimethod in focus (Flick, 2002, pp. 226–227). However, the use of multiple methods, or triangulation, reflects an attempt to secure an in-depth understanding of the phenomenon in question. Objective reality can never be captured. We know a thing only through its representations. Triangulation is not a tool or a strategy of validation, but an alternative to validation (Flick, 2002, p. 227). The combination of multiple methodological practices, empirical materials, perspectives, and observers in a single study is best understood, then, as a strategy that adds rigor, breadth, complexity, richness, and depth to any inquiry (see Flick, 2002, p. 229).

In Chapter 15 of this volume, Richardson and St. Pierre dispute the usefulness of the concept of triangulation, asserting that the central image for qualitative inquiry should be the crystal, not the triangle. Mixed-genre texts in the postexperimental moment have more than three sides. Like crystals, Eisenstein's montage, the jazz solo, or the pieces in a quilt, the mixed-genre text "combines symmetry and substance with an infinite variety of shapes, substances, transmutations. . . . Crystals grow, change, alter. . . . Crystals are prisms that reflect externalities and refract within themselves, creating different colors, patterns, arrays, casting off in different directions" (Richardson, 2000, p. 934).

In the crystallization process, the writer tells the same tale from different points of view. For example, in *A Thrice-Told Tale* (1992), Margery Wolf uses fiction, field notes, and a scientific article to give three different accounts of the same set of experiences in a native village. Similarly, in her play *Fires in the Mirror* (1993), Anna Deavere Smith presents a series of performance pieces based on interviews with people who were involved in a racial conflict in Crown Heights, Brooklyn, on August 19, 1991. The play has multiple speaking parts, including conversations with gang members, police officers, and anonymous young girls and boys. There is no one "correct" telling of this event. Each telling, like light hitting a crystal, reflects a different perspective on this incident.

Viewed as a crystalline form, as a montage, or as a creative performance around a central theme, triangulation as a form of, or alternative to, validity thus can be extended. Triangulation is the simultaneous display of multiple, refracted realities. Each of the metaphors "works" to create simultaneity rather than the sequential or linear. Readers and audiences are then invited to explore competing visions of the context, to become immersed in and merge with new realities to comprehend.

The methodological *bricoleur* is adept at performing a large number of diverse tasks, ranging from interviewing to intensive self-reflection and introspection. The theoretical *bricoleur* reads widely and is knowledgeable about the many interpretive paradigms (feminism, Marxism, cultural studies, constructivism, queer theory) that can be brought to any particular problem. He or she may not, however, feel that paradigms can be mingled or synthesized. That is, one cannot easily move between paradigms as overarching philosophical systems denoting particular ontologies, epistemologies, and methodologies. They represent belief systems that attach users to particular worldviews. Perspectives, in contrast, are less well-developed systems, and one can move between them more easily. The researcher as *bricoleur*-theorist works between and within competing and overlapping perspectives and paradigms.

The interpretive *bricoleur* understands that research is an interactive process shaped by his or her own personal history, biography, gender, social class, race, and ethnicity, and by those of the people in the setting. The critical *bricoleur* stresses the dialectical and hermeneutic nature of interdisciplinary inquiry, knowing that the boundaries that previously separated traditional disciplines no longer hold (Kincheloe, 2001, p. 683). The political *bricoleur* knows that science is power, for all research findings have political implications. There is no value-free science. This researcher seeks a civic social science based on a politics of hope (Lincoln, 1999). The gendered, narrative *bricoleur* also knows that researchers all tell stories about the worlds they have studied. Thus the narratives, or stories, scientists tell are accounts couched and framed within specific storytelling traditions, often defined as paradigms (e.g., positivism, postpositivism, constructivism).

The product of the interpretive *bricoleur*'s labor is a complex, quiltlike bricolage, a reflexive collage or montage—a set of fluid, interconnected images and representations. This interpretive structure is like a quilt, a performance text, a sequence of representations connecting the parts to the whole.

*Qualitative Research as a Site of Multiple Interpretive Practices*

Qualitative research, as a set of interpretive activities, privileges no single methodological practice over another. As a site of discussion, or discourse, qualitative research is difficult to define clearly. It has no theory or paradigm that is distinctly its own. As the contributions to Part II of Volume 1 reveal, multiple theoretical paradigms claim use of qualitative research methods and strategies, from constructivist to cultural studies, feminism, Marxism, and ethnic models of study. Qualitative research is used in many separate disciplines, as we will discuss below. It does not belong to a single discipline.

Nor does qualitative research have a distinct set of methods or practices that are entirely its own. Qualitative researchers use semiotics, narrative, content, discourse, archival and phonemic analysis, even statistics, tables, graphs, and numbers. They also draw on and utilize the approaches, methods, and techniques of ethnomethodology, phenomenology, hermeneutics, feminism, rhizomatics, deconstructionism, ethnography, interviewing, psychoanalysis, cultural studies, survey research, and participant observation, among others.[11] All of these research practices "can provide important insights and knowledge" (Nelson et al., 1992, p. 2). No specific method or practice can be privileged over any other.

Many of these methods, or research practices, are used in other contexts in the human disciplines. Each bears the traces of its own disciplinary history. Thus there is an extensive history of the uses and meanings of ethnography and ethnology in education (see Ladson-Billings & Donnor, Volume 1, Chapter 11; Kincheloe & McLaren, Volume 1, Chapter 12); of participant observation and ethnography in anthropology (see Foley & Valenzuela, Volume 1, Chapter 9; Tedlock, Volume 2, Chapter 5; Brady, Chapter 16, this volume), sociology (see Holstein & Gubrium, Volume 2, Chapter 6; Fontana & Frey, Chapter 4, this volume; Harper, Chapter 6, this volume), communications (see Alexander, Volume 2, Chapter 3; Holman Jones, Chapter 7, this volume), and cultural studies (see Saukko, Volume 1, Chapter 13); of textual, hermeneutic, feminist, psychoanalytic, arts-based, semiotic, and narrative analysis in cinema and literary studies (see Olesen, Volume 1, Chapter 10; Finley, Chapter 3, this volume; Brady, Chapter 16, this volume); and of narrative, discourse, and conversational analysis in sociology, medicine, communications, and education (see Miller & Crabtree, Volume 2, Chapter 11; Chase, Chapter 2, this volume; Peräkylä, Chapter 11, this volume).

The many histories that surround each method or research strategy reveal how multiple uses and meanings are brought to each practice. Textual analyses in literary studies, for example, often treat texts as self-contained systems. On the other hand, a researcher working from a cultural studies or feminist perspective reads a text in terms of its location within a historical moment marked by a particular gender, race, or class ideology. A cultural studies use of ethnography would bring a set of understandings from feminism, postmodernism, and poststructuralism to the project. These understandings would not be shared by mainstream postpositivist sociologists. Similarly, postpositivist and poststructural historians bring different understandings and uses to the methods and findings of historical research (see Tierney, 2000). These tensions and contradictions are all evident in the chapters in this volume.

These separate and multiple uses and meanings of the methods of qualitative research make it difficult for scholars to agree on any essential definition of the field, for it is never just one thing.[12] Still, we must establish a definition for purposes of this discussion. We borrow from, and paraphrase, Nelson et al's (1992, p. 4) attempt to define cultural studies:

> Qualitative research is an interdisciplinary, transdisciplinary, and sometimes counterdisciplinary field. It crosscuts the humanities and the social and physical sciences. Qualitative research is many things at the same time. It is multiparadigmatic in focus. Its practitioners are sensitive to the value of the multimethod approach. They are committed to the naturalistic perspective and to the interpretive understanding of human experience. At the same time, the field is inherently political and shaped by multiple ethical and political positions.
>
> Qualitative research embraces two tensions at the same time. On the one hand, it is drawn to a broad, interpretive, postexperimental, postmodern, feminist, and critical sensibility. On the other hand, it is drawn to more narrowly defined positivist, postpositivist, humanistic, and naturalistic conceptions of human experience and its analysis. Further, these tensions can be combined in the same project, bringing both postmodern and naturalistic, or both critical and humanistic, perspectives to bear.

This rather awkward statement means that qualitative research, as a set of practices, embraces within its own multiple disciplinary histories constant tensions and contradictions over the project itself, including its methods and the forms its findings and interpretations take. The field sprawls between and cuts across all of the human disciplines, even including, in some cases, the physical sciences. Its practitioners are variously committed to modern, postmodern, and postexperimental sensibilities and the approaches to social research that these sensibilities imply.

## Resistances to Qualitative Studies

The academic and disciplinary resistances to qualitative research illustrate the politics embedded in this field of discourse. The challenges to qualitative research are many. As Seale, Gobo, Gubrium, and Silverman (2004) observe, we can best understand these criticisms by "distinguish[ing] analytically the political (or external) role of [qualitative] methodology from the procedural (or internal) one" (p. 7). Politics situate methodology within and outside the academy. Procedural issues define how qualitative methodology is used to produce knowledge about the world.

Often, the political and the procedural intersect. Politicians and "hard" scientists sometimes call qualitative researchers journalists or soft scientists. The work of qualitative scholars is termed unscientific, or only exploratory, or subjective. It is called criticism rather than theory or science, or it is interpreted politically, as a disguised version of Marxism or secular humanism (see Huber, 1995; see also Denzin, 1997, pp. 258–261).

These political and procedural resistances reflect an uneasy awareness that the interpretive traditions of qualitative research commit the researcher to a critique of the positivist or postpositivist project. But the positivist resistance to qualitative research goes beyond the "ever-present desire to maintain a distinction between hard science and soft scholarship" (Carey, 1989, p. 99; see also Smith & Hodkinson,

Chapter 13, this volume). The experimental (positivist) sciences (physics, chemistry, economics, and psychology, for example) are often seen as the crowning achievements of Western civilization, and in their practices it is assumed that "truth" can transcend opinion and personal bias (Carey, 1989, p. 99; Schwandt, 1997b, p. 309). Qualitative research is seen as an assault on this tradition, whose adherents often retreat into a "value-free objectivist science" (Carey, 1989, p. 104) model to defend their position. They seldom attempt to make explicit, or to critique, the "moral and political commitments in their own contingent work" (Carey, 1989, p. 104; see also Guba & Lincoln, Volume 1, Chapter 8).

Positivists further allege that the so-called new experimental qualitative researchers write fiction, not science, and that these researchers have no way of verifying their truth statements. Ethnographic poetry and fiction signal the death of empirical science, and there is little to be gained by attempting to engage in moral criticism. These critics presume a stable, unchanging reality that can be studied using the empirical methods of objective social science (see Huber, 1995). The province of qualitative research, accordingly, is the world of lived experience, for this is where individual belief and action intersect with culture. Under this model there is no preoccupation with discourse and method as material interpretive practices that constitute representation and description. Thus is the textual, narrative turn rejected by the positivists.

The opposition to positive science by the poststructuralists is seen, then, as an attack on reason and truth. At the same time, the positivist science attack on qualitative research is regarded as an attempt to legislate one version of truth over another.

### Politics and Reemergent Scientism

The scientifically based research (SBR) movement initiated in recent years by the National Research Council (NRC) has created a hostile political environment for qualitative research. Connected to the federal legislation known as the No Child Left Behind Act of 2001, SBR embodies a reemergent scientism (Maxwell, 2004), a positivist, evidence-based epistemology. The movement encourages researchers to employ "rigorous, systematic, and objective methodology to obtain reliable and valid knowledge" (Ryan & Hood, 2004, p. 80). The preferred methodology employs well-defined causal models and independent and dependent variables. Researchers examine causal models in the context of randomized controlled experiments, which allow for replication and generalization of their results (Ryan & Hood, 2004, p. 81).

Under such a framework, qualitative research becomes suspect. Qualitative research does not require well-defined variables or causal models. The observations and measurements of qualitative scholars are not based on subjects' random assignment to experimental groups. Qualitative researchers do not generate "hard evidence" using such methods. At best, through case study, interview, and ethnographic methods, researchers can gather descriptive materials that can be tested with experimental methods. The epistemologies of critical race, queer, postcolonial, feminist, and postmodern theories are rendered useless by the SBR perspective, relegated at best to the category of scholarship, not science (Ryan & Hood, 2004, p. 81; St. Pierre, 2004, p. 132).

Critics of the SBR movement are united on the following points. "Bush science" (Lather, 2004, p. 19) and its experimental, evidence-based methodologies represent a racialized, masculinist backlash to the proliferation of qualitative inquiry methods over the past two decades. The movement endorses a narrow view of science (Maxwell, 2004) that celebrates a "neoclassical experimentalism that is a throwback to the Campbell-Stanley era and its dogmatic adherence to an exclusive reliance on quantitative methods" (Howe, 2004, p. 42). The movement represents "nostalgia for a simple and ordered universe of science that never was" (Popkewitz, 2004, p. 62). With its emphasis on only one form of scientific rigor, the NRC ignores the value of using complex historical, contextual, and political criteria to evaluate inquiry (Bloch, 2004).

As Howe (2004) observes, neoclassical experimentalists extol evidence-based "medical research as the model for educational research, particularly the random clinical trial" (p. 48). But dispensing a pill in a random clinical trial is quite unlike "dispensing a curriculum," and the "effects" of an educational experiment cannot be easily measured, unlike a "10-point reduction in diastolic blood pressure" (p. 48; see also Miller & Crabtree, Volume 2, Chapter 11).

Qualitative researchers must learn to think outside the box as they critique the NRC and its methodological guidelines (Atkinson, 2004). They must apply their imaginations and find new ways to define such terms as *randomized design, causal model, policy studies,* and *public science* (Cannella & Lincoln, 2004a, 2004b; Lincoln & Cannella, 2004a, 2004b; Lincoln & Tierney, 2004; Weinstein, 2004). More deeply, qualitative researchers must resist conservative attempts to discredit qualitative inquiry by placing it back inside the box of positivism.

### Mixed-Methods Experimentalism

As Howe (2004) notes, the SBR movement finds a place for qualitative methods in mixed-methods experimental designs. In such designs, qualitative methods may be "employed either singly or in combination with quantitative methods, including the use of randomized experimental designs" (p. 49). Mixed-methods designs are direct descendants of classical experimentalism. They presume a methodological hierarchy in which quantitative methods are at the top and qualitative methods are relegated to "a largely auxiliary role in pursuit of the *technocratic* aim of accumulating knowledge of 'what works'" (pp. 53–54).

The mixed-methods movement takes qualitative methods out of their natural home, which is within the critical, interpretive framework (Howe, 2004, p. 54; but see Teddlie & Tashakkori, 2003, p. 15). It divides inquiry into dichotomous categories: exploration versus confirmation. Qualitative work is assigned to the first category, quantitative research to the second (Teddlie & Tashakkori, 2003, p. 15). Like the classic experimental model, it excludes stakeholders from dialogue and active participation in the research process. This weakens its democratic and dialogical dimensions and decreases the likelihood that previously silenced voices will be heard (Howe, 2004, pp. 56–57). As Howe (2004) cautions, it is not just the "'methodological fundamentalists' who have bought into [this] approach. A sizable number of rather influential . . . educational researchers . . . have also signed on. This might be a compromise to the current political climate; it might be a backlash against the perceived excesses of postmodernism; it might be both. It is an ominous development, whatever the explanation" (p. 57).

### Pragmatic Criticisms of Antifoundationalism

Seale et al. (2004) contest what they regard as the excesses of an antimethodological, "anything goes," romantic postmodernism that is associated with our project. They assert that too often the approach we value produces "low quality qualitative research and research results that are quite stereotypical and close to common sense" (p. 2). In contrast, they propose a practice-based, pragmatic approach that places research practice at the center. They note that research involves an engagement "with a variety of things and people: research materials . . . social theories, philosophical debates, values, methods, tests . . . research participants" (p. 2). (Actually, this approach is quite close to our own, especially our view of the *bricoleur* and bricolage.) Seale et al.'s situated methodology rejects the antifoundational claim that there are only partial truths, that the dividing line between fact and fiction has broken down (p. 3). These scholars believe that this dividing line has not collapsed, and that qualitative researchers should not accept stories if they do not accord with the best available facts (p 6).

Oddly, these pragmatic procedural arguments reproduce a variant of the evidence-based model and its criticisms of poststructural, performative sensibilities. They can be used to provide political support for the methodological marginalization of the positions advanced by many of the contributors to this volume.

▣  ▣  ▣

The complex political terrain described above defines the many traditions and strands of qualitative research: the British tradition and its presence in other national contexts; the American pragmatic, naturalistic, and interpretive traditions in sociology, anthropology, communications, and education; the German and French phenomenological, hermeneutic, semiotic, Marxist, structural, and poststructural perspectives; feminist studies, African American studies, Latino studies, queer studies, studies of indigenous and aboriginal cultures. The politics of qualitative research creates a tension that informs each of these traditions. This tension itself is constantly being reexamined and interrogated as qualitative research confronts a changing historical world, new intellectual positions, and its own institutional and academic conditions.

To summarize: Qualitative research is many things to many people. Its essence is twofold: a commitment to some version of the naturalistic, interpretive approach to its subject matter and an ongoing critique of the politics and methods of postpositivism. We turn now to a brief discussion of the major differences between qualitative and quantitative approaches to research. We then discuss ongoing differences and tensions within qualitative inquiry.

## ▣ QUALITATIVE VERSUS QUANTITATIVE RESEARCH

The word *qualitative* implies an emphasis on the qualities of entities and on processes and meanings that are not experimentally examined or measured (if measured at all) in terms of quantity, amount, intensity, or frequency. Qualitative researchers stress the socially constructed nature of reality, the intimate relationship between the researcher and what is studied, and the situational constraints that shape inquiry. Such researchers emphasize the value-laden nature of inquiry. They seek answers to questions that stress *how* social experience is created and given meaning. In contrast, quantitative studies emphasize the measurement and analysis of causal relationships between variables, not processes. Proponents of such studies claim that their work is done from within a value-free framework.

### Research Styles: Doing the Same Things Differently?

Of course, both qualitative and quantitative researchers "think they know something about society worth telling to others, and they use a variety of forms, media and means to communicate their ideas and findings" (Becker, 1986, p. 122). Qualitative research differs from quantitative research in five significant ways (Becker, 1996). These points of difference, discussed in turn below, all involve different ways of addressing the same set of issues. They return always to the politics of research and to who has the power to legislate correct solutions to social problems.

*Uses of positivism and postpositivism.* First, both perspectives are shaped by the positivist and postpositivist traditions in the physical and social sciences (see the discussion below). These two positivist science traditions hold to naïve and critical realist positions concerning reality and its perception. In the positivist version it is contended that there is a reality out there to be studied, captured, and understood, whereas the postpositivists argue that reality can never be fully apprehended, only approximated (Guba, 1990, p. 22). Postpositivism relies on multiple methods as a way of capturing as much of reality as possible. At the same time, it emphasizes the discovery and verification of theories. Traditional evaluation criteria, such as internal and external validity, are stressed, as is the use of qualitative procedures that lend themselves to structured (sometimes statistical) analysis. Computer-assisted methods of analysis that permit frequency counts, tabulations, and low-level statistical analyses may also be employed.

The positivist and postpositivist traditions linger like long shadows over the qualitative research project. Historically, qualitative research was defined within the positivist paradigm, where qualitative researchers attempted to do good positivist research with less rigorous methods and procedures. Some mid-20th-century qualitative researchers reported participant observation findings in terms of quasi-statistics (e.g., Becker, Geer, Hughes, & Strauss, 1961). As recently as 1998, Strauss and Corbin, two leading proponents of the grounded theory approach to qualitative research, attempted to modify the usual canons of good (positivist) science to fit their own postpositivist conception of rigorous research (but see Charmaz, Volume 2, Chapter 7; see also Glaser, 1992). Some applied researchers, while claiming to be atheoretical, often fit within the positivist or postpositivist framework by default.

Flick (2002) usefully summarizes the differences between these two approaches to inquiry, noting that the quantitative approach has been used for purposes of isolating "causes and effects ... operationalizing theoretical relations ... [and] measuring and ... quantifying phenomena ... allowing the generalization of findings" (p. 3). But today doubt is cast on such projects: "Rapid social change and the resulting diversification of life worlds are increasingly confronting social researchers with new social contexts and perspectives. ... traditional deductive methodologies ... are failing. ... thus research is increasingly forced to make use of inductive strategies instead of starting from theories and testing them. ... knowledge and practice are studied as *local* knowledge and practice" (p. 2).

Spindler and Spindler (1992) summarize their qualitative approach to quantitative materials: "Instrumentation and quantification are simply procedures employed to extend and reinforce certain kinds of data, interpretations and test hypotheses across samples. Both must be kept in their place. One must avoid their premature or overly extensive use as a security mechanism" (p. 69).

Although many qualitative researchers in the postpositivist tradition use statistical measures, methods, and documents as a way of locating a group of subjects within a larger population, they seldom report their findings in terms of the kinds of complex statistical measures or methods to which quantitative researchers are drawn (e.g., path, regression, and log-linear analyses).

*Acceptance of postmodern sensibilities.* The use of quantitative, positivist methods and assumptions has been rejected by a new generation of qualitative researchers who are attached to poststructural and/or postmodern sensibilities. These researchers argue that positivist methods are but one way of telling stories about societies or social worlds. These methods may be no better or no worse than any other methods; they just tell different kinds of stories.

This tolerant view is not shared by all qualitative researchers (Huber, 1995). Many members of the critical theory, constructivist, poststructural, and postmodern schools of thought reject positivist and postpositivist criteria when evaluating their own work. They see these criteria as irrelevant to their work and contend that such criteria reproduce only a certain kind of science, a science that silences too many voices. These researchers seek alternative methods for evaluating their work, including verisimilitude, emotionality, personal responsibility, an ethic of caring, political praxis, multivoiced texts, and dialogues with subjects. In response, positivists and postpositivists argue that what they do is good science, free of individual bias and subjectivity. As noted above, they see postmodernism and poststructuralism as attacks on reason and truth.

*Capturing the individual's point of view.* Both qualitative and quantitative researchers are concerned with the individual's point of view. However, qualitative investigators think they can get closer to the actor's perspective through detailed interviewing and observation. They argue that quantitative researchers are seldom able to capture their subjects' perspectives because they have to rely on more remote, inferential empirical methods and materials. Many quantitative researchers regard the empirical materials produced by interpretive methods as unreliable, impressionistic, and not objective.

*Examining the constraints of everyday life.* Qualitative researchers are more likely to confront and come up against the constraints of the everyday social world. They see this world in action and embed their findings in it. Quantitative researchers abstract from this world and seldom study it directly. They seek a nomothetic or etic science based on probabilities derived from the study of large numbers of randomly selected cases. These kinds of statements stand above and outside the constraints of everyday life. Qualitative researchers, on the other hand, are committed to an emic, idiographic, case-based position that directs attention to the specifics of particular cases.

*Securing rich descriptions.* Qualitative researchers believe that rich descriptions of the social world are valuable, whereas quantitative researchers, with their etic, nomothetic commitments, are less concerned with such detail. Quantitative researchers are deliberately unconcerned with rich descriptions because such detail interrupts the process of developing generalizations.

▣ ▣ ▣

The five points of difference described above reflect qualitative and quantitative scholars' commitments to different styles of research, different epistemologies, and different forms of representation. Each work tradition is governed by a different set of genres; each has its own classics, its own preferred forms of representation, interpretation, trustworthiness, and textual evaluation (see Becker, 1986, pp. 134–135). Qualitative researchers use ethnographic prose, historical narratives, first-person accounts, still photographs, life histories, fictionalized "facts," and biographical and autobiographical materials, among others. Quantitative researchers use mathematical models, statistical tables, and graphs, and they usually write about their research in impersonal, third-person prose.

## ▣ TENSIONS WITHIN QUALITATIVE RESEARCH

It is erroneous to presume that all qualitative researchers share the same assumptions about the five points of difference described above. As the following discussion reveals, positivist, postpositivist, and poststructural differences define and shape the discourses of qualitative research. Realists and postpositivists within the interpretive, qualitative research tradition criticize poststructuralists for taking the textual, narrative turn. These critics contend that such work is navel gazing. It produces the conditions "for a dialogue of the deaf between itself and the community" (Silverman, 1997, p. 240). Critics accuse those who attempt to capture the point of view of the interacting subject in the world of naïve humanism, of reproducing "a Romantic impulse which elevates the experiential to the level of the authentic" (Silverman, 1997, p. 248).

Still others assert that those who take the textual, performance turn ignore lived experience. Snow and Morrill (1995) argue that "this performance turn, like the preoccupation with discourse and storytelling, will take us further from the field of social action and the real dramas of everyday life and thus signal the death knell of ethnography as an empirically grounded enterprise" (p. 361). Of course, we disagree.

### Critical Realism

For some, there is a third stream, between naïve positivism and poststructuralism. Critical realism is an antipositivist movement in the social sciences closely associated with the works of Roy Bhaskar and Rom Harré (Danermark, Ekström, Jakobsen, & Karlsson, 2002). Critical realists use the word *critical* in a particular way. This is not "Frankfurt school" critical theory, although there are traces of social criticism here and there (see Danermark et al., 2002, p. 201). Instead, *critical* in this context refers to a transcendental realism that rejects methodological individualism and universal claims to truth. Critical realists oppose logical positivist, relativist, and antifoundational epistemologies. Critical realists agree with the positivists that there is a world of events out there that is observable and independent of human consciousness. They hold that knowledge about this world is socially constructed. Society is made up of feeling, thinking human beings, and their interpretations of the world must be studied (Danermark et al., 2002, p. 200). Critical realists reject a correspondence theory of truth. They believe that reality is arranged in levels and that scientific work must go beyond statements of regularity to analysis of the mechanisms, processes, and structures that account for the patterns that are observed.

Still, as postempiricist, antifoundational, critical theorists, we reject much of what the critical realists advocate. Throughout the past century, social science and philosophy have been continually tangled up with one another. Various "isms" and philosophical movements have crisscrossed sociological and educational discourses, from positivism to postpositivism, to analytic and linguistic philosophy, to hermeneutics, structuralism, poststructuralism, Marxism, feminism, and current post-post versions of all of the above. Some have said that the logical positivists steered the social sciences on a rigorous course of self-destruction.

We do not think that critical realism will keep the social science ship afloat. The social sciences are normative disciplines, always already embedded in issues of value, ideology, power, desire, sexism, racism, domination, repression, and control. We want a social science that is committed up front to issues of social justice, equity, nonviolence, peace, and universal human rights. We do not want a social science that says it can address these issues if it wants to. For us, that is no longer an option.

With these differences within and between interpretive traditions in hand, we must now briefly discuss the history of qualitative research. We break this history into eight historical moments, mindful that any history is always somewhat arbitrary and always at least partially a social construction.

## ▣ THE HISTORY OF QUALITATIVE RESEARCH

The history of qualitative research reveals that the modern social science disciplines have taken as their mission "the analysis and understanding of the patterned conduct and social processes of society" (Vidich & Lyman, 2000, p. 37). The notion that social scientists could carry out this task presupposed that they had the ability to observe this world objectively. Qualitative methods were a major tool of such observations.[13]

Throughout the history of qualitative research, qualitative investigators have defined their work in terms of hopes and values, "religious faiths, occupational and professional ideologies" (Vidich & Lyman, 2000, p. 39). Qualitative research (like all research) has always been judged on the "standard of whether the work communicates or 'says' something to us" (Vidich & Lyman, 2000, p. 39), based on how we conceptualize our reality and our images of the world. *Epistemology* is the word that has historically defined these standards of evaluation. In the contemporary period, as we have argued above, many received discourses on epistemology are now being reevaluated.

Vidich and Lyman's (2000) work on the history of qualitative research covers the following (somewhat) overlapping stages: early ethnography (to the 17th century), colonial ethnography (17th-, 18th-, and 19th-century explorers), the ethnography of the American Indian as "Other" (late-19th- and early 20th-century anthropology), community studies and ethnographies of American immigrants (early 20th century through the 1960s), studies of ethnicity and assimilation (midcentury through the 1980s), and the present, which we call the *eighth moment*.

In each of these eras, researchers were and have been influenced by their political hopes and ideologies, discovering findings in their research that confirmed their prior theories or beliefs. Early ethnographers confirmed the racial and cultural diversity of peoples throughout the globe and attempted to fit this diversity into a theory about the origins of history, the races, and civilizations. Colonial ethnographers, before the professionalization of ethnography in the 20th century, fostered a colonial pluralism that left natives on their own as long as their leaders could be co-opted by the colonial administration.

European ethnographers studied Africans, Asians, and other Third World peoples of color. Early American ethnographers studied the American Indian from the perspective of the conqueror, who saw the lifeworld of the primitive as a window to the prehistoric past. The Calvinist mission to save the Indian was soon transferred to the mission of saving the "hordes" of immigrants who entered the United States with the beginnings of industrialization. Qualitative community studies of the ethnic Other proliferated from the early 1900s to the 1960s and included the work of E. Franklin Frazier, Robert Park, and Robert Redfield and their students, as well as William Foote Whyte, the Lynds, August Hollingshead, Herbert Gans, Stanford Lyman, Arthur Vidich, and Joseph Bensman. The post-1960 ethnicity studies challenged the "melting pot" hypotheses of Park and his followers and corresponded to the emergence of ethnic studies programs that saw Native Americans, Latinos, Asian Americans, and African Americans attempting to take control over the study of their own peoples.

The postmodern and poststructural challenge emerged in the mid-1980s. It questioned the assumptions that had organized this earlier history in each of its colonizing moments. Qualitative research that crosses the "postmodern divide" requires the scholar, Vidich and Lyman (2000) argue, to "abandon all established and preconceived values, theories, perspectives . . . and prejudices as resources for ethnographic study" (p. 60). In this new era the qualitative researcher does more than observe history; he or she plays a part in it. New tales from the field will now be written, and they will reflect the researchers' direct and personal engagement with this historical period.

Vidich and Lyman's analysis covers the full sweep of ethnographic history. Ours is confined to the 20th and 21st centuries and complements many of their divisions. We begin with the early foundational work of the British and French as well as the Chicago, Columbia, Harvard, Berkeley, and British schools of sociology and anthropology. This early foundational period established the norms of classical qualitative and ethnographic research (see Gupta & Ferguson, 1997; Rosaldo, 1989; Stocking, 1989).

## ▣ THE EIGHT MOMENTS OF QUALITATIVE RESEARCH

As we have noted above, we divide our history of qualitative research in North America in the 20th century and beyond into eight phases, which we describe in turn below.

## The Traditional Period

We call the first moment the traditional period (this covers the second and third phases discussed by Vidich & Lyman, 2000). It begins in the early 1900s and continues until World War II. In this period, qualitative researchers wrote "objective," colonizing accounts of field experiences that were reflective of the positivist scientist paradigm. They were concerned with offering valid, reliable, and objective interpretations in their writings. The "Other" whom they studied was alien, foreign, and strange.

Here is Malinowski (1967) discussing his field experiences in New Guinea and the Trobriand Islands in the years 1914–1915 and 1917–1918. He is bartering his way into field data:

> Nothing whatever draws me to ethnographic studies. . . . On the whole the village struck me rather unfavorably. There is a certain disorganization . . . the rowdiness and persistence of the people who laugh and stare and lie discouraged me somewhat. . . . Went to the village hoping to photograph a few stages of the *bara* dance. I handed out half-sticks of tobacco, then watched a few dances; then took pictures—but results were poor. . . . they would not pose long enough for time exposures. At moments I was furious at them, particularly because after I gave them their portions of tobacco they all went away. (quoted in Geertz, 1988, pp. 73–74)

In another work, this lonely, frustrated, isolated field-worker describes his methods in the following words:

> In the field one has to face a chaos of facts. . . . in this crude form they are not scientific facts at all; they are absolutely elusive, and can only be fixed by interpretation. . . . *Only laws and generalizations are scientific facts,* and field work consists only and exclusively in the interpretation of the chaotic social reality, in subordinating it to general rules. (Malinowski, 1916/1948, p. 328; quoted in Geertz, 1988, p. 81)

Malinowski's remarks are provocative. On the one hand they disparage fieldwork, but on the other they speak of it within the glorified language of science, with laws and generalizations fashioned out of this selfsame experience.

During this period the field-worker was lionized, made into a larger-than-life figure who went into the field and returned with stories about strange peoples. Rosaldo (1989) describes this as the period of the Lone Ethnographer, the story of the man-scientist who went off in search of his native in a distant land. There this figure "encountered the object of his quest . . . [and] underwent his rite of passage by enduring the ultimate ordeal of 'fieldwork'" (p. 30). Returning home with his data, the Lone Ethnographer wrote up an objective account of the culture studied. This account was structured by the norms of classical ethnography. This sacred bundle of terms (Rosaldo, 1989, p. 31) organized ethnographic texts around four beliefs and commitments: a commitment to objectivism, a complicity with imperialism, a belief in monumentalism (the ethnography would create a museumlike picture of the culture studied), and a belief in timelessness (what was studied would never change). The Other was an "object" to be archived. This model of the researcher, who could also write complex, dense theories about what was studied, holds to the present day.

The myth of the Lone Ethnographer depicts the birth of classic ethnography. The texts of Malinowski, Radcliffe-Brown, Margaret Mead, and Gregory Bateson are still carefully studied for what they can tell the novice about fieldwork, taking field notes, and writing theory. But today the image of the Lone Ethnographer has been shattered. Many scholars see the works of the classic ethnographers as relics from the colonial past (Rosaldo, 1989, p. 44). Whereas some feel nostalgia for this past, others celebrate its passing. Rosaldo (1989) quotes Cora Du Bois, a retired Harvard anthropology professor, who lamented this passing at a conference in 1980, reflecting on the crisis in anthropology: "[I feel a distance] from the complexity and disarray of what I once found a justifiable and challenging discipline. . . . It has been like moving from a distinguished art museum into a garage sale" (p. 44).

Du Bois regards the classic ethnographies as pieces of timeless artwork contained in a museum. She feels uncomfortable in the chaos of the garage sale. In contrast, Rosaldo (1989) is drawn to this metaphor because "it provides a precise image of the postcolonial situation where cultural artifacts flow between unlikely places, and nothing is sacred, permanent, or sealed off. The image of anthropology as a garage sale depicts our present global situation" (p. 44). Indeed, many valuable treasures may be found in unexpected places, if one is willing to look long and hard. Old standards no longer hold. Ethnographies do not produce timeless truths. The commitment to objectivism is now in doubt. The complicity with imperialism is openly challenged today, and the belief in monumentalism is a thing of the past.

The legacies of this first period begin at the end of the 19th century, when the novel and the social sciences had become distinguished as separate systems of discourse (Clough, 1998, pp. 21–22). However, the Chicago school, with its emphasis on the life story and the "slice-of-life" approach to ethnographic materials, sought to develop an interpretive methodology that maintained the centrality of the narrated-life-history approach. This led to the production of texts that gave the researcher-as-author the power to represent the subject's story. Written under the mantle of straightforward, sentiment-free social realism, these texts used the language of ordinary people. They articulated a social science version of literary naturalism, which often produced the sympathetic illusion that a solution to a social problem had been found. Like the Depression-era juvenile delinquent and other "social problems" films (Roffman & Purdy, 1981), these accounts romanticized the subject. They turned the deviant into a sociological version of a screen hero. These sociological stories, like their film counterparts, usually had happy endings, as they followed individuals through the three stages of the classic morality tale: being in a state of grace, being seduced by evil and falling, and finally achieving redemption through suffering.

## Modernist Phase

The modernist phase, or second moment, builds on the canonical works from the traditional period. Social realism, naturalism, and slice-of-life ethnographies are still valued. This phase extended through the postwar years to the 1970s and is still present in the work of many (for reviews, see Wolcott, 1990, 1992, 1995; see also Tedlock, Volume 2, Chapter 5). In this period many texts sought to formalize qualitative methods (see, e.g., Bogdan & Taylor, 1975; Cicourel, 1964; Filstead, 1970; Glaser & Strauss, 1967; Lofland, 1971, 1995; Lofland & Lofland, 1984, 1995; Taylor & Bogdan, 1998).[14] The modernist ethnographer and sociological participant observer attempted rigorous qualitative studies of important social processes, including deviance and social control in the classroom and society. This was a moment of creative ferment.

A new generation of graduate students across the human disciplines encountered new interpretive theories (ethnomethodology, phenomenology, critical theory, feminism). They were drawn to qualitative research practices that would let them give a voice to society's underclass. Postpositivism functioned as a powerful epistemological paradigm. Researchers attempted to fit Campbell and Stanley's (1963) model of internal and external validity to constructionist and interactionist conceptions of the research act. They returned to the texts of the Chicago school as sources of inspiration (see Denzin, 1970, 1978).

A canonical text from this moment remains *Boys in White* (Becker et al., 1961; see also Becker, 1998). Firmly entrenched in mid-20th-century methodological discourse, this work attempted to make qualitative research as rigorous as its quantitative counterpart. Causal narratives were central to this project. This multimethod work combined open-ended and quasi-structured interviewing with participant observation and the careful analysis of such materials in standardized, statistical form. In his classic article "Problems of Inference and Proof in Participant Observation," Howard S. Becker (1958/1970) describes the use of quasi-statistics:

> Participant observations have occasionally been gathered in standardized form capable of being transformed into legitimate statistical data. But the exigencies of the field usually prevent the collection of data in such a form to meet the assumptions of statistical tests, so that the observer deals in what have been called "quasi-statistics." His conclusions, while implicitly numerical, do not require precise quantification. (p. 31)

In the analysis of data, Becker notes, the qualitative researcher takes a cue from more quantitatively oriented colleagues. The researcher looks for probabilities or support for arguments concerning the likelihood that, or frequency with which, a conclusion in fact applies in a specific situation (see also Becker, 1998, pp. 166–170). Thus did work in the modernist period clothe itself in the language and rhetoric of positivist and postpositivist discourse.

This was the golden age of rigorous qualitative analysis, bracketed in sociology by *Boys in White* (Becker et al., 1961) at one end and *The Discovery of Grounded Theory*

(Glaser & Strauss, 1967) at the other. In education, qualitative research in this period was defined by George and Louise Spindler, Jules Henry, Harry Wolcott, and John Singleton. This form of qualitative research is still present in the work of scholars such as Strauss and Corbin (1998) and Ryan and Bernard (2000).

The "golden age" reinforced the picture of qualitative researchers as cultural romantics. Imbued with Promethean human powers, they valorized villains and outsiders as heroes to mainstream society. They embodied a belief in the contingency of self and society, and held to emancipatory ideals for "which one lives and dies." They put in place a tragic and often ironic view of society and self, and joined a long line of leftist cultural romantics that included Emerson, Marx, James, Dewey, Gramsci, and Martin Luther King, Jr. (West, 1989, chap. 6).

As this moment came to an end, the Vietnam War was everywhere present in American society. In 1969, alongside these political currents, Herbert Blumer and Everett Hughes met with a group of young sociologists called the "Chicago Irregulars" at the American Sociological Association meetings held in San Francisco and shared their memories of the "Chicago years." Lyn Lofland (1980) describes this time as a

> moment of creative ferment—scholarly and political. The San Francisco meetings witnessed not simply the Blumer-Hughes event but a "counter-revolution." . . . a group first came to . . . talk about the problems of being a sociologist and a female. . . . the discipline seemed literally to be bursting with new . . . ideas: labelling theory, ethnomethodology, conflict theory, phenomenology, dramaturgical analysis. (p. 253)

Thus did the modernist phase come to an end.

## Blurred Genres

By the beginning of the third phase (1970–1986), which we call the moment of blurred genres, qualitative researchers had a full complement of paradigms, methods, and strategies to employ in their research. Theories ranged from symbolic interactionism to constructivism, naturalistic inquiry, positivism and postpositivism, phenomenology, ethnomethodology, critical theory, neo-Marxist theory, semiotics, structuralism, feminism, and various racial/ethnic paradigms. Applied qualitative research was gaining in stature, and the politics and ethics of qualitative research—implicated as they were in various applications of this work—were topics of considerable concern. Research strategies and formats for reporting research ranged from grounded theory to the case study, to methods of historical, biographical, ethnographic, action, and clinical research. Diverse ways of collecting and analyzing empirical materials were also available, including qualitative interviewing (open-ended and quasi-structured) and observational, visual, personal experience, and documentary methods. Computers were entering the situation, to be fully developed as aids in the analysis of qualitative data in the next decade, along with narrative, content, and semiotic methods of reading interviews and cultural texts.

Two books by Clifford Geertz, *The Interpretation of Cultures* (1973) and *Local Knowledge* (1983), defined the beginning and the end of this moment. In these two works, Geertz argued that the old functional, positivist, behavioral, totalizing approaches to the human disciplines were giving way to a more pluralistic, interpretive, open-ended perspective. This new perspective took cultural representations and their meanings as its points of departure. Calling for "thick description" of particular events, rituals, and customs, Geertz suggested that all anthropological writings are interpretations of interpretations.[15] The observer has no privileged voice in the interpretations that are written. The central task of theory is to make sense out of a local situation.

Geertz went on to propose that the boundaries between the social sciences and the humanities had become blurred. Social scientists were now turning to the humanities for models, theories, and methods of analysis (semiotics, hermeneutics). A form of genre diaspora was occurring: documentaries that read like fiction (Mailer), parables posing as ethnographies (Castañeda), theoretical treatises that look like travelogues (Lévi-Strauss). At the same time, other new approaches were emerging: poststructuralism (Barthes), neopositivism (Philips), neo-Marxism (Althusser), micro-macro descriptivism (Geertz), ritual theories of drama and culture (V. Turner), deconstructionism (Derrida), ethnomethodology (Garfinkel). The golden age of the social sciences was over, and a new age of blurred, interpretive genres was upon us. The essay as an art form was replacing the scientific article. At issue now was the author's presence in the interpretive text (Geertz, 1988). How can the researcher speak with authority in an age when there are no longer any firm rules concerning the text, including the author's place in it, its standards of evaluation, and its subject matter?

The naturalistic, postpositivist, and constructionist paradigms gained power in this period, especially in education, in the works of Harry Wolcott, Frederick Erickson, Egon Guba, Yvonna Lincoln, Robert Stake, and Elliot Eisner. By the end of the 1970s, several qualitative journals were in place, including *Urban Life and Culture* (now *Journal of Contemporary Ethnography*), *Cultural Anthropology, Anthropology and Education Quarterly, Qualitative Sociology,* and *Symbolic Interaction,* as well as the book series *Studies in Symbolic Interaction.*

## Crisis of Representation

A profound rupture occurred in the mid-1980s. What we call the fourth moment, or the crisis of representation, appeared with *Anthropology as Cultural Critique* (Marcus & Fischer, 1986), *The Anthropology of Experience* (Turner & Bruner, 1986), *Writing Culture* (Clifford & Marcus, 1986), *Works and Lives* (Geertz, 1988), and *The Predicament of Culture* (Clifford, 1988). These works made research and writing more reflexive and called into question the issues of gender, class, and race. They articulated the consequences of Geertz's "blurred genres" interpretation of the field in the early 1980s.[16]

Qualitative researchers sought new models of truth, method, and representation (Rosaldo, 1989). The erosion of classic norms in anthropology (objectivism, complicity with colonialism, social life structured by fixed rituals and customs, ethnographies as monuments to a culture) was complete (Rosaldo, 1989, pp. 44–45; see also Jackson, 1998, pp. 7–8). Critical theory, feminist theory, and epistemologies of color now competed for attention in this arena. Issues such as validity, reliability, and objectivity, previously believed settled, were once more problematic. Pattern and interpretive theories, as opposed to causal, linear theories, were now more common, as writers continued to challenge older models of truth and meaning (Rosaldo, 1989).

Stoller and Olkes (1987, pp. 227–229) describe how they felt the crisis of representation in their fieldwork among the Songhay of Niger. Stoller observes: "When I began to write anthropological texts, I followed the conventions of my training. I 'gathered data,' and once the 'data' were arranged in neat piles, I 'wrote them up.' In one case I reduced Songhay insults to a series of neat logical formulas" (p. 227). Stoller became dissatisfied with this form of writing, in part because he learned "everyone had lied to me and . . . the data I has so painstakingly collected were worthless. I learned a lesson: Informants routinely lie to their anthropologists" (Stoller & Olkes, 1987, p. 9). This discovery led to a second—that he had, in following the conventions of ethnographic realism, edited himself out of his text. This led Stoller to produce a different type of text, a memoir, in which he became a central character in the story he told. This story, an account of his experiences in the Songhay world, became an analysis of the clash between his world and the world of Songhay sorcery. Thus Stoller's journey represents an attempt to confront the crisis of representation in the fourth moment.

Clough (1998) elaborates this crisis and criticizes those who would argue that new forms of writing represent a way out of the crisis. She argues:

> While many sociologists now commenting on the criticism of ethnography view writing as "downright central to the ethnographic enterprise" [Van Maanen, 1988, p. xi], the problems of writing are still viewed as different from the problems of method or fieldwork itself. Thus the solution usually offered is experiments in writing, that is a self-consciousness about writing. (p. 136)

It is this insistence on the difference between writing and fieldwork that must be analyzed. (Richardson & St. Pierre are quite articulate about this issue in Chapter 15 of this volume.)

In writing, the field-worker makes a claim to moral and scientific authority. This claim allows the realist and experimental ethnographic texts to function as sources of validation for an empirical science. They show that the world of real lived experience can still be captured, if only in the writer's memoirs, or fictional experimentations, or dramatic readings. But these works have the danger of directing attention away from the ways in which the text constructs sexually situated individuals in a field of social difference. They also perpetuate "empirical science's hegemony" (Clough, 1998, p. 8), for these new writing technologies of the subject become the site "for the production of knowledge/power . . . [aligned] with . . . the capital/state axis" (Aronowitz, 1988, p. 300; quoted in Clough, 1998, p. 8). Such experiments come up against, and then back away from, the difference between empirical science and social criticism. Too often they fail to engage fully a new politics of textuality that would "refuse the identity of empirical science" (Clough, 1998, p. 135). This new social criticism "would intervene in the relationship of information economics, nation-state politics, and technologies of mass communication, especially in terms of the empirical sciences" (Clough, 1998, p. 16). This, of course, is the terrain occupied by cultural studies.

In Chapter 15 of this volume, Richardson and St. Pierre develop the above arguments, viewing writing as a method of inquiry that moves through successive stages of self-reflection. As a series of written representations, the field-worker's texts flow from the field experience, through intermediate works, to later work, and finally to the research text, which is the public presentation of the ethnographic and narrative experience. Thus fieldwork and writing blur into one another. There is, in the final analysis, no difference between writing and fieldwork. These two perspectives inform one another throughout every chapter in this volume. In these ways the crisis of representation moves qualitative research in new and critical directions.

## A Triple Crisis

The ethnographer's authority remains under assault today (Behar, 1995, p. 3; Gupta & Ferguson, 1997, p. 16; Jackson, 1998; Ortner, 1997, p. 2). A triple crisis of representation, legitimation, and praxis confronts qualitative researchers in the human disciplines. Embedded in the discourses of poststructuralism and postmodernism (Vidich & Lyman, 2000; see also Richardson & St. Pierre, Chapter 15, this volume), these three crises are coded in multiple terms, variously called and associated with the *critical, interpretive, linguistic, feminist,* and *rhetorical* turns in social theory. These new turns make problematic two key assumptions of qualitative research. The first is that qualitative researchers can no longer directly capture lived experience. Such experience, it is argued, is created in the social text written by the researcher. This is the representational crisis. It confronts the inescapable problem of representation, but does so within a framework that makes the direct link between experience and text problematic.

The second assumption makes problematic the traditional criteria for evaluating and interpreting qualitative research. This is the legitimation crisis. It involves a serious rethinking of such terms as *validity, generalizability,* and *reliability,* terms already retheorized in postpositivist (Hammersley, 1992), constructionist-naturalistic (Guba & Lincoln, 1989, pp. 163–183), feminist (Olesen, Volume 1, Chapter 10), interpretive and performative (Denzin, 1997, 2003), poststructural (Lather, 1993; Lather & Smithies, 1997), and critical discourses (Kincheloe & McLaren, Volume 1, Chapter 12). This crisis asks, How are qualitative studies to be evaluated in the contemporary, poststructural moment? The first two crises shape the third, which asks, Is it possible to effect change in the world if society is only and always a text? Clearly these crises intersect and blur, as do the answers to the questions they generate (see Ladson-Billings, 2000; Schwandt, 2000; Smith & Deemer, 2000).

The fifth moment, the postmodern period of experimental ethnographic writing, struggled to make sense of these crises. New ways of composing ethnography were explored (Ellis & Bochner, 1996). Theories were read as tales from the field. Writers struggled with different ways to represent the "Other," although they were now joined by new representational concerns (Fine, Weis, Weseen, & Wong, 2000; see also Fine & Weis, Volume 1, Chapter 3). Epistemologies from previously silenced groups emerged to offer solutions to these problems. The concept of the aloof observer was abandoned. More action, participatory, and activist-oriented research was on the horizon. The search for grand narratives was being replaced by more local, small-scale theories fitted to specific problems and specific situations.

The sixth moment, postexperimental inquiry (1995–2000), was a period of great excitement, with AltaMira Press, under the direction of Mitch Allen, taking the lead. AltaMira's book series titled *Ethnographic Alternatives*, for which Carolyn Ellis and Arthur Bochner served as series editors, captured this new excitement and brought a host of new authors into the interpretive community. The following description of the series from the publisher reflects its experimental tone: "Ethnographic Alternatives publishes experimental forms of qualitative writing that blur the boundaries between social sciences and humanities. Some volumes in the series . . . experiment with novel forms of expressing lived experience, including literary, poetic, autobiographical, multivoiced, conversational, critical, visual, performative and co-constructed representations."

During this same period, two major new qualitative journals began publication: *Qualitative Inquiry* and *Qualitative Research*. The editors of these journals were committed to publishing the very best new work. The success of these ventures framed the seventh moment, what we are calling the methodologically contested present (2000–2004). As discussed above, this is a period of conflict, great tension, and, in some quarters, retrenchment.

The eighth moment is now, the future (2005– ). In this moment scholars, as reviewed above, are confronting the methodological backlash associated with "Bush science" and the evidence-based social movement.

## Reading History

We draw several conclusions from this brief history, noting that it is, like all histories, somewhat arbitrary. First, each of the earlier historical moments is still operating in the present, either as legacy or as a set of practices that researchers continue to follow or argue against. The multiple and fractured histories of qualitative research now make it possible for any given researcher to attach a project to a canonical text from any of the above-described historical moments. Multiple criteria of evaluation compete for attention in this field. Second, an embarrassment of choices now characterizes the field of qualitative research. Researchers have never before had so many paradigms, strategies of inquiry, and methods of analysis to draw upon and utilize. Third, we are in a moment of discovery and rediscovery, as new ways of looking, interpreting, arguing, and writing are debated and discussed. Fourth, the qualitative research act can no longer be viewed from within a neutral or objective positivist perspective. Class, race, gender, and ethnicity shape inquiry, making research a multicultural process. Fifth, we are clearly not implying a progress narrative with our history. We are not saying that the cutting edge is located in the present. We are saying that the present is a politically charged space. Complex pressures both within and outside of the qualitative community are working to erase the positive developments of the past 30 years.

## ▣ QUALITATIVE RESEARCH AS PROCESS

Three interconnected, generic activities define the qualitative research process. They go by a variety of different labels, including *theory, analysis, ontology, epistemology,* and *methodology.* Behind these terms stands the personal biography of the researcher, who speaks from a particular class, gender, racial, cultural, and ethnic community perspective. The gendered, multiculturally situated researcher approaches the world with a set of ideas, a framework (theory, ontology) that specifies a set of questions (epistemology) that he or she then examines in specific ways (methodology, analysis). That is, the researcher collects empirical materials bearing on the question and then analyzes and writes about those materials. Every researcher speaks from within a distinct interpretive community that configures, in its special way, the multicultural, gendered components of the research act.

In this volume we treat these generic activities under five headings, or phases: the researcher and the researched as multicultural subjects, major paradigms and interpretive perspectives, research strategies, methods of collecting and analyzing empirical materials, and the art of interpretation. Behind and within each of these phases stands the biographically situated researcher. This individual enters the research process from inside an interpretive community. This community has its own historical research traditions, which constitute a distinct point of view. This perspective leads the researcher to adopt particular views of the "Other" who is studied. At the same time, the politics and the ethics of research must also be considered, for these concerns permeate every phase of the research process.

## ▣ THE OTHER AS RESEARCH SUBJECT

Since its early 20th-century birth in modern, interpretive form, qualitative research has been haunted by a double-faced ghost. On the one hand, qualitative researchers have assumed that qualified, competent observers can, with objectivity, clarity, and precision, report on their own observations of the social world, including the experiences of others. Second, researchers have held to the belief in a real subject, or real individual, who is present in the world and able, in some form, to report on his or her experiences. So armed, researchers could blend their own observations with the self-reports provided by subjects through interviews and life story, personal experience, and case study documents.

These two beliefs have led qualitative researchers across disciplines to seek a method that will allow them to record accurately their own observations while also uncovering the meanings their subjects bring to their life experiences. Such a method would rely on the subjective verbal and written expressions of meaning given by the individuals studied as windows into the inner lives of these persons. Since Dilthey (1900/1976), this search for a method has led to a perennial focus in the human disciplines on qualitative, interpretive methods.

Recently, as noted above, this position and its beliefs have come under assault. Poststructuralists and postmodernists have contributed to the understanding that there is no clear window into the inner life of an individual. Any gaze is always filtered through the lenses of language, gender, social class, race, and ethnicity. There are no objective observations, only observations socially situated in the worlds of—and between—the observer and the observed. Subjects, or individuals, are seldom able to give full explanations of their actions or intentions; all they can offer are accounts, or stories, about what they have done and why. No single method can grasp all the subtle variations in ongoing human experience. Consequently, qualitative researchers deploy a wide range of interconnected interpretive methods, always seeking better ways to make more understandable the worlds of experience they have studied.

Table 1.1 depicts the relationships we see among the five phases that define the research process. Behind all but one of these phases stands the biographically situated researcher. These five levels of activity, or practice, work their way through the biography of the researcher. We take them up briefly in order here; we discuss these phases more fully in our introductions to the individual parts of this volume.

## Phase 1: The Researcher

Our remarks above indicate the depth and complexity of the traditional and applied qualitative research perspectives into which a socially situated researcher enters. These traditions locate the researcher in history, simultaneously guiding and constraining the work that is done in any specific study. This field has always been characterized by diversity and conflict, and these are its most enduring traditions (see Greenwood & Levin, Volume 1, Chapter 2). As a carrier of this complex and contradictory history, the researcher must also confront the ethics and politics of research (see Fine & Weis, Volume 1, Chapter 3; Smith, Volume 1, Chapter 4; Bishop, Volume 1, Chapter 5; Christians, Volume 1, Chapter 6). Researching the native, the indigenous Other, while claiming to engage in value-free inquiry for the human disciplines is over. Today

**Table 1.1.**     The Research Process

*Phase 1: The Researcher as a Multicultural Subject*

History and research traditions
Conceptions of self and the Other
The ethics and politics of research

*Phase 2: Theoretical Paradigms and Perspectives*

Positivism, postpositivism
Interpretivism, constructivism, hermeneutics
Feminism(s)
Racialized discourses
Critical theory and Marxist models
Cultural studies models
Queer theory

*Phase 3: Research Strategies*

Design
Case study
Ethnography, participant observation, performance ethnography
Phenomenology, ethnomethodology
Grounded theory
Life history, *testimonio*
Historical method
Action and applied research
Clinical research

*Phase 4: Methods of Collection and Analysis*

Interviewing
Observing
Artifacts, documents, and records
Visual methods
Autoethnography
Data management methods
Computer-assisted analysis
Textual analysis
Focus groups
Applied ethnography

*Phase 5: The Art, Practices, and Politics of Interpretation and Evaluation*

Criteria for judging adequacy
Practices and politics of interpretation
Writing as interpretation
Policy analysis
Evaluation traditions
Applied research

researchers struggle to develop situational and transsituational ethics that apply to all forms of the research act and its human-to-human relationships. We no longer have the option of deferring the decolonization project.

## Phase 2: Interpretive Paradigms

All qualitative researchers are philosophers in that "universal sense in which all human beings . . . are guided by highly abstract principles" (Bateson, 1972, p. 320). These principles combine beliefs about ontology (What kind of being is the human being? What is the nature of reality?), epistemology (What is the relationship between the inquirer and the known?), and methodology (How do we know the world, or gain knowledge of it?) (see Guba, 1990, p. 18; Lincoln & Guba, 1985, pp. 14–15; see also Guba & Lincoln, Volume 1, Chapter 8). These beliefs shape how the qualitative researcher sees the world and acts in it. The researcher is "bound within a net of epistemological and ontological premises which—regardless of ultimate truth or falsity—become partially self-validating" (Bateson, 1972, p. 314).

The net that contains the researcher's epistemological, ontological, and methodological premises may be termed a *paradigm,* or an interpretive framework, a "basic set of beliefs that guides action" (Guba, 1990, p. 17). All research is interpretive; it is guided by the researcher's set of beliefs and feelings about the world and how it should be understood and studied. Some beliefs may be taken for granted, invisible, only assumed, whereas others are highly problematic and controversial. Each interpretive paradigm makes particular demands on the researcher, including the questions the researcher asks and the interpretations he or she brings to them.

At the most general level, four major interpretive paradigms structure qualitative research: positivist and postpositivist, constructivist-interpretive, critical (Marxist, emancipatory), and feminist-poststructural. These four abstract paradigms become more complicated at the level of concrete specific interpretive communities. At this level it is possible to identify not only the constructivist, but also multiple versions of feminism (Afrocentric and poststructural),[17] as well as specific ethnic, Marxist, and cultural studies paradigms. These perspectives, or paradigms, are examined in Part II of Volume 1.

The paradigms examined in Part II work against and alongside (and some within) the positivist and postpositivist models. They all work within relativist ontologies (multiple constructed realities), interpretive epistemologies (the knower and known interact and shape one another), and interpretive, naturalistic methods.

Table 1.2 presents these paradigms and their assumptions, including their criteria for evaluating research, and the typical form that an interpretive or theoretical statement assumes in each paradigm.[18] These paradigms are explored in considerable detail in the chapters in Volume 1, Part II by Guba and Lincoln (Chapter 8), Olesen (Chapter 10), Ladson-Billings and Donnor (Chapter 11), Kincheloe and McLaren (Chapter 12), Saukko (Chapter 13), and Plummer (Chapter 14). We have discussed the

**Table 1.2.**      Interpretive Paradigms

| Paradigm/Theory | Criteria | Form of Theory | Type of Narration |
|---|---|---|---|
| Positivist/ postpositivist | Internal, external validity | Logical-deductive, grounded | Scientific report |
| Constructivist | Trustworthiness, credibility, transferability, confirmability | Substantive-formal | Interpretive case studies, ethnographic fiction |
| Feminist | Afrocentric, lived experience, dialogue, caring, accountability, race, class, gender, reflexivity, praxis, emotion, concrete grounding | Critical, standpoint | Essays, stories, experimental writing |
| Ethnic | Afrocentric, lived experience, dialogue, caring, accountability, race, class, gender | Standpoint, critical, historical | Essays, fables, dramas |
| Marxist | Emancipatory theory, falsifiability dialogical, race, class, gender | Critical, historical, economic | Historical, economic, sociocultural analyses |
| Cultural studies | Cultural practices, praxis, social texts, subjectivities | Social criticism | Cultural theory-as criticism |
| Queer theory | Reflexivity, deconstruction | Social criticism, historical analysis | Theory as criticism, autobiography |

positivist and postpositivist paradigms above. They work from within a realist and critical realist ontology and objective epistemologies, and they rely on experimental, quasi-experimental, survey, and rigorously defined qualitative methodologies. Ryan and Bernard (2000) have developed elements of this paradigm.

The constructivist paradigm assumes a relativist ontology (there are multiple realities), a subjectivist epistemology (knower and respondent cocreate understandings), and a naturalistic (in the natural world) set of methodological procedures. Findings are usually presented in terms of the criteria of grounded theory or pattern theories (see Guba & Lincoln, Volume 1, Chapter 8; Charmaz, Volume 2, Chapter 7; see also Ryan & Bernard, 2000). Terms such as *credibility, transferability, dependability,* and *confirmability* replace the usual positivist criteria of internal and external validity, reliability, and objectivity.

Feminist, ethnic, Marxist, cultural studies, and queer theory models privilege a materialist-realist ontology; that is, the real world makes a material difference in terms of race, class, and gender. Subjectivist epistemologies and naturalistic methodologies (usually ethnographies) are also employed. Empirical materials and theoretical arguments are evaluated in terms of their emancipatory implications. Criteria from gender and racial communities (e.g., African American) may be applied (emotionality and feeling, caring, personal accountability, dialogue).

Poststructural feminist theories emphasize problems with the social text, its logic, and its inability ever to represent the world of lived experience fully. Positivist and postpositivist criteria of evaluation are replaced by other criteria, including the reflexive, multivoiced text that is grounded in the experiences of oppressed peoples.

The cultural studies and queer theory paradigms are multifocused, with many different strands drawing from Marxism, feminism, and the postmodern sensibility (see Saukko, Volume 1, Chapter 13; Plummer, Volume 1, Chapter 14; Richardson & St. Pierre, Chapter 15, this volume). There is a tension between a humanistic cultural studies, which stresses lived experiences (meaning), and a more structural cultural studies project, which stresses the structural and material determinants (race, class, gender) and effects of experience. Of course, there are two sides to every coin, and both sides are needed—indeed, both are critical. The cultural studies and queer theory paradigms use methods strategically—that is, as resources for understanding and for producing resistances to local structures of domination. Scholars may do close textual readings and discourse analyses of cultural texts (see Olesen, Volume 1, Chapter 10; Saukko, Volume 1, Chapter 13; Chase, Chapter 2, this volume) as well as local, online, reflexive, and critical ethnographies, open-ended interviewing, and participant observation. The focus is on how race, class, and gender are produced and enacted in historically specific situations.

Paradigm and personal history in hand, focused on a concrete empirical problem to examine, the researcher now moves to the next stage of the research process—namely, working with a specific strategy of inquiry.

## Phase 3: Strategies of Inquiry and Interpretive Paradigms

Table 1.1 presents some of the major strategies of inquiry a researcher may use. Phase 3 begins with research design, which, broadly conceived, involves a clear focus on the research question, the purposes of the study, and "what information most appropriately will answer specific research questions, and which strategies are most effective for obtaining it" (LeCompte & Preissle, 1993, p. 30; see also Cheek, Volume 2, Chapter 2). A research design describes a flexible set of guidelines that connect theoretical paradigms first to strategies of inquiry and second to methods for collecting empirical materials.

A research design situates the researcher in the empirical world and connects him or her to specific sites, persons, groups, institutions, and bodies of relevant interpretive material, including documents and archives. A research design also specifies how the investigator will address the two critical issues of representation and legitimation.

A strategy of inquiry comprises a bundle of skills, assumptions, and practices that the researcher employs as he or she moves from paradigm to the empirical world. Strategies of inquiry put paradigms of interpretation into motion. At the same time, strategies of inquiry also connect the researcher to specific methods of collecting and analyzing empirical materials. For example, the case study strategy relies on interviewing, observing, and document analysis. Research strategies implement and anchor paradigms in specific empirical sites or in specific methodological practices, such as making a case an object of study. These strategies include the case study, phenomenological and ethnomethodological techniques, and the use of grounded theory, as well as biographical, autoethnographic, historical, action, and clinical methods. Each of these strategies is connected to a complex literature, and each has a separate history, exemplary works, and preferred ways of putting the strategy into motion.

## Phase 4: Methods of Collecting and Analyzing Empirical Materials

Qualitative researchers employ several methods for collecting empirical materials.[19] These methods, which are taken up in this volume, Part I (Part IV in the *Handbook*), include interviewing; direct observation; the analysis of artifacts, documents, and cultural records; the use of visual materials; and the use of personal experience. The researcher may also read and analyze interviews or cultural texts in a variety of different ways, including content, narrative, and semiotic strategies. Faced with large amounts of qualitative materials, the investigator seeks ways of managing and interpreting these documents, and here data management methods and computer-assisted models of analysis may be of use.

## Phase 5: The Art and Politics of Interpretation and Evaluation

Qualitative research is endlessly creative and interpretive. The researcher does not just leave the field with mountains of empirical materials and then easily write up his or her findings. Qualitative interpretations are constructed. The researcher first creates a field text consisting of field notes and documents from the field, what Roger Sanjek (1990, p. 386) calls "indexing" and David Plath (1990, p. 374) calls "filework." The writer-as-interpreter moves from this text to a research text: notes and interpretations based on the field text. This text is then re-created as a working interpretive document that contains the writer's initial attempts to make sense of what he or she has learned. Finally, the writer produces the public text that comes to the reader. This final tale from the field may assume several forms: confessional, realist, impressionistic, critical, formal, literary, analytic, grounded theory, and so on (see Van Maanen, 1988).

The interpretive practice of making sense of one's findings is both artistic and political. Multiple criteria for evaluating qualitative research now exist, and those that we emphasize stress the situated, relational, and textual structures of the ethnographic experience. There is no single interpretive truth. As we argued earlier, there are multiple interpretive communities, each with its own criteria for evaluating interpretations.

Program evaluation is a major site of qualitative research, and qualitative researchers can influence social policy in important ways. The chapters by Greenwood and Levin (Volume 1, Chapter 2), Kemmis and McTaggart (Volume 2, Chapter 10), Miller and Crabtree (Volume 2, Chapter 11), Tedlock (Volume 2, Chapter 5), Smith and Hodkinson (this volume, Chapter 13), and House (this volume, Chapter 19) trace and discuss the rich history of applied qualitative research in the social sciences. This is the critical site where theory, method, praxis, action, and policy all come together. Qualitative researchers can isolate target populations, show the immediate effects of certain programs on such groups, and isolate the constraints that operate against policy changes in such settings. Action-oriented and clinically oriented qualitative researchers can also create spaces where those who are studied (the Other) can speak. The evaluator becomes the conduit for making such voices heard.

## ▣ Bridging the Historical Moments: What Comes Next?

In Chapter 15 of this volume, Richardson and St. Pierre argue that we are already in the post-"post" period—post-poststructuralism, post-postmodernism, post-postexperimentalism. What this means for interpretive ethnographic practices is still not clear, but it is certain that things will never again be the same. We are in a new age where messy, uncertain, multivoiced texts, cultural criticism, and new experimental works will become more common, as will more reflexive forms of fieldwork, analysis, and intertextual representation. The subject of our final essays in this volume is these sixth, seventh, eighth, and ninth moments. It is true that, as the poet said, the center no longer holds. We can reflect on what should be at the new center.

Thus we come full circle. Returning to our bridge metaphor, the chapters that follow take the researcher back and forth through every phase of the research act. Like a good bridge, the chapters provide for two-way traffic, coming and going between moments, formations, and interpretive communities. Each chapter examines the relevant histories, controversies, and current practices that are associated with each paradigm, strategy, and method. Each chapter also offers projections for the future, where a specific paradigm, strategy, or method will be 10 years from now, deep into the formative years of the 21st century.

In reading the chapters that follow, it is important to remember that the field of qualitative research is defined by a series of tensions, contradictions, and hesitations. These tensions work back and forth between and among the broad, doubting postmodern sensibility; the more certain, more traditional positivist, postpositivist, and naturalistic conceptions of this project; and an increasingly conservative, neoliberal global environment. All of the chapters that follow are caught in and articulate these tensions.

# ▣ NOTES

1. Recall bell hooks's (1990, p. 127) reading of the famous photo of Stephen Tyler doing fieldwork in India that appears on the cover of *Writing Culture* (Clifford & Marcus, 1986). In the picture, Tyler is seated at some distance from three dark-skinned persons. One, a child, is poking his or her head out of a basket. A woman is hidden in the shadows of the hut. A man, a checkered white-and-black shawl across his shoulder, elbow propped on his knee, hand resting along the side of his face, is staring at Tyler. Tyler is writing in a field journal. A piece of white cloth is attached to his glasses, perhaps shielding him from the sun. This patch of whiteness marks Tyler as the white male writer studying these passive brown and black persons. Indeed, the brown male's gaze signals some desire, or some attachment to Tyler. In contrast, the female's gaze is completely hidden by the shadows and by the words of the book's title, which are printed across her face.

2. Qualitative research has separate and distinguished histories in education, social work, communications, psychology, history, organizational studies, medical science, anthropology, and sociology.

3. Some definitions are in order here. *Positivism* asserts that objective accounts of the real world can be given. *Postpositivism* holds that only partially objective accounts of the world can be produced, for all methods for examining such accounts are flawed. According to *foundationalism,* we can have an ultimate grounding for our knowledge claims about the world, and this involves the use of empiricist and positivist epistemologies (Schwandt, 1997a, p. 103). *Nonfoundationalism* holds that we can make statements about the world without "recourse to ultimate proof or foundations for that knowing" (Schwandt, 1997a, p. 102). *Quasi-foundationalism* holds that we can make certain knowledge claims about the world based on neorealist criteria, including the correspondence concept of truth; there is an independent reality that can be mapped (see Smith & Hodkinson, Chapter 13, this volume).

4. Jameson (1991, pp. 3–4) reminds us that any periodization hypothesis is always suspect, even one that rejects linear, stagelike models. It is never clear to what reality a stage refers, and what divides one stage from another is always debatable. Our eight moments are meant to mark discernible shifts in style, genre, epistemology, ethics, politics, and aesthetics.

5. Several scholars have termed this model a *progress narrative* (Alasuutari, 2004, pp. 599–600; Seale et al., 2004, p. 2). Critics assert that we believe that the most recent moment is the most up-to-date, the avant-garde, the cutting edge (Alasuutari, 2004, p. 601). Naturally, we dispute this reading. Teddlie and Tashakkori (2003, pp. 5–8) have modified our historical periods to fit their historical analysis of the major moments in the emergence of the use of mixed methods in social science research in the past century.

6. Some additional definitions are needed here. *Structuralism* holds that any system is made up of a set of oppositional categories embedded in language. *Semiotics* is the science of signs or sign systems—a structuralist project. According to *poststructuralism,* language is an unstable system of referents, thus it is impossible ever to capture completely the meaning of an

action, text, or intention. *Postmodernism* is a contemporary sensibility, developing since World War II, that privileges no single authority, method, or paradigm. *Hermeneutics* is an approach to the analysis of texts that stresses how prior understandings and prejudices shape the interpretive process. *Phenomenology* is a complex system of ideas associated with the works of Husserl, Heidegger, Sartre, Merleau-Ponty, and Alfred Schutz. *Cultural studies* is a complex, interdisciplinary field that merges critical theory, feminism, and poststructuralism.

7. Of course, all settings are natural—that is, places where everyday experiences take place. Qualitative researchers study people doing things together in the places where these things are done (Becker, 1986). There is no field site or natural place where one goes to do this kind of work (see also Gupta & Ferguson, 1997, p. 8). The site is constituted through the researcher's interpretive practices. Historically, analysts have distinguished between experimental (laboratory) and field (natural) research settings, hence the argument that qualitative research is naturalistic. Activity theory erases this distinction (Keller & Keller, 1996, p. 20; Vygotsky, 1978).

8. According to Weinstein and Weinstein (1991), "The meaning of *bricoleur* in French popular speech is 'someone who works with his (or her) hands and uses devious means compared to those of the craftsman.' . . . the *bricoleur* is practical and gets the job done" (p. 161). These authors provide a history of the term, connecting it to the works of the German sociologist and social theorist Georg Simmel and, by implication, Baudelaire. Hammersley (1999) disputes our use of this term. Following Lévi-Strauss, he reads the *bricoleur* as a mythmaker. He suggests that the term be replaced with the notion of the boatbuilder. Hammersley also quarrels with our "moments" model of the history of qualitative research, contending that it implies some sense of progress.

9. Brian De Palma reproduced this baby carriage scene in his 1987 film *The Untouchables*.

10. In the harbor, the muzzles of the *Potemkin's* two huge guns swing slowly toward the camera. Words on the screen inform us, "The brutal military power answered by guns of the battleship." A final famous three-shot montage sequence shows first a sculpture of a sleeping lion, then a lion rising from his sleep, and finally the lion roaring, symbolizing the rage of the Russian people (Cook, 1981, p. 167). In this sequence Eisenstein uses montage to expand time, creating a psychological duration for this horrible event. By drawing out this sequence, by showing the baby in the carriage, the soldiers firing on the citizens, the blood on the mother's glove, the descending carriage on the steps, he suggests a level of destruction of great magnitude.

11. Here it is relevant to make a distinction between techniques that are used across disciplines and methods that are used within disciplines. Ethnomethodologists, for example, employ their approach as a method, whereas others selectively borrow that method as a technique for their own applications. Harry Wolcott (personal communication, 1993) suggests this distinction. It is also relevant to make distinctions among topic, method, and resource. Methods can be studied as topics of inquiry; that is how a case study gets done. In this ironic, ethnomethodological sense, method is both a resource and a topic of inquiry.

12. Indeed, any attempt to give an essential definition of qualitative research requires a qualitative analysis of the circumstances that produce such a definition.

13. In this sense all research is qualitative, because "the observer is at the center of the research process" (Vidich & Lyman, 2000, p. 39).

14. See Lincoln and Guba (1985) for an extension and elaboration of this tradition in the mid-1980s, and for more recent extensions see Taylor and Bogdan (1998) and Creswell (1998).

15. Greenblatt (1997, pp. 15–18) offers a useful deconstructive reading of the many meanings and practices Geertz brings to the term *thick description.*

16. These works marginalized and minimized the contributions of standpoint feminist theory and research to this discourse (see Behar, 1995, p. 3; Gordon, 1995, p. 432).

17. Olesen (Volume 1, Chapter 10) identifies three strands of feminist research: mainstream empirical, standpoint and cultural studies, and poststructural, postmodern. She places Afrocentric and other models of color under the cultural studies and postmodern categories.

18. These, of course, are our interpretations of these paradigms and interpretive styles.

19. *Empirical materials* is the preferred term for what traditionally have been described as data.

## ▣ REFERENCES

Alasuutari, P. (2004). The globalization of qualitative research. In C. Seale, G. Gobo, J. F. Gubrium, & D. Silverman (Eds.), *Qualitative research practice* (pp. 595–608). London: Sage.

Aronowitz, S. (1988). *Science as power: Discourse and ideology in modern society.* Minneapolis: University of Minnesota Press.

Atkinson, E. (2004). Thinking outside the box: An exercise in heresy. *Qualitative Inquiry, 10,* 111–129.

Bateson, G. (1972). *Steps to an ecology of mind.* New York: Ballantine.

Battiste, M. (2000). Introduction: Unfolding lessons of colonization. In M. Battiste (Ed.), *Reclaiming indigenous voice and vision* (pp. xvi–xxx). Vancouver: University of British Columbia Press.

Becker, H. S. (1970). Problems of inference and proof in participant observation. In H. S. Becker, *Sociological work: Method and substance.* Chicago: Aldine. (Reprinted from *American Sociological Review,* 1958, *23,* 652–660)

Becker, H. S. (1986). *Doing things together.* Evanston, IL: Northwestern University Press.

Becker, H. S. (1996). The epistemology of qualitative research. In R. Jessor, A. Colby, & R. A. Shweder (Eds.), *Ethnography and human development: Context and meaning in social inquiry* (pp. 53–71). Chicago: University of Chicago Press.

Becker, H. S. (1998). *Tricks of the trade: How to think about your research while you're doing it.* Chicago: University of Chicago Press.

Becker, H. S., Geer, B., Hughes, E. C., & Strauss, A. L. (1961). *Boys in white: Student culture in medical school.* Chicago: University of Chicago Press.

Behar, R. (1995). Introduction: Out of exile. In R. Behar & D. A. Gordon (Eds.), *Women writing culture* (pp. 1–29). Berkeley: University of California Press.

Bloch, M. (2004). A discourse that disciplines, governs, and regulates: The National Research Council's report on scientific research in education. *Qualitative Inquiry, 10,* 96–110.

Bochner, A. P., & Ellis, C. (Eds.). (2002). *Ethnographically speaking: Autoethnography, literature, and aesthetics.* Walnut Creek, CA: AltaMira.

Bogdan, R., & Taylor, S. J. (1975). *Introduction to qualitative research methods: A phenomenological approach to the social sciences.* New York: John Wiley.

Campbell, D. T., & Stanley, J. C. (1963). *Experimental and quasi-experimental designs for research.* Chicago: Rand McNally.

Cannella, G. S., & Lincoln, Y. S. (2004a). Dangerous discourses II: Comprehending and countering the redeployment of discourses (and resources) in the generation of liberatory inquiry. *Qualitative Inquiry, 10,* 165–174.

Cannella, G. S., & Lincoln, Y. S. (2004b). Epilogue: Claiming a critical public social science— reconceptualizing and redeploying research. *Qualitative Inquiry, 10,* 298–309.

Carey, J. W. (1989). *Communication as culture: Essays on media and society.* Boston: Unwin Hyman.

Cicourel, A. V. (1964). *Method and measurement in sociology.* New York: Free Press.

Clifford, J. (1988). *The predicament of culture: Twentieth-century ethnography, literature, and art.* Cambridge, MA: Harvard University Press.

Clifford, J., & Marcus, G. E. (Eds.). (1986). *Writing culture: The poetics and politics of ethnography.* Berkeley: University of California Press.

Clough, P. T. (1998). *The end(s) of ethnography: From realism to social criticism* (2nd ed.). New York: Peter Lang.

Cook, D. A. (1981). *A history of narrative film.* New York: W. W. Norton.

Creswell, J. W. (1998). *Qualitative inquiry and research design: Choosing among five traditions.* Thousand Oaks, CA: Sage.

Danermark, B., Ekström, M., Jakobsen, L., & Karlsson, J. C. (2002). *Explaining society: Critical realism in the social sciences.* London: Routledge.

de Certeau, M. (1984). *The practice of everyday life.* Berkeley: University of California Press.

Denzin, N. K. (1970). *The research act.* Chicago: Aldine.

Denzin, N. K. (1978). *The research act: A theoretical introduction to sociological methods* (2nd ed.). New York: McGraw-Hill.

Denzin, N. K. (1997). *Interpretive ethnography: Ethnographic practices for the 21st century.* Thousand Oaks, CA: Sage.

Denzin, N. K. (2003). *Performance ethnography: Critical pedagogy and the politics of culture.* Thousand Oaks, CA: Sage.

Dilthey, W. L. (1976). *Selected writings.* Cambridge: Cambridge University Press. (Original work published 1900)

Diversi, M. (1998). Glimpses of street life: Representing lived experience through short stories. *Qualitative Inquiry, 4,* 131–137.

Ellis, C. (2004). *The ethnographic I: A methodological novel about autoethnography.* Walnut Creek, CA: AltaMira.

Ellis, C., & Bochner, A. P. (Eds.). (1996). *Composing ethnography: Alternative forms of qualitative writing.* Walnut Creek, CA: AltaMira.

Filstead, W. J. (Ed.). (1970). *Qualitative methodology.* Chicago: Markham.

Fine, M., Weis, L., Weseen, S., & Wong, L. (2000). For whom? Qualitative research, representations, and social responsibilities. In N. K. Denzin & Y. S. Lincoln (Eds.), *Handbook of qualitative research* (2nd ed., pp. 107–131). Thousand Oaks, CA: Sage.

Flick, U. (2002). *An introduction to qualitative research* (2nd ed.). London: Sage.

Geertz, C. (1973). *The interpretation of cultures: Selected essays.* New York: Basic Books.

Geertz, C. (1983). *Local knowledge: Further essays in interpretive anthropology.* New York: Basic Books.

Geertz, C. (1988). *Works and lives: The anthropologist as author.* Stanford, CA: Stanford University Press.

Glaser, B. G. (1992). *Emergence vs. forcing: Basics of grounded theory.* Mill Valley, CA: Sociology Press.

Glaser, B. G., & Strauss, A. L. (1967). *The discovery of grounded theory: Strategies for qualitative research.* Chicago: Aldine.

Goodall, H. L., Jr. (2000). *Writing the new ethnography.* Walnut Creek, CA: AltaMira.

Gordon, D. A. (1995). Culture writing women: Inscribing feminist anthropology. In R. Behar & D. A. Gordon (Eds.), *Women writing culture* (pp. 429–441). Berkeley: University of California Press.

Greenblatt, S. (1997). The touch of the real. In S. B. Ortner (Ed.), The fate of "culture": Geertz and beyond [Special issue]. *Representations, 59,* 14–29.

Guba, E. G. (1990). The alternative paradigm dialog. In E. G. Guba (Ed.), *The paradigm dialog* (pp. 17–30). Newbury Park, CA: Sage.

Guba, E. G., & Lincoln, Y. S. (1989). *Fourth generation evaluation.* Newbury Park, CA: Sage.

Gupta, A., & Ferguson, J. (Eds.). (1997). Discipline and practice: "The field" as site, method, and location in anthropology. In A. Gupta & J. Ferguson (Eds.), *Anthropological locations: Boundaries and grounds of a field science* (pp. 1–46). Berkeley: University of California Press.

Hammersley, M. (1992). *What's wrong with ethnography? Methodological explorations.* London: Routledge.

Hammersley, M. (1999). Not bricolage but boatbuilding: Exploring two metaphors for thinking about ethnography. *Journal of Contemporary Ethnography, 28,* 574–585.

Harper, D. (1987). *Working knowledge: Skill and community in a small shop.* Chicago: University of Chicago Press.

Holman Jones, S. (1999). Torch. *Qualitative Inquiry, 5,* 235–250.

hooks, b. (1990). *Yearning: Race, gender, and cultural politics.* Boston: South End.

Howe, K. R. (2004). A critique of experimentalism. *Qualitative Inquiry, 10,* 42–61.

Huber, J. (1995). Centennial essay: Institutional perspectives on sociology. *American Journal of Sociology, 101,* 194–216.

Jackson, M. (1998). *Minima ethnographica: Intersubjectivity and the anthropological project.* Chicago: University of Chicago Press.

Jameson, F. (1991). *Postmodernism; or, The cultural logic of late capitalism.* Durham, NC: Duke University Press.

Keller, C. M., & Keller, J. D. (1996). *Cognition and tool use: The blacksmith at work.* New York: Cambridge University Press.

Kincheloe, J. L. (2001). Describing the bricolage: Conceptualizing a new rigor in qualitative research. *Qualitative Inquiry, 7,* 679–692.

Ladson-Billings, G. (2000). Socialized discourses and ethnic epistemologies. In N. K. Denzin & Y. S. Lincoln (Eds.), *Handbook of qualitative research* (2nd ed., pp. 257–277). Thousand Oaks, CA: Sage.

Lather, P. (1993). Fertile obsession: Validity after poststructuralism. *Sociological Quarterly, 35,* 673–694.

Lather, P. (2004). This *is* your father's paradigm: Government intrusion and the case of qualitative research in education. *Qualitative Inquiry, 10,* 15–34.

Lather, P., & Smithies, C. (1997). *Troubling the angels: Women living with HIV/AIDS.* Boulder, CO: Westview.

LeCompte, M. D., & Preissle, J. (with Tesch, R.). (1993). *Ethnography and qualitative design in educational research* (2nd ed.). New York: Academic Press.

Lévi-Strauss, C. (1966). *The savage mind* (2nd ed.). Chicago: University of Chicago Press.

Lincoln, Y. S. (1999, June). *Courage, vulnerability and truth.* Keynote address delivered at the conference "Reclaiming Voice II: Ethnographic Inquiry and Qualitative Research in a Postmodern Age," University of California, Irvine.

Lincoln, Y. S., & Cannella, G. S. (2004a). Dangerous discourses: Methodological conservatism and governmental regimes of truth. *Qualitative Inquiry, 10,* 5–14.

Lincoln, Y. S., & Cannella, G. S. (2004b). Qualitative research, power, and the radical Right. *Qualitative Inquiry, 10,* 175–201.

Lincoln, Y. S., & Guba, E. G. (1985). *Naturalistic inquiry.* Beverly Hills, CA: Sage.

Lincoln, Y. S., & Tierney, W. G. (2004). Qualitative research and institutional review boards. *Qualitative Inquiry, 10,* 219–234.

Lofland, J. (1971). *Analyzing social settings.* Belmont, CA: Wadsworth.

Lofland, J. (1995). Analytic ethnography: Features, failings, and futures. *Journal of Contemporary Ethnography, 24,* 30–67.

Lofland, J., & Lofland, L. H. (1984). *Analyzing social settings: A guide to qualitative observation and analysis* (2nd ed.). Belmont, CA: Wadsworth.

Lofland, J., & Lofland, L. H. (1995). *Analyzing social settings: A guide to qualitative observation and analysis* (3rd ed.). Belmont, CA: Wadsworth.

Lofland, L. H. (1980). The 1969 Blumer-Hughes Talk. *Urban Life and Culture, 8,* 248–260.

Malinowski, B. (1948). *Magic, science and religion, and other essays.* New York: Natural History Press. (Original work published 1916)

Malinowski, B. (1967). *A diary in the strict sense of the term* (N. Guterman, Trans.). New York: Harcourt, Brace & World.

Marcus, G. E., & Fischer, M. M. J. (1986). *Anthropology as cultural critique: An experimental moment in the human sciences.* Chicago: University of Chicago Press.

Maxwell, J. A. (2004). Reemergent scientism, postmodernism, and dialogue across differences. *Qualitative Inquiry, 10,* 35–41.

Monaco, J. (1981). *How to read a film: The art, technology, language, history and theory of film* (Rev. ed.). New York: Oxford University Press.

Nelson, C., Treichler, P. A., & Grossberg, L. (1992). Cultural studies: An introduction. In L. Grossberg, C. Nelson, & P. A. Treichler (Eds.), *Cultural studies* (pp. 1–16). New York: Routledge.

Ortner, S. B. (1997). Introduction. In S. B. Ortner (Ed.), The fate of "culture": Geertz and beyond [Special issue]. *Representations, 59,* 1–13.

Pelias, R. J. (2004). *A methodology of the heart: Evoking academic and daily life.* Walnut Creek, CA: AltaMira.

Plath, D. W. (1990). Fieldnotes, filed notes, and the conferring of note. In R. Sanjek (Ed.), *Fieldnotes: The makings of anthropology* (pp. 371–384). Ithaca, NY: Cornell University Press.

Popkewitz, T. S. (2004). Is the National Research Council committee's report on scientific research in education scientific? On trusting the manifesto. *Qualitative Inquiry, 10,* 62–78.

Richardson, L. (1997). *Fields of play: Constructing an academic life.* New Brunswick, NJ: Rutgers University Press.

Richardson, L. (2000). Writing: A method of inquiry. In N. K. Denzin & Y. S. Lincoln (Eds.), *Handbook of qualitative research* (2nd ed., pp. 923–948). Thousand Oaks, CA: Sage.

Richardson, L., & Lockridge, E. (2004). *Travels with Ernest: Crossing the literary/sociological divide.* Walnut Creek, CA: AltaMira.

Roffman, P., & Purdy, J. (1981). *The Hollywood social problem film.* Bloomington: Indiana University Press.

Ronai, C. R. (1998). Sketching with Derrida: An ethnography of a researcher/erotic dancer. *Qualitative Inquiry, 4,* 405–420.

Rosaldo, R. (1989). *Culture and truth: The remaking of social analysis.* Boston: Beacon.

Ryan, G. W., & Bernard, H. R. (2000). Data management and analysis methods. In N. K. Denzin & Y. S. Lincoln (Eds.), *Handbook of qualitative research* (2nd ed., pp. 769–802). Thousand Oaks, CA: Sage.

Ryan, K. E., & Hood, L. K. (2004). Guarding the castle and opening the gates. *Qualitative Inquiry, 10,* 79–95.

St. Pierre, E. A. (2004). Refusing alternatives: A science of contestation. *Qualitative Inquiry, 10,* 130–139.

Sanjek, R. (1990). On ethnographic validity. In R. Sanjek (Ed.), *Fieldnotes: The makings of anthropology* (pp. 385–418). Ithaca, NY: Cornell University Press.

Schwandt, T. A. (1997a). *Qualitative inquiry: A dictionary of terms.* Thousand Oaks, CA: Sage.

Schwandt, T. A. (1997b). Textual gymnastics, ethics and angst. In W. G. Tierney & Y. S. Lincoln (Eds.), *Representation and the text: Re-framing the narrative voice* (pp. 305–311). Albany: State University of New York Press.

Schwandt, T. A. (2000). Three epistemological stances for qualitative inquiry: Interpretivism, hermeneutics, and social constructionism. In N. K. Denzin & Y. S. Lincoln (Eds.), *Handbook of qualitative research* (2nd ed., pp. 189–213). Thousand Oaks, CA: Sage.

Seale, C., Gobo, G., Gubrium, J. F., & Silverman, D. (2004). Introduction: Inside qualitative research. In C. Seale, G. Gobo, J. F. Gubrium, & D. Silverman (Eds.), *Qualitative research practice* (pp. 1–11). London: Sage.

Semali, L. M., & Kincheloe, J. L. (1999). Introduction: What is indigenous knowledge and why should we study it? In L. M. Semali & J. L. Kincheloe (Eds.), *What is indigenous knowledge? Voices from the academy* (pp. 3–57). New York: Falmer.

Silverman, D. (1997). Towards an aesthetics of research. In D. Silverman (Ed.), *Qualitative research: Theory, method and practice* (pp. 239–253). London: Sage.

Smith, A. D. (1993). *Fires in the mirror: Crown Heights, Brooklyn, and other identities.* New York: Anchor.

Smith, J. K., & Deemer, D. K. (2000). The problem of criteria in the age of relativism. In N. K. Denzin & Y. S. Lincoln (Eds.), *Handbook of qualitative research* (2nd ed., pp. 877–896). Thousand Oaks, CA: Sage.

Smith, L. T. (1999). *Decolonizing methodologies: Research and indigenous peoples.* Dunedin, New Zealand: University of Otago Press.

Snow, D., & Morrill, C. (1995). Ironies, puzzles, and contradictions in Denzin and Lincoln's vision of qualitative research. *Journal of Contemporary Ethnography, 22,* 358–362.

Spindler, G., & Spindler, L. (1992). Cultural process and ethnography: An anthropological perspective. In M. D. LeCompte, W. L. Millroy, & J. Preissle (Eds.), *The handbook of qualitative research in education* (pp. 53–92). New York: Academic Press.

Stocking, G. W., Jr. (1986). Anthropology and the science of the irrational: Malinowski's encounter with Freudian psychoanalysis. In G. W. Stocking, Jr. (Ed.), *Malinowski, Rivers, Benedict and others: Essays on culture and personality* (pp. 13–49). Madison: University of Wisconsin Press.

Stocking, G. W., Jr. (1989). The ethnographic sensibility of the 1920s and the dualism of the anthropological tradition. In G. W. Stocking, Jr. (Ed.), *Romantic motives: Essays on anthropological sensibility* (pp. 208–276). Madison: University of Wisconsin Press.

Stoller, P., & Olkes, C. (1987). *In sorcery's shadow: A memoir of apprenticeship among the Songhay of Niger.* Chicago: University of Chicago Press.

Strauss, A. L., & Corbin, J. (1998). *Basics of qualitative research: Techniques and procedures for developing grounded theory* (2nd ed.). Thousand Oaks, CA: Sage.

Taylor, S. J., & Bogdan, R. (1998). *Introduction to qualitative research methods: A guidebook and resource* (3rd ed.). New York: John Wiley.

Teddlie, C., & Tashakkori, A. (2003). Major issues and controversies in the use of mixed methods in the social and behavioral sciences. In A. Tashakkori & C. Teddlie (Eds.), *Handbook of mixed methods in social and behavioral research* (pp. 3–50). Thousand Oaks, CA: Sage.

Tierney, W. G. (2000). Undaunted courage: Life history and the postmodern challenge. In N. K. Denzin & Y. S. Lincoln (Eds.), *Handbook of qualitative research* (2nd ed., pp. 537–553). Thousand Oaks, CA: Sage.

Trujillo, N. (2004). *In search of Naunny's grave: Age, class, gender, and ethnicity in an American family.* Walnut Creek, CA: AltaMira.

Turner, V., & Bruner, E. (Eds.). (1986). *The anthropology of experience.* Urbana: University of Illinois Press.

Van Maanen, J. (1988). *Tales of the field: On writing ethnography.* Chicago: University of Chicago Press.

Vidich, A. J., & Lyman, S. M. (1994). Qualitative methods: Their history in sociology and anthropology. In N. K. Denzin & Y. S. Lincoln (Eds.), *Handbook of qualitative research* (pp. 23–59). Thousand Oaks, CA: Sage.

Vidich, A. J., & Lyman, S. M. (2000). Qualitative methods: Their history in sociology and anthropology. In N. K. Denzin & Y. S. Lincoln (Eds.), *Handbook of qualitative research* (2nd ed., pp. 37–84). Thousand Oaks, CA: Sage.

Vygotsky, L. S. (1978). *Mind in society: The development of higher psychological processes* (M. Cole, V. John-Steiner, S. Scribner, & E. Souberman, Eds.). Cambridge, MA: Harvard University Press.

Weinstein, D., & Weinstein, M. A. (1991). Georg Simmel: Sociological flaneur bricoleur. *Theory, Culture & Society, 8,* 151–168.

Weinstein, M. (2004). Randomized design and the myth of certain knowledge: Guinea pig narratives and cultural critique. *Qualitative Inquiry, 10,* 246–260.

West, C. (1989). *The American evasion of philosophy: A genealogy of pragmatism.* Madison: University of Wisconsin Press.

Wolf, M. A. (1992). *A thrice-told tale: Feminism, postmodernism, and ethnographic responsibility.* Stanford, CA: Stanford University Press.

Wolcott, H. F. (1990). *Writing up qualitative research.* Newbury Park, CA: Sage.

Wolcott, H. F. (1992). Posturing in qualitative inquiry. In M. D. LeCompte, W. L. Millroy, & J. Preissle (Eds.), *The handbook of qualitative research in education* (pp. 3–52). New York: Academic Press.

Wolcott, H. F. (1995). *The art of fieldwork.* Walnut Creek, CA: AltaMira.

# Part I

# METHODS OF COLLECTING AND ANALYZING EMPIRICAL MATERIALS

Nothing stands outside representation. Research involves a complex politics of representation. The socially situated researcher creates, through interaction and material practices, those realities and representations that are the subject matter of inquiry. In such sites, the interpretive practices of qualitative research are implemented. These methodological practices represent different ways of generating and representing empirical materials grounded in the everyday world. Part IV of the *Handbook* examines the multiple practices and methods of analysis that qualitative researchers-as-methodological *bricoleurs* now employ.

## ▣ NARRATIVE INQUIRY

Today narrative inquiry is flourishing; it is everywhere. We know the world through the stories that are told about it. Even so, as Susan Chase (Chapter 2, this volume) reminds us, narrative inquiry as a particular type of qualitative inquiry is a field in the making. Chase defines narrative as retrospective meaning making and defines narrative inquiry as an "amalgam of interdisciplinary lenses, diverse disciplinary approaches, and both traditional and innovative methods—all revolving around an interest in biographical particulars as narrated by the one who lives them." She provides an excellent historical overview of this field, moving from the sociologists and anthropologists in the first half of the 20th century who championed the life history method, to the second-wave feminists who "poured new life into the study of personal narratives," to sociolinguists who treated oral narrative as a form of discourse, to contemporary scholars who turn the use of interviews into the study of how persons perform and tell stories about themselves.

Narratives are socially constrained forms of action, socially situated performances, ways of acting in and making sense of the world. Narrative researchers often write in the first person, thus "emphasizing their own narrative action." Chase identifies several distinct approaches to narrative analysis, including psychological, sociological, anthropological, autoethnographic, and performances studies of identity. She then outlines a series of issues that must be addressed in any narrative inquiry. These involve interpretive authority and "hearing" the story that is being told.

Narrative inquiry can advance a social change agenda. Wounded storytellers can empower others to tell their stories. *Testimonios,* as emergency narratives, can mobilize a nation against social injustice, repression, and violence. Collective stories can form the basis of a social movement. Telling the stories of marginalized people can help to create a public space requiring others to hear what they do not want to hear.

## ▣ Arts-Based Inquiry

Arts-based inquiry uses the aesthetics, methods, and practices of the literary, performance, and visual arts as well as dance, theater, drama, film, collage, video, and photography. Arts-based inquiry is intertextual. It crosses the borders of art and research. Susan Finley (Chapter 3, this volume) writes a history of this methodology, locating it in the postcolonial postmodern context. She assesses the usefulness of activist art (e.g., photographs of refugees of war, children and street art, street theater) when political activism is the goal. She shows how activist art can be used to address issues of political significance, including engaging community participants in acts of political self-expression.

When grounded in a critical performance pedagogy, arts-based work can be used to advance a progressive political agenda that addresses issues of social inequity. Thus do researchers take up their "cameras, paintbrushes, bodies, and voices" in the name of social justice projects. Such work exposes oppression, targets sites of resistance, and outlines a transformative praxis that performs resistance texts. Finley shows how she makes this commitment to transformative praxis work by offering moving examples from her At Home At School (AHAS) program for kindergarten through eighth-grade (K–8) children who live in shelter and transitional housing.

## ▣ THE INTERVIEW

We live in an interview society, in a society whose members seem to believe that interviews generate useful information about lived experience and its meanings. The interview has become a taken-for-granted feature of our mediated mass culture. But the interview is a negotiated text—a site where power, gender, race, and class intersect. Stealing a narrative line from the film *Memento*, which begins at the end with a murder, Fontana and Frey (Chapter 4, this volume) begin their review of the history of the interview in the social sciences by starting in the present. They work back and forth in time from Kong, Mahoney, and Plummer's (2002) essay, "Queering the Interview." This essay shows how the interview became a tool of modernist democratization and ultimately of social reform.

Working back from the present, Fontana and Frey note the interview's major forms—structured, unstructured, and open-ended—while showing how the tool is modified and changed during use. They also discuss the group (or focused) interview, the oral history interview, creative interviewing, online interviewing, and gendered, feminist, and postmodern (or multivoiced) active interviewing.

The interview is a conversation—the art of asking questions and listening. It is not a neutral tool, for at least two people create the reality of the interview situation. In this situation, answers are given. Thus, the interview produces situated understandings grounded in specific interactional episodes. This method is influenced by the personal characteristics of the interviewer, including race, class, ethnicity, and gender.

Fontana and Frey review the important work of feminist scholars on the interview, especially the arguments of Behar, Reinharz, Hertz, Richardson, Clough, Collins, Smith, and Oakley. The British sociologist Oakley (1981) and other feminist scholars have identified a major contradiction between scientific positivistic research, which requires objectivity and detachment, and feminist-based interviewing, which requires openness, emotional engagement, and the development of a potentially long-term trusting relationship between the interviewer and the subject.

A feminist interviewing ethic, as Fontana and Frey suggest, redefines the interview situation. This ethic transforms interviewers and respondents into coequals who are carrying on a conversation about mutually relevant, often biographically critical, issues. This narrative, performative, storytelling framework challenges the informed consent and deception models of inquiry discussed by Christians (Volume 1, Chapter 6) in Volume 1, Part I. This ethic changes the interview into an important tool for the types of clinical and applied action research discussed by Kemmis and McTaggart (Volume 2, Chapter 10) and Miller and Crabtree (Volume 2, Chapter 11). This ethic also turns the interview into a vehicle for social change, as noted in Chase's (Chapter 2, this volume) discussion of the interview as a site for storytelling.

## ▣ RECONTEXTUALIZING OBSERVATIONAL METHODS

Going into a social situation and looking is another important way of gathering materials about the social world. Drawing on previous arguments (Angrosino & Pérez, 2000), Michael Angrosino (Chapter 5, this volume) fundamentally rewrites the methods and practices of naturalistic observation. All observation involves participation in the world being studied. There is no pure, objective, detached observation; the effects of the observer's presence can never be erased. Furthermore, the colonial concept of the subject (the object of the observer's gaze) is no longer appropriate. Observers now function as collaborative participants in action inquiry settings. Angrosino and Pérez (2000) argue that observational interaction is a tentative situational process. It is shaped by shifts in gendered identity as well as by existing structures of power. As relationships unfold, participants validate the cues generated by others in the sitting. Finally, during the observational process, people assume situational identities that might not be socially or culturally normative.

Like Christians (Volume 1, Chapter 6), Angrosino offers compelling criticisms of institutional review boards (IRBs), noting that positivistic social scientists seldom recognize the needs of observational ethnographers. At many universities, the official IRBs are tied to the experimental, hypothesis-testing, so-called scientific paradigm. This paradigm creates problems for the postmodern observer, for the scholar who becomes part of the world that is being studied. To get approval for their research, scholars might have to engage in deception (in this instance of the IRB). This leads some ethnographers to claim that their research will not be intrusive and, hence, will not cause harm. Yet interactive observers are by definition intrusive. When collaborative inquiry is undertaken, subjects become stakeholders, persons who shape the inquiry itself. What this means for consent forms—and for forms of participatory inquiry more broadly—is not clear. Alternative forms of ethnographic writing, including the use of fictionalized stories, represent one avenue for addressing this ethical quandary.

Angrosino offers an ethic of "proportionate reason." This utilitarian ethic attempts to balance the benefits, costs, and consequences of actions in the field, asking whether the means to an end are justified by the importance and value of the goals attained. This ethic is then translated into a progressive social agenda. This agenda stresses social (not commutative), distributive, or legal justice. A social justice ethic asks the researcher to become directly involved with the poor and the marginalized, to become an advocate, and to facilitate empowerment in communities. A pedagogy for social justice based on a service learning model is outlined.

Angrosino demystifies the observation method. Observation is no longer the key to some grand analysis of culture or society. Instead, observational research now becomes a method that focuses on differences, on the lives of particular people in concrete, but constantly changing, human relationships. The relevance and need for a feminist ethics of care and commitment become even more apparent.

## ▣   Reimagining Visual Methods

Today visual sociologists and anthropologists use photography, motion pictures, the World Wide Web, interactive CDs, CD–ROMs, and virtual reality as ways of forging connections between human existence and visual perception. These forms of visual representation represent different ways of recording and documenting what passes as social life. Often called the mirror with a memory, photography takes the researcher into the everyday world, where the issues of observer identity, the subject's point of view, and what to photograph become problematic. Douglas Harper (Chapter 6, this volume) examines the status of visual thinking in the sociological community, the impact of new technologies on visual methods, the continuing development of traditional forms of visual documentary, and problematic issues surrounding ethics in the visual research world. Journals have become more sophisticated in the presentation of visual materials, and new technologies and skills using Web sites have created new ways of presenting visual materials. These methods have been taken up by experimental, reflexive digital ethnographers. Harper wisely notes that these developments exist within an unstable and constantly changing electronic world. The software and the computers that deliver these developments have short lives.

Historically, visual sociology began within the postpositivist tradition, providing visual information to support the realist tales of traditional ethnography. Photographs were a part of the unproblematic "facts" that constituted the "truth" of these tales. Now visual sociology, like ethnography, is in a period of deep questioning and great change. Visual sociology, Harper contends, must find a place in this new ethnography. Drawing from his own research, Harper illustrates the value of photo elicitation in the study of the meaning of change in the dairy industry in northern New York State. In photo elicitation studies, photos are used to stimulate a quality of memory that word-based interviewing does not.

Harper discusses the use of photographs to observe public life. IRBs have been reluctant to give permission to photograph the public without informed consent. But many visual sociologists base their photographic research on the model of documentary photography and photojournalism, where the right to photograph the public has been guaranteed by amendments to the Constitution dealing with the freedom of expression. Visual sociologists point to these precedents and argue that harm to subjects is unlikely to occur from "showing normal people doing normal things" in public.

IRBs insist that confidentiality be maintained, that subjects remain anonymous. But in many cases, subjects are both willing and pleased to be identified; furthermore, their very identifiability may be critical to the research project. In such situations, the researcher is urged to develop an ethical covenant with those being studied so that only mutually agreed-on materials will be published.

We need to learn how to experiment with visual (and nonvisual) ways of thinking. We need to develop a critical visual sensibility, a sensibility that will allow us to bring the gendered material world into play in critically different ways. We need to interrogate critically the hyperlogics of cyberspace and its virtual realities. The rules and methods for establishing truth that hold these worlds together must also be better understood.

## ▣ AUTHOETHNOGRAPHY: MAKING THE PERSONAL POLITICAL

Stacy Holman Jones (Chapter 7, this volume) shows how autoethnography can be used to make the personal political. Her essay is about autoethnography as a radical democratic practice, a political practice intended to create a space for dialogue and debate about issues of injustice. Her chapter, like Madison's (Volume 2, Chapter 7) contribution on ethnography as street performance tells by showing. Autoethnographic performances breathe life into life ethnographies.

Personal experience reflects the flow of thoughts and meanings people have in their immediate situations. These experiences can be routine or problematic. They occur within the life of a person. When they are talked about, they assume the shape of a story or a narrative. Lived experience cannot be studied directly because language, speech, and systems of discourse mediate and define the very experience one attempts to describe. We study the representations of experience, not experience itself. We examine the stories people tell one another about the experiences they have had. These stories may be personal experience narratives or self stories, interpretations made up as the person goes along.

Many now argue that we can study only our own experiences. The researcher becomes the research subject. This is the topic of autoethnography. Holman Jones's text reflexively presents the arguments for writing reflexive personal narratives. Indeed, her multivoiced text is an example of such writing; it performs its own narrative reflexivity. Holman Jones masterfully reviews the arguments for studying personal experience narratives, anchoring her text in the discourses of feminist poststructuralism and postmodernism, especially the works of Ronai, Ellis, Bochner, and Richardson.

Holman Jones reviews the history of and arguments for this writing form, the challenge to create texts that unfold in the life of the writer while embodying tactics that enact a progressive politics of resistance. Such texts, when performed (and writing is a form of performance), enact a politics of possibility. They shape a critical awareness, they disturb the status quo, and they probe questions of identity. Holman Jones writes out of her own history with this method, and in so doing she takes readers to the Alexander (Volume 2, Chapter 3) and Madison (Volume 2, Chapter 7) contributions on performance ethnography and critical ethnography. In a moving passage, she shares a poem/letter she wrote to and for her dead grandfather.

In her concluding sections, Holman Jones embeds the performance turn in the history of progressive theater. She then invites readers to perform the testimony and witnessing of personal stories, to stage improbable impossible encounters of possibility, to create disturbances and chaos, to stage arguments, and to use words in ways that move the world.

## ◙ ONLINE ETHNOGRAPHY

Annette Markham (Chapter 8, this volume) argues that computer-mediated construction of self, other, and social structure constitutes a unique phenomenon of study. Offline, the body is present and can be responded to by others. Identity construction is a situated, face-to-face process. Online, in contrast, the body is absent and interaction is mediated by computer technology and the production of written discourse. Markham examines many of the issues that can arise in the qualitative study of Internet-mediated situations. These are issues connected to definitions of what constitutes the field or boundaries of a text as well as what counts as text or empirical material. How the other is interpreted and given a textual presence is also problematic, as are ethical issues that are complex.

Ethical guidelines for Internet research vary sharply across disciplines and nations. Markham contrasts the utilitarian IRB ethical model predominant in the United States with the deontological or communitarian stance predominant in Europe. In some nations, citizens enjoy a greater protection of privacy regarding data collection and use. Under the usual IRB model, online ethnographers wrestle with securing informed consent, and with maintaining subject anonymity, while protecting subjects from harm. Under a communitarian, feminist ethical model, researchers enter into a collaborative relationship with a moral community of online interactants. Attempts are made to establish agreed-on understandings concerning privacy, ownership of materials, the use of personal names, and the meaning of broad principles such as justice and beneficence.

Markham wisely concludes, "Because the Internet is new, is widespread, and has the potential for changing the way in which people live their everyday professional and personal lives in a global society, it is essential to reflect carefully on the ethical frames that influence our studies and the political possibilities of our research."

## ◙ ANALYTIC PERSPECTIVES

In a powerful programmatic statement, Paul Atkinson and Sara Delamont (Chapter 9, this volume) argue that social activity and representation have their own indigenous modes of organization. These modes include language, discourse, narratives, visual styles, and semiotic and cultural codes. Qualitative researchers must remain faithful to this indigenous organization and deploy analytic strategies that are fitted to it. We need rigorous work that pays systematic attention to the systemic relations among the interaction order, orders of talk, representational orders, and the organized properties of material culture. Atkinson and Delamont endorse the disciplined use of such analytic perspectives and approaches as discourse, narrative, and semiotic analysis.

Inquiry must also be concerned with forms of collective—not individual—social action. Furthermore, an engaged social science should remain faithful to the world and its organization. Atkinson and Delamont reject certain postmodern positions that free qualitative analysis from the conventions of academic writing. We need more principled and disciplined ways of accounting for the world and its organization. The authors' perspective restores a particular sense of tradition and continuity to the qualitative research project, connecting it back, at one level, to the Chicago School of the 1930s and 1940s.

## ▣ FOUCAULT'S METHODOLOGIES

It goes without saying that Michel Foucault was one of the giant intellectuals of the 20th century. The meanings of his legacy for the humanities and the social sciences are multiple and unfolding (see Holstein & Gubrium [Volume 2, Chapter 6] and Peräkylä [Chapter 11, this volume]). At one level, as Kamberelis and Dimitriadis (Chapter 12, this volume) note in their contribution on focus groups, Foucault's project represents an attempt to understand how any object has been constituted out of a particular intersection of forces, discourses, and institutions. A genealogy maps the complex and contradictory ways in which forces and processes come together to produce a certain set of effects. Foucault's genealogies are not histories of causes; rather, they are histories of effects of consequences.

Foucault's work has traditionally been divided into three sequential phases: archaeology, genealogy, and care of the self. James Scheurich and Kathryn Bell McKenzie (Chapter 10, this volume) focus on the first two phases, offering a masterful reading of Foucault's methodologies and his use of archaeology and genealogy. Foucault offered nothing less than a sweeping critique of the modernist view of the human sciences and of the human subject (man) as the object of inquiry. He moved back and forth between systems of discourse, what he called *savoir* (e.g., implicit knowledge, everyday opinions, commercial practices), and formal bodies of learning (*connaissance*), including specific disciplines such as Freudian psychoanalysis. Savoir provides the discursive conditions for the development of connaissance. For example, an understanding of the history of psychiatry as a discipline requires the study of the relations among rules of jurisprudence, norms of industrial labor and bourgeois morality, and opinions of madness in daily life. Foucault's archaeology focused on the analysis of these local discourses, whereas his genealogy focused on the transformation of such knowledge into more formal disciplinary systems. Scheurich and McKenzie usefully outline the interpretive rules advocated by Foucault in his archaeologies and genealogies.

## ▣ ANALYZING TALK AND TEXT

Qualitative researchers study spoken and written records of human experience, including transcribed talk, films, novels, and photographs. Interviews give researchers accounts of the issues being studied. The topics of research are not interviews themselves. Research studies using naturally occurring empirical materials—tape recordings of mundane interaction—constitute topics of inquiry in their own right. This is the topic of Anssi Peräkylä's (Chapter 11, this volume) contribution.

With Chase (Chapter 2, this volume), Fontana and Frey (Chapter 4, this volume), and Holstein and Gubrium (Volume 2, Chapter 6), Peräkylä treats interview materials as narrative accounts rather than as true pictures of reality. Texts are based on transcriptions of interviews and other forms of talk. These texts are social facts; they are produced, shared, and used in socially organized ways. Peräkylä discusses semiotics, discourse analysis, critical discourse analysis, and historical discourse analysis as approaches to understanding naturally occurring textual materials.

Peräkylä also discusses membership categorization analysis (MCA) as a less familiar form of narrative analysis. Drawing on the work of Harvey Sacks (Silverman, 1998), Peräkylä illustrates the logic of MCA. With this method, the researcher asks how persons use everyday terms and categories in their interactions with others.

Peräkylä turns next to the analysis of talk. There are two main social science traditions that inform the analysis of transcripts: conversation analysis (CA) and discourse analysis (DA). He reviews and offers examples of both traditions, arguing that talk is socially organized action that creates and maintains intersubjective reality. Drawing from his own research on AIDS and its treatment, Peräkylä notes that in observing the "skillful practices through which AIDS counselors encourage their clients to talk about their subjective experiences, we were also observing the operation of an institution, involving powerful relations and bodies of knowledge, at a particular moment in its historical development."

In sum, text-based documents of experience are complex. But if talk constitutes much of what we have, then the forms of analysis outlined by Peräkylä represent significant ways of making the world and its words more visible.

## ▣ FOCUS GROUPS: PEDAGOGY, POLITICS, AND INQUIRY

Kamberelis and Dimitriadis (Chapter 12, this volume) significantly advance the discourse on focus group methodology by showing how focus groups have been used in market and military research, in emancipatory pedagogy, and in first-, second-, and third-generation feminist inquiry. Building on Foucault, they place these three genealogies of focus group activity in dialogue with one another.

Kamberelis and Dimitriadis contrast the dialogical, critical theory approach to focus groups with the use of such groups in propaganda and market research. In the marketing context, focus groups are used to extract information from people on a given topic. This information is then used to manipulate people more effectively. Critical pedagogy theorists, such as Freire and Kozol, use focus groups for imagining and enacting the "emancipatory political possibilities of collective work."

Kamberelis and Dimitriadis contrast these two approaches with the history of focus groups in feminist inquiry, noting the use of such groups in first-, second-, and third-wave feminist formations for consciousness-raising purposes. They draw on Madriz (2000), who offered a model of focus group interviewing that emphasizes a feminist ethic of empowerment, moral community, emotional engagement, and the development of long-term trusting relationships. This method gives a voice to women of color who have long been silenced. Focus groups facilitate women writing culture together. As a Latina feminist, Madriz placed focus groups within the context of collective testimonies and group resistance narratives. Focus groups reduce the distance between the researcher and the researched. The multivocality of the participants limits the control of the researcher over the research process.

Within this history, focus groups have been used to elicit and validate collective testimonies, to give a voice to the previously silenced by creating a safe space for sharing one's life experiences. The critical insights and practices of consciousness-raising groups have helped us to move more deeply into the praxis-oriented commitments of the seventh and eighth moments. In these spaces, as the work of Radway and Lather and Smithies documents, focus groups can become the vehicle for allowing participants to take over and own the research. In these ways, focus groups become the sites where pedagogy, politics, and interpretive inquiry intersect and inform one another.

When this happens, as in the projects discussed by Fine and Weis (Chapter 3) in Volume 1, Part I, inquiry becomes directly involved in the complexities of political activism and policymaking.

Madriz, Olesen, Ladson-Billings, and Donnor remind us that women of color experience a triple subjugation based on class, race, and gender oppression. Critical focus groups, as discussed by Kamberelis and Dimitriadis, create the conditions for the emergence of a critical race consciousness, a consciousness focused on social change. It seems that with critical focus groups, critical race theory and progressive politics have found their methodology.


## ▣ CONCLUSION

The researcher-as-methodological bricoleur should have a working familiarity with each of the methods of collecting and analyzing empirical materials presented in this part of the *Handbook*. This familiarity includes understanding the history of each method and technique as well as possessing hands-on experience with each. Only in this way can the limitations and strengths of each method and technique be fully appreciated. At the same time, the investigator will see more clearly how each, as a set of material interpretive practices, creates its own subject matter.

In addition, it must be understood that each paradigm and perspective, as presented in Part II, has a distinct history with these methods of research. Although methods-as-tools are somewhat universal in application, they are not used uniformly by researchers from all paradigms, and when they are used they are fitted and adapted to the particularities of the paradigm in question. However, researchers from all paradigms and perspectives can profitably make use of each of these methods of collecting and analyzing empirical materials.

## ▣ References

Angrosino, M. V., & Pérez, K. A. (2000). Rethinking observation: From method to context. In N. K. Denzin & Y. S. Lincoln (Eds.), *Handbook of qualitative research* (2nd ed., pp. 673–702). Thousand Oaks, CA: Sage.

Kong, T. S. K., Mahoney, D., & Plummer, K. (2002). Queering the interview. In J. Gubrium & J. Holstein (Eds.), *Handbook of qualitative research: Context and method* (pp. 239–258). Thousand Oaks, CA: Sage.

Madriz, E. (2000). Focus groups in feminist research. In N. K. Denzin & Y. S. Lincoln (Eds.), *Handbook of qualitative research* (2nd ed., pp. 835–850). Thousand Oaks, CA: Sage.

Oakley, A. (1981). Interviewing women: A contradiction in terms. In H. Roberts (Ed.), *Doing feminist research* (pp. 30–61). London: Routledge.

Silverman, D. (1998). *Harvey Sacks: Social science and conversation analysis.* Oxford, UK: Polity.

# 2

# NARRATIVE INQUIRY

*Multiple Lenses,*
*Approaches, Voices*

Susan E. Chase

D uring the early 1990s, as I struggled to interpret and represent *as narrative* my interviews with women school superintendents, I relied on a rich interdisciplinary tradition defending the study of individuals in their social and historical context. That tradition includes works as diverse as Thomas and Znaniecki's (1918/1927) *The Polish Peasant in Europe and America,* Garfinkel's (1967) ethnomethodological study of Agnes, and the Personal Narratives Group's (1989) feminist explorations of women's journals, life histories, and autobiographies. In this tradition, researchers begin with the biographical leg of Mills's (1959) famous trilogy—biography, history, and society. Mills called these three "the co-ordinate points of the proper study of man" (p. 143). Of course, I was also writing after the narrative turn, and so Barthes's (1977) dramatic words— "narrative is present in every age, in every place, in every society" (p. 79)—had already infiltrated sociological theory. And yet I found few empirical sociological studies based on interview material that could serve as methodological models for the particular way in which I wanted to treat the women's interviews as narratives. Most helpful to me was Riessman's (1990) approach to interview material in *Divorce Talk.*[1]

These days, narrative inquiry in the social sciences is flourishing. Signs of this burgeoning interest include an interdisciplinary journal called *Narrative Inquiry,* a book series on *The Narrative Study of Lives,* and professional conferences specifically showcasing narrative work.[2] Nonetheless, I still get the sense that narrative inquiry is a field in the making. Researchers new to this field will find a rich but diffuse tradition, multiple methodologies in various stages of development, and plenty of opportunities for exploring new ideas, methods, and questions.

In preparation for writing this chapter, I gathered and read as many examples of what might be called narrative inquiry as I could, and I wrestled with various ways of defining the contours of narrative inquiry, both past and present. Although qualitative researchers now routinely refer to any prosaic data (as opposed to close-ended or short-answer data) as "narrative" (Polkinghorne, 1995), I present narrative *inquiry* as a particular type—a subtype—of qualitative inquiry. Contemporary narrative inquiry can be characterized as an amalgam of interdisciplinary analytic lenses, diverse disciplinary approaches, and both traditional and innovative methods—all revolving around an interest in biographical particulars as narrated by the one who lives them.

In what follows, I begin by defining some pivotal terms and then discuss the predecessors of contemporary narrative researchers: sociologists and anthropologists who championed the life history method during the first half of the 20th century, second-wave feminists who poured new life into the study of personal narratives, and sociolinguists who treated oral narrative as a form of discourse worthy of study in itself. After that historical overview, I turn to contemporary narrative inquiry, articulating a set of analytic lenses through which narrative researchers view empirical material and outlining several current approaches to narrative research. Next come explorations of specific methodological issues in contemporary narrative inquiry. For researchers who collect narratives through intensive interviews, a central question is how to treat the interviewee as a narrator, both during interviews and while interpreting them. For all narrative researchers, a central question revolves around which voice or voices researchers should use as they interpret and represent the voices of those they study. And although all qualitative researchers address the question of the relationship between the relatively small "sample" they study and some larger whole, this question is particularly poignant for narrative researchers, who often present the narratives of a very small number of individuals—or even of just one individual—in their published works. The subsequent section addresses the relationship between narrative inquiry and social change. In the concluding paragraphs, I sketch some questions that arose for me as I worked on this chapter, questions that I hope narrative inquirers will explore during the coming years.

## ▣ FOUNDATIONAL MATTERS AND HISTORICAL BACKGROUND

### Pivotal Terms

The terms that narrative researchers use to describe the empirical material they study have flexible meanings, beginning with *narrative* itself. A narrative may be oral or written and may be elicited or heard during fieldwork, an interview, or a naturally occurring conversation. In any of these situations, a narrative may be (a) a short topical story about a particular event and specific characters such as an encounter with a friend, boss, or doctor; (b) an extended story about a significant aspect of one's life such as schooling, work, marriage, divorce, childbirth, an illness, a trauma, or participation in a war or social movement; or (c) a narrative of one's entire life, from birth to the present.

*Life history* is the more specific term that researchers use to describe an extensive autobiographical narrative, in either oral or written form, that covers all or most of a life. But *life history* can also refer to a social science text that presents a person's biography. In that case, *life story* may be used to describe the autobiographical story in the person's own words (for the complexity of these terms, see Bertaux, 1981; Frank, 2000). Yet some researchers treat the terms *life history* and *life story* as interchangeable, defining both as birth-to-present narratives (Atkinson, 2002). For still others, a life story is a narrative about a specific significant aspect of a person's life, as in the second definition (b) in the preceding paragraph. A life story may also revolve around an epiphanal event (Denzin, 1989) or a turning point (McAdams, Josselson, & Lieblich, 2001) in one's life. Instead of *life story*, some researchers use *personal narrative* to describe a compelling topical narration (Riessman, 2002a). They may use this term to indicate that they are not talking about literary narratives or folklore (but see Narayan & George, 2002, for the intermingling of personal narrative and folklore). *Personal narrative* can also refer in a more generic sense to diaries, journals, and letters as well as to autobiographical stories (Personal Narratives Group, 1989).

Historians use *oral history* to describe interviews in which the focus is not on historical events themselves—historians' traditional interest—but rather on the meanings that events hold for those who lived through them (McMahan & Rogers, 1994; Thompson, 1978/2000). A *testimonio* is a type of oral history, life history, or life story; it is an explicitly political narrative that describes and resists oppression (Beverley, 2000; Tierney, 2000; see also Beverley, Volume 2, Chapter 9). For the past few decades, *testimonio* has been especially associated with the (usually oral) narratives of Latin American activists in revolutionary movements (e.g., Menchú, 1984; Moyano, 2000; Randall, 1981, 1994, 2003). Finally, a *performance narrative* transforms any oral or written narrative into a public performance, either on stage (Madison, 1998; McCall & Becker, 1990) or in alternative textual forms such as poems and fiction (Denzin, 1997, 2000, 2003; Richardson, 2002).

## Sociology and Early Life Histories

The predecessors of today's narrative researchers include the Chicago School sociologists who collected life histories and other personal documents during the 1920s and 1930s.[3] Thomas and Znaniecki's (1918/1927) *The Polish Peasant* is frequently cited as the first significant sociological use of life history. In the final 300 pages of the second volume, Thomas and Znaniecki presented the "life record" of a Polish immigrant, Wladek Wiszniewski, whom they paid to write his autobiography

(p. 1912). The sociologists' voice preceded the life record with nearly 800 pages on the disorganization and reorganization of social life in Poland as well as the organization and disorganization of social life after immigration to the United States. They also added explanatory footnotes throughout Wiszniewski's life record.

In explaining their interest in life records, Thomas and Znaniecki (1918/1927) stated,

> A social institution can be fully understood only if we do not limit ourselves to the abstract study of its formal organization, but analyze the way in which it appears in the personal experience of various members of the group and follow the influence which it has upon their lives. (p. 1833)

Indeed, they claimed, "Personal life records, as complete as possible, constitute the *perfect* type of sociological material" (p. 1832). In their view, social scientists turned to other materials and methods because of practical difficulties; it is too time-consuming to get sufficient numbers of life records on every sociological issue, and it is too time-consuming to analyze them. Nonetheless, some sociologists, especially in Poland, made the effort. Józef Chalasiński, a follower of Znaniecki, championed the method of using public competitions to solicit hundreds of ordinary people's autobiographies. His research demonstrated that "the formation and transformations of whole social classes (peasants, workers) could be described and understood by analyzing sets of autobiographies" (Bertaux, 1981, p. 3; see also Chalasiński, 1981).[4]

*The Polish Peasant* was followed by other Chicago School studies based on life histories, especially of juvenile delinquents and criminals (e.g., Shaw, 1930/1966; Sutherland, 1937). These sociologists had some interest in the individual's subjective experience, but they were primarily interested in explaining the individual's behavior as an interactive process between the individual and his or her sociocultural environment. Although studies of urban boys' and men's lives are frequently cited in reviews of the life history method, Hagood's (1939) *Mothers of the South: Portraiture of the White Tenant Farm Woman* also offers an example of early narrative methods.[5]

During the 1940s and 1950s, mainstream American sociology favored abstract theory along with survey and statistical research methods, and the life history method was marginalized. At this point, sociologists were more interested in positivist methods that use single studies to confirm or disconfirm predetermined hypotheses than in research based on the "mosaic" model offered by the Chicago School—studies that may produce no definitive conclusions of their own but that contribute to a larger collective research endeavor (Becker, 1966, pp. viii–ix, xvi–xviii; Bertaux, 1981, p. 1; Denzin, 1970, p. 219).

## Anthropology and Early Life Histories

Anthropological use of the life history method emerged early in the 20th century, mostly as a way of recording American Indian cultures that were assumed to be nearly extinct.[6] During the 1920s, life history became a rigorous anthropological method with the publication of Radin's (1926) *Crashing Thunder* (Langness & Frank, 1981, pp. 17–18, 20). Crashing Thunder, a middle-aged Winnebago man in financial difficulty, wrote his autobiography for a fee in two sessions (Lurie, 1961, p. 92). Radin (1926) supplied the cultural context and heavy annotations of the life record.

During the early period, anthropologists gathered life histories as a way of understanding cultural facts, choosing to study people who they assumed were representative of their cultural group (Langness & Frank, 1981, p. 24). By the mid-1940s, under the influence of Edward Sapir, Ruth Benedict, and Margaret Mead, many anthropologists had developed a stronger interest in individuals per se and especially in the relationship between cultural context and distinct personality types (Langness, 1965, pp. 11, 19; see also DuBois, 1944/1960; Kardiner, 1945). Anthropologists also used life histories to present insiders' views of culture and daily life, as exemplified by Lewis's (1961) publication of the life stories of the members of one Mexican family in *The Children of Sánchez*. In this and other works, Lewis also developed the controversial concept of "the culture of poverty" (Langness & Frank, 1981, pp. 24–25). Finally, anthropologists have used life histories to study cultural change, as brought about either by contact between different cultural groups or as the result of revolutionary movements (Langness, 1965, p. 16; Langness & Frank, 1981, pp. 24–27). Although the majority of early anthropological life histories were studies of men, some anthropologists—mostly women—used life history methods to study women's lives (Watson & Watson-Franke, 1985, chap. 6).

## Feminism and Personal Narratives

The liberation movements of the 1960s and 1970s helped to reinvigorate the life history method. For example, the civil rights movement led to renewed interest in slave narratives, many of which had been collected from 1936 to 1938 by unemployed writers working with the Federal Writers' Project of the Works Project Administration. More than 2,000 oral histories of former slaves had been deposited in the Library of Congress, but only a glimpse of them was available to the public in Botkin's (1945) *Lay My Burden Down: A Folk History of Slavery*. Two and a half decades later, activists and academics returned to these narratives, and sociologist Rawick (1972) published them in their entirety in 18 volumes of *The American Slave: A Composite Autobiography*. In the introductory volume, he offered a beginning toward a social history of black community life under slavery, based on the narratives, countering previous academic treatment of slaves as voiceless victims (p. xiv).[7]

The second wave of the women's movement played a major role in the renaissance of life history methods and the study of personal narratives such as journals and autobiographies.[8] As feminists critiqued the androcentric assumptions of social science—that men's lives and activities are more important than those of women and/or constitute the norm from which women's lives and activities deviate—they began to treat women's personal narratives as "essential primary documents for feminist research" (Personal Narratives Group, 1989, p. 4). By listening to previously silenced voices, feminist researchers challenged social science knowledge about society, culture, and history (Belenky, Clinchy, Goldberger, & Tarule, 1986; Franz & Stewart, 1994; Gluck, 1979; Gluck & Patai, 1991; Personal Narratives Group, 1989; Reinharz, 1992, chap. 7; Reinharz & Chase, 2002; Watson & Watson-Franke, 1985, chap. 6). Through the influence of working-class feminists and feminists of color (among others), race, ethnicity, nationality, social class, sexual orientation, and disability came to the fore as central aspects of women's lives (for an extensive overview, see Geiger, 1986; see also Olesen, Volume 1, Chapter 10). The first decade or so of second-wave academic feminism produced many examples of feminist research based on life histories and personal narratives (e.g., Babb & Taylor, 1981; Hunt & Winegarten, 1983; Jacobs, 1979; Ruddick & Daniels, 1977; Sexton, 1981; Sidel, 1978; for an extensive list, see Reinharz, 1992, chap. 7).

The explosion of interest in women's personal narratives was accompanied by feminist challenges to conventional assumptions about research relationships and research methods. Thomas and Znaniecki (1918/1927), and many who followed in their footsteps, had said little about how they gathered their materials, noting only that they motivated people to write their life histories through monetary rewards or public contests (Langness & Frank, 1981; Watson & Watson-Franke, 1985). In addition, despite the early life historians' apparently humanistic bent (e.g., Shaw's [1930/1966] interest in ameliorating the miserable conditions of Stanley's life as a juvenile delinquent and anthropologists' interest in recording what they assumed were disappearing cultures), from a feminist point of view, the people in these life histories appeared as distant "others" or deviant "objects" of social scientist interest. It is important to keep in mind, of course, that the early life historians were writing in positivist times, during which the social sciences were struggling to gain recognition as sciences.[9]

Feminists resisted the idea that life histories and other personal narratives were primarily useful for gathering information about historical events, cultural change, or the impact of social structures on individuals' lives. Rather, they were interested in women as social actors in their own right and in the subjective meanings that women assigned to events and conditions in their lives. Importantly, these feminist lenses opened up new understandings of historical, cultural, and social processes. Furthermore, as feminists approached women as subjects rather than as objects, they also began to consider *their* subjectivity—the role that researchers' interests and social locations play in the research relationship. Whose questions should get asked and answered? Who should get the last say? How does power operate in the research relationship? And as feminists incorporated postmodern influences, they began to ask questions—which are still pertinent today—about voice, authenticity, interpretive authority, and representation. What does it mean to hear the other's voice? In what sense do—or don't—women's life histories and personal narratives "speak for themselves"? How do interactional, social, cultural, and historical conditions mediate women's stories? In what ways are women's voices muted, multiple, and/or contradictory? Under what conditions do women develop "counternarratives" as they narrate their lives? How should researchers represent all of these voices and ideas in their written works (Anderson & Jack, 1991; McCall & Wittner, 1990; Personal Narratives Group, 1989; Ribbens & Edwards, 1998)?

## Sociolinguistics and Oral Narratives

The mid-1960s saw the development of another line of inquiry that has influenced contemporary narrative research. At this time, anthropologists, sociologists, and sociolinguists (e.g., Erving Goffman, Harold Garfinkel, John Gumperz, Dell Hymes, Harvey Sacks, Emanuel Schegloff, William Labov) were exploring a "range of subject matters at the intersection of language, interaction, discourse, practical action, and inference" (Schegloff, 1997, p. 98).

A 1967 article by Labov and Waletzky, "Narrative Analysis: Oral Versions of Personal Experience," is often cited as a groundbreaking presentation of the idea that ordinary people's oral narratives of everyday experience (as opposed to full-fledged life histories, written narratives, folklore, and literary narratives) are worthy of study in themselves. In this article, Labov and Waletzky (1967/1997) argued that oral narratives are a specific form of discourse characterized by certain structures serving specific social functions. Using data from individual and focus group interviews, they claimed that narrative discourse consists of clauses that match the temporal sequence of reported events. They also identified five sociolinguistic features of oral narratives: Orientation (which informs listeners about actors, time, place, and situation), Complication (the main body of the narrative—the action), Evaluation (the point of the story), Resolution (the result of the action), and Coda (which returns the listener to the current moment).

In 1997, the *Journal of Narrative and Life History* reprinted Labov and Waletzky's 1967 article along with 47 then-current assessments of how it had influenced linguistically informed narrative inquiry since it was first published. Bruner (1997), for instance, suggested that Labov and Waletzky's "fivefold characterization of overall narrative structure transformed the study of narrative profoundly. It set many of us thinking about the cognitive representation of reality imposed by narrative structure on our experience of the world and how we evaluate that experience" (p. 64). Referring to his own influential distinction between logico–scientific and narrative modes of thought—which he had articulated in *Actual Minds, Possible Worlds* (Bruner, 1986)— Bruner (1997) added, "I happily admit that it set me thinking about narrative not simply as a form of text but as a mode of thought" (p. 64).

Many of the assessments of the 1967 article point to the limits of Labov and Waletzky's narrowly structuralist formulation. For example, Riessman (1997) gave them credit for helping her attend to the fundamental structures and functions of oral narratives in her research on people's experiences of divorce. But she found their definition of narrative much too narrow, and so she developed a typology of narrative genres such as the habitual narrative and the hypothetical narrative (pp. 155–156). These helped Riessman to show how people recount their divorce experiences differently and to discuss the connection between the form and function of their speech.

In a different vein, Schegloff (1997) critiqued Labov and Waletzky's failure to take into account the interactional context in which oral narratives are elicited and received. Over the past three decades, conversation analysts such as Schegloff have explored (among other things) how stories arise and how they function in naturally occurring conversations (for an overview, see Holstein & Gubrium, 2000, chap. 7). Other sociolinguistically oriented researchers have investigated the research interview itself as a particular kind of discourse or communicative event in which narratives may be discouraged or encouraged (Briggs, 1986, 2002; Mishler, 1986). Furthermore, although Labov and Waletzky assumed a one-to-one correspondence between a narrative and the events it describes—between narrative and reality—most researchers since then have resisted this referential view of language. A central tenet of the narrative turn is that speakers *construct* events through narrative rather than simply refer to events.[10]

Despite the limitations of the original formulation, the attention that Labov and Waletzky devoted to the linguistic structures and functions of ordinary people's oral narratives served as a launching pad for diverse explorations of the sociolinguistic features of oral discourse. Many contemporary narrative researchers embrace the idea that how individuals narrate experience is as important to the meanings they communicate as is what they say.

## ▣ CONTEMPORARY NARRATIVE INQUIRY

Turning to the present, I begin by outlining a set of five analytic lenses through which contemporary researchers approach empirical material. These lenses reflect the influence of the histories just reviewed and, taken as a whole, suggest the distinctiveness of narrative inquiry—how it is different from (if connected to) other forms of qualitative research.

### Analytic Lenses

First, narrative researchers treat narrative—whether oral or written—as a distinct form of discourse. Narrative is retrospective meaning making—the shaping or ordering of past experience. Narrative is a way of understanding one's own and others' actions, of organizing events and objects into a meaningful whole, and of connecting and seeing the consequences of actions and events over time (Bruner, 1986; Gubrium & Holstein, 1997; Hinchman & Hinchman, 2001; Laslett, 1999; Polkinghorne, 1995). Unlike a chronology, which also reports events over time, a narrative communicates the narrator's point of view, including why the narrative is worth telling in the first place. Thus, in addition to describing what happened, narratives also express emotions, thoughts, and interpretations. Unlike editorials, policy statements, and doctrinal statements of belief, all of which also express a point of view, a narrative makes the self (the narrator) the protagonist, either as actor or as interested observer of others' actions. Finally, unlike scientific discourse, which also explains or presents an understanding of actions and events, narrative discourse highlights the uniqueness of each human action and event rather than their common properties (Bruner, 1986; Polkinghorne, 1995).

Second, narrative researchers view narratives as verbal action—as doing or accomplishing something. Among other things, narrators explain, entertain, inform, defend, complain, and confirm or challenge the status quo. Whatever the particular action, when someone tells a story, he or she shapes, constructs, and performs the self, experience, and reality. When researchers treat narration as actively creative in this way, they emphasize the narrator's voice(s). The word *voice* draws our attention to what the narrator communicates and how he or she communicates it as well as to the subject positions or social locations from which he or she speaks (Gubrium & Holstein, 2002). This combination of what, how, and where makes the narrator's voice particular. Furthermore, when researchers treat narration as actively creative and the narrator's voice as particular, they move away from questions about the factual nature of the narrator's statements. Instead, they highlight the versions of self, reality, and experience that the storyteller produces through the telling. Although narrators are accountable for the credibility of their stories, narrative researchers treat credibility and believability as something that storytellers accomplish (Holstein & Gubrium, 2000; Lincoln, 2000).

Third, narrative researchers view stories as both enabled and constrained by a range of social resources and circumstances. These include the possibilities for self and reality construction that are intelligible within the narrator's community, local setting, organizational and social memberships, and cultural and historical location. While acknowledging that every instance of narrative is particular, researchers use this lens to attend to similarities and differences across narratives. For example, they emphasize patterns in the storied selves, subjectivities, and realities that narrators create during particular times and in particular places (Brockmeier & Carbaugh, 2001; Bruner, 2002; Hatch & Wisniewski, 1995; Holstein & Gubrium, 2000).

Fourth, narrative researchers treat narratives as socially situated interactive performances—as produced in this particular setting, for this particular audience, for these particular purposes. A story told to an interviewer in a quiet relaxed setting will likely differ from the "same" story told to a reporter for a television news show, to a private journal that the writer assumes will never be read by others, to a roomful of people who have had similar experiences, to a social service counselor, or to the same interviewer at a different time. Here, researchers emphasize that the narrator's story is flexible, variable, and shaped in part by interaction with the audience. In other words, a narrative is a joint production of narrator and listener, whether the narrative arises in naturally occurring talk, an interview, or a fieldwork setting (Bauman, 1986; Briggs, 1986, 2002; Mishler, 1986).

Fifth, narrative researchers, like many other contemporary qualitative researchers, view *themselves* as narrators as they develop interpretations and find ways in which to present or publish their ideas about the narratives they studied (Denzin & Lincoln, 2000). This means that the four lenses just described make as much sense when applied to the researcher as they do when applied to the researched. Breaking from traditional social science practice, narrative researchers are likely to use the first person when presenting their work, thereby emphasizing their own narrative action. As narrators, then, researchers develop meaning out of, and some sense of order in, the material they studied; they develop their own voice(s) as they construct others' voices and realities; they narrate "results" in ways that are both enabled and constrained by the social resources and circumstances embedded in their disciplines, cultures, and historical moments; and they write or perform their work for particular audiences. The idea that researchers are narrators opens up a range of complex issues about voice, representation, and interpretive authority (Emihovich, 1995; Hertz, 1997; Josselson, 1996a; Krieger, 1991; Tierney, 2002; Tierney & Lincoln, 1997).

Theoretically, it is possible to treat these five analytic lenses as distinct. However, as researchers go about the business of hearing, collecting, interpreting, and representing narratives, they are well aware of the interconnectedness of the lenses. As they do their work, researchers may emphasize one or another lens or their intersections, or they may shift back and forth among the lenses, depending on their specific approaches to empirical narrative material.

## Diverse Approaches

Although narrative inquiry as a whole is interdisciplinary, specific approaches tend to be shaped by interests and assumptions embedded in researchers' disciplines. Without claiming to be comprehensive or exhaustive in my categories, I briefly outline five major approaches in contemporary narrative inquiry.[11] It is here that we see diversity and multiplicity in this field of inquiry.

Some psychologists have developed an approach that focuses on the relationship between individuals' life stories and the quality of their lives, especially their psychosocial development.[12] In addition to gathering extensive life stories,[13] these researchers sometimes use conventional psychological tests. For example, in a study of adults' narratives about turning points in their lives, McAdams and Bowman (2001) found that those who score high on conventional measures of psychological well-being and generativity (i.e., commitment to caring for and contributing to future generations) are likely to tell "narratives of redemption," that is, to construct negative events as having beneficial consequences. Conversely, those who score low in terms of psychological well-being and generativity are more likely to tell "narratives of contamination," that is, to present good experiences as having negative outcomes. While acknowledging that biographical, social, cultural, and historical circumstances condition the stories that people tell about themselves, narrative psychologists look for evidence (e.g., in a person's score on conventional measures) that the stories that people tell affect how they live their lives. They emphasize "the formative effects of narratives" and propose that some stories cripple, and others enable, an efficacious sense of self in relation to life problems or traumas (Rosenwald & Ochberg, 1992, p. 6).

In their interpretations, these psychological researchers tend to emphasize *what* the story is about—its plot, characters, and sometimes the structure or sequencing of its content. Along these lines, McAdams (1997) argued that the content of a life story embodies a person's identity and that both develop and change over time. This idea was exemplified by Josselson's (1996b) longitudinal study of how women revise their stories *and* their lives as they move through their 20s, 30s, and 40s.

A second approach has been developed by sociologists who highlight the "identity work" that people engage in as they construct selves within specific institutional, organizational, discursive, and local cultural contexts. Unlike the psychologists just described, who conceptualize the life story as distinguishable from—yet having an impact on—the life, these researchers often treat narratives *as* lived experience. Thus, they are as interested in the *hows* of storytelling as they are in the *whats* of storytelling—in the narrative practices by which storytellers make use of available resources to construct recognizable selves. They often study narratives that are produced in specific organizational settings such as prisons, courts, talk shows, human service agencies, self-help groups, and therapy centers (Gubrium & Holstein, 2001; Holstein & Gubrium, 2000; Miller, 1997; Pollner & Stein, 1996). For example, in her study of support groups for women who have experienced domestic violence, Loseke (2001) showed how group facilitators often encourage battered women to transform their narratives into "formula stories" about wife abuse. She found that many women resist the counselors' version of their experience and resist identifying themselves as "battered women," and she suggested that the problem may lie less in women's psychological denial of their victimization and more in the formula story's failure to encompass the complexities of lived experience (p. 122). As part of everyday lived experience, narratives themselves are messy and complex.

A major conceptual touchstone in this sociological approach is the "deprivatization" of personal experience. This approach highlights the wide range of institutional and organizational settings—some more and some less coercive—that shape "the selves we live by." A person's movement across a variety of settings creates further constraints as well as a plethora of options for narrating the self in a postmodern world (Holstein & Gubrium, 2000).

The third approach is also sociological.[14] Here, narrative researchers share the interest in the *hows* and *whats* of storytelling but base their inquiry on intensive interviews about specific aspects of people's lives rather than on conversations in specific organizational contexts. These researchers are interested in how people communicate meaning through a range of linguistic practices, how their stories are embedded in the interaction between researcher and narrator, how they make sense of personal experience in relation to culturally and historically specific discourses, and how they draw on, resist, and/or transform those discourses as they narrate their selves, experiences, and realities.

Examples of this approach include Langellier's (2001) study of how a woman performs the self and resists medical discourse as she comes to terms with breast cancer, Mishler's (1999) exploration of adult identity formation in craft artists' work histories, Foley and Faircloth's (2003) study of how midwives both use and resist medical discourse to legitimize their work, Riessman's (1990) examination of women's and men's divorce stories in relation to discourse about marriage and gender, Bell's (1999) exploration of how diethylstilbestrol (DES)-exposed daughters negotiate tensions between scientific and feminist discourses, Luttrell's (1997) analysis of the gendered and racialized identities of working-class mothers who return to school to get general equivalency diplomas (GEDs), and Lempert's (1994) analysis of how a woman survivor of domestic violence narrates self-transformation in relation to her physical, psychological, social, and cultural environments.

These researchers often produce detailed transcripts to study interactional processes in the interview as well as linguistic and thematic patterns throughout the narrative. A major goal of this sociological approach is showing that people create a range of narrative strategies in relation to their discursive environments, that is, that individuals' stories are constrained but not determined by hegemonic discourses. Another goal is showing that narratives provide a window to the contradictory and shifting nature of hegemonic discourses, which we tend to take for granted as stable monolithic forces.

Anthropologists have led the way in a fourth approach to narrative inquiry. Some call this approach *narrative ethnography,* which is a transformation of both the ethnographic and life history methods. Like traditional ethnography, this approach involves long-term involvement in a culture or community; like life history, it focuses heavily on one individual or on a small number of individuals. What makes narrative ethnography distinct is that both the researcher and the researched "are presented together within a single multivocal text focused on the character and process of the human encounter" (Tedlock, 1992, p. xiii).

Myerhoff's (1979/1994) *Number Our Days* is an early example. In this study of a community of elderly immigrant Jews in California, Myerhoff highlighted the life of Shmuel Goldman, a tailor and one of the most learned members of the community. At the same time, she analyzed her subjectivity as well as her relationship with those she studied. Although Myerhoff presented page after page of Shmuel's life stories "verbatim," she also showed how her questions and interruptions shaped Shmuel's narrative. And she went further. She described her distaste on observing selfish bickering over food at a community lunch, and then—with the help of a dream—she reinterpreted those actions as reflecting the social and psychological conditions of community members' lives (pp. 188–189). When Shmuel died during the course of the study, Myerhoff wrote a conversation that she imagined she and Shmuel would have had about another community member's death (pp. 228–231). Finally, she told her own story of how her grandmother's stories influenced her own life and research (pp. 237–241).

In more recent narrative ethnographies, researchers are even more explicit about the intersubjectivity of the researcher and the researched as they work to understand the other's voice, life, and culture (Behar, 1993/2003; Frank, 2000; Shostak, 2000b). A major goal of narrative ethnography is moving to the center of empirical anthropological work the issues of voice, intersubjectivity, interpretive authority, and representation.

A fifth approach to narrative inquiry is found in *autoethnography*, where researchers also turn the analytic lens on themselves and their interactions with others, but here researchers write, interpret, and/or perform their own narratives about culturally significant experiences (Crawley, 2002; Ellis & Berger, 2002; Ellis & Bochner, 1996; Ellis & Flaherty, 1992; see also Holman Jones, Chapter 7, this volume). Autoethnographers who share an interest in a topic sometimes engage in collaborative research by conducting interviews with each other, tape-recording conversations with each other, and/or writing separate accounts of their experiences. For example, Ellis and Bochner (1992) narrated separate and joint accounts of their experience of Ellis's unwanted pregnancy and subsequent abortion. And Ellis, Kiesinger, and Tillmann-Healy (1997) used an interactive interviewing method to investigate Kiesinger's and Tillmann-Healy's experiences of bulimia and Ellis's responses to their accounts.

Autoethnographers often present their work in alternative textual forms such as layered accounts (Ellis & Berger, 2002; Ellis & Bochner, 1996), and many have experimented with performing their narratives as plays, as poems, or in various other forms (Denzin, 1997, 2000, 2003; McCall & Becker, 1990; Richardson, 2002). Sometimes autoethnographers resist analysis altogether, leaving interpretation up to the audiences of their performances (Hilbert, 1990). The goal of autoethnography, and of many performance narratives, is to *show* rather than to *tell* (Denzin, 2003, p. 203) and, thus, to disrupt the politics of traditional research relationships, traditional forms of representation, and traditional social science orientations to audiences.[15]

---

▣ Methodological Issues in Contemporary Narrative Inquiry

## The Research Relationship: Narrator and Listener in Interview-Based Studies

All narrative researchers attend to the research relationship, but those whose studies are based on in-depth interviews aim specifically at transforming the interviewer–interviewee relationship into one of narrator and listener. This involves a shift in understanding the nature of interview questions and answers. These researchers often illustrate this shift by telling about how they initially ignored, grew impatient with, or got thrown off track by interviewees' stories—and later realized their mistake (Anderson & Jack, 1991; Mishler, 1986; Narayan & George, 2002; Riessman, 1990, 2002a). For instance, in *Narrating the Organization,* Czarniawska (1997) described how she used to ask questions that encouraged interviewees to generalize and compare their experiences, for example, "What are the most acute problems you are experiencing today?" and "Can you compare your present situation with that of 2 years ago?" She found, however, that most people "would break through my structure" by offering stories about the background of current circumstances. "This used to bring me to the verge of panic—'How to bring them to the point?'—whereas now I have at least learned that this *is* the point" (p. 28).

The moral of Czarniawska's account, and of similar accounts, is that the stories people tell *constitute* the empirical material that interviewers need if they are to understand how people create meanings out of events in their lives. To think of an interviewee as a narrator is to make a conceptual shift away from the idea that interviewees have answers to researchers' questions and toward the idea that interviewees are narrators with stories to tell and voices of their own.

Let me pause to say that this idea need not reflect the romantic notion, critiqued by Atkinson and Silverman (1997), that "the open-ended interview offers the opportunity for an authentic gaze into the soul of another" (p. 305). Similarly, Gubrium and Holstein (2002) critiqued the notion of a narrator's "own" voice, which implies that narrators' stories are not socially mediated. I contend that conceiving of an interviewee as a narrator is not an interest in the other's "authentic" self or unmediated voice but rather an interest in the other as a narrator of his or her particular biographical experiences as he or she understands them. Although any narration is always enabled and constrained by a host of social circumstances, *during interviews* the narrative researcher needs to orient to the particularity of the narrator's story and voice.

This conceptual shift has consequences for data collection (as well as for interpretive processes, which I will get to next). When researchers conceive of interviewees as narrators, they not only attend to the stories that people *happen* to tell during interviews but also work at *inviting* stories. Although some interviewees tell stories whether or not researchers want to hear them, other interviewees might not take up the part of narrator unless they are specifically and carefully invited to do so.

Paradoxically, assumptions embedded in our "interview society" may discourage interviewees from becoming narrators in the sense that I am developing that idea here. Denzin and Lincoln (2000) suggested that we live "in a society whose members seem to believe that interviews generate useful information about lived experience and its meanings" (p. 633; see also Atkinson & Silverman, 1997; Gubrium & Holstein, 2002). Yet interviewees often speak in generalities rather than specifics, even when talking about their experiences, because they assume (often accurately) that researchers are interested in what is general rather than particular about their experience (Weiss, 1994). As Czarniawska (1997) stated, researchers often "ask people in the field to compare, to abstract, to generalize" (p. 28). Sacks (1989) called these "sociological questions"—questions that are organized around the researcher's interest in general social processes—even though the questions may be couched in everyday language (p. 88). When researchers ask sociological questions, they are likely to get sociological answers—generalities about the interviewee's or others' experiences. The interview questions that qualitative researchers include in appendixes to their studies show how often they encourage interviewees to speak generally and abstractly.[16]

How, then, do narrative researchers invite interviewees to become narrators, that is, to tell stories about biographical particulars that are meaningful to them? I have described this as a matter of framing the interview as a whole with a broad question about whatever story the narrator has to tell about the issue at hand (Chase, 1995b, 2003). This requires a certain kind of preparation before interviewing; it requires knowing what is "storyworthy" in the narrator's social setting, an idea that is most easily grasped through examples from non-Western cultures. Grima (1991), for instance, found that Paxtun women in Northwest Pakistan attributed the most value to stories of suffering and personal hardship and that these stories were intimately connected to an honorable identity. If a woman had no such experiences, she had no story to tell. Similarly, in Rosaldo's (1976) anthropological fieldwork with Tukbaw, an Ilongot man in the Philippines, the researcher told of realizing that he had come close to "assuming that every man has his life story within him" and that the narrator himself "should be the subject of the narrative" (pp. 121–122). Although Tukbaw had plenty of stories to tell, these Western assumptions about narratives were unfamiliar to him.

Although broad cultural assumptions condition narrators' voices and the stories they have to tell, so do specific institutional, organizational, and/or discursive environments (Gubrium & Holstein, 2001). In my study of women school superintendents, for example, the fact that they are highly successful women in an overwhelmingly white- and male-dominated occupation shapes their work narratives and makes them storyworthy in a particular way. Their work narratives revolve around the juxtaposition between their individual accomplishments, on the one hand, and the gendered and racial inequities they face in their profession, on the other, and this juxtaposition makes their work narratives interesting not only to researchers and the general public but also to themselves (Chase, 1995a, pp. 14–15). Once a researcher has a sense of the broad parameters of the story that the narrator has to tell—of what is storyworthy given the narrator's social location in his or her culture, community, and/or organizational setting—the researcher can prepare for narrative interviews by developing a broad question that will invite the other to tell his or her story (Chase, 1995b). The point, of course, is not to ask for a "formula story" (Loseke, 2001); instead, the researcher needs to know the parameters of the story that others similarly situated *could* tell so as to invite *this* person's story.

In some cases, it may be easy to figure out how to frame the interview as a whole; it may be easy to articulate a broad open question that will invite a personal narrative. In my study of women superintendents, the question about their career histories turned out to be pivotal. (I confess that I did not understand it this way at the time and that my coresearcher, Colleen Bell, and I asked plenty of sociological questions along the way.) But it is not always so easy to know what the broad question will be. For example, Sacks (1989), in her ethnographic study of working-class women's militancy and leadership in the workplace, conducted interviews to understand the connection between what women learned from their families and from their workplace militancy. After her sociological interview questions produced dead ends, she finally began to ask "how they learned about work and what it meant to them." She realized that this question invited stories that showed how "family learning empowered women to rebel" (p. 88).

Being prepared to invite a story, however, is only part of the shift in the research relationship. Burgos (1989) described a transformation that may occur when an interviewee takes up the invitation to become a narrator:

> A life story comes off successfully when its narrator exercises her power upon the person who is ostensibly conducting the interview by derealising his interventions, capturing his attention, neutralizing his will, arousing his desire to learn something else, or something more, than what would be allowed by the logic of the narrative itself. (p. 33)

This statement offers a strong version of the narrator's voice as well as of the researcher's listening; in speaking from and about biographical particulars, a narrator may disrupt the assumptions that the interviewer brings to the research relationship. Thus, narrative interviewing involves a paradox. On the one hand, a researcher needs to be well prepared to ask good questions that will invite the other's particular story; on the other hand, the very idea of a particular story is that it cannot be known, predicted, or prepared for in advance. The narrator's particular story is not identical to—and may even depart radically from—what is "storyworthy" in his or her social context.

An example can be found in my own research. As Colleen Bell and I interviewed a woman superintendent who was leaving her job for a less prestigious and less stressful position, she showed us family photographs and began to tell stories about a family member who had a serious physical disability. At the time, I experienced this as a digression from her work narrative, and I waited patiently for her to get back to it. Later, as I reviewed the interview tapes, I realized that her sharing of family photos and stories was integral, not peripheral, to her work narrative; her career move "down," away from the exhausting and very public work of the superintendency, was for her a move toward a more balanced work–family relationship. If I had been open to understanding the family photos and stories as central to her work narrative, I might have prompted for and heard a fuller account of the particular way in which this woman narrated her career history. She was speaking in a different voice, or from a different subject position, from what I had anticipated; she disrupted my assumption about the "logic" of a career narrative.

## The Interpretive Process in Interview-Based Studies

When it comes to interpreting narratives heard during interviews, narrative researchers begin with narrators' voices and stories, thereby extending the narrator–listener relationship and the active work of listening into the interpretive process. This is a move away from a traditional theme-oriented method of analyzing qualitative material. Rather than locating distinct themes *across* interviews, narrative researchers listen first to the voices *within* each narrative.[17]

I realized the importance of this shift as I interpreted the women superintendents' interviews. At first, I tried to organize the transcripts into themes about work (e.g., aspirations, competence, confidence) and themes about inequality (e.g., barriers, discrimination, responses). But I soon found that it was difficult to separate a woman's talk about work and her talk about inequality. Finally it dawned on me that there was a connection between a woman's construction of self in one story (e.g., about her individual strength as a competent leader) and her construction of self in other stories (e.g., about her individual strength in fighting discrimination). Thus, I began to focus on connections among the various stories that a woman told over the course of the interview. I used the term *narrative strategy* to refer to the specific way in which each woman juxtaposed her stories about achievement and her stories about gendered and/or racial inequalities, that is, how she navigated the disjunction between individualistic discourse about achievement and group-oriented discourse about inequality (Chase, 1995a, pp. 23–25). The term *narrative strategy* draws attention to the complexity within each woman's voice—to the various subject positions each woman takes up—as well as to diversity among women's voices because each woman's narrative strategy is particular.

Narrative researchers who base their work on interviews use a variety of methods for listening to—for interpreting—complexity and multiplicity within narrators' voices. For example, in their study of adolescent girls "at risk" for early pregnancy and dropping out of school, Taylor, Gilligan, and Sullivan (1995) described an explicitly feminist Listening Guide that requires reading each interview four times. First, they attended to "the overall shape of the narrative and the research relationship"; second, to the narrator's first-person voice—how and where she uses "I"; third and fourth, to "contrapuntal voices"—voices that express psychological development, on the one hand, and psychological risk and loss, on the other (pp. 29–31). In contrast, Bamberg (1997) focused on three levels of narrative positioning: how narrators position self and others (e.g., as protagonists, as antagonists, as victims, as perpetrators), how narrators position self in relation to the audience, and how narrators "position themselves to themselves," that is, construct "a [local] answer to the question 'Who am I?'" (p. 337).

In one way or another, then, narrative researchers listen to the narrator's voices—to the subject positions, interpretive practices, ambiguities, and complexities—*within* each narrator's story. This process usually includes attention to the "narrative linkages" that a storyteller develops between the biographical particulars of his or her life, on the one hand, and the resources and constraints in his or her environment for self and reality construction, on the other (Holstein & Gubrium, 2000, p. 108). Rather than unitary, fixed, or authentic selves, these researchers suggest that narrators construct "nonunitary subjectivities" (Bloom & Munro, 1995), "revised" identities (Josselson, 1996b), "permanently unsettled identities" (Stein, 1997), and "troubled identities" (Gubrium & Holstein, 2001).

## Researchers' Voices and Narrative Strategies

Implicit in my discussion of how the researcher listens to the narrator's voice—both during the interview and while interpreting it—is the *researcher's* voice. Here, I return to issues I raised under the fifth analytic lens—issues of voice, interpretive authority, and representation. To sort out a range of possibilities, I develop a typology of three voices or narrative strategies that contemporary narrative researchers deploy as they wrestle with the question of how to use their voice(s) to interpret and represent the narrator's voice(s). My typology is not an exhaustive and rigid classification of every possible narrative strategy; rather, it is a flexible device for understanding the diversity in narrative researchers' voices. In practice, researchers may move back and forth among them.

### The Researcher's Authoritative Voice

Many narrative researchers develop an authoritative voice in their writing, including those I just described in the section on interpretive processes in interview-based studies and those I described previously in the section on diverse approaches as taking psychological and sociological approaches (the first three approaches). This narrative strategy connects and separates the researcher's and narrator's voices in a particular way. Sociologists usually present long stretches from narrators' stories or long excerpts of naturally occurring conversation, followed by their interpretations. Psychologists are more likely to offer long summaries of narrators' stories, followed by their interpretations. In each case, in the texts they create, researchers connect or intermingle their voices with narrators' voices.

At the same time, these researchers separate their voices from narrators' voices through their interpretations. They assert an authoritative interpretive voice on the grounds that they have a different interest from the narrators in the narrators' stories. For example, during an interview, both narrator and listener are interested in developing the fullness and particularity of the narrator's story, but when it comes to interpreting, the researcher turns to *how* and *what* questions that open up particular ways of understanding what the narrator is communicating through his or her story. These questions are about narrative processes that narrators typically take for granted as they tell their stories such as their use of cultural, institutional, or organizational discourses for making sense of experience, their development of narrative strategies or narrative linkages in relation to conflicting discourses, their communication of meaning through linguistic features of talk, and/or their reconstruction of psychological issues through particular metaphors or subjugated storylines (Brockmeier & Carbaugh, 2001; Capps & Ochs, 1995; Chase, 1996; Gubrium & Holstein, 1997; Hinchman & Hinchman, 2001; Holstein & Gubrium, 2000; Ochberg, 1996; Rosenwald & Ochberg, 1992).

By writing with an authoritative voice, these researchers are vulnerable to the criticism that they "privilege the analyst's listening ear" at the narrator's expense (Denzin, 1997, p. 249). After all, as narrators work to make sense of their experiences through narration, they do not talk about "the selves we live by," "identity work," "nonunitary subjectivities," "discursive constraints," or "hegemonic discourses." Nor do researchers talk this way as they narrate stories in *their* everyday lives. But I prefer (in part because my work fits here) to understand these researchers as making visible and audible taken-for-granted practices, processes, and structural and cultural features of our everyday social worlds. The sociological concepts that researchers develop serve that aim. Ochberg (1996) articulated this point from a psychological perspective: "Interpretation reveals what one [the narrator] might say if only one could speak freely, but we can see this only if we are willing to look beyond what our informants tell us in so many words" (p. 98).

By taking up an authoritative sociological or psychological voice, the researcher speaks differently from, but not disrespectfully of, the narrator's voice. Czarniawska (2002) suggested that "the justice or injustice done to the original narratives depends on the attitude of the researcher and on the precautions he or she takes" (p. 743). In discussing "narrative responsibility and respect," she recommended that researchers attend to diversity in the stories that various narrators tell, to dominant and marginal readings of narrators' stories, and to narrators' responses (including opposition) to the researchers' interpretations (pp. 742–744).[18] It bears emphasizing that when these researchers present extensive quotations from narrators' stories, they make room for readers' alternative interpretations (Laslett, 1999; Riessman, 2002).

### The Researcher's Supportive Voice

At the other end of an imaginary continuum, some narrative researchers develop a supportive voice that pushes the narrator's voice into the limelight. This is characteristic of Latin American testimonios. For example, in *I Rigoberta Menchú: An Indian Woman in Guatemala* (Menchú, 1984), the translator, Ann Wright, offered a short preface, and anthropologist Elisabeth Burgos-Debray wrote an introduction in which she described how she conducted and edited the interviews with Menchú. But the majority of the book consists of Menchú's uninterrupted stories. Diana Miloslavich Tupac developed a similarly supportive voice as editor and annotator of the work and autobiography of martyred Peruvian activist Maria Elena Moyano (Moyano, 2000). Significantly, these two testimonios named the narrators—Menchú and Moyano—as the books' authors. Other testimonios, especially those that include two or more narrators, name the researchers as the authors (e.g., Randall, 1981, 1994, 2003).

Researchers who publish oral histories or life histories may also use a muted supportive voice. For instance, in Shostak's (1981/2000a) introduction and epilogue to *Nisa: The Life and Words of a !Kung Woman,* she described her research with Nisa and the !Kung people, and she began each chapter with anthropological commentary. But the majority of the book consists of Nisa's stories (see also Blauner, 1989; Gwaltney, 1980/1993; Terkel, 1995).

When researchers present performance narratives, they may also deploy supportive voices. For example, Madison (1998) described a theatrical performance of the personal narratives of two women cafeteria workers who led a strike for better pay and working conditions at the University of North Carolina. Although the strike took place in 1968, the public performance of the narratives took place 25 years later to a packed audience during the university's bicentennial celebration. Both women were in the audience, and after the performance they received "a thunderous and lengthy standing ovation" (p. 280) as well as attention from the local media. On the occasion of the performance, the researcher's voice as interviewer and editor of the women's narratives was muted; the performance highlighted the women's voices and opened possibilities for political and civic engagement on the part of the women, the audience, and the performers.[19]

In each of these cases—testimonio, oral history, life history, and performance narrative—the researcher (and translator, who is sometimes—but not always—the same person) makes decisions about how to translate and transcribe the narrator's story, which parts of the story to include in the final product, and how to organize and edit those parts into a text or performance. And yet, because the goal of this narrative strategy is to bring the narrator's story to the public—to get the narrator's story heard—researchers do not usually dwell on how they engaged in these interpretive processes. Or if they do, they do so elsewhere. For example, in an article written after *Nisa* was published, Shostak (1989) discussed the complexities of these interpretive decisions, including the way in which she presented three voices in the book: Nisa's first-person voice, Shostak's anthropological voice, and Shostak's voice "as a young American woman experiencing another world" (pp. 230–231). Along somewhat different lines, Madison (1998, pp. 277–278) explained the idea of the "performance of possibilities," which underlies performance narratives and which provides a strong framework during the performance itself.

These researchers may encounter the criticism that they romanticize the narrator's voice as "authentic" (Atkinson & Silverman, 1997). At its best, however, this narrative strategy aims not for establishing authenticity but rather for creating a self-reflective and respectful distance between researchers' and narrators' voices. There is a time and there is a place, these researchers might say, for highlighting narrators' voices and for moving temporarily to the margins the ways in which researchers (along with a host of social, cultural, and historical circumstances) have already conditioned those voices.

*The Researcher's Interactive Voice*

A third narrative strategy displays the complex interaction—the intersubjectivity—between researchers' and narrators' voices. These researchers examine *their* voices—their subject positions, social locations, interpretations, and personal experiences—through the refracted medium of narrators' voices. This narrative strategy characterizes narrative ethnographies as well as some autoethnographies.

Frank (2000) used this narrative strategy in *Venus on Wheels: Two Decades of Dialogue on Disability, Biography, and Being Female in America,* in which she presented her long-term relationship with Diane DeVries, a woman who was born without arms and legs. Frank not only presented DeVries's stories about living with her disability but also investigated her own interest in DeVries's stories:

> In choosing to write about the life of Diane DeVries, I had to ask myself how it was that, as an anthropologist, I chose not to travel to some remote place, but to stay at home and study one individual, one with a congenital absence of limbs. (p. 85)

Through reflection on her experiences of others' disabilities, her own disabilities, and emotional lack and loss in her own life, Frank realized that "I had expected to find a victim in Diane" but instead found "a survivor" (p. 87).

Interestingly, in *Return to Nisa,* Shostak (2000b) developed the same narrative strategy while moving in the opposite geographic direction. Whereas Frank needed to understand why she chose to "stay at home," Shostak needed to understand why, after being diagnosed with breast cancer, she felt compelled to leave her husband and three young children to spend a month in Botswana with Nisa and the other !Kung people whom she had not seen for 14 years. In *Return to Nisa,* Shostak wrote not only about Nisa's life during the intervening years but also about her own complex interest in reconnecting with Nisa, who (among other things) is a well-respected healer.

In narrative ethnographies and autoethnographies, researchers make themselves vulnerable in the text (Behar, 1996; Krieger, 1991). They include extensive discussions of their emotions, thoughts, research relationships, and their unstable interpretive decisions. They include embarrassing and even shameful incidents. Indeed, these researchers are vulnerable to the criticism that they are self-indulgent and that they air dirty laundry that nobody wants to see. Yet they ground these practices in the idea that researchers need to understand themselves if they are to understand how they interpret narrators' stories *and* that readers need to understand *researchers'* stories (about their intellectual and personal relationships with narrators as well as with the cultural phenomena at hand) if readers are to understand narrators' stories. These researchers aim to undermine the myth of the invisible omniscient author (Tierney, 2002; Tierney & Lincoln, 1997).

## The Particular and the General

Despite differences in their narrative strategies for interpreting and representing narrators' voices, narrative researchers have in common the practice of devoting much more space in their written work to fewer individuals than do other qualitative researchers. Many anthropologists have written books based on one individual's life story (e.g., Behar, 1993/2003; Crapanzano, 1980; Frank, 2000; Shostak, 1981/2000a, 2000b).[20] And many sociologists, psychologists, and other narrative researchers have based books, book chapters, and articles on a small number of narratives (e.g., Bell, 1999; Bobel, 2002, chap. 1; Capps & Ochs, 1995; Chase, 1995a, 2001; DeVault, 1999, chap. 5; Ferguson, 2001, pp. 135–161; Josselson, 1996b, chaps. 4–7; Langellier, 2001; Lempert, 1994; Liebow, 1993, pp. 251–309; Luttrell, 2003, chap, 4; Mishler, 1999; Riessman, 1990, chap. 3; Rosier, 2000; Stromberg, 1993, chaps. 3–6; Wozniak, 2002, chaps. 2 and 9).

The question of whether and how an individual's narrative (or a small group of individuals' narratives) represents a larger population goes back to *The Polish Peasant.* Thomas and Znaniecki (1918/1927) argued that sociologists should gather life histories of individuals who represent the population being studied (pp. 1834–1835). They defended their extensive use of Wiszniewski's life record by claiming that he was "a typical representative of the culturally passive mass which, under the present conditions and at the present stage of social evolution, constitutes in every civilized society the enormous majority of the population" (p. 1907). In evaluating *The Polish Peasant,* however, Blumer (1939/1979) claimed that Thomas and Znaniecki had failed to demonstrate Wiszniewski's representativeness and that it would have been difficult for them to do so anyway (p. 44).

Contemporary narrative researchers occupy a different social and historical location. Under the auspices of the narrative turn, they reject the idea that the small number of narratives they present must be generalizable to a certain population. Some researchers do this by highlighting the particularity of the narratives they present and by placing them in a broader frame. For example, Shostak's *Nisa* is about one woman's narrative, but Shostak (1989) used the stories of the other !Kung women she interviewed, as well as previous anthropological studies of the !Kung people, to show how Nisa's story is at once unique in some respects and similar to other !Kung women's stories in other ways.

Many contemporary narrative researchers, however, make a stronger break from Thomas and Znaniecki's (1918/1927) positivist stance regarding representativeness. Given "narrative elasticity" and the range of "narrative options" in any particular setting (Holstein & Gubrium, 2000), as well as constant flux in social and historical conditions, these researchers propose that the range of narrative possibilities within any group of people is potentially limitless. To make matters more complex, as Gubrium and Holstein (2002) suggested, "Treating subject positions and their associated voices seriously, we might find that an ostensibly single interview could actually be, in practice, an interview with several subjects, whose particular identities may be only partially clear" (p. 23).

Thus, many contemporary narrative researchers approach *any* narrative as an *instance* of the possible relationships between a narrator's active construction of self, on the one hand, and the social, cultural, and historical circumstances that enable and constrain that narrative, on the other. Researchers often highlight a range of possible narratives to show that no one particular story is determined by a certain social location, but they do not claim that their studies exhaust the possibilities within that context (see, e.g., Auerbach, 2002; Bell, 1999; Chase, 1995a; Mishler, 1999). From this perspective, any narrative is significant because it embodies—and gives us insight into—what is possible and intelligible within a specific social context.[21]

## ▣ NARRATIVE INQUIRY AND SOCIAL CHANGE

As outlined by Denzin and Lincoln, a major goal of this series based on the *Handbook* is exploring how qualitative research can "advance a democratic project committed to social justice in an age of uncertainty" (personal communication, July 7, 2002). With that goal in mind, I now turn to questions about the relationship between narrative inquiry and social change. What kinds of narratives disrupt oppressive social processes? How and when do researchers' analyses and representations of others' stories encourage social justice and democratic processes? And for whom are these processes disrupted and encouraged? Which audiences need to hear which researchers' and narrators' stories?

For some people, the act of narrating a significant life event itself facilitates positive change. In discussing a breast cancer survivor's narrative, Langellier (2001) wrote, "The wounded storyteller reclaims the capacity to tell, and hold on to, her own story, resisting narrative surrender to the medical chart as the official story of the illness" (p. 146; see also Capps & Ochs, 1995; Frank, 1995). Along similar lines, Rosenwald and Ochberg (1992) claimed that self-narration can lead to personal emancipation—to "better" stories of life difficulties or traumas. In these cases, the narrator is his or her own audience, the one who needs to hear alternative versions of his or her identity or life events, and the one for whom changes in the narrative can "stir up changes" in the life (p. 8; see also Mishler, 1995, pp. 108–109).

For other narrators, the urgency of storytelling arises from the need and desire to have *others* hear one's story. Citing René Jara, Beverley (2000) described testimonios as "emergency narratives" that involve

a problem of repression, poverty, marginality, exploitation, or simply survival. . . . The voice that speaks to the reader through the text . . . [takes] the form of an I that demands to be recognized, that wants or needs to stake a claim on our attention. (p. 556)

But it is not only Latin American testimonios that are narrated with this urgent voice. The stories of many marginalized groups have changed the contemporary narrative landscape—to name just a few, the stories of transgendered people, people with disabilities, and the survivors of gendered, racial/ethnic, and sexual violence. Indeed, "giving voice" to marginalized people and "naming silenced lives" have been primary goals of narrative research for several decades (McLaughlin & Tierney, 1993; Personal Narratives Group, 1989).

If a previously silenced narrator is to challenge an audience's assumptions or actions effectively, the audience must be ready to hear the narrator's story—or must be jolted into listening to it. In writing about empathetic listening, Frank (2000) stated, "Taking the other's perspective is a necessary step in constructive social change" (p. 94). In a similar vein, Gamson (2002) argued that storytelling "promotes empathy across different social locations" (p. 189). Although he was writing about media discourse on abortion, Gamson's argument is relevant to the narrative approaches I have been discussing. Gamson resisted the critique of American popular media (e.g., newspapers, television) that they are too infused with personal narratives. Because an unwanted pregnancy is ultimately a woman's problem, excluding stories about that "existential dilemma" from media and policy discourse silences women in particular. Thus, he argued that "personalization . . . opens discursive opportunities" (p. 189). Gamson had in mind "deliberation and dialogue in a narrative mode," which (unlike abstract argument) "lends itself more easily to the expression of moral complexity." In this sense, "storytelling facilitates a healthy democratic, public life" (p. 197).

During recent years, many narrative researchers have pushed beyond the goal of eliciting previously silenced narratives. Tierney's (2000) description of the goal of life history research applies to other forms of narrative research as well:

> Life histories are helpful not merely because they add to the mix of what already exists, but because of their ability to refashion identities. Rather than a conservative goal based on nostalgia for a paradise lost, or a liberal one of enabling more people to take their places at humanity's table, a goal of life history work in a postmodern age is to break the stranglehold of metanarratives that establishes rules of truth, legitimacy, and identity. The work of life history becomes the investigation of the mediating aspects of culture, the interrogation of its grammar, and the decentering of its norms. (p. 546)

These statements offer a strong version of what I described earlier as the researcher's authoritative voice. When researchers' interpretive strategies reveal the stranglehold of oppressive metanarratives, they help to open up possibilities for social change. In this sense, audiences need to hear not only the narrator's story, but also the researcher's explication of how the narrator's story is constrained by, and strains against, the mediating aspects of culture (and of institutions, organizations, and sometimes the social sciences themselves). Audiences whose members identify with the narrator's story might be moved by the researcher's interpretation to understand *their* stories in new ways and to imagine how they could tell their stories differently. Audiences whose members occupy social locations different from the narrator's might be moved through empathetic listening to think and act in ways that benefit the narrator or what he or she advocates (Madison, 1998, pp. 279–282).

What if the audience is hostile? DeVault and Ingraham (1999) broached this issue: "A radical challenge to silencing is not only about having a say, but about talking back in the strongest sense—saying the very things that those in power resist hearing" (p. 184). When the audience is both powerful and invested in the status quo—invested in oppressive metanarratives—narrators and narrative researchers may turn to "collective stories," which connect an individual's story to the broader story of a marginalized social group (Richardson, 1990). In discussing the collective stories of sexual abuse survivors and gays and lesbians, Plummer (1995) wrote, "For narratives to flourish, there must be a community to hear. . . . For communities to hear, there must be stories which weave together their history, their identity, their politics. The one—community—feeds upon and into the other—story" (p. 87). In the face of a hostile and powerful audience, narrators strengthen their communities through narratives and simultaneously seek to broaden their community of listeners. Thus, collective stories—or testimonios—become integral to social movements (see also Davis, 2002). However, it is important to heed Naples's (2003) cautionary note. In her analysis of how personal narratives function in the social movement of childhood sexual abuse survivors, she argued that we must determine when and where various strategies of speaking from personal experience are more effective and less effective in challenging oppression (p. 1152).

Although discussion of social movements and testimonios evokes the need for large-scale social change, we also need to consider the role of narratives and narrative research in small-scale, localized social change. For example, in Auerbach's (2002) study of Latino/Latina parent involvement in a college access program for their high school children, she heard many parents tell of poor treatment at the hands of school personnel. Auerbach also observed that the program gave parents some opportunities to share their stories publicly with each other and that sometimes this public performance of their stories led to collective problem solving (p. 1381). Equally important, Auerbach pointed to the need for such programs to create "a third space" that "disrupts the official discourse and scripted behavior that normally dominates school events for parents, just as it does in classrooms for students" (p. 1386). In other words, such programs hold the promise of creating conditions that would allow school administrators, teachers, and counselors to hear parents' narratives so that school staff can be jolted into resisting metanarratives that usually prevail in their work environments—immigrant families of color are uninterested in their children's education, immigrant children of color have limited educational potential, and so forth (see also Rosier, 2000). Auerbach suggested that researchers can help to create public spaces in which marginalized people's narratives can be heard even by those who normally do not want to hear them.

## ▣ NARRATIVE INQUIRY: A FIELD IN THE MAKING

In *my* narrative, I have attempted to give shape to the massive material that can be called narrative inquiry, identifying its contours and complexities and arguing for the idea that it constitutes a subfield within qualitative inquiry even amid its multiplicity. Here I raise some issues—in the form of a set of relationships—that I believe are pivotal to the future of this field.

First is the relationship between theoretical and methodological work within narrative inquiry. Narrative theorists point out that narrative research is embedded in and shaped by broad social and historical currents, particularly the ubiquity of personal narratives in contemporary Western culture and politics—from television talk shows, to politicians' speeches, to self-help groups. Clough (2000) warned, however, that the "trauma culture" we currently inhabit encourages proliferation of personal narratives about trouble and suffering without offering a theory and politics of social change. Along similar lines, Atkinson and Silverman (1997) and Gubrium and Holstein (2002) pointed to the powerful tug of our "interview society," and they warned researchers against the romantic assumption that narrators reveal "authentic" selves and speak in their "own" voices, as if their selves and voices were not already mediated by the social contexts in which they speak. I argued earlier that treating interviewees as narrators does not mean succumbing to those problematic assumptions. Here, however, I suggest that narrative researchers need to do more, collectively, to integrate a critique of the trauma culture/interview society with discussion of methodological issues involved in conducting empirical research (e.g., inviting and interpreting narrators' stories). How do these two activities—one theoretical and the other methodological—support each other and serve a joint purpose? What specific research practices produce narrative research informed by a broad social critique and a politics of social change? Given the centrality of personal narrative in many political, cultural, and social arenas, narrative researchers have much work to do and much to offer by way of empirically grounded analysis and social critique (Crawley & Broad, 2004; Naples, 2003). No one theoretical or empirical project can do everything, of course, but it seems to me that one key lies in more conversation among narrative researchers across theoretical and methodological interests.

Second is the relationship between Western and non-Western narrative theories and practices. Gubrium and Holstein (2002) suggested that the interview society has gone global—that people around the globe know what it means to be interviewed. Even Nisa, a member of the (until recently) hunting and gathering !Kung people, knows how to place herself at the center of a life story (Shostak, 1981/2000a, 2000b). At the same time, narrative researchers need to understand cross-cultural differences more fully. What do Western narrative researchers (and Westerners in general) have to learn from the ways in which non-Westerners narrate the self, narrate group identities, or integrate folklore narratives into personal narratives (Grima, 1991; Narayan &

George, 2002; Riessman, 2002b)? If self or identity is not the central construct in (at least some) non-Western narratives (Rosaldo, 1976), what is? What do non-Western narrative researchers have to teach their Western counterparts about the kinds of narratives that need to be heard and about interpretive and narrative strategies for presenting and performing them? What is the relationship among narrative, narrative research, and social change in non-Western societies? For example, what impact do Latin American testimonios have in the local communities from which they arise? I am not suggesting that Western narrative researchers should take up residence in non-Western locales; rather, I am suggesting that we need to understand more fully how our research is imbued with Western assumptions about self and identity. Anthropologists may be ahead of the game here, but much American narrative research remains unreflective about its Western character.

The third issue revolves around the relationship between narrative inquiry and technological innovation. Although it is hard to imagine narrative researchers giving up the domain of face-to-face interviewing and on-site gathering of naturally occurring conversation, some researchers have already moved into the domain of virtual research and many others will follow in their footsteps (Mann & Stewart, 2002; see also Markham, Chapter 8, this volume). How are e-mail, chat groups, online support groups, and instant messaging changing the meaning of "naturally occurring conversation"? How are they creating new arenas for narrating the self and for constructing identities, realities, relationships, and communities? As narrative researchers explore these new opportunities to hear people converse and to interview individuals and groups, what new risks and ethical issues will they encounter? What new forms of knowledge will emerge?

Fourth, researchers interested in the relationship between narrative and social change need to do more to address the issue of audience (Lincoln, 1997). We need to think more about who could benefit from, and who needs to hear, *our* research narratives. Marginalized people in the communities we study? Power brokers and gatekeepers in the communities we study? Policymakers? Students in our classes? The public at large? Other researchers within our disciplines and substantive fields of study? Equally important, in my view, is the need for narrative researchers to explore the possible points of contact between *narrators'* stories and various audiences who need to hear them. What kinds of stories (and what kinds of research narratives) incite collective action? And to what effect? When do previously silenced narrators jolt powerful—and initially hostile—audiences to join in breaking the stranglehold of oppressive metanarratives? And how can researchers help to create the conditions of empathetic listening across social locations?

Along these lines, what do we have to learn from Ensler's (2001) wildly successful *Vagina Monologues*? How did Ensler transform interviews with women about their bodies into performances that have sparked a massive international movement against violence against women?[22] Similarly, what do we have to learn about writing for the public from Ehrenreich's (2001) best-seller, *Nickel and Dimed: On (Not) Getting By in America*?

In this mixture of undercover reporting and narrative ethnography, Ehrenreich wrote both seriously and humorously about her efforts to make ends meet for a month at a time as a waitress in Florida, a house cleaner in Maine, and a Wal-Mart employee in Minnesota. Many of my students claim that this text disrupts their attachment to individualist ideologies in ways that other texts do not. I am not suggesting that we should all aspire to off-Broadway performances or to best-sellerdom for our work; rather, I am suggesting that we need to think more concertedly and broadly about whom we write for and speak to—and how we do so. For many of us, this may mean thinking about how to create public spaces in our local communities where the personal narratives and collective stories of marginalized people can be heard by—and can jolt out of their complacency—those who occupy more powerful subject positions and social locations.

Finally, narrative researchers need to attend to the relationship between our work and that of our social science colleagues who work within other traditions of inquiry. We need to treat other social science scholars as an important audience for our work. We need to demonstrate that immersion in the biographical leg of Mills's trilogy—biography, history, and society—produces new significant concepts and analyses that other researchers in our substantive areas and disciplines *need* to do their work well. For example, Loseke's (2001) concept of the "formula story" of wife abuse, and her analysis of its inadequacy in capturing women's complex stories of domestic violence, is crucial to the work of other social scientists—whether quantitative or qualitative—who study the success or failure of battered women's shelters in helping women to leave abusive partners. Generally speaking, narrative inquiry's contributions to social science have to do with concepts and analyses that demonstrate two things: (a) the creativity, complexity, and variability of individuals' (or groups') self and reality constructions and (b) the power of historical, social, cultural, organizational, discursive, interactional, and/or psychological circumstances in shaping the range of possibilities for self and reality construction in any particular time and place. Narrative researchers need to confidently assert their contributions to, their interventions in, and their transformations of social science scholarship.

As narrative researchers grapple with these and myriad other issues and questions, it is hard to imagine Mills's argument for the joint investigation of biography, society, and history going out of style. What exactly that means, however, will likely undergo many further permutations, disrupting assumptions that many of us now hold dear.

▣ NOTES

1. I thank Norman Denzin, Yvonna Lincoln, James Holstein, Ruthellen Josselson, and Catherine Riessman for their comments on earlier drafts of this chapter.

2. The *Journal of Narrative and Life History* was created in 1990, and it became *Narrative Inquiry* in 1998. As just two examples of conferences, in February 2003 the American Educational Research Association held a Winter Institute on Narrative Inquiry in Social

Science Research at the Ontario Institute for Studies in Education, and in May 2004 the second biannual Narrative Matters conference was held at St. Thomas University in New Brunswick.

3. For overviews of early life history methods in sociology, see Becker (1966), Bertaux (1981), Denzin (1970), and Plummer (1983).

4. The life history and life story approaches continue to be international in scope. The 2003 Board of Biography and Society, a research committee of the International Sociological Association, included researchers from many European countries as well as from Japan, South Africa, and Russia.

5. In addition to summarizing the interview data that she gathered from 129 women about childbearing, child rearing, marriage, housework, fieldwork, and community participation, Hagood (1939) presented two women's life stories in depth. This allows readers to see the impact on these two women's lives of the social and economic conditions described earlier in the book.

6. For overviews of early life history methods in anthropology, see Langness (1965), Langness and Frank (1981), and Watson and Watson-Franke (1985).

7. Two volumes of *The American Slave* consist of interviews conducted at Fisk University before the Federal Writers' Project was created. During the late 1960s and early 1970s, Lester (1968) and Yetman (1970), among others, were publishing parts of and writing about the slave narratives. After the publication of *The American Slave,* Rawick (1977) and other researchers searched for, found, and published many other slave narratives that had been deposited in state collections and libraries. Not surprisingly, they found evidence that some of the narratives had been tampered with, presumably to suppress negative portrayals of whites.

8. For overviews of early second-wave feminist use of life history and personal narratives, see Armitage (1983), Geiger (1986), Gluck (1979, 1983), Personal Narratives Group (1989), and Reinharz (1992, chap. 7).

9. Even before feminism became a major influence in social science research, there were exceptions to this pattern of methodological indifference and objectification of research participants. For example, in *Mountain Wolf Woman: Sister of Crashing Thunder,* Lurie (1961) addressed many methodological issues and described in detail her relationship with Mountain Wolf Woman.

10. See Mishler (1995, pp. 90–102) on various ways in which narrative researchers connect the "telling" and the "told."

11. Polkinghorne (1995) and Mishler (1995) also made distinctions among types of narrative research in the social sciences, but because they excluded some kinds of work that I want to include (and because they included some kinds that I want to exclude), I construct my own categories here.

12. Because quantitative modes of inquiry are so dominant in psychology, some psychologists treat narrative inquiry as synonymous with qualitative inquiry (Josselson, Lieblich, & McAdams, 2003). Nonetheless, I have tried to separate out a psychological approach that uses the analytic lenses I have articulated and so is not identical to qualitative research in general.

13. For interview guides used by psychological researchers who take a narrative approach, see McAdams and Bowman (2001, pp. 12–13) and Josselson (1996b, pp. 265–272).

14. Some of the researchers I include in this approach are not sociologists. For example, Mishler is a psychologist and Langellier is a communication scholar. Nonetheless, their approach is sociological in the ways described here.

15. Sometimes memoirs, even those not written by social scientists, have autoethnographic characteristics. For example, in *Crossing the Color Line: Race, Parenting, and Culture*, Reddy (1994) investigated her experiences as a white woman married to an African American man and as the mother of two biracial children. She showed how these racialized relationships disrupted her identity as a white woman and her understanding of racial issues in the social world. The writing itself, however, is not experimental in the same way that much autoethnographic writing is.

16. See Chase (1995b, 2003) for a comparison of sociological interview questions and questions oriented to inviting narratives.

17. The influence of narrative inquiry can be seen in the difference between Rubin's (1976) *Worlds of Pain: Life in the Working Class Family* and Rubin's (1994) *Families on the Faultline: America's Working Class Speaks About the Family, the Economy, Race, and Ethnicity*. In the earlier book, Rubin (1976) presented anonymous excerpts from a range of interviewees to represent various themes. In contrast, Rubin (1994) organized the more recent book around the stories of specific families, beginning and ending the book with the same four families.

18. See also Ochberg (1996) on the ways in which researchers "convert what we have been told from one kind of account into another" (p. 110). In addition, Josselson (1996a) offered an interesting discussion of the anxiety, guilt, and shame that may arise when "writing other people's lives" and sharing interpretations with those people.

19. Ferguson's (2001) *Bad Boys: Public Schools in the Making of Black Masculinity* offers an example of a researcher mixing narrative strategies. For the most part, Ferguson wrote with an authoritative voice. But in the middle of the book, she shifted to a supportive voice when she included a 27-page transcript from an interview with an African American mother whose attempt to discipline her son was itself disciplined by police, courts, and social service agencies. Ferguson stated, "You must read what Mariana had to say aloud. You cannot understand it unless you hear the words" (p. 135).

20. For many other examples, see Koehler (1981, pp. 89–93), Langness and Frank (1981), and Watson and Watson-Franke (1985).

21. Focusing on instances rather than representative cases is not unique to narrative inquiry, but the issue may seem more urgent in narrative research because of the small number of narratives that researchers present. For broader discussions of the relation between the particular and the general, see Blum and McHugh (1984, p. 37), Denzin (1997, p. 245), and Psathas (1995, p. 50).

22. *The Vagina Monologues* was originally an off-Broadway production based on interviews with 200 American women. It has been performed in many cities and communities across the United States as well as around the globe. When performed in conjunction with the "V-day" movement, profits are donated to organizations fighting violence against women.

## ▣ REFERENCES

Anderson, K., & Jack, D. C. (1991). Learning to listen: Interview techniques and analyses. In S. B. Gluck & D. Patai (Eds.), *Women's words: The feminist practice of oral history* (pp. 11–26). New York: Routledge.

Armitage, S. H. (1983). The next step. *Frontiers: A Journal of Women's Studies, 7*, 3–8.

Atkinson, P., & Silverman, D. (1997). Kundera's *Immortality:* The interview society and the invention of the self. *Qualitative Inquiry, 3,* 304–325.

Atkinson, R. (2002). The life story interview. In J. F. Gubrium & J. A. Holstein (Eds.), *Handbook of interview research: Context and method* (pp. 121–140). Thousand Oaks, CA: Sage.

Auerbach, S. (2002). "Why do they give the good classes to some and not to others?" Latino parent narratives of struggle in a college access program. *Teachers College Record, 104,* 1369–1392.

Babb, J., & Taylor, P. E. (1981). *Border healing woman: The story of Jewel Babb.* Austin: University of Texas Press.

Bamberg, M. G. W. (1997). Positioning between structure and performance. *Journal of Narrative and Life History, 7,* 335–342.

Barthes, R. (1977). *Image, music, text* (S. Heath, Trans.). New York: Hill & Wang.

Bauman, R. (1986). *Story, performance, and event: Contextual studies in oral narrative.* Cambridge, UK: Cambridge University Press.

Becker, H. S. (1966). Introduction. In C. R. Shaw, *The jack-roller: A delinquent boy's own story.* Chicago: University of Chicago Press.

Behar, R. (1996). *The vulnerable observer: Anthropology that breaks your heart.* Boston: Beacon.

Behar, R. (2003). *Translated woman: Crossing the border with Esperanza's story.* Boston: Beacon. (Original work published 1993)

Belenky, M. F., Clinchy, B. M., Goldberger, N. R., & Tarule, J. M. (1986). *Women's ways of knowing: The development of self, voice, and mind.* New York: Basic Books.

Bell, S. E. (1999). Narratives and lives: Women's health politics and the diagnosis of cancer for DES daughters. *Narrative Inquiry, 9,* 347–389.

Bertaux, D. (Ed.). (1981). *Biography and society: The life history approach in the social sciences.* Beverly Hills, CA: Sage.

Beverley, J. (2000). Testimonio, subalternity, and narrative authority. In N. K. Denzin & Y. S. Lincoln (Eds.), *Handbook of qualitative research* (2nd ed., pp. 555–565). Thousand Oaks, CA: Sage.

Blauner, B. (1989). *Black lives, white lives: Three decades of race relations in America.* Berkeley: University of California Press.

Bloom, L. R., & Munro, P. (1995). Conflicts of selves: Nonunitary subjectivity in women administrators' life history narratives. In J. A. Hatch & R. Wisniewski (Eds.), *Life history and narrative* (pp. 99–112). London: Falmer.

Blum, A., & McHugh, P. (1984). *Self-reflection in the arts and sciences.* Atlantic Highlands, NJ: Humanities Press.

Blumer, H. (1979). *Critiques of research in the social sciences: An appraisal of Thomas and Znaniecki's* The Polish Peasant in Europe and America. New Brunswick, NJ: Transaction Books. (Original work published 1939)

Bobel, C. (2002). *The paradox of natural mothering.* Philadelphia: Temple University Press.

Botkin, B. A. (Ed.). (1945). *Lay my burden down: A folk history of slavery.* Chicago: University of Chicago Press.

Briggs, C. L. (1986). *Learning how to ask: A sociolinguistic appraisal of the role of the interview in social science research.* Cambridge, UK: Cambridge University Press.

Briggs, C. L. (2002). Interviewing, power/knowledge, and social inequality. In J. F. Gubrium & J. A. Holstein (Eds.), *Handbook of interview research: Context and method* (pp. 911–922). Thousand Oaks, CA: Sage.

Brockmeier, J., & Carbaugh, D. (Eds.). (2001). *Narrative and identity: Studies in autobiography, self, and culture.* Amsterdam, Netherlands: John Benjamins.

Bruner, J. (1986). *Actual minds, possible worlds.* Cambridge, MA: Harvard University Press.

Bruner, J. (1997). Labov and Waletzky: Thirty years on. *Journal of Narrative and Life History, 7,* 61–68.

Bruner, J. (2002). *Making stories: Law, literature, life.* New York: Farrar, Straus, & Giroux.

Burgos, M. (1989). Life stories, narrativity, and the search for the self. *Life Stories* [*Récits de vie*], 5, 27–38.

Capps, L., & Ochs, E. (1995). *Constructing panic: The discourse of agoraphobia.* Cambridge, MA: Harvard University Press.

Chalasiński, J. (1981). The life records of the young generation of Polish peasants as a manifestation of contemporary culture. In D. Bertaux (Ed.), *Biography and society: The life history approach in the social sciences* (pp. 119–132). Beverly Hills, CA: Sage.

Chase, S. E. (1995a). *Ambiguous empowerment: The work narratives of women school superintendents.* Amherst: University of Massachusetts Press.

Chase, S. E. (1995b). Taking narrative seriously: Consequences for method and theory in interview studies. In R. Josselson & A. Lieblich (Eds.), *Interpreting experience: The narrative study of lives* (pp. 1–26). Thousand Oaks, CA: Sage.

Chase, S. E. (1996). Personal vulnerability and interpretive authority in narrative research. In R. Josselson (Ed.), *Ethics and process in the narrative study of lives* (pp. 45–59). Thousand Oaks, CA: Sage.

Chase, S. E. (2001). Universities as discursive environments for sexual identity construction. In J. F. Gubrium & J. A. Holstein (Eds.), *Institutional selves: Troubled identities in a postmodern world* (pp. 142–157). New York: Oxford University Press.

Chase, S. E. (2003). Learning to listen: Narrative principles in a qualitative research methods course. In R. Josselson, A. Lieblich, & D. P. McAdams (Eds.), *Up close and personal: The teaching and learning of narrative research* (pp. 79–99). Washington, DC: American Psychological Association.

Clough, P. T. (2000). Comments on setting criteria for experimental writing. *Qualitative Inquiry, 6,* 278–291.

Crapanzano, V. (1980). *Tuhami: Portrait of a Moroccan.* Chicago: University of Chicago Press.

Crawley, S. L. (2002). "They still don't understand why I hate wearing dresses!" An autoethnographic rant on dresses, boats, and butchness. *Cultural Studies, Critical Methodologies, 2,* 69–92.

Crawley, S. L., & Broad, K. L. (2004). "Be your(real lesbian)self": Mobilizing sexual formula stories through personal (and political) storytelling. *Journal of Contemporary Ethnography, 33,* 39–71.

Czarniawska, B. (1997). *Narrating the organization: Dramas of institutional identity.* Chicago: University of Chicago Press.

Czarniawska, B. (2002). Narrative, interviews, and organizations. In J. F. Gubrium & J. A. Holstein (Eds.), *Handbook of interview research: Context and method* (pp. 733–749). Thousand Oaks, CA: Sage.

Davis, J. E. (Ed.). (2002). *Stories of change: Narrative and social movements.* Albany: State University of New York Press.

Denzin, N. K. (1970). *The research act: A theoretical introduction to sociological methods.* Chicago: Aldine.

Denzin, N. K. (1989). *Interpretive biography.* Newbury Park, CA: Sage.

Denzin, N. K. (1997). *Interpretive ethnography: Ethnographic practices for the 21st century.* Thousand Oaks, CA: Sage.

Denzin, N. K. (2000). The practices and politics of interpretation. In N. K. Denzin & Y. S. Lincoln (Eds.), *Handbook of qualitative research* (2nd ed., pp. 897–922). Thousand Oaks, CA: Sage.

Denzin, N. K. (2003). The call to performance. *Symbolic Interaction, 26,* 187–207.

Denzin, N. K., & Lincoln, Y. S. (2000). Introduction: The discipline and practice of qualitative research. In N. K. Denzin & Y. S. Lincoln (Eds.), *Handbook of qualitative research* (2nd ed., pp. 1–28). Thousand Oaks, CA: Sage.

DeVault, M. L. (1999). *Liberating method: Feminism and social research.* Philadelphia: Temple University Press.

DeVault, M. L., & Ingraham, C. (1999). Metaphors of silence and voice in feminist thought. In M. L. DeVault, *Liberating method: Feminism and social research* (pp. 175–186). Philadelphia: Temple University Press.

DuBois, C. (1960). *The people of Alor: A social-psychological study of an East Indian island.* Cambridge, MA: Harvard University Press. (Original work published 1944)

Ehrenreich, B. (2001). *Nickel and dimed: On (not) getting by in America.* New York: Metropolitan Books.

Ellis, C., & Berger, L. (2002). Their story/My story/Our story: Including the researcher's experience in interview research. In J. F. Gubrium & J. A. Holstein (Eds.), *Handbook of interview research: Context and method* (pp. 849–875). Thousand Oaks, CA: Sage.

Ellis, C., & Bochner, A. P. (1992). Telling and performing personal stories: The constraints of choice in abortion. In C. Ellis & M. G. Flaherty (Eds.), *Investigating subjectivity: Research on lived experience* (pp. 79–101). Newbury Park, CA: Sage.

Ellis, C., & Bochner, A. P. (Eds.). (1996). *Composing ethnography: Alternative forms of qualitative writing.* Walnut Creek, CA: AltaMira.

Ellis, C., & Flaherty, M. G. (Eds.). (1992). *Investigating subjectivity: Research on lived experience.* Newbury Park, CA: Sage.

Ellis, C., Kiesinger, C. E., & Tillmann-Healy, L. M. (1997). Interactive interviewing: Talking about emotional experience. In R. Hertz (Ed.), *Reflexivity and voice* (pp. 119–149). Thousand Oaks, CA: Sage.

Emihovich, C. (1995). Distancing passion: Narratives in social science. In J. A. Hatch & R. Wisniewski (Eds.), *Life history and narrative* (pp. 37–48). London: Falmer.

Ensler, E. (2001). *The vagina monologues: The V-day edition.* New York: Villard/Random House.

Ferguson, A. A. (2001). *Bad boys: Public schools in the making of black masculinity.* Ann Arbor: University of Michigan Press.

Foley, L., & Faircloth, C. A. (2003). Medicine as discursive resource: Legitimation in the work narratives of midwives. *Sociology of Health & Illness, 25,* 165–184.

Frank, A. W. (1995). *The wounded storyteller: Body, illness, and ethics.* Chicago: University of Chicago Press.

Frank, G. (2000). *Venus on wheels: Two decades of dialogue on disability, biography, and being female in America.* Berkeley: University of California Press.

Franz, C. E., & Stewart, A. J. (Eds.). (1994). *Women creating lives: Identities, resilience, and resistance.* Boulder, CO: Westview.

Gamson, W. A. (2002). How storytelling can be empowering. In K. A. Cerulo (Ed.), *Culture in mind: Toward a sociology of culture and cognition* (pp. 187–198). New York: Routledge.

Garfinkel, H. (1967). *Studies in ethnomethodology.* Englewood Cliffs, NJ: Prentice Hall.

Geiger, S. N. G. (1986). Women's life histories: Method and content. *Signs: Journal of Women in Culture and Society, 11,* 334–351.

Gluck, S. (1979). What's so special about women? Women's oral history. *Frontiers: A Journal of Women's Studies, 2,* 3–11.

Gluck, S. B. (1983). Women's oral history: The second decade. *Frontiers: A Journal of Women's Studies, 7,* 1–2.

Gluck, S. B., & Patai, D. (Eds.). (1991). *Women's words: The feminist practice of oral history.* New York: Routledge.

Grima, B. (1991). The role of suffering in women's performance of *paxto.* In A. Appadurai, F. J. Korom, & M. A. Mills (Eds.), *Gender, genre, and power in South Asian expressive traditions* (pp. 78–101). Philadelphia: University of Pennsylvania Press.

Gubrium, J. F., & Holstein, J. A. (1997). *The new language of qualitative method.* New York: Oxford University Press.

Gubrium, J. F., & Holstein, J. A. (Eds.). (2001). *Institutional selves: Troubled identities in a postmodern world.* New York: Oxford University Press.

Gubrium, J. F., & Holstein, J. A. (2002). From the individual interview to the interview society. In J. F. Gubrium & J. A. Holstein (Eds.), *Handbook of interview research: Context and method* (pp. 3–32). Thousand Oaks, CA: Sage.

Gwaltney, J. L. (Ed.). (1993). *Drylongso: A self-portrait of Black America.* New York: New Press. (Original work published 1980)

Hagood, M. J. (1939). *Mothers of the South: Portraiture of the white tenant farm woman.* New York: Greenwood.

Hatch, J. A., & Wisniewski, R. (Eds.). (1995). *Life history and narrative.* London: Falmer.

Hertz, R. (Ed.). (1997). *Reflexivity and voice.* Thousand Oaks, CA: Sage.

Hilbert, R. A. (1990). The efficacy of performance science: Comment on McCall and Becker. *Social Problems, 37,* 133–135.

Hinchman, L. P., & Hinchman, S. K. (Eds.). (2001). *Memory, identity, community: The idea of narrative in the human sciences.* Albany: State University of New York Press.

Holstein, J. A., & Gubrium, J. F. (2000). *The self we live by: Narrative identity in a postmodern world.* New York: Oxford University Press.

Hunt, A. M., & Winegarten, R. (1983). *I am Annie Mae: An extraordinary black Texas woman in her own words.* Austin: University of Texas Press.

Jacobs, R. H. (1979). *Life after youth: Female, forty—What next?* Boston: Beacon.

Josselson, R. (1996a). On writing other people's lives: Self-analytic reflections of a narrative researcher. In R. Josselson (Ed.), *Ethics and process in the narrative study of lives* (pp. 60–71). Thousand Oaks, CA: Sage.

Josselson, R. (1996b). *Revising herself: The story of women's identity from college to midlife.* New York: Oxford University Press.

Josselson, R., Lieblich, A., & McAdams, D. P. (Eds.). (2003). *Up close and personal: The teaching and learning of narrative research.* Washington, DC: American Psychological Association.

Kardiner, A. (1945). *The psychological frontiers of society.* Westport, CT: Greenwood.

Koehler, L. (1981). Native women of the Americas: A bibliography. *Frontiers: A Journal of Women's Studies, 6,* 73–101.

Krieger, S. (1991). *Social science and the self: Personal essays on an art form.* New Brunswick, NJ: Rutgers University Press.

Labov, W., & Waletzky, J. (1997). Narrative analysis: Oral versions of personal experience. *Journal of Narrative and Life History, 7,* 3–38. (Original work published 1967)

Langellier, K. M. (2001). You're marked: Breast cancer, tattoo, and the narrative performance of identity. In J. Brockmeier & D. Carbaugh (Eds.), *Narrative and identity: Studies in autobiography, self, and culture* (pp. 145–184). Amsterdam, Netherlands: John Benjamins.

Langness, L. L. (1965). *The life history in anthropological science.* New York: Holt, Rinehart & Winston.

Langness, L. L., & Frank, G. (1981). *Lives: An anthropological approach to biography.* Novato, CA: Chandler & Sharp.

Laslett, B. (1999). Personal narratives as sociology. *Contemporary Sociology, 28,* 391–401.

Lempert, L. B. (1994). A narrative analysis of abuse: Connecting the personal, the rhetorical, and the structural. *Journal of Contemporary Ethnography, 22,* 411–441.

Lester, J. (1968). *To be a slave.* New York: Scholastic.

Lewis, O. (1961). *The children of Sánchez: Autobiography of a Mexican family.* New York: Random House.

Liebow, E. (1993). *Tell them who I am: The lives of homeless women.* New York: Penguin.

Lincoln, Y. S. (1997). Self, subject, audience, text: Living at the edge, writing in the margins. In W. G. Tierney & Y. S. Lincoln (Eds.), *Representation and the text: Re-framing the narrative voice* (pp. 37–55). Albany: State University of New York Press.

Lincoln, Y. S. (2000). Narrative authority vs. perjured testimony: Courage, vulnerability, and truth. *Qualitative Studies in Education, 13,* 131–138.

Loseke, D. R. (2001). Lived realities and formula stories of "battered women." In J. F. Gubrium & J. A. Holstein (Eds.), *Institutional selves: Troubled identities in a postmodern world* (pp. 107–126). New York: Oxford University Press.

Lurie, N. O. (Ed.). (1961). *Mountain Wolf Woman: Sister of Crashing Thunder.* Ann Arbor: University of Michigan Press.

Luttrell, W. (1997). *School-smart and mother-wise: Working-class women's identity and schooling.* New York: Routledge.

Luttrell, W. (2003). *Pregnant bodies, fertile minds: Gender, race, and the schooling of pregnant teens.* New York: Routledge.

Madison, D. S. (1998). Performance, personal narratives, and the politics of possibility. In S. J. Dailey (Ed.), *The future of performance studies: Visions and revisions* (pp. 276–286). Annandale, VA: National Communication Association.

Mann, C., & Stewart, F. (2002). Internet interviewing. In J. F. Gubrium and J. A. Holstein (Eds.), *Handbook of interview research: Context and method* (pp. 603–627). Thousand Oaks, CA: Sage.

McAdams, D. P. (1997). *The stories we live by: Personal myths and the making of the self.* New York: Guilford.

McAdams, D. P., & Bowman, P. J. (2001). Narrating life's turning points: Redemption and contamination. In D. P. McAdams, R. Josselson, & A. Lieblich (Eds.), *Turns in the road: Narrative studies of lives in transition* (pp. 3–34). Washington, DC: American Psychological Association.

McAdams, D. P., Josselson, R., & Lieblich, A. (Eds.). (2001). *Turns in the road: Narrative studies of lives in transition.* Washington, DC: American Psychological Association.

McCall, M. M., & Becker, H. S. (1990). Performance science. *Social Problems, 37,* 117–132.

McCall, M. M., & Wittner, J. (1990). The good news about life history. In H. S. Becker & M. M. McCall (Eds.), *Symbolic interaction and cultural studies* (pp. 46–89). Chicago: University of Chicago Press.

McLaughlin, D., & Tierney, W. G. (Eds.). (1993). *Naming silenced lives: Personal narratives and processes of educational change.* New York: Routledge.

McMahan, E. M., & Rogers, K. L. (Eds.). (1994). *Interactive oral history interviewing.* Hillsdale, NJ: Lawrence Erlbaum.

Menchú, R. (1984). *I, Rigoberta Menchú: An Indian woman in Guatemala* (with an introduction by E. Burgos-Debray, Ed.; A. Wright, Trans.). London: Verso.

Miller, G. (1997). *Becoming miracle workers: Language and meaning in brief therapy.* New York: Aldine de Gruyter.

Mills, C. W. (1959). *The sociological imagination.* London: Oxford University Press.

Mishler, E. G. (1986). *Research interviewing: Context and narrative.* Cambridge, MA: Harvard University Press.

Mishler, E. G. (1995). Models of narrative analysis: A typology. *Journal of Narrative and Life History, 5,* 87–123.

Mishler, E. G. (1999). *Storylines: Craft artists' narratives of identity.* Cambridge, MA: Harvard University Press.

Moyano, M. E. (2000). *The autobiography of María Elena Moyano: The life and death of a Peruvian activist* (D. M. Tupac, Ed. and Annot.). Gainesville: University Press of Florida.

Myerhoff, B. (1994). *Number our days: Culture and community among elderly Jews in an American ghetto.* New York: Meridian/Penguin. (Original work published 1979)

Naples, N. (2003). Deconstructing and locating survivor discourse: Dynamics of narrative, empowerment, and resistance for survivors of childhood sexual abuse. *Signs: Journal of Women in Culture and Society, 28,* 1151–1185.

Narayan, K., & George, K. M. (2002). Personal and folk narrative as cultural representation. In J. F. Gubrium & J. A. Holstein (Eds.), *Handbook of interview research: Context and method* (pp. 815–831). Thousand Oaks, CA: Sage.

Ochberg, R. L. (1996). Interpreting life stories. In R. Josselson (Ed.), *Ethics and process in the narrative study of lives* (pp. 97–113). Thousand Oaks, CA: Sage.

Personal Narratives Group. (Eds.). (1989). *Interpreting women's lives: Feminist theory and personal narratives.* Bloomington: Indiana University Press.

Plummer, K. (1983). *Documents of life: An introduction to the problems and literature of a humanistic method.* London: George Allen & Unwin.

Plummer, K. (1995). *Telling sexual stories: Power, change, and social worlds.* London: Routledge.

Polkinghorne, D. E. (1995). Narrative configuration in qualitative analysis. In J. A. Hatch & R. Wisniewski (Eds.), *Life history and narrative* (pp. 5–23). London: Falmer.

Pollner, M., & Stein, J. (1996). Narrative mapping of social worlds: The voice of experience in Alcoholics Anonymous. *Symbolic Interaction, 19,* 203–223.

Psathas, G. (1995). *Conversation analysis: The study of talk-in-interaction.* Thousand Oaks, CA: Sage.

Radin, P. (Ed.). (1926). *Crashing Thunder: The autobiography of an American Indian.* New York: Appleton.

Randall, M. (1981). *Sandino's daughters: Testimonies of Nicaraguan women in struggle.* Vancouver, British Columbia: New Star Books.

Randall, M. (1994). *Sandino's daughters revisited: Feminism in Nicaragua.* New Brunswick, NJ: Rutgers University Press.

Randall, M. (2003). *When I look into the mirror and see you: Women, terror, and resistance.* New Brunswick, NJ: Rutgers University Press.

Rawick, G. P. (1972). *The American slave: A composite autobiography,* Vol. 1: *From sundown to sunup—The making of the black community.* Westport, CT: Greenwood.

Rawick, G. P. (1977). General introduction. In G. Rawick, J. Hillegas, & K. Lawrence (Eds.), *The American slave: A composite autobiography,* Supplement, Ser. 1, Vol. 1: *Alabama narratives* (pp. ix–li). Westport, CT: Greenwood.

Reddy, M. T. (1994). *Crossing the color line: Race, parenting, and culture.* New Brunswick, NJ: Rutgers University Press.

Reinharz, S. (1992). *Feminist methods in social research.* New York: Oxford University Press.

Reinharz, S., & Chase, S. E. (2002). Interviewing women. In J. F. Gubrium & J. A. Holstein (Eds.), *Handbook of interview research: Context and method* (pp. 221–238). Thousand Oaks, CA: Sage.

Ribbens, J., & Edwards, R. (Eds.). (1998). *Feminist dilemmas in qualitative research: Public knowledge and private lives.* London: Sage.

Richardson, L. (1990). Narrative and sociology. *Journal of Contemporary Ethnography, 19,* 116–135.

Richardson, L. (2002). Poetic representation of interviews. In J. F. Gubrium & J. A. Holstein (Eds.), *Handbook of interview research: Context and method* (pp. 877–892). Thousand Oaks, CA: Sage

Riessman, C. K. (1990). *Divorce talk: Women and men make sense of personal relationships.* New Brunswick, NJ: Rutgers University Press.

Riessman, C. K. (1997). A short story about long stories. *Journal of Narrative and Life History, 7,* 155–158.

Riessman, C. K. (2002a). Analysis of personal narratives. In J. F. Gubrium & J. A. Holstein (Eds.), *Handbook of interview research: Context and method* (pp. 695–710). Thousand Oaks, CA: Sage.

Riessman, C. K. (2002b). Positioning gender identity in narratives of infertility: South Indian women's lives in context. In M. C. Inhorn & F. van Balen (Eds.), *Infertility around the globe: New thinking on childlessness, gender, and reproductive technologies* (pp. 152–170). Berkeley: University of California Press.

Rosaldo, R. (1976). The story of Tukbaw: "They listen as he orates." In F. E. Reynolds & D. Capps (Eds.), *The biographical process: Studies in the history and psychology of religion* (pp. 121–151). The Hague, Netherlands: Mouton.

Rosenwald, G. C., & Ochberg, R. L. (Eds.). (1992). *Storied lives: The cultural politics of self-understanding.* New Haven, CT: Yale University Press.

Rosier, K. B. (2000). *Mothering inner-city children: The early school years.* New Brunswick, NJ: Rutgers University Press.

Rubin, L. B. (1976). *Worlds of pain: Life in the working-class family.* New York: Basic Books.

Rubin, L. B. (1994). *Families on the faultline: America's working class speaks about the family, the economy, race, and ethnicity.* New York: HarperPerennial.

Ruddick, S., & Daniels, P. (Eds.). (1977). *Working it out: 23 women writers, artists, scientists, and scholars talk about their lives and work.* New York: Pantheon.

Sacks, K. B. (1989). What's a life story got to do with it? In Personal Narratives Group (Eds.), *Interpreting women's lives: Feminist theories and personal narratives* (pp. 85–95). Bloomington: University of Indiana Press.

Schegloff, E. A. (1997). "Narrative analysis" thirty years later. *Journal of Narrative and Life History, 7,* 97–106.

Sexton, P. C. (1981). *The new Nightingales: Hospital workers, unions, new women's issues.* New York: Enquiry Press.

Shaw, C. R. (1966). *The jack-roller: A delinquent boy's own story.* Chicago: University of Chicago Press. (Original work published 1930)

Shostak, M. (1989). "What the wind won't take away": The genesis of *Nisa—The life and words of a !Kung woman.* In Personal Narratives Group (Eds.), *Interpreting women's lives: Feminist theory and personal narratives* (pp. 228–240). Bloomington: Indiana University Press.

Shostak, M. (2000a). *Nisa: The life and words of a !Kung woman.* Cambridge, MA: Harvard University Press. (Original work published 1981)

Shostak, M. (2000b). *Return to Nisa.* Cambridge, MA: Harvard University Press.

Sidel, R. (1978). *Urban survival: The world of working-class women.* Boston: Beacon.

Stein, A. (1997). *Sex and sensibility: Stories of a lesbian generation.* Berkeley: University of California Press.

Stromberg, P. G. (1993). *Language and self-transformation: A study of the Christian conversion narrative.* Cambridge, UK: Cambridge University Press.

Sutherland, E. H. (1937). *The professional thief.* Chicago: University of Chicago Press.

Taylor, J. M., Gilligan, C., & Sullivan, A. M. (1995). *Between voice and silence: Women and girls, race and relationship.* Cambridge, MA: Harvard University Press.

Tedlock, B. (1992). *The beautiful and the dangerous: Encounters with the Zuni Indians.* New York: Viking/Penguin Books.

Terkel, S. (1995). *Coming of age: The story of our century by those who've lived it.* New York: New Press.

Thomas, W. I., & Znaniecki, F. (1927). *The Polish peasant in Europe and America* (Vol. 2). New York: Alfred A. Knopf. (Original work published 1918)

Thompson, P. (2000). *The voice of the past: Oral history* (3rd ed.). New York: Oxford University Press. (Original work published 1978)

Tierney, W. G. (2000). Undaunted courage: Life history and the postmodern challenge. In N. K. Denzin & Y. S. Lincoln (Eds.), *Handbook of qualitative research* (2nd ed., pp. 537–553). Thousand Oaks, CA: Sage.

Tierney, W. G. (2002). Get real: Representing reality. *Qualitative Studies in Education, 15,* 385–398.

Tierney, W. G., & Lincoln, Y. S. (Eds.). (1997). *Representation and the text: Re-framing the narrative voice.* Albany: State University of New York Press.

Watson, L. C., & Watson-Franke, M-B. (1985). *Interpreting life histories: An anthropological inquiry.* New Brunswick, NJ: Rutgers University Press.

Weiss, R. S. (1994). *Learning from strangers: The art and method of qualitative interview studies.* New York: Free Press.

Wozniak, D. F. (2002). *They're all my children: Foster mothering in America.* New York: New York University Press.

Yetman, N. R. (1970). *Life under the "peculiar institution": Selections from the slave narrative collection.* New York: Holt, Rinehart & Winston.

# 3

# ARTS-BASED INQUIRY

## *Performing*
## *Revolutionary Pedagogy*

Susan Finley

T he focus of this chapter is the usefulness of arts-based approaches to doing
qualitative inquiry when political activism is the goal. References were chosen
to include both theoretical discussions about arts-based inquiry methodologies and examples of arts-based representations as well as to underscore the notions of
usefulness and political activism that are served by arts-based inquiry. In this review,
special attention is given to arts-based research that is positioned toward future developments in the field of socially responsible, politically activist, and locally useful
research methodologies. From an historical perspective and for the purpose of defining arts-based research, the chapter addresses concerns and issues that have dominated discussions about arts-based research methodologies. Ultimately, it is argued
that arts-based research can contribute greatly to "a radical ethical aesthetic . . . [that]
grounds its representations of the world in a set of interpretive practices that implement critical race, queer, and Third World postcolonial theory" (Denzin, 2000, p. 261).

This chapter begins with a description of characteristics of arts-based research
that render it unique among the various forms of postmodern qualitative inquiry.
Following this characterization of arts-based research, it presents a skeletal outline of
broader social features that provide a contextual backdrop for a radical, ethical, and
revolutionary arts-based inquiry. Finally, the chapter concludes with an example of
community-based, activist, arts-based inquiry. The genealogy of arts-based research

that I have chosen to follow is couched in the widely shared belief that social science inquiry is always moral and political, and I further interpret this as a timely proclamation that its practitioners should, therefore, be purposeful in performing inquiry that is activist, engages in public criticism, and is resistant to neoconservative discourses that threaten social justice. Moreover, I believe that this purposeful turn to a revolutionary, performative research aesthetics facilitates critical race, indigenous, queer, feminist, and border studies.

## ▣ POSTMODERN INTEGRATIONS OF ACTIVISM, SOCIAL SCIENCE, AND ART: DEFINING THE FEATURES OF ARTS-BASED INQUIRY

Arts-based inquiry has emerged in postcolonial postmodern contexts, woven from complex threads of social, political, and philosophical shifts in perspectives and practices across multiple discourse communities. It has surfaced in the context of a reflexive turn that marked the social sciences, philosophy and literary criticism, science, education, and the arts, and it is evidenced in particular by the narrative turn in sociological discourse.

Arts-based inquiry is one methodological and theoretical genre among many new forms of qualitative inquiry. It is situated within what Lincoln (1995) described as an emerging tradition of participatory critical action research in social science. Practitioners of inquiry in this line propose reinterpretation of the methods and ethics of human social research and seek to construct action-oriented processes for inquiry that are useful within the local community where the research originates. Arts-based inquiry, as it is practiced by academics doing human social research, fits historically within a postmodern framework that features a developing activist dynamic among both artists and social researchers.

Three historical stories are used here to recount the genealogy of a radical aesthetic inquiry: (a) the turn to activist social science, (b) the emergence of arts-based research (and the turn to activist arts), and (c) the turn to a radical, ethical, and revolutionary arts-based inquiry (and the emergence of revolutionary pedagogy).

### The Turn to Activist Social Science

Postmodern foundational shifts brought about new conceptualizations of how research works, how meanings are made, and what social purposes research might serve. Social scientists began to act on their realization that traditional techniques of research were not adequate to handle the many questions that needed to be asked when the frame was shifted to take on new and diverse perspectives. For instance, writers such as Guba (1967) identified the proliferation of new questions as a profound movement in social research away from questions concerning technique to questions concerning theory, and he foresaw a reformist movement that would bring "art" to inquiry (p. 64) as researchers sought ways in which to merge theory and practice. New questions prompted new ways of looking, and the transformation of social science research to include qualitative methodologies began full bore by the early 1970s (Schwandt, 2000).

Two primary issues arose to create a space for arts-based social science inquiry. First, the dialogue turned to ethical issues that occur in the relationship between researchers and the communities in which they work. Qualitative researchers had embraced new practices that redefined the roles of researchers and research participants—who no longer were subjects but instead were collaborators or even coresearchers—so that the lines between the researcher and the researched blurred. In the context of this type of locally meaningful inquiry, researchers and participants were actively developing an ethics of care that ultimately became a quality standard in the new paradigm for social science research (Lincoln & Reason, 1996). Rather than following the quantitative scientific model of objectivity, qualitative social science inquiry was increasingly defined as action-based inquiry that takes its forms through interpersonal, political, emotional, moral, and ethical relational skills that develop and are shared between researchers and research participants (Lincoln, 1995; Lincoln & Reason, 1996).

Second, questions and issues arose in this new stance of researchers as community partners and initiated a "crisis of representation" (Denzin & Lincoln, 1994) that prompted questions from researchers. How should research be reported? Are the traditional approaches to dissemination adequate for an expanding audience that includes a local community? How do researchers "write up" their understandings without "othering" their research partners, exploiting them, or leaving them voiceless in the telling of their own stories? What forms should research take? How can researchers make their work available and useful to participants rather than produce reports in the tradition of academics writing for other academics or policymakers?

Nontraditional methods and revised standards for evaluating research emerged from these questions and in 1995 gave rise to the publication of the journal *Qualitative Inquiry* (edited by Norman Denzin and Yvonna Lincoln) as a location for ongoing discussions about the practices and methodologies that take place in participatory, critical action forms of research (for a review of the first 7 years of publication of *Qualitative Inquiry,* see Finley, 2003a). Writing in *Qualitative Inquiry,* Lincoln (1995) and Lincoln and Reason (1996) identified particular skills that had emerged in the new tradition of inquiry. The skills that were increasingly necessary to new paradigm researchers included interpersonal, political, emotional, moral, and ethical competence; intellectual openness and creativity; and spiritual qualities related to empathy and understanding when confronted with human experience.

In this context of research reform, Eisner (e.g., 1991/1998) also argued that successful researchers in the new social science genre require a different kind of skill base than was previously expected among social researchers. He proposed a graduate school curriculum that values students' developing skills of imagination, perception, and interpretation of the qualities of things as well as mastery of skills of artistic representation. To address the representational crisis, Eisner encouraged reaching into the existing fields of arts and letters: "Art, music, dance, prose, and poetry are some of the forms that have been invented to perform this function" (p. 235). Likewise, Seale (1999) visualized a studio apprenticeship model for learning a wide variety of research skills "in much the same way as artists learn to paint, draw, or sculpt" (p. 476). Similarly, Tierney (1998, 1999) acknowledged that authors' attempts to include multiple textual voices called for narrative range as wide and experimental as offered in literature. Writing in a special issue of *Qualitative Inquiry* devoted to life history research that took its forms in literary genres, Tierney (1999) observed, "What these authors are struggling over is how to get out of the representational straightjacket that social scientists have been in for most of this century" (p. 309). He continued, "The authors want to create greater narrative flexibility in time, space, and voice. Their assumption is that rather than a standard proof akin to the natural scientists, readers make meaning from emotive and affective aspects of a text" (pp. 309–310).

Thus, the turn to activist social science was simultaneous and mutual with the turn to narrative social science research. Casey (1995) explained that methodological shifts in research approaches are tied to political or theoretical interests charged by social and historical circumstances and that narrative research is politically situated in that it "deliberately defies the forces of alienation, anomie, annihilation, authoritarianism, fragmentation, commodification, deprecation, and dispossession" (p. 213). In the context of activism, what is called for is expressive research that portrays the multidimensionality of human life as compared with truth finding, proofs, and conclusivity in traditional social science. Recognition of the power dynamic between the researcher and the researched called for the adaptation of literary forms to serve the purpose of research texts that represent, as vividly as possible, the words as well as the worlds of participants. The prevailing ethics of care among new social science researchers moved narrative discourse (i.e., storytelling) to the forefront of social science research.

Working in this politically and ethically charged context of border crossing, activist researchers broke new ground, offering research narratives in multiple literary forms. Denzin (2004) wrote,

> Experimental, reflexive ways of writing first-person ethnographic texts are now commonplace. Critical narrative perspectives have become a central feature of counter-hegemonic, decolonizing methodologies (Mutua and Swadener, 2004, p. 16). Sociologists, anthropologists, and educators continue to explore new ways of composing ethnography, and cultural criticism is now accepted practice. (p. 1)

Indeed. Columbia University now offers its medical students courses in literature, literary theory, and creative writing as part of its Program in Narrative Medicine (Thernstrom, 2004).

## The Emergence of Arts-Based Research

Within the context of burgeoning new practices that merged activist social science and narrative art forms, Eisner (1981) expounded on the differences between scientific and artistic approaches to qualitative research, giving rise to arts-based educational research. One of Eisner's important contributions was his insistence on the power of form to inform that included a call to use many different art forms (e.g., dance, film, plastic arts) as well as the various narrative forms that have proliferated in the new social science paradigm. Eisner's theories are couched in the historical antecedents of artists and social scientists whose works seem virtually interchangeable—art that is social science and social science that is artful. They are especially respectful of the contributions that artists have made to understanding social life. In the new construction of social science, borders were crossed, but boundaries were similarly breached by postmodern artists seeking political voice and power and audience-participant influence in the construction of social values.

Cultural, historical, and political contexts that shaped the reform of social science research similarly invigorated political activism among artists. For example, Felshin (1995) argued that activist art took hold in the context of feminist-driven paradigmatic shifts that emerged during the 1970s and then expanded and institutionalized over the subsequent 20 years. Felshin traced the particular influence of paradigmatic shifts on the role of artists in society. She pointed out, for instance, that whereas activist art addresses a broad spectrum of social issues—homelessness, AIDS, violence against women, environmental neglect, sexism, racism, illegal immigration, and other topics common methodologies, formal strategies, and activist goals are shared by new paradigm activist artists.

Activist art, in this self-reflective, early postmodern phase, according to Felshin (1995), is characterized by six traits:

- Innovative use of public space to address issues of sociopolitical and cultural significance
- Encouragement of community or public participation in arts making as a means of effecting social change
- Engagement of community participants in acts of self-expression or self-representation as a way of promoting voice and visibility among participants and of making the personal political
- Use of mainstream media techniques (e.g., billboards, posters, subway and bus advertising, newspaper inserts) to connect to a wider audience and to subvert the usual uses of commercial forms
- Immersion in community for preliminary research and collaborations among artists and communities/constituencies that share a personal stake in the issues addressed
- Conscious use of public spaces to contextualize artworks and to encourage audiences to define themselves not as passive spectators but rather as active participants in the artworks

In sum, Felshin defined "new public art" in terms that recollect Lincoln's (1995) descriptions of developing trends in "new social science." In this border-crossing dynamic, new work that has been created stands neither inside nor outside the realms of social science or art; instead, this work is located in the spaces formed by emotionality, intellect, and identity.

In arts-based research, paradigms for making meaning in the contextual realms of art and social science collide, coalesce, and restructure to become something that is not strictly identifiable as either art or science. As Ulmer (1994) observed, "To do heuretics is to cross the discourses of art and theory" (p. 81). *Heuretics* refers to creative processes of discovery and invention such as those that have been enjoyed by arts-based researchers who have consciously brought the methodologies of the arts to define new practices of human social inquiry. Eisner offered seven organizing premises that make explicit his definition of arts-based inquiry, and his formative book, *The Enlightened Eye* (Eisner, 1991/1998), is presented as an argument in support of each of the seven foundations:

1. There are multiple ways in which the world can be known. Artists, writers, and dancers, as well as scientists, have important things to tell about the world.

2. Human knowledge is a constructed form of experience and, therefore, is a reflection of mind as well as of nature. Knowledge is made and not simply discovered.

3. The terms through which humans represent their conception of the world have a major influence on what they are able to say about it.

4. The effective use of any form through which the world is known and represented requires intelligence.

5. The selection of a form through which the world is to be represented not only influences what humans can say but also influences what they are likely to experience.

6. Educational inquiry will be more complete and informative as humans increase the range of ways in which they describe, interpret, and evaluate the educational world.

7. The particular forms of representation that become acceptable in the educational research community are as much a political matter as they are an epistemological one. New forms of representation, when acceptable, will require new competencies.

Eisner's argument rests in a multiple-intelligences stance that holds that there are varied ways in which the world can be known and that broadening the range of perspectives available for constructing knowledge increases the informative value of research. Arts-based researchers are increasingly using art forms that include visual and performing arts as well as forms borrowed from literature. This presents a boundary crossing among arts-based researchers; it critiques the privilege of language-based ways of knowing, and it further challenges status quo responses to the question "what is research?" There is a political challenge in Eisner's foundational construction. Here again, he noted that who does research and whether it is recognized as research when it is presented in art forms is a political issue linked to education. If research is to become a site for the implementation of critical race, feminist, and Third World methodologies (among others), researchers need to emphasize and confront the power issues underscored in Eisner's foundations. There are multiple socially constructed ways of knowing the world, and diversity is achieved in and through the voices of diverse people brought forward in the act of doing research as well as in representing it. As I have said elsewhere,

> It is an act of political emancipation from the dominant paradigm of science for new paradigm researchers to say "I am doing art" and to mean "I am doing research"—or vice versa. In either utterance, that art and research are common acts makes a political statement. (Finley, 2003a, p. 290)

On the one hand, a communal experience of research requires that the information-gathering and analytical processes of inquiry be communal in nature and open to participation among members of the community that the research intends to serve. On the other hand, the community of care encompassed in the research experience also includes the audiences to research. Making art is a passionate visceral activity that creates opportunities for communion among participants, researchers, and the various audiences who encounter the research text. Arts-based research crosses the boundaries of art and research as defined by conventions formed in historically, culturally bounded contexts of the international art market and in the knowledge market dominated by higher education.

It is important to acknowledge here that both art with political purpose and social inquiry with artistic qualities have long and rich histories. In the arts-based research example, however, what is profoundly different and starkly political is the effort to claim that art is equal to   indeed, sometimes even profoundly more appropriate than—science as a way of understanding. Arts-based research is one of many systemic studies of phenomena undertaken to advance human understanding—not exactly art and certainly not science. As Slattery and Langerock (2002) stated, arts-based research takes place in "synthetical moments—experiences of profound insight that merge time, space, and self in seamless transhistorical moments [not] . . . easily discernible and not clearly categorized within the rigid disciplinary boundaries" of art and science (p. 350). A primary concern for arts-based researchers is how to make the best use of their hybrid, boundary-crossing approaches to inquiry to bring about culturally situated, political aesthetics that are responsive to social dilemmas. The response has been to create and encourage open hermeneutic texts that create spaces for dialogues that blur boundaries among researchers, participants, and audiences so that, ideally, roles reverse and participants lead researchers to new questions, audiences revert to questioning practitioners, and so forth as all interact within the text. In this instance, the text is defined in its broadest possible terms and invokes all of the actions in the world that can be "read."

Intertextuality refers to a kind of play (fullness) between texts. One text plays with the next text; that is, the play of intertextuality is the process of reading through which one text refers to another text in the process of cultural production (Barthes, 1970/1974). Intertextuality in research display points to the more dynamic aspects of cultural production. The meaning texts of social science include all things that can be read, can be interpreted, or are the referents to which people make meanings about their world. Thus, personal identity is created within social structures that are themselves "performance texts" that play into ongoing and always changing social and cultural constructions. For example, Garoian (1999) and Finley (2001) have separately produced examples of collage–assemblage artworks that are self-consciously autobiographical, drawing into their representative forms textual referents to social constructions such as ethnicity, gender, socioeconomic status, and cultural history. Although these works are profoundly personal accounts of "becoming" the people we are, they are also commentaries on cultural histories and the texts that shaped and formed us. The concept of intertextuality goes a long way in explaining why culture and other social constructions are always dynamic.

Aspects of intertextuality form the basis for arts-based inquiry. In the hyphen that connects "arts" and "based" is a textual reference to the arts as a basis for something else, something that is "not art." Connecting activist movements in art and research is one of the fundamental acts of intertextual reading that forms the foundation for arts-based research. Among the particular skills of the arts-based researcher is the ability to play or, perhaps more accurately, to construct a field for play; there is a physical dimension to making something, a confluence of mind and body applied in efforts to understand (see also Butler, 1997, 1999; Finley, 2001; Fox & Geichman, 2001). For Richardson, this physical dimension to cognition implies a "kinesthetic balance" that moves the audience/reader to some kind of action (Richardson & Lockridge, 1998). Moving people to action can be the purpose of arts-based research. The primary characteristics of arts-based research provide a formula for a radical, ethical, and revolutionary qualitative inquiry.

This genealogy of arts-based inquiry exists in the identification of intertextual connections and tensions (i.e., disconnections) among "new wave" social science researchers and storytellers, poets, dancers, painters, weavers, dramatists, and filmmakers who have situated themselves and their work in dynamic and diverse postmodern social structures. A postmodern rewriting of the story of arts-based inquiry methodologies plays out in discontinuous, discordant, and intertextual constructions. That there is a shared urge to use their work to promote revolutionary social justice that brings artists and social scientists into collective discourse is just one such construction.

As Barone (2001a) noted, arts-based inquiry evidences elements of design that are aesthetic in character and that, with variation according to art form, are "selected for their usefulness in recasting the contents of experience into a form with the potential for challenging (sometimes deeply held) beliefs and values" (p. 26).

Imagination, community, and communal experience, as well as perceptual, emotional, and sensual awareness, all contribute to the aesthetic dimensions of arts-based research. In arts-based research, the artfulness to be found in everyday living composes the aesthetic (Barone, 2001a; Barone & Eisner, 1997; Dewey, 1934/1958). Denzin (2000) and others have encouraged researchers to focus on the vernacular and to capture the visceral ephemeral moments in daily life. Vernacular, expressive, and contextualized language forms open narratives that promote empathy and care (Barone, 2001b). These entreaties to the vernacular for the purpose of broader audience/participant voice, representation, and appeal, as well as the philosophical appeal to regarding people equally, recall Tolstoy's (1946/1996) comments about art:

> We are accustomed to understand art to be only what we hear and see in theaters, concerts, and exhibitions, together with buildings, statues, poems, and novels. . . . [But] all human life is filled with works of art of every kind—from cradlesong, jest, mimicry, the ornamentation of houses, dress, and utensils, to church services, building monuments, and triumphal processions. It is all artistic activity. (p. 66)

In its use of everyday, localized, and personal language, and in its reliance on texts that are ambiguous and open to interpretation, arts-based research draws people into dialogue and opens the possibility for critical critique of social structures (Barone, 2001a, 2001b). *Performativity* is the writing and rewriting of meanings that continually disrupts the authority of texts. Resistance is a kind of performance that holds up for critique hegemonic texts that have become privileged stories told and retold. All knowledge claims are dependent on ascription within power structures (stories) that are performed within cultural boundaries.

This connection among political resistance, pedagogy, and performance has emerged as a way of understanding, and it represents an arts-based methodological approach for interpreting and taking action (for a more comprehensive discussion of the "dramaturgical turn," see Denzin, 1997, 2003). Dramaturgy as a research form draws from the rich history of politically motivated, activist theater used to resist oppression. Garoian (1999) argued that performances in this genre can be used to "critique dominant cultural assumptions, to construct identity, and to attain political agency" (p. 2). Garoian defined the human body as a "contested site" (p. 23) where the activity of the play enables culturally disenfranchised actors to push against tradition, hegemony, and dominant standpoints. With echoes of Felshin (1995), Garoian drew on the feminist arts movement as a site of activist performance art, particularly with references to the performance artist Suzanne Lacy. Broadening his definition of performance as pedagogy, Garoian observed,

> [Lacy's] art work is performative curriculum because it opens a liminal space, within which a community can engage a critical discourse, a space wherein decisions are contingent upon the collective desires of its citizens, as well as an ephemeral space because it is

applicable to the particular time and place for which it has been designed. Thus, for Lacy, communities are contested sites, and performance art is a function of community development. (p. 128)

The community aspects of Lacy's work are accomplished by the involvement of diverse communities of participants as experts and actors examining their own oppression, where expertise is defined by participants' lives in the community. The participants in her work are coresearchers, critiquing and challenging themselves to understand their community and to overcome cultural oppressions that occur there. Thus, art, politics, pedagogy, and inquiry are brought together in performance.

In tracing the evolution of performance as a primary site for revolutionary research methodology, Denzin (2003) explained,

> Ethnography had to be taken out of a purely methodological framework and located first within a performative arena and then within the spaces of pedagogy, where it was understood that the pedagogical is always political. We can now see that interpretive ethnography's subject matter is set by a dialectical pedagogy. This pedagogy connects oppressors and the oppressed in capital's liminal, epiphanic spaces. (p. 31)

## The Turn to a Radical, Ethical, and Revolutionary Arts-Based Inquiry

With reference to writers who have advanced the notion of critical performance pedagogy, such as Freire (1970/2001), Giroux (2000, 2001), Kincheloe and McLaren (2000), Conquergood (1998), Garoian (1999), Pineau (1998), and Hill (1998), Denzin (2003) put forward a model of performance ethnography "that moves from interpretation and emotional evocation to praxis, empowerment, and social change" (p. 133).

This turn by Denzin (1999) to critical performance delivered on his charge to critical ethnographers that performative pedagogy is needed to confront race relations and inequalities in the globalized capitalist democratic system. Denzin (2003) explained that, through an evolutionary process, the field of ethnography has reached its current critical, performative pedagogical moment; it is a point in time when performative ethnography can be enacted as critical social practice. A critical performance pedagogy should enable oppressed persons to "unveil the world of oppression and through praxis commit themselves to its transformation" (Freire, 1970/2001, p. 54, cited in Denzin, 2003, p. 30).

It is a shift in perspective and a call to action demanded by the cultural, social, and governmental epoch in which we live. As McLaren (2003) stated, there is renewed intensity in pleas to take reformative action today in the face of globalized oppression and repressive political structures. These "dark times" as McLaren (1999) called them, demand that practitioners and theorists who base their work in an ethics of care and social responsibility will take critical pedagogy to the heights of political action. Revolutionary performance pedagogy must move beyond the dialogical tasks of reframing, refunctioning, and reposing questions and formulations of knowledge that characterize critical pedagogy in preference for action (p. 8). Instead, the call to revolution is ethical: "to make liberation and the abolition of human suffering the goal of the educative enterprise" (p. 5).

Revolutionary pedagogy, as described by McLaren (1999, 2001, 2003), does the following:

- Resists heterogeneity in discourses and representations of history, culture, and politics that ignore the tensions and contradictions lived through raced and gendered difference
- Names and gives voice to nonparticipants in the power structures derived from world capitalism and colonialist practices
- Contests various assaults on protections for the poor, for women, and for people of color
- Challenges the assumptions and ideologies enacted in schooling and attempts to refashion a politics of education to the larger universal values of social democracy
- Offers a provisional glimpse of a new society freed from the bondage of the past
- Creates narrative spaces set against the subjectification of everyday experience and gives rise to an empowered way of being by recognizing and naming, in an uncompromising critique, the everyday signifiers of power and practices of concealment that typically prevent self-knowledge and by discouraging naming the tensions and contradictions wrought by capitalist colonialist practices
- Directly confronts differentiated totalities of contemporary society and their historical imbrications in the world system of global capitalism by engagement in revolutionary transformation (conceived as an opposition to social justice reforms)

From a postmodern perspective, Ulmer (1994) similarly argued for a revolutionary pedagogy that makes its task the transformation of institutions by using the formalizing structures of the institution itself to experimentally rearrange reality for critical effect. He cited Eco (1984, p. 409) to make his case for engaging in "revolutionary" interventionist works that entertain the possibility, as in an ideal "guerilla" semiotics, of "changing the circumstances by virtue of which the receivers choose their own codes of reading. . . . This pragmatic energy of semiotic consciousness shows how a descriptive discipline can also be an active project" (Ulmer, 1994, p. 86).

Social crisis suggests that the next phase in the development of arts-based research will bring into focus the potential for arts-based inquiry to confront postmodern political issues such as diversity and globalization and for its practitioners to implement critical race, queer, and postcolonial epistemologies.

In performance, the emphasis is on doing. Thus, performance creates a specialized (open and dialogic) space that is simultaneously asserted for inquiry and expression. Performance requires some sort of imaginative interpretation of events and the contexts of their occurrences. A performance text redirects attention to the process of doing research rather than looking for truth, answers, and expert knowledge in a final report of findings from the researcher. "Open texts cannot be decontextualized; their (now unpredictable) meanings emerge within the sociology of space and are connected within the reciprocal relationships that exist between people and the political, dynamic qualities of place" (Finley, 2003a, p. 288).

Such performances are possible in any art form, including visual arts, music, dance, poetry, and narrative. In posing questions, analyzing information, making discoveries, and/or engaging in political action, the performative text is a politically, socially, and contextually grounded work (in the example of music, see Daspit, 2000; Frith, 1996).

It is in this liminal space that distinctions are made between private and public spheres, thereby rendering personal identity, culture, and social order unstable, indeterminate, inchoate, and amenable to change. Giroux (1995) argued, "It is within the tension between what might be called the trauma of identity formation and the demands of public life that cultural work is both theorized and made performative" (p. 5, cited in Garoian, 1999, pp. 40–41). From within the openings that are created by arts research, people—just ordinary people, you and me, researchers as participants as audiences—can implement new visions of dignity, care, democracy, and other postcolonial ways of being in the world.

## ▣ ARTS-BASED INQUIRY AS "GUERRILLA WARFARE": TAKING BACK THE STREETS

Denzin (1999) urged a new movement in qualitative inquiry in which researchers take up their pens (and their cameras, paintbrushes, bodies, and voices) so that we might "conduct our own ground-level guerrilla warfare against the oppressive structures of our everyday lives" (pp. 568, 572). Following Freire (1970/2001; see also discussion of this point in Denzin, 2003), there are two primary tasks that are the specific aims of human social inquiry in the context of a revolutionary arts-based pedagogy: (a) to unveil oppression and (b) to transform praxis. What follows is a discussion of those two tasks and an example of radical, ethical, and revolutionary arts-based inquiry. This inquiry has taken place (and is continuing) among various diverse communities of economically poor children and their families (both sheltered and unsheltered), street youths (unaccompanied minors, runaway and throwaway children, travelers, and other people between 17 and 24 years of age who live on the streets), and tent communities where unhoused people govern their own lives. It also includes the experience of field-based, community-centered research among college students, teachers, shelter workers, and other social services providers as well as the community more broadly. The discourse community is intentionally broad so as to involve as many individuals and role representatives as I can draw into dialogue, critical critique, inquiry, and social action around issues of poverty and homelessness as they influence the educational lives and experiences of children, youths, and adults. (For examples, see Finley, 2000a, 2000b, 2003b; Finley & Finley, 1999. For a discussion of Finley, 2000a, as participatory performance inquiry, see Denzin, 2003. For an adaptation into a stage performance of these and other research publications in this line of social research, see Saldaña, Finley, & Finley, in press. For discussions of ethnomethodology, see Saldaña, 1999, 2003.)

## "Mystory" Performances

With the intention of empowering children living in shelter and transitional housing to become active learners in classrooms, the At Home At School (AHAS) program that I organize brings together K–8 (kindergarten through eighth grade) children, their families, and preservice and inservice teachers in a field-based community project. All of us are students; we are both the researchers and the researched following an arts-based inquiry model of new paradigm human studies. Children experience arts-based literacy instruction (broadly conceived) throughout the school year during after-school educational enrichment and in an intensive 6-week summer school program. Doing drama, literature, visual arts, gardening, and computer technology are the mainstays of the children's program. Teachers learn firsthand what it means for children to live in a shelter or temporary apartment, they experience the encumbrances of poverty to education more closely than most have experienced previously, and they learn methods for integrating arts across the disciplines. Children in this setting have experienced the criminalization of homelessness in America, marginalization in schools, and disrupted lives in changing homes and schools as they and their families search for affordable housing. Of course, some are further inured to the vagaries of addictions, imprisonments of parents and siblings, and other social manifestations of poverty in a minimum-wage economy.

While enrolled in AHAS, children who reside in shelter and transitional housing live in a system that regulates their time—with rules for when they can bathe, sleep, eat, and so forth—simply because of their status as unhoused (longtime or recently) and economically poor persons.

Variously, in addition to strengthening academic performance as a means to build self-esteem, my goal with the children who attend AHAS is to draw their attention to the relationship between themselves and society so as to help them redirect the anger that they sometimes feel at themselves and their parents back toward the system of sustained poverty that subverts them. The goal is for the children to embrace their understandings of themselves and society in terms of political struggle and, in so doing, to encourage them to imagine all that they can do and be in their lives—and to dispute what might seem to be a destiny of lifelong poverty. My task is to provide tools for constructing new autobiographical images and then to encourage ongoing practices that these children and their families might use to transform their lives.

Equally important is my goal of providing tools for K–12 educators to recognize that their own compliance with a system that degrades and disenfranchises these children leaves "blood on their hands." The goal is to encourage them to find ways in which to assist students toward newly formed life stories built on the notion of a caring community that includes educators who, while part of the system, will use the system in its own trans-formation. Because art is a visceral and personal experience that gives expression to affective ways of being and knowing, I introduce arts-based inquiry in this curriculum as a way for the children and their teachers to create their own "mystories." Mystory performances are personal cultural texts (e.g., narratives, paintings, poetry, music) that contextualize important personal experiences and problems within the institutional settings and historical moments where their authors (e.g., painters, collagists, drama-tists) find themselves. They attempt to make sense of seemingly senseless moments in life, to capture frustrations and turmoil and open them for critical critique. They open a liminal space, and create an open and dialogic text, where a diverse group of people can be brought to collective understanding of the sites of power, of conflicts between the empowered and the powerless, and from this point of understanding can begin to address the need for social change (for further discussions of the functions of mystory, see Denzin, 2003; Ulmer, 1989).

Teacher-led projects in which children have created mystories that have taken place in the context of AHAS include an extended effort at portraiture during which children painted their life histories first by learning to work within the symbolic lan-guage of colors, lines, and space and brush work while working with charcoal, pens, and water and acrylic paints. Over a period of roughly 3 months (shelter stays are lim-ited to 90 days, so there was a changing population of children, with some attending all of the sessions and some attending only a few), during weekly sessions children painted self-portraits, pictures of objects, and so forth to tell life stories. The project culminated with a day of communal painting of five mural panels (4 feet by 4 feet) with the theme of "the story of us." Again, the children followed up the session by ver-bally processing the meanings they intended when they began painting and by defin-ing the meanings they constructed during the process.

Amid likenesses of "Sponge Bob," trees, peace symbols, and American flags, per-sonal and community stories emerged. One child who had practiced and then painted a very pleasing tree blacked it out with other paint so that it was no longer even visi-ble on the canvas, and two other boys joined him in his "scorched earth" efforts. When the child expressed his anger and frustration with multiple heart surgeries that left him physically smaller than his peers—a personal story, but one that had community ties—his teachers were better prepared to understand his occasional displays of seemingly unfounded temper. Telling his life story, he found compassion and under-standing among his peers and teachers, and he began to attend tutoring sessions each week with absolute regularity, had fewer outbursts, and began (over a period of sev-eral months) to improve his school performance.

In this same setting, three girls had painted a scene in which two (gender-neutral) couples walked among trees and flowers. On close inspection, one couple held hands while the other couple did not, and the couple not holding hands had tears flowing from their eyes. These girls' storytelling turned to personal remembrances of divorce, of grandparents left in other states as a result of moves, and of feelings of being disconnected from peers when at school. From that point, beginning with the girls who had painted the scene but also involving other children, a conversation grew about loving their own mothers but wanting to build lasting relationships in their own lives. Because the scene took a mural space very close to a U.S. flag, next to which another student had written "give peace a chance" and several had drawn peace signs, conversation shifted again, now having moved from the realm of personal experiences of divorce and separation, to a discussion of world instability and U.S. dominance, and the instability to children's lives introduced by war. Nothing was resolved—there were disagreements as to whether the United States was right or wrong to go to war—but most important was that there was a conversation about the war at all; children were expressing their opinions about world events and were confident that their ideas mattered. I could not help but think that students' understandings wrought by telling mystories would carry over, at least in minimal ways, to life at school.

Painted portraits are just one way for the children to tell "the story of us." We also have had occasions for movie making, writing, and performing rap and blues, and we have constructed a community in which personal storytelling is rewarded. Against this backdrop of unveiling personal and systemic events that have shaped the lives of the children, two events that have occurred convince me that we are achieving transformative praxis in AHAS.

First, a rule prohibited people living in the shelter from fraternizing with people living in transitional housing by going back and forth to each other's places of residence. Two 12-year-old girls—one who lived in a transitional housing apartment and the other who was housed at the shelter—became very close friends during tutoring. While the girls were making plans to visit one another after the program at the apartment of one of the girls, another student reminded them of the rule and that if it were enforced, the girls' families would be asked to leave. This was followed by a discussion among the children in which they recognized how unfair the situation was. They decided that they had to do something about it. Their solution was to write in their journals about the situation and then to show me what they had written and enlist my help in challenging the rule. They disputed the system, and they took action to try and change the rule. In the end, because of their problem solving, the rule was changed.

Second, the painted murals were hung, along with excerpts from the narrative sessions, in the gallery of the Student Services building at the university where I teach. I took a class of 11 practicing teachers (who were enrolled in my advanced children's literature course) to see the display. Of these 11 teachers, 5 began volunteer tutoring on a weekly basis and several carried over beyond the end of the semester. In addition, they conducted book drives at their schools so that every child could take a book home with him or her. Most important, all of the teachers made statements similar to this comment offered by one:

I have always had these children in my classes, and I have always resented them being there. I have seen them as unprepared, [as] underparented, and as a waste of my time. I have changed. I'm a good teacher to a lot of the children. My goal now is—truly, not just as mere rhetoric—to become a teacher of all of the children in my classroom. These children are now my children.

In sum, although the painting of the portraits affected these children's perceptions of themselves as learners and in both their current and future participation in society, what is perhaps more profound is the impact that the children have had, through their paintings and stories, on other children in similar circumstances who will attend classes taught by the teachers and preservice teachers who have adopted activist pedagogies and practices.

As an educator, I want to encourage children to learn early to become lifelong activists who are equipped for guerrilla warfare against oppression by virtue of their ability to name their oppressors, dispute oppressive practices that are stereotyped or systematized into seeming normality, imagine a life lived otherwise, and then construct and enact a script that shifts them into an alternative space. Art, in any of its various forms, provides media for self-reflection, self-expression, and communication between and among creators and audiences. Performing social change begins with artful ways of seeing and knowing ourselves and the world in which we live.

The AHAS example demonstrates that art can be the catalyst for audiences to see themselves differently, to receive messages, and to find a level of understanding about people that they would have ignored in different circumstances. Knowing these children through their artful expressions of themselves motivated a group of adults to embrace their empathetic emotions and to give something of their time and expertise as teachers. Yet once they were in direct contact with the artists, the teachers became students of the social structures they helped to perpetuate and began to write small scripts based on the need for change, with book drives and gifts of books being the foundation for change in the emotional and physical spaces in which teaching and learning occur in their schools and classrooms. For the teachers, it takes a sustained effort at learning to use the tools that are available to create and revise their own self-portraits; practice is required. Artful performance in the community will occur if teachers look deeply enough into themselves and can paint their way to a more humanistic and communal portraiture than schools typically allow.

In these examples, the children have become researchers and artists of their own lives. Other examples, not given here because of space considerations, would demonstrate the arts-based inquiry that teachers have experienced in this context. Still another group of examples would be my own inquiries into the experiences of AHAS, some of which have been coauthored and copresented with K–12 students, teachers, street youths, and street artists. In this schema, arts-based research makes possible the erasure of distinctions between the researcher and the researched. We all are inquirers into our experiences and collaborators in efforts to create a better space to share our lives.

A major dilemma for arts-based researchers has emerged around definitions of quality criteria. What is good arts-based research? Is it incumbent on arts-based research to demonstrate the best in terms of artistic skill and craftsmanship? And, if demonstrations of artistic skill are necessary to arts-based research, can quality arts-based inquiry be achieved by community-members (e.g., children and teachers, as well as university researchers) who are not educated in the art-form chosen as the representational text? How far can arts-based researchers go in becoming "community partners" where distinctions between the roles of researcher and researched converge? Who is an artist? Who is a researcher? These are questions that underscore the postmodern turn in sociological research, but they have become somewhat polarizing issues among arts-based researchers. Some practitioners of arts-based inquiry argue for the need to develop an established research tradition that has coherence and integrity in its methodological and epistemological commitments, whereas others take the position I have taken in this chapter—that quality control efforts force a singular way of knowing and shut off the possibilities for diverse voices and expressions. Performativity is the quality criterion I have emphasized in this chapter as being necessary to achieve arts-based approaches to inquiry that is activist, engages in public criticism, is resistant to threats to social justice, and purposefully intends to facilitate critical race, indigenous, queer, and feminist and border studies as entrée to multiple, new, and diverse ways of understanding and living in the world.

## ▣ REFERENCES

Barone, T. (2001a). Science, art, and the predispositions of educational researchers. *Educational Researcher, 30*(7), 24–28.

Barone, T. (2001b). *Teaching eternity: The enduring outcomes of teaching.* New York: Columbia University, Teachers College Press.

Barone, T., & Eisner, E. (1997). *Handbook on complementary methods for educational research* (R. Yeager, Ed.). Washington, DC: American Educational Research Association.

Barthes, R. (1974). *S/Z* (R. Miller, Trans.). New York: Hill & Wang. (Original work published 1970)

Butler, J. (1997). *Excitable speech: A politics of the performative.* New York: Routledge.

Butler, J. (1999). Revisiting bodies and pleasures. *Theory, Culture, and Society, 16,* 11–20.

Casey, K. (1995). The new narrative research in education. *Review of Research in Education, 21,* 211–253.

Conquergood, D. (1998). Beyond the text: Toward a performative cultural politics. In S. J. Dailey (Ed.), *The future of performance studies: Visions and revisions* (pp. 25–36). Washington, DC: National Communication Association.

Denzin, N. K. (1997). Performance texts. In W. G. Tierney & Y. S. Lincoln (Eds.), *Representation and the text: Re-framing the narrative voice* (pp. 179–217). Albany: State University of New York Press.

Denzin, N. K. (1999). Two-stepping in the 90s. *Qualitative Inquiry, 5,* 568–572.

Denzin, N. K. (2000). Aesthetics and the practices of qualitative inquiry. *Qualitative Inquiry, 6,* 256–265.

Denzin, N. K. (2003). *Performance ethnography: Critical pedagogy and the politics of culture.* Thousand Oaks, CA: Sage.

Denzin, N. K. (2004). *The First International Congress of Qualitative Inquiry.* Retrieved November 15, 2004, from www.qi2005.org/index.html

Denzin, N. K., & Lincoln, Y. S. (Eds.). (1994). *Handbook of qualitative research.* Thousand Oaks, CA: Sage.

Despit, T. (2000). Rap pedagogies: Bringing the noise of knowledge born in the microphone to radical education. In T. Despit & J. A. Weaver (Eds.), *Popular culture and critical pedagogy: Reading, constructing, connecting* (pp. 163–182). New York: Garland.

Dewey, J. (1958). *Art as experience.* New York: Capricorn. (Original work published 1934)

Eco, U. (1984). *La structure absente: Introduction a la recherché semiotique* (U. Esposito-Torrigiani, Trans.). Paris: Mercured de France.

Eisner, E. W. (1981). On the difference between scientific and artistic approaches to qualitative research. *Educational Researcher, 10*(4), 5–9.

Eisner, E. W. (1998). *The enlightened eye: Qualitative inquiry and the enhancement of educational practice.* Upper Saddle River, NJ: Prentice Hall. (Original work published 1991)

Felshin, N. (Ed.). (1995). *But is it art? The spirit of art as activism.* Seattle, WA: Bay Press.

Finley, S. (2000a). "Dream child": The role of poetic dialogue in homeless research. *Qualitative Inquiry, 6,* 432–434.

Finley, S. (2000b). From the streets to the classrooms: Street intellectuals as teacher educators, collaborations in revolutionary pedagogy. In K. Sloan & J. T. Sears (Eds.), *Democratic curriculum theory and practice: Retrieving public spaces* (pp. 98–113). Troy, NY: Educator's International Press.

Finley, S. (2001). Painting life histories. *Journal of Curriculum Theorizing, 17*(2), 13–26.

Finley, S. (2003a). Arts-based inquiry in *QI:* Seven years from crisis to guerrilla warfare. *Qualitative Inquiry, 9,* 281–296.

Finley, S. (2003b). The faces of dignity: Rethinking the politics of homelessness and poverty America. *Qualitative Studies in Education, 16,* 509–531.

Finley, S., & Finley, M. (1999). Sp'ange: A research story. *Qualitative Inquiry, 5,* 313–337.

Fox, C. T., with Geichman, J. (2001). Creating research questions from strategies and perspectives of contemporary art. *Curriculum Inquiry, 31,* 33–49.

Freire, P. (2001). *Pedagogy of the oppressed.* New York: Continuum. (Original work published 1970)

Frith, S. (1996). *Performing rites: On the value of popular music.* Cambridge, MA: Harvard University Press.

Garoian, C. R. (1999). *Performing pedagogy: Toward an art of politics.* Albany: State University of New York Press.

Giroux, H. A. (1995). Borderline artists, cultural workers, and the crisis of democracy. In C. Becker (Ed.), *The artist in society: Rights, rules, and responsibilities* (pp. 4–14). Chicago: New Art Examiner.

Giroux, H. A. (2000). *Impure acts: The practical politics of cultural studies.* New York: Routledge.

Giroux, H. A. (2001). Cultural studies as performative politics. *Cultural Studies–Critical Methodologies, 1,* 5–23.

Guba, E. (1967). The expanding concept of research. *Theory Into Practice, 6*(2), 57–65.

Hill, R. T. G. (1998). Performance pedagogy across the curriculum. In S. J. Dailey (Ed.), *The future of performance studies: Visions and revisions* (pp. 141–144). Washington, DC: National Communication Association.

Kincheloe, J. L., & McLaren, P. (2000). Rethinking critical theory and qualitative research. In N. K. Denzin & Y. S. Lincoln (Eds.), *Handbook of qualitative research* (2nd ed., pp. 279–313). Thousand Oaks, CA: Sage.

Lincoln, Y. S. (1995). Emerging criteria for quality in qualitative and interpretive research. *Qualitative Inquiry, 1,* 275–289.

Lincoln, Y. S., & Reason, P. (Eds.). (1996). Quality in human inquiry [special issue]. *Qualitative Inquiry, 2*(1).

McLaren, P. (1999). Contesting capital: Critical pedagogy and globalism. *Current Issues in Comparative Education, 1*(2). Retrieved January 3, 2004, from www.tc.columbia.edu/cice/v01lnr2/a1152.htm

McLaren, P. (2001). Che Guevara, Paulo Freire, and the politics of hope: Reclaiming critical pedagogy. *Cultural Studies–Critical Methodologies, 1,* 108–131.

McLaren, P. (2003). Towards a critical revolutionary pedagogy: An interview with Peter McLaren by Michael Pozo (Ed.). *St. John's University Humanities Review, 2*(1). Retrieved December 16, 2004, from www.axisoflogic.com/cgibin/exec/view.pl?archive=38&num=3801

Mutua, K., & Swadener, B. B. (2004). Introduction. In K. Mutua & B. B. Swadener (Eds.), *Decolonizing research in cross-cultural contexts: Critical personal narratives* (pp. 1–23). Albany: State University of New York Press.

Pineau, E. L. (1998). Performance studies across the curriculum: Problems, possibilities, and projections. In S. J. Dailey (Ed.), *The future of performance studies: Visions and revisions* (pp. 128–135). Washington, DC: National Communication Association.

Richardson, L., & Lockridge, E. (1998). Fiction and ethnography: A conversation. *Qualitative Inquiry, 4,* 328–336.

Saldaña, J. (1999). Playwriting with data: Ethnographic performance texts. *Youth Theatre Journal, 13,* 60–71.

Saldaña, J. (2003). Dramatizing data: A primer. *Qualitative Inquiry, 9,* 218–236.

Saldana, J., Finley, S., & Finley, M. (in press). Street rat. In J. Saldaña (Ed.), *Ethnodrama: An anthology of reality theatre.* Walnut Creek, CA: AltaMira.

Schwandt, T. (2000). Three epistemological stances for qualitative inquiry. In N. K. Denzin & Y. S. Lincoln (Eds.), *Handbook of qualitative research* (2nd ed., pp. 189–213). Thousand Oaks, CA: Sage.

Seale, C. (1999). Quality in arts-based research. *Qualitative Inquiry, 5,* 465–478.

Slattery, P., & Langerock, N. (2002). Blurring art and science: Synthetical moments on the borders. *Curriculum Inquiry, 32,* 349–356.

Thernstrom, M. (2004, April 18). The writing cure: Can understanding narrative make you a better doctor? *The New York Times Magazine,* pp. 42–47.

Tierney, W. G. (1998). Life history's history: Subjects foretold. *Qualitative Inquiry, 4,* 49–70.

Tierney, W. G. (1999). Guest editor's introduction. Writing life's history. *Qualitative Inquiry, 5,* 307–312.

Tolstoy, L. (1996). *What is art?* (A. Maude, Trans.). New York: Penguin. (Original work published 1946)

Ulmer, G. (1989). *Teletheory.* New York: Routledge.

Ulmer, G. (1994). The heuretics of deconstruction. In P. Brunette & D. Wills (Eds.), *Deconstruction and the visual arts: Art, media, architecture* (pp. 80–96). New York: Cambridge University Press.

# 4

# THE INTERVIEW

## *From Neutral Stance to Political Involvement*

### Andrea Fontana and James H. Frey

T he movie *Memento* begins at the end, showing a killing and then backing up to the beginning scene by scene. We do not go that far here; after all, this is not a thriller but rather a chapter about interviewing. Yet we cut to the chase, beginning with the razor-edge state of interviewing and then backing up to the old days and progressing to our days through the chapter, with full knowledge of where we are going. If you think that this will spoil the ending, skip the first section and read it last.

We have no actual killing here, but metaphorically, traditional interviewing—as it is commonly understood—does get killed. The perpetrators (or liberators, depending on your point of view) are Kong, Mahoney, and Plummer (2002), the coauthors of "Queering the Interview." They focus on the changing public perception of gays and lesbians in the United States during the past few decades and on how that changing perception altered the tone of interviewing those groups. Decades ago, when gays were "homosexuals," the interview "was clearly an instrument of pathological diagnosis," yet when the milieu became one of social reform, "the interview became a tool of modernist democratization and ultimately of social reform" (p. 240).

What this tells us about interviewing is that it is inextricably and unavoidably historically, politically, and contextually bound. This boundedness refutes the whole tradition of the interview of gathering objective data to be used neutrally for scientific purposes.

If *queering* the interview denies its primary goal, what should be done? We could reject interviewing altogether. That is hardly feasible in today's society, which has been tabbed as "the interview society," where everyone gets interviewed and gets a moment in the sun, even if only to reveal dastardly aberrations on the *Jerry Springer* show. We certainly do not want to trivialize the interview in the same way as the mass media have tended to do. What should we do? Very simply, some sociologists have turned the timetable and returned the scope of the interview to that of the predecessors of interactionism, the pragmatists, focusing on social amelioration. If the interview cannot be a neutral tool (and we will see that it never really was), why not turn it into a walking stick to help some people get on their feet? This is where the interview is now, and we outline this development next.

## ◨ EMPATHETIC INTERVIEWING

"Empathetic" emphasizes taking a stance, contrary to the scientific image of interviewing, which is based on the concept of neutrality. Indeed, much of traditional interviewing concentrates on the language of scientific neutrality and the techniques to achieve it. Unfortunately, these goals are largely mythical.

As many have argued convincingly (Atkinson & Silverman, 1997; Fontana, 2002; Hertz, 1997b; Holstein & Gubrium, 1995; Scheurich, 1995), interviewing is not merely the neutral exchange of asking questions and getting answers. Two (or more) people are involved in this process, and their exchanges lead to the creation of a collaborative effort called *the interview*. The key here is the "active" nature of this process (Holstein & Gubrium, 1995) that leads to a contextually bound and mutually created story—the interview. Some have highlighted the problematics of the interview. Atkinson and Silverman (1997) drew attention to the asymmetric nature of the interview and to the fact that the final product is a pastiche that is put together by fiat. Scheurich (1995) observed that the interviewer is a person, historically and contextually located, carrying unavoidable conscious and unconscious motives, desires, feelings, and biases—hardly a neutral tool. Scheurich maintained, "The conventional, positivist view of interviewing vastly underestimates the complexity, uniqueness, and indeterminateness of each one-to-one human interaction" (p. 241).

If we proceed from the belief that neutrality is not possible (even assuming that it would be desirable), then taking a stance becomes unavoidable. An increasing number of social scientists have realized that they need to interact as persons with the interviewees and acknowledge that they are doing so. Long ago, Douglas (1985) advocated revealing personal feelings and private situations to the interviewee as a quid pro quo of good faith. Yet Douglas, despite his openness, still placed primary importance on the traditional notion of obtaining better and more comprehensive responses; he failed to see that his openness was merely a technique to persuade the interviewee to reveal more and be more honest in his or her responses.

New empathetic approaches in interviewing differ from the conventional approach; they see that it is time to stop treating the interviewee as a "clockwork orange," that is, looking for a better juicer (techniques) to squeeze the juice (answers) out of the orange (living person/interviewee). Scheurich (1995) concurred: "The modernist representation is not sheer fabrication, but all of the juice of the lived experience has been squeezed out" (p. 241). The new empathetic approaches take an ethical stance in favor of the individual or group being studied. The interviewer becomes an advocate and partner in the study, hoping to be able to use the results to advocate social policies and ameliorate the conditions of the interviewee. The preference is to study oppressed and underdeveloped groups.

Kong and colleagues (2002), as mentioned earlier, showed that the change toward empathy might not be so much of an individual decision as it is the result of changing historical, political, and cultural perspectives. They discussed changes in interviewing regarding same-sex experiences. They showed that during the past few decades, as Americans underwent a profound change from "homosexuals" to "gays," *"the sensibilities of interviewing are altered with the changing social phenomena that constitute the "interview"* (p. 240, italics in original). Thus, interviews changed from "instruments of pathological diagnosis" (p. 240) to become much more humanized in the wake of social reform. Interviews became "a methodology of friendship" (p. 254). Kong and colleagues concluded that the interview is bound in historical, political, and cultural moments and that as those moments change, so does the interview. The work by these three coauthors was radical in that it collapsed decades of alleged "objective interview findings." As they clearly stated, framing the interview within specific parameters (i.e., "We are interviewing pathological, sick, deviant individuals" vs. "We are interviewing individuals who should not be ostracized because of their diverse sexual sensibilities") will lead to entirely different results. These results will be anything but neutral; they will be politically laden and used for or against the group studied.

Researchers have strongly emphasized the removal of barriers between the interviewer and the interviewee in the process of interviewing women. Many female researchers advocate a partnership between the researcher and respondents, who should work together to create a narrative—the interview—that could be beneficial to the group studied. Most researchers address factors beyond that of gender. Hertz and Ferguson (1997) addressed the plight of single mothers—both heterosexuals and lesbians. Weston (1998) also attended to groups of same-sex preferences in academia. Collins (1990) added the element of being black to that of being female. Denzin (2003a, 2003b) extended the interest in amelioration of oppressed groups to that in reporting the results of the study. He maintained that traditional reporting modes are ill equipped to capture the attention and hearts of the readers (see also Behar, 1996). Denzin (2003a) issued a "manifesto" calling for performance ethnography: "We need to explore performance ethnography as a vehicle for enacting a performative cultural politics of hope" (p. 202).

Some researchers are becoming keenly attuned to the fact that in knowing "others," we come to know "ourselves." Holstein and Gubrium (1995) urged researchers to be reflexive not only about *what* the interview accomplishes but also about *how* the interview is accomplished, thereby uncovering the ways in which we go about creating a text. Wasserfall (1993) noted that even when the researcher and respondents are women, if there is a discordant view of the world (in her study, a political one), there is a great divide between the two. She added that, despite claims to "friendship and cooperation," it is the researcher who ultimately cuts and pastes together the narrative, choosing what will become a part of it and what will be cut. Similarly, El-Or (1992) pointed to a gap between the researcher and respondents created by religious differences (in her study, when a nonreligious ethnographer studies an ultra-orthodox group). El-Or also reflexively addressed the notion of "friendship" between the researcher and respondents and concluded that it is fleeting and somewhat illusory: "We can't be friends because she [the respondent] was the object and we both know it" (p. 71). Atkinson and Silverman (1997) also emphasized self-restraint and self-reflexivity in warning that researchers should not replace a false god (the authorial monologue of classical sociology) with another (the monologue of a privileged speaking respondent). Researchers should not privilege any ways of looking at the world or at a particular technique but should instead continue to question, question, and question.

Atkinson and Silverman's (1997) chilly warning can be turned on the proponents of the empathetic approach because they strongly privilege a method of inquiry over all others. Yet as Denzin (2003a) observed, "Symbolic interactionism is at a crossroad. We need to reclaim the progressive heritage given to us by DuBois, Mead, Dewey, and Blumer" (p. 202). As Fontana (2003) pointed out, perhaps Denzin (and we could add all of the others) is being a postmodern Don Quixote in his approach, yet the windmills of racism, sexism, and ageism are not mere shadows in our minds; rather, they are very real and very oppressive. The empathetic approach is not merely a "method of friendship"; it is a method of morality because it attempts to restore the sacredness of humans before addressing any theoretical or methodological concerns.

We too have "queered" the chapter to follow by framing it in the light of today's development and new awareness in interviewing. Let us turn the time back and see how interviewing has come to be where it is.

## ▣ INTERVIEWING IN PERSPECTIVE

Asking questions and getting answers is a much harder task that it may seem at first. The spoken or written word always has a residue of ambiguity, no matter how carefully we word the questions and how carefully we report or code the answers. Yet interviewing is one of the most common and powerful ways in which we try to understand our fellow humans. Interviewing includes a wide variety of forms and a multiplicity of uses.

The most common form of interviewing involves individual, face-to-face verbal inter-change, but interviewing can also take the form of face-to-face group interchange and telephone surveys. It can be structured, semistructured, or unstructured. Interviewing can be used for marketing research, political opinion polling, therapeutic reasons, or academic analysis. It can be used for the purpose of measurement, or its scope can be the understanding of an individual or a group perspective. An interview can be a one-time brief exchange, such as 5 minutes over the telephone, or it can take place over multiple lengthy sessions, at times spanning days as in life history interviewing.

The use of interviewing to acquire information is so extensive today that it has been said that we live in an "interview society" (Atkinson & Silverman, 1997; Silverman, 1993). Increasingly, qualitative researchers are realizing that interviews are not neutral tools of data gathering but rather active interactions between two (or more) people leading to negotiated, contextually based results. Thus, the focus of interviews is moving to encompass the *hows* of people's lives (the constructive work involved in producing order in everyday life) as well as the traditional *whats* (the activities of everyday life) (Cicourel, 1964; Dingwall, 1997; Gubrium & Holstein, 1997, 1998; Holstein & Gubrium, 1995; Kvale, 1996; Sarup, 1996; Seidman, 1991; Silverman, 1993, 1997a). Interviews are moving toward new electronic forms and have seen a return to the pragmatic ideal of political involvement.

In this chapter, after discussing the interview society, we examine interviews by beginning with structured methods of interviewing and gradually moving to more qualitative types, examining interviews as negotiated texts and ending with electronic interviews and new trends in interviewing. We begin by briefly outlining the history of interviewing and then turn to a discussion of the academic uses of interviewing. Although the focus of this volume is qualitative research, to demonstrate the full import of interviewing, we need to discuss the major types of interviewing (structured, group, and unstructured) as well as other ways in which to conduct interviews. One caveat is that, in discussing the various interview methods, we use the language and rationales employed by practitioners of these methods; we note our differences with these practitioners and our criticisms later in the chapter in our discussion of gendered and other new types of qualitative interviewing. Following our examination of structured interviewing, we address in detail the various elements of qualitative interviewing. We then discuss the problems related to gendered interviewing, as well as issues of interpretation and reporting, as we broach some considerations related to ethical issues. Finally, we note some of the new trends in qualitative interviewing.

## ▣ THE INTERVIEW SOCIETY

Before embarking on our journey through interviewing per se, we comment briefly on the tremendous reliance on interviewing in the U.S. society today. This reliance on interviewing has reached such a level that a number of scholars have referred to the United States as "the interview society" (Atkinson & Silverman, 1997; Silverman, 1993).

Both qualitative and quantitative researchers tend to rely on the interview as the basic method of data gathering whether the purpose is to obtain a rich, in-depth experiential account of an event or episode in the life of the respondent or to garner a simple point on a scale of 2 to 10 dimensions. There is inherent faith that the results are trustworthy and accurate and that the relation of the interviewer to the respondent that evolves during the interview process has not unduly biased the account (Atkinson & Silverman, 1997; Silverman, 1993). The commitment to, and reliance on, the interview to produce narrative experience reflects and reinforces the view of the United States as an interview society.

It seems that everyone—not just social researchers—relies on the interview as a source of information, with the assumption that interviewing results in a true and accurate picture of the respondents' selves and lives. One cannot escape being interviewed; interviews are everywhere in the form of political polls, questionnaires about visits to doctors, housing applications, forms regarding social service eligibility, college applications, talk shows, news programs—the list goes on and on. The interview as a means of data gathering is no longer limited to use by social science researchers and police detectives; it is a "universal mode of systematic inquiry" (Holstein & Gubrium, 1995, p. 1). It seems that nearly any type of question—whether personal, sensitive, probing, upsetting, or accusatory—is fair game and permissible in the interview setting. Nearly all interviews, no matter their purposes (and these can be varied—to describe, to interrogate, to assist, to test, to evaluate, etc.), seek various forms of biographical description. As Gubrium and Holstein (1998) noted, the interview has become a means of contemporary storytelling in which persons divulge life accounts in response to interview inquiries. The media have been especially adept at using this technique.

As a society, we rely on the interview and, by and large, take it for granted. The interview and the norms surrounding the enactment of the respondent and researcher roles have evolved to the point where they are institutionalized and no longer require extensive training; rules and roles are known and shared. (However, there is a growing group of individuals who increasingly question the traditional assumptions of the interview, and we address their concerns later in our discussion of gendered interviewing and new trends in interviewing.) Many practitioners continue to use and take for granted traditional interviewing techniques. It is as if interviewing is now part of the mass culture, so that it has actually become the most feasible mechanism for obtaining information about individuals, groups, and organizations in a society characterized by individuation, diversity, and specialized role relations. Thus, many believe that it is not necessary to "reinvent the wheel" for each interview situation given that "interviewing has become a routine technical practice and a pervasive, taken-for-granted activity in our culture" (Mishler, 1986, p. 23).

This is not to say, however, that the interview is so technical and the procedures are so standardized that interviewers can ignore contextual, societal, and interpersonal elements. Each interview context is one of interaction and relation, and the result is as much a product of this social dynamic as it is the product of accurate accounts and replies. The interview has become a routine and nearly unnoticed part of everyday life. Yet response rates continue to decline, indicating that fewer people are willing to disclose their "selves" or that they are so burdened by requests for interviews that they are much more selective in their choices of which interviews to grant. Social scientists are more likely to recognize, however, that interviews are interactional encounters and that the nature of the social dynamic of the interview can shape the nature of the knowledge generated. Interviewers with less training and experience than social scientists might not recognize when interview participants are "actively" constructing knowledge around questions and responses (Holstein & Gubrium, 1995).

We now turn to a brief history of interviewing to frame its roots and development.

## THE HISTORY OF INTERVIEWING

At least one form of interviewing or another has been with us for a very long time. Even ancient Egyptians conducted population censuses (Babbie, 1992). During more recent times, the tradition of interviewing evolved from two trends. First, interviewing found great popularity and widespread use in clinical diagnosis and counseling where the concern was with the quality of responses. Second, during World War I, interviewing came to be widely employed in psychological testing, with the emphasis being on measurement (Maccoby & Maccoby, 1954).

The individual generally credited with being the first to develop a social survey relying on interviewing was Charles Booth (Converse, 1987). In 1886, Booth embarked on a comprehensive survey of the economic and social conditions of the people of London, published as *Life and Labour of the People in London* (Booth, 1902–1903). In his early study, Booth embodied what were to become separate interviewing methods because he not only implemented survey research but also triangulated his work by relying on unstructured interviews and ethnographic observations:

> The data were checked and supplemented by visits to many neighborhoods, streets, and homes, and by conferences with various welfare and community leaders. From time to time Booth lived as a lodger in districts where he was not known, so that he could become more intimately acquainted with the lives and habits of the poorer classes. (Parten, 1950, pp. 6–7)

Many other surveys of London and other English cities followed, patterned after Booth's example. In the United States, a similar pattern ensued. In 1895, a study attempted to do in Chicago what Booth had done in London (Converse, 1987). In 1896, the American sociologist W. E. B. DuBois, who admittedly was following Booth's lead, studied the black population of Philadelphia (DuBois, 1899). Surveys of cities and small towns followed, with the most notable among them being the Lynds' *Middletown* (Lynd & Lynd, 1929) and *Middletown in Transition* (Lynd & Lynd, 1937).

Opinion polling was another early form of interviewing. Some polling took place well before the start of the 20th century, but it really came into its own in 1935 with the forming of the American Institute of Public Opinion by George Gallup. Preceding Gallup, in both psychology and sociology during the 1920s, there was a movement toward the study (and usually the measurement) of attitudes. W. I. Thomas and Florian Znaniecki used the documentary method to introduce the study of attitudes in social psychology. Thomas's influence along with that of Robert Park, a former reporter who believed that sociology was to be found out in the field, sparked a number of community studies at the University of Chicago that came to be known collectively as the works of the Chicago School. Many other researchers, such as Albion Small, George H. Mead, E. W. Burgess, Everett C. Hughes, Louis Wirth, W. Loyd Warner, and Anselm Strauss, were also greatly influential (for a recent discussion of the relations and influence of various Chicago School members, see Becker, 1999).

Although the members of the Chicago School are reputed to have used the ethnographic method in their inquiries, some disagree and have noted that many of the Chicago School studies lacked the analytic component of modern-day ethnography and so were, at best, "firsthand descriptive studies" (Harvey, 1987, p. 50). Regardless of the correct label for the Chicago School members' fieldwork, they clearly relied on a combination of observation, personal documents, and informal interviews in their studies. Interviews were especially in evidence in the work of Thrasher (1927/1963), who in his study of gang members relied primarily on some 130 qualitative interviews, and in that of Anderson (1923), whose classic study of hobos relied on informal indepth conversations.

It was left to Herbert Blumer and his former student, Howard Becker, to formalize and give impetus to sociological ethnography during the 1950s and 1960s, and interviewing began to lose both the eclectic flavor given to it by Booth and the qualitative accent of the Chicago School members. Understanding gang members or hobos through interviews lost importance; instead, what became relevant was the use of interviewing in survey research as a tool to quantify data. This was not new given that opinion polls and market research had been doing it for years. But during World War II, there was a tremendous increase in survey research as the U.S. armed forces hired great numbers of sociologists as survey researchers. More than a half million American soldiers were interviewed in one manner or another (Young, 1966), and their mental and emotional lives were reported in a four-volume survey, *Studies in Social Psychology in World War II,* the first two volumes of which were directed by Samuel Stouffer and titled *The American Soldier.* This work had tremendous impact and led the way to widespread use of systematic survey research.

What was new, however, was that quantitative survey research moved into academia and came to dominate sociology as the method of choice for the next three decades. An Austrian immigrant, Paul Lazarsfeld, spearheaded this move. He welcomed *The American Soldier* with great enthusiasm. In fact, Lazarsfeld and Robert

Merton edited a book of reflections on *The American Soldier* (Merton & Lazarsfeld, 1950). Lazarsfeld moved to Columbia in 1940, taking with him his market research and other applied grants, and he became instrumental in directing the Bureau of Applied Social Research. Two other "survey organizations" were also formed: the National Opinion Research Center (formed in 1941 by Harry Field, first at the University of Denver and then at the University of Chicago) and the Survey Research Center (formed in 1946 by Rensis Likert and his group at the University of Michigan).

Academia at the time was dominated by theoretical concerns, and there was some resistance toward this applied, numbers-based kind of sociology. Sociologists and other humanists were critical of Lazarsfeld and the other survey researchers. Herbert Blumer, C. Wright Mills, Arthur Schlesinger, Jr., and Pitirin Sorokin were among those who voiced their displeasure. According to Converse (1987), Sorokin felt that "the new emphasis on quantitative work was obsessive, and he called the new practitioners 'quantophrenics'—with special reference to Stouffer and Lazarsfeld" (p. 253). Converse also quoted Mills: "Those in the grip of the methodological inhibition often refuse to say anything about modern society unless it has been through the fine little mill of the Statistical Ritual" (p. 252). Converse noted that Schlesinger called the survey researchers "social relations hucksters" (p. 253).

But the survey researchers also had powerful allies such as Merton, who joined the Bureau of Applied Social Research at Columbia in 1943, and government monies were becoming increasingly available for survey research. The 1950s saw a growth of survey research in the universities and a proliferation of survey research texts. Gradually, survey research increased its domain over sociology, culminating in 1960 with the election of Lazarsfeld to the presidency of the American Sociological Association. The methodological dominance of survey research continued unabated throughout the 1970s, 1980s, and 1990s, although other methods began to erode the prominence of survey research.

Qualitative interviewing continued to be practiced hand in hand with participant observation methods, but it too assumed some of the quantifiable scientific rigor that preoccupied survey research to a great extent. This was especially visible in grounded theory (Glaser & Strauss, 1967), with its painstaking emphasis on coding data, and in ethnomethodology, with its quest for invariant properties of social action (Cicourel, 1970). Other qualitative researchers suggested variations. Lofland (1971) criticized grounded theory for paying too little attention to data-gathering techniques. Douglas (1985) suggested lengthy, existential one-on-one interviews that lasted at least 1 day. Spradley (1980) tried to clarify the difference between ethnographic observation and ethnographic interviewing.

Recently, postmodernist ethnographers have concerned themselves with some of the assumptions present in interviewing and with the controlling role of the interviewer. These concerns have led to new directions in qualitative interviewing focusing on increased attention to the voices of the respondents (Marcus & Fischer, 1986), the interviewer–respondent relationship (Crapanzano, 1980), the importance of the researcher's gender in interviewing (Gluck & Patai, 1991), and the role of other elements such as race, social status, and age (Seidman,1991).

Platt (2002), in her recent chapter on the history of interviewing, correctly noted that the interview encompasses so many different practices that it is extremely hard to derive meaningful generalization about it and that the changes that have taken places over time are driven partly by methodological concerns and partly by sociopolitical motives.

## ▣ STRUCTURED INTERVIEWING

In structured interviewing, the interviewer asks all respondents the same series of preestablished questions with a limited set of response categories. There is generally little room for variation in response except where open-ended questions (which are infrequent) may be used. The interviewer records the responses according to a coding scheme that has already been established by the project director or research supervisor. The interviewer controls the pace of the interview by treating the questionnaire as if it were a theatrical script to be followed in a standardized and straightforward manner. Thus, all respondents receive the same set of questions asked in the same order or sequence by an interviewer who has been trained to treat every interview situation in a like manner. There is very little flexibility in the way in which questions are asked or answered in the structured interview setting. Instructions to interviewers often include some of the following guidelines:

- Never get involved in long explanations of the study; use the standard explanation provided by the supervisor.
- Never deviate from the study introduction, sequence of questions, or question wording.
- Never let another person interrupt the interview; do not let another person answer for the respondent or offer his or her opinion on the question.
- Never suggest an answer or agree or disagree with an answer. Do not give the respondent any idea of your personal views on the topic of the question or survey.
- Never interpret the meaning of a question; just repeat the question and give instructions or clarifications that are provided in training or by the supervisor.
- Never improvise such as by adding answer categories or making wording changes.

Telephone interviews, face-to-face interviews in households, intercept interviews in malls and parks, and interviews generally associated with survey research are most likely to be included in the structured interview category.

This interview context calls for the interviewer to play a neutral role, never interjecting his or her opinion of a respondent's answer. The interviewer must establish what has been called "balanced rapport"; he or she must be casual and friendly, on the one hand, but must be directive and impersonal, on the other. The interviewer must perfect a style of "interested listening" that rewards the respondent's participation but does not evaluate these responses (Converse & Schuman, 1974).

It is hoped that in a structured interview, nothing is left to chance. However, response effects, or nonsampling errors, that can be attributed to the questionnaire administration process commonly evolve from three sources. The first source of error is respondent behavior. The respondent may deliberately try to please the interviewer or to prevent the interviewer from learning something about him or her. To do this, the respondent will embellish a response, give what is described as a "socially desirable" response, or omit certain relevant information (Bradburn, 1983, p. 291). The respondent may also err due to faulty memory. The second source of error is found in the nature of the task, that is, the method of questionnaire administration (face-to-face or telephone) or the sequence or wording of the questions. The third source of error is the interviewer, whose characteristics or questioning techniques might impede proper communication of the question (Bradburn, 1983). It is the degree of error assigned to the interviewer that is of greatest concern.

Most structured interviews leave little room for the interviewer to improvise or exercise independent judgment, but even in the most structured interview situation, not every contingency can be anticipated and not every interviewer behaves according to the script (Bradburn, 1983; Frey, 1989). In fact, a study of interviewer effects found that interviewers changed the wording of as many as one third of the questions (Bradburn, Sudman, & Associates, 1979).

In general, research on interviewer effects has shown interviewer characteristics such as age, gender, and interviewing experience to have a relatively small impact on responses (Singer & Presser, 1989). However, there is some evidence to show that student interviewers produce a larger response effect than do nonstudent interviewers, higher status interviewers produce a larger response effect than do lower status interviewers, and the race of interviewers makes a difference only on questions specifically related to race (Bradburn, 1983; Hyman, 1954; Singer, Frankel, & Glassman, 1983).

The relatively minor impact of the interviewer on response quality in structured interview settings is directly attributable to the inflexible, standardized, and predetermined nature of this type of interviewing. There is simply little room for error. However, those who are advocates of structured interviewing are not unaware that the interview is a social interaction context and that it is influenced by that context. Good interviewers recognize this fact and are sensitive to how interaction can influence response. Converse and Schuman (1974) observed, "There is no single interview style that fits every occasion or all respondents" (p. 53). This means that interviewers must be aware of respondent differences and must be able to make the proper adjustments called for by unanticipated developments. As Gorden (1992) stated, "Interviewing skills are not simple motor skills like riding a bicycle; rather, they involve a high-order combination of observation, emphatic sensitivity, and intellectual judgment" (p. 7).

It is not enough to understand the mechanics of interviewing; it is also important to understand the respondent's world and forces that might stimulate or retard responses (Kahn & Cannell, 1957). Still, the structured interview proceeds under a stimulus–response format, assuming that the respondent will truthfully answer questions previously determined to reveal adequate indicators of the variable in question so long as those questions are phrased properly. This kind of interview often elicits rational responses, but it overlooks or inadequately assesses the emotional dimension.

Developments in computer-assisted interviewing (Couper et al., 1998) have called into question the division between traditional modes of interviewing such as the survey interview and the mail survey. Singleton and Straits (2002) noted that today we are really looking at a continuum of data-collecting methods rather than clearly divided methods; in fact, as these authors observed, many surveys today incorporate a variety of data-gathering methods driven by concerns such as time constraints, financial demands, and other practical elements.

## ▣ GROUP INTERVIEWING

The group interview is essentially a qualitative data-gathering technique that relies on the systematic questioning of several individuals simultaneously in a formal or informal setting. Thus, this technique straddles the line between formal and informal interviewing.

The use of the group interview has ordinarily been associated with marketing research under the label of *focus group,* where the purpose is to gather consumer opinions on product characteristics, advertising themes, and/or service delivery. This format has also been used to a considerable extent by political parties and candidates who are interested in voter reactions to issues and policies. The group interview has also been used in sociological research. Bogardus (1926) tested his social distance scale during the mid-1920s, Zuckerman (1972) interviewed Nobel laureates, Thompson and Demerath (1952) looked at management problems in the military, Morgan and Spanish (1984) studied health issues, Fontana and Frey (1990) investigated reentry into the older worker labor force, and Merton and his associates studied the impact of propaganda using group interviews (see Frey & Fontana, 1991). In fact, Merton, Fiske, and Kendall (1956) coined the term "focus group" to apply to a situation where the researcher/ interviewer asks very specific questions about a topic after having completed considerable research. There is also some evidence that established anthropologists such as Malinowski used this technique but did not report it (Frey & Fontana, 1991). Today, all group interviews are generically designated *focus group* interviews, even though there is considerable variation in the nature and types of group interviews.

In a group interview, the interviewer/moderator directs the inquiry and the interaction among respondents in a very structured fashion or in a very unstructured manner, depending on the interviewer's purpose. The purpose may be exploratory; for example, the researcher may bring several persons together to test a methodological technique, to try out a definition of a research problem, or to identify key informants. An extension of the exploratory intent is to use the group interview for the purpose of pretesting questionnaire wording, measurement scales, or other elements of a survey design. This is now quite common in survey research (Desvousges & Frey, 1989). Group interviews can also be used successfully to aid respondents' recall or to stimulate embellished descriptions of specific events (e.g., a disaster, a celebration) or experiences shared by members of the group. Group interviews can also be used for triangulation purposes or used in conjunction with other data-gathering techniques. For example, group interviews could be helpful in the process of "indefinite triangulation" by putting individual responses into a context (Cicourel, 1974). Finally, phenomenological purposes may be served whether group interviews are the sole basis for gathering data or are used in association with other techniques.

Group interviews take different forms, depending on their purposes. They can be brainstorming interviews with little or no structure or direction from the interviewer, or they can be very structured such as those in nominal/delphi and marketing focus groups. In the latter cases, the role of the interviewer is very prominent and directive. Fieldwork settings provide both formal and informal occasions for group interviews. The field researcher can bring respondents into a formal setting in the field context and ask very directed questions. Or, a natural field setting, such as a street corner or a neighborhood tavern, can be conducive to casual but purposive inquiries.

Group interviews can be compared on several dimensions. First, the interviewer can be very formal, taking a very directive and controlling posture, guiding discussion strictly, and not permitting digression or variation from topic or agenda. This is the mode of focus and nominal/delphi groups. In the latter case, participants are physically isolated but share views through a coordinator/interviewer. The nondirective approach is more likely to be implemented in a naturally established field setting (e.g., a street corner) or in a controlled setting (e.g., a research laboratory) where the research purpose is phenomenological to establish the widest range of meaning and interpretation for the topic. Groups can also be differentiated by question format and purpose, which in the case of group interviews usually means exploration, phenomenological, or pretest purposes. Exploratory interviews are designed to establish familiarity with a topic or setting; the interviewer can be very directive (or the opposite), but the questions are usually unstructured or open-ended. The same format is used in interviews with phenomenological purposes, where the intent is to tap intersubjective meaning with depth and diversity. Pretest interviews are generally structured in a question format, with the interview being directive in style. Table 4.1 compares the types of group interviews on various dimensions.

The skills that are required to conduct the group interview are not significantly different from those needed for the individual interview. The interviewer must be flexible,

**Table 4.1**     Types of Group Interviews and Dimensions

| Type | Setting Purpose | Role of Interviewer | Question Format | Purpose |
|---|---|---|---|---|
| Focus group | Formal, preset | Directive | Structured | Exploratory, pretest |
| Brainstorming | Formal or informal | Nondirective | Unstructured | Exploratory |
| Nominal/Delphi exploratory | Formal | Directive | Structured | Exploratory, pretest |
| Field, natural | Informal, spontaneous | Moderately nondirective | Very unstructured | Exploratory Phenomenological |
| Field, formal | Preset In field | Somewhat directive | Semistructured | Phenomenological |

Source: Frey and Fontana (1991, p. 184).

objective, empathetic, persuasive, a good listener, and so forth. But the group interview does present some problems not found in the individual interview. Merton and colleagues (1956) noted three specific problems, namely, that (a) the interviewer must keep one person or small coalition of persons from dominating the group, (b) the interviewer must encourage recalcitrant respondents to participate, and (c) the interviewer must obtain responses from the entire group to ensure the fullest coverage of the topic. In addition, the interviewer must balance the directive interviewer role with the role of moderator, and this calls for management of the dynamics of the group being interviewed. Furthermore, the group interviewer must simultaneously worry about the script of questions and be sensitive to the evolving patterns of group interaction.

Group interviews have some advantages over individual interviews, namely, that (a) they are relatively inexpensive to conduct and often produce rich data that are cumulative and elaborative, (b) they can be stimulating for respondents and so aid in recall, and (c) the format is flexible. Group interviews are not, however, without problems. The results cannot be generalized, the emerging group culture may interfere with individual expression (a group can be dominated by one person), and "groupthink" is a possible outcome. The requirements for interviewer skills are greater than those for individual interviewing because of the group dynamics that are present. Nevertheless, the group interview is a viable option by both qualitative and quantitative research.

Morgan (2002) advocated a systematic approach to focus group interviewing so as to create a methodological continuity and the ability to assess the outcomes of focus group research. Morgan suggested that, just as social scientists were originally inspired to use focus groups by the example of marketing, it might be time to look at marketing again to see what is being done and use the marketing example to innovate in the field of social sciences.

## ▣ UNSTRUCTURED INTERVIEWING

Unstructured interviewing can provide greater breadth than do the other types given its qualitative nature. In this section, we discuss the traditional type of unstructured interview—the open-ended, in-depth (ethnographic) interview. Many qualitative researchers differentiate between in-depth (ethnographic) interviewing and participant observation. Yet, as Lofland (1971) pointed out, the two go hand in hand, and much of the data gathered in participant observation come from informal interviewing in the field. Consider the following report from Malinowski's (1967/1989) diary:

> Saturday 8 [December 1917]. Got up late, felt rotten, took enema. At about 1 I went out; I heard cries; [people from] Kapwapu were bringing *uri* to Teyava. I sat with the natives, talked, took pictures. Went back. Billy corrected and supplemented my notes about *wasi*. At Teyava, an old man talked a great deal about fishes, but I did not understand him too well. Then we moved to his *bwayama*. Talked about *lili'u*. They kept questioning me about the war—In the evening I talked to the policeman about *bwaga'u, lili'u,* and *yoyova*. I was irritated by their laughing. Billy again told me a number of interesting things. Took quinine and calomel. (p. 145)

Malinowski's (1967/1989) "day in the field" shows how very important unstructured interviewing is in the conduct of fieldwork and clearly illustrates the difference between structured interviewing and unstructured interviewing. Malinowski had some general topics he wanted to know about, but he did not use close-ended questions or a formal approach to interviewing. What is more, he committed (as most field-workers do) what structured interviewers would see as two "capital offenses." First, he answered questions asked by the respondents. Second, he let his personal feelings influence him (as all field-workers do); thus, he deviated from the "ideal" of a cool, distant, and rational interviewer.

Malinowski's example captures the difference in structured versus unstructured interviewing. The former aims at capturing precise data of a codable nature so as to explain behavior within preestablished categories, whereas the latter attempts to understand the complex behavior of members of society without imposing any a priori categorization that may limit the field of inquiry.

In a way, Malinowski's interviewing is still structured to some degree; there is a setting, there are identified informants, and the respondents are clearly discernible. In other types of interviewing, there might be no setting; for instance, Hertz (1995,

1997b, 1997c) focused on locating women in a historic moment rather than in a place. In addition, in their study of single mothers, Hertz and Ferguson (1997) interviewed women who did not know each other and who were not part of a single group or village. At times, informants are not readily accessible or identifiable, but anyone the researcher meets may become a valuable source of information. Hertz and Ferguson relied on tradespeople and friends to identify single mothers in the study. Fontana and Smith (1989) found that respondents were not always readily identifiable. In studying Alzheimer's disease patients, they discovered that it was often possible to confuse caregivers and patients during the early stages of the disease. Also, in Fontana's (1977) research on the poor elderly, the researcher had no fixed setting at all; he simply wandered from bench to bench in the park where the old folks were sitting, talking to any disheveled old person who would talk back.

Spradley (1979) aptly differentiated among various types of interviewing. He described the following interviewer–respondent interaction, which would be unthinkable in traditional sociological circles yet is the very essence of unstructured interviewing—the establishment of a human-to-human relation with the respondent and the desire to *understand* rather than to *explain:*

> Presently she smiled, pressed her hand to her chest, and said: "Tsetchwe." It was her name. "Elizabeth," I said, pointing to myself. "Nisabe," she answered. . . . Then, having surely suspected that I was a woman, she put her hand on my breast gravely, and, finding out that I was, she touched her own breast. Many Bushmen do this; to them all Europeans look alike. "Tasu si" (women), she said. Then after a moment's pause, Tsetchwe began to teach me. (pp. 3–4)

Spradley (1979) went on to discuss all of the things that an interviewer learns from the natives—their culture, their language, their ways of life. Although each and every study is different, these are some of the basic elements of unstructured interviewing. These elements have been discussed in detail already, and we need not elaborate on them too much here (for detailed accounts of unstructured interviewing, see Adams & Preiss, 1960; Lofland, 1971; Spradley, 1979). Here we provide brief synopses. Remember that these are presented only as heuristic devices; every study uses slightly different elements and often in different combinations.

It is important to keep in mind that the following description of interviewing is highly modernistic in that it presents a structured format and definite steps to be followed. In a way, it mimics structured interviewing in an attempt to "scientize" the research, albeit by using very different steps and concerns. Later in this chapter, in discussing new trends, we deconstruct these notions as we frame the interview as an active emergent process. We contend that our interview society gives people instructions on how to comply with these heuristics (Silverman, 1993, 1997a, 1997b). Similarly, Scheurich (1995, 1997) was openly critical of both positivistic and interpretive interviewing because they are based on modernistic assumptions.

For Scheurich (1997), rather than being a process "by the numbers," interviewing (and its language) is "persistently slippery, unstable, and ambiguous from person to person, from situation to situation, from time to time" (p. 62).

Although postmodern researchers follow Scheurich, more traditional sociologists and researchers from other disciplines still follow this "how to" approach to interviewing, where the illusion exists that the better they execute the various steps, the better they will apprehend the reality that they assume is out there, ready to be plucked.

*Accessing the Setting.* How do we "get in"? That, of course, varies according to the group that one is attempting to study. One might have to disrobe and casually stroll in the nude if he or she is doing a study of nude beaches (Douglas, Rasmussen, & Flanagan, 1977), or one might have to buy a huge motorbike and frequent seedy bars in certain locations if he or she is attempting to befriend and study the Hell's Angels (Thompson, 1985). The different ways and attempts to get in vary tremendously, but they all share the common goal of gaining access to the setting. Sometimes there is no setting per se, as when Fontana (1977) attempted to study the poor elderly on the streets and had to gain access anew with each and every interviewee.

*Understanding the Language and Culture of the Respondents.* Wax (1960) gave perhaps the most poignant description of learning the language and culture of the respondents in her study of "disloyal" Japanese in concentration camps in America between 1943 and 1945. Wax had to overcome a number of language and cultural problems in her study. Although respondents may be fluent in the language of the interviewer, there are different ways of saying things—or indeed, certain things that should not be said at all— linking language and cultural manifestations. Wax made this point:

> I remarked that I would like to see the letter. The silence that fell on the chatting group was almost palpable, and the embarrassment of the hosts was painful to see. The *faux pas* was not asking to see a letter, for letters were passed about rather freely. It rested on the fact that one did not give a Caucasian a letter in which the "disloyal" statement of a friend might be expressed. (p. 172)

Some researchers, especially in anthropological interviews, tend to rely on interpreters and so become vulnerable to added layers of meanings, biases, and interpretations, and this may lead to disastrous misunderstandings (Freeman, 1983). At times, specific jargon, such as the medical metalanguage of physicians, may be a code that is hard for nonmembers to understand.

*Deciding How to Present Oneself.* Do we present ourselves as representatives from academia studying medical students (Becker, 1956)? Do we approach the interview as a woman-to-woman discussion (Spradley, 1979)? Do we "dress down" to look like the respondents (Fontana, 1977; Thompson, 1975)? Do we represent the colonial culture

(Malinowski, 1922), or do we humbly present ourselves as "learners" (Wax, 1960)? This is very important because once the interviewer's presentational self is "cast," it leaves a profound impression on the respondents and has a great influence of the success of the study (or lack thereof). Sometimes inadvertently, the researcher's presentational self may be misrepresented, as Johnson (1976) discovered in studying a welfare office when some of the employees assumed that he was a "spy" for management despite his best efforts to present himself to the contrary.

*Locating an Informant.* The researcher must find an insider—a member of the group being studied—who is willing to be an informant and act as a guide and translator of cultural mores and, at times, of jargon or language. Although the researcher can conduct interviews without an informant, he or she can save much time and avoid mistakes if a good informant becomes available. The "classic" sociological informant was Doc in Whyte's (1943) *Street Corner Society.* Without Doc's help and guidance, it is doubtful that Whyte would have been able to access his respondents to the level he did. Rabinow's (1977) discussion of his relation with his main informant, Abd al-Malik ben Lahcen, was very instructive. Malik acted as a translator but also provided Rabinow with access to the cultural ways of the respondents, and by his actions he provided Rabinow with insights into the vast differences between a University of Chicago researcher and a native Moroccan.

*Gaining Trust.* Survey researchers asking respondents whether they would or would not favor the establishment of a nuclear dump in their state (Frey, 1993) do not have too much work to do in the way of gaining trust; respondents have opinions about nuclear dumps and are very willing to express them, sometimes forcefully. But it is clearly a different story if one wants to ask about people's frequency of sexual intercourse or preferred method of birth control. The interviewer needs to establish some trust with the respondents (Cicourel, 1974). Rasmussen (1989) had to spend months as a "wallflower" in the waiting room of a massage parlor before any of the masseuses gained enough trust in him to divulge to him, in unstructured interviews, the nature of their "massage" relation with clients. Gaining trust is essential to the success of the interviews, and once it is gained, trust can still be very fragile. Any faux pas by the researcher may destroy days, weeks, or months of painfully gained trust.

*Establishing Rapport.* Because the goal of unstructured interviewing is *understanding,* it is paramount to establish rapport with respondents; that is, the researcher must be able to take the role of the respondents and attempt to see the situation from their viewpoint rather than superimpose his or her world of academia and preconceptions on them. Although a close rapport with the respondents opens the doors to more informed research, it may create problems in that the researcher may become a spokesperson for the group studied, losing his or her distance and objectivity, or may "go native" and become a member of the group and forgo his or her academic role. At times, what the researcher might feel is a good rapport turns out not be, as Thompson (1985) found out in a nightmarish way when he was subjected to a brutal beating by the Hell's Angels just as his study of them was coming to a close. At the other end of the spectrum, some researchers might never feel that they have established a good rapport with their respondents. Malinowski (1967/1989), for example, always mistrusted the motives of the natives and at times was troubled by their brutish sensuality or angered by their outright lying or deceptions: "After lunch I [carried] yellow calico and spoke about the *baloma*. I made a small *sagali*, Navavile. I was *fed up* with the *niggers*" (p. 154).

*Collecting Empirical Material.* Being out in the field does not afford one the luxury of video cameras, soundproof rooms, and high-quality recording equipment. Lofland (1971) provided detailed information on doing and writing up interviews and on the types of field notes that one ought to take and how to organize them. Yet fieldworkers often must make do with what they can have in the field; the "tales" of their methods used range from holding a miniature tape recorder as inconspicuously as possible to taking mental notes and then rushing to the privacy of a bathroom to jot down notes—at times on toilet paper. We agree with Lofland that, regardless of the circumstances, researchers ought to (a) take notes regularly and promptly, (b) write down everything no matter how unimportant it might seem at the time, (c) try to be as inconspicuous as possible in note taking, and (d) analyze notes frequently.

## Other Types of Unstructured Interviewing

We consider the issue of interpreting and reporting empirical material later in the chapter. In this subsection, we briefly outline some different types of unstructured interviews.

### Oral History

The oral history differs from other unstructured interviews in purpose but not methodologically. The oral collection of historical materials goes back to ancient times, but its modern-day formal organization can be traced to 1948 when Allan Nevins began the Oral History Project at Columbia University (Starr, 1984, p. 4). The oral history captures a variety of forms of life, from common folks talking about their jobs in Terkel's (1975) *Working* to the historical recollections of President Harry Truman in Miller's (1974) *Plain Speaking* (see also Starr, 1984, p. 4). Often oral history transcripts are not published, but many may be found in libraries. They are like silent memoirs waiting for someone to rummage through them and bring their testimony to life. Recently, oral history has found great popularity in the feminist movement (Gluck & Patai, 1991), where it is seen as a way of understanding and bringing forth the history of women in a culture that has traditionally relied on masculine interpretation: "Refusing to be rendered historically voiceless any longer, women are creating a new history—using our own voices and experiences" (Gluck, 1984, p. 222).

Relevant to the study of oral history (and, in fact, to all interviewing) is the study of memory and its relation to recall. For instance, Schwartz (1999) examined the ages at which we recall critical episodes in our lives, concluding that "biographical memory . . . is better understood as a social process" and that "as we look back, we find ourselves remembering our lives in terms of our experience with others" (p. 15; see also Schwartz, 1996). Ellis (1991) resorted to the use of "sociological introspection" to reconstruct biographical episodes of her past life. Notable among Ellis's work in this genre was her reconstruction of her 9-year relationship with her partner, Gene Weinstein. Ellis (1995) described the emotional negotiations the two of them went through as they coped with his downward-spiraling health until the final negotiation with death.

### Creative Interviewing

Close to oral history, but used more conventionally as a sociological tool, is Douglas's (1985) "creative interviewing." Douglas argued against the "how to" guides to conducting interviews because unstructured interviews take place in the largely situational everyday world of members of society. Thus, interviewers must necessarily be creative, must forget "how to" rules, and must adapt to the ever-changing situations they face. Similar to oral historians, Douglas described interviewing as collecting oral reports from the members of society. In creative interviewing, these reports go well beyond the length of conventional unstructured interviews and may become "life histories," with interviewing taking place in multiple sessions over many days with the respondents.

## ▣ POSTMODERN INTERVIEWING

Douglas's (1985) concern with the important role played by the interviewer as human, a concern that is also shared by the feminist oral historians, became a paramount element in the interviewing approaches of postmodern anthropologists and sociologists during the mid-1980s. Marcus and Fischer (1986) addressed ethnography at large, but their discussion was germane to unstructured interviewing because, as we have seen, such interviewing constitutes the major way of collecting data in fieldwork. Marcus and Fischer voiced reflexive concerns about the ways in which the researcher influences the study, both in the methods of data collection and in the techniques of reporting findings. This concern led to new ways of conducting interviews in the hope of minimizing, if not eliminating, the interviewer's influence. One such way is through *polyphonic* interviewing, where the voices of the respondents are recorded with minimal influence from the researcher and are not collapsed together and reported as one through the interpretation of the researcher. Instead, the multiple perspectives of the various respondents are reported, and differences and problems encountered are discussed, rather than glossed over (Krieger, 1983). *Interpretive interactionism* follows in the footsteps of creative and polyphonic interviewing, but borrowing from James Joyce, it adds a new element—that of epiphanies, which Denzin (1989) described as "those interactional moments that leave marks on people's lives [and] have the potential for creating transformational experiences for the person" (p. 15). Thus, the topic of inquiry becomes dramatized by the focus on existential moments in people's lives, possibly producing richer and more meaningful data. Finally, as postmodernists seek new ways of understanding and reporting data, we note the concept of "oralysis," which refers to "the ways in which oral forms, derived from everyday life, are, with the recording powers of video, applied to the analytical tasks associated with literate forms" (Ulmer, 1989, p. xi). In oralysis, the traditional product of interviewing, talk, is coupled with the visual, providing a product consonant with a society that is dominated by the medium of television (Ulmer, 1989).

## ▣ GENDERED INTERVIEWING

> The housewife goes into a well-stocked store to look for a frying pan. Her thinking probably does not proceed exactly this way, but it is helpful to think of the many possible two-way choices she might make: Cast iron or aluminum? Thick or thin? Metal or wooden handle? Covered or not? Deep or shallow? Large or small? This brand or that? Reasonable or too high in price? To buy or not? Cash or charge? Have it delivered or carry it? . . . The two-way question is simplicity itself when it comes to recording answers and tabulating them (Payne, 1951, pp 55–56)

The preceding quote represents the prevalent paternalistic attitude toward women in interviewing (Oakley, 1981, p. 39) as well as the paradigmatic concern with coding answers and, therefore, with presenting limited dichotomous choices. Apart from a tendency to be condescending to women, the traditional interview paradigm does not account for gendered differences. In fact, Babbie's (1992) classic text, *The Practice of Social Research*, briefly referenced gender only three times and did not even mention the influence of gender on interviews. As Oakley (1981) cogently pointed out, both the interviewer and the respondent are considered to be faceless and invisible, and they must be if the paradigmatic assumption of gathering value-free data is to be maintained. Yet, as Denzin (1989) told us, "gender filters knowledge" (p. 116); that is, the sex of the interviewer and the sex of the respondent make a difference because the interview takes place within the cultural boundaries of a paternalistic social system in which masculine identities are differentiated from feminine ones.

In the typical interview, there exists a hierarchical relation, with the respondent being in the subordinate position. The interviewer is instructed to be courteous, friendly, and pleasant:

The interviewer's manner should be friendly, courteous, conversational, and unbiased. He should be neither too grim nor too effusive; neither too talkative nor too timid. The idea should be to put the respondent at ease, *so that he will talk freely and fully.* (Selltiz, Jahoda, Deutsch, & Cook, 1965, p. 576, emphasis added)

Yet, as the last line of this quote shows, this demeanor is a ruse to gain the trust and confidence of the respondent without reciprocating those feelings in any way. The interviewer is not to give his or her own opinions and is to evade direct questions. What seems to be a conversation is really a one-way pseudoconversation, raising an ethical dilemma (Fine, 1983–1984) inherent in the study of people for opportunistic reasons. When the respondent is female, the interview presents added problems because the preestablished format directed at information relevant for the study tends both to ignore the respondent's own concerns and to curtail any attempts to digress and elaborate. This format also stymies any revelation of personal feelings and emotions.

Warren (1988) discussed problems of gender in both anthropological and sociological fieldwork, and many of these problems are also found in the ethnographic interview. Some of these problems are the traditional ones of entrée and trust that may be heightened by the sex of the interviewer, especially in highly sex-segregated societies:

I never witnessed any ceremonies that were barred to women. Whenever I visited compounds, I sat with the women while the men gathered in the parlors or in front of the compound. . . . I never entered any of the places where men sat around to drink beer or palm wine and to chat. (Sudarkasa, 1986, quoted in Warren, 1988, p. 16)

Solutions to the problem have been to view the female anthropologist as androgyny or to grant her honorary male status for the duration of her research. Warren (1988) also pointed to some advantages of the researcher being female and, therefore, being seen as harmless or invisible. Other problems are associated with the researcher's status and race and with the context of the interview, and again these problems are magnified for female researchers in a paternalistic world. Female interviewers at times face the added burden of sexual overtures or covert sexual hassles (p. 33).

Feminist researchers are suggesting ways in which to circumvent the traditional interviewing paradigm. Oakley (1981) noted that interviewing is a masculine paradigm that is embedded in a masculine culture and stresses masculine traits while at the same time excluding traits, such as sensitivity and emotionality, that are culturally viewed as feminine traits. However, there is a growing reluctance, especially among female researchers (Oakley, 1981; Reinharz, 1992; Smith, 1987), to continue interviewing women as "objects" with little or no regard for them as individuals. Although this reluctance stems from moral and ethical reasons, it is also relevant methodologically. As Oakley (1981) pointed out, in interviewing there is "no intimacy without reciprocity" (p. 49). Thus, the emphasis is shifting to allow the development of a closer relation between the interviewer and the respondent. Researchers are attempting to minimize status differences and are doing away with the traditional hierarchical situation in interviewing. Interviewers can show their human side and can answer questions and express feelings. Methodologically, this new approach provides a greater spectrum of responses and a greater insight into the lives of the respondents—or "participants," to avoid the hierarchical pitfall (Reinharz, 1992, p. 22)—because it encourages them to control the sequencing and language of the interview while also allowing them the freedom of open-ended responses (Oakley, 1981; Reinharz, 1992; Smith, 1987). To wit, "Women were always . . . encouraged to 'digress' into details of their personal histories and to recount anecdotes of their working lives. Much important information was gathered in this way" (Yeandle, 1984, quoted in Reinharz, 1992, p. 25).

Hertz (1997a) made the self of the researcher visible and suggested that it is only one of many selves that the researcher takes to the field. She asserted that interviewers need to be reflexive; that is, they need to "have an ongoing conversation about experience while simultaneously living in the moment" (p. viii). By doing so, they will heighten the understanding of differences of ideologies, culture, and politics between interviewers and interviewees.

Hertz also underscored the importance of "voices"—how we (as authors) express and write our stories, which data we include and which data we exclude, whose voices we choose to represent and whose voices we choose not to represent. The concern with voices is also found, very powerfully, in Vaz's (1997) edited *Oral Narrative Research With Black Women*. One of the contributors, Obbo (1997), stated,

> This chapter is a modest exercise in giving expression to women's voices and in rescuing their perceptions and experiences from being mere murmurs or backdrop to political, social, and cultural happenings. Women's voices have been devalued by male chronicles of cultural history even when the men acknowledge female informants; they are overshadowed by the voice of male authority and ascendance in society. (pp. 42–43)

This commitment to maintaining the integrity of the phenomena and preserving the viewpoint of the respondents, as expressed in their everyday language, is very akin to phenomenological and existential sociologies (Douglas & Johnson, 1977; Kotarba & Fontana, 1984) and also reflects the concern of postmodern ethnographers (Marcus & Fischer, 1986). The differences are (a) the heightened moral concern for respondents/ participants, (b) the attempt to redress the male/female hierarchy and existing paternalistic power structure, and (c) the paramount importance placed on membership because the effectiveness of male researchers in interviewing female respondents has been largely discredited.

Behar (1996) addressed the ambiguous nature of the enterprise of interviewing by asking the following questions. Where do we locate the researcher in the field? How much do we reveal about ourselves? How do we reconcile our different roles and positions? Behar made us see that interviewer, writer, respondent, and interview are not clearly distinct entities; rather, they are intertwined in a deeply problematic way.

Behar and Gordon (1995) also cogently pointed out that the seminal work by Marcus and Fischer (1986) broke ground with modernistic ethnography but remains an example of paternalistic sociology because it did not address women's concerns.

Some feminist sociologists have gone beyond the concern with interviewing or fieldwork in itself. Richardson (1992a) strove for new forms of expression to report the findings and presented some of her fieldwork in the form of poetry. Clough (1998) questioned the whole enterprise of fieldwork under the current paradigm and called for a reassessment of the whole sociological enterprise and for a rereading of existing sociological texts in a light that is not marred by a paternalistic bias. Their voices echoed the concern of Smith (1987), who eloquently stated,

> The problem (of a research project) and its particular solution are analogous to those by which fresco painters solved the problems of representing the different temporal moments of a story in the singular space of the wall. The problem is to produce in a two-dimensional space framed as a wall a world of action and movement in time. (p. 281)

A growing number of researchers believe that we cannot isolate gender from other important elements that also "filter knowledge." For example, Collins (1990) wrote eloquently about the filtering of knowledge through memberships—of being black and female in American culture, in her case. Weston (1998) made just as powerful a case for sexuality, contending that it should not be treated as a compartmentalized subspecialty because it underlies and is integral to the whole of social sciences. It is clear that gender, sexuality, and race cannot be considered in isolation; race, class, hierarchy, status, and age (Seidman, 1991) all are part of the complex, yet often ignored, elements that shape interviewing.

## ▣ FRAMING AND INTERPRETING INTERVIEWS

Aside from the problem of framing real-life events in a two-dimensional space, we face the added problems of how the framing is being done and who is doing the framing. In sociological terms, this means that the type of interviewing selected, the techniques used, and the ways of recording information all come to bear on the results of the study. In addition, data must be interpreted, and the researcher has a great deal of influence over what part of the data will be reported and how the data will be reported.

### Framing Interviews

Numerous volumes have been published on the techniques of structured interviewing (see, e.g., Babbie, 1992; Bradburn et al., 1979; Gorden, 1980; Kahn & Cannell, 1957). There is also a voluminous literature on group interviewing, especially on marketing, and survey research (for a comprehensive review of literature in this area, see Stewart & Shamdasani, 1990). The uses of group interviewing have also been linked to qualitative sociology (Morgan, 1988). Unstructured interviewing techniques also have been covered thoroughly (Denzin, 1989; Lofland, 1971; Lofland & Lofland, 1984; Spradley, 1979).

As we have noted, unstructured interviews vary widely given their informal nature and depending on the type of the setting, and some eschew the use of any preestablished set of techniques (Douglas, 1985). Yet there are techniques involved in interviewing whether the interviewer is just being "a nice person" or he or she is following a format. Techniques can be varied to meet various situations, and varying one's techniques is known as using tactics. Traditionally, the researcher is involved in an informal conversation with the respondent; thus, the researcher must maintain a tone of "friendly" chat while trying to remain close to the guidelines of the topics of inquiry that he or she has in mind. The researcher begins by "breaking the ice" with general questions and gradually moves on to more specific ones while also—as inconspicuously as possible—asking questions intended to check the veracity of the respondent's statements. The researcher should avoid getting involved in a "real" conversation in which he or she answers questions asked by the respondent or provides personal opinions on the matters discussed. The researcher can avoid "getting trapped" by shrugging off the relevance of his or her opinions (e.g., "It doesn't matter how I feel; it's your opinion that's important") or by feigning ignorance (e.g., "I really don't know enough about this to say anything; you're the expert"). Of course, as we have seen in the case of gendered interviewing, the researcher may reject these techniques and "come down" to the level of the respondent to engage in a "real" conversation with give and take and shared empathetic understanding.

The use of language, particularly that of specific terms, is important to create a "sharedness of meanings" in which both interviewer and the respondent understand the contextual nature of specific referents. For instance, in studying nude beaches, Douglas and Rasmussen (1977) discovered that the term "nude beach virgin" had nothing to do with chastity; rather, it referred to the fact that a person's buttocks were white, indicating to others that he or she was a newcomer to the nude beach. Language is also important in delineating the type of question (e.g., broad, narrow, leading, instructive).

Nonverbal techniques are also important in interviewing. There are four basic modes of nonverbal communication:

> *Proxemic* communication is the use of interpersonal space to communicate attitudes, *chronemic* communication is the use of pacing of speech and length of silence in conversation, *kinesic* communication includes any body movements or postures, and *paralinguistic* communication includes all the variations in volume, pitch, and quality of voice. (Gorden, 1980, p. 335)

All four of these modes represent important techniques for the researcher. In addition, the researcher should carefully note and record respondents' use of these modes because interview data are more than verbal records and should include, as much as possible, nonverbal features of the interaction. Finally, techniques vary with the group being interviewed; for instance, interviewing a group of children requires a different approach from the one that the interviewer may use when interviewing a group of elderly widows (Lopata, 1980).

An interesting proposal for framing interviews came from Saukko (2000), who asked, "How can we be true and respect the inner experiences of people and at the same time critically assess the cultural discourses that form the very stuff from which our experiences are made?" (p. 299). Using the metaphor of patchwork quilts (which have no center), Saukko patched and stitched together the stories of five anorexic women. Thus, she rejected the idea of framing characters as monological and instead, borrowing from Bakhtin (1986), presented them as "dialogic characters" (Saukko, 2000, p. 303).

## Interpreting Interviews

Many studies that use unstructured interviews are not reflexive enough about the interpreting process. Common platitudes proclaim that data speak for themselves and that the researcher is neutral, unbiased, and "invisible." The data reported tend to flow nicely, there are no contradictory data, and there is no mention of what data were excluded and why. Improprieties never happen, and the main concern seems to be the proper (if unreflexive) filing, analyzing, and reporting of events. But anyone who has engaged in fieldwork knows better. No matter how organized the researcher may be, he or she slowly becomes buried under an increasing mountain of field notes, transcripts, newspaper clippings, and audiotapes. Traditionally, readers were presented with the researcher's interpretation of the data, cleaned and streamlined and collapsed in a rational noncontradictory account. More recently, sociologists have come to grips with the reflexive, problematic, and sometimes contradictory nature of data and with the tremendous, if unspoken, influence of the researcher as author. What Van Maanen (1988) called "confessional style" began in earnest during the 1970s (Johnson, 1976) and has continued unabated to our days in a soul cleansing by researchers of problematic feelings and sticky situations in the field. Although perhaps somewhat overdone at times, these "confessions" are very valuable because they make readers aware of the complex and cumbersome nature of interviewing people in their natural settings and lend a tone of realism and veracity to studies. Malinowski (1967/1989) provided a good example: "Yesterday I slept very late. Got up around 10. The day before I had engaged Omaga, Koupa, and a few others. They didn't come. Again I fell into a rage" (p. 67).

Showing the human side of the researcher and the problematics of unstructured interviewing has taken new forms in deconstructionism (Derrida, 1976). Here, the influence of the author is brought under scrutiny. Thus, the text created by the rendition of events by the researcher is "deconstructed"; the author's biases and taken-for-granted notions are exposed, and sometimes alternative ways of looking at the data are introduced (Clough, 1998).

Postmodern social researchers, as we have seen, attempt to expose the role of the researcher as field-worker and minimize his role as author. For instance, Crapanzano

(1980) reported Tuhami's accounts, whether they were sociohistorical renditions, dreams, or outright lies, because they all constituted a part of this Moroccan Arab respondent's sense of self and personal history. In interviewing Tuhami, Crapanzano learned not only about his respondent but also about himself:

> As Tuhami's interlocutor, I became an active participant in his life history, even though I rarely appear directly in his recitations. Not only did my presence, and my questions, prepare him for the text he was to produce, but they produced what I read as a change of consciousness in him. They produced a change of consciousness in me too. We were both jostled from our assumptions about the nature of the everyday world and ourselves and groped for common reference points within this limbo of interchange. (p. 11)

No longer pretending to be a faceless respondent and an invisible researcher, Tuhami and Crapanzano were portrayed as individual humans with their own personal histories and idiosyncrasies, and the readers learn about two people and two cultures.

Gubrium and Holstein (2002) actually considered the interview as a contextually based, mutually accomplished story that is reached through collaboration between the researcher and the respondent. Thus, just to tell what happened (the *what*) is not enough because the what depends greatly on the ways, negotiations, and other interactive elements that take place between the researcher and the respondent (the *how*). Others have addressed the same concerns, at times enlarging the one-to-one interaction to interaction between the researcher and a whole community or outlining the various types of collaborative interviewing (Ellis & Berger, 2002).

The discovery of reflexivity proved to be an epiphanic moment for Banister (1999). Once she was able to realize that her study of midlife women resonated strong personal notes with her midlife experience, Banister acknowledged that the she was not just a witness to her respondents and came to see the liminality of her position. Thus, she was able to understand the women's midlife experience as well as her own and to reach a deep ethnographic understanding.

Another powerful way in which to accentuate reflexivity in interviewing is through narrative, where in trying to understand the "other" we learn about (our)"selves," reaching the hermeneutic circle, that is, the circle of understanding (Rabinow & Sullivan, 1987; Warren, 2002). Denzin (2003b) noted that writers can gain knowledge about themselves by bringing forth their autobiographical past; in a way, they are bringing the past into the present (Pinar, 1994). Denzin (2003a) proposed that this perhaps can best be achieved through the use of performances rather than traditional writing modes as a way in which to reach across the divide and extend a hand to those who have been oppressed. In performance, we infuse powerful feelings and try to recreate a way in which to understand those we study and ourselves in our relationship to them, that is, not merely to create new sociological knowledge but also to use that hand to grasp and pull the downtrodden out of the mire in which they are suffocating.

## ▣ ETHICAL CONSIDERATIONS

Because the objects of inquiry in interviewing are humans, extreme care must be taken to avoid any harm to them. Traditionally, ethical concerns have revolved around the topics of *informed consent* (receiving consent by the respondent after having carefully and truthfully informed him or her about the research), *right to privacy* (protecting the identity of the respondent), and *protection from harm* (physical, emotional, or any other kind).

No sociologists or other social scientists would dismiss these three ethical concerns, yet there are other ethical concerns that are less unanimously upheld. The controversy over overt/covert fieldwork is more germane to participant observation but could include the surreptitious use of tape-recording devices. Warwick (1973) and Douglas (1985) argued for the use of covert methods because they mirror the deceitfulness of everyday-life reality, whereas others, including Erickson (1967), vehemently opposed the study of uninformed respondents.

Another problematic issue stems from the researcher's degree of involvement with the group under study. Whyte (1943) was asked to vote more than once during the same local elections (i.e., to vote illegally) by the members of the group to which he had gained access and befriended, thereby gaining the group members' trust. He used "situational ethics," that is, judging the legal infraction to be minor in comparison with the loss of his fieldwork if he refused to vote more than once. Thompson (1985) was faced with a more serious possible legal breach. He was terrified at the prospect of having to witness one of the alleged rapes for which the Hell's Angels had become notorious, but as he reported, none took place during his research. The most famous, and widely discussed, case of questionable ethics in qualitative sociology took place during Humphreys's (1970) research for *Tearoom Trade*. Humphreys studied homosexual encounters in public restrooms in parks ("tearooms") by acting as a lookout ("watch queen"). Although this fact in itself may be seen as unethical, it is the following one that raised many academic eyebrows. Humphreys, unable to interview the men in the tearoom, recorded their cars' license plate numbers, which led him to find their residences with the help of police files. He then interviewed many of the men in their homes without being recognized as having been their watch queen.

A twist in the degree of involvement with respondents came from a controversial article by Goode (2002) in which he summarily dismissed years of research with the fat civil rights organization as a "colossal waste of time." Goode discussed the problematics of sexual intimacy between researchers and respondents and acknowledged that he had casual sexual liaisons with some of the respondents. In fact, he fathered a child with a person he had met at research meetings. Goode's article was published along with a number of responses, all of them very critical (in different ways) of Goode's cavalier approach (Bell, 2002; Manning, 2002; Sagui, 2002; Williams, 2002). Perhaps the following quote from Williams (2002) best summarized the feelings of the scholars responding to Goode: "I would hope and expect that sociologists and their audiences could understand public discrimination without sleeping with its victims" (p. 560).

Another ethical problem is raised by the veracity of the reports made by researchers. For example, Whyte's (1943) famous study of Italian street corner men in Boston has come under severe scrutiny (Boelen, 1992) as some have alleged that Whyte portrayed the men in demeaning ways that did not reflect their visions of themselves. Whyte's case is still unresolved; it illustrates the delicate issue of ethical decisions in the field and in reporting field notes, even more than 50 years later (Richardson, 1992b).

A growing number of scholars, as we have seen (Oakley, 1981), feel that most of traditional in-depth interviewing is unethical, whether wittingly or unwittingly. The techniques and tactics of interviewing, they say, are really ways of manipulating the respondents while treating them as objects or numbers rather than as individual humans. Should the quest for objectivity supersede the human side of those we study? Consider the following:

> One day while doing research at the convalescent center, I was talking to one of the aides while she was beginning to change the bedding of one of the patients who had urinated and soaked the bed. He was the old, blind, ex-wrestler confined in the emergency room. Suddenly, the wrestler decided he was not going to cooperate with the aide and began striking violently at the air about him, fortunately missing the aide. Since nobody else was around, I had no choice but to hold the patient pinned down to the bed while the aide proceeded to change the bedding. It was not pleasant: The patient was squirming and yelling horrible threats at the top of his voice; the acid smell of urine was nauseating; I was slowly losing my grip on the much stronger patient, while all along feeling horribly like Chief Bromden when he suffocates the lobotomized MacMurphy in Ken Kesey's novel. *But there was no choice; one just could not sit back and take notes while the patient tore apart the aide.* (Fontana, 1977, p. 187, emphasis added)

A chapter (Edwards & Mauthner, 2002) in a recent edited volume (Mauthner, Birch, Jessop, & Miller, 2002) presented new insight on the ethics of feminist research. Edwards and Mauthner (2002) outlined the various models of ethics currently existing: the universalist models based on "universal principles such as honesty, justice, and respect" or based on "'goodness' of outcomes of research" (p. 20). In contrast, a third model is based on "contextual or situational ethical position" (p. 20). The authors noted that a majority of feminist researchers (if not all of them) have focused on care and responsibility, that is, on contextually based "feminist-informed social *values*" (p. 21). The authors lauded the work of Denzin (1997) for applying these feminist principles to social research. However, they found that some of Denzin's ideas could be refined to some degree. For instance, Denzin (1997) advocated a symmetrical relation between researchers and respondents, whereas others (e.g., Young, 1997) criticized this as "neither possible nor desirable" (Edwards & Mauthner, 2002, p. 26) and called instead for "asymmetrical reciprocity." In the words of the Edwards and Mauthner (2002), "Rather than ignoring or blurring power positions, ethical practice needs to pay attention to them" (p. 27).

Clearly, as we move forward with sociology, we cannot—to paraphrase what Blumer said so many years ago—let the methods dictate our images of humans. As Punch (1986) suggested, as field-workers we need to exercise common sense and responsibility—and, we would like to add, to our respondents first, to the study next, and to ourselves last. As Johnson (2002) empathically proclaimed, regardless of what criteria we wish to adopt for interviewing, "the most important ethical imperative is to tell the truth" (p. 116).

## ▣ NEW TRENDS IN INTERVIEWING

The latest trends in interviewing have come some distance from structured questions; we have reached the point of the interview as negotiated text. Ethnographers have realized for quite some time that researchers are not invisible neutral entities; rather, they are part of the interaction they seek to study, and they influence that interaction. At last, interviewing is being brought in line with ethnography. There is a growing realization that interviewers are not the mythical neutral tools envisioned by survey research. Interviewers are increasingly seen as active participants in an interaction with respondents, and interviews are seen as negotiated accomplishments of both interviewers and respondents that are shaped by the contexts and situations in which they take place. As Schwandt (1997) noted, "It has become increasingly common in qualitative studies to view the interview as a form of discourse between two or more speakers or as a linguistic event in which the meanings of questions and responses are contextually grounded and jointly constructed by interviewer and respondent" (p. 79). We are beginning to realize that we cannot lift the results of interviews out of the contexts in which they were gathered and claim them as objective data with no strings attached.

### The Interview as a Negotiated Accomplishment

Let us briefly recap the two traditional approaches to the interview, following Holstein and Gubrium (1995, 1997). The authors use Converse and Schuman's (1974) *Conversations at Random* as an exemplar of the interview as used in survey research. In this context, the interviewer is carefully instructed to remain as passive as possible so as to reduce his or her influence; the scope of the interviewer's function is to access the respondent's answers. This is a *rational* type of interviewing; it assumes that there is an objective knowledge out there and if that one can access it if he or she is skilled enough, just as a skilled surgeon can remove a kidney from a donor and use it in a different context (e.g., for a patient awaiting a transplant).

Holstein and Gubrium (1995, 1997) regarded Douglas's (1985) creative interviewing as a romanticist type of interviewing. Douglas's interviewing is based on *feelings;* it assumes that researchers, as interviewers, need to "get to know" the respondents beneath their rational facades and that researchers can reach respondents' deep well of emotions by engaging them and by sharing feelings and thoughts with them. Douglas's interviewer is certainly more active and far less neutral than Converse and Schuman's interviewer, but the assumptions are still the same—that the *skills* of the interviewer will provide access to knowledge and that there is a *core knowledge* that the researcher can access.

Holstein and Gubrium (1995) finally considered the new type of interviewing, although "new" isn't exactly accurate given that their reference for this is the work of Ithiel de Sola Pool, published in 1957. To wit, "Every interview is . . . an interpersonal drama with a developing plot" (Pool, 1957, p. 193, quoted in Holstein & Gubrium 1995, p. 14). Holstein and Gubrium went on to discuss that so far we have focused on the *whats* of the interview (the substantive findings) and that it is now time to pay attention to the *hows* of the interview (the context, particular situation, nuances, manners, people involved, etc., in which interview interactions take place). This concept harks back to ethnomethodology, according to Holstein and Gubrium: "To say that the interview is an interpersonal drama with a developing plot is part of a broader claim that reality is an ongoing, interpretive accomplishment" (p. 16). Garfinkel, Sacks, and others clearly stated during the late 1960s that reality is an ever-changing, ongoing accomplishment based on the practical reasoning of the members of society. It is time to consider the interview as a practical production, the meaning of which is accomplished at the intersection of the interaction of the interviewer and the respondent.

In a later essay, Gubrium and Holstein (1998) continued their argument by looking at interviews as storytelling, which they saw as a practical production used by members of society to accomplish coherence in their accounts. Once more, they encouraged us to examine the *hows* as well as the *whats* of storytelling. Similarly, Sarup (1996) told us,

> Each narrative has two parts, a story (*histoire*) and a discourse (*discourse*). The story is the content, or chain of events. The story is the "what" in a narrative, the discourse is the "how." The discourse is rather like a plot, how the reader becomes aware of what happened, [and] the order of appearance of the events. (p. 17)

Gubrium and Holstein are not alone in advocating this reflexive approach to interviews. Both Silverman (1993) and Dingwall (1997) credited Cicourel's (1964) classic work, *Method and Measurement in Sociology,* with pointing to the interview as a social encounter. Dingwall (1997) noted,

> If the interview is a social encounter, then, logically, it must be analysed in the same way as any other social encounter. The products of an interview are the outcome of a socially situated activity where the responses are passed through the role-playing and impression management of both the interviewer and the respondent. (p. 56)

Seidman (1991) discussed interviewing as a relationship by relying on a principal intellectual antecedent of the ethnomethodologist Alfred Schutz. Seidman analyzed the interviewer–respondent relation in terms of Schutz's (1967) "I–Thou" relation, where the two share a reciprocity of perspective and, by both being "thou" oriented, create a "we" relationship. Thus, the respondent is no longer "an object or a type" (Seidman, 1991, p. 73); rather, the respondent becomes an equal participant in the interaction.

To recapitulate, we must find someone willing to talk to us (Arksey & Knight, 2002). Then we go through many creative stratagems to find more respondents (Warren, 2002; Weiss, 1994). Then, we talk to the respondents and attend to the meaning of the stories they weave while interjecting our own perspectives. Warren (2002) puts it beautifully: "In the social interaction of the qualitative interview, the perspectives of the interviewer and the respondent dance together for the moment but also extend outward in social space and backward and forward in time" (p. 98). Finally, we try to piece together the kaleidoscope of shapes and colors into a coherent story— something that has some meaning and, in the common understanding that we achieve, brings us all closer together (Atkinson, 2002).

## The Problematics of New Approaches

Some of the proponents of the ethnomethodologically informed interview are critical of both interactionist and positivist interview methods. Dingwall (1997), as well as others, spoke of the romantic movement in ethnography (and interviewing)—the idea that the nearer we come to the respondent, the closer we are to apprehending the "real self." This assumption neglects the fact that the self is a process that is ever negotiated and accomplished in the interaction. Dingwall also faulted the "postmodern" turn; that is, if there is no real self, then there is no real world and so we can create one of our own. Finally, Dingwall was troubled by the "crusading" nature of the romantics and asked, "What is the value of a scholarly enterprise that is more concerned with being 'right on' than with being right?" (p. 64).

In a similar vein, Atkinson and Silverman (1997) rejected the postmodern notion of "polyphonic voices," correctly noting that the interviewer and the respondent collaborate together to create an essentially monologic view of reality. This same rejection could be made by using Schutz's (1967) argument, that is, "I" and "thou" create a unified "we" rather than two separate versions of it.

Ethnomethodologically informed interviewing is not, however, immune from criticism itself. Schutz (1967) assumed a reciprocity of perspective that might not exist. Granted, in our interview society, we all know the commonsense routines and ground rules of interviewing, but in other societies this might not be the case. Bowler (1997) attempted to interview Pakistani women about their experience with maternity services and found a total lack of understanding of the value of social research and interviewing:

I had told them that I was writing a book on my findings. Yams, who spoke the better English, translated this with a look of disbelief on her face, and then they both dissolved into laughter. The hospitals were very good. There weren't any problems. All was well. (p. 72)

Bowler was forced to conclude that interviewing might not work when there is no "shared notion of the process of research" (p. 66).

Silverman (1993) envisioned a different problem. He seemed to feel that some ethnomethodologists have suspended their interest in substantive concerns of everyday life, claiming that they cannot address them until they knew more about the ways in which these realities are accomplished. He noted, "Put simply, according to one reading of Cicourel, we would focus on the conversational skills of the participants rather than on the content of what they are saying and its relation to the world outside the interview" (p. 98).

Cicourel (1970) stated that sociologists need to outline a workable model of the actor before engaging in the study of self and society. Garfinkel held similar beliefs. For instance, in his famous study of a transsexual named Agnes, Garfinkel (1967) examined the routines by which societal members pass as males or females; he had little or no interest in issues of transsexuality per se. Thus, it would follow that, according to Silverman's reading of ethnomethodology, we should learn the conversational methods before attempting to learn substantive matters in interviewing.

## ▣ FUTURE DIRECTIONS

To borrow from Gubrium and Holstein (1997), "Where do we go from here?" (p. 97). We share with these two authors a concern with appreciating the new horizons of postmodernism while simultaneously remaining conservatively committed to the empirical description of everyday life. Gubrium and Holstein (1998) introduced a technique called "analytic bracketing" to deal with the multiple levels of interviewing (and ethnography):

We may focus, for example on *how* a story is being told, while temporarily deferring our concern for the various *whats* that are involved—for example, the substance, structure, or plot of the story, the context within which it is told, or the audience to which it is accountable. We can later return to these issues. (p. 165)

The use of this analytic bracketing allows the authors to analyze interviewing in its coherence and diversity as an event that is collaboratively achieved and in which product and process are mutually constituted.

A pressing problem in interviewing concerns the kinds of standards that we should apply to these new and different types of interviews. To assume absolute relativism is not the solution because it would lead, in Silverman's (1997b) words, to the "sociology of navel-gazing" (p. 240). Silverman proposed an aesthetics for research, rejecting attempts to use literary forms in sociology: "If I want to read a good poem, why on earth should I turn to a social science journal?" (p. 240). Silverman's critique of inter-actionist sociology and proposal for aesthetic values seemed to focus on the following three points. First, he attacked the grandiose political theorizing of British sociology and invoked a return to more modest, more minute goals. Second, he rejected the romanticist notion of equating experience (from the members' viewpoint) with authenticity. Third, he noted that in sociology we mimic the mass media of the interview society, thereby succumbing to the trivial, the kitschy, the gossipy, and the melodramatic and ignoring simplicity and profundity.

Silverman's (1997b) notions that we should pay attention to minute details in sociological studies, rather than embarking on grandiose abstract projects, in a way was not dissimilar to Lyotard's (1984) appeal for a return to local elements and away from metatheorizing. For Silverman, the "minute" details are the small details that go on in front of our eyes in our everyday life—very similar to Garfinkel's mundane routines that allow us to sustain the world and interact with each other.

We agree with Silverman that we need to stop deluding ourselves that in our particular method (whichever it may be), we have the key to the understanding of the self. We also agree that it is imperative that we look for new standards given that we are quickly digressing into a new form of the theater of the absurd (and without the literary flair, we fear). But we cannot wait to find a model of the methods used by participants in interviews or in everyday life before we proceed; Cicourel's (1970) invariant properties of interaction turned out to be so general as to be of little use to sociological inquiry.

We need to proceed by looking at the substantive concerns of the members of society while simultaneously examining the constructive activities used to produce order in everyday life and, all along, remaining reflexive about how interviews are accomplished (Gubrium & Holstein, 1997, 1998). For instance, as Baker (1997) pointed out, a researcher telling a respondent that "I am a mother of three" versus telling the respondent that "I am a university professor" accesses different categories and elicits different accounts. We need to move on with sociological inquiry, even though we realize that conditions are less than perfect. To paraphrase Robert Solow, as cited by Geertz (1973), just because complete asepsis is impossible does not mean that we may just as well perform surgery in a sewer.

A different kind of future direction for interviewing stems largely from the new feminist interviewing practices. The traditional interview has painstakingly attempted to maintain neutrality and achieve objectivity and has kept the role of the interviewer as invisible as possible. Feminists instead are rebelling against the practice of *exploiting* respondents and wish to use interviewing for ameliorative purposes. To wit, "As researchers with a commitment to change, we must decenter ourselves from the 'ivory tower' and construct more participatory, democratic practices. *We must keep people and politics at the center of our research*" (Benmayor, 1991, pp. 172–173, emphasis added). Denzin (1997) referred to this approach as the "feminist, communitarian ethical model" (see also Lincoln, 1995) and told us,

> The feminist, communitarian researcher does not invade the privacy of others, use informed consent forms, select subjects randomly, or measure research designs in terms of their validity. This framework presumes a researcher who builds collaborative, reciprocal, trusting, and friendly relations with those studied.... It is also understood that those studied have claims of ownership over any materials that are produced in the research process, including field notes. (Denzin, 1997, p. 275)

Combining the roles of the scholar and the feminist may be problematic and sometimes may lead to conflict if the researcher has a different political orientation from that of the people studied (Wasserfall, 1993), but this approach may also be very rewarding in allowing the researcher to see positive results stemming from the research (Gluck, 1991).

A third kind of future direction, one that is already here but is likely to expand greatly in the near future, is that of performance and poetics. I combine the two because they stem from the same concerns for speaking with the voices of the respondents and taking a helping stance toward them. Also, they both possess an expressional trope that goes beyond the traditional one of social sciences—prose. Denzin (2003a) championed performance to the exclusion of other modes of relating social science (ethnography and interview). Performance does not become fixed in a written text to be read later; rather, performance is doing, is now, and has feelings, passions, joy, tears, despair, and hope. Performance can reach people's hearts and not only their minds. Performance can be a powerful instrument for social reform, for righting some wrongs, and for helping those in need. Performance relates to people in our media society; it draws interest, draws attention, and leads to questioning.

Poetics operates in a similar way by encapsulating in a welter of feelings and emotions a life story, an epiphanic moment in the life, a tragedy, a moment of sorrow, or a moment of utter joy. Consider the reply of Louisa May, a sort of average woman from Tennessee, when her partner asked her to terminate her pregnancy:

Jody May's father said,

"Get an Abortion."

I told him,

"I would never marry you.

I would never marry you.

I would never.

I am going to have this child.

I am going to.

I am. I am."

Richardson's (1997) masterful poem captured the soul of Louisa May, and through the poem we come to know that woman, we know her feelings, and our heart goes out to her.

Richardson (2002), in speaking about poetry pointed out that prose is privileged only because it is empowered by the current system, yet it is only one of many tropes of expression, including performance and poetry, in a newly fragmented world in which not only metatheories but also modes of expression have been fragmented, and we can now speak in many voices and in different tropes.

## Electronic Interviewing

Another direction currently being taken in interviewing is related to the changing technologies available. The reliance on the interview as a means of information gathering most recently has expanded to electronic outlets, with questionnaires being administered by fax, electronic mail, and Web sites. Estimates suggest that nearly 50% of all households have computers and that nearly half of these use the Internet. Software that allows researchers to schedule and archive interview data gathered by chat room interviews is now available. The limited population of potential respondents with access to computers makes surveys of the general population infeasible, but electronic interviewing can reach 100% of some specialized populations (Schaefer & Dillman, 1998).

It is now possible to engage in "virtual interviewing," where Internet connections are used synchronously or asynchronously to obtain information. The advantages include low cost (no telephone or interviewer charges) and speed of return. Of course, face-to-face interaction is eliminated, as is the possibility of both the interviewer and the respondent reading nonverbal behavior or of cueing from gender, race, age, class, or other personal characteristics. Thus, establishing an interviewer–interviewee "relationship" and "living the moment" while gathering information (Hertz, 1997a) is difficult if not impossible. Internet surveys make it easy for respondents to manufacture fictional social realities without anyone knowing the difference (Markham, 1998). Of course, interviewers can deceive respondents by claiming to have experiences or characteristics that they do not have in hopes of establishing better rapport. They can feign responses for the same purpose by claiming "false nonverbals," for example, telling respondents that they "laughed at" or "were pained by" particular comments. Markham (1998), in her autoethnography of Internet interviewing, reported that electronic interviews take longer than their traditional counterparts and that responses are more cryptic and less in depth; however, the interviewer has time to phrase follow-up questions or probes properly.

It is also virtually impossible to preserve anonymity in Internet e-mail surveys, but chat rooms and similar sites permit the use of pseudonyms. Although electronic interviews are currently used primarily for quantitative research and usually employ structured questionnaires, it is only a matter of time before researchers adapt these techniques to qualitative work, just as they have adapted electronic techniques of data analysis. For example, Markham (1998) immersed herself in the process of engaging with various electronic or Internet formats (e.g., chat rooms, listservs) to interview other participants and to document her journey in the virtual world, learning the experience of cyberspace and the meanings that participants attached to their online lifestyles. She asked an intriguing question: "Can I have a self where my body does not exist?" (p. 8).

The future may see considerable ethnography by means of computer-mediated communication, where virtual space—rather than a living room or workplace—is the setting of the interview. It remains to be seen whether electronic interviewing will allow researchers to obtain "thick descriptions" or accounts of subjective experiences or whether such interviewing will provide the "process context" that is so important to qualitative interviews. In addition, researchers conducting such interviewing can never be sure that they are receiving answers from desired or eligible respondents. Interviewing by way of the Internet is so prominent today that researchers are studying its effects on response quality. Schaefer and Dillman (1998), for example, found that e-mail surveys achieved response rates similar to those of mail surveys but yielded better quality data in terms of item completion and more detailed responses to open-ended questions.

There are clearly many unanswered questions and problems related to the use of electronic interviewing. This mode of interviewing will obviously increase during the new millennium as people rely increasingly on electronic modes of communication. But just how much Internet communication will displace face-to-face interviewing is a matter that only time will tell.

## ◨ CONCLUSION

In this chapter, we have examined the interview, from structured types of interview to the interview as negotiated text. We outlined the history of interviewing, with its qualitative and quantitative origins. We looked at structured, group, and various types of unstructured interviewing. We examined the importance of gender in interviewing and the ways in which framing and interpreting affect interviews. We examined the importance of ethics in interviewing. Finally, we discussed the new trends in interviewing.

We have included discussion of the whole gamut of the interview, despite the fact that this book is concerned with qualitative research, because we believe that researchers must be cognizant of all the various types of interviews, both modern and postmodern, if they are to gain a clear understanding of interviewing. Clearly, certain types of interviewing are better suited to particular kinds of situations, and researchers *must be aware of the implications, pitfalls, and problems of the types of interview they choose.* If we wish to find out how many people oppose the establishment of a nuclear repository in their area, then a structured type of interview, such as that used in survey research, is our best tool; we can quantify and code the responses and can use mathematical models to explain our findings. If we are interested in opinions about a given product, then a focus group interview will provide us with the most efficient results. If we wish to know about the lives of Palestinian women in the resistance (Gluck, 1991), then we need to interview them at length and in depth in an unstructured way. In the first example just cited, and perhaps in the second, we can speak in the formal language of scientific rigor and verifiability of findings. In the third example, we can speak of understanding a negotiated way of life.

More scholars are realizing that to pit one type of interviewing against another is a futile effort—a leftover from the paradigmatic quantitative/qualitative hostility of past generations. Thus, an increasing number of researchers are using a multimethod approach to achieve broader and often better results. This multimethod approach is referred to as *triangulation* (Denzin, 1989; Flick, 1998) and allows researchers to use different methods in different combinations. For instance, group interviewing has long been used to complement survey research and is now being used to complement participant observation (Morgan, 1988). Humans are complex, and their lives are ever changing. The more methods we use to study them, the better our chances will be to gain some understanding of how they construct their lives and the stories they tell us about them.

The brief journey we have taken through the world of interviewing should allow us to be better informed about, and perhaps more sensitized to, the problematics of asking questions for sociological reasons. We must remember that each individual has his or her own social history and an individual perspective on the world. Thus, we cannot take our task for granted. As Oakley (1981) noted, "Interviewing is rather like a marriage: Everybody knows what it is, an awful lot of people do it, and yet behind each closed front door there is a world of secrets" (p. 41). She was quite correct. We all think that we know how to ask questions and talk to people, from common everyday folks to highly qualified quantophrenic experts. Yet to learn about people, we must treat them as people, and they will work with us to help us create accounts of their lives. So long as many researchers continue to treat respondents as unimportant faceless individuals whose only contributions are to fill more boxed responses, the answers that researchers will get will be commensurable with the questions they ask and the way in which they ask them. As researchers, we are no different from Gertrude Stein, who, while on her deathbed, asked her lifelong companion Alice B. Toklas, "What is the answer?" When Alice could not bring herself to speak, Gertrude asked, "In that case, what is the question?"

## ▣ REFERENCES

Adams, R. N., & Preiss, J. J. (Eds.). (1960). *Human organizational research: Field relations and techniques.* Homewood, IL: Dorsey.

Anderson, N. (1923). *The hobo: The sociology of the homeless man.* Chicago: University of Chicago Press.

Arksey, H., & Knight, P. (2002). *Interviewing for social scientists: An introductory resource with examples.* Thousand Oaks, CA: Sage.

Atkinson, P. (2002). The life story interview. In J. Gubrium & J. Holstein (Eds.), *Handbook of interview research: Context and method* (pp. 121–140). Thousand Oaks, CA: Sage.

Atkinson, P., & Silverman, D. (1997). Kundera's *Immortality:* The interview society and the invention of the self. *Qualitative Inquiry, 3,* 304–325.

Babbie, E. (1992). *The practice of social research* (6th ed.). Belmont, CA: Wadsworth.

Baker, C. (1997). Membership categorization and interview accounts. In D. Silverman (Ed.), *Qualitative research: Theory, method, and practice* (pp. 130–143). London: Sage.

Bakhtin, M. (1986). *Speech genres and other late essays.* Austin: University of Texas Press.

Banister, E. M. (1999). Evolving reflexivity: Negotiating meaning of women's midlife experience. *Qualitative Inquiry, 5,* 3–23.

Becker, H. S. (1956). Interviewing medical students. *American Journal of Sociology, 62,* 199–201.

Becker, H. S. (1999). The Chicago School, so-called. *Qualitative Sociology, 22,* 3–12.

Behar, R. (1996). *The vulnerable observer: Anthropology that breaks your heart.* Boston: Beacon.

Behar, R., & Gordon, D. (Eds.). (1995). *Women writing culture.* Berkeley: University of California Press.

Bell, S. (2002). Sexualizing research: Response to Erich Goode. *Qualitative Sociology, 25,* 535–539.

Benmayor, R. (1991). Testimony, action research, and empowerment: Puerto Rican women and popular education. In S. B. Gluck & D. Patai (Eds.), *Women's words: The feminist practice of oral history* (pp. 159–174). New York: Routledge.

Boelen, W. A. M. (1992). Street corner society: Cornerville revisited. *Journal of Contemporary Ethnography, 21,* 11–51.

Bogardus, E. S. (1926). The group interview. *Journal of Applied Sociology, 10,* 372–382.

Booth, C. (1902–1903). *Life and labour of the people in London.* London: Macmillan.

Bowler, I. (1997). Problems with interviewing: Experiences with service providers and clients. In G. Miller & R. Dingwall (Eds.), *Context and method in qualitative research* (pp. 66–76). Thousand Oaks, CA: Sage.

Bradburn, N. M. (1983). Response effects. In P. H. Rossi, J. D. Wright, & A. B. Anderson (Eds.), *Handbook of survey research* (pp. 289–328). New York: Academic Press.

Bradburn, N. M., Sudman, S., & Associates. (1979). *Improving interview method and questionnaire design.* San Francisco: Jossey–Bass.

Cicourel, A. (1964). *Method and measurement in sociology.* New York: Free Press.

Cicourel, A. (1970). The acquisition of social structure: Toward a developmental sociology of language and meaning. In J. D. Douglas (Ed.), *Understanding everyday life: Toward a reconstruction of social knowledge* (pp. 136–168). Chicago: Aldine.

Cicourel, A. (1974). *Theory and method in a study of Argentine fertility.* New York: John Wiley.

Clough, P. T. (1998). *The end(s) of ethnography: From realism to social criticism* (2nd ed.). New York: Peter Lang.

Collins, P. H. (1990). *Black feminist thought: Knowledge, consciousness, and the politics of empowerment.* New York: Routledge.

Converse, J. M. (1987). *Survey research in the United States: Roots and emergence 1890–1960.* Berkeley: University of California Press.

Converse, J. M., & Schuman, H. (1974). *Conversations at random: Survey research as interviewers see it.* New York: John Wiley.

Couper, M., Baker, R., Bethlehem, J., Clark, C., Nicholls, W., II, & O'Reilly, J. (Eds.). (1998). *Computer-assisted survey information collection.* New York: John Wiley.

Crapanzano, V. (1980). *Tuhami: Portrait of a Moroccan.* Chicago: University of Chicago Press.

Denzin, N. K. (1989). *The research act: A theoretical introduction to sociological methods* (3rd ed.). Englewood Cliffs, NJ: Prentice Hall.

Denzin, N. K. (1997). *Interpretive ethnography: Ethnographic practices for the 21st century.* London: Sage.

Denzin, N. K. (2003a). The call to performance. *Symbolic Interaction, 26,* 187–208.

Denzin, N. K. (2003b). *Performance ethnography: Critical pedagogy and the politics of culture.* Thousand Oaks, CA: Sage.

Derrida, J. (1976). *Of grammatology* (G. C. Spivak, Trans.). Baltimore, MD: Johns Hopkins University Press.

Desvousges, W. H., & Frey, J. H. (1989). Integrating focus groups and surveys: Examples from environmental risk surveys. *Journal of Official Statistics, 5,* 349–363.

Dingwall, R. (1997). Accounts, interviews, and observations. In G. Miller & R. Dingwall (Eds.), *Context and method in qualitative research* (pp. 51–65). Thousand Oaks, CA: Sage.

Douglas, J. D. (1985). *Creative interviewing.* Beverly Hills, CA: Sage.

Douglas, J. D., & Johnson, J. M. (1977). *Existential sociology.* Cambridge, UK: Cambridge University Press.

Douglas, J. D., Rasmussen, P., with Flanagan, C. A. (1977). *The nude beach.* Beverly Hills, CA: Sage.

DuBois, W. E. B. (1899). *The Philadelphia Negro: A social study.* Philadelphia: Ginn.

Edwards, R., & Mauthner, M. (2002). Ethics and feminist research: Theory and practice. In M. Mauthner, M. Birch, J. Jessop, & T. Miller (Eds.), *Ethics in qualitative research* (pp. 14–31). London: Sage.

Ellis, C. (1991). Sociological introspection and emotional experience. *Symbolic Interaction, 14,* 23–50.

Ellis, C. (1995). *Final negotiation: A story of love, loss, and chronic illness.* Philadelphia: Temple University Press.

Ellis, C., & Berger, L. (2002). Their story/My story/Our story: Including the researcher's experience in interview research. In J. Gubrium & J. Holstein (Eds.), *Handbook of interview research: Context and method* (pp. 849–876). Thousand Oaks, CA: Sage.

El-Or, T. (1992). Do you really know how they make love? The limits on intimacy with ethnographic informants. *Qualitative Sociology, 15,* 53–72.

Erickson, K. T. (1967). A comment on disguised observation in sociology. *Social Problems, 14,* 366–373.

Fine, M. (1983–1984). Coping with rape: Critical perspectives on consciousness. *Imagination, Cognition, and Personality, 3,* 249–267.

Flick, U. (1998). *An introduction to qualitative research: Theory, method, and applications.* London: Sage.

Fontana, A. (1977). *The last frontier: The social meaning of growing old.* Beverly Hills, CA: Sage.

Fontana, A. (2002). Postmodern trends in interviewing. In J. Gubrium & J. Holstein (Eds.), *Handbook of qualitative research: Context and method* (pp. 161–175). Thousand Oaks, CA: Sage.

Fontana, A. (2003). The windmills of morality. *Symbolic Interaction, 26,* 209–216.

Fontana, A., & Frey, J. H. (1990). Postretirement workers in the labor force. *Work and Occupations, 17,* 355–361.

Fontana, A., & Smith, R. (1989). Alzheimer's disease victims: The "unbecoming" of self and the normalization of competence. *Sociological Perspectives, 32,* 35–46.

Freeman, D. (1983). *Margaret Mead and Samoa: The making and unmaking of an anthropological myth.* Cambridge, MA: Harvard University Press.

Frey, J. H. (1989). *Survey research by telephone* (2nd ed.). Newbury Park, CA: Sage.

Frey, J. H. (1993). Risk perception associated with a high-level nuclear waste repository. *Sociological Spectrum, 13,* 139–151.

Frey, J. H., & Fontana, A. (1991). The group interview in social research. *Social Science Journal, 28,* 175–187.

Garfinkel, H. (1967). *Studies in ethnomethodology.* Englewood Cliffs, NJ: Prentice Hall.

Geertz, C. (1973). Thick descriptions: Toward an interpretive theory of culture. In C. Geertz, *The interpretation of cultures: Selected essays* (pp. 3–30). New York: Basic Books.

Glaser, B., & Strauss, A. (1967). *The discovery of grounded theory: Strategies for qualitative research.* Chicago: Aldine.

Gluck, S. B. (1984). What's so special about women: Women's oral history. In D. Dunaway & W. K. Baum (Eds.), *Oral history: An interdisciplinary anthology* (pp. 221–237). Nashville, TN: American Association for State and Local History.

Gluck, S. B. (1991). Advocacy oral history: Palestinian women in resistance. In S. B. Gluck & D. Patai (Eds.), *Women's words: The feminist practice of oral history* (pp. 205–220). New York: Routledge.

Gluck, S. B., & Patai, D. (Eds.). (1991). *Women's words: The feminist practice of oral history.* New York: Routledge.

Goode, E. (2002). Sexual involvement and social research in a fat civil rights organization. *Qualitative Sociology, 25,* 501–534.

Gorden, R. L. (1980). *Interviewing: Strategy, techniques, and tactics.* Homewood, IL: Dorsey.

Gorden, R. 1. (1992). *Basic interviewing skills.* Itasca, IL: Peacock.

Gubrium, J., & Holstein, J. (1997). *The new language of qualitative methods.* New York: Oxford University Press.

Gubrium, J., & Holstein, J. (1998). Narrative practice and the coherence of personal stories. *Sociological Quarterly, 39,* 163–187.

Gubrium, J., & Holstein, J. (Eds.). (2002). *Handbook of interview research: Context and method.* Thousand Oaks, CA: Sage.

Harvey, L. (1987). *Myths of the Chicago School of Sociology.* Aldershot, UK: Avebury.

Hertz, R. (1995). Separate but simultaneous interviewing of husbands and wives: Making sense of their stories. *Qualitative Inquiry , 1,* 429–451.

Hertz, R. (1997a). Introduction: Reflexivity and voice. In R. Hertz (Ed.), *Reflexivity and voice* (pp. vii–xviii). Thousand Oaks, CA: Sage.

Hertz R. (1997b). *Reflexivity and voice.* Thousand Oaks, CA: Sage.

Hertz, R. (1997c). A typology of approaches to childcare: The centerpiece of organizing family life for dual-earner couples. *Journal of Family Issues, 18,* 355–385.

Hertz, R., & Ferguson, F. (1997). Kinship strategies and self-sufficiency among single mothers by choice: Postmodern family ties. *Qualitative Sociology, 20,* 13–37.

Holstein, J., & Gubrium, J. (1995). *The active interview.* Thousand Oaks, CA: Sage.

Holstein, J., & Gubrium, J. (1997). Active interviewing. In D. Silverman (Ed.), *Qualitative research: Theory, method, and practice* (pp. 113–129). Thousand Oaks, CA: Sage.

Humphreys, L. (1970). *Tearoom trade: Impersonal sex in public places.* Chicago: Aldine.

Hyman, H. H. (1954). *Interviewing in social research.* Chicago: University of Chicago Press.

Johnson, J. (1976). *Doing field research.* New York: Free Press.

Johnson, J. (2002). In-depth interviewing. In J. Gubrium & J. Holstein (Eds.), *Handbook of interview research: Context and method* (pp. 103–119). Thousand Oaks, CA: Sage.

Kahn, R., & Cannell, C. F. (1957). *The dynamics of interviewing: Theory, techniques, and cases.* New York: John Wiley.

Kong, T. S. K., Mahoney, D., & Plummer, K. (2002). Queering the interview. In J. Gubrium & J. Holstein (Eds.), *Handbook of qualitative research: Context and method* (pp. 239–258). Thousand Oaks, CA: Sage.

Kotarba, J. A., & Fontana, A. (Eds.). (1984). *The existential self in society.* Chicago: University of Chicago Press.

Krieger, S. (1983). *The mirror dance: Identity in a women's community.* Philadelphia: Temple University Press.

Kvale, S. (1996). *InterViews: An introduction to qualitative research interviewing.* Thousands Oaks, CA: Sage.

Lincoln, Y. S. (1995). The sixth moment: Emerging problems in qualitative research. *Studies in Symbolic Interaction, 19,* 37–55.

Lofland, J. (1971). *Analyzing social settings.* Belmont, CA: Wadsworth.

Lofland, J., & Lofland, L. (1984). *Analyzing social settings: A guide to qualitative observation and analysis* (2nd ed.). Belmont, CA: Wadsworth.

Lopata, H. Z. (1980). Interviewing American widows. In W. Shaffir, R. Stebbins, & A. Turowetz (Eds.), *Fieldwork experience: Qualitative approaches to social research* (pp. 68–81). New York: St. Martin's.

Lynd, R. S., & Lynd, H. M. (1929). *Middletown: A study in American culture.* New York: Harcourt, Brace.

Lynd, R. S., & Lynd, H. M. (1937). *Middletown in transition: A study in cultural conflicts.* New York: Harcourt, Brace.

Lyotard, J. F. (1984). *The postmodern condition: A report on knowledge* (G. Bennington & B. Massumi, Trans.). Minneapolis: University of Minnesota Press.

Maccoby, E. E., & Maccoby, N. (1954). The interview: A tool of social science. In G. Lindzey (Ed.), *Handbook of social psychology,* Vol. 1: *Theory and method* (pp. 449–487). Reading, MA: Addison-Wesley.

Malinoswki, B. (1922). *Argonauts of the Western Pacific.* New York: E. P. Dutton.

Malinowski, B. (1989). *A diary in the strict sense of the term.* Stanford, CA: Stanford University Press. (Original work published 1967)

Manning, P. (2002). Fat ethics: Response to Erich Goode. *Qualitative Sociology, 25,* 541–547.

Marcus, G. E., & Fischer, M. M. J. (1986). *Anthropology as cultural critique: An experimental moment in the human sciences.* Chicago: University of Chicago Press.

Markham, A. N. (1998). *Life online: Researching real experience in virtual space.* Walnut Creek, CA: AltaMira.

Mauthner, M., Birch, M., Jessop, J., & Miller, T. (Eds.). (2002). *Ethics in qualitative research.* London: Sage.

Merton, K., Fiske, M., & Kendall, P. (1956). *The focused interview: A manual of problems and procedures.* Glencoe, IL: Free Press.

Merton, R. K., & Lazarsfeld, P. F. (Eds.). (1950). *Continuities in social research: Studies in the scope and method of "The American soldier."* Glencoe, IL: Free Press.

Miller, M. (1974). *Plain speaking: An oral biography of Harry S. Truman.* New York: Putnam.

Mishler, E. G. (1986). *Research interviewing: Context and narrative.* Cambridge, MA: Harvard University Press.

Morgan, D. (1988). *Focus groups as qualitative research.* Newbury Park, CA: Sage.

Morgan, D. (2002). Focus group interviewing. In J. Gubrium & J. Holstein (Eds.), *Handbook of interview research: Context and method* (pp. 141–159). Thousand Oaks, CA: Sage.

Morgan, D., & Spanish, M. T. (1984). Focus groups: A new tool for qualitative research. *Qualitative Sociology, 7,* 253–270.

Oakley, A. (1981). Interviewing women: A contradiction in terms. In H. Roberts (Ed.), *Doing feminist research* (pp. 30–61). London: Routledge & Kegan Paul.

Obbo, C. (1997). What do women know? . . . "As I was saying!" In K. M. Vaz (Ed.), *Oral narrative research with black women* (pp. 41–63). Thousand Oaks, CA: Sage.

Parten, M. (1950). *Surveys, polls, and samples.* New York: Harper.

Payne, S. L. (1951). *The art of asking questions.* Princeton, NJ: Princeton University Press.

Pinar, W. (1994). *Autobiography, politics, and sexuality: Essays in curriculum theory 1972–1992.* New York: Peter Lang.

Platt, J. (2002). The history of the interview. In J. Gubrium & J. Holstein (Eds.), *Handbook of interview research: Context and method* (pp. 33–54). Thousand Oaks, CA: Sage.

Pool, I. S. (1957). A critique of the twentieth anniversary issue. *Public Opinion Quarterly, 21,* 190–198.

Punch, M. (1986). *The politics and ethics of fieldwork.* Newbury Park, CA: Sage.

Rabinow, P. (1977). *Reflections on fieldwork in Morocco.* Berkeley: University of California Press.

Rabinow, P., & Sullivan, W. (Eds.). (1987). *Interpretive social science: A second look.* Berkeley: University of California Press.

Rasmussen, P. (1989). *Massage parlor prostitution.* New York: Irvington.

Reinharz, S. (1992). *Feminist methods in social research.* New York: Oxford University Press.

Richardson, L. (1992a). The poetic representation of lives: Writing a postmodern sociology. *Studies in Symbolic Interaction, 13,* 19–28.

Richardson, L. (1992b). Trash on the corner: Ethics and technocracy. *Journal of Contemporary Sociology, 21,* 103–119.

Richardson, L. (1997). *Fields of play: Constructing an academic life.* New Brunswick, NJ: Rutgers University Press.

Richardson, L. (2002). Poetic representation of interviews. In J. Gubrium & J. Holstein (Eds.), *Handbook of interview research: Context and method* (pp. 877–892). Thousand Oaks, CA: Sage.

Sagui, A. (2002). Sex, inequality, and ethnography: Response to Erich Goode. *Qualitative Sociology, 25,* 549–556.

Sarup, M. (1996). *Identity, culture, and the postmodern world.* Athens: University of Georgia Press.

Saukko, P. (2000). Between voice and discourse: Quilting interviews on anorexia. *Qualitative Inquiry, 6,* 299–317.

Schaefer, D. R., & Dillman, D. A. (1998). Development of a standard e-mail methodology. *Public Opinion Quarterly, 62,* 378–397.

Scheurich, J. J. (1995). A postmodernist critique of research interviewing. *Qualitative Studies in Education, 8,* 239–252.

Scheurich, J. (1997). *Research method in the postmodern.* London: Falmer.

Schutz, A. (1967). *The phenomenology of the social world.* Evanston, IL: Northwestern University Press.

Schwandt, T. A. (1997). *Qualitative inquiry: A dictionary of terms.* Thousand Oaks, CA: Sage.

Schwartz, B. (1999). Memory and the practice of commitment. In B. Glassner & R. Hertz (Eds.), *Qualitative sociology as everyday life* (pp. 159–168). Thousand Oaks, CA: Sage.

Schwartz, B. (Ed.). (1996). Collective memory [special issue]. *Qualitative Sociology, 19*(3).

Seidman, I. E. (1991). *Interviewing as qualitative research.* New York: Columbia University, Teachers College Press.

Selltiz, C., Jahoda M., Deutsch, M., & Cook, S. W. (1965). *Research methods in social relations.* London; Methuen.

Silverman, D. (1993). *Interpreting qualitative data: Methods for analysing talk, text, and interaction.* London: Sage.

Silverman, D. (Ed.). (1997a). *Qualitative research: Theory, method, and practice.* London: Sage.

Silverman, D. (1997b). Towards an aesthetics of research. In D. Silverman (Ed.), *Qualitative research: Theory, method, and practice* (pp. 239–253). London: Sage.

Singer, E., Frankel M., & Glassman, M. B. (1983). The effect of interviewer characteristics and expectations on response. *Public Opinion Quarterly, 47,* 68–83.

Singer, E., & Presser, S. (1989). *Survey research methods.* Chicago: University of Chicago Press.

Singleton, R. A., Jr., & Straits, B. (2002). Survey interviewing. In J. Gubrium & J. Holstein (Eds.), *Handbook of interview research: Context and method* (pp. 59–82). Thousand Oaks, CA: Sage.

Smith, D. E. (1987). *The everyday world as problematic: A feminist sociology.* Boston: Northeastern University Press.

Spradley, J. P. (1979). *The ethnographic interview.* New York: Holt, Rinehart & Winston.

Spradley, J. P. (1980). *Participant observation.* New York: Holt, Rinehart & Winston.

Starr, L. (1984). Oral history. In D. Dunaway & W. K. Baum (Eds.), *Oral history: An interdisciplinary anthology* (pp. 3–26). Nashville, TN: American Association for State and Local History.

Stewart, D., & Shamdasani, P. (1990). *Focus groups: Theory and practice.* Newbury Park, CA: Sage.

Sudarkasa, N. (1986). In a world of women: Field work in a Yoruba community. In P. Golde (Ed.), *Women in the field: Anthropological experiences* (pp. 167–191). Berkeley: University of California Press.

Terkel, S. (1975). *Working.* New York: Avon.

Thompson, H. (1985). *Hell's Angels.* New York: Ballantine.

Thompson, J., & Demerath, M. J. (1952). Some experiences with the group interview. *Social Forces, 31,* 148–154.

Thrasher, F. M. (1963). *The gang: A study of 1,313 gangs in Chicago.* Chicago: University of Chicago Press. (Original work published 1927)

Ulmer, G. (1989). *Teletheory: Grammatology in an age of video.* New York: Routledge.

Van Maanen, J. (1988). *Tales of the field: On writing ethnography.* Chicago: University of Chicago Press.

Vaz, K. M. (Ed.). (1997). *Oral narrative research with black women.* Thousand Oaks, CA: Sage.

Warren, C. A. B. (1988). *Gender issues in field research.* Newbury Park, CA: Sage.

Warren, C. A. B. (2002). Qualitative interviewing. In J. Gubrium & J. Holstein (Eds.), *Handbook of interview research: Context and meaning* (pp. 83–101). Thousand Oaks, CA: Sage.

Warwick, D. P. (1973). Tearoom trade: Means and ends in social research. *Hastings Center Studies, 1,* 27–38.

Wasserfall, R. (1993). Reflexivity, feminism, and difference. *Qualitative Sociology, 16,* 23–41.

Wax, R. (1960). Twelve years later: An analysis of field experiences. In R. N. Adams & J. J. Preiss (Eds.), *Human organization research: Field relations and techniques* (pp. 166–178). Homewood, IL: Dorsey.

Weiss, R. S. (1994). *Learning from strangers: The art and method of qualitative interview studies.* New York: Free Press.

Weston, K. (1998). *Longslowburn: Sexuality and social science.* New York: Routledge.

Whyte, W. F. (1943). *Street corner society: The social structure of an Italian slum.* Chicago: University of Chicago Press.

Williams, C. (2002). To know me is to love me? Response to Erich Goode. *Qualitative Sociology, 25,* 557–560.

Yeandle, S. (1984). *Women's working lives: Patterns and strategies.* New York: Tavistock.

Young, I. M. (1997). *Intersecting voices: Dilemmas of gender, political philosophy, and policy.* Princeton, NJ: Princeton University Press.

Young, P. (1966). *Scientific social surveys and research* (4th ed.). Englewood Cliffs, NJ: Prentice Hall.

Zuckerman, H. (1972). Interviewing an ultra-elite. *Public Opinion, 36,* 159–175.

# 5

# RECONTEXTUALIZING OBSERVATION

## Ethnography, Pedagogy, and the Prospects for a Progressive Political Agenda

Michael V. Angrosino

O bservation has been characterized as "the fundamental base of all research methods" in the social and behavioral sciences (Adler & Adler, 1994, p. 389) and as "the mainstay of the ethnographic enterprise" (Werner & Schoepfle, 1987, p. 257). Even studies that rely mainly on interviewing as a data collection technique employ observational methods to note body language and other gestural cues that lend meaning to the words of the persons being interviewed. Social scientists are

**Author's Note.** This chapter builds on the essay, "Rethinking Observation: From Method to Context" (Angrosino & Pérez, 2000), which appeared in the second edition of the *Handbook*. In that chapter, we argued that observation-based ethnographic research is not so much a specific method of inquiry as a context in which new ways of conducting qualitative research are emerging. I suggested that researchers' activities were developing in response to a greater consciousness of situational identities, the ethical demands of the modern research enterprise, and relationships of relative power in the field setting, particularly in reference to studies dealing with gender, sexuality, and people on the sociocultural margins (e.g., people with disabilities). The current chapter explores the ramifications of seeing observational research as context, with an emphasis on a convergence of pedagogy and political action in service to a progressive social agenda.

observers both of human activities and of the physical settings in which such activities take place. Some such observation may take place in a laboratory or clinic, in
which case the activity may be the result of a controlled experiment. On the other
hand, it is also possible to conduct observations in settings that are the "natural" loci
of those activities. Some scholars have criticized the very concept of the "natural"
setting, particularly when fieldwork is conducted in Third World locations (or in
domestic inner-city sites) that are the products of inherently "unnatural" colonial
relationships (Gupta & Ferguson, 1996, p. 6), but the designation is still prevalent
throughout the literature. In that case, it is proper to speak of "naturalistic observation," or fieldwork, which is the focus of this chapter.

Observations in natural settings can be rendered as descriptions either through
open-ended narrative or through the use of published checklists or field guides
(Rossman & Rallis, 1998, p. 137; for an historical overview of this dichotomy, see
Stocking, 1983a). In either case, in the past it was generally assumed that naturalistic
observation should not interfere with the people or activities under observation. Most
social scientists have long recognized the possibility of observers affecting what they
observe; nonetheless, careful researchers were supposed to adhere to rigorous standards of objective reporting designed to overcome potential bias. Even cultural anthropologists, who have usually thought of themselves as "participant observers" and who
have deliberately set out to achieve a degree of subjective immersion in the cultures
they study (Cole, 1983, p. 50; Wolcott, 1995, p. 66), still claim to be able to maintain their
scientific objectivity. Failure to do so would mean that they had "gone native," with their
work consequently being rendered suspect as scientific data (Pelto & Pelto, 1978, p. 69).
The achievement of the delicate balance between participation and observation
remains the ideal of anthropologists (Stocking, 1983b, p. 8), even though it is no longer
"fetishized" (Gupta & Ferguson, 1996, p. 37). Objectivity remains central to the self-
images of most practitioners of the social and behavioral sciences. Objective rigor has
most often been associated with quantitative research methods, and the harmoniza-
tion of empathy and detachment has been so important that even those dedicated to
qualitative methods have devoted considerable effort to organizing their observational
data in the most nearly objective form (i.e., the form that looks most quantitative) for
analysis (see, e.g., Altheide & Johnson, 1994; Bernard, 1988; Miles & Huberman, 1994;
Silverman, 1993).

Adler and Adler (1994), in fact, suggested that in the future observational research
will be found as "part of a methodological spectrum," but that in this spectrum it will
serve as "the most powerful source of validation" (p. 389). Observation, they claimed,
rests on "something researchers can find constant," meaning "their own direct knowledge and their own judgment" (p. 389). In social science research, as in legal cases, eyewitness testimony from trustworthy observers has been seen as a particularly
convincing form of verification (Pelto & Pelto, 1978, p. 69). In actuality, the production
of a convincing narrative report of the research has most often served as de facto

validation, even if the only thing it validates is the ethnographer's writing skill and not his or her observational capacities (Kuklick, 1996, p. 60).

Postmodernist analysts of society and culture certainly did not invent the current critique of assumptions about the objectivity of science and its presumed authoritative voice, but the prevalence of that analysis in contemporary scholarship has raised issues that all qualitative researchers need to address. The postmodernist critique is not necessarily directed toward the conduct of field-based observational research, but it is impossible to consider postmodern discourse on the production and reproduction of knowledge without taking into account the field context from which so much of our presumed "data" are said to emerge. Earlier criticism of field-workers might have been directed at particular researchers, with the question being whether they had lived up to the expected standards of objective scholarship. In the postmodernist milieu, in contrast, the criticism is directed at the standards themselves. In effect, it is now possible to question whether observational objectivity is either desirable or feasible as a goal. Clifford (1983a), who has written extensively and critically about the study of culture and society, even called into question the work of the revered Bronislaw Malinowski, the archetype of the scientific participant observer who, according to Stocking (1983a), is the scholar most directly responsible for the "shift in the conception of the ethnographer's role, from that of inquirer to that of participant 'in a way' in village life" (p. 93). Perhaps more surprisingly, Clifford (1983a) also questioned the research of the very influential contemporary interpretivist Clifford Geertz, whom he took to task for suggesting that the ethnographer, through empathy, can describe a culture in terms of the meanings specific to members of that culture. In other words, the ethnographer, as a distinct person, disappears—just as he or she was supposed to do in Malinowski's more openly positivistic world. This assessment was echoed by Sewell (1997), who pointed out that Geertz did not expect field-workers to "achieve some miracle of empathy with the people whose lives they briefly and incompletely share; they acquire no preternatural capacity to think, feel, and perceive like a native" (p. 40). The problem is not that Geertz failed to achieve some sort of idealized empathetic state; rather, the question is whether such a state is even relevant to ethnographic research and whether it is desirable to describe and/or interpret cultures as if those depictions could exist without the ethnographer's being part of the action.

The postmodernist critique, which emphasizes the importance of understanding the ethnographer's "situation" (his or her gender, class, ethnicity, etc.) as part of interpreting the ethnographic product, is particularly salient because the remote, traditional folk societies that were the anthropologist's stock-in-trade have virtually disappeared. Most cultural anthropology now is carried out in communities that, if not literate themselves, are parts of larger literate societies that are themselves parts of global communication and transportation networks. Like sociologists, anthropologists now "study up" (i.e., they conduct research among elites), if only to help them understand

the predicament of the poor and marginalized people who remain their special concern. Doing so overcomes some of the problems associated with the lingering colonialist bias of traditional ethnography (Wolf, 1996, p. 37), but it raises new issues regarding
the position and status of the observational researcher. For one thing, ethnographers
can no longer claim to be the sole arbiters of knowledge about the societies and cultures they study because they are in a position to have their analyses read and contested
by those for whom they presume to speak (Bell & Jankowiak, 1992; Larcom, 1983,
p. 191). In effect, objective truth about a society or culture cannot be established because
there are inevitably going to be conflicting versions of what happened. Sociologists and
other social scientists were working in such settings long before anthropologists came
onto the scene and were already beginning to be aware of the problems inherent in
claiming the privilege of objective authoritative knowledge when there are all too many
"natives" ready and able to challenge them. As Wolf (1992) wryly commented,

> We can no longer assume that an isolated village will not within an amazingly short period
> of time move into the circuit of rapid social and economic change. A barefoot village kid who
> used to trail along after you *will* one day show up on your doorstep with an Oxford degree
> and your book in hand. (p. 137)

The validity of the traditional assumption—that the truth can be established
through careful cross-checking of ethnographers' and insiders' reports—is no longer
universally granted because contemporary social and behavioral scientists are increasingly inclined to expect differences in testimony grounded in gender, class, ethnicity,
and other factors that are not easy to mix into a consensus. Ethnographic truth has
come to be seen as a thing of many parts, and no one perspective can claim exclusive
privilege in the representation thereof. Indeed, the result of ethnographic research "is
never reducible to a form of knowledge that can be packaged in the monologic voice of
the ethnographer alone" (Marcus, 1997, p. 92).

Ethnographers of various disciplines have responded to this new situation by revising the ways in which they conduct observation-based research and present their analyses of this research. No longer can it be taken for granted that ethnographers operate
at a distance from their human subjects. Indeed, the very term *subject*, with its implicit
colonialist connotations, is no longer appropriate. Rather, there is said to be a *dialogue*
between researchers and those whose cultures/societies are to be described. "Dialogue"
in this sense does not literally mean a conversation between two parties; in practice, it
often consists of multiple, even contradictory, voices. As a result, discussions of ethnographers' own interactions, relationships, and emotional states while in the field have
been moved from their traditional discreet place in acknowledgments or forewords to
the centers of the ethnographies themselves. The increasing acceptance of autoethnography and performance-based ethnography has also resulted in a greater personalization of the activities of the researchers (see, e.g., Bochner & Ellis, 2002; see also Holman
Jones, Chapter 7, this volume). Although these practices have certainly opened up new

horizons in ethnographic reportage, they raise further issues of their own. For example, because it is likely to be the ethnographers who write up (or at least collate or edit) the results of field studies, do they not continue to claim the implicit status of arbiters/mediators of social/cultural knowledge (Wolf, 1992, p. 120)? Ethnographers may assert that they represent the many voices involved in the research, but we still have only their assurance that such is the case.

Nonetheless, we now function in a context of "collaborative" research. *Collaboration* no longer refers only to the conduct of multidisciplinary teams of professional researchers; it often means the presumably equal participation of professional researchers and their erstwhile "subjects" (Kuhlmann, 1992; Wolf, 1996, p. 26). Matsumoto (1996), for example, sent a prepared list of questions to the people she was interested in interviewing for an oral history project. She assured them that any questions to which they objected would be eliminated. The potential respondents reacted favorably to this invitation to participate in the formulation of the research design. As such situations become more common, it is important that we rethink our current notions about "observation"—what it is, how it is done, what role it plays in the generation of ethnographic knowledge. To that end, it might be useful to shift from a concentration on observation as a "method" per se to a perspective that emphasizes observation as a context for interaction among those involved in the research collaboration.

## ▣ OBSERVATION-BASED RESEARCH: TRADITIONAL ASSUMPTIONS

Observational researchers traditionally have attempted to see events through the eyes of the people being studied. They have been attentive to seemingly mundane details and to take nothing in the field setting for granted. They were taught to contextualize data derived from observation in the widest possible social and historical frame, all without overgeneralizing from a necessarily limited (and probably statistically nonrepresentative) sample. Their research design usually involved the use of as many means of data collection as were feasible to supplement purely observational data. Although observational research has played a part in many different schools of social theory, it has been most prominently associated with those orientations that seek to construct explanatory frameworks only after careful analysis of objectively recorded data.

There are three main ways in which social scientists have conducted observation-based research. Despite considerable overlap, it is possible to distinguish among (a) participant observation, grounded in the establishment of considerable rapport between the researcher and the host community and requiring the long-term immersion of the researcher in the everyday life of that community; (b) reactive observation, associated with controlled settings and based on the assumption that the people being studied are aware of being observed and are amenable to interacting with the researcher only in response to elements in the research design; and (c) unobtrusive (nonreactive) observation, conducted with people who are unaware of being studied.

All forms of observational research involve three procedures of increasing levels of specificity: (a) descriptive observation (the annotation and description of all details by an observer who assumes a nearly childlike stance, eliminating all preconceptions and taking nothing for granted), a procedure that yields a large amount of data, some of which will prove to be irrelevant; (b) focused observation (where the researcher looks only at material that is pertinent to the issue at hand, often concentrating on well-defined categories of group activity such as religious rituals and political elections); and (c) selective observation (focusing on a specific form of a more general category such as initiation rituals and city council elections). (For an elaboration of these points, see Werner & Schoepfle, 1987, pp. 262–264.)

Underlying these various methodological points was the assumption that it is both possible and desirable to develop standardized procedures that can "maximize observational efficacy, minimize investigator bias, and allow for replication and/or verification to check out the degree to which these procedures have enabled the investigator to produce valid, reliable data that, when incorporated into his or her published report, will be regarded by peers as objective findings" (Gold, 1997, p. 397). True objectivity was held to be the result of agreement between participants and observers as to what is really going on in a given situation. Such agreement was obtained by the elicitation of feedback from those whose behaviors were being reported. Ethnography's "self-correcting investigative process" has typically included adequate and appropriate sampling procedures, systematic techniques for gathering and analyzing data, validation of data, avoidance of observer bias, and documentation of findings (Clifford, 1983b, p. 129; Gold, 1997, p. 399). The main difference between sociological and anthropological practitioners of ethnography seems to be that the former have generally felt the need to validate their eyewitness accounts through other forms of documentation, whereas the latter have tended to use participant observation—"relatively unsystematized" as it might be—as the ultimate reality check on "all the other, more refined research techniques" (Pelto & Pelto, 1978, p. 69).

One classic typology (Gold, 1958) divided naturalistic researchers into "complete participants" (highly subjective and, hence, scientifically questionable), "participants-as-observers" (insiders with a little bit of scientific training but still not truly acceptable as scientists), "observers-as-participants," and "complete observers." Gold (1997) went on to advocate a form of ethnographic research that seeks to collect data that are "grounded in the informants' actual experience" (p. 399). He insisted on the continuing importance of maintaining standards of reliability and validity through "adequate and appropriate sampling procedures, systematic techniques for gathering and analyzing data, validation of data, avoidance of observer bias, and documentation of findings," although he admitted that such goals are met in ethnographic research "in ways that differ from conventional (statistical) procedures" (p. 399).

A somewhat different perspective is represented by Adler and Adler (1987), who emphasized a range of "membership roles" as opposed to roles defined relative to some presumed ideal of pure observation. This shift was occasioned by the realization that pure observation was, first, nearly impossible to achieve in practice and, second, ethically questionable, particularly in light of the evolving professional concern with informed consent. Therefore, Adler and Adler wrote about (a) peripheral member researchers (those who believe they can develop a desirable insider's perspective without participating in those activities that constitute the core of group membership), (b) active member researchers (those who become involved with the central activities of the group, sometimes even assuming responsibilities that advance the group without necessarily fully committing themselves to members' values and goals), and (c) complete member researchers (those who study settings in which they are already members or with which they become fully affiliated during the course of research). In the scholarly world prior to the ascendancy of the postmodernist critique, even complete member researchers, who were expected to celebrate the "subjectively lived experience," were still enjoined to avoid using their insider status to "alter the flow of interaction unnaturally" (Adler & Adler, 1994, p. 380).

▣ OBSERVATION-BASED RESEARCH: CURRENT ASSUMPTIONS

Contemporary observation-based social research may be characterized by the following trends. First, there is an increasing willingness on the part of ethnographers to affirm or develop a "membership" identity in the communities they study. Second, researchers recognize the possibility that it may be neither feasible nor possible to harmonize observer and insider perspectives so as to achieve a consensus about "ethnographic truth." Thus, there is a recognition that our erstwhile "subjects" have become collaborators, although they often speak in a voice different from that of hegemonic authoritative science.

Traditional researchers' concern with process and method, therefore, has been supplemented with (but by no means supplanted by) an interest in the ways in which ethnographic observers interact with, or enter into a dialogic relationship with, members of the group being studied. In light of these trends, an earlier incarnation of this chapter suggested that observation-based ethnographic research was not so much a specific method of inquiry as a context in which new roles for the qualitative researcher were emerging. Research roles were said to be developing in response to a greater consciousness of situational identities and to the perception of relative power, particularly in reference to studies dealing with gender, sexuality, and people on the sociocultural margins (e.g., people with disabilities). (For a detailed review of research illustrating these trends, see Angrosino & Pérez, 2000, pp. 678–690.)

At this point, however, it no longer seems fruitful to go on arguing the case for rethinking observation. The numerous studies cited by Angrosino and Pérez (2000) demonstrate quite plainly that the new perspective is already part and parcel of the conceptual framework and methodological toolkits of a wide range of contemporary qualitative researchers.[1] If the battle cannot be said to have been definitively won, there is no longer any doubt that the traditional view—with its fixation on objectivity, validation, and replicability—is now simply one point on a continuum and not the unique voice of reputable social research. The pressing question that now faces us is the following: How do we move this new perspective beyond the confines of academic discourse and ensure its relevance in ways that help us to advance a progressive social agenda?

## ▣ The Ethical Dimension of Observation-Based Research

Before answering the question at the end of the previous section directly, we must first consider the matter of ethics as it bears on the conduct of observation-based research. Ethics concerns us on two levels. First, we must take into account the current standards operative in most universities and other research institutions that govern the ways in which we work. Second, and perhaps more important in the long run, is the matter of what we mean by a "progressive social agenda." In other words, what values may we invoke to explain and justify the ways in which we seek to use our ethnographic knowledge?

### Institutional Structures

Observation was once thought of as a data collection technique employed primarily by ethnographers who thought of themselves as objective researchers extrinsic to the social settings they studied. It has become a context in which researchers who define themselves as members of those social settings interact with other members of those settings. This transition has also effected a shift in the parameters of research ethics.

For good or ill, virtually all social research in our time is governed by the structure of institutional review boards (IRBs), which grew out of federal regulations, beginning in the 1960s, that mandated informed consent for all those participating in federally funded research. Rules governing the use of human subjects are "rooted in scandal" (Gunsalus, 2002, p. B24), specifically the scandal of experiments that led to injury or even death of participants. The perceived threat was from "intrusive" research (usually biomedical). The new rules were designed so that participation in such research would be under the control of the "subjects," who had a right to know what was going to happen to them and who were expected to agree formally to all provisions of the research. The right of informed consent, and the IRBs that were eventually created to enforce it at all institutions receiving federal moneys (assuming a function originally carried out centrally by the U.S. Office of Management and Budget), radically altered the power relationship between the researcher and the human subject, allowing both parties to have a say in the conduct and character of research. (For more detailed reviews of this history, see Fluehr-Lobban, 2003; Wax & Cassell, 1979.) Although few would criticize the move toward protection of human subjects and the concern for their privacy, the increasingly cautious approach of IRBs and their tendency to expand their jurisdiction over all aspects of the research process have turned IRBs into "de facto gatekeepers for a huge amount of scholarly inquiry" (Gunsalus, 2002, p. B24).

Ethnographic researchers, however, have always been uncomfortable with this situation—not because they wanted to conduct covert harmful research but rather because they did not believe that their research was intrusive. Such a claim stemmed from the assumptions typical of the observers-as-participants role, although it is certainly possible to interpret it as a relic of the "paternalism" that traditional researchers often adopted with regard to their human subjects (Fluehr-Lobban, 2003, p. 172). Ethnographers were also concerned that the proposals sent to IRBs had to be fairly complete when it came to explicating the methodology so that all possibilities of doing harm could be adequately assessed. Their research, they argued, often grew and changed as it went along and could not always be set out with the kind of predetermined specificity that the legal experts seemed to expect. They further pointed out that the statements of professional ethics promulgated by the relevant disciplinary associations already provided for informed consent; thus, the IRBs were being redundant in their oversight.

During the 1980s, social scientists won from the U.S. Department of Health and Human Services an exemption from review for all social research except that dealing with children, people with disabilities, and others defined as members of "vulnerable" populations (Fluehr-Lobban, 2003, p. 167). Nevertheless, legal advisers at many universities (including the University of South Florida [USF], where I am based) have opted for caution and been very reluctant to allow this near blanket exemption to be applied. Indeed, at USF, proposals that may meet the general federal criteria for exemption must still be reviewed, although they may be deemed eligible for an "expedited" review. Even proposals that are completely exempt (e.g., studies relying on on-the-record interviews with elected officials about matters of public policy) must still be filed with the IRB. It is ironic that one type of observational research is explicitly mentioned in the "exempt" category—research that is "public" (e.g., studying patterns of where people sit in airport waiting rooms). This is one of the increasingly rare remaining classic "pure observer" types of ethnography. The exemption, however, is disallowed if the researcher intends to publish photos or otherwise identify the people who make up the "public" being researched.

USF now has two IRBs: one for biomedical research and one for "behavioral research." Because the latter is dominated by psychologists (by far the largest department in the social sciences division of the College of Arts and Sciences), this separate status rarely works to the satisfaction of ethnographic researchers. The psychologists, who are used to dealing with hypothesis-testing, experimental clinical or lab-based research, have been reluctant to recognize a subcategory of "observational" research design. As a result, the form currently required by the behavioral research IRB is couched in terms of the individual human subject rather than in terms of populations or communities, and it mandates the statement of a hypothesis to be tested and a "protocol for the experiment." Concerned ethnographers at USF have discovered that some other institutions have developed forms more congenial to their particular needs, but as of this writing they have had no success in convincing the USF authorities to adopt any of them as an alternative to the current "behavioral research" form for review. Indeed, the bias in favor of clinical research seems to have hardened. For example, of the many hundreds of pages in the federal handbook for IRBs, only 11 paragraphs are devoted to behavioral research (Gunsalus, 2002, p. B24). Moreover, it is now mandated that all principal investigators on IRB-reviewed research projects take continuing education on evolving federal ethical standards. It is possible to do so over the Internet, but during the 2001–2002 academic year, all of the choices of training modules were drawn from the realm of health services research.

### Issues for Contemporary Observational Researchers

Ethical ethnographers who adopt more clearly "membership"-oriented identities, therefore, are caught between two equally untenable models of research. On the one hand is the official IRB, which is tied to the hypothesis-testing, experimental clinical model. On the other hand are those ethnographers who, in their zeal to win exemption from irrelevant and time-consuming strictures, appear to be claiming that their research is not—or should not be considered—intrusive at all. Yet the interactive, membership-oriented researchers *are by definition* intrusive—not in the negative sense of the word, to be sure, but they are still deeply involved in the lives and activities of the community members they study, a stance fraught with all sorts of possibilities for "harm." The dilemma becomes particularly difficult when we attempt to move beyond academic research to the application of research in service to a social agenda. Such action would seem to require intervention and advocacy—or even conflict in some cases—to bear fruit. As such, there is certainly the possibility of harm, but it is difficult to anticipate what form that harm might take. In principle at least, it might be possible to say that because research collaborators are no longer "subjects," by definition they have as much power as do researchers in shaping the research agenda; they do not need to be warned or protected. But in reality, the researcher is still in a privileged position, at least where actually conducting the research and disseminating its results are concerned. The contemporary researcher probably does not want to retreat to the objective cold of the classic observer, but neither does he or she want to shirk the responsibility for doing everything possible to avoid hurting or embarrassing people who have been trusting partners in the research endeavor. (For another perspective on these matters, see Kemmis & McTaggart, Volume 2, Chapter 10.)

▣ VALUES AND THE SOCIAL AGENDA

Observational research, as it has evolved during recent times, is essentially a matter of interpersonal interaction and only rarely is a matter of objective hypothesis testing. As Fluehr-Lobban (2003) suggested, this turn of events makes it more imperative that we be mindful of the relational ethics implied by the informed consent process (pp. 169–172). Ethnographers should not try to exempt themselves from monitoring; we can, in contrast, work toward a less burdensome and more appropriate set of ethical standards. It is important to keep in mind, however, that human action must always be interpreted in situational context and not in terms of universally applicable objective "codes." Angrosino and Pérez (2000) suggested a method of "proportionate reason" as one way in which to link social research to an ethical framework (pp. 692–695). This position, associated with the philosophical writings of Cahill (1981), Curran (1979), Hoose (1987), and Walter (1984), assesses "the relation between the specific value at stake and the . . . limitations, the harm, or the inconvenience which will inevitably come about in trying to achieve that value" (Gula, 1989, p. 273). In other words, although it is certainly important to weigh the consequences of an action, we must keep in mind that consequences are only one part of the total meaning of an action. Proportionate reason defines what a person is doing in an action (e.g., an ethnographer engaged in an observational context); the person and the action are inseparable. (The opposite, of course, would be the old notion of the ethnographic observer as extrinsic to the action he or she is recording.)

There are three criteria that help us to decide whether a proper relationship exists between the specific value and the other elements of the act (McCormick, 1973; McCormick & Ramsey, 1978). First, *the means used will not cause more harm than necessary to achieve the value.* In traditional moral terms, the ends cannot be said to justify the means. If we take "the value" to refer to the production of some form of ethnography, we must be careful to ensure that the means used (e.g., inserting oneself into a social network, using photographs or other personal records) do not cause disproportionate harm. We might all agree that serving as *comadre* or *compadre* to a child of the community that one is studying is sufficiently proportionate; in contrast, we might well argue about whether becoming the lover of someone in that community (particularly if that sexual liaison is not intended to last beyond the time of the research) does more harm than an ethnographic book, article, or presentation might be worth. Volunteering as a classroom tutor in a program that serves adults with mental retardation whom one is interested in observing and interviewing is probably sufficiently proportionate; in contrast, becoming a bill-paying benefactor to induce cooperation among such adults in a group home would be morally questionable.

The second criterion is that *no less harmful way to protect the value currently exists.* Some might argue that observational research always and inevitably compromises personal privacy, such that no form of research can ethically protect that cherished value. But most researchers would probably reject such an extreme view and instead take the position that there is real value in disseminating the fruits of ethnographic research so as to increase our knowledge and understanding of cultural diversity, the nature of coping strategies, or any number of currently salient social justice issues. Granted that *all* methods have the potential to harm, we must be sure to choose those that do the *least* amount of harm but that still enable us to come up with the sort of product that will be effective in communicating the valuable message. The strategy of writing ethnographic fiction, for example, might be one way in which to make sure that readers do not know exactly who is being described.

The third criterion is that *the means used to achieve the value will not undermine it.* If one sets out, for example, to use research to promote the dignity of people defined as mentally disabled, one must make sure that the research techniques do not subject those people to ridicule. Videotaping a group of people with mental retardation as they play a game of softball might conceivably result in confirming the popular stereotypes of such people as clumsy or inept—objects of pity (at best) or of scorn (at worst)—rather than as dignified individuals. Videotaping as an adjunct to observational research is itself ethically neutral; its appropriateness must be evaluated in this proportionate context.

McCormick (1973) suggested three modes of knowing whether there is a proportionate reason to carry out a suggested action. First, we know that a proper relation exists between a specific value and all other elements of an act through *experience,* which sometimes amounts to plain common sense. For example, although we may think that it is important to encourage individual expression, we know from experience that doing so in the context of a traditional community, where the individual is typically subordinate to the group, will do real violence to the precepts by which the people we are intent on studying have historically formed themselves into a cohesive society. Experience might suggest that we rethink a decision to collect personal life histories of people in such communities in favor of focusing on the collective reconstruction of remembered common activities or events.

Second, we might know that a proper relationship exists through our own *intuition* that some actions are inherently disproportionate, even if we do not have personal experience of their being so. For example, we should intuitively know that publishing information of a personal nature collected from undocumented migrant workers might mean that such information could be used against them. Our righteous goal of improving the lot of the migrants might well be undermined by giving authorities the ammunition to harass them further. A perception of what *could* happen (the result of intuition) is, of course, different from a perception of what *will* happen (the result of experience), and we are clearly not well served by dreaming up every conceivable disaster. It serves no purpose to allow ourselves to be paralyzed beforehand by overactive guilty consciences. But there is certainly a commonsensical hierarchy of plausibility that occurs in such cases; some things that *could* happen are more likely to come about than are others.

Third, we know through *trial and error*. This is a mode of knowing that would be completely impossible under current institutional ethical guidelines. But the fact is that we do not, and cannot, know all possible elements in any given human social interaction, and the idea that we can predict—and thereby forestall—all harm is naïve in the extreme. An ethical research design would omit (or seek to modify) that which experience and intuition tell us is most likely to do harm. We can then proceed, but only on the understanding that the plan will be modified during the course of the action when it becomes clear what is feasible and desirable in the real-life situation. For those uncomfortable with the indeterminacy of the term "trial and error," Walter (1984) suggested "rational analysis and argument" (p. 38). By gathering evidence and formulating logical arguments, we try to give reasons to support our choices for certain actions over others. But this way of knowing does indeed involve the possibility of committing errors, perhaps some that may have unexpected harmful consequences. It is nonetheless disingenuous to hold that all possibilities of harm can be anticipated and that any human action, including a research project based on interpersonal interaction, can be made risk free. The moral advantage of the proportionate reasoning strategy is that it encourages researchers to admit to errors once they have occurred, to correct the errors so far as possible, and to move on. The "objective" mode of research ethics, in contrast, encourages researchers to believe that they have eliminated all such problems, and so they are disinclined to own up to problems that crop up and, hence, are less capable of repairing the damage. Those who work with people with developmental disabilities are familiar with the expression "the dignity of risk," which is used to describe the habilitation of clients for full participation in the community. To deny clients the possibility of making mistakes (by assuming that all risks can be eliminated beforehand and by failing to provide training in reasonable problem-solving techniques) is to deny them one of the fundamental characteristics of responsible adult living. One either lives in a shelter, protected from risk by objectified codes, or lives real life. The ethical paradigm suggested here does nothing more than allow the observational researcher the dignity of risk.

The logic of proportionate reason as a foundation for an ethical practice of social research might seem, at first glance, to slide into subjective relativism. Indeed, the conscience of the individual researcher plays a very large part in determining the morality of a given interaction. But proper proportionalism cannot be reduced to a proposition that an action can mean anything an individual wants it to mean or that ethics is simply a matter of personal soul searching. Rather, the strategy is based on a sense of community; the individual making the ethical decision must ultimately be guided by a kind of "communal discernment" (Gula, 1989, p. 278). When we speak of "experience," for example, we refer not only to personal experience but also to the "wisdom of the past" embodied in a community's traditions. As such, it

> demands broad consultation to seek the experience and reflection of others in order to prevent the influence of self-interest from biasing perception and judgment. Using proportionalism

requires more moral consultation with the community than would ever be required if the morality of actions were based on only one aspect . . . apart from its relation to all the . . . features of the action. (Gula, 1989, p. 278)

That being the case, the ideal IRB would not be content with a utilitarian checklist of presumed consequences. Rather, it would constitute a circle of "wise" peers with whom the researcher could discuss and work out the (sometimes conflicting) demands of experience, intuition, and the potential for rational analysis and argument. The essential problem with current ethical codes, from the standpoint of the qualitative observational researcher, is that they set up an arbitrary—and quite unnecessary—adversarial relationship between researchers and the rest of the scholarly community. The framework of proportionate reason implies that ethical research is the product of shared discourse and not of a species of prosecutorial inquisition.

## ◙ ELEMENTS IN A SUGGESTED PROGRESSIVE SOCIAL AGENDA

The abstractions of the proportionate reason framework can be translated into a progressive social agenda to guide the researcher. Progressive politics seeks a just society, although traditional moral philosophy speaks of four different types of justice: (a) commutative justice, which is related to the contractual obligations between individuals involving a strict right and the obligation of restitution (e.g., when one person lends another person a sum of money, the borrower is obliged to return that money according to the terms of the agreement); (b) distributive justice, which is related to the obligation of a government toward its citizens with regard to its regulation of the burdens and benefits of societal life (e.g., a government may tax its citizens but must do so fairly, according to their ability to pay, and must distribute the proceeds according to need); (c) legal justice, which is related to citizens' obligation toward the government or society in general (e.g., citizens are obligated to pay taxes, serve on juries, and possibly serve in the military, although they reserve the right to engage in conscientious objection— or even civil disobedience—if they deem the demands of the government unjust); and (d) social justice, which is related to the obligation of all people to apply moral principles to the systems and institutions of society (e.g., individuals and groups are urged to take an active interest in necessary social and economic reforms). My own personal vision tends to emphasize the element of social justice, and I suggest three ways in which researchers can work toward the principles embodied in the concept of social justice.

First, the researcher should be directly connected to the poor and marginalized. Helping the latter might well involve intensive study of power elites, but a progressive agenda goes by the boards if the researcher comes to identify with those elites and sees the poor simply as a "target population." Direct connection necessarily involves becoming a part of the everyday life of a community. The middle-class researcher who *chooses* to live with the poor and otherwise marginalized in our society (or with entire societies that are poor and marginalized vis-à-vis larger global powers) is, of course, in a very different position compared with residents of such communities who have no choice in the matter. But research in service to a progressive agenda flows from a degree of empathy (not simply "rapport" in the way that term was used by traditional participant observers) that is not available to those who do not even try to maintain such ongoing contact.[2]

Second, the researcher should ask questions and search for answers. This might seem like an obvious thing for a researcher to do, but we are in the habit of asking questions based primarily on our scholarly knowledge of the literature. We move in a more productive direction if we begin to ask questions based on our experience of life among the poor and marginalized rather than on our experience of what others have written or said about them. By the same token, we must avoid the sentimental conclusion that "the people" have all the answers, just as we shun the assumption that "the experts" know what is best for the people. Asking the relevant questions might lead us to look within the community for answers drawing on its own untapped resources, or it might lead us to explore options beyond the community.

Third, the researcher should become an advocate. Advocacy might mean becoming a spokesperson for causes or issues already defined by the community. It also might mean helping the people to discern and articulate issues that may have been inchoate to that point. Advocacy often means engaging in some sort of conflict (either among factions within the community or between the community and the powers-that-be), but it can also mean finding ways in which to achieve consensus in support of an issue that has the potential to unite. In either case, one ends up working *with* the community as opposed to working *for* the community (with the latter implying a more distanced stance).

The overall goal of this process is to empower the community to take charge of its own destiny to whatever extent is practical. The researcher might well retain a personal agenda (e.g., collecting data to complete a dissertation), but his or her main aim is to work with the community to achieve shared goals. Such a philosophy can be difficult to convey to students or other apprentice researchers (e.g., how does it all work out "on the ground"?). To that end, it might be instructive to consider a form of pedagogy that, although not specifically designed for this purpose, certainly serves these ends.

## Pedagogy for Social Justice: Service Learning

The concept of "service learning" was given a boost by the Johnson Foundation/ Wingspread report titled *Principles of Good Practice for Combining Service and Learning*. Service learning is more than simply a way in which to incorporate some local field research into social science courses. As a strategy adopted by USF and others in response to the *Principles* report, service learning is the process of integrating volunteer community service combined with active guided reflection into the curriculum to enhance and enrich student learning of course material. It is designed to reinvigorate the spirit of activism and volunteerism that energized campuses during the 1960s but that waned during subsequent decades. Colleges and universities that accepted this challenge formed a support network (Campus Compact) to develop and promote service learning as a pedagogical strategy. Service learning is now a national movement.

The philosophical antecedent and academic parent of service learning is experiential learning (e.g., cooperative education, internships, field placements), which was based on the direct engagement of the learner in the phenomenon being studied. The critical difference and distinguishing characteristic of service learning is its emphasis on enriching student learning while also revitalizing the community. To that end, service learning involves students in course-relevant activities that address real community needs. Course materials (e.g., textbooks, lectures, discussions, reflection) inform students' service, and the service experience is brought back to the classroom to inform the academic dialogue and the quest for knowledge. This reciprocal process is based on the logical continuity between experience and knowledge.

The pedagogy of service learning reflects research indicating that we retain 60% of what we do, 80% of what we do with active guided reflection, and 90% of what we teach or give to others. The pedagogy is also based on the teaching of information-processing skills rather than on the mere accumulation of information. In a complex society, it is nearly impossible to determine what information will be necessary to solve particular problems. All too often the content that students learn in class is obsolete by the time they obtain their degrees. Service learning advocates promote the importance of "lighting the fire" (i.e., teaching students how to think for themselves) as opposed to "filling the bucket" (i.e., giving students predigested facts and figures). Learning is not a predictable linear process. It may begin at any point during a cycle, and students might have to apply their limited knowledge in a service situation before consciously setting out to gain or comprehend a body of facts related to that situation. The discomfort arising from the lack of knowledge is supposed to encourage further accumulation of facts or the evolutionary development of a personal theory for future application. To ensure that this kind of learning takes place, however, skilled guidance in reflection on the experience must occur. By providing students with the opportunity to have a concrete experience and then assisting them in the intellectual processing of that experience, service learning not only takes advantage of a natural learning cycle but also allows students to provide a meaningful contribution to the community.

It is important to note that the projects that form the basis of the students' experience are generated by agencies or groups in the community. The projects can be either specific one-time efforts (e.g., a Habitat for Humanity home-building project) or longer term initiatives (e.g., the development of an after-school recreation and tutoring program based at an inner-city community center). Given the theme of this chapter, it is significant that all such activities build on the fundamentals of observational research. Student volunteers gradually adopt membership identities in the community and must nurture their skills as observers of unfamiliar interactions so as to carry out the specific mandates of the chosen projects and to act as effective change agents in the community. In this way, service learning projects affiliated with courses outside the social and behavioral sciences require students to become practitioners of observational research methods, although such an outcome is not a specifically identified goal of the course. Recently at USF, service learning has been a key feature of a diverse set of courses, including an anthropology seminar on community development, a sociology course on the effects of globalization, an interdisciplinary social science course on farm-worker and other rural issues, a psychology course on responses to the HIV/AIDS epidemic, a social work course on racial and ethnic relations, and a business seminar on workplace communication.

In sum, service learning, which affects the professional educator as well as the novice/student, is more than simply traditional "applied social science," which often had the character of "doing for" the community. Service learning, which begins with the careful observation of a community on the part of a committed student adopting a membership identity, is active engagement in and with the community in ways that foster the goals of a social justice–oriented progressive political and social agenda.

## Prospects for Observational Research

Although it is certainly true that "forecasting the wax and wane of social science research methods is always uncertain" (Adler & Adler, 1994, p. 389), it is probably safe to say that observation-based research is going to be increasingly committed to what Abu-Lughod (1991) called "the ethnography of the particular" (p. 154). Rather than attempting to describe the composite culture of a group or to analyze the full range of institutions that supposedly constitute the society, the observational ethnographer will be able to provide a rounded account of the lives of particular people, with the focus being on individuals and their ever-changing relationships rather than on the supposedly homogeneous, coherent, patterned, and (particularly in the case of traditional anthropologists) timeless nature of the supposed "group." Currently the "ethnography of the particular" coexists uneasily with more quantitative and positivistic schools of sociology, anthropology, and social psychology. There is, however, considerable doubt as to how long that link can survive given the very different aims and approaches of the diverging branches of the once epistemologically unified social sciences. It seems likely that observational techniques will find a home in a redefined genre of cultural studies, leaving their positivist colleagues to carry on in a redefined social science discipline.

Observation once implied a notebook and pencil and perhaps a sketch pad and simple camera. The conduct of observational research was revitalized by the introduction of movie cameras and then video recorders. Note taking has been transformed by the advent of laptop computers and software programs that assist in the analysis of narrative data. But as our technological sophistication increases, we face an increasing intellectual dilemma in doing research. On the one hand, we speak the theoretical language of "situatedness," indeterminacy, and relativism; on the other hand, we rely more and more on technology that suggests the capture of "reality" in ways that could be said to transcend the individual researcher's relatively limited capacity to interpret. The technology makes it possible for the ethnographer to record and analyze people and events with a degree of particularity that would have been impossible just a decade ago, but it also has the potential to privilege what is captured on the record at the expense of the lived experience as the ethnographer has personally known it. It would be foolish to suggest that, for the sake of consistency, observation-based ethnographers should eschew further traffic with sophisticated recording and analytic technology. But it would be equally foolish to assume that the current strong trend in the direction of individualized particularism can continue without significant modification in the face of technology that has the perceived power to objectify and turn into "data" everything it encounters. Perhaps it will become necessary for us to turn our observational powers on the very process of observation, that is, to understand ourselves not only as psychosocial creatures (which is the current tendency) but also as users of technology. As Postman (1993) pointed out, technological change is never merely additive or subtractive; it is never simply an aid to doing what has always been done. Rather, it is "ecological" in the sense that a change in one aspect of behavior has ramifications for the entire system of which that behavior is a part. Under those circumstances, perhaps the most effective use of observational techniques we can make in the near future will be to discern the ethos of the technology that we can no longer afford to think of as a neutral adjunct to our business-as-usual mentality. It is a technology that itself has the capacity to define our business. We need to turn our observational powers to what happens not only when "we" encounter "them" but also when we do so with a particular kind of totalizing technology.

No technological revolution has been more challenging to the traditions of observational research than the rise of the Internet and with it the increasing prevalence and salience of the "virtual community." Ethnographers have long observed communities that are defined by some sort of geographic "reality," although we have also recognized the importance of social networks that are not place bound. Contemporary virtual communities are an extension of such older "communities of interest," although they depend on computer-mediated communication and are characterized by online interactions. Research needs to be developed to explore the nature of these virtual communities. How are they similar to traditional communities or social networks? How are they different? How does electronic communication make new kinds of community possible? How does it facilitate existing communities? (Regarding questions such as these, see Gabrial, 1998; Hine, 2000; Jones, 1998, 1999; Markham, 1996; Miller & Slater, 2000). As Bird and Barber (2002) noted, "Life on-line is becoming simply another part of life in the twenty-first century. On-line communities may replicate many of the features of other non-place-based communities, but they also make available new possibilities and new kinds of connections" (p. 133).

The increasing salience of electronic media poses some special ethical challenges for the ethnographic observer. It goes without saying that the traditional norms of informed consent and protection of privacy and confidentiality continue to be important, even though we are observing and otherwise dealing with people we do not see face to face. It is true that the Internet is a kind of public space, but the people who inhabit its virtual terrain are still individuals entitled to enjoy the same rights as are people in more traditional communities. There are as yet no comprehensive guidelines applicable to online research, but a few principles seem to be emerging by consensus. First, research based on a content analysis of a public Web site need not pose an ethical problem, and "it is probably acceptable to quote messages posted on public message boards" (Bird & Barber, 2002, p. 134). But the attribution of such quotes to identifiable correspondents would be a breach of privacy. Second, when observing an online community, the researcher should inform the members of his or her presence and of his or her intentions. The members should be assured that the researcher will not use real names, e-mail addresses, or any other identifying markers in any publication based on the research. Third, many online groups have their own rules for entering and participating. The "virtual" community should be treated with the same respect as if it were a "real" community, and its norms of courtesy should be observed carefully. Some researchers conducting online ethnographies, therefore, have accepted as standard procedure the sharing of drafts of research reports for comments by members of the online community. By allowing members to help decide how their comments will be used, this practice realizes the larger ethical goal (discussed earlier) of turning research "subjects" into truly empowered collaborators.

Bird and Barber (2002) pointed out that "electronic communication is stripped of all but the written word" (p. 134). As such, the ethnographer is at somewhat of a disadvantage given that the traditional cues of gestures, facial expressions, and tones of voice—all of which give nuances of meaning to social behavior—are missing. By the same token, the identity of the person with whom the researcher is communicating can be concealed—or even deliberately falsified—in ways that would not be possible in face-to-face communication. Therefore, it is necessary to develop a critical sense, to evaluate virtual sources carefully, and to avoid making claims of certainty that cannot be backed up by other means.

Whether in the virtual world or the real world, observation-based researchers continue to grapple with the ethical demands of their work. In light of comments in this chapter, it is heartening to learn that a recent report from the Institute of Medicine (IOM) has presented us with the challenge of rethinking the whole notion of research ethics. Ethical regulations, as discussed previously, have tended to ask basically negative questions (e.g., What is misconduct? How can it be prevented?). The IOM report, however, invites us in the near term future to consider the positive (e.g., What is integrity? How do we find out whether we have it? How can we encourage it?). According to Frederick Grinnell, a member of the IOM committee that produced the report, the promotion of researcher integrity has both individual and institutional components, namely "encouraging individuals to be intellectually honest in their work and to act responsibly, and encouraging research institutions to provide an environment in which that behavior can thrive" (Grinnell, 2002, p. B15). Grinnell went so far as to claim that qualitative social researchers have a central role to play in this proposed evolution of the structures of research ethics because they are particularly well equipped to conduct studies that would identify and assess the factors that influence integrity in research in both individuals and large social institutions.

## ▣ A CLOSING WORD

It seems clear that the once unquestioned hegemony of positivistic epistemology that encompassed even so fundamentally humanistic a research technique as observation has now been shaken to its roots. One telling indication of the power of that transition—and a challenging indication of things to come—was a comment by the late Stephen Jay Gould, the renowned paleontologist and historian of science, who ruefully admitted,

> No faith can be more misleading than an unquestioned personal conviction that the apparent testimony of one's eyes must provide a purely objective account, scarcely requiring any validation beyond the claim itself. Utterly unbiased observation must rank as a primary myth and shibboleth of science, for we can only see what fits into our mental space, and all description includes interpretation as well as sensory reporting. (1998, p. 72)

## ▣ NOTES

1. In the chapter that appeared in the second edition of the *Handbook,* Pérez and I discussed a number of such studies. One of the authors we cited, James Mienczakowski, has asked that we clarify some of the remarks we made about his work. Noting his use of "alternative" means of reporting ethnographic data, we linked him with others experimenting with ethnographic writing, including autoethnographers. In so doing, we might have unwittingly left the impression that Mienczakowski's work fell into the category of autoethnography. Although that work is not dealt with in this chapter, I feel honor bound to allow Mienczakowski to present what he believes is a more accurate representation of his work. In a personal communication (May 17, 2004), he noted, "My work unequivocally describes not self-location or autoethnography but a very different form of ethnographic research construction. In fact, . . . my personal experiences or location . . . are not relevant to, or the focus of, my published researches in detoxification therapy."

2. "Empathy" in this context should be interpreted in a political sense; that is, the researcher takes on a commitment to the community's agenda. Use of the term in this way should not be taken to imply anything about the totality of the community's culture or about the ability of the researcher to achieve a capacity to enter totally into the ethos of that community—if such a thing as an enveloping community ethos even exists.

## ▣ REFERENCES

Abu-Lughod, L. (1991). Writing against culture. In R. G. Fox (Ed.), *Recapturing anthropology: Working in the present* (pp. 137–162). Santa Fe, NM: School of American Research.

Adler, P. A., & Adler, P. (1987). *Membership roles in field research.* Newbury Park, CA: Sage.

Adler, P. A., & Adler, P. (1994). Observational techniques. In N. K. Denzin & Y. S. Lincoln (Eds.), *Handbook of qualitative research* (pp. 377–392). Thousand Oaks, CA: Sage.

Altheide, D. L., & Johnson, J. M. (1994). Criteria for assessing interpretive validity in qualitative research. In N. K. Denzin & Y. S. Lincoln (Eds.), *Handbook of qualitative research* (pp. 485–499). Thousand Oaks, CA: Sage.

Angrosino, M. V., & Pérez, K. (2000). Rethinking observation: From method to context. In N. K. Denzin & Y. S. Lincoln (Eds.), *Handbook of qualitative research* (2nd ed., pp. 673–702). Thousand Oaks, CA: Sage.

Bell, J., & Jankowiak, W. R. (1992). The ethnographer vs. the folk expert: Pitfalls of contract ethnography. *Human Organization, 51,* 412–417.

Bernard, H. R. (1988). *Research methods in cultural anthropology.* Newbury Park, CA: Sage.

Bird, S. E., & Barber, J. (2002). Constructing a virtual ethnography. In M. V. Angrosino (Ed.), *Doing cultural anthropology* (pp. 129–137). Prospect Heights, IL: Waveland.

Bochner, A. P., & Ellis, C. (Eds.). (2002). *Ethnographically speaking: Autoethnography, literature, and aesthetics.* Walnut Creek, CA: AltaMira.

Cahill, L. S. (1981). Teleology, utilitarian, and Christian ethics. *Theological Studies, 41,* 601–629.

Clifford, J. (1983a). On ethnographic authority. *Representations, 1,* 118–146.

Clifford, J. (1983b). Power and dialogue in ethnography: Marcel Griaule's initiation. In G. W. Stocking (Ed.), *Observers observed: Essays on ethnographic fieldwork* (pp. 121–156). Madison: University of Wisconsin Press.

Cole, D. (1983). "The value of a person lies in his *Herzenbildung*": Franz Boas' Baffinland letter-diary, 1883–1884. In G. W. Stocking (Ed.), *Observers observed: Essays on ethnographic fieldwork* (pp. 13–52). Madison: University of Wisconsin Press.

Curran, C. E. (1979). Utilitarianism and contemporary moral theology: Situating the debates. In C. E. Curran & R. A. McCormick (Eds.), *Readings in moral theology* (pp. 341–362). Ramsey, NJ: Paulist Press.

Fluehr-Lobban, C. (2003). Informed consent in anthropological research: We are not exempt. In C. Fluehr-Lobban (Ed.), *Ethics and the profession of anthropology* (2nd ed., pp. 159–178). Walnut Creek, CA: AltaMira.

Gabrial, A. (1998). Assyrians: "3,000 years of history, yet the Internet is our only home." *Cultural Survival Quarterly, 21,* 42–44.

Gold, R. L. (1958). Roles in sociological field observation. *Social Forces, 36,* 217–223.

Gold, R. L. (1997). The ethnographic method in sociology. *Qualitative Inquiry, 3,* 388–402.

Gould, S. J. (1998). The sharp-eyed lynx, outfoxed by nature (Part 2). *Natural History, 107,* 23–27, 69–73.

Grinnell, F. (2002, October 4). The impact of ethics on research. *Chronicle of Higher Education,* p. B15.

Gula, R. M. (1989). *Reason informed by faith.* New York: Paulist Press.

Gunsalus, C. K. (2002, November 15). Rethinking protections for human subjects. *Chronicle of Higher Education,* p. B24.

Gupta, A., & Ferguson, J. (1996). Discipline and practice: "The field" as site, method, and location in anthropology. In A. Gupta & J. Ferguson (Eds.), *Anthropological locations: Boundaries and grounds of a field science* (pp. 1–46). Berkeley: University of California Press.

Hine, C. (2000). *Virtual ethnography.* London: Sage.

Hoose, B. (1987). *Proportionalism.* Washington, DC: Georgetown University Press.

Jones, S. G. (Ed.). (1998). *Cybersociety 2.0.* London: Sage.

Jones, S. G. (1999). *Doing Internet research: Critical issues and methods for examining the Net.* London: Sage.

Kuhlmann, A. (1992). Collaborative research among the Kickapoo tribe of Oklahoma. *Human Organization, 51,* 274–283.

Kuklick, H. (1996). After Ishmael: The fieldwork tradition and its future. In A. Gupta & J. Ferguson (Eds.), *Anthropological locations: Boundaries and grounds of a field science* (pp. 47–65). Berkeley: University of California Press.

Larcom, J. (1983). Following Deacon: The problem of ethnographic reanalysis, 1926–1981. In G. W. Stocking (Ed.), *Observers observed: Essays on ethnographic fieldwork* (pp. 175–195). Madison: University of Wisconsin Press.

Marcus, G. E. (1997). The uses of complicity in the changing mise-en-scène of anthropological fieldwork. *Reflections, 59,* 85–108.

Markham, A. (1996). *Life on-line: Researching real experience in virtual space.* Walnut Creek, CA: AltaMira.

Matsumoto, V. (1996). Reflections on oral history: Research in a Japanese-American community. In D. L. Wolf (Ed.), *Feminist dilemmas in fieldwork* (pp. 160–169). Boulder, CO: Westview.

McCormick, R. A. (1973). *Ambiguity and moral choice.* Milwaukee, WI: Marquette University Press.

McCormick, R. A., & Ramsey, P. (1978). *Doing evil to achieve good.* Chicago: Loyola University Press.

Miles, M. B., & Huberman, A. M. (1994). *Qualitative data analysis: An expanded sourcebook* (2nd ed.). Thousand Oaks, CA: Sage.

Miller, D., & Slater, D. (2000). *The Internet: An ethnographic approach.* New York: Berg.

Pelto, P. J., & Pelto, G. H. (1978). *Anthropological research: The structure of inquiry* (2nd ed.). New York: Cambridge University Press.

Postman, N. (1993). *Technopoly: The surrender of culture to technology.* New York: Vintage.

Rossman, G. B., & Rallis, S. F. (1998). *Learning in the field: An introduction to qualitative research.* Thousand Oaks, CA: Sage.

Sewell, W. H. (1997, Summer). Geertz and history: From synchrony to transformation. *Representations,* pp. 35–55.

Silverman, D. (1993). *Interpreting qualitative data: Strategies for analysing talk, text, and interaction.* London: Sage.

Stocking, G. W. (1983a). The ethnographer's magic: Fieldwork in British anthropology from Tylor to Malinowski. In G. W. Stocking (Ed.), *Observers observed: Essays on ethnographic fieldwork* (pp. 70–120). Madison: University of Wisconsin Press.

Stocking, G. W. (1983b). History of anthropology: Whence/whither. In G. W. Stocking (Ed.), *Observers observed: Essays on ethnographic fieldwork* (pp. 3–12). Madison: University of Wisconsin Press.

Walter, J. (1984). Proportionate reason and its three levels of inquiry: Structuring the ongoing debate. *Louvain Studies, 10,* 30–40.

Wax, M. L., & Cassell, J. (1979). *Federal regulations: Ethical issues and social research.* Boulder, CO: Westview.

Werner, O., & Schoepfle, G. M. (1987). *Systematic fieldwork,* Vol. 1: *Foundations of ethnography and interviewing.* Newbury Park, CA: Sage.

Wolcott, H. F. (1995). *The art of fieldwork.* Walnut Creek, CA: AltaMira.

Wolf, D. L. (1996). Situating feminist dilemmas in fieldwork. In D. L. Wolf (Ed.), *Feminist dilemmas in fieldwork* (pp. 1–55). Boulder, CO: Westview.

Wolf, M. A. (1992). *A thrice-told tale: Feminism, postmodernism, and ethnographic responsibility.* Stanford, CA: Stanford University Press.

# 6

# WHAT'S NEW VISUALLY?

## Douglas Harper

O ne faces the task of a chapter on the same subject for the third edition of the *Handbook* with a certain amount of trepidation. After all, not that much changes in the social sciences, especially within such a few brief years. Yet there are new themes, technologies, and practices mixed into the gradual evolutions of established patterns in visual methods. With that in mind, my goal in this chapter is to minimize overlap with the chapters in the earlier editions, with the modest proposal of seeing what indeed is new in visually inspired qualitative research.

Thus, readers interested in the postmodern critique of visual ethnography; the relationship among visual sociology, visual anthropology, and documentary photography; and the development of a research typology of visual thinking in visual research should consult the earlier chapters (Harper, 1993, 2000). I suggested that visual sociology offered the opportunity to address the postmodern critiques of ethnography and documentary photography and, in so doing, to fashion a new method based on the understanding of the social construction of the image and the need for collaboration between the subject and the photographer.

This chapter examines the status of visual thinking in the sociological community, the impact of new technologies on visual methods, the continuing development of visual documentary and visual sociology, and problematical ethics questions in the visual research world.

In the background is a much discussed separation in the visual studies movement between the study of social life using images, which is often referred to as the empirical wing of visual sociology, and the study of the meanings of visual culture, which is usually called cultural studies. Some have argued that this clouds the fact that we share a fundamental interest in the meanings of visual imagery.

As an example of visually oriented cultural studies, Fuery and Fuery (2003) explore Foucault's imaging of the body, Lacanian theories of abjection and reflection, Kristeva's ideas about body fragmentation and visual culture, Derrida's notions about social reproduction and the semiotics of imagery, and Barthes's semiotics of photography. Their book contains only one image—a reproduction of a 1992 *Calvin and Hobbes* cartoon to illustrate Kristeva's theory of the abjection of the self. However, the arguments are grounded in examples of visual imagery on Web sites that are listed at the ends of the chapters. Thus, the reader can refer to the images of Magritte, Dali, Warhol, Caravaggio, and Bernini, to the photographs of Newton, and to the films of Hitchcock without the expense and inconvenience of having the images in the book itself. Of course, reading the book implies access to a computer and the Internet, and referencing Web sites in this way assumes that the images will still be available online for as long as the book is used. Because the images are not esoteric, this is probably a safe bet. So, the book presents itself as a postmodern argument against the hegemony of its own form.

But more to the point of this chapter, Fuery and Fuery (2003) show how cultural studies use images to advance theories of the self, society, existence itself, and/or symbolism. I have suggested elsewhere (Harper, n.d.) that cultural studies generally use images (from fine arts to mass media, from architectural shapes to fashion, from body decoration and shapes to imagery of nightmares) as a referent for the development of theory. One can argue that these cultural studies are ethnographic in an indirect manner; they are based on the analysis of the visual culture writ large.

This chapter has a different orientation because I believe that a handbook of qualitative research should focus on field research. From my perspective, the emphasis should be on the practical, that is, using imagery to study specific questions and issues in sociology, anthropology, communications, and the like. Much of what I discuss in the following draws on photography, although there are several other suitable ways in which to visually represent the world in social research. For example, in my own study of the work of a rural artisan (Harper, 1987), drawings complemented photographs. The drawings allowed a more subjective take; elements could be left out, and interiors of objects could be invaded with cutaways. So, there is no reason why photography must dominate empirical visual sociology beyond the fact that it has proven to be enormously useful.

Most of the visual sociology discussed in this chapter depends on photographs—processed, juxtaposed, deconstructed, and captioned, but still evidence of something seen. It is a reminder, once again, of photography as both empirical and constructed. It has become something of a ritual to repeat this idea in all articles or chapters on visual sociology, but it appears to be necessary.

## ▣ INNOVATIONS IN JOURNAL PUBLICATION

Sociological research that relies on visual data is being published with increasing frequency. Journals such as *Qualitative Inquiry* and *Symbolic Interaction* include imagery—not exactly routinely, but more and more frequently nonetheless. Several new visually oriented journals have joined established visual social science journals, such as *Visual Anthropology* and *Visual Sociology* (renamed *Visual Studies* in 2001), as outlets for visual research.

A promising development within American sociology was the introduction of the American Sociological Association's (ASA) journal, *Contexts*, in 2001. *Contexts*, intended to popularize sociology for a mass audience, is the first American sociology journal to forefront visual information, albeit with not entirely consistent results.

Visual illustration in *Contexts* is used in three ways. I call the first the "illustrated research article," with an example being Rank's (2003) study of the incidence of poverty in the United States. Rank uses photographs to portray a spectrum of the poor, including well-dressed job seekers, some using cell phones, in an unemployment line in New York; a group of perhaps 200 disheveled homeless people gathering for shelter in San Francisco; a young homeless family in Eugene, Oregon, sitting on a curb across the street from a grocery store; and an African American woman and an aged white immigrant in the daily routines of their poverty. The images put a face on statistical data, but what do they add beyond that?

First, they contextualize poverty with other sociological variables such as family life, unemployment, and global migration. Visual documentation becomes a part of research triangulation, confirming theories using different forms of data. In these instances, the photographs argue that visual traces of the world adequately describe the phenomenon under question.

The photographs also subjectively connect the viewer to the argument. The well-dressed job seekers in New York connect poverty directly to employment. The homeless couple and child in Oregon do not look like the stereotyped vision of poverty; we would expect to see their attractive faces in a typical middle-class home. The immigrant in poverty is an elderly man from the Netherlands, showing us that nonminority immigrants also struggle to make ends meet in the United States.

But although these photographs are important to the text, they remain secondary. The visual dimension is not integrated into the research; the images are added by an editor who has the challenging job of securing photos from a variety of sources. The result is that useful photos are often found and published, but so are images that fall short of their mandate to visually tell a sociological story.

*Contexts* also publishes photo essays, where sociological thinking emerges directly from images rather than reinforcing and elaborating on word-based thinking. Gold's (2003) photo essay on the Israeli diaspora is a good example. The body of the article consists of 12 photographs and captions organized around the themes of "Individual and Community Business," "Designing and Finding Communities," and "Transnational Networks and Identities." The photographs locate people in various environments—from their homes, to businesses, to public settings—interacting in the routines of various social scenes. The images are organized conceptually and are the main way in which the ideas are presented. Gold's photo essay (and others published in *Contexts*) shows the possibility of sociological thinking that derives nearly entirely from images. The intention is that sociologists will regard the photographs in these essays as visual data, that is, that sociologists will engage the photographs with active intellectual "looking." Because photographs saturate popular culture and are generally treated superficially, this is a big leap.

As hinted at previously, asking sociologists to take photographs seriously raises the matter of their truth status—or their validity, in sociological terminology. Here, as has been stated many times previously and has already been mentioned in this chapter, rests a central irony of the photograph: It is both true and constructed. It is true in the sense that it reflects light falling on a surface, but it is also constructed by the technical, formalistic, and other selections that go into making the image and by the contexts (from historical to presentational format) in which it is viewed. In this way, photos are similar to all forms of data—both qualitative and quantitative.

It is hoped that the *Contexts* photo essays will elevate sociologists' understanding of this essential similarity between photographic data and other forms of data.

*Contexts* also publishes photo essays on social change, that is, images that show the same social scene at an earlier time and a more contemporary time. Photography is especially helpful in studies of social change because photographs can be matched with earlier images to reveal extraordinarily detailed renditions of changes in human habitation, landscape, and/or traces of human interaction. This approach draws on the work of a single sociologist, Jon Rieger, who has applied the fine arts and documentary "rephotography" movement to the study of social change in northern Michigan (Rieger, 1996, 2003) and other settings.

Although *Contexts* has broken new ground in sociology, it remains to be seen whether the journal will successfully make the case for visual data in research or whether it will be considered less rigorous precisely because the journal relies heavily on visual displays. For *Contexts* to redefine visual thinking in sociological publishing, it must initiate a discussion of the role of visual information in sociological thinking and presentation.

The journal must also improve its means of attaining images; it is simply not feasible to assume that good-hearted photographers will donate the use of their photos. It is also not feasible to assume that volunteer staff members (despite their success so far) can do what professional photo editors do, that is, find and get access to the very best photos to develop visual arguments.

## ▣ NEW TECHNOLOGIES; NEW WAYS OF THINKING

What is genuinely new in visual sociology is the use of technology in recording, organizing, presenting, and analyzing visual information. Emerging technologies have revolutionized the use of imagery in social science, and some intrepid researchers have already provided convincing examples. The basis of the revolution is the computer, but more specifically it is software programs such as Macromedia's *Director* and, in some cases, the Web. All of these technologies are several generational offsprings of *HyperCard*, a program bundled with early Apple computers that allowed information to be organized in a nonlinear manner. In what follows, I briefly examine four projects that demonstrate the range of these new ways of thinking and doing field research visually.

Jay Ruby's ethnographic study of Oak Park, Illinois, uses the Web to disseminate the ongoing results of a field study (Ruby, n.d.). The Web site (http://astro.ocis.temple.edu/~ruby/opp/) includes interviews, photographs, observations, historical commentary, and video segments in various forms of completion. Ruby also established a listserv of residents of Oak Park, inviting people who are the subject of the study to disagree, elaborate, or simply comment on the ongoing study. According to Ruby's Web site,

> Oak Park Stories is a series of experimental, reflexive, and digital ethnographics that attempt to explore a forty-year-old social experiment in Oak Park, a Chicago suburb. It is experimental in that I have not followed the traditional method of producing a book or film but instead made an interactive and nonlinear work that has both video and text. It is reflexive in that the subject of my research is my hometown. . . . It is digital in its form of delivery—on a DVD using QuickTime movies and html documents. I have constructed these Stories in a nonlinear fashion; that is, unlike a book or a film, there is no defined beginning, middle, or end. Viewers/Readers are free to begin anywhere. They can ignore anything that doesn't interest them. I have provided many links to materials that will allow anyone interested to pursue a topic in more depth. I have found writing in a nonlinear fashion to be amazingly freeing.

The Web site is organized around "modules," which are broad categories with scroll-down subcategories. These include an extensive discussion of ethnography, histories of families that represent the community, the black migration to Chicago and Oak Park itself, biographies of individuals who have played an important role in the community, and other modules that explore themes such as racial integration.

The module organization is similar to chapters in a book but also is distinctly different. The modules include subcategories of photo essays (often from archival sources) that show, for example, images of race riots in 1919 and images of a single African American on an otherwise all-white championship football team. The module format establishes a logic for the overall project: The first-order categories are the modules themselves, the second-order categories are scrollable items beneath the module title, and the third-order information exists in the many linked articles, photo essays, newspapers, and other archival documents that are sprinkled liberally throughout. This is similar to the organization of a book with a chapter structure, text, and endnotes, but it is markedly different because of the freedom allowed to go into more depth than a particular subject in a book might allow or to add material that might be too tangential for a scholarly study. For example, Ruby's study develops a central theme of racial and ethnic integration. Subcategories of the integration module present the history of African Americans in Chicago in more detail than would likely be included in an academic monograph. Ruby's pages-long overview of housing policies, race politics, and shifting demographic information can, however, easily be included in the Web presentation. It is contextualizing information that some, but certainly not all, viewers/readers will use. Links to additional sites further these possibilities.

Ruby posts quarterly reports from the field and asks for feedback by way of Web discussions. His importance in visual anthropology and prominence in a visual communication listserv generates a Web-based audience for his work.

The attractiveness of this mode of dissemination is precisely that a variety of communication modes—text, still images, and moving images—can be integrated. However, the memory-hungry nature of video makes it (so far) impractical to include more than a few seconds of video clips, with the moving images being bracketed into a small thumbnail on the screen. The final project is intended as a number of DVDs, where longer video segments can be included.

The sharing of the project-in-progress by way of an evolving Web site has not, to my knowledge, been done before. The project could be left in this form and updated on a continual basis through the near future. However, Ruby intends to finalize the project as one or more DVDs distributed in the same way as other emerging visual anthropology multimedia projects are distributed, that is, through commercial or academic publishers.

Other visually oriented sociologists have begun to develop the potential of advanced interactivity with Macromedia's *Director*. The first of these projects was Biella, Chagnon, and Seaman's (1997) *Yanamamo Interactive*, which is an interactive version of Chagnon and Asch's classic ethnographic film, *The Ax Fight*.[1] *The Ax Fight* is a 10-minute film showing a hostile interaction between two groups of Yanamamo tribespeople in Venezuela. The film has become an important teaching tool as well as an important research tool. It is a commonly cited example of how minimally edited ethnographic film can tell several layers of ethnographic stories. So, the Biella project is based on expanding the potential of a classic in visual anthropology, primarily (but not exclusively) for teaching.

The traditional means of teaching this material has been to show the film, assign readings on the Yanamamo, and integrate these materials in lectures and discussions. Researchers use a similar strategy—close study of the film and consideration of visual material in the context of written sources.

By packaging the film with different kinds of information (still photographs, graphs, tables, and extensive texts) so that various parts can be connected in novel ways, *Yanamamo Interactive* opens up heretofore unexplored pedagogical and research possibilities.

The *Yanamamo Interactive* CD-ROM includes three versions of the film (unedited and edited in two forms), 380 paragraphs that describe the events as they unfold in the film (these are viewed alongside the scrolling film), more than 100 captioned photographs of the participants in the ax fight, genealogical charts that plot the participants' relationships, and maps of the village and the interaction of the fight. As noted, the software architecture allows viewers to move among filmed events, biographical sketches, maps of important places, and ethnographic explanations freely and creatively. The format invites theory testing, both formally and informally. The CD-ROM defines film as being integral to ethnography rather than as a form of ethnography itself. As a result, the film can be seen as ethnographic information that is deconstructed by reading the anthropology that gives background information.

My experience with the CD-ROM has been nothing short of inspiring. I am well aware of how difficult it is to teach ethnographic film; students see the film in one parcel of time and then read or discuss it in another parcel of time. Thus, the emotional and subjective experience of studying film is separated from the more analytical experience of studying texts. This separation often leads to stereotyping precisely because emotions and analysis become ever more distant from each other.

The interactivity potential of the CD-ROM allows the viewer to, for example, stop the video, select a particular participant in the fight, and trace the participant's genealogy in the village and his social position vis-á-vis his participation in village groups and activities. Thus, students and researchers can study the contexts of social action and begin to understand the layers of meaning that reside under the surface of the fight. In fact, the organization of the material invites students and researchers to ask new questions and to investigate new lines of reasoning.

The project has been distributed with an introductory anthropology textbook and is widely used in university anthropology courses. The CD-ROM allows students from a wide range of backgrounds to actually encounter ethnographic information and, thus, to do visual research at a fairly sophisticated level.

It is likely that the format introduced in *Yanamamo Interactive* will soon become common in visual anthropology, extending the usefulness of ethnographic film for both teaching and research. Several projects by the authors of this CD-ROM and others are under way.

Macromedia's *Director* has also been used to produce a searchable archive of the work of documentary photographer Jean Mohr. Mohr is best known for his collaborations with John Berger (Berger & Mohr, 1967, 1975, 1982) and for his work in the area of international human rights for several international organizations (Mohr's first photographs, taken during the early 1950s, documented the everyday lives of Palestinian refugees). He has also photographed less known projects involving the Chicago police on patrol and international tours of a European symphony.

The CD-ROM titled *Jean Mohr: A Photographer's Journey* (Mohr, n.d.) collects more than 1,200 of Mohr's black-and-white and color photographs (from more than 1 million taken during his 50-year career) and includes brief interviews with Mohr and others about the meaning of his work as well as brief texts that explain and elaborate on the projects from which the images were drawn.

The core of the project is the photographs, which are organized in five categories, the most important of which are "image type," "subjects," and "regions." Each of these categories includes several subcategories accessible as drop-down menus. For example, the image category of "subjects" includes the subcategories of "migrants," "music," "refugees," and several others. Thus, the viewer is able to create a corpus of images by clicking on one subcategory in each main category. For example, I direct the CD-ROM to gather Mohr's black-and-white portraits of refugees who were photographed in Africa. Or, the viewer could direct the CD-ROM to select color images on the general subject of music that Mohr photographed in the Middle East. Combining a different subelement from each of the main categories allows the viewer to construct hundreds of individualized archives.

These advanced searching capabilities allow the viewer to use Mohr's work efficiently and creatively. I found that, after several hours of working with the archive, the only limitation that suggested itself was the number of photographs that it included. A total of 1,200 images might seem like a lot at first glance, but they are a tiny percentage of Mohr's life work. Most searches cross-referenced across several categories yield 20 to 30 images, whereas Mohr's full corpus would include several times that number. The most challenging aspect of this project was clearly in programming the navigation; one senses that more images could have easily been scanned and added to the archive. Thus, if the project had included three to four times the number of images, the archive would be that much more useful.

Electronic and searchable photograph archives from newspapers or public collections are increasingly available. Mohr's project, however, might be the first to present the life work of a sociologically oriented photographer with information that describes his career, publications, self-reflections, and commentary on his relationship with Berger. As an overview of the work of a single photographer, it sketches the working methods of an artist. It also provides visual evidence on sociological themes such as refugees as well as visual area studies of the places where Mohr concentrated his efforts. Short video clips also humanize Mohr.

One would hope that the considerable effort represented in this CD-ROM project will lead others to synthesize their photographic work, especially when the work so broadly addresses subject matters of interest to sociological researchers.

Two projects with a smaller scope show the potential of interactive media in visual research. Ricabeth Steiger photographed an aspect of daily life—a train commute she makes several times a week from Basel to Zurich, Switzerland, to construct a visual ethnography of a taken-for-granted aspect of daily life (Steiger, 2000) (Figure 6.1). The images are both impressionistic (showing blurred landscapes through the train windows—the world speeding by as viewed from inside the train) and ethnographic (showing the tacit social scripts—how people interact on a train—that underlie the public behavior in Switzerland).

Steiger's project was published in *Visual Sociology* as a research article in two forms. The article text and photo sequence were published as thumbnail-sized images in the print journal and on a CD-ROM that housed a *Director*-based movie version of the project. The CD-ROM format allowed Steiger to transform still photographs into a new mode of communication—a virtual movie consisting of an automatically

**Figure 6.1.** Inside the Train

Source: Photograph by Ricabeth Steiger.

advancing slide show. This was an ideal solution; the images were too numerous to work as an article but were too few to constitute a book, and they needed to be viewed in sequence to achieve the intended effect. Although the thumbnail images published in the journal are a catalog of the photos, the virtual movie clearly constitutes the actual article.

The publication of the project in *Visual Sociology* was a breakthrough in the presentation of visual research. The development of the CD-ROM required the journal designer to have knowledge of relevant software and cross-platform development. The International Visual Sociology Association (IVSA), the sponsoring academic organization of the journal, devoted considerable resources to fund the CD-ROM and to package and distribute it as a regular part of the journal. It did so with the hope that the project's revolutionary character would help to encourage a new way in which to see and do visual research.

Finally, Dianne Hagaman recently published a photographic project using the same software, with considerably more elaborate development (Hagaman, 2002). As in the case of Steiger's project, the subject is a visual ethnography of daily life, in this case her life with her husband, the sociologist Howard S. Becker.

The photographs are organized into 14 "sonnets," with each sonnet named after a jazz standard such as "Night and Day," "Slow Boat to China" (Figure 6.2), or "One Morning in May." Jazz has been an important part of Becker's life; he was (and

**Figure 6.2.**     From "Slow Boat to China" Sonnet of the CD-ROM *Howie Feeds Me*

Source: Photographs by Dianne Hagaman.

remains) a practicing musician, and his studies of jazz are important contributions to cultural sociology. The photographs also have a jazzy quality; they are subtle and present reality from an oblique angle, transforming otherwise unremarkable subject matter, such as window frames and beds, into poetic visual statements. Likewise, jazz presents familiar melodies in unusual and provocative frames of musical reference.

The photographs are about place (the couple's homes in Seattle and San Francisco and the couple's travels to Paris and other locations where Becker lectures), landscape (Hagaman is a master at rendering sky as a part of landscape, often inhabited by birds on the wing), social gatherings (often with well-known sociologists), and (most centrally) their own relationship. According to Hagaman's introduction,

> We weren't kids when we met and decided to live together, and we didn't have our whole lives ahead of us. . . .
>
> He played the piano and knew hundreds of songs from his days when he played clubs in Chicago. And he could cook. And liked to do it. He told me that after his wife Nan died, he made himself three full meals a day, every day, in order to establish a routine and structure in his life in a time of change and grief.
>
> I, however, had never learned to cook. It wasn't deliberate. I just somehow fell through the cracks. But, maybe as a consequence, I've never taken the preparation or the social aspects of food for granted: how central eating is and preparing the food that you eat (that magical skill) is, who we eat with and where.

Thus, the project is titled *Howie Feeds Me,* and the photographs allude to a relationship rooted in caring for and nourishing the body and spirit. In this way, the project is an ethnography of the daily life of a couple and their loving relationship, as told from the perspective of one partner. The only similar attempts to communicate this theme are Laura Letinsky's photo essay *Venus Inferred* (Letinsky, 2000), which focuses on the

banalities of the sexual lives of several couples, and Pernette and Leeuwenberg's (2001) photo essay on their intimate relationship. But whereas Letinsky (2000) focuses on the obvious (i.e., a series of couples looking embarrassed in the act of coupling) and Pernette and Leeuwenberg (2001), both photographers in their early 30s, use the camera to record the energy and lovingness of sexual union, Hagaman (2002) communicates the mundane aspects of nonsexual intimacy with subtlety and humor that suggests the stuff of daily life.

Much of the message of Hagaman's essay is in the medium. The project is rooted in 35-millimeter black-and-white photos, but from the beginning it was intended for the computer. Hagaman organized the CD-ROM–mounted photo sequences in what she calls sonnets: "I took the idea of the fourteen lines of a sonnet and used it to organize my photographs, a group of fourteen images making a kind of poem: rhyming, repeating, alluding, and suggesting, the way photographs do when you put them into groups."

The sonnets are of two forms. One is a series of individual images presented on the computer screen against a white background, like images on the wall of a gallery. These have short captions that usually identify the place or action depicted. The viewer studies these images individually and in sequence as well as in the context of the story hinted at by the title of the sonnet (a jazz standard).

Other sonnets are continuous visual loops of joined images that the viewer scrolls through. The images adjoin each other completely; the viewer creates new images composed of parts of the adjoining images by stopping the scroll bar in other than the borders of the photographs. Thus, when the viewer scrolls, images suddenly combine exteriors of a room from one image and exteriors of a street from another; other images contain both night and day, and so forth. The continually joined images add a dimension that could not be achieved if the images stood alone either on a gallery wall or on a computer screen.

The photographs are also presented as thumbnails with detailed descriptions of location, people, and events that are useful points of reference.

New developments such as those described heretofore have revolutionary potential in visual studies. There are, however, several issues that may affect their contributions.

The first issue concerns longevity. The software that runs the various programs is under constant development, and the systems that run the computers are as well. For example, Apple's recent operating system, OS-X (already in its third iteration), has required full redesign of participating software. Similar developments in PC operating systems have led to the same challenges. With the rate of current development, it is nearly impossible to predict the hardware, operating system, and/or software compatibility for today's projects that will be in use 10 or even 5 years from now. Of course, the book that I just removed from the shelf will be there, in exactly the same form, 50 years from now.

The second issue is that, as noted previously, electronic delivery and organization of material often allows information to be packaged in a way that could not be presented in print form. But the opposite is also true: Old-fashioned media, including books, articles, and handmade images, have been shown to have a remarkable resiliency precisely because of the very qualities that the electronic forms transcend. The illustrated book or journal article, for example, imposes limitations that the Web does not and that might lead to more judicious editing or organization. The linearity of old-fashioned presentations remains meaningful as a frame by which ideas and images can be organized.

There is also the matter by which various forms of information find their way to consumers. Books and articles are published and distributed through a system that draws on well-articulated institutional structures and a public that consumes in a certain way. This is a multilayered and conservative system. Nontextual media, such as CD-ROMs and DVDs, have only recently begun to get a foothold in this system.

This is not to say that the old forms are necessarily better or worse than newer competing forms of visual communication. It is simply to say that some aspects of change come slowly. This must be said in the context of the increasing success of the Web and multimedia platforms.

## ▣ THE CONTINUATION OF THE OLD

Certain themes and forms of visual research, however, continue to produce useful visual research. One is the visual critical analysis, such as Margolis's (1998, 1999) studies of education and labor processes. This work traces its roots to studies such as Stein's (1983) critical investigation of early social reform–oriented photography. Stein's study focuses on how the sponsorship, photographic technology, and forms of dissemination influenced what the photos communicated. These arguments often suggest that the photographs have latent meanings that reinforce the very structures they seem to be criticizing.

A more informal use of images to ask critical questions of the past is Norfleet's (2001) *When We Liked Ike.* Norfleet, who may have been the first practicing visual sociologist (she worked in photography and sociology for several decades at Harvard University), here assembles photographs from archives from the 1950s that document everyday life—families, institutions, organizations, leisure life, and so forth. She captions these images with excerpts from popular sociological texts of the time (e.g., those of David Reisman and Vance Packard), excerpts from novelists (e.g., J. D. Salinger), and quotes from the popular press (e.g., *Ladies Home Journal*). The viewer is taken to the everyday world that became the basis of sociological analysis.

Empirical visual sociology lives on as well. For example, Rich and Chalfen (1999) use visual methods in a study of disease phenomenology. In their research, chronic asthma sufferers in their teens or younger made and analyzed videos of their personal worlds under the influence of asthma. The films and discussions opened a window into the private world of a disease at a particular stage of the life cycle. The visual dimension served as a means of discovery by the disease victims (they filmed their worlds to tell the story of their disease experience), and it also served as the basis of dialogue among asthma sufferers, adults in their social worlds (e.g., parents, teachers), and the medical community. The videos described social isolation, parental irresponsibility, and other themes that led to a fuller understanding of how the teens and younger children manage a debilitating disease.

Rich and Chalfen's use of native-produced imagery draws originally from Worth, Adair, and Chalfen's (1972/1997) Navajo project of the late 1960s, where anthropologists taught reservation Navajo to use 16-millimeter cameras to tell their cultural stories. Many other examples followed.

Native-produced still images, however, have also become important visual research tools in social science. An early example was Ewald's work with Appalachian youth. Her approach was to teach young children to photograph their families and surroundings, develop the black-and-white film, and print the images. She asked the children she taught what they imagined and dreamed about and how they interpreted their daily surroundings. Ewald's initial success led to several similar projects in South America, Holland, and other settings (Ewald, 1985, 1992, 1996).

Photo elicitation is another approach that belongs exclusively to the visual. In a recent description of the method (Harper, 2002), I found photo elicitation to be the primary method in 40 studies, including doctoral theses, books, articles, and reports. Several studies have been finished during the period since the article was published, and certainly many were missed in the review. The disciplines represented in these studies include anthropology, communication, education, sociology (especially urban, rural, and communities studies), photojournalism, cultural studies, ethnic studies, and industrial management. In these vastly dissimilar kinds of research, the common desire to understand the world as defined by the subject led to wide applications of the photo elicitation method.

In what follows, I explain one way in which photo elicitation operates in a brief review of a study of the meaning of change in dairy farming in northern New York (Harper, 2001). In this project, my goal was to understand how agriculture had changed and what these changes meant for those who lived through them. To this end, I showed elderly farmers' photographs from the 1940s, (a period when they had been teens or young adult farmers) and asked them to remember events, stories, or commonplace activities that the photos brought to mind. The success of the project rested on the coincidence of the availability of an extraordinary archive of documentary photographs (the Standard Oil of New Jersey archive) from just the era that elderly farmers had experienced at the beginnings of their careers and the fact that these photographs were of such a quality as to inspire detailed and often deep memories.

The farmers described the mundane aspects of farming, including the social life of shared work (Figure 6.3). But more important, they explained what it meant to have participated in agriculture that had been neighbor based, environmentally friendly, and oriented toward animals more as partners than as exploitable resources.

**Figure 6.3.**     A Farm Work Crew Eating Dinner

Source: Photograph by Sol Libsohn. Used by permission of the Ekstrom Library, University of Louisville.

In this and other photo elicitation studies, photographs proved to be able to stimulate memories that word-based interviewing did not. The result was discussions that went beyond "what happened when and how" to themes such as "this was what this had meant to us as farmers."

Visual methods have also been applied to approaches that have not previously been thought to be visual. A recent issue of *Visual Studies* (Volume 18, Issue 1) was devoted to ethnomethodology. The visual worlds that ethnomethodologists studied included the textual materials in various administrative jobs (Carlin, 2003) and the work objects of scientific endeavors (Kawatoko & Ueno, 2003). These studies draw on Sudnow's (1993) pioneering ethnomethodological studies of jazz performance that were communicated partly through photographic imagery.

Several texts on visual methods have been published during recent years. The most useful are Pink's (2001) *Doing Visual Ethnography,* Banks's (2001) *Visual Methods in Social Research,* and van Leeuwen and Jewitt's (2001) edited *Handbook of Visual Analysis.* Pink has studied visual research broadly, whereas Banks has concentrated on visual anthropology. Van Leeuwen and Jewitt's handbook is a useful collection of cultural studies and empirical research. Their contributors describe content analysis, visual anthropology, cultural studies, semiotics, ethnomethodology, and film analysis. Although most contributors downplay approaches that favor "researchers making photos to analyze reality," the collection is a useful starting place. Less useful is Emission and Smith's (2000) *Researching the Visual,* which is largely a polemic against the photocentric orientation of visual sociology.

It is especially interesting that those who have synthesized the strains and traditions of visual social studies have come largely from outside the United States and, most significant during the past few years, from the United Kingdom. The "U.K. School" emphasizes cultural studies but is increasingly eclectic, with recent and forthcoming collections that center on visual ethnography (e.g., Knowles & Sweetman, 2004).

The other significant European movement in visual sociology is situated in Italy, primarily at the University of Bologna. Beginning in the early 1990s, Patrizia Faccioli and her colleagues have conducted visual research on a wide range of topics using photo elicitation, documentary photography, content analysis, and semiotics (for an overview, see Faccioli & Losacco, 2003). Losacco's (2003) recent monograph uses family photography to understand the negotiation of cultural identities of Italian immigrants in Canada.

That the IVSA meets regularly in Europe helps to facilitate the growth of visual methods internationally. The development of visual social science in the remaining areas of the world where social sciences are taught is a critical next development.

However, although there are many recent texts on visual methods, there are few new in-depth studies based on visual data or visual analysis. Quinney has written and photographed a series of introspective ethnographies of place, with the most recent (Quinney, 2001) exploring the meaning of what he refers to the "borderland"—Hamlin Garland's "middle border," which he presents as a landscape, a state of mind, and a basis for philosophical orientation. Barndt (2002) uses photographs to both gather and present information in a study of the globalization of the food. *Changing Works* (Harper, 2001) is one of the few recent ethnographic studies based on photographs.

However, photo documentary studies continue to be published. Recent examples include Coles and Nixon's (1998) *School,* which explores the social realities of three schools in Boston; Goodman's (1999) *A Kind of History,* which documents 20 years in the life of an ordinary American town; and Wilson's (2000) photo study of the *Hutterites of Montana.* Yet the documentary tradition remains the scope or attention of most social scientists. Unfortunately, Becker's suggestion back in 1974 that documentary photographers and sociologists with an interest in photography should explore their overlap and get on with learning from each other is still largely underrealized (Becker, 1974).

## ▣ UNRESOLVED ISSUES: ETHICS OF VISUAL RESEARCH— SPECIAL ISSUES AND SPECIAL CONSIDERATIONS

The scientific world, of which sociology is a part, has become increasingly concerned with research ethics. This preoccupation is partly due to past misuses of scientific research. This has, in turn, led to the increased use of institutional review boards (IRBs) as legally mandated monitors of all research at U.S. universities. These issues are also the subjects of codes of ethics of professional societies such as the ASA.

Qualitative researchers, however, often have a difficult time in defining their work in terms that meet the expectations of IRBs. This is especially the case for photographic researchers. The primary issue concerns the matter of subject informed consent and subject anonymity. The problems for qualitative researchers, and the special case of sociological photographers, are detailed in what follows.

The first concerns the observation of public life and, in the case of visual sociology, the photography of public life. Observation of public life has been a part of sociology since Georg Simmel's studies of generic forms of social interaction, based in part on his observations of public life from his Berlin apartment window, or since Irving Goffman's observations of the nuances of human interaction in social gatherings. Anderson (2003) refers to this style of sociological observation as "folk ethnography." Anderson's method involves observing the public on bus trips and walks through a city as well as overhearing conversations in restaurants and other instances of public life.

In large part, IRBs appear to be ready to accept that observation of public life may take place without informed consent. But the right to photograph the public without the subjects' consent has, by and large, not been tested by passage of research proposals by members of the visual sociological community. Many visual sociologists model our photographic research on documentary photography and photojournalism, where the right to photograph in public has been guaranteed by amendments to the U.S. Constitution dealing with freedom of expression. In these studies, it is precisely the clearly portrayed face of a stranger doing the things people normally do that leads to compelling documentary statements or sociologically meaningful insights.

Visual sociologists point to the precedent of photojournalism and documentary and argue that harm to subjects is unlikely to occur from showing normal people doing normal things. In a personal example, I was photographed unawares at a recent Pittsburgh Pirates baseball game by a photographer working for the *Pittsburgh Post Gazette,* and I was presented in a half-page photograph to support the message of an article that alleged low attendance at the Pirates games. In fact, I had chosen to sit by myself in an otherwise empty section because I like the vantage point of that section and I enjoy the solitude in a baseball stadium early in the season. Having the photo in the *Post Gazette* made me a celebrity for a day, but it also opened up other questions. Was I skipping work? Was I a social isolate? And so forth. However, the public accepts that being in a public space makes one susceptible to public photography. I was not harmed by my momentary celebrity status, and the ethics of photojournalism were not violated. I was portrayed accurately in the mundane performance of my life.

Those of us who want to use photography in sociology believe that it is logical to argue that we have the same rights as those who work in the closely related worlds of photojournalism and photodocumentary. Indeed, some of us have come to define ourselves as documentary photographers, rather than as visual sociologists, to avoid IRB scrutiny, although this is surely not a solution to this issue.

The second matter concerns the loss of confidentiality in photos that portray people clearly. The language of the current ethics literature (in the ASA code of conduct or the IRB guidelines) is strongly aligned with protecting the anonymity of subjects. That is commendable if subjects wish to remain anonymous. But what about subjects who are pleased and willing to be subjects (and who sign releases to this effect)? The identifiability of subjects is critical to the sociological usefulness of the images; these include elements such as subjects' expressions, gestures, hairstyles, clothing, and other personal attributes.

There has been little written about the ethics of photographic research. Several years ago, Gold (1989) argued that the biomedical model did not sufficiently address the ethical issues of visually based research, arguing instead for a "research outlook—sensitivity—that is rooted in the covenantal ethical position . . . as a means of addressing the ethical problems of visual sociology" (p. 100). This sensitivity "requires the researcher to develop an in-depth understanding of subjects so that he or she may determine which individuals and activities may be photographed, in what ways it is appropriate to do so, and how the resulting images should be used" (p. 103). This involves understanding the point of view of subjects, especially their thoughts on how and where the images will be used. According to Gold, "Unlike a contract that simply specifies rights and duties, a covenant requires the researcher to consider his or her relationship with subjects on a much wider level, accepting the obligations that develop between involved, interdependent persons" (p. 104).

The practical implications are that one will sometimes find oneself in research situations where photography would violate the norms of the setting or the feelings of the subjects; in such cases, photography should not be done. Gold (1989) suggests that sociologists use their knowledge as well as their ethical sensitivities to guide their actions. Whether this can be the basis of an acceptable method remains to be seen.

For visual ethnography to come out of the closet, these issues need to be resolved. Visual researchers must have their work sanctioned by boards that eventually will accept research that varies radically from the formal experiment and that depends on the right to document life in glaring exactitude.

## ▣ SUMMARY

My hope is that visual methods will become ever more important in the various research traditions where it already has a foothold and that this growth will take place in a way that acknowledges the potential of new media, while preserving what is useful in the old media, and acknowledges the subjects' rights but calls forth a larger ethical stance than the biomedical contractual model determines as appropriate. I hope that during the next decade, visual social studies will become a world movement and, thus, a means to long overdue internationalization of sociology.

For visual social science to develop, professional rules and norms concerning ethics must acknowledge the rights of photographers/researchers to photograph in public and to present identifiable subjects, but in the context of ethical considerations that consider photographers/researchers as connected by webs of obligation and moral regard.

## ▣ NOTE

1. Biella and colleagues' (1997) project, as well as Steiger's (2000) article (which had just been released when the second iteration of this chapter was written), both were mentioned briefly in my chapter in the second edition of the *Handbook*.

## ▣ REFERENCES

Anderson, E. (2003, November). *Folk ethnography*. Paper presented at the conference Being Here/Being There: Fieldwork Encounters and Ethnographic Discoveries, University of Pennsylvania, Philadelphia, PA.

Banks, M. (2001). *Visual methods in social research*. London: Sage.

Barndt, D. (2002). *Tangled routes: Women, work, and globalization of the tomato trail*. Lanham, MD: Rowman & Littlefield.

Becker, H. S. (1974). Photography and sociology. *Studies in the Anthropology of Visual Communication, 1*(1), 3–26.

Berger, J., & Mohr, J. (1967). *A fortunate man.* New York: Pantheon.

Berger, J., & Mohr, J. (1975). *A seventh man.* New York: Viking.

Berger, J., & Mohr, J. (1982). *Another way of telling.* New York: Pantheon.

Biella, P., Chagnon, N., & Seaman, G. (1997). *Yanamamo interactive: The ax fight* [CD-ROM]. New York: Harcourt Brace.

Carlin, A. P. (2003). Pro forma arrangements: The visual availability of textual artefacts. *Visual Studies, 18*(1), 6–20.

Coles, R., & Nixon, N. (1998). *School.* Boston: Little, Brown.

Emission, M., & Smith, P. (2000). *Researching the visual.* London: Sage.

Ewald, W. (1985). *Portraits and dreams.* New York: Writers and Readers.

Ewald, W. (1992). *Magic eyes: Scenes from an Andean girlhood.* Seattle, WA: Bay Press.

Ewald, W. (1996). *I dreamed I had a girl in my pocket: The story of an Indian village.* New York: DoubleTake Books.

Faccioli, P., & Losacco, G. (2003). *Manuale di Sociologia Visuale.* Milan, Italy: Angeli.

Fuery, P., & Fuery, K. (2003). *Visual cultures and critical theory.* Oxford, UK: Oxford University Press.

Gold, S. (1989). Ethical issues in visual field work. In G. Blank, J. L. McCartney, & E. Brent (Eds.), *Practical applications in research and work* (pp. 99–112). New Brunswick, NJ: Transaction Publishers.

Gold, S. (2003). Israeli diaspora. *Contexts, 2*(3), 50–57. (American Sociological Association)

Goodman, M. (1999). *A kind of history.* San Francisco: Markerbooks.

Hagaman, D. (2002). *Howie feeds me* [CD-ROM]. Rochester, NY: Visual Studies Workshop.

Harper, D. (1987). *Working knowledge: Skill and community in a small shop.* Chicago: University of Chicago Press.

Harper, D. (1993). On the authority of the image: Visual sociology at the crossroads. In N. K. Denzin & Y. Lincoln (Eds.), *Handbook of qualitative research* (pp. 403–412). Newbury Park, CA: Sage.

Harper, D. (2000). Reimagining visual methods: Galileo to *Neuromancer.* In N. Denzin & Y. Lincoln (Eds.), *Handbook of qualitative research* (2nd ed., pp. 717–732). Thousand Oaks, CA: Sage.

Harper, D. (2001). *Changing works: Visions of a lost agriculture.* Chicago: University of Chicago Press.

Harper, D. (2002). Talking about pictures: A case for photo elicitation. *Visual Studies, 17*(1), 13–26.

Harper, D. (n.d.). Cultural studies and the photograph. Manuscript.

Kawatoko, Y., & Ueno, N. (2003). Talking about skill: Making objects, technologies, and communities visible. *Visual Studies, 18*(1), 47–57.

Knowles, C., & Sweetman, P. (2004). *Picturing the social landscape.* London: Routledge.

Letinsky, L. (2000). *Venus inferred.* Chicago: University of Chicago Press.

Losacco, G. (2003). *Wop o Mangicake, Consumi e identita etnica: La negoziazione dell'italianita a Toronto.* Milan, Italy: Angeli.

Margolis, E. (1998). Picturing labor: A visual ethnography of the coal mine labor process. *Visual Sociology, 13*(2), 5–36.

Margolis, E. (1999). Class pictures: Representations of race, gender, and ability in a century of school photography. *Visual Sociology, 14*(1), 7–38.

Mohr, J. (n.d.). *Jean Mohr: A photographer's journey.* Geneva, Switzerland: Association Memoires de Photographes.

Norfleet, B. (2001). *When we liked Ike: Looking for postwar America.* New York: Norton.

Pernette, W., & Leeuwenberg, F. (2001). *Twogether.* Zurich, Switzerland: Edition Stemmle.

Pink, S. (2001). *Doing visual ethnography.* London: Sage.

Quinney, R. (2001). *Borderland: A midwest journal.* Madison: University of Wisconsin Press.

Rank, M. (2003). As American as apple pie: Poverty and welfare. *Contexts, 2*(3), 41–50. (American Sociological Association)

Rich, M., & Chalfen, R. (1999). Showing and telling asthma: Children teaching physicians with visual narrative. *Visual Sociology, 14*(1), 51–72.

Rieger, J. H. (1996). Photographing social change. *Visual Sociology, 11*(1), 5–49.

Rieger, J. H. (2003). A retrospective visual study of social change: The pulp-logging industry in an upper peninsula Michigan county. *Visual Studies, 18*(2), 157–178.

Ruby, J. (n.d.). *Oak Park.* [Online.] Available: http://astro.temple.edu~ruby/opp

Steiger, R. (2000). Enroute: An interpretation through images. *Visual Sociology, 15.* [CD ROM.]

Stein, S. (1983, May). Making connections with the camera: Photography and social mobility in the career of Jacob Riis. *Afterimage, 14.*

Sudnow, D. (1993). *Ways of the hand: The organization of improvised conduct.* Cambridge: MIT Press.

van Leeuwen, T., & Jewitt, C. (Eds.). (2001). *Handbook of visual analysis.* London: Sage.

Wilson, L. (2000). *Hutterites of Montana.* New Haven, CT: Yale University Press.

Worth, S., Adair, J., & Chalfen, R. (1997). *Through Navajo eyes: An exploration in film communication and anthropology.* Albuquerque: University of New Mexico Press. (Original work published 1972)

# AUTOETHNOGRAPHY

## Making the Personal Political

Stacy Holman Jones

*The next moment in qualitative inquiry will be one at which the practices of qualitative research finally move, without hesitation or encumbrance, from the personal to the political.*

—Norman Denzin,
"Aesthetics and the Practices of Qualitative Inquiry," 2000, p. 261

*We cannot move theory into action unless we can find it in the eccentric and wandering ways of our daily life. . . . [Stories] give theory flesh and breath.*

—Minnie Bruce Pratt, *S/HE,* 1995, p. 22

*I think theater is primarily a site for liberation stories and a sweaty laboratory to model possible strategies for empowerment.*

—Tim Miller,
"Solo Performing as Call to Arms," 2002, para. 3

This is a chapter about the personal text as critical intervention in social, political, and cultural life. Please do not read it alone.

This chapter is more than a little utopian in its call to disrupt, produce, and imagine a breakthrough in—and not a respite from—the way things are and perhaps should be (Ricoeur, 1986, pp. 265–266). It cannot stand alone in the world.

This is a chapter about how looking at the world from a specific, perspectival, and limited vantage point can tell, teach, and put people in motion. It is about autoethnography as a radical democratic politics—a politics committed to creating space for dialogue and debate that instigates and shapes social change (Reinelt, 1998, p. 286). It does not act alone.

This is a chapter about how a personal text can move writers and readers, subjects and objects, tellers and listeners into this space of dialogue, debate, and change. It does not speak alone.

This chapter is meant for more than one voice, for more than personal release and discovery, and for more than the pleasures of the text. It is not a text alone.

This chapter is meant for public display, for an audience. It is not meant to be left alone.

This chapter is an ensemble piece. It asks that you read it with other texts, in other contexts, and with others. It asks for a performance, one in which we might discover that our autoethnographic texts are not alone. It is a performance that asks how our personal accounts count.

## ▣ TURNING TO NARRATIVE:
## CRISES, HISTORIES, AND MOVEMENTS

### Demanding a Response

"Don't read this until you steady yourself. This isn't just the third essay on the list of assigned reading for next week. It will make you cringe. It will haunt you. It will change you."

This is what I said to friends in my team ethnography graduate course at California State University, Sacramento.[1] It was, for me, a novel course in many ways: We were working together as a research team; we were writing Van Maanen's (1988) realist, impressionist, and confessional tales; and we were creating a text together as a class.[2] In the midst of the creativity and camaraderie we experienced in this course, Ronai's (1995) "Multiple Reflections of Child Sex Abuse: An Argument for a Layered Account" altered us and the way in which we approached our work. In the essay, Ronai juxtaposed reflections on being sexually abused as a child with an argument for a layered account—a telling that creates a "continuous dialectic of experience, emerging from the multitude of reflexive voices that simultaneously produce and interpret . . . text[s]" (p. 396).

"Multiple Reflections" is autoethnography, although I did not know it then. Ronai (1995) offered up her own terrifying experience in the name of saying something startling and intricate about sexual abuse and the force and import of her scholarly and personal efforts to make sense of this experience. Ronai's story had a powerful effect on me. My thinking—about sexual abuse, about writing and scholarship, about the power of texts—shifted. Her language and story accomplished something that, up until that point, I had believed to be the business of music, novels, and film; they invited me into a lived felt experience. I could not stand outside of her words at safe remove. Ronai's story demanded that I respond and react. I marveled at the beauty of her language. I talked about her essay with my colleagues and listened as they recounted their own experiences of sexual abuse. I was enraged about what happened to Ronai and to my friends.

This is the story of my first encounter with autoethnography as a communication scholar. Of course, I had been experiencing autoethnographic texts all my life—in Raymond Carver's short stories, Silvia Plath's poetry, Milan Kundera's novels, and Billie Holiday's singing. Until I read "Multiple Reflections," however, I did not make the connection between what these works and acts accomplished and what I believed scholarship to be about.

## Autoethnography Is . . .

A balancing act. Autoethnography and writing about autoethnography, that is.[3] Autoethnography works to hold self and culture together, albeit not in equilibrium or stasis. Autoethnography writes a world in a state of flux and movement—between story and context, writer and reader, crisis and denouement. It creates charged moments of clarity, connection, and change.

Writing about autoethnography is also a balancing act. In a handbook chapter that wants to move theory and method to action, what do I leave in and leave out? How do I balance *telling* (about autoethnography's history, methods, responsibilities, and possibilities) with *showing* (doing the work of autoethnography here on these pages)? How much of my self do I put in and leave out?

I begin with another sort of balancing act, sifting though books and essays, looking for words that others have used to describe the doing of autoethnography. Autoethnography is . . .

"research, writing, and method that connect the autobiographical and personal to the cultural and social. This form usually features concrete action, emotion, embodiment, self-consciousness, and introspection . . . [and] claims the conventions of literary writing." (Ellis, 2004, p. xix)

"a self-narrative that critiques the situatedness of self with others in social contexts." (Spry, 2001, p. 710)

"texts [that] democratize the representational sphere of culture by locating the particular experiences of individuals in a tension with dominant expressions of discursive power." (Neumann, 1996, p. 189)

Soon, however, I find myself wanting to bend the rules, to reinscribe words about other endeavors—autobiographies, personal narratives, memoirs, short fiction, performances—as defining moments for autoethnography. I tell myself that this is not a selfish impulse—wanting beautiful phrases of other origins for autoethnography—because autoethnography is not a practice alone in the world. Autoethnography does have a story, one that was told in loving detail by Reed-Danahay (1997, pp. 4–9), Ellis and Bochner (2000, pp. 739–743), and Neumann (1996, pp. 188–193), among others. But because autoethnography is what Geertz (1983) referred to as a blurred genre, it overlaps with, and is indebted to, research and writing practices in anthropology, sociology, psychology, literary criticism, journalism, and communication (for these histories, see Denzin, 1997, pp. 203–207; Ellis, 2004, pp. 12–18; Neumann, 1996, pp. 193–195), to say nothing of our favorite storytellers, poets, and musicians.

And so I allow words about other sorts of personal texts to make themselves heard in the dance of my fingers on the keys. Autoethnography is . . .

"a catastrophic encounter, a moment of vulnerability and ambiguity that is sensuous, embodied, and profoundly implicated in the social and ideological structures of their life-worlds." (Marilyn Brownstein, quoted in Grumet, 2001, p. 177)

"the kind [of art] that takes you deeper inside yourself and ultimately out again." (Friedwald, 1996, p. 126)

"storytelling [that] can change the world." (Wade Davis, quoted in Chadwick, 2003).

Taking these words as a point of departure, I create my own responses to the call: Autoethnography is . . .

Setting a scene, telling a story, weaving intricate connections among life and art, experience and theory, evocation and explanation . . . and then letting go, hoping for readers who will bring the same careful attention to your words in the context of their own lives.

Making a text present. Demanding attention and participation. Implicating all involved. Refusing closure or categorization.

Witnessing experience and testifying about power without foreclosure—of pleasure, of difference, of efficacy.

Believing that words matter and writing toward the moment when the point of creating autoethnographic texts *is* to change the world.

I return to the books balanced on my lap. I keep looking, unsatisfied with my textual portrait. It feels tentative and unfinished. And perhaps it should be. I decide on one final entry because it says something I have not managed to put into my collected words. Autoethnography is . . .

"[a] performance text . . . turning inward waiting to be staged." (Denzin, 1997, p. 199)

I decide to stop here, knowing that this is not the end of a story about autoethnography, only a beginning. I return to my own story of autoethnographic history and my encounter with Ronai's (1995) story. More than creating connections and shifts in my thinking, more than inspiring both rage and desire, this story also signals a crisis, one that began long before Ronai's story or my reading of it and one that continues as we speak, as we write and are written on these pages and on the stages of our experience.

## ▣ CRISIS

It is a triple crisis, a triple threat, a triple crown of thorns: representation, legitimation, and praxis. These crises, which mark and coincide with a turn toward interpretive, qualitative, narrative, and critical inquiry in the human disciplines, are summoned in an oft-recited line in a familiar play: How much does a scholar know, how does she know it, and what can she do with this knowledge in the world?[4]

The idea of a triple crisis implies that it is something new and something different. But these crises are not new (Denzin, 1997, p. 203). Crisis itself is not new. It is simply the result of forces in conflict, the dramatic nature of human action, and the choices (conscious and unconscious) we make in a world full of possibilities (Pelias, 1992, p. 7). The drama of representation, legitimation, and praxis is part of an ongoing dialogue between self and world about questions of ontology, epistemology, method, and praxis: What is the nature of knowing, what is the relationship between knower and known, how do we share what we know and with what effect? What makes this triple crisis feel urgent is the ways in which this dialogue has increasingly questioned the stability and coherence of our lives as we live and tell about them. This dialogue asks how, in lifeworlds that are partial, fragmented, and constituted and mediated by language, we can tell or read our stories as neutral, privileged, or in any way complete. In answering these questions, we have looked to the personal, concrete, and mundane details of experience as a window to understanding the relationships between self and other or between individual and community. We use the contingent and skeptical languages of poststructuralism and postmodernism (among others) to tell and understand our lives and our world, hoping to confront questions of "self, place, [and] power" in ways that are more satisfying and—yes—more subversive than in previous performances (Neumann, 1996, p. 195; see also Denzin, 1997; Reinelt, 1998, p. 285).

A crisis is a turning point, a moment when conflict must be dealt with even if we cannot resolve it. It is a tension that opens a space of indeterminacy, threatens to destabilize social structures, and enables a creative uncertainty (Reinelt, 1998, p. 284). Interpretive, qualitative, narrative, and critical inquiry have had many such moments, all of which led to shifts in genres and methods. We have traveled from . . .

the impossibility of careful, faithful, and authoritative cataloguing of an exotic other . . .

to partial, reflexive, and local narrative accounts . . .

to texts that work to create a space for an ethics committed to dialogue.

In the current moment . . .

we confront the impossibility of representing lived experience by troubling the link between life and text . . .

we develop (and question the development of) criteria for understanding and evaluating the work we do to narrate the conditions of our lives . . .

we resolve to do work that makes a difference by writing the social imaginary in inciteful and revolutionary ways.[5]

We rise to the challenge of movement. . . .

## ▣ MOVEMENT

Even though I was able to place "Multiple Reflections" within the larger context of turns and movements in interpretive, qualitative, narrative, and critical inquiry, I did not know what to do with the rage I felt on the day I read Ronai's (1995) essay. I looked for a place to put my anger, a way to assuage it, and a means to act on it without forgetting or dismissing it. In her chapter in the second edition of the *Handbook,* Olesen (2000) wrote, "Rage is not enough" (p. 215). Olesen's challenge—to me, to you—is to move from rage to "progressive political action, to theory and method that connect politics, pedagogy, and ethics to action in the world" (N. Denzin & Y. Lincoln, personal communication, September 23, 2002).

This is a challenge that autoethnographers have been working to meet slowly and incrementally. It is the challenge of creating texts that unfold in the intersubjective space of individual and community and that embrace tactics for both *knowing* and *showing* (Jackson, 1993; Kemp, 1998, p. 116). Responding to this challenge means asking questions about the following:

■ How knowledge, experience, meaning, and resistance are expressed by embodied, tacit, intonational, gestural, improvisational, coexperiential, and covert means (Conquergood, 2002, p. 146). Autoethnographic texts focus on how subordinated people use deliberately subtle and opaque forms of communication—forms that are not textual or visual—to express their thoughts, feelings, and desires by performing these practices on the page and on stage (Daly & Rogers, 2001; Jones, 1997a; Stewart, 1996).

■ How emotions are important to understanding and theorizing the relationship among self, power, and culture. Autoethnographic texts focus on creating a palpable emotional experience as it connects to, and separates from, other ways of knowing, being, and acting in/on the world (Bochner, 2001; Ellis, 1995, 1997; Jago, 2002; Spry, 2001).

■ How body and voice are inseparable from mind and thought as well as how bodies and voices move and are privileged (and are restricted and marked) in very particular and political ways. Autoethnographic texts seek to invoke the corporeal, sensuous, and political nature of experience rather than collapse text into embodiment or politics into language play (Alexander, 2000; Gingrich-Philbrook, 1997; Jackson, 1998; Jones, 1997b; Pineau, 2002; Stoller, 1997).

■ How selves are constructed, disclosed, and implicated in the telling of personal narratives as well as how these narratives move in and change the contexts of their telling.[6] Texts aspire to purposeful and tension-filled "self-investigation" of an author's (and a reader's) role in a context, a situation, or a social world. Such self-investigation generates what Gornick (2001) termed "self-implication," that is, seeing "one's own part in the situation"—particularly "one's own frightened or cowardly or self-deceived part" (pp. 35–36)—in creating the dynamic and movement of a text (see also Bochner, 2001; Ellis, 2002; Garrick, 2001; Hartnett, 1998; Langellier, 1999; Park-Fuller, 2000; Spry, 2002; Vickers, 2002).

■ How stories help us to create, interpret, and change our social, cultural, political, and personal lives. Autoethnographic texts point out not only the necessity of narrative in our world but also the power of narrative to reveal and revise that world, even when we struggle for words, when we fail to find them, or when the unspeakable is invoked but not silent (Bochner, 2001; Denzin, 2000; Hartnett, 1999; Lockford, 2002; Neumann, 1996; Pelias, 2002; Richardson, 1997).

These questions challenge us to create work that acts through, in, and on the world and to shift our focus from representation to presentation, from the rehearsal of new ways of being to their performance. These questions posit the challenge of *movement*—to talk and share in new and difficult ways, to think and rethink our positions and commitments, to push through resistance in search of hope (Becker, 2000, pp. 523, 541–542). Responding to these questions has led me and others to turn to performance. In making this turn, we must consider how the practices of autoethnography are informed by a rich history in performance, a history that needs to be written into accounts of autoethnographic theory and practices (Denzin, 2003; Ellis & Bochner, 1996). Our abiding interest in performance ethnography, performative writing, and personal performance narratives is telling. These endeavors point to how personal stories become a means for interpreting the past, translating and transforming contexts, and envisioning a future.

◨ TURNING TO PERFORMANCE: LETTERS OF/FOR/ON CHANGE

## The Impossibility of Iser

I went to the University of Texas at Austin to study organizational culture and to learn more about ethnography, writing, and scholarship. When I looked through the graduate course offerings in the Department of Communication, I kept coming back to a course titled Reading and Performing. I was intrigued. I wanted to learn about performance studies, and I wanted to explore theories and practices of reading. But performing? I was not sure I was ready for that.

The professor[7] encouraged me to come to the first class to see what it was all about, and so I did. The material was compelling, the students were engaging, and the professor was witty and commanding. But what about the performances? My last—and only—performance experience was playing the baby Jesus in the church Christmas pageant. I was not sure whether I should stay, but I knew I wanted to stay. Then the professor began assigning reading reports, and I began to sweat. And then it was my turn. He looked at me and said, "Well, I don't *know* you, but you look like a nice person. I am assigning you Wolfgang Iser because *he* is a nice person."

I had to stay. I had to report on Iser. It is what a nice person would do. I read *The Fictive and the Imaginary* (Iser, 1993), and I understood that Iser was talking about reading and also about writing and performing. He stated,

> The impossibility of being present to ourselves becomes our possibility to play ourselves out to the fullness that knows no bounds, because no matter how vast the range, none of the possibilities will "make us tick." This impossibility suggests a purpose for literary staging. . . . Literature becomes a panorama of what is possible, because it is not hedged in by either the limitations or the considerations that determine the institutionalized organizations within which human life otherwise takes its course. (p. xviii)

As I wrote my report, I kept coming back to this passage because it speaks to the fertile space within which we confront the impossibility of full or complete knowledge (of self, of others, and of the relationships between the two). Because we cannot know, write, or stage it "all," we are free to create a vision of what is possible. Reading Iser, I was convinced that texts both written and read might engage and exceed these constraints in liberatory ways. I was also convinced that performance offered a possibility for realizing this goal.

## Performance Rising

Conquergood (1991) traced the rise of performance in ethnographic research[8] and writing in his essay, "Rethinking Ethnography."[9] He tracked the turn to performance to Victor Turner's characterization of humankind as *homo performans*—humanity as performer—"a culture-inventing, social-performing, self-making, and self-transforming creature" (p. 187). Turner's move to link ethnography with performance as a lived and living practice accomplishes four goals. First, it turns our attention to how bodies and voices are situated in contexts—in and of "time, place, and history" (p. 187). Second, the performative turn moves researchers and researched toward a relationship of embodied "intimate involvement and engagement of 'coactivity' or co-performance with historically situated, named, 'unique individuals'" (p. 187; see also Kisliuk, 2002, pp. 105–106). Third, performance-centered ethnography points up the visual, linguistic, and textual bias of Western civilization and redirects our attention to an aural, bodily, and postmodern expression of culture and lifeworld, fieldwork and writing (Conquergood, 1991, p. 189; see also Tyler, 1986). Fourth, in highlighting the "polysemic" and constitutive nature of social life and cultural performances, the performance paradigm asks us to focus on how texts can be created, communicated, and most notably critiqued on multiple levels (Conquergood, 1991, p. 189).

Conquergood[10] (1991) was not suggesting that ethnography abandon text or field in favor of performance; rather, he was suggesting that we use performance as a metaphor, means, and method for thinking about and sharing what is lost and left out of our fieldwork and our texts as well as thinking about how performance complements, alters, supplements, and critiques these texts (p. 191).[11]

## Ekphrastic Criticism

A thief drives to the museum in his black van. The night
watchman says, Sorry, closed, you have to come back tomorrow.
The thief sticks the point of his knife in the guard's ear.
I haven't got all evening, he says, I need some art.
Art is for pleasure, the guard says, not possession, you can't
something, and then the duct tape is going across his mouth.
Don't worry, the thief says, we're both on the same side.
He finds the Dutch Masters and goes right for a Vermeer:
"Girl Writing a Letter." The thief knows what he's doing.
He has a Ph.D. He slices the canvas on one edge from
the shelf holding the salad bowls right down to the
square of sunlight on the black and white checked floor.
The girl doesn't hear this, she's too absorbed in writing
her letter, she doesn't notice him until too late.[12]

I chose Carpenter's (1993) "Girl Writing a Letter" for my first performance for Reading and Performing. I chose this poem because it is smart and funny and has a happy ending. I thought these things, that is, until I began to work on the performance. There were too many characters, too many stories, too many voices and attitudes to attend to all at once. But it was too late. I stayed the course. I reported on Iser. Now I had to perform.

I finished my performance of "Girl Writing a Letter," and the professor was silent. I waited, my heart pulsing in my head. He walked to the chalkboard and wrote "Ekphrastic." Ekphrastic? What does that mean? Was it good? Awful? He explained that ekphrastic works, such as my poem, are meditations on others' creative acts (Scott, 1994, p. xi), usually texts considering a visual or aural work of art. Think John Keats's "Ode to a Grecian Urn." Ekphrastic texts attempt to invoke "the picture-making capacity of words in poems" (Krieger, 1992, p. 1).

After this brief lesson, the professor moved on, inviting the next performance. I was left to wonder—about the poem, about the performance, about ekphrasis. Later that week, I saw my professor in the hallway outside of his office. He said, "Nice work the other day. Great poem. Great performance. I thought you said you weren't a performer."

"I'm not."

"*You* are a *performer.*"

I spent the next several weeks reading and thinking about performance, texts, and ekphrasis. Although it is typically the domain of the poet and literary scholar, ekphrasis describes our attempts to translate and transmute an experience to text and text to experience. Ekphrasis "breathes words into the mute picture; it makes pictures out of the suspended words of its text. It is as much about urgency as it is about rest, as much voyage as interlude" (Scott, 1994, p. xii). And what happens when we perform an ekphrastic text? What happens when we perform the artist performing the artist, repeating the act of connection and creation, breaking that experience out of one form and context and remaking it in another? Perhaps we create a critical ekphrasis, a performance that moves through *mimesis* (imitation) and *poiesis* (creation) to *kinesis* (movement) (Conquergood, 1992, p. 84).[13]

## Inventory

I was hooked. I changed parties and turned to performance studies. I enrolled in Performance History, Autobiography, and Performance and in Performance Ethnography. On the first day of Performance Ethnography, the professor[14] asked students to pair up and said, "Without speaking, write three observations or assumptions about your partner and then discuss."

There were an odd number of students, so I was paired with the professor. I wrote, "Sings well, writes poetry, believes in reincarnation." She wrote, "Married or in a committed relationship, precise and particular, doesn't relax easily." We shared our lists and laughed over the entries. Some of them were on target, and others were not. But each item on our lists spoke to our projections, our hopes, things we wanted for ourselves, and things we did not want.

At the end of class, the professor asked us to do a self-inventory, answering questions about our physical, emotional, spiritual, intellectual, artistic, and artifactual selves:

What are three of your typical gestures?

When you cried last, what was it about?

What spiritual activities do you engage in each day?

What was the last book you read that was not assigned for a class?

In what activities are you the most creative?

How do you typically adorn your body?

Answering these questions and others, I thought about how performance ethnography is an inventory of both self and other, an act of interpretation and a performance of that assessment, and a journey through imitation and creation into movement. I wondered where this journey would take me.

## Doing Bodies Doing Culture

Jones (2002) wrote that performance ethnography is "most simply, how culture is done in the body" (p. 7). The process of creating and staging performance ethnography, however, is not simply placing, and then playing, bodies in cultures. Rather, performance ethnography seeks to *implicate* researchers and audiences by creating an experience that brings together theory and praxis in complicated, contradictory, and meaningful ways.

Performance ethnography is grounded in two primary ideas: (a) that our identities and daily practices are a series of performance choices (conscious and unconscious) that we improvise within cultural and social guidelines and (b) that we learn though participation or through performance (p. 7; see also Denzin, 2003, pp. 14–16). Performance ethnography can take many forms, ranging from recreating cultural performances for audiences invested and interested in understanding, preserving, and/or challenging particular identities and ways of life (Conquergood, 1985, 1994) to presenting individual (autoethnographic) experiences as a means for pointing out the subjective and situated nature of identity, fieldwork, and cultural interpretation (Jones, 1996; Spry, 2001). Performance ethnography can also be presented in various ways, ranging from traditionally "theatrical" settings complete with fourth wall conventions (in which the audience observes the action on stage) to installations and scenes in which audience members are invited/compelled to participate in the creation of the performance. Whatever the form or process, performance ethnographies seek to "explore bodily knowing, to stretch the ways in which ethnography might share knowledge of a culture, and to puzzle through the ethical and political dilemmas of fieldwork and representation" (Jones, 2002, p. 7). Jones (2002) asserted that performance ethnography achieves these goals by focusing on four principles: (a) creating a specific context for the performance, (b) working in collaboration with and being accountable to a fieldwork community, (c) highlighting the performer's "situated and interested role" in the interpretation of culture, and (d) providing a multitude of perspectives that audience members must actively synthesize (pp. 8–9).

Doing bodies doing culture can be these things if we are willing to remember and perform context, accountability, subjectivity, and multivocality, that is, if we create work that is both "community-based and community active" (Kisliuk, 2002, p. 116). We must be willing not only to implicate our audiences but also to incite them to participate, to act, and to take risks.

## Girl Writing (Another) Letter

During the second semester of my Ph.D. program, insomnia came to live with me. I would lie in bed with my mind racing. I rehashed rehearsals and classroom conversations. I wondered whether I had paid the electric bill. I agonized over who or what to choose as my subject for Performance Ethnography. I considered sites and contexts as well as organizations and individuals, but nothing seemed right. I changed positions, tried to focus on the hum of the air conditioner and the steady pulse of the highway traffic, and then fell into a shallow sleep and dreamed of my grandfather.

A few months before insomnia came to stay, my grandfather had died. I was in the heat of my first semester at Texas when my mother called to tell me. My grandfather had spent the past 2 years mourning the death of my grandmother, and a heart attack had rescued him from living alone without her.

I did not go to the funeral. My mother convinced me to stay in school. That was where my grandfather had wanted me, where he was proud of me. Months later, my sleepless nights began and ended with dreams of my grandfather and the hazy edges of my unlived grief. One night after my eyes flew open to greet the red glare of 2 o'clock, I decided that I had had enough. I decided that I would meet my grandfather in the space he cared about most and to live my grief at school in Performance Ethnography. I got up and composed another letter—another poem for performance.

*Dear Grandpa*

I didn't hear you leave.

I was too busy writing,

your college girl,

never noticing until too late.

Grandma phoned from her hospital bed

asked me to look in on you.

Said last night you were hit by a car,

walking home in the rain.

I drive to you teeth clenched.

Fear works the doorbell and

twists into my breathing

until I hear you call over barking dogs.

The door opens and you shrink in its frame.

Angry bruises glow violent beneath pale skin,

your left eye pinched shut against the pain.

My own vision blurs as we embrace.

You don't want to see a doctor, don't want

to lie down, don't want to rest.

You need to get to the hospital, to her.

You've been gone too long.

I take you to her, but say I can't stay.

That's right, I'm your college girl.

I watch you touch her face and stroke her hair.

I am furious you don't want to live without her.

I tell you both good-bye, not knowing

this is the last time, not knowing

I left you together. Is this how you wanted it?

I didn't hear you leave.

I wove this letter into a performance that included my grandfather's letters to me, family photos, reflections on his life and death, and arguments for the performance of grief.[15] I used monologue, epic, and "everyday life" performance techniques to show my grandfather, myself, and the process of performing an other (Hopper, 1993; Stucky, 1993). I felt closer to my grandfather; more in tune with his presence in my life, dreams, and grief; and proud to share both with an audience.

This performance was my response to the project of performance ethnography. It was my subjective and vulnerable experience. It did not produce "findings"; it was not generalizable outside of asking audience members to recall and reinhabit their own moments of grieving (Goodall, 2000, p. 2). It generated whatever credibility it earned out of my fumbling attempts to make sense of my loss. This is a hallmark of autoethnography and autoethnographic performance—speaking in and through experiences that are unspeakable as well as inhabiting and animating the struggle for words and often our failure to find them (A. Bochner & C. Ellis, personal communication, September 6, 2003). These are risky performances for all involved, and not only because they testify to the spaces of failure, silence, and loss. They are risky because in the rush to identification, empathy, and our desire for an "authentic" experience, audiences and performers can give and receive testimony in ways that move too quickly from a connected yet distinctive "you" and "me" to an unquestioned and violent "we" (Salverson, 2001, p. 124; see also Diamond, 1992). This collapsing of me into you and you into me can work to shut down engagement and responsibility. It can fail to recognize the ethical move required to make autoethnography and autoethnographic performances "a doorway, an instrument of encounter, a place of public and private negotiations—where the goal is not just to empathize, but to *attend*" (Salverson, 2001, p. 125, emphasis added). My performance of my grief for my grandfather stopped short of asking my audience and myself to take a greater risk, to move through *mimesis* (reflection) to *poiesis* (creation) and *kinesis* (movement). That performance—the performance of critique and change—required another letter.

## Connecting

I flew to St. Louis, Missouri, and met an old friend. We drove into a new territory, with her convertible twisting and winding into the state park, where we breathed in the scents of pine and sunlight. We were there for a conference on performative writing. We collected there to share the work—the words—we believed to be performative writing. I was nervous, tentative, and unsure. Should *I* be here? Should it be someone else instead? Of course. I felt guilty about leaving work on a dissertation about torch singing as a feminist performance practice. Should I be *here*? Should I be at home writing—focused on finishing—instead? Of course. But I was here to listen, to read my words, and to experience. And I knew that when we embody stories and identities, there is always danger and always risk,[16] so I went.

We began by talking about performative writing. What is it? How do we know it? What does it aspire to be? How do we judge? What does performance have to do with it? We talked and questioned and made notes, never deciding but instead piling on detail and nuance. Performative writing . . .

"[is a] kind of writing where the body and the spoken word, performance practice and theory, the personal and the scholarly, come together." (Miller & Pelias, 2001, p. v)

"requires faith that language inked on a page can 'do' as well as 'be'." (Stucky, 2001, p. vii)

"depends upon the performative body believing in language." (Gingrich-Philbrook, 2001, p. vii)

"*creates* a performance, rather than describes one." (Barthes, 1977, p. 114)

The hurried and rich discussion left me breathless and nervous. Did my words embody a belief in the power of language? Move beyond the pages of their inscription? Invoke, conjure, and create a new world? As much as the warm atmosphere and kind eyes of the participants told me to relax—to enjoy this performance—I was afraid of how my work would be read, heard, and judged.

Reading, reception, and judgment—conversations about why and how to evaluate alternative auto/ethnographic work abound.[17] For example, Richardson (2000) offered five criteria that she uses when reviewing what she calls creative analytic practices (CAP) ethnography: (a) substantive contribution to an understanding of social life, (b) aesthetic merit, (c) reflexivity, (d) emotional and intellectual impact, and (e) a clear expression of a cultural, social, individual, or communal sense of reality (p. 937). Using Richardson's and others' models, I have developed a list of actions and accomplishments that I look for in my work and in the work of others. They are changing. They are generated in the doing of this writing rather than outside or prior to it:

- *Participation as reciprocity.* How well does the work construct participation of authors/readers and performers/audiences as a *reciprocal* relationship marked by mutual responsibility and obligation (Elam, 1997, p. 78; hooks, 1995, p. 221)?

- *Partiality, reflexivity, and citationality as strategies for dialogue (and not "mastery").* How well does the work present a partial and self-referential tale that connects with other stories, ideas, discourses, and contexts (e.g., personal, theoretical, ideological, cultural) as a means of creating a dialogue among "authors, readers, and subjects written/read" (Pollock, 1998, p. 80; see also Denzin, 1997, pp. 224–227, Lather, 2001, p. 216; Richardson, 1997, p. 91)?

- *Dialogue as a space of debate and negotiation.* How well does the work create a space for and engage in meaningful dialogue among different bodies, hearts, and minds (Conquergood, 1985, p. 9; Denzin, 1997, p. 247)?

- *Personal narrative and storytelling as an obligation to critique.* How do narrative and story enact an ethical obligation to critique subject positions, acts, and received notions of expertise and justice within and outside of the work (Conquergood, 2002, p. 152; Denzin, 1997, p. 200; Langellier, 1999, 128–131)?

- *Evocation and emotion as incitements to action.* How well does the work create a plausible and visceral lifeworld and charged emotional atmosphere as an incitement to act within and outside the context of the work (Bochner, 2000, p. 271; Denzin, 1997, p. 209)?

- *Engaged embodiment as a condition for change.* How does the work place/embody/interrogate/intervene in experience in ways that make political action and change possible in and outside of the work? In other words, how does the work "make writing *do*" (Diamond, 1996, p. 2; Pollock, 1998, pp. 95–96)?

I brought these actions and accomplishments with me to the gathering on performative writing. As the first author/performer began, I heard them sound and reverberate on his tongue and in his words and through his story. I heard them sound and reverberate as we listened to each other that weekend, writing and telling and remaking selves in the words on our pages, in our mouths, on our bodies, and in the room with the green window on the world.[18]

## (Re)Making the Self

Miller (1998)[19] maintained that the gathering interest in autobiographical performance has much to do with a shift in performance studies from aesthetic performance to "a more integral paradigm for explaining, critiquing, and experiencing how contemporary life is lived" (p. 318). This shift, like the move toward interpretive, qualitative, narrative, and critical inquiry in other human disciplines, was precipitated by a rethinking of the relationships among texts, performers, audiences, and contexts; a proliferation in the number and nature of communication technologies; and a postmodern decentering of the authority, autonomy, and stability of institutions, subjectivities, and texts (pp. 319–320). Out of this shift emerged an emphasis on personal narrative as a situated, fluid, and emotionally and intellectually charged *engagement* of self and other (performer and witness) made possible in the "evolving, revelatory dance between performer and spectator" (Miller, 1995, p. 49). In such exchanges, audiences and performers (often composed of people who are classified by virtue of race, class, age, sexual preference, gender identity, and experience as "others") create and constitute a shared history and, thus, break into and diminish their marginalization. These performances create highly personal encounters within an increasingly impersonal public sphere.

Autobiographical performances provide an opportunity to "educate, empower, and emancipate" (Langellier, 1999, p. 129). Langellier (1999) located a means of mitigating and complicating the "either/or" logic of celebration (resistance) and suspicion (dominance) within personal narrative performance, specifically in the interaction between performance and performativity. Langellier asserted that "stories are made, not found" in performances that mediate between experience and story, between the doing and the done (p. 128; see also Denzin, 2003, p. 10).

These distinctions between experience and story, between the doing and the done, rely on a notion of performativity that states that a life story—an identity—is not something an author/performer "elects to do, but . . . [rather] is *performative* in the sense that it constitutes an effect of the very subject it appears to express" (Butler, 1991, p. 24). Performativity points to how identities, and thus life stories, are not easily adopted or changed (as a role taken on by an actor) but instead accrue "gradually, yet [do] not attach [themselves] to some blank, some actor cast in a play she's not yet read; [such identities] come into being by virtue of being performed" (Solomon, 1997, p. 169). That is, life stories are created and recreated in the moments of their telling.

Performativity points to the impossibility of separating our life stories from the social, cultural, and political contexts in which they are created and the ways in which performance as a site of dialogue and negotiation is itself a contested space (Diamond, 1996, p. 2). Langellier (1999) wrote,

> Identity and experience are a symbiosis of performed story and the social relations in which they are materially embedded. . . . This is why personal narrative performance is especially crucial to those communities left out of the privileges of dominant culture, those bodies without voice in the political sense. (p. 129)

The challenge is to consider how particular performances of personal stories "need performativity to comprehend [their] constitutive effects" as well as how performativity "relies upon performance to show itself" (Langellier, 1999, p. 136). In the iterative and unstable move between performance and performativity, "questions of embodiment, of social relations, of ideological interpellations, of emotional and political effects, all become discussable" (Diamond, 1996, p. 4). It is a discussion that moves discourse to storytelling performance, from autonomous texts to situated practices, from received storylines to emergent dramas with numerous possible "endings," and from omniscient narrators to a proliferation of unreliable reflexive voices. It is a discussion that creates and challenges social relations "within the performance event and perhaps even beyond it" (Langellier, 1999, p. 132; see also Denzin, 2003, pp. 10–11).

Performative writing brings the performance–performativity dynamic to the moment of texting in which identities and experiences are constructed, interpreted, and changed. It occurs when we encounter the page with the intention of entering into a discussion marked by contest and negotiation, embodied knowledge and vociferous exchange, emotional and intellectual charge. It occurs when we invite an audience into dialogue as we write, speak, and perform the words on the page, in our mouths, on our bodies, and in the world. Because the performance–performativity dynamic asserts that performances are inseparable from performers and that performativity is inseparable from politics, autobiographical performance, personal narrative, and performative auto/ethnography enmesh the personal within the political and the political within the personal in ways that can, do, and must matter.

## A Love Letter

It was my turn. I moved from my seat on the floor and into the chair beneath the window. All eyes—expectant and encouraging—were on me. I took a breath and began a story about torch singers and ghosts.

On the flight from Detroit to Paris, I read about the Edith Piaf Museum in the guidebook:

> Paris. Open by appointment 1–6 p.m. Closed Friday, Saturday, Sunday, and bank holidays. Private museum in an apartment. Memorabilia of the singer. China collection. Free.

I circle the phone number. I turn the dog-eared page. I close my eyes and begin listening for Piaf as she haunts Paris, as she haunts me, a present history singing her invisibility. . . .

I arrive at the apartment museum at 1 p.m. Melissa accompanies me as translator. The proprietor, Bernard Marchois, invites us in. Standing immediately in front of us is a black-and-white cardboard cutout of Piaf. Marchois tells us that the cutout was created as a lobby display for one of her last concerts at the Paris Olympia. He smiles. This is a life-sized portrait, he says. He puts his arm around the cardboard statue. He is not a tall man, but Edith looks like a tiny bird under his arm—yes, a sparrow.

He shows us into the sitting room, and Melissa and I look around. This place, like all of the others, is packed tight with Piaf memorabilia. These are *her* things—her records, her jewelry, her hastily scrawled letters, her black dress, her china. We sit on a couch. (Is it hers? Did she sit here?) Marchois pulls up a chair. Melissa explains that we're interested in hearing about Piaf's performances, about Piaf the woman. He nods and smiles. I ask him to tell us how they met. Melissa asks again, in French. He laughs. He explains that he met Piaf when he was a teenager. An older couple—friends of the family—invited him to see Piaf at the Olympia. Before the show, the couple took Marchois backstage to meet her. He was disappointed. She was frail and plain. She looked like a cleaning lady.

"Surprised?" she asked.

Marchois nodded sheepishly.

She laughed a round, full laugh. "You come back and see me after the show, eh?"

He was sure he had seen enough, but he nodded again.

"The show was electrifying. By the end of the show, I was smitten. I could barely contain my excitement as we made our way backstage. When we entered the dressing room, she turned that lightning smile on me."

"So, what do you think of me now?"

"She saw everything in my eyes."

She laughed. "Come," she said, and she pulled me into her embrace.

Marchois's eyes glisten. He sighs. He says they were friends, never lovers. He says she loved life, loved to laugh and play music, loved to sing. He says her songs were full of heartache, but that heartache was never hopeless. It was simply part of the equation of living. Her songs were signposts of the places she was in between—spaces of contradiction, tension, and immanent possibilities.[20] He says she loved sharing these places, these wounds of feeling. He says, again, she loved life.

I see the cardboard likeness of Piaf in the next room. I see the picture of Marchois with his arm around her—not the life-sized photo but [rather] what is pressing in from the other side of the image displayed within her tiny frame.[21] I see him sitting here, in an apartment filled with her teacups and earrings and stationery. I glance down at my notebook. My next question is, "Why do this? Why invite strangers into your home to talk about Edith Piaf?" I look up at him and I have my answer. He is an amateur, a careful collector of memories. He does this so that he might breathe life back in where only a vague memory or a bare trace was visible to those who bothered to look.[22] He lives among her things because looking at them and showing them to others is his lover's discourse.[23] He is writing ghost stories in a language of commonplace things that take on an immense power.[24] And with each day, with each conversation, he proclaims his love and writes his memories anew.

We leave the museum and walk toward the Metro station. Melissa asks if I got what I wanted. I say, Yes. No. I'm not sure, and maybe that's the point. I came to Paris looking for the real Edith Piaf, and I'm leaving with her ghost.

Melissa stops. Why do this? Why follow her ghost around Paris?

I have my answer: Because following a ghost is about making contact, and that contact changes you.[25]

Later, when I sit down to write this story of my encounter with Piaf and her ghost, I feel her watching over my shoulder as I move my fingers along the keys, always with me, the questioning, critical ghost of my text. She leaves wounds of feeling on my language; never hopeless, just part of living. My stories are love letters, invitations to hear the unspoken, unheard voices of the singer and myself.

## Performing Possibilities

I finished my story, and the audience was still and silent. Then the discussion began, pulling my story and me into a new performance. We talked of rhythm and thick description, theory and practice, haunting and writing. I was challenged and energized by our conversation. I envisioned new possibilities for my story and for the power of narrative to inscribe and embody a horizon of movement. I left the chair under the window and returned to my place on the floor.

I flew home from the conference and spent a few days writing and reading about performance, personal narrative, and performativity. I made note of what Madison (1998a) stated about the "performance of possibilities," that is, the "active, creative work that weaves the life of the mind with being mindful of life, of 'merging text and world,' of critically traversing the margin *and* the center, of opening more and different paths for enlivening relations and spaces" (p. 277).

Performances of possibilities are created in the momentum of movement from silence to voice and from margin to center. They provide a gathering place for narratives that seek change in "systems and processes that limit possibilities" (Madison, 1998a, p. 279). The space and movement of performances of possibilities are infused with the responsibility to ethically engage with selves and others in ways that do not forestall or foreclose dialogue. Performances of possibilities provide both the means and the method for an alterative, alternative ethnography. They are, to use Sandoval's (2000) description, subjunctive; they join together the possible and what is, they provide the medium "through which difference both arises and is undone; [they] join together through *movement*" (p. 180).

Then I returned to my dissertation, my love letter to torch singing. I brought these questions with me to my writing.

## Intimate Provocation

Madison's questions link the personal with the political and suggest how the turn toward performative narratives and narrative performances creates a politically efficacious poetics in and through movement (see also Conquergood, 2002; Langellier, 1999; Hartnett, 1998; Jones, 2002; Spry, 2001).

The lessons and challenges for autoethnography in the turn toward performance, performative writing, and personal narrative are clear. Autoethnographic texts are personal stories that are both constitutive and performative. They are charged exchanges of presence or "mutual presentness" (Dolan, 1993, p. 151). They are love letters—processes and productions of desire—for recognition, for engagement, and for change. Tedlock (1991) characterized the ethnographer's process as that of an amateur, which derives from the Latin *amatus* or "to love" (p. 82). Written and experienced in this way, autoethnography becomes an intimate provocation, a critical ekphrasis, a story of and with movement.

But like all stories, my account is partial, fragmented, and situated in the texts and contexts of my own learning, interpretations, and practices. Rather than end here in the intersections and interactive possibilities of narrative and performance, I want to tell you one more story, invent one more history, invoke one more discussion of the intricacies of theory and praxis. I want to tell you about socially resistive performance as a site and means of intimate provocation. I want to ask you to consider the place of autoethnography in this story.

## ▣ TURNING AGAIN: PERFORMING SOCIAL RESISTANCE

### Watching and Writing

When I was young—4 and 5 and 6 years old—I loved staying over on Saturday nights with my grandparents. I relished staying up late nights and having their undivided attention. But most of all, I loved watching *The Lawrence Welk Show*. My grandmother marveled at my fixation on the set. At first, she thought it was the bubbles that held my attention, but I watched everything—the musical numbers, the singers, the dancing. I clapped in time with the movement of Bobby and Sissy. I clapped in time with my grandfather's typewriter click-clacking in the other room.

My grandmother would call him in to see my performance, and the typing—the writing of letters, histories, and wild fictions—would stop. My grandfather would stroll into the living room to watch me. He would smile and pick me up, swinging me high over his head and onto his shoulders. He would hold my hands and spin me in time to Bobby and Sissy's waltz, swing, or foxtrot. And when the number was over, he would return me to my spot on the floor in front of the television and then return to his typewriter.

Out of sight, he would place his fingers on the keys and furiously tap out his own rhythm, vision, and story. And I would return to the dancing, the music, the singing, and the bubbles.

## Hopeful Openness

First, consider several ideas about theater and social change:

- That art does not mirror or transcend experience but rather is a means for creating and experiencing the world
- That what happens in a performance can influence, and can *change,* what happens in the world
- That the performer–spectator relationship is not fixed but rather malleable—that a spectator can be an active agent (e.g., cocreator, participant) *in* a performance rather than a passive consumer *of* a performance
- That performance creates a space in which participants not only glimpse who and what they are and desire but also come into contact with different identities, positions, and desires
- That such encounters can demand and facilitate response and action

Now, imagine these ideas as they are played out on stages and street corners, in lecture halls, and in coffee shops. Can you see and hear these performances? Can you imagine that each "models a hopeful openness to the diverse possibilities of democracy" (Dolan, 2001b, p. 2)?

Wait. Do not answer yet. I want to tell you one more story.

Performance has long been a site and means for negotiating social, cultural, and political dialogue (for two historical accounts of this process in different contexts, see Denning, 1997, and Scott, 1990). In the United States, activist theater has coalesced around social movements such as the labor movement of the 1930s, the civil rights and feminist movements of the 1960s and 1970s, and the AIDS activism of the 1980s (Cohen-Cruz, 2001, p. 95). The associations between social movements and activist performance, however, are opportunistic, tenuous, and changing. Such associations do not adequately describe the changing nature of social change theater. Instead, as Cohen-Cruz (2001) proposed, movements in the form and function of activist performance correspond to shifts in the ways in which performance posits the performer–audience–text–context relationship.[26]

During the late 1960s and early 1970s, the conditions for activist theater were ripe. Actors formed radical collectives that produced both realist drama and original work. The goals of these "actor-based, movement-linked" companies "were plain: get the United States out of Vietnam, enforce equal rights for all people regardless of race or ethnicity, boycott grapes" (Cohen-Cruz, 2001, p. 98). Although techniques were many, much of this work drew on Bertolt Brecht's concept of epic theater—performances that create a distinction among—and distance between— actor and character, text and context. Epic theater asks audiences to critically engage with and evaluate the performance and its social implications rather than get swept away in the emotional and nonevaluative force of theater-as-entertainment. Distinction and distance are what make theater an occasion for enlightened and involved citizenship as well as a powerful site and means for breaking into and refiguring our world (Brecht, 1957/1998, p. 125).

As the national movements with which these performances were allied began to fracture and shift, socially resistant performance also began to change (Cohen-Cruz, 2001, p. 99). Performers turned their attention to issues in their own communities and began to grapple with the need to express not only solidarity and unity but also the intricacies of identity, difference, and identification (pp. 98–99). During the 1980s, identity politics (e.g., efforts focused specifically on gay rights or gender equality) emphasized personal storytelling and creating an environment and process in which community members could participate in performances. Whereas 1960s "political theater was more consistently radical in *content*, community-based theater is more consistently radical in, and focused on, *process*" (p. 100, emphasis added). The force and power of this work inheres in creating reciprocity among artists and community members, linking the personal with the political, and instigating specific, local actions. Working with untrained participants meant that community-based theater relied heavily on workshops for developing and rehearsing performances. Workshop techniques, such as those developed by Augusto Boal, facilitated this process. Boal (1979/1985), whose work draws and builds on Brechtian principles, outlined several techniques to assist community members in creating "theater [as] a rehearsal for revolution" (p. 122). Whereas Brecht advocated a critically active spectator, Boal asserted that spectators must learn to become "spect-actors" and, as such, to actively participate in the unfolding drama on stage. In so doing, spect-actors train themselves for real action in the world (p. 122).

Participants did learn to become active participants on stage and in the world. They benefited from the performance in definable and material ways. Challenges surrounding the need to balance aesthetic concerns with the sharing of experience, the splintering effects of identity-based dialogues, and the need to connect local action to larger contexts precipitated a shift from community-based performance to theater and civic dialogue (Cohen-Cruz, 2001, p. 104). Theater and civic dialogue is focused on realigning and reconnecting the politics surrounding gender, race, class, and sexuality (among other identities and positions) in a way that does not obfuscate or collapse differences but instead puts these identities and positions in conflict and conversation with one another around an issue of civic importance (Dolan, 2001a, p. 90). The goal of civic dialogue performance is to "engage the public more fully with contemporary issues" (p. 106). As such, civic dialogue returns to the broad social, cultural, and political contexts and issues "reminiscent of 1960s theater, but from multiple perspectives" (p. 106). Civic dialogue performance is inspired and informed by an impetus to involve audiences in the wake of actual events to create critical engagement (hooks, 1995, p. 214).

Whereas the techniques of both Brecht and Boal formed the cornerstone for much theater practice in movement- and community-based theater, civic dialogue theater embraces a fluid and opportunistic approach to performative paradigms and styles (hooks, 1995, p. 219). Civic dialogue performance also takes advantage of the multiple sites available for engagement—live theater and street performance, television and the Internet, dance parties and spectacles (Orenstein, 2001, pp. 149–150). These performances must, as Orenstein (2001) asserted, "appeal to a broad audience by offering frameworks for protest that leave room for individual creativity and by eschewing overly restrictive or exclusive ideologies" (p. 151).

What lessons does this history offer for autoethnography? First, it provides another context for the turn to performance, performative writing, and personal performance narratives in interpretive, qualitative, critical, and narrative inquiry. Second, this history traces the movement between and among art and politics, individual and community, representation and participation. In the shifts toward reflexivity, inclusion, personal stories, local actions, multiple perspectives, and civic dialogue, social protest theater demonstrates how paradigms and techniques can be used in the service of making art matter and generating action in the world. Social protest theater's history also speaks to how the stories *we* tell can and do reflect back on, become entangled in, and critique this current historical moment and its discontents (Denzin, 1997, p. 200).

## Journalist . . . Artist

When I got a little older, my Saturday night stays with my grandparents in the company of Lawrence Welk were extended to weeklong visits over summer vacation. I would visit them at their lake house, with its screened porch, sloping lawn, and dense stand of trees. Inside the house, there was a guest bedroom with a white iron twin bed, just for me. There was my grandmother's electric organ, with its waltz, foxtrot, and bossa nova accompaniment. There were shelves of books and stacks of board games—Monopoly, Scrabble, and Parcheesi. There were all of these things to keep my hands and mind busy, and after 20 minutes or so I would whine that there was absolutely nothing to do.

I would start wondering how much longer it would be until my parents came to pick me up.

I would sprawl on the couch and sulk.

I would wander into the kitchen and watch my grandmother peeling potatoes. I would watch her so intently that she would turn around and ask, "What's the matter?"

"I'm *bored.*"

"Do you want to read?"

"No."

"Want to go outside and play?"

"Nope."

"Want Grandpa to play Scrabble with you?"

"No."

"Well then, dear, what do you want to do?"

And I would stare back at her, expressionless, until she would shrug and return to the potatoes.

We enacted this scene nearly every day during my visits. And then one day, my grandmother turned to me and said, "Why don't you write something?"

"*What?*" I had not heard that one before.

"Why don't you pretend you're a reporter and you're going to write a story for the evening edition of the paper?"

"But I don't know how to be a reporter."

"I'll show you."

And with that, my grandmother set off to look for my reporter's costume. She gave me a small pad and pencil. She gave me an old hat of my grandfather's. She wrote "Press" on a slip of paper and stuck it in the hatband. Then she said, "Why don't you interview Grandpa for your story?"

At least I think that is what she said. I was already looking for my grandfather.

He was sitting at the dining room table, staring at his typewriter. His hands were clasped behind his head. He was reading the newly typed sheet in front of him, silently mouthing the words. He looked up from his work and said, "Well, who is this?"

"I'm a reporter and I'm here to interview you for the evening edition!"

"Sure. Pull up a chair. Care for a drink?"

"Can't. I'm on the job."

"Very well, then. What can I do for you?"

I asked my grandfather how old he was, how much he weighed, and how tall he was.

I asked about his favorite color, record, and book. I asked him why he loved Grandma and whether he wished he could live forever. I asked him why he sat at his typewriter all afternoon and into the darkness, typing. He said that he was writing stories.

"Stories about what?"

"Stories about what I see when I close my eyes and listen very, very carefully."

"Listen to what?"

"To the radio. To the mourning doves. To you playing the organ. To the beating of my own heart."

He smiled and asked me whether I had any other questions. I said, "No, that does it." He went back to staring at the page and reading his words to himself. And then he put his fingers on the keys and began typing.

I stayed there, very still in my chair and wrote down the things I noticed about my grandfather as he worked—the way his glasses glinted when the light hit them, the way his right hand would raise up from the keys and push the return key and land back on the keys in one fluid motion, the way he smiled at being watched and documented.

I worked on my story for several days. When I was done, my grandmother pasted it onto a large sheet of construction paper. Both of my grandparents said that they liked my story very much.

The story I wrote at my grandparents' house that summer did not come out of nowhere. I intended to write it. I donned the costume of a reporter and played the role as I remembered it—watching carefully, asking questions, and writing things down. I do not recall how the story went, but I do know that it was about my grandfather's performance as an artist—as a writer. It was my attempt to document music, movement, and the beating of his heart. And although I did not know it then, this story was my attempt to write a text that enacted the very art it sought to inscribe.

## On Location

The "documentary idea" in solo performance, as Kalb (2001) put it, is to give an audience the impression of having been there "*on location*" (p. 20, emphasis added). For Kalb, the actual fact of being there is not as important as the rhetorical power of solo performance to generate "powerful topical narratives that are not easily dismissed or second-guessed, and for performance circumstances" in which Brecht's epic theater[27] "becomes a living concept again because the reality of the performer-researcher has been made an active part of the art" (p. 16). Documentary solo performance subscribes to an inherent duplicity—of fact and fiction, imagination and realism, objectivity and partisanship—that "recognizes the audience's sophistication regarding stories" (p. 22). It is this duplicity, along with a performer's ability to bridge and exploit the possibilities inherent in the move between documentary realism and fictionalization, that makes a performance compelling.

Anna Deavere Smith's performances *Fires in the Mirror* (regarding the 1991 riots in Crown Heights, Brooklyn, New York, following the death of a black boy struck by a rabbi's motorcade and the retaliatory stabbing of a Jewish student) and *Twilight: Los Angeles* (regarding the 1992 riots in Los Angeles following the acquittal of the police officers accused of beating Rodney King) offer striking examples of the duplicity of solo documentary performance.[28] Smith constructed these performances by interviewing people directly and indirectly involved in the events and delivered, "verbatim, their words and the essence of their physical beings in characterizations which fall somewhere between caricature, Brechtian epic gestures, and mimicry" (Reinelt, 1996, p. 609). Reinelt (1996) characterized Smith's performance technique as "a bridge that makes the unlikely seem connected. She ghosts her portraits with her own persona, signifying sympathy, fairness, and also her own subject position" (p. 615). Reinelt argued[29] that, in filtering the voices of (many) others through her own voice and oscillating between identification and difference,

> Smith needs to have it both ways. . . . She needs to be identified as both journalist and artist. In a sense, Smith dares to speak [for others] . . . *not* because she is objective, fair-minded, and even-handed, but because she demonstrates the process of bridging difference, seeking information and understanding, and finessing questions of identity. Since the audience is positioned in the direct address sequences to "be" Smith, they are positioned to experience the activity of bridging, working with difference. This effect is the most radical element of Smith's work—it engages the spectator in radical political activity to the extent that the spectator grapples with this epistemological process. (p. 615)

Smith's work enacts this bridging in the performance of personal stories. Rather than use these stories as a mirror for a subject's or an audience's unexamined experience, Smith's solo performances "turn the mirror into a political tool" (Kalb, 2001, p. 23; see also Dolan, 2001a, p. 89; Kondo, 2000). Smith noted, "My project is about . . . the gap between . . . the performer and the other and . . . the gap between the performer and the text" (quoted in Capo and Langellier, 1994, p. 68). By remaining critically present in her portrayal of others and their stories, Smith brings the performative to her performance. She eschews politically disengaged, reductive, and static *representation(s)* of events and participants in favor of work that *presents*—creates—a "generative engagement between performer and audience" in the negotiation among stories, selves, texts, and contexts (Salverson, 2001, p. 123). She moves through *mimesis* to *poiesis* and *kinesis.*

What happens when performers present their own stories? Solo performers often offer their personal stories as testimony about "real" events. Audiences witness such testimony and, as such, become implicated in the encounters. As Hughes and Román (1998) noted,

> When we attend a solo piece it's knowing that there is a good chance the performer is also the writer and the stories we will hear "really happened." There is some level of safety that disappears for the audience: we can't hide behind "it's only art." (p. 4; see also Miller, 1995)

Personal narrative performances deny any easy distinction between "art" and "life." Such performances retain their performative, political power in and through the ways in which they foreground the constitutive and shifting nature of giving testimony and witnessing. Rather than present experience as authentic (true) and untouchable (immune to critical commentary), solo performers create intimate provocations in which they testify and audiences bear witness to their stories (Gray & Sinding, 2002).

Robbie McCauley is a performer who writes, directs, and performs personal narrative, making explicit the social conditions in which her stories are situated (Whyte, 1993, p. 282). In telling personal narratives, McCauley "intends that her onlookers . . . , in witnessing the experiences she invokes in her performances, will begin to understand their own implication in the situations that she presents" (p. 282). In her work *Sally's Rape: The Whole Story,* McCauley explores how her own story is shaped by the stories of others, including her "great-great-grandmother Sally, a slave on the Monticello estate of Thomas Jefferson" (p. 280).[30] The work includes a scene in which McCauley stands naked on an auction block. Her white partner Jeannie Hutchins[31] instructs the audience to create the scene of a slave market by chanting "Bid 'em in, bid 'em in." McCauley performs a monologue in which the voice of Sally and her own voice are intertwined as her body is examined and violated. Whyte (1993) described her experience of this scene:

> For the onlooker there is an awe-ful fascination in this representation of the slave auction, this scene of victimage. The pleasure of looking at the naked body of the black woman is . . . made guilty by the awareness of being inescapably positioned as a potential buyer in the slave market. . . . Similarly, whether or not you join the chanting you are trapped by the sympathetic magic of sound which reanimates the past, and no matter how much you tell yourself you had nothing to do with this scene, you are made vicariously complicit in the auction system that McCauley's staging represents. (p. 278)

McCauley's work illustrates the ways in which giving testimony and witnessing can and must be situated in larger contexts and shared histories. Her performances ask audiences and performers to come together differently and deeply "without collapsing either the 'I' or the 'other' into a totalizing 'we'" (Salverson, 2001, p. 120). McCauley taps into the vulnerability required to tell personal stories to move audiences past simple, essentialist identification and toward a generative engagement with their differences. She noted, "When you engage your vulnerability around . . . issues that are both political and personal, then you can have something powerful happen between people" (quoted in Becker, 2000, p. 530).

Where does bridging the political and personal in solo performance move (and leave) performers and audiences? Hughes and Román (1998) wrote,

> "The personal is political" remain[s] a vital challenge for solo performers. . . . Consequently, few performance artists—no matter how skilled or funny—intend to simply entertain: they mean to provoke, to raise questions, to implicate their audiences. (pp. 8–9)

Thus, the idea of being *on location* as a solo performer means using personal stories to create "calculated disturbances" in social, cultural, and political networks of power

(Lane, 2002, p. 61). Writer, performer, and director Tim Miller commented on the exacting nature of these disturbances: "The whole reason for being an artist in this particular realm (performance) . . . is to respond quickly, effectively, and surgically to what you want to do" (quoted in Burnham, 1998, p. 35).

Miller's solo performances focus on gay rights and identities as these issues are reflected in/through the critical lens of his personal experience. His recent work *Glory Box* protests the failure of immigration laws to recognize gay and lesbian relationships, using the experience of his own relationship with his Australian Scottish partner. Writing about his experience traveling in the United States and performing *Glory Box*, Miller (2002) noted,

> I am trying to make my case to the communities I engage that this violence and injustice against lesbian and gay couples must stop. . . . I think theater is primarily a site for liberation stories and a sweaty laboratory to model possible strategies for empowerment. (para. 4)

For Miller, these strategies include explicit calls to action both within and outside of the performance. In each community in which he performs, Miller joins forces with national and local organizations invested in an issue, encourages community members to lobby their congressional representatives, asks audience members to sign petitions that support changes in legislation, and uses the performance as a catalyst for media coverage that will raise awareness about the issue (para. 7–11).

In addition to this "nuts-and-bolts activism," Miller asks his audience to engage in the more individual work of consciousness raising, which he terms "emotional and psychic . . . adjustments." For example, Miller's performance asks straight audience members to acknowledge their heterosexual privilege and asks gay and lesbian audience members to recognize the institutional and symbolic degradation of their lives (para. 12). In both its activist and consciousness-raising impulses, Miller's work "retains a personal and political investment that blurs the borders between public and private" (Dolan, 2001a, p. 114).

By taking their stories on location and using the duplicity of artistry and journalism, expert testimony and witnessing, solo performers teach us how to create, enact, and incite performances full of possibilities.

## Torch Stories

In my dream, I see my grandfather on my university campus. I am walking to the library when I see him. He is reading a newspaper in the coffee shop. I call to him, and he looks up from the pages. He stands and waves, and when I reach him we embrace. He buys me a cup of coffee, and we settle in for a long talk.

He says, "What are you writing about?"

"I'm writing about how we are called to participate in music, in texts. I'm writing about torch singing as a sounding of personal and political desire."

He raises his eyebrows. "Really?"

"I guess what I'm really doing is writing a series of stories about torch singing."

He nods. "That sounds like fun."

"It is."

We turn our attention to our coffee and other topics, although I keep the conversation about writing torch stories going in my head. They are stories about what happens in between binaries, stories about what occurs between participation and provocation, emotion and politics, subject and object, body and voice, intended meaning and literal meaning, form and function, monologue and dialogue, connection and distance, conclusions and possibilities. They are stories that begin with the idea that performance, because it is imbricated in a culture and vast spiral of relationships, is necessarily and thoroughly *political* (Colleran & Spencer, 1998, p. 1). They are stories that look into the gaps and contradictions between a modernist/realist perspective on performance that imagines that "stable meanings can . . . be 'shared' between author and reader, actor and audience, stage and auditorium" and a postmodern/anti-realist approach that deconstructs the "process of meaning-making itself" (Kershaw, 1999, p. 12).

Because of this, torch stories are stories that ask what happens when I try to understand performance by straddling the fence—with one foot planted in the realm of uncovering and celebrating difference, multiple subject positions, and ideological and political pluralism and with the other foot firmly placed inside the possibility of a community experience, a shared sense of agency, and concerted action directed at social change. They are, just as important, stories that ask what happens when audiences engage with texts that are overtly resistant not in form or content but rather in their activity as a subtle and indirect voicing (Holderness, 1992, p. 10). They are stories that want to have it both ways, to say that it depends.

In the gaps and fissures of cultural production and politics, these stories create, to use theater scholar Kershaw's (1999) term, a source of *freedom*. This freedom is doubled—"not just freedom from oppression, repression, [and] exploitation . . . but also freedom *to reach beyond* existing systems of formalized power, freedom to create currently unimaginable forms of association and action" (p. 18). The freedom found in performance—found in telling stories—creates a resistive and transgressive radicalism.

Kershaw (1999) preferred "radical" to "political" because "radical has no necessary ideological tendency. . . . It gestures . . . towards kinds of freedom that currently cannot be envisaged" (p. 18). These stories also "invite an ideological investment that it cannot itself determine"; they are a "performative process in need of direction" (p. 20). *One* direction that readers and audience members might take is to actively engage what Brecht (1957/1998) termed a "complex seeing" and hearing that allows for multiple perspectives within the tangle of identifications and difference without forgetting the need to expose systems of oppression or the desire to find new ways of being in the world (p. 44). Even so, the source and object of these desires vary; they depend on readers' and audience members' perspectives and ideological investments. These stories promise a performative field of dreams—if you want to hear a critique, it will come.

Because these stories create an open and indeterminate space for interpretation and action, tracing their political efficacy is something like tracking the movement of an unspoken idea. The accounts, ideas, and explanations that these stories contain are points of contact, although they do not connect in a direct route or on a logical course. They are spaces of hope—*destinations* that can be arrived at from any number of locations.

"About these stories you're writing," my grandfather says, pulling me back into the conversation. "Does anything radical happen in them?"[32]

"Well, I think so. Yes."

"Tell me."

## ◻ PERFORMATIVE PRAXIS: AUTOETHNOGRAPHY AS A POLITICS (FULL) OF POSSIBILITY

I began this chapter asking you to consider how our autoethnographic texts do not stand, speak, or act alone; are not texts alone; and do not want to be left alone. I wanted to create a noisy and fractious dialogue on and about personal stories, performance, and social change. I wanted to stage this dialogue in and through the flesh and breath of my own experience. I wanted to create a text that shows—performs—a writing practice that tries to respond to the crisis of praxis. I wanted to engage you in a conversation that says and does something about autoethnography. I wanted to suggest how we make our personal accounts count.

I want to close by asking you to keep this conversation going in your own texts, contexts, and praxes. I want you to take this conversation into the next turn, crisis, and moment in autoethnography and to move your work, "without hesitation or encumbrance from the personal to the political" (Denzin, 2000, p. 261). Drawing on the lessons that the turn toward personal narrative and performance has taught us, write your stories as they are constructed in and through the stories of others. Look at the intersections in the work of personal storytellers, performance ethnographers, and social protest performers described in this chapter and elsewhere as examples of how you might radically contextualize your texts and your subjectivity; embody personal and community accountability; attend to connection without collapsing or foreclosing debate, dialogue, and difference; move people to understand their world and its oppressions in new ways; and create the possibility of resistance, hope, and—*yes*—freedom (Denzin, 2003, pp. 33, 268). Ask how your texts can create and constitute social action—how your words can make a *difference* in and outside of individual processes of knowing and coming to know—and then *write* them and *share* them (B. Alexander, personal communication, August 2003). This, I believe, is the future of autoethnography.

It is the challenge of telling and showing, to borrow from Ellis (2000), stories that are not only necessary but also full of possibilities (p. 275). In the spirit of moving into this future, I want to challenge you to do the following:

■ *Recognize the power of the in-between.* Recognize the power of having it "both ways," of insisting on the interaction of message and aesthetics, process and product, the individual and the social. Recall how the crises, turns, and movements in and toward narrative, performance, and social protest theater are generated in the radical possibilities that exist in these in-betweens. Make work that "struggles to open the space between analysis and action, and to pull the pin on the binary opposition between theory and practice" (Conquergood, 2002, p. 145).

■ *Stage impossible encounters.* Create texts that stage what Cohen-Cruz (2001) termed "impossible encounters" in their "capacity to bring people in contact with ideas, situations, or others that appear to be totally different" (p. 105). Use these encounters as occasions to negotiate a debate and dialogue about issues of importance to you and the world. Remember that, as McCauley stated, "Dialogue is an act. . . . It is not before or after the act. Saying the words, allowing the dialogue, making dialogue happen is an act, a useful act in the moment" (quoted in Mahone, 1994, p. 213).

■ *Contextualize giving testimony and witnessing.* Perform the testimony and witnessing of personal stories in, through, and with larger social contexts. Consider that when we bring our texts to contexts, we can make work that constitutes a first step toward social change. Strive to make work that "might act as a doorway, an instrument of encounter, a place of public and private negotiations" (Salverson, 2001, p. 125) where the goal is to witness "within the context of the meeting with the person who testifies" (p. 121).

■ *Create disturbances.* Value texts that "mean to provoke, to raise questions, [and] to implicate" authors and audiences, texts that create disturbances (Hughes & Román, 1998, p. 9). Capitalize on the complicity wrought in writing and reading autoethnographic texts—in how, when we place our lives and bodies in the texts that we create, engage, and perform, they are "no longer just our own; for better or worse they have become part of a community experience" (Nudd, Schriver, & Galloway, 2001, p. 113). Write texts that insist that to be there—on location—"is to be implicated" (p. 115).

■ *Make texts of an explicit nature.* Respond to the need to be explicit in moving your readers and audiences intellectually, emotionally, and toward concerted social, cultural, and political action. Use your texts to "stage arguments, to embody knowledge and politics, to open a community to itself and the world in ways that are dangerous, visceral, compelling, and moving" (Dolan, 2001a, p. 62). Ask not only whether your texts are moving but also *how* they create movement and toward what *ends?* (Salverson, 2001, p. 122, emphasis added).

These are your challenges, and they are my own. In a handbook chapter that wants to move theory and method to action, it is the charge to make the personal political in your work and in my own. Will the chapter on autoethnography in the next edition of the *Handbook* ask whether there is a place for autoethnography in our conversations about a radical democratic politics, a poetics of change, or a performance of possibilities? Will this chapter end with this query, or will it constitute a beginning, an opening into a conversation about where we have been and how far we have come—in being willing and able to say that we are in a moment when the point of creating autoethnographic texts is to change the world?

## ▣ EPILOGUE: THERE ARE LIVING FORCES IN POETRY

You deal in dangerous and intimate provocations.
Yelling "Change!" in crowded theaters, committing efficacy to writing
believing that
there are living forces in . . . poetry.[33]

You take your politics personally
and make the personal political.
You stake your life story on re-presenting, not imitating;
bringing movement, not mirrors, to reality.

You understand how
theater, art, text, experience is what
we make of it
and we are made by that making.[34]

You play the imaginary
line between artist and activist.
You give flesh and breath to the theory that there are countless ways
of making do . . . and getting through.[35]

Is there a place for autoethnography in this poem?
You tell me.

## ▣ NOTES

1. Titled "Communication Studies 298: Colloquium in Communication," this special topics course was designed and taught by my mentor, Nick Trujillo, as a team ethnography course that focuses on studies of organizational culture. Trujillo (2003) discussed this course and

others in his essay, "Reflections on a Career in Academia." See also my essay, "What We Save: A Bricolage On/About Team Ethnography" (Holman Jones, 2003).

2. This text was published as "Fragments of Self at the Postmodern Bar" by Communication Studies 298 (1997).

3. This section has an obvious debt, and owes a sincere thanks, to Pelias's (1999) "Performance Is" (pp. 109–111).

4. For a discussion of how these questions anticipate the crises of representation, legitimation, and praxis, see Denzin (1997, pp. 3–14) and Lather (1993, pp. 673–674).

5. For a summary of these responses, see Denzin (1997, pp. 16–21).

6. The interest in personal narratives as auto/ethnographic texts owes a clear debt to the long-standing practice of telling personal stories among women anthropologists and the traditions and conventions of feminist ethnography. See, for example, Abu-Lughod (1990), Gordon (1988), Tedlock (2000), and Visweswaran (1997).

7. Paul Gray was the director of graduate studies and professor of performance studies at the University of Texas, Austin when I began my Ph.D. studies there in 1996. Reading and Performing was the first of several courses I took with him. Gray was the first (but certainly not the only) faculty member to encourage my interest in both performance and performing. He is an astute critic, powerful intellect, and enthusiastic mentor, and he is a teacher to whom I am happily indebted.

8. Ethnography is both a method for studying performance (projects that focus on the performance practices of particular individuals and cultures [Conquergood, 1992; Jackson, 1993; Jones, 2002; Madison, 1998b]) and a performance practice in its own right (a means of sharing the results of fieldwork [Gray, 2003; Mienczakowski & Morgan, 1993; Paget, 1995; Welker & Goodall, 1997]).

9. In Conquergood's (1991) essay, he explored four themes generated in and through the "deep epistemological, methodological, and ethical self-questioning" of the crisis of representation and an increased emphasis on critical approaches and theory.

10. Conquergood and Turner are not alone here. Clifford Geertz, Dell Hymes, Erving Goffman, Richard Bauman, Kenneth Burke, and other anthropologists, sociologists, folklorists, and linguists all are interested and involved in the performative turn (Stucky & Wimmer, 2002, pp. 12–13; see also Denzin, 1997, pp. 102–104).

11. This is adapted from Conquergood (1991), who wrote, "I want to think about performance as a complement, alternative, supplement, and critique of inscribed texts" (p. 191).

12. Carpenter (1993, p. 125).

13. I am drawing on Conquergood's (1992) description of the "varying meanings of the key word 'performance' as it has emerged with increasing prominence in cultural studies. This critical genealogy can be traced from performance as mimesis to poiesis to kinesis, performance as imitation, construction, dynamism" (pp. 83–84).

14. Joni Jones taught Performance Ethnography. Her work on performance and identity in the academy and her fieldwork with the Yoruba in Nigeria are central to the discussion and practice of performance ethnography and are an inspiration for my own work. Jones directed my dissertation, an ethnographic and performative study of torch singing. This work bears the mark and trace of her thoughtful, sincere, and challenging guidance.

15. This performance was my response to the assignment designed by Joni Jones. This assignment asked us to create what Pineau (2002) described as the use of performance as methodology (p. 50). She wrote, "Performance methodology means learning by doing and

might include any experiential approach that asks students to struggle bodily with course content" (p. 50; see also Alexander, 1999).

16. I am referencing Langellier's (1999) essay in which she wrote, "When personal narrative performance materializes performativity—when a narrator embodies identity and experience—there is always danger and risk" (p. 129).

17. I have found touchstones in Conquergood (1985, 1991, 2002), Denzin (1997), Lather (1993, 2001), Lincoln (1990), Pollock (1998), Richardson (2000), and Stewart (1996); see also Bochner (2000); Clough (2000); and Ellis (2000).

18. The conference was titled the Giant City Conference on Performative Writing and took place in April 2001 at Giant City Park in Makanda, Illinois. Each writer presented his or her work "under a small window that opened to the green woods" (Miller & Pelias, 2001, p. v). In this passage, I make reference to the "green window" (as the conference proceedings came to be titled) and to the piece shared by Gingrich-Philbrook (2001) that began this work.

19. I had the pleasure of taking courses titled Performing Autobiography and Writing and Performance Art with Lynn Miller while I attended the University of Texas as well as of having her help on my dissertation committee. Miller's passion for and knowledge about autobiographical performance has influenced my work and informed my understanding of how and why personal narrative performance matters in autoethnography.

20. Scott (1990, p. xii).

21. Gordon (1997, p. 107).

22. Gordon (1997, p. 22).

23. Barthes (1977/1978).

24. Carver (2001) wrote, "It's possible, in a poem or short story, to write about commonplace things and objects using commonplace but precise language, and to endow those things—a chair, a window curtain, a fork, a stone, a woman's earring—with immense, even startling power" (p. 89).

25. Gordon (1997, p. 22).

26. The shifts in form and process discussed here do not correspond neatly or entirely to chronological or sequential logic. The social protest theater strategies I describe (following Jan Cohen-Cruz) are not mutually exclusive, and all of these techniques are used in contemporary performance.

27. Kalb (2001) focused specifically on Brecht's notion of *Verfremdung* (alienation) in which audiences are encouraged to move beyond simple identification (empathy) with characters to a critical orientation in which actors are separate from characters and context is clearly connected to the text being presented.

28. See also Kalb's (2001) discussion of Marc Wolf, Danny Hoch, and Sarah Jones.

29. Reinelt (1996) was commenting on both the stage performance and video of *Fires in the Mirror,* produced for American Playhouse.

30. Whyte (1993) noted that McCauley's great-great-grandmother was not Sally Hemings, although Whyte pointed out that McCauley's performance "plays on the similarities between the lives of these two Sallies and those of other women slaves" (p. 292).

31. Portions of *Sally's Rape* were based on conversations with Hutchins about race, class, gender, history, and contexts. See Becker (2000, p. 520).

32. This is drawn from Kershaw (1999), who asserted that the questions we should ask about performance—and I would include stories—are "Has anything radical happened?" and "How was it done?" (p. 218).

33. Artaud (1958, p. 85).
34. Nudd, Schriver, and Galloway (2001, p. 15).
35. DeCerteau (1984, p. 29).

## ▣ References

Abu-Lughod, L. (1990). Can there be a feminist ethnography? *Women and Performance, 5*(1), 7–27.

Alexander, B. K. (1999). Moving toward a critical poetic response. *Theatre Topics, 9*(2), 107–125.

Alexander, B. K. (2000). *Skin Flint* (or, *The Garbage Man's Kid*): A generative autobiographical performance based on Tami Spry's *Tattoo Stories. Text and Performance Quarterly, 20,* 97–114.

Artaud, A. (1958). *The theater and its double* (M. C. Richards, Trans.). New York: Grove Press.

Barthes, R. (1977). *Image–music–text* (S. Heath, Trans.). New York: Hill & Wang.

Barthes, R. (1978). *A lover's discourse: Fragments* (R. Howard, Trans.). New York: Hill & Wang. (Originally work published in 1977)

Becker, B. (2000). Robbie McCauley: A journey toward movement. *Theatre Journal, 52,* 519–542.

Boal, A. (1985). *Theatre of the oppressed* (C. A. McBride & M. O. McBride, Trans.). New York: Theatre Communications Group. (Original work published 1979)

Bochner, A. P. (2000). Criteria against ourselves. *Qualitative Inquiry, 6,* 266–272.

Bochner, A. P. (2001). Narrative's virtues. *Qualitative Inquiry, 7,* 131–157.

Brecht, B. (1998). *Brecht on theatre: The development of an aesthetic* (J. Willett, Ed. & Trans.). New York: Hill & Wang. (Original work published 1957)

Burnham, L. F. (1998). Interview with Tim Miller. In G. Harper (Ed.), *Interventions and provocations: Conversations on art, culture, and resistance* (pp. 31–40). Albany: State University of New York Press.

Butler, J. (1991). Imitation and gender insubordination. In D. Fuss (Ed.), *Inside/Out: Lesbian theories, gay theories* (pp. 13–31). New York: Routledge.

Capo, K. E., & Langellier, K. M. (1994). Anna Deavere Smith on *Fires in the Mirror. Text and Performance Quarterly, 14,* 62–76.

Carpenter, W. (1993). Girl writing a letter. *Iowa Review, 23*(2), 125.

Carver, R. (2001). On writing. In W. L. Stull (Ed.), *Call if you need me: The uncollected fiction and other prose* (pp. 87–92). New York: Vintage Contemporaries.

Chadwick, A. (2003, May 27). *Researcher heads to Sahara to study ancient cultures (Part 1).* [Online.] Washington, DC: National Geographic Radio Expeditions and National Public Radio. Available: www.npr.org/templates/story/story.php?storyid=1275887

Clough, P. (2000). Comments on setting criteria for experimental writing. *Qualitative Inquiry, 6,* 278–291.

Cohen-Cruz, J. (2001). Motion of the ocean: The shifting face of U.S. theater for social change since the 1960s. *Theater, 31*(3), 95–107.

Colleran, J., & Spencer, J. S. (1998). Introduction. In J. Colleran & J. S. Spencer (Eds.), *Staging resistance: Essays on political theater* (pp. 1–10). Ann Arbor: University of Michigan Press.

Communication Studies 298. (1997). Fragments of self at the postmodern bar. *Journal of Contemporary Ethnography, 26*, 251–292.

Conquergood, D. (1985). Performing as a moral act. *Literature and Performance, 5*(2), 1–13.

Conquergood, D. (1991). Rethinking ethnography: Towards a critical cultural politics. *Communication Monographs, 58*, 179–194.

Conquergood, D. (1992). Ethnography, rhetoric, and performance. *Quarterly Journal of Speech, 78*, 80–123.

Conquergood, D. (1994). For the nation! How street gangs problematize patriotism. In H. W. Simons & M. Billig (Eds.), *After postmodernism: Reconstructing ideology critique* (pp. 200–221). London: Sage.

Conquergood, D. (2002). Performance studies: Interventions and radical research. *Drama Review, 46*(2), 145–156.

Daly, A., & Rogers, A. (2001). Carolee Schneemann: A life drawing. *Drama Review, 45*(2), 9–54.

DeCerteau, M. (1984). *The practice of everyday life* (S. F. Rendall, Trans.). Berkeley: University of California Press.

Denning, M. (1997). *The cultural front: The laboring of American culture in the twentieth century.* London: Verso.

Denzin, N. (1997). *Interpretive ethnography: Ethnographic practices for the 21st century.* Thousand Oaks, CA: Sage.

Denzin, N. (2000). Aesthetics and the practices of qualitative inquiry. *Qualitative Inquiry, 6*, 256–265.

Denzin, N. (2003). *Performance ethnography: Critical pedagogy and the politics of culture.* Thousand Oaks, CA: Sage.

Diamond, E. (1992). The violence of "we." In J. G. Reinelt & J. R. Roach (Eds.), *Critical theory and performance* (pp. 390–398). Ann Arbor: University of Michigan Press.

Diamond, E. (1996). Introduction. In E. Diamond (Ed.), *Performance and cultural politics* (pp. 1–12). London: Routledge.

Dolan, J. (1993). *Presence and desire: Essays on gender, sexuality, performance.* Ann Arbor: University of Michigan Press.

Dolan, J. (2001a). *Geographies of learning: Theory and practice, activism and performance.* Middleton CT: Wesleyan University Press.

Dolan, J. (2001b). Rehearsing democracy: Advocacy, public intellectuals, and civic engagement in theatre and performance studies. *Theatre Topics, 11*(1), 1–17.

Elam, H. J., Jr. (1997). *Taking it to the streets: The social protest theater of Luis Valdez and Amiri Baraka.* Ann Arbor: University of Michigan Press.

Ellis, C. (1995). *Final negotiations: A story of love, loss, and chronic illness.* Philadelphia: Temple University Press.

Ellis, C. (1997). Evocative autoethnography: Writing emotionally about our lives. In W. Tierney & Y. Lincoln (Eds.), *Representation and the text: Reframing the narrative voice* (pp. 116–139). Albany: State University of New York Press.

Ellis, C. (2000). Creating criteria: An ethnographic short story. *Qualitative Inquiry, 6*, 273–277.

Ellis, C. (2002). Shattered lives: Making sense of September 11th and its aftermath. *Journal of Contemporary Ethnography, 31*, 375–410.

Ellis, C. (2004). *The ethnographic I: A methodological novel about teaching and doing auto-ethnography.* Walnut Creek, CA: AltaMira.

Ellis, C., & Bochner, A. P. (1996). Introduction: Talking over ethnography. In C. Ellis & A. P. Bochner (Eds.), *Composing ethnography: Alternative forms of qualitative writing* (pp. 13–48). Walnut Creek, CA: AltaMira.

Ellis, C., & Bochner, A. P. (2000). Autoethnography, personal narrative, reflexivity: Researcher as subject. In N. K. Denzin & Y. S. Lincoln (Eds.), *Handbook of qualitative research* (2nd ed., pp. 733–768). Thousand Oaks, CA: Sage.

Friedwald, W. (1996). *Jazz singing: America's great voices from Bessie Smith to bebop and beyond.* New York: Da Capo.

Garrick, D. A. (2001). Performances of self-disclosure. *Drama Review, 45*(4), 94–105.

Geertz, C. (1983). *Local knowledge: Further essays in interpretive anthropology.* New York: Basic Books.

Gingrich-Philbrook, C. (1997). Refreshment. *Text and Performance Quarterly, 17,* 352–360.

Gingrich-Philbrook, C. (2001). Preface to the proceedings. In L. Miller & R. J. Pelias (Eds.), *The green window: Proceedings of the Giant City conference on performative writing* (p. vii). Carbondale: Southern Illinois University Press.

Goodall, H. L. (2000). *Writing the new ethnography.* Walnut Creek, CA: AltaMira.

Gordon, A. F. (1997). *Ghostly matters: Haunting and the sociological imagination.* Minneapolis: University of Minnesota Press.

Gordon, D. (1988). Writing culture, writing feminism: The poetics and politics of experimental ethnography. *Inscriptions, 3*(4), 7–24.

Gornick, V. (2001). *The situation and the story: The art of personal narrative.* New York: Farrar, Straus & Giroux.

Gray, R. (2003). Performing on and off the stage: The place(s) of performance in arts-based approaches to qualitative inquiry. *Qualitative Inquiry, 9,* 254–267.

Gray, R., & Sinding, C. (2002). *Standing ovation: Performing social science research about cancer.* Walnut Creek, CA: AltaMira.

Grumet, M. R. (2001). Autobiography: The mixed genre of public and private. In D. H. Holdstein & D. Bleich (Eds.), *Personal effects: The social character of scholarly writing* (pp. 165–177). Logan: Utah State University Press.

Hartnett, S. (1998). Democracy is difficult: Poetry, prison, and performative citizenship. In S. J. Dailey (Ed.), *The future of performance studies: Visions and revisions* (pp. 287–297). Annandale, VA: National Communication Association.

Hartnett, S. (1999). Four meditations on the search for grace amidst terror. *Text and Performance Quarterly, 19,* 196–216.

Holderness, G. (1992). Introduction. In G. Holderness (Ed.), *The politics of the theatre and drama* (pp. 1–17). New York: St. Martin's.

Holman Jones, S. (2003). What we save: A bricolage on/about team ethnography. *American Communication Journal, 6*(2). [Online]. Available: www.acjournal.org

hooks, b. (1995). Performance practice as a site of opposition. In C. Ugwu (Ed.), *Let's get it on: The politics of black performance* (pp. 210–221). Seattle: Bay Press.

Hopper, R. (1993). Conversational dramatism and everyday life performance. *Text and Performance Quarterly, 13,* 181–183.

Hughes, H., & Román, D. (1998). O solo homo: An introductory conversation. In H. Hughes & D. Román (Eds.), *O solo homo: The new queer performance* (pp. 1–15). New York: Grove Press.

Iser, W. (1993). *The fictive and the imaginary: Charting literary anthropology.* Baltimore, MD: Johns Hopkins University Press.

Jackson, S. (1993). Ethnography and the audition: Performance as ideological critique. *Text and Performance Quarterly, 13,* 21–43.

Jackson, S. (1998). White noises: On performing white, on writing performance. *Drama Review, 42*(1), 49–65.

Jago, B. (2002). Chronicling an academic depression. *Journal of Contemporary Ethnography, 31,* 729–757.

Jones, J. L. (1996). The self as other: Creating the role of Joni Jones the ethnographer for Broken Circles. *Text and Performance Quarterly, 16,* 131–145.

Jones, J. L. (1997a). Performing Osun without bodies: Documenting the Osun Festival in print. *Text and Performance Quarterly, 17,* 69–93.

Jones, J. L. (1997b). Sista docta: Performance as critique of the academy. *Drama Review, 41,* 51–67.

Jones, J. L. (2002). Performance ethnography: The role of embodiment in cultural authenticity. *Theatre Topics, 21,* 1–15.

Kalb, J. (2001). Documentary solo performance. *Theater, 31*(3), 13–29.

Kemp, A. (1998). This black body in question. In P. Phelan & J. Lane (Eds.), *The ends of performance* (pp. 116–129). New York: New York University Press.

Kershaw, B. (1999). *The radical in performance: Between Brecht and Baudrillard.* London: Routledge.

Kisliuk, M. (2002). The poetics and politics of practice: Experience, embodiment, and the engagement of scholarship. In N. Stucky & C. Wimmer (Eds.), *Teaching performance studies* (pp. 99–117). Carbondale: Southern Illinois University Press.

Kondo, D. (2000). (Re)Visions of race: Contemporary race theory and the cultural politics of racial crossover in documentary theater. *Theatre Journal, 52,* 81–107.

Krieger, M. (1992). *Ekphrasis: The illusion of the natural sign.* Baltimore, MD: Johns Hopkins University Press.

Lane, J. (2002). Reverend Billy: Preaching, protest, and postindustrial flânerie. *Drama Review, 46*(1), 60–84.

Langellier, K. M. (1999). Personal narrative, performance, performativity: Two or three things I know for sure. *Text and Performance Quarterly, 19,* 125–144.

Lather, P. (1993). Fertile obsession: Validity after poststructuralism. *Sociological Quarterly, 34,* 673–693.

Lather, P. (2001). Postbook: Working the ruins of feminist ethnography. *Signs, 26*(4), 199–227.

Lincoln, Y. S. (1990). The making of a constructivist. In E. C. Guba & Y. S. Lincoln (Eds.), *The paradigm dialog* (pp. 67–87). Newbury Park, CA: Sage.

Lockford, L. (2002). From silence to siren to silence: A personal tale of political consequence. *Qualitative Inquiry, 8,* 622–631.

Madison, D. S. (1998a). Performance, personal narratives, and the politics of possibility. In S. J. Dailey (Ed.), *The future of performance studies: Visions and revisions* (pp. 276–285). Annandale, VA: National Communication Association.

Madison, D. S. (1998b). That was my occupation: Oral narrative, performance, and black feminist thought. In D. Pollock (Ed.), *Exceptional spaces: Essays in performance and history* (pp. 319–342). Chapel Hill: University of North Carolina Press.

Mahone, S. (1994). *Moon marked and touched by the sun.* New York: Theatre Communications Group.

Mienczakowski, J., & Morgan, S. (1993). *Busting: The challenge of the drought spirit.* Brisbane, Australia: Griffith University.

Miller, L. C. (1995). "Polymorphous perversity" in women's performance art: The case of Holly Hughes. *Text and Performance Quarterly, 15,* 44–58.

Miller, L. C. (1998). Witness to the self: The autobiographical impulse in performance studies. In J. S. Trent (Ed.), *Communication: Views from the helm for the 21st century* (pp. 318–322). Boston: Allyn & Bacon.

Miller, L. C., & Pelias, R. J. (2001). A beginning preface. In L. C. Miller & R. J. Pelias (Eds.), *The green window: Proceedings of the Giant City conference on performative writing* (pp. v–vi). Carbondale: Southern Illinois University Press.

Miller, T. (2002). *Solo performing as call to arms.* [Online.] Available: www.communityarts.net/readingroom/archie/32miller.php

Neumann, M. (1996). Collecting ourselves at the end of the century. In C. Ellis & A. P. Bochner (Eds.), *Composing ethnography: Alternative forms of qualitative writing* (pp. 172–198). Walnut Creek, CA: AltaMira.

Nudd, D. M., Schriver, K., & Galloway, T. (2001). Is this theater queer? The Micke Faust Club and the performance of community. In S. C. Haedick & T. Nellhaus (Eds.), *Performing democracy: International perspectives on urban community-based performance* (pp. 104–116). Ann Arbor: University of Michigan Press.

Olesen, V. (2000). Feminisms and qualitative research at and into the millennium. In N. K. Denzin & Y. S. Lincoln (Eds.), *Handbook of qualitative research* (2nd ed., pp. 215–255). Thousand Oaks, CA: Sage.

Orenstein, C. (2001). Agitational performance, now and then. *Theater, 31*(3), 139–151.

Paget, M. A. (1995). Performing the text. In J. Van Maanen (Ed.), *Representation in ethnography* (pp. 222–272). Thousand Oaks, CA: Sage.

Park-Fuller, L. M. (2000). Performing absence: The staged personal narrative as testimony. *Text and Performance Quarterly, 20,* 20–42.

Pelias, R. J. (1992). *Performance studies: The interpretation of aesthetic texts.* New York: St. Martin's.

Pelias, R. J. (1999). *Writing performance: Poeticizing the researcher's body.* Carbondale: Southern Illinois University Press.

Pelias, R. J. (2002). For father and son: An ethnodrama with no catharsis. In A. P. Bochner & C. Ellis (Eds.), *Ethnographically speaking: Autoethnography, literature, and aesthetics* (pp. 35–43). Walnut Creek, CA: AltaMira.

Pineau, E. L. (2002). Critical performative pedagogy: Fleshing out the politics of liberatory education. In N. Stucky & C. Wimmer (Eds.), *Teaching performance studies* (pp. 41–54). Carbondale: Southern Illinois University Press.

Pollock, D. (1998). Performing writing. In P. Phelan & J. Lane (Eds.), *The ends of performance* (pp. 73–103). New York: New York University Press.

Pratt, M. B. (1995). *S/HE.* Ithaca, NY: Firebrand Books.

Reed-Danahay, D. E. (1997). *Auto/Ethnography: Rewriting the self and the social.* Oxford, UK: Berg.

Reinelt, J. (1996). Performing race: Anna Deavere Smith's *Fires in the Mirror. Modern Drama, 39,* 609–617.

Reinelt, J. (1998). Notes for a radical democratic theater: Productive crisis and the challenge of indeterminacy. In J. Colleran & J. S. Spencer (Eds.), *Staging resistance: Essays on political theater* (pp. 283–300). Ann Arbor: University of Michigan Press.

Richardson, L. (1997). *Fields of play: Constructing an academic life.* New Brunswick, NJ: Rutgers University Press.

Richardson, L. (2000). Writing: A method of inquiry. In N. K. Denzin & Y. S. Lincoln (Eds.), *Handbook of qualitative research* (2nd ed., pp. 923–948). Thousand Oaks, CA: Sage.

Ricoeur, P. (1986). *Lectures on ideology and utopia* (G. H. Taylor, Ed.). New York: Columbia University Press.

Ronai, C. R. (1995). Multiple reflections of child sex abuse: An argument for a layered account. *Journal of Contemporary Ethnography, 23,* 395–426.

Salverson, J. (2001). Change on whose terms? Testimony and an erotics of inquiry. *Theater, 31*(3), 119–125.

Sandoval, C. (2000). *Methodology of the oppressed.* Minneapolis: University of Minnesota Press.

Scott, G. F. (1994). *The sculpted word: Keats, ekphrasis, and the visual arts.* Hanover, NH: University Press of New England.

Scott, J. C. (1990). *Domination and the arts of resistance: Hidden transcripts.* New Haven, CT: Yale University Press.

Solomon, A. (1997). *Re-dressing the canon: Essays on theatre and gender.* London: Routledge.

Spry, T. (2000). Tattoo stories: A postscript to *Skins. Text and Performance Quarterly, 20,* 84–96.

Spry, T. (2001). Performing autoethnography: An embodied methodological praxis. *Qualitative Inquiry, 7,* 706–732.

Stewart, K. (1996). *A space on the side of the road: Cultural poetics in an "other" America.* Princeton, NJ: Princeton University Press.

Stoller, P. (1997). *Sensuous scholarship.* Philadelphia: University of Pennsylvania Press.

Stucky, N. (1993). Toward an aesthetics of natural performance. *Text and Performance Quarterly, 13,* 168–180.

Stucky, N. (2001). Preface to the proceedings. In L. Miller & R. J. Pelias (Eds.), *The green window: Proceedings of the Giant City conference on performative writing* (p. vii). Carbondale: Southern Illinois University Press.

Stucky, N., & Wimmer, C. (2002). The power of transformation in performance studies pedagogy. In N. Stucky & C. Wimmer (Eds.), *Teaching performance studies* (pp. 1–29). Carbondale: Southern Illinois University Press.

Tedlock, B. (1991). From participant observation to the observation of participation: The emergence of narrative ethnography. *Journal of Anthropological Research, 47,* 69–94.

Tedlock, B. (2000). Ethnography and ethnographic representation. In N. K. Denzin & Y. S. Lincoln (Eds.), *Handbook of qualitative research* (2nd ed., pp. 455–486). Thousand Oaks, CA: Sage.

Trujillo, N. (2003). Reflections on a career in academia: A response. *American Communication Journal, 6*(2). [Online.] Available: www.acjournal.org

Tyler, S. A. (1986). Post-modern ethnography: From document of the occult to occult document. In J. Clifford & G. E. Marcus (Eds.), *Writing culture: The poetics and politics of ethnography* (pp. 122–140). Berkeley: University of California Press.

Van Maanen, J. (1988). *Tales of the field.* Chicago: University of Chicago Press.

Vickers, M. H. (2002). Researchers as storytellers: Writing on the edge—without a safety net. *Qualitative Inquiry, 8,* 608–621.

Visweswaran, K. (1997). Histories of feminist ethnography. *Annual Review of Anthropology, 26,* 591–621.

Welker, L. S., & Goodall, H. L. (1997). Representation, interpretation, and performance: Opening the text of *Casing a Promised Land. Text and Performance Quarterly, 17,* 109–122.

Whyte, R. (1993). Robbie McCauley: Speaking history other-wise. In L. Hart & P. Phelan (Eds.), *Acting out: Feminist performances* (pp. 277–293). Ann Arbor: University of Michigan Press.

# 8

# THE METHODS, POLITICS, AND ETHICS OF REPRESENTATION IN ONLINE ETHNOGRAPHY

Annette N. Markham

*in cyberspace, one dwells in language. and through language
i exist as myself in language online . . . it feels more like being me
than i sometimes feel offline. . . I think myself in language is more
communicative of who i am. and because i'm a good writer, eloquence makes me beautiful . . .*

—Sherie, online interview participant

*Here, I can edit what I think before I say it. This makes communi-
cation easier between my friends and I. There are fewer errors in
meaning when our thoughts have been written clearly.*

—Robin, online interview participant

*My ambiguity makes you nervous. I can be many things at once
here. Are they all 'me'? Who am I? 'He' . . . 'Her' . . . 'Per' . . .
'It' . . . 'We' . . . ? Can't you tell? Why do you want to know???*

—DominOH!, online interview participant

Whether one studies the Internet as a social structure or utilizes Internet-based technologies as tools for research, Internet-based technologies change the research scenario. Computer mediation has a significant influence on many aspects of communication practice and theory. The internet has similarities to many earlier media for communication, such as letter writing, telephone, telegraph, Post-It Notes, and so forth. At the same time, the capacities and uses of Internet communication are unique in configuration and shape a user's (and thus the researcher's) perceptions and interactions. These influences extend beyond the interpersonal; outcomes of these communication processes have the potential to shift sensemaking practices at the cultural level. We are, as Gergen (1991) notes, saturated in technologies. The Internet and associated communication media permeate and alter interactions and the possible outcomes of these interactions at the dyadic, group, and cultural level.[1] Equally, Internet technologies have the potential to shift the ways in which qualitative researchers collect, make sense of, and represent data.

In technologically mediated environments, self, other, and social structures are constituted through interaction, negotiated in concert with others. The extent to which information and communication technology (ICT) can mediate one's identity and social relations should call us to epistemological attention. Whether or not we do research of physical or online cultures, new communication technologies highlight the dialogic features of social reality, compelling scholars to reexamine traditional assumptions and previously taken-for-granted rubrics of social research.

In the early 1990s, as the capacities of the Internet became more publicly known and accessed, the use of the Internet for the development of personal relationships and social structures grew, as did the study of computer-mediated subjectivity and community. Through a phone line, access to the Internet, and specialized software, people could meet and develop relationships with others from the privacy of their homes. People could do this anonymously if they chose, creating personae that were similar to or highly distinctive from what they perceived their physical personae to be. They could create or join communities based on like-mindedness rather than physical proximity.

During these early years when Internet and virtual reality technologies caught public and scholarly interest, the study of computer-mediated communication (CMC) worked from theoretical extremes: On the one hand, computer-mediated communication was lauded as a means of transcending the limits associated with human embodiment. By erasing sociocultural markers such as race and gender or escaping the body altogether, virtual communication would lead to a utopian society whereby democratic participation in public discourse was unhindered by physicality and corresponding stereotypes. At the other extreme, skeptics critiqued CMC because it removed essential socioemotional or nonverbal cues and would result in impoverished, low-trust relationships at best and social withdrawal, at worst. Citizens would resemble hackers: pale, reclusive, and prone to eating pizza and Chinese take-out. As time passed, use grew, novelty diminished, and more measured accounts emerged based less on theoretical speculation and more on study of actual contexts.[2] It became clear that meaningful and significant relationships and social structures could thrive in text-only online environments. This capacity is now taken for granted. The past decade of communication has included forms new to many of us: email, mailing lists, Multi User Dimensions (MUDs or MOOs), real time chatrooms, instant messaging, Web sites, blogs, and so forth. We are now familiar with the concepts of cybersex, online marriages, Friendster, and other creative uses of technology to enact identity and relationships through computer-mediation. Many of us can probably name close colleagues and friends whom we would not recognize in person.

The computer-mediated construction of self, other, and social structure constitutes a unique phenomenon for study. In online environments, the construction of identity is a process that must be initiated more deliberately or consciously. Offline, the body can simply walk around and be responded to by others, providing the looking glass with which one comes to know the self. Online, the first step toward existence is the production of discourse, whether in the form of words, graphic images, or sounds. But as many scholars have taught us (e.g., Bakhtin, 1981; Blumer, 1969; Buber, 1958; Laing, 1969), we understand our Self only in concert with Other, a continual dialogic process of negotiation and a great deal of faith in shared meaning (Rommetveit, 1980).

In most computer-mediated environments, this process requires a more deliberate exchange of information because people are not co-present in the same physical space and the nonverbal aspects of the process are, for the most part, missing. The process is obfuscated because a person typically takes knowledge of self for granted with little reflection on the social, interactive process by which the self is negotiated with others in context. Mostly overlooked by users, the production of the message is only the first part of the process: Whether by receiving a reply message or by tracking a virtual footprint of a visitor to one's Web site, one can only know if one has been acknowledged through some sort of response. MacKinnon's insights in this matter (1995) warrant repeating here. He notes that the common phrase "I think, therefore I am" is woefully inadequate in cyberspace. Even "I speak, therefore I am" is not enough. In cyberspace, the more appropriate phrase is "I am perceived, therefore I am." (p. 119). Implied in this last phrase is the fact that online, perception of another's attention is only known by overt response. So we can usefully note this by adding the phrase "I am responded to, therefore I am" (Markham, 2003a).

The participant statements (from my previous research of Internet users) at the beginning of this chapter represent well the importance of text to a person's construction and negotiation of identity in online text-based environments. Sherie expresses a desire to be known solely as text (not through, but *as* text). For Sherie, computer-mediated communication is a way of being. Robin always uses correct punctuation and strives to make the meaning as clear as possible. Text is perceived as a powerful means of controlling, through editing and backspacing, the way the self is presented to others. DominOH!, unlike the other two, does not pay much attention to the textual, linguistic aspects of the medium. Rather, DominOH! uses the technology as an interaction space which protects anonymity and allows the social self to be less firmly attached to the body. Yet the text is vital to the researcher's understanding of DominOH!'s persona online.

For all three personae interviewed, text remains the means through which each performs and negotiates the self. None of these textual entities exists in isolation. Their existence is made possible by direct or perceived interaction with others. They are communicative through and through; their social being is initiated through a process of creating and sending a message and negotiated through a process of interaction.

Although we recognize that reality is socially negotiated through discursive practice, the dialogic nature of identity and culture is thrown into high relief in computer-mediated environments. This gives rise to many possibilities and paradoxes in social research. For any researcher studying life online, the traditional challenge of understanding other-in-context is complicated by the blatant interference of the researcher into the frame of the field and by the power of the researcher in representing the culture. Researchers have always interfered with the context in some way while conducting research. In the past three or more decades, scholars have problematized this feature of research, as well as highlighted the blurring of boundaries between researcher and researched. Still, these issues become startlingly apparent—and challenging—in the context of CMC environments.

These issues call not only for adjustment of traditional methods to online environments or the creation of new methods, but also for across-the-board reassessment and interrogation of the premises of qualitative inquiry in general. Interestingly, the specific logistic and analytic problems associated with the interpretive study of computer-mediated personae reveal many weaknesses in qualitative methods and epistemologies, generally. In the years I have spent trying to figure out how to make sense of participants whose gender, name, body type, age, ethnicity, class, and location remain inexplicable, I have been compelled to seriously examine certain practices of Othering which, despite efforts to be reflexive, hide in everyday, embodied ways of knowing. Put more positively, studying computer-mediated interactions allows and encourages exploration of what is happening in "the hyphen that both separates and merges personal identities with our inventions of Others" (Fine, 1994, p. 70).

New communication technologies privilege and highlight certain features of interaction while obscuring others, confounding traditional methods of capturing and examining the formative elements of relationships, organizations, communities and cultures. Additionally, a person's conceptual framework of any new communication technology will predetermine, to a certain extent, that person's understanding of, response to, and interaction with the technology. This complicates the researcher's ability to assume commonalities among participants' communicative practices via CMC, or to presume that participants understand and use the technology in the same way the researcher does. The challenge for the qualitative researcher in the computer-mediated environment is to attend to the details of how one is going about the process of getting to know something about the context and the persons being studied.

At the same time, examining one's own influence in the shape of the outcome is a vital practice. Grappling with both the practical and the epistemological implications of this influence can help researchers make more socially responsible decisions. In a very real sense, every method decision is an ethics decision, in that these decisions have consequences for not just research design but also the identity of the participants, the outcomes of our studies, and the character of knowledge which inevitably grows from our work in the field.

In this chapter, I describe some of the tensions and complications that can arise in the qualitative study of Internet-mediated contexts when decisions must be made about (a) defining the boundaries of the field, (b) determining what constitutes data, (c) interpreting the other as text, (d) using embodied sensibilities to interpret textuality, and (e) representing the other ethically in research reports. My overall object in this discussion is to illustrate some of the challenges of doing research in computer-mediated environments and to display the significance of the researcher's choices on the field's structure, on the other's embodied or reported Being, and ultimately, on the social knowledge derived from the research project. The discussion is intended to help researchers generate questions which can be used to interrogate their own epistemological and axiological assumptions throughout the design and enactment of the inquiry. In addition to this primary train of thought, I talk briefly about how the Internet is conceptualized, review some of the main shifts in thinking about qualitative Internet research, and discuss some of the major ethical considerations which are entwined with this type of inquiry.

To clarify what this chapter does and does not do: First, this chapter focuses on textuality. The examples throughout this chapter draw primarily on text-based computer-mediated discourse and interactions among participants or between participant and researcher. Although technologies facilitate visual and audio simulations and representations and the capacities of the traditional PC are moving to mobile or convenience devices, text remains a primary unit of analysis for the qualitative researcher. Put differently, the issues raised here apply equally to multi-media and mobile aspects of CMC because these are, for the most part, analyzed as texts, broadly speaking.

Second, even though this chapter focuses on computer-mediated contexts, the spirit of these arguments applies to other forms of interaction, both online and offline. The intriguing thing about CMC is that it calls attention to the ways we literally see and make sense of the world and points out many of the biases inherent in our traditional ways of seeing and knowing. Therefore, one should not dismiss the challenges discussed herein even if doing radically different types of qualitative research.

Third, this chapter does not seek to provide an overview of how qualitative research is conducted on or via the Internet, but rather, addresses key epistemological and methodological questions facing ethnographers researching in social spaces constituted in part or wholly through new communication technologies. Many sources exist to aid the researcher with specific procedures and methods for qualitative studies (this volume) and qualitative Internet studies (e.g., Johns, Chen, & Hall, 2003; Mann & Stewart, 2000).

Finally, this chapter focuses more on problems and challenges than opportunities and potential of CMC-related research environments. This imbalance is not indicative of my own or a general attitude toward qualitative Internet research. Here, however, I want to build a case for cautious, reflexive, and prepared research which, while celebrating those aspects of new communication technologies that make them well suited for qualitative inquiry, remains attentive to the consequences of one's research choices.

## ▣ SHIFTING LENSES

The study of CMC spans virtually every academic discipline and methodological approach. Research objects and lenses have shifted rapidly in the past decade or so, commensurate with the rapid development and dissemination of information and communication technologies (ICT). Qualitative study of ICT in the past decade has tended to shift in two ways. First, though not a universal trend, research has tended to shift from strongly polarized depictions and predictions in the early 1990s, to more descriptive accounts in the mid-late 1990s and, in the new century, to more theoretically grounded, comparative, or theory-building studies.

Accounts of CMC, identity, and culture throughout the early 1990s were heavily influenced by pop culture descriptions of and personal experience with novel and exciting forms of interaction. Gibson's term *Cyberspace*, coined in his science fiction novel *Neuromancer*, offered the elusive but intriguing definition of online experience as "a consensual hallucination experienced daily by billions of legitimate operators, in every nation, by children being taught mathematical concepts. . . . A graphical representation of data abstracted from the banks of every computer in the human system. Unthinkable complexity. Lines of light ranged in the non-space of the mind, clusters and constellations of data. Like city lights, receding" (1984). About virtual reality, Rheingold (1991) told readers "*we have to decide fairly soon what it is we as humans ought to become, because we're on the brink of having the power of creating any experience we desire*" (p. 386, emphasis in original). Wright (1994) told us simply that it would "deeply change politics, culture, and the fabric of society—if not, indeed, the very metaphysics of human existence" (p. 101). Barlow offered a vision of Cyberspace as the Wild West, a final frontier to be claimed: "Cyberspace . . . is presently inhabited almost exclusively by mountain men, desperadoes and vigilantes, kind of a rough bunch. . . . And as long as that's the case, it's gonna be the Law of the Wild in there" (cited in Woolley, 1992, pp. 122–123). Keeps (1993) suggested that virtuality through computer-mediated communication "announces the end of the body, the apocalypse of corporeal subjectivity" (p. 4).

These ideas caught the imagination of scholars and influenced significantly the tone of research. This is not surprising: With the invention or new use of every communication technology in the past century, claims regarding media effects tend to be overestimated and exaggerated as long as the technology remained novel. Although this period was not without empirically based and theoretically grounded research, there was a feeling of utopianism in descriptions of how technology might (or should) free us from the constraints of worldwide shackles like hierarchy, traditional social stereotypes, embodiment, and even death. Rheingold's *Virtual Community* (1993) and Benedikt's edited collection *Cyberspace: First Steps* (1991) represent this trend well. To give these authors credit, their ideas sparked the interest of many scholars whose work followed.

Simultaneously, research was influenced by news coverage, movies, and pop culture accounts that predicted negative, even dire consequences of this new Internet era. *Time Magazine* offered a cover story on "Cyberporn," wherein readers learned that the Internet threatened our children's safety (from adult sexual predators) and innocence (from easy access to pornography). Vastly exaggerated claims incited sound criticism; the magazine editors had relied exclusively on evidence supplied by an undergraduate student's non-peer-reviewed study. Critiqued or not, this issue of *Time* was quoted by legislators, parents, and scholars. "Internet Addiction Disorder" entered the medical lexicon in 1996. Popular films spelled out the dangers of identity theft, hackers, and spending too much time in front of one's computer. Pundits predicted that face-to-face interactions would become impoverished as people forgot the intricacies and delicacies of human interaction in physical environments.

These swings have evened out in the last few years, resulting in published accounts which exhibit many of the more traditional characteristics of social research. Scholars are explaining their approach and methods more carefully, grounding their work in previous research more thoroughly, and attending more closely to the history of communication technologies as well as the history of qualitative inquiry. The targets of research continue to follow shifts in technological development. Herring (2004) aptly notes that researchers have tended to follow novelty; researchers quickly flock to each new technology. Research in the 1980s tended to focus on the use and impact of computers, email, and networking in the workplace (overviewed well by Sproull & Kiesler, 1991). In the 1990s, research waves moved progressively through various forms of CMC, such as Email, Usenet, MUDs and MOOs, the World Wide Web, IM (Instant Messaging), SMS (Short Messaging Service via mobile telephone), and Blogs.

Various social interaction practices and social structures received empirical attention over the past decade: Flaming and other forms of emotionally charged or violent acts (e.g., Dery, 1994; Dibbell, 1996; MacKinnon, 1998); the use of emoticons to compensate for the absence of nonverbals (Witmer & Katzman, 1998); the social construction of virtual communities via mailing lists (e.g., Baym, 2000; Bromseth, 2002; Rheingold, 1993; Sveningsson, 2001), MUDs or MOOs (e.g., Kendall, 1998; Reid, 1995) or Web sites (Johnson, 2003); the intersection of technology and identity (e.g., Lupton, 1995; Markham, 1998; Senft & Horn, 1996; Sondheim, 1996; Stone, 1996; Turkle, 1995); sexuality (e.g., Keisler, 1997; Waskul, Douglass, & Edgley, 2000); gender and participation in CMC (e.g., Herring, 1993); and race (Kolko, Nakamura, & Rodman, 2000). Ethnographically informed studies have focused on online groups (e.g., Baym, 2000; Eichhorn, 2001; Kendall, 1998; Orgad, 2002; Reid, 1995); use of Internet in traditional, physically based cultures (e.g., Miller & Slater, 2000); cultural formation around particular topics (e.g., Hine, 2000); and sensemaking in specialized environments such as virtual work teams (e.g., Shane, 2001).

Multiple anthologies offered accounts of cyberculture (e.g., *High Noon on the Electronic Frontier* [Ludlow, 1996]; *the Cybercultures Reader* [Bell & Kennedy, 2000]). Utilizing both pop culture and academic accounts, these texts provide a useful overview of the 1990s viewpoints about computer-mediated communication and cultural practice. Few resources existed during the 1990s to specifically guide qualitative researchers. Although researchers offered context-specific discussions of research methods (represented well in *Internet Research*, edited by Jones, 1999), a comprehensive treatment did not appear until 2000, when Mann and Stewart's volume provided principles and practices for conducting qualitative inquiry using Internet communication as a tool of research.

As research in this evolving field grows more refined, the conceptualization of computer-mediated communication has shifted from sweeping universalized encapsulations to more specific, context-based definitions. As well, some have noted a move from exaggerated to mundane accounts. A recent article (Herring, 2004) entitled "Slouching Toward the Ordinary" notes the trend to minimize the impact of new communication technologies on identity, subjectivity, and social practices and structures. In this same vein, ethnographic inquiry appears to be shifting from the study of online-only environments and virtual identity to the intersection of computer-mediated communication with everyday life. Scholars are now calling for increased attention to the multiple uses and definitions of "Internet" in context, as well as increased attention to how the online and offline intersect (Baym, Zhang, & Lin, 2002; Orgad, 2002).

Overtly political analyses of computer-mediated communication are diverse in scope and range. I mention just two areas: research in developing countries and research interrogating the role of the researcher. Work exploring the use of Internet technologies in developing countries is important and increasing. Kolko conducted in-depth interviews in Uzbekistan as a means of grounding her NSF-funded study of how ICT affects life in central Asia (personal communication, October 15, 2002). Miller and Slater have conducted the most widely known ethnography of a developing country to date, exploring the ways in which the Internet is perceived and used in Trinidad (2000). Theresa Senft's recent work in Ghana illustrates a politically motivated effort to use interpretive participatory action research to help the cause of women and the poor in that region of the world (personal communication, October 2004).

Research exploring the researcher's role in Internet studies is also expanding: My own work was acknowledged as an explicitly reflexive discussion of the researcher's role in Internet ethnography (1998). Later works also discuss directly the ethical and political stance of the researcher and the relationship between researcher and participants (e.g., Ryen, 2002). Bromseth (2002, 2003) discusses in depth the ethical dilemmas of collecting data in groups where people are reluctant to be studied. Gajjala (2002) explores her own study of a group wherein the members were overtly and actively resistant to her intent as a researcher. Along different lines, Eichhorn's study of a virtual group (2001) astutely addresses the paradox of using offline interviews to understand online subjectivities. Orgad's work (2002) illustrates the opposite paradox: using only online interviews with women in a virtual support group to understand how these women make sense of their illness. In both cases, these researchers recognized during the course of their research that giving voice to the participants meant selecting the medium based on what was most appropriate for the participants, not the researcher.

A final note about the shifting trends in qualitative research over the past decade of Internet studies. Many studies have been labeled "ethnography" when the more appropriate term would be interview study, case study, phenomenology, grounded theory, narrative analysis, biography or life history, and so forth. "Ethnography" seems to be a term that is applied by scholars who do not know what else to call their work or, in my case (1998), by scholars whose study of new forms of ethnography broadens the umbrella of what can be considered "ethnography." Closely related, the quality of work in Internet studies from an ethnographer's or qualitative methodologist's perspective has varied widely; some scholars come to the field of inquiry having been trained in qualitative methods, while others have topic- or technology-specific expertise or interest but no familiarity or training in the diversity of qualitative approaches (Mann, 2002, 2003).

## ▣ CRITICAL JUNCTURES IN RESEARCH DESIGN AND PROCESS

The idea of studying the Internet or using Internet technologies to facilitate qualitative research is beguiling: A researcher's reach is potentially global, data collection is economical, and transcribing is no more difficult than cutting and pasting. But in the virtual field, as one interacts with anonymous participants, tracks disjointed, non-linear, multiple participant conversations, and analyzes hundreds of screens worth of cultural texts, one can begin to feel like the Internet might cause more headaches than it cures. Deceptive in its apparent simplicity, qualitative inquiry in this environment requires careful attention to the traditional means by which social life is interpreted and the adjustments that must be made to give value to the online experience and internal consistency to one's methods. The absence of visual information about the participant functions more paradoxically than one might realize. Socioeconomic markers such as body type, gender, race, and class are used consciously or unconsciously by researchers to make sense of participants in physical settings. Online, these frames are still used but without visual information, they function invisibly. This warrants close examination, both to consider how this happens and to explore how the researcher's default premises and unconscious choices can influence the shape of the participant and the reality of the outcome.

This complexity of knowing anything certain about the other is paradoxical, yet to acknowledge the uncertainty or even impossibility of knowing Other is to risk paralysis in the research process, loss of authority in the presentation of research, and diminishment of one's academic role as observer/interpreter/archivist of social life. How, then, does one proceed? "With caution" is a trite yet reasonable response which calls for sensitivity to the context, interrogation of one's own presumptions, and flexible adaptation to a new era in social research, one in which we recognize the limitations bred by our traditional five senses and take the risks necessary to reconsider how and why we seek and create knowledge. Proceeding thus is a political move. It does not retreat from understanding Other on the grounds that the researcher cannot know anything except his or her own experiences. It also does not rest on the laurels of traditional methods, trying to shore up ways of knowing that are crumbling before our eyes as digital and convergent media saturate cultural practices and forms. It faces the complexity and interrogates the way we analyze people for purposes of academic inquiry. If one examines deeply the way new communication technologies influence the research project, one is likely to stumble into issues which question the fundamental reasons for doing research in the first place. Allowing oneself to explore those issues can vitally contribute to the creation of reflexive and socially responsible research practice.

At several junctures during the research project, we have the opportunity and responsibility to reflexively interrogate our roles, methods, ethical stances, and interpretations. When studying computer-mediated environments, this need is intensified because the traditional frames of reference we use to guide our premises and procedures are entrenched in physical foundations and modernist ontologies. Questions one might address include the following:

- What can we say we know about the Other when self, other, and the context may be constructed solely through the exchange of messages?
- In social situations derived from discursive interaction, is it possible to simply observe? Is it desirable?
- How does the researcher's participation in the medium affect the identity of the participant and the shape of the culture?
- How can one balance the traditional scientific impulse to uncover the "real" while interacting with people who may or may not have any correspondence to their physical counterparts?
- In what ways do one's research traditions delimit and limit the possibilities for sensemaking in environments which are not overtly physical, visual, and aural?

Whether or not the researcher pays attention to them, the issues raised by these questions operate throughout any ethnographically based project. They identify logistic challenges but also display problematic working assumptions that must be addressed. Reflexive research practice requires a constant disruption of the seemingly placid surface of inquiry. Stopping to identify critical decision junctures and reflect on the consequences of specific actions constitutes an honest presence in the research process and active engagement in the ethical grounding of one's inquiry.[3]

Defining the boundaries of the field.

Determining what constitutes data.

Interpreting the other as text.

Using embodied sensibilities to interpret textuality.

Representing others ethically in research reports.

Each of these categories identifies a critical decision juncture within the research project. Neither exhaustive nor separate, these categories can be used as examples to help one think through some of the decisions made during the course of a study which have meaningful consequences for the identity of the participants, the representation of self and other in research reporting, and the shape of the body of scientific knowledge built on multiple ethnographically informed studies. The actual questions one might ask are particular to the researcher and the project, as variable as one's worldviews and methodological approaches.

## Defining the Boundaries of the Field

Drawing boundaries around the research context, or "identifying the field" involves a series of decisions that both presuppose and reveal the researcher's underlying ontological and epistemological assumptions. Obviously, reflecting on our own biases is not just useful but ethically necessary, even if our academic training did not identify the necessity for such reflection. When studying physically based cultures, the location of the field is typically predetermined, so the logistical challenges lie in gaining access and building rapport with informants. For the Internet ethnographer, the process of locating and defining sensible boundaries of the field can be convoluted and elusive.

Because the Internet is geographically dispersed, the researcher has the option to disregard location and distance to communicate instantaneously and inexpensively with people. Logistically, the distance-collapsing capacity of the Internet allows the researcher to connect to participants around the globe. The researcher can include people previously unavailable for study. This not only increases the pool of participants but also provides the potential for cross-cultural comparisons that were not readily available previously for practical and financial reasons. In a world where potential participants are only a keyboard click and fibre optic or wireless connection away, distance become almost meaningless as a pragmatic consideration in research design; the Internet serves as an extension of the researcher's and participant's bodies. Research can be designed around questions of interaction and social behavior unbound from the restrictions of proximity or geography. Participants can be selected on the basis of their appropriate fit within the research questions rather than their physical location or convenience to the researcher.

### From Geographic to Discursive Boundaries

As we shift from geographic to computer-mediated spaces, we are shifting focus from place to interaction, from location to locomotion (Markham, 2003a). Consequently, communities and culture are not neatly mapped before entering the field, but instead are created as part of the ethnographic process. Christine Hine (2000) argues that the ethnographer's notion of cultural boundary must be reconsidered given this capacity of the Internet. Rather than relying on traditional, geographically based means of encapsulating the culture under study, such as national boundaries or town limits, ethnographers might find more accuracy in using discourse patterns to find boundaries. "The ethnographer must read the texts and interactions of interest, much like trail signs, and make defensible decisions about which paths to follow, which paths to disregard, and thereby which boundaries to draw" (Markham, 2003b).

Seemingly mundane decisions become crucial criteria that are used, consciously or not, to create boundaries around the field of inquiry. Boundary markers are underwritten by the researcher's choice about how to find data sites, which search engine to use to sample, whom to interact with, what to say in interaction with participants, what language to speak, when to seek and conduct interviews (including both time of day and considering time zones), and so forth. Computer-mediated cultural contexts are shifting contexts. Their discursive construction occurs in global as well as local patterns. Membership can be transient. This becomes more meaningful when one realizes the boundary-forming work that is being accomplished when one contributes messages to a group, defines the boundaries of a cultural phenomenon through one's own surfing choices, and sifts or funnels the data set by using a particular search engine or set of databases. Each action taken by the researcher in this vast information sphere contributes directly to the construction of the structures that eventually get labeled "field" or "data."

Indeed, the global potential of this medium is often conflated with global reach, an achievement that relies on global access (Markham, 2004b). Arguably, people in industrialized countries tend to overestimate the degree to which the world has access to computers and electronic communication technologies. Access is not universal and those populations being studied via the Internet represent a very privileged and small portion of the world's population. In many ways, then, the boundaries may be flexible, seemingly arbitrary, and discursively constructed, but nonetheless remain within larger political and economic structures that are not universally experienced.

*Participation in the Discursive Construction of the Field*

As I have noted previously (Markham 1998), interacting with anyone formally or informally marks a significant shift from observer to participant, from archivist to accomplice. Online, as one participates in the context, one co-constructs the spaces under investigation. Interactions with participants are not simple events in these online spaces, they are organizing elements of these spaces.

By the very nature of their actions and interactions, researchers in any cultural environment are involved in the construction of what becomes the object of analysis. This is highlighted in technologically mediated environments because both the production and consumption of communication can be global, non-sequential, fragmented, disembodied, and decentered. In contexts where the boundaries of self, other, and social world are created and sustained solely through the exchange of information, being is therefore relational and dialectic. Social constructions are less connected to their physical properties. Boundaries are not so much determined by "location" as they are by "interaction."

The boundaries of the field become more a matter of choice than in physically located spaces. Researchers are more obviously participative. Addressing a seemingly simple question of "should I participate or observe" then, gives rise to an entirely more complicated set of issues that shape the research design and complicate our concepts of how media function socially. The deceptively easy act of choosing a particular community of Web sites creates an audience that previously did not exist and indicates to the larger academic community that this context is meaningful. Thus, choice of field becomes a politically charged process because of the inherent ethicality of one's decisions.

Ethnography that ignores these issues can remain at the edges of the cultural context and more importantly, can become mired in the now much critiqued notion that the researcher observes but does not interfere with or influence that which is studied. Moreover, the decisions that a researcher makes at this level directly influence the way the researcher later represents the context and the participants, which ultimately impacts our academic conversations of and knowledge about computer-mediated communication environments. These are issues laden with ethical responsibility, yet the questions themselves appear to be so straightforward they are often only addressed as simple logistics problems.

This discussion necessarily takes us forward to later stages of the research process. The effort or unconscious decision to absent oneself from the field will not remove the researcher from the process and product. Thinking ahead to the outcome of inquiry—the research report—one must acknowledge that the interpretation of culture will change depending on the form of the telling. Interpretative focus and the nature of the "findings" shift with the passage of time, the venue for publication, the credibility of the author or notoriety of the subject, and innumerable other factors.

Frankly, whether or not the researcher participates or simply observes, the construction of the research report will present a particular reality of the object of analysis that is influenced by the identity and participation of the researcher. It may be more productive to acknowledge one's participative role early, so that every aspect of the research design can effectively incorporate the researcher's presence in the construction of the field under study. As Internet Studies evolves as an interdisciplinary field of inquiry, further research depth and credibility will be gained through realistic and contemporary conceptualizations of the ways in which the researcher, reader, and object of analysis intersect.

## Determining What Constitutes Data

A researcher's representation of others is inextricably bound up with the way data are collected and distinguished as meaningful versus meaningless. Computer-mediated communication contexts complicate the researcher's decisions, not only because the contexts are constructed interactively, comprised of mostly disembodied participants, or because the researcher has little access to typical sensemaking devices used to identify and collect data. The researcher's decisions are further complicated because we are always and constantly struck with stimuli in any research environment, stimuli that must be filtered in and out in order to create sensible categories for interpretation. Interacting in text-only online environments diminishes the most prominent of our senses: vision. CMC separates more obviously the wholeness of a person's being into component parts; that which was previously made sense of as a whole is consequently made sense of at different points of time using different combinations of senses. This feature of technology promotes highly focused and divided attention on the content, the producer, the carrier, and the meaning of discursive activity in context. Even in more overtly visual research environments, where the researcher may have access to photos, Web cams, Web sites, hyperlink behavior, and blogs, the issue is not resolved because traditional research training is designed for physically co-present environments.

Methodologically, one must reflect carefully on what collected information is considered as "data." Just as interaction constructs and reflects the shape of the phenomena being studied, interaction also delineates the being doing the research in the field. Obviously, we cannot pay attention to everything—our analytical lens is limited by what we are drawn to, what we are trained to attend to, and what we want to find. Borrowing from Goffman (1959), our understanding is determined as much by our own frames of reference as the frames supplied by the context. Our selection of data and rejection of non-data presents a critical juncture within which to interrogate the possible consequences of our choices on the representation of others through our research.

An example of online discourse from prior research (Markham, 1998) illustrates the implications of this point. Matthew, as with all the participants in my study, is a self-described "heavy user" of the Internet. The interview occurred in a MOO, an online environment which is designed to facilitate the enactment and appearance of particular forms of communication. By writing different commands or using particular punctuation, one can speak, exclaim, question, whisper, emote, or think, so that dialogue appears as a verbal statement (Annette says, "Hi." Annette exclaims, "Hi!" Annette asks "Hi?") a cartoon-like thought bubble . o O (Annette wonders if the reader sees that this is a thought bubble), a description of one's nonverbal behaviors or thoughts (Annette scratches her head thoughtfully), and so forth.

Initially archiving Matthew's interview, I included the entire log of the conversation. As I began the analysis process, I removed extraneous, repetitive, or system-specific commands in order to minimize distractions. The following sample is from this latter phase, where the commands are removed. From this log, I conducted the initial analysis of data:

Matthew:     "Now madison, that's a nice town."

Markham:   "okay here's some official stuff for you Matthew."

Markham:   "I guarantee that I will not ever reveal your address/name/location."

Matthew:     "Fine about the secrecy stuff."

Markham:   "Matthew, I guarantee that I will delete any references that might give a reader clues about where you live, who you are, or where you work."

Markham:   "do you mind that I archive this interview?"

Matthew:     "Log away, Annette" . . .

Markham:   "what do you do mostly when you're online? Where do you go?"

Matthew:     "Mostly I'm doing one of two things. Firstly I do research. If I'm looking for academic research in software engineering, my specialty, a lot of it is on the Web . . ."

Matthew:     "And a lot of tools to play with are there, too."

Matthew:     "Also, I use it for news and information, the way I used to use the radio. (I'm an unrepentant . . ."

Matthew:     "real-lifer). For instance, if I'm going to go run (or bike or do something else outside) . . . "

Matthew:     "I check the weather on the Web when in years past I would turn on the radio. Ditto for news" . . .

Markham:   "how would you compare your sense of self as a person online to your sense of self offline?"

Matthew:      "More confident online, because I'm a better editor than writer/speaker. I do well when I can backspace."

Matthew:      "But I'm the same me in both places. I guess I've been me too long to be anybody else without a lot more practice than I have time for."

Markham:     "hmmm . . . How would you describe your self?"

Markham:     "i mean, what's the 'me' you're talking about?"

Matthew:      "Kind of androgenous. Plenty of women for friends. But I was never good at dating or any of the romantic/sexual stuff."

Matthew:      "Also, somewhat intellectual."

Matthew:      has a delayed blushing reaction to the androgeny comment.

Matthew:      "And a fitness nut."

Markham:     o O ( I wonder why Matthew is blushing . . . )

Markham:     "tell me about your most memorable online experience"

Matthew:      "OK, it was a couple years ago and I was just getting on the Web and starting to realize all"

After conducting initial coding and analysis, I found that I was struggling with this interview. I returned to the original transcript and realized I had made an error in my delineation of "meaningful" from "nonessential" data. The following excerpt illustrates what I saw when I returned to the original interview (the pieces I had removed are underlined):

Matthew says, "Now madison, that's a nice town."

Matthew spills popcorncrumbs into his keyboard :-(

Markham says, "bummer, Matthew."

Matthew says, "If you see me going away for a while, you know I went to make more popcorn ;-)"

Markham says, "okay here's some official stuff for you Matthew."

Markham says, "I guarantee that I will not ever reveal your address/name/location."

Matthew says, "Fine about the secrecy stuff."

Markham says, "Matthew, I guarantee that I will delete any references that might give a reader clues about where you live, who you are, or where you work."

Markham asks, "do you mind that I archive this interview?"

Matthew salutes and says "Yes'm

Matthew says, "Log away, Annette"

Markham says, "okay. i have a tendency to ask questions too quickly."

Matthew doesn't answer because he's too busy opening a box of rice cakes. . . .

Markham asks, "what do you do mostly when you're online? Where do you go?"

Matthew says, "Mostly I'm doing one of two things. Firstly I do research. If I'm looking for academic research in software engineering, my specialty, a lot of it is on the Web . . . "

Matthew says, "And a lot of tools to play with are there, too."

Matthew says, "Also, I use it for news and information, the way I used to use the radio. (I'm an unrepentent . . . "

Matthew says, "real-lifer). For instance, if I'm going to go run (or bike or do something else outside) . . . "

Matthew says, "I check the weather on the Web when in years past I would turn on the radio. Ditto for news" . . .

Markham asks, "how would you compare your sense of self as a person online to your sense of self offline?"

Matthew says, "More confident online, because I'm a better editor than writer/speaker. I do well when I can backspace."

Matthew says, "But I'm the same me in both places. I guess I've been me too long to be anybody else without a lot more practice than I have time for."

Markham asks, "hmmm . . . How would you describe your self?"

Markham asks, "i mean, what's the 'me' you're talking about?"

Matthew says, "Kind of androgenous. Plenty of women for friends. But I was never good at dating or any of the romantic/sexual stuff."

Matthew says, "Also, somewhat intellectual."

Matthew says, has a delayed blushing reaction to the androgeny comment.

Matthew says, "And a fitness nut."

Markham . o O (I wonder why Matthew is blushing . . .)

Matthew does pushups.

Markham stares

Markham . o O ( should I be doing something too? )

Matthew says, "You should be asking me questions (the interviewee becomes the interviewer)"

Markham sighs and refocuses

Markham says, "tell me about your most memorable online experience"

Matthew gets very jealous of people who have sleep.

Matthew enters state of deep thought.

Matthew goes to raid the nearby refrigerator while composing reply in head

Matthew says, "OK, it was a couple years ago and I was just getting on the Web and starting to realize all"

My interpretation shifted as I realized the extent to which Matthew made certain to include his embodied activities in the conversation. Regardless of the interpretation one elects to make about these underlined enactments (Matthew is hungry, bored, creative, using conventions learned in culture), the fact remains that the "data" are different from one transcript to the next.

One can elect to bracket or set aside the form and focus only on the content. This decision would be guided by the premise that the meaning of one's utterances is only understood in context and therefore the medium is less important than the content. On the other hand, to ignore the form in this interview could also be seen as a poor choice, given the well-founded premise that nonverbal behaviors function discursively in the presentation of self, negotiation of identity, and eventual symbolic construction of culture. In this case, my analysis would suffer without the inclusion of Matthew's delineation of his embodied activities. It also raises the question of what constitutes form and what constitutes content.

One's choice in this situation should be guided by the research questions or the overall goal of research, which in this case was to explore how people experience the Internet and how their identities are presented and negotiated. Yet, this edict is laden with ambiguity when put into practice. Multiple dilemmas present themselves: How much does text represent the reality of the person? Put more personally, how much would I want to be bound by what I wrote at any particular time? To what extent does or should the researcher include spelling or typing ability as meaningful information in the understanding of identity or culture? How much are my own preconceptions and stereotypes influencing how I elect to categorize data from non-data?

One might wonder whether or not I ever asked Matthew to participate in the decision about what constituted "data," as this would seem a relatively easy way to answer some of the questions asked above. What would Matthew categorize as meaningful data from unessential non-data? On the other hand, why and under what circumstances would I want Matthew to determine what ought to be analyzed and what ought to be ignored?

These questions are important in that they directly shape what is examined by the researcher. This is not an unfamiliar point, as it raises the importance of interrogating the researcher's role in writing culture (Clifford and Marcus, 1986). In this case (and any, I would suggest), while the analysis may indeed emerge from the data, *the researcher determines a priori what constitutes data in the first place*, making this decision point a crucial reflection point.

## Interpreting the Other Through Their Text

As one addresses these issues and shifts from data collection to analysis, another critical juncture arises, sponsored by the following question: To what extent is the Other defined by his or her texts? When the participant, researcher, and context are nothing but text and everything beyond mere language, our perceptual filters must be adjusted to accommodate complexities of human expression. Discursive practices are the heart of our enterprise as ethnographic researchers. When the discourse is limited to the exchange of texts, one might think that the methods of analysis are likewise limited to what is seen in the text, but this is not the case. Rather, an array of interpretive tools are used to make sense of these texts and it becomes a worthwhile task to reflect on some of the more hidden or unacknowledged analytical methods being used to interpret the Other.

The following two examples usefully illustrate the extent to which participants can be judged in multiple ways by the form of their texts. The samples of discourse in these examples represent well the writing tendencies of two participants: Sheol and DominOH!.

> <Sheol> I am intrested in talking to:) Could you be more spesific about what questions you will ask? Just let me know when you want to talk, and I will try to accomidate! :)

> <Sheol> I became a very popular (I know that sounds conseeded) figuar on the line I called home. I am ruled by the right side of my brain so I liked the diea of being that personality.

In this interview with Sheol, it was impossible to bracket the spelling, use of graphic accents, tag lines, and so forth. From the beginning, I had been determined to conduct systematic analyses that remained close to the text. I was using a blend of content-oriented analytical tools to code, thematize, and make sense of the interactions with participants. Reflecting on my inability to ignore the form in my analysis of content jarred me out of the false stability granted by method-specific procedures and caused me to identify some of the ways I was putting Sheol into categories without noticing what I was doing.

For example, very early on, I categorized Sheol as female because a gendered language style was very evident in tags, qualifiers, expressions of emotion, and heavy use of graphic accents (Sheol turned out to be male). Sheol was also: Young (spelling was phonetic, attention to language misuse was not at all evident); Perhaps not very intelligent (multiple spelling errors, unreadable messages, apparent lack of ability to be a real hacker); and, of course, Caucasian (default characteristic because of mainstream cultural assumptions about use of the Internet as well as the tendency to make the online other look more like the self). Additionally and solely based on my own frame of reference, Sheol was heterosexual, middle class, and American.

In a different study, a participant called DominOH! also used phonetic spelling, but in a different way:

> <DominOH!> Sumtymz i am lost in my online identiteez . . . well, the aktuel problem? i feel more 'found' in my online selvvz . . . kicky, spun out, reeler than real. More atooned to the energee and more atooned to those i'm talking with . . .

> <DominOH!> . . . so much fun 2 play . . . YOU, and EVERYONE else, kannot reely no mee. And y do you feeeeel that you need 2?! So, online I'm a nerdy college professor with a quirky sense of humor, or I'm a professhunal athlete with a career ending injuree, and sumtymz i'm handsum, or i'm beauteous . . . and if peepole wanna hang with mee, i'm alwaze up for play.

In my conversations with this persona, I found it easier to bracket the misspellings because they appeared obvious and deliberate. DominOH! seemed to revel in the ability to remain elusive during our various interactions. DominOH!'s discourse was marked with aggressive and challenging statements. I was cautious with this participant to not make assumptions about gender but found myself categorizing DominOH! as male, young, well-educated, and Caucasian.

As the researcher, I have numerous choices regarding the interpretation of these interviews. My choices will build cultural knowledge about Sheol and DominOH! as individuals and about how people interact in cyberspace. In interpretive inquiry, the integrity of one's interpretation is tied directly to reflexivity. Frequently, though, reflexivity happens *after* the analysis is in progress or the project is completed. I mentally attached a number of social labels to both these participants during the course of our conversations and long after, as I was interpreting the discourse. Some of the labels I did not recognize until others pointed them out. The importance is not in the accuracy of the labels, but in the type of evidence used to derive the category. Without reflection, I initially gave a negative attribution to Sheol's phonetic spelling (deficient abilities) while giving a positive attribution to DominOH!'s (cleverness). Without reflection, I categorized Sheol as female and DominOH! as male, based solely on their use of accommodating or aggressive language.

This example illustrates that one's interpretation is founded in the text but simultaneously not limited to the text. While systematic procedures of analysis are vital tools for the social scientist, they are not fail safe if followed to the letter. Procedures can actually blind one to the actual interpretive processes occurring. In Internet-based environments, the existence of the online persona being studied is often encap-sulated by their pixels on a computer screen. The choices made to attend to, ignore, or edit these pixels has real consequences for the persons whose manifestations are being altered beyond and outside their control. if a subject types solely in lowercase and uses nonstandard.grammatical.conventions the reeders correction of *errors* may inappropriately ignore and thus misrepresent a participant's deliberate presenta-tion of self. ;-) if someone spells atroshiously or uniQueLY and the researcher corrects it in the research report for readAbility, alteration of a person's desired online identity may be the price of smooth reading (Markham, 2003a, 2003b).

On the other hand, Sheol may be working with a sticky keyboard, ignoring the errors in the interest of speed, or multi-tasking such that he is not devoted fully to our interaction. DominOH! may be more comfortable with phonetic spelling. Maybe she or he was aggressive in response to something I had said early on. Certainly, to make the interpretive task both easier and more grounded in the participant's experi-ence, one could ask the participants to clarify their own writing tendencies. One could also gather additional demographic information. My point, however, is not to articu-late how to make the interpretations more accurate or truthful, but to identify one of many moments in the research project when the researcher faces, consciously or not, certain decisions about what to include as part of the interpretive consideration, only some of which can be identified or controlled.

To make this task more difficult, the most ethically sensitive approach to analysis is complicated—and impeded—by academic conventions and training. Most social science approaches teach the researcher to distill the complexity of human experience into discrete variables that are easily measured. Interpretive methods seek to ease these restrictions but involve ways of knowing that continually strive to simplify rather than complexify human experience. To shift the gaze from the subject of research to the gaze itself is one step in the evolution of human sciences. To stop there, however, is to risk losing sight of the larger goals of inquiry. Rather than seeking to describe or reflect reality, researchers must consider the political act of promoting, activating, or engendering realities.

## The Search for Authenticity[4]

Particularly notable in disembodied research environments, the researcher's body continues to be privileged as the site of experience, the best measure of authenticity, and the residence of knowledge. This is sensible, literally, because we make sense of our world through our eyes, ears, noses, mouths, and sense of touch. We abstract our embodied knowledge to convey it through logic, language, and print, but as Ackerman (1995) notes, our primary level of understanding remains firmly entwined with our senses. "There is no way in which to understand the world without first detecting it through the radar-net of our senses. . . . The senses . . . tear reality apart into vibrant morsels and reassemble them into a meaningful pattern. . . . Reasoning we call it, as if it were a mental spice" (pp. xv–xvii).

The implications of this are significant in scientific research; in most traditions, the interpretive act is characterized as an analytical, logical, mental procedure. Separated from the body in theory, the embodied practice of interpretation lingers. Online, this underlying disjuncture is highlighted precisely because the body of the participant is *notably* absent.

### Searching for the Body Behind the Text

The question often asked about participants in online contexts is "Who are they, really?" By this, one often means, who are they, as I can see, verify, and know them in a body? From students, reviewers, and publishers, I have heard the suggestion many times: "You should have interviewed the participants offline as well as online. Then, you would have a better idea of who they are." Shifting one's perspective slightly, one might ask questions that get at the underlying issues: How much do we rely on our bodies and the bodies of participants to establish presence and know other? Is this reliance warranted or desirable? Will our picture of other, in person, make our understanding of them more whole? More directly: Does the embodiment of a participant gauge their authenticity?

The answers depend not only on the question one is seeking to address but also on the researcher's underlying epistemological assumptions. If one is simply using the Internet as a tool to expand one's reach to participants and interviewing them online is merely a convenience, one should consider the extent to which people can and do express themselves well, truly, or fully in text. But if one is studying Internet contexts as cultural formations or social interaction in computer-mediated communication contexts, the inclusion of embodied ways of knowing may be unwarranted and even counterproductive.

In chat rooms, on mobile phones, through personal Web sites, and other media, identity is produced and consumed in a form abstracted from actual presence. Cultural understanding is literally constructed discursively and interactively. We know from both popular press and scholarly studies that many people seek interaction and community on the Internet because it provides the perceived means to escape the confines of embodied social markers to engage in what many refer to as a "meeting of the minds." Whether or not this is truly possible (and some have argued (e.g., Ess, 2003; Kolko, Nakamura, & Rodman, 2000) that it is not), a user's desire to present and be perceived as a confluence of texts without body might best be read by researchers as a request for us to acknowledge text as ample and sufficient evidence of being and to study it as such (Markham, 2003a, 2004a).

Yet social scientists persist in seeking the authentic by privileging the concept of the body. The desire to add validity to findings often results in research design that holds up the textual representation of the participants next to their physical personae. The goal is to see the extent to which the images match. Researchers deciding to interview participants both online and f2f (face to face) may claim that their efforts will add authenticity to their interpretation—by adding paralinguistic or nonverbal cues to the words people speak—and thereby add more credibility to their findings (Markham, 2003a).

For good biologically based reasons, researchers rely on and trust their traditional senses of sight, smell, touch, taste, and hearing to provide verification of concrete reality. We are conditioned to rely particularly on our visual sensibilities: "Seventy percent of the body's sense receptors cluster in the eyes, and it is mainly through seeing the world that we appraise and understand it" (Ackerman, 1995, p. 230). Ecologist and philosopher David Abram adds that perception is a reciprocity between the body and the entities that surround it. Considering Merleau-Ponty's idea that perception itself is embodied, Abram notes that "[Perception] is a sort of silent conversation that I carry on with things, a continuous dialogue that unfolds far below my verbal awareness" (1997, p. 52). Although "we conceptually mobilize or objectify the phenomenon . . . by mentally absenting ourselves from this relation" (Abram, 1997, p. 56), our understanding of the world is sensual. While it makes sense that researchers use embodied sensibilities, this is not mentioned much, if at all, in methods textbooks. It therefore becomes a critical juncture to address in a very conscious manner.

### Removing the Researcher's Body

In essentially disembodied relationships and cultures, one must wonder if the intrusion of certain embodied sense-making faculties bleeds integrity from the project of knowing the other in context. Yet, as mentioned above, perception always involves embodiment, and this cannot be set aside in the context of studying life online. Hence, a paradox emerges that may not be overcome but should be considered, acknowledged, or accounted for in the research design or research report.

Irony follows, however, when one notes the marked absence of the researcher's own embodiment in many studies of text-based cultural contexts. Although a researcher may give his or her participants' bodied forms and make sense of their identities through his or her own body, this sensibility is rarely noted in the published paper. Considerable privilege is given to the researcher to make his or her own embodiment a choice or even a non-issue while simultaneously questioning the authenticity of the participants' choices regarding their own embodiment. Ethically as well as epistemologically, it is vital to reflect carefully on the extent to which the research design privileges the researcher at the expense of both understanding the other and operating with a keen awareness of the context (Markham, 2003a, p. 152).

The online persona may be much more fluid and changeable than we imagine as we catch them in particular moments or only a fraction of the virtual venues they populate. Anonymity in text-based environments gives one more choices and control in the presentation of self, whether or not the presentation is perceived as intended. Understanding the potential for flexible, ad hoc negotiation of identity in technologically mediated social spaces may foster another critical juncture at which the researcher can ask an intriguing set of questions about the representation of other: "As researchers and members of various communities and cultures, what do we use to construct a sense of who the Other really is?" "In what ways do our methods of comprehending life as interwoven with new communication technologies ignore, deny, or validate shifting constructions of identity and social world?"

### Interpreting Within
### Socioeconomic Comfort Zones

It makes sense that researchers visualize their participants even in non-visual text-based media. Yet, it is not only the visual bias that must be critically analyzed by researchers, but also the imagination with which one visualizes the participant. Pioneers on the research frontier of online ethnography continually juxtapose embodiment with other modes of presentation and knowing. When we rely on our embodied sensibilities of knowing, we are not necessarily getting a better or more "accurate" picture of the subjects of our studies; we may be simply reflecting our own comfort zones of research. Critical reflection on the product of our gaze can reveal some of these comfort zones for introspection and interrogation. Researchers should be wary of the tendency to perceive the world in familiar, close-to-home categories. What do the participants look like in the mind's eye? How likely is the researcher to give the participant an ethnic category different from his or her own? What information is used to make judgments about the embodied person behind the screen?

Typing speed, spelling and grammar usage, choice of (nick)name; linear or fragmented progression of ideas: These all influence the way a participant is understood by the researcher. As the researcher visually appraises the discursive practices of the participants, the form wafts through the sense-making like an invisible but compelling scent on the breeze. Whether one notices that the text is idiosyncratic or not, either in its error or uniqueness or blandness or precision, the form influences meaning and helps give a bodied shape to the participant. Form composes new stereotypes that must be acknowledged and interrogated.

As researchers, we carry our own predilections concerning race, gender, and bodied appearance of virtual participants. For no obvious reasons, I identified the participant mentioned above, Sheol, as white, female, heterosexual, young, and average in body weight and height. After about two hours of the interview, Sheol mentioned "girlfriend," and I recognized that I had made an invisible (but obviously in operation) assumption that she was heterosexual. Forced to reconcile the contradiction between my a priori assumption and the use of the word "girlfriend," I began to look for clues of gender I must have missed earlier. I also began to wonder at my invisible use of sexuality and gender as categories.

I did not reflect on the fact that I was giving Sheol a body in my mind until this disjuncture occurred and I realized the body in my mind no longer fit the body being presented by the participant. To note, Sheol was simply chatting with me, not presenting a body in any deliberate fashion. I had given shape to the person. A few minutes later, when Sheol referred to himself as a male, I realized she was not a lesbian but that 'he' had a 'girlfriend.' I had made yet another blunder. The form of the message had led me to an initial assumption that Sheol was female. The name, if read at a very surface level, hinted that Sheol was female (here, "Sheol" is a double-pseudonym but the original name was similar in that if read quickly, part of the spelling could be mistaken as an obviously female name or marker, like "Susanerd" or "21She132"). I also knew from previous research that women tend to use more tag lines, offer more caveats, and augment their texts with more emoticons and punctuation.

Recent inquiry of race in cyberspace contends that users transform online others into images of themselves but that these images are limited by media representations of identity, so that most visualizations will conform to mass media images of beauty, race, gender, ethnicity, and size (Nakamura, 1995). What impact does this have for qualitative researchers conducting ethnographically informed research in anonymous or virtual environments?

In teaching computer-mediated courses, my assumptions turn my students white and nondescript. If they use an interesting name, I find myself trying to find a body that suits what I perceive the name implies about the appearance of their persona. When I reflect on my visual images, I realize that even though race is supposedly absent from the research lens, it becomes a category which defaults to "white" (Nakamura, 2003). My experience is not atypical. It illustrates how much we rely on and use our own parameters to categorize others into something we can comfortably address. Scholarly discussion of race and the Internet is growing, particularly concerning how the Internet has been created and perceived naïvely as a raceless space (Kendall, 1998; Kolko, Nakamura, & Rodman, 2000; Poster, 1998). These discussions will help researchers better reflect on the spaces studied as well as the assumptions made during the collection and interpretation phases of the project.

Again, traditional academic training complicates the issues of embodiment for researchers in that this training seeks to make the researcher invisible. Traditional academic training encourages the researcher to focus on the theory and method as the locus of control in the study. Good research design, in the scientific tradition, eliminates bias, allows the method to strictly guide the findings, and ignores non-scientific measures such as hunches. The researcher's senses should be removed from the analysis of data and the researcher's voice should be removed from the final report. This training creates habits—even among strongly resistant researchers—to ignore or deny the impact of one's conscious or unconscious embodied sensibilities on the research outcome. It is difficult even in qualitative research to peel back one's own complicated layers of interpretation.

## Considering Methods as Ethics

As mentioned early in this article, any method decision is an ethics decision. The political potential and consequences of our research should not be underestimated. Every choice we make about how to represent the self, participants, and the cultural context under study contributes to how these are understood, framed, and responded to by readers, future students, policy makers, and the like.

The process of studying culture is one of comprehension, encapsulation, and control. To say otherwise is to deny our impulses and roles as scholars and scientists. At a very basic level, we go there to learn something about Other and—when we think we have something figured out, to decide how to tell others what we think we know. To accomplish this goal, we must stop for a moment the flood of experience, extract a sample of it for inspection, and re-present it in academic terms with no small degree of abstraction. The researcher is afforded a tremendous degree of control in representing the realities of the people and contexts under study. This control need not be characterized in a completely negative fashion, as we could also consider the image of a Möbius strip, where seemingly opposing sides are eventually realized as part of the same path. Our capacity to represent cultural knowledge is a great responsibility, with many traps and difficulties. But it is also a gift, well earned through education, well honed through experience, and well intended through ethical reflexivity.

### Editing Choices

Consider the way research reports present, frame, and embody the people being studied: A person's very being has the potential to be literally reconfigured when edited by the researcher and put into a context of a research account rather than left in the context of experience.

This dilemma does not apply only to the study of virtual environments, but any study of human behavior, of course. But computer-mediated environments seem to highlight this dilemma of research reporting because it's so clear that text can be the primary, if not sole means of producing and negotiating self, other, body, and culture. Common practices of editing are rarely questioned. What happens when we transform the participant's utterances from disjunctive sentence fragments to smooth paragraphs? How are we presenting the social reality of these spaces when we correct grammar, spelling, and punctuation? How might we be changing their identities when we transform the appearance of their fonts to meet the acceptable standards for various publishing venues? Study participants can appear to be as smooth as movie characters after the writer has cleaned up everyday talk. Of course, the writer must make the report readable, but this need must be balanced with what is possibly silenced in this process. Online, this project takes a somewhat different form than in physically based research contexts. Highly disjunctive online conversations get reproduced as tidy exchanges of messages. A conversation developing over the course of six months can appear as a single paragraph in the written report. Deliberate fragmentation of ideas can be spliced into linear logic. Key to the ethical representation of the participant is sensitivity to the context and the individual. Certain editing choices may not alter the meaning of the utterances, interaction, or identity of the textual being embodied through these utterances. Other editing choices can function to devalue, ignore, or silence a fundamental aspect of a persona (Markham, 2003a).

On the other side of the coin, when presenting dialogue with participants, how many writers present a version of reality wherein they themselves talk and think in a hyper-organized fashion? Researchers are not likely to do this deliberately. Rather, the habit is an ingrained part of our training; it goes along with other practices, such as using passive voice and third person in the traditional academic paper. In the search for understanding the discursive construction of reality in computer-mediated environments, overediting may be misleading and limiting. The reader may have difficulty reading non-linear, disjunctive, or seriously misspelled examples of dialogue, but just like the visual elements of a personal Web site, these features of discourse illustrate vividly how it is experienced.

Generally speaking, as soon as an interaction occurs, the study of it becomes an abstraction. This is a fact of research. Even so, simplification or dismissal of the challenge of representation is not warranted. The task is to design research which allows human subjects to retain their autonomy and identity—whether or not their uniqueness is intentional or unintentional.

### In Whose Interests?

Shifting from ideas about re-presenting participants to ideas about advocacy, the political aspects of research become more visible. The question of advocacy can be asked in many ways: "Whose interests does the research serve?" "Why am I doing this research anyway?" "What groups need speaking for?" "How can my analysis help someone?" "How can my writing and publishing give voice to those who might remain otherwise silent?"

These are not simply political or ethical questions. These are methods questions that must be embedded in design, in that they impact directly the way information is collected and analyzed and how research findings are written and distributed. Yet questions such as these are not typically included in research methods textbooks as a part of the primary methodological discussion. If included at all, these questions are relegated to a separate unit or chapter entitled "Ethics" or separated from the main text, along with other special, non-typical considerations.

Even if one's research goals do not include serving as an advocate for participants, I suggest that not only will research design be more ethically grounded and reflexive but also the results will have more integrity if these questions are considered throughout the course of the study. They serve as important reminders that researchers often take more than they give, that the researcher's choices are always privileged, and that even when wanting to give voice to participants, the researcher can unintentionally end up as the hidden ventriloquist, speaking for, rather than with, others (Fine, Weis, Weseen, & Wong, 2000).

### Ethics and Institutional Review Boards

Ethical guidelines for Internet research vary sharply across disciplines and countries, depending on the premises and assumptions used to develop the criteria from which actions are judged as ethical or not. In this section, I've chosen to outline the features of Internet interaction that give rise to ethical controversies and to sketch the major distinctions between the "utilitarian" (predominant in the United States) and the "deontological" or "communitarian" stances (predominant in certain parts of the EU, particularly Nordic countries). This discussion is intended to give researchers alternative ways of thinking about projects, so that decisions are made not just based on what is legally required but also on what constitutes the right course of action in particular research and social contexts.

For Internet researchers, ethical challenges and controversy arise in the following circumstances:

- Some users perceive publicly accessible discourse sites as private.
- Some users have a writing style that is readily identifiable in their online community, so that the researcher's use of a pseudonym does not guarantee anonymity.
- Online discussion sites can be highly transient. Researchers gaining access permission in June may not be studying the same population in July.
- Search engines are often capable of finding statements used in research reports, making anonymity in certain venues almost impossible to guarantee.
- Age is difficult if not impossible to verify in certain online environments.
- Vulnerable persons are difficult to identify in certain online environments.
- Informed consent of the actual participant (the persona corresponding to the driver's license) is difficult to attain in writing if the participant desires anonymity from the researcher.

Some of the above generate general ethical issues; others generate official red flags for institutional research boards, which govern research of human subjects at institutions of higher education.

### Utilitarian and Communitarian Approaches

Are Institutional Review Boards (IRBs) in the United States more interested in protecting the institution than the human subject? Do the regulations really serve the interest of the human subject? Christians (2000) and Thomas (2003) argue that the system of regulation may be counterproductive, though it was designed to protect the participant, because these regulations are embedded in positivist, capitalist, and utilitarian social structures.

Officially, IRBs require researchers to preserve the autonomy of human subjects (respect for persons), distribute fairly both the benefits and burdens of research (justice), and secure the well-being of subjects by avoiding or minimizing harm (beneficence). Pragmatically, to adhere to the general IRB regulations, a researcher would ask: First, does the research protect the autonomy of the human subject? Second, do the potential benefits of study outweigh the risks posed to the human subject? Operationalized in the United States, if the potential benefit of the proposed research is "good" enough, the risk is acceptable, therefore making the second question a prioritized criterion.

Doing enough "good," according to Christians (2000), becomes a matter of determining what makes the majority of people happy. Combined with a strong tradition in positivism, which values neutrality and validity through scientifically verifiable measures, determinations of "happiness" are largely restricted to those domains that are extrinsic, observable, and measurable (pp. 138–142). "In its conceptual structure, IRB policy is designed to produce the best ration of benefits to costs. IRBs ostensibly protect the subjects who fall under the protocols they approve. However, given the interlocking utilitarian functions of social science, the academy, and the state . . . , IRBs in reality protect their own institutions rather than subject populations in society at large" (see Vanderpool, 1996, chaps. 2–6). Thomas (2003) adds to this, noting: "Too often, [IRB] decisions seem driven not so much by protecting research subjects, but by following federally mandated bureaucratic procedures that will protect the institution from sanctions in the event of a federal audit" (p. 196). IRBs are designed to provide guidelines where they might otherwise be ignored; in that, the regulations are sensible. But when these guidelines are used as an exclusive means of defining the ethical boundaries of one's work, the spirit of the regulation has been replaced by unreflexive adherence to the letter of the law.

This stance gets turned upside down (or right side up, depending on how you look at it) when we examine the ethical sphere of other countries. Ess (2003) outlines a European perspective as one that is more deontological. Citizens enjoy a much greater protection of privacy regarding data collection and use. Research stresses the protection of individual rights, "first of all, the right to privacy—even at the cost of thereby losing what might be research that promises to benefit the larger whole" (Ess & AOIR working committee on ethics, 2002, p. 20).

If we take a look at the contrast between U.S. and European approaches to ethics in research, this recommendation takes shape as a viable and proactive stance. The Association of Internet Researchers has addressed the issue of ethics in Internet research in some depth (2002). They offer key questions which can help guide researchers in making ethically grounded decisions regarding the particularities of online environments outlined above. Some of these questions include:

- What ethical expectations are established by the venue?
- When should one ask for informed consent?
- What medium for informed consent (email, fax, Instant Messaging) would best protect the human subject?
- In studying groups with a high turnover rate, is obtaining permission from the moderator/facilitator/list owner, etc., sufficient?
- What are the initial ethical expectations/assumptions of the authors/subjects being studied? For example: Do participants in this environment assume/believe that their communication is private?
- Will the material be referred to by direct quotation or paraphrased?
- Will the material be attributed to a specified person? Referred to by his/her real name? Pseudonym? "Double-pseudonym?" (i.e., a pseudonym for a frequently used pseudonym?)

Chris Mann (2002), a British sociologist specializing in the study of ethics, distills the issues into a set of three very simple questions:

- Are we seeking to magnify the good?
- Are we acting in ways that do not harm others?
- Do we recognize the autonomy of others and acknowledge that they are of equal worth to ourselves and should be treated so?

These criteria shift the focus away from utility and regulation and place the emphasis squarely on the purpose of the research, a point made clearly by Denzin (1997, 2003) in discussing a feminist communitarian stance. An example illustrating the difference between these stances and possible outcomes is the U.S. researcher asking:

"Am I working with human subjects or public documents?"

This question arises in a study wherein the scholar is using publicly accessed archives of online discourse. Many Internet scholars contend that publicly accessible online discourse does not require human subject approval because the domains in which these texts are produced are public (Walther, 2002). This determination is derived from arguments about the regulatory definitions of what constitutes human subjects research. Walther further notes that while participants might perceive that the space is private and therefore their texts are private, this perception is "extremely misplaced" (p. 3).

Posed to a colleague in Scandinavia, the question was not sensible (Bromseth, personal communication, February 19, 2004). She understood the question, but indicated that her colleagues would not frame the question in the same way. Among other things, Bromseth noted that the question focuses on the researcher's legalistic dilemma and not the participants in the study. The question polarizes the issue into an "either/or" false dichotomy to be solved by definition-based, legalistic clarification, rather than through the input of and interaction with the human subject(s).

To further clarify the distinction, note that the title of this current section of this chapter highlights ethics alongside their regulatory body for academics, the IRB. My choice in heading reflects a utilitarian stance. On the contrary, when describing the ethical issues facing Internet researchers, Bromseth (2003) never mentions a regulatory body at all, instead focusing on the respondent. She writes within the communitarian or deontological stance, "Researchers have been forced to rethink basic issues . . . to be able to develop and apply approaches that work for ourselves and our research goals and that would be ethically defensible in relation to our informants" (p. 68).

With deeply rooted standpoints and few universal principles, how should one treat texts and Web sites, which may or may not be vital to the subjectivity of the author; which may or may not be considered private by the author; which may or may not be important to our individual research goals? There are no simple conclusions to be drawn in the arena of ethical Internet research. Institutional research boards will continue to regulate the activities of scholars. National, regional, and cultural principles will undoubtedly remain distinct; ethical guidelines are entrenched in larger socio-political-economic structures of meaning. Internet researchers will continue to argue the issues of publicly accessible documents; anonymity; copyright; presentation of other; and privacy. Excellent overviews of opposing positions can be found in various journals, online reports, and conference/workshop proceedings.[5]

Given the variations in ethical stances as well as the diversity of methodological choices, each researcher must explore and define research within their own integral frameworks. Thomas (2003) recommends a more proactive approach to ethical behavior than simply adhering to rules set out by IRBs. "In this view, we recognize the potential ambiguity of social situations in which most value decisions are made and commit ourselves not to rules, but to broad principles of justice and beneficence" (p. 197). As to how one might determine what these broad principles actually are, Stephen L. Carter (1996) reminds us of what it means to have integrity. It involves not only discerning what is right and what is wrong, but also acting on this discernment, even at personal cost, and publicly acknowledging and defending one's stance and choices. Acting with integrity, Carter adds, "demands that we take the time for genuine reflection to be certain that the [morality] we are pressing is right" (p. 204).

## ▣ RETHINKING THE PURPOSE OF RESEARCH

My ten years of experience as an Internet researcher lead me to believe that it is time to reassess our priorities and processes as researchers. Instead of asking "how we can protect human subjects through various types of research design?" we will frame better questions and find richer answers by shifting our focus toward the participant. Putting the human subject squarely in the center of the research both shifts the ethical considerations and allows for socially responsible research.

All ethnographically informed research, particularly in computer-mediated environments, includes decisions about how to draw boundaries around groups, what to leave in as meaningful data and what to dismiss as unimportant, and how to explain what we think we know to our audiences. These research design decisions, which are often dismissed as simple logistics and not often mentioned in methods texts or ethics discussions, influence the representation of research participants, highlight particular findings while dismissing others, create ideologically charged bases of knowledge and, ultimately, impact legislation and policy making. This chain of events requires astute, reflexive methodological attention. We make choices, either consciously or unconsciously, throughout the research process. Researchers must grapple with natural and necessary change engendered by vivid awareness of the constructed nature of science, knowledge, and culture.

One way to meet the future is to learn from but not rely on the past. Practically speaking, this involves a return to the fundamental question: Why are we doing research? Politically speaking, this involves taking risks that will productively stretch the academy's understanding of what inquiry intends to produce.

The Internet continues to provide a unique space for the construction of identity in that it offers anonymity in an exclusively discursive environment. The difficulty of observing and interviewing in these contexts is that our expectations remain rooted in embodied ways of collecting, analyzing and interpreting information. Simply put, our methods are still more suitable for research in physically proximal contexts. Moreover, although the technology of the internet has afforded us greater reach to participants and provided a space for researchers to interact with participants in creative ways, our epistemological frameworks have not yet shifted to match this reality. It is necessary not only to accommodate the features of computer-mediated communication into our basic assumptions, but also to interrogate and rework the underlying premises we use to make sense of the world.

Computer mediated communication highlights key paradoxes of social research in that personae being represented are already one step removed from their bodies when encountered by the researcher. Doing research of life online has compelled me to recognize that I have always taken for granted my ability to parse human experience by carefully paying attention to people's activities in context. Engaging in meaningful experiences with anonymous beings and interviewing people I cannot see face to face, I can identify many of the weaknesses of qualitative research processes in general. Interviewing or observing in natural settings, researchers rely on the ability to judge a face, looking for visual signs of authentic emotion and inauthentic pretense. We make immediate categorizing decisions based on first impressions, listening to the tenor of a voice on the phone or looking at body type, ethnic markers, hair style and color, and clothing brands. Even the most astute and cautious researchers unconsciously rely on habitual patterns of sense making in everyday interactions with others.

We must directly engage the fact that the questions driving the research must change to accommodate the enduring partiality of scientific knowing. Political action is a sensible shift, therefore, in that it does not seek to find the truth, but to create the possibilities for people to enjoy a better life.

In whatever ways we utilize the potential of Internet-mediated communication to facilitate our social inquiry, ethically sensitive approaches are complicated, even impeded, by our methodological training. Depending on the academic discipline we find ourselves working within, we will be encouraged in varying degrees to oversimplify the complexity of human experience, transforming the mysteries of interaction into discrete variables that are easily measured. This is done for admirable reason and by no means am I recommending a complete dismissal of traditional means of collecting and analyzing data. At the same time, Internet contexts prompt us to reconsider the foundations of our methods and compel us to assess the extent to which our methods are measuring what we think they are, or getting to the heart of what we have assumed they did. Through the Internet, we have the opportunity to observe how written discourse functions to construct meaning and how textual dialogue can form the basis of cultural understanding. The taken-for-granted methods we use to make sense of participants in our research projects need thorough reexamination in light of our growing comprehension of how intertextuality literally occurs.

Even within a contemporary framework of sociological inquiry—whereby the distinction between the researcher and researched is problematized, the researcher's role is acknowledged, and bias is accepted as a fundamental fact of interpretation— our obligation to the participant remains. We make decisions, conscious or unconscious, about what constitutes the virtual field and subject of study. Often dismissed as logistical, research design decisions, these choices make a great difference in what is studied, how it is studied, and eventually, how society defines and frames computer-mediated communication environments. Because Internet-based technologies for communication are still new and potentially changing the way people live their everyday professional and personal lives in a global society, it is essential to reflect carefully on the ethical frames influencing our studies and the political possibilities of our research.

## ▣ NOTES

1. It is important to note that although this chapter focuses on computer-mediated communication, the capacities and consequences extend well beyond the desktop or laptop. For excellent discussions of the ways in which mobile telephones influence identity and cultural constructions, see Howard Rheingold (2002) or Katz and Aakhus (2002).

2. The trend is exaggerated here to illustrate the extremes. Speculative and exaggerated accounts are important to consider because they influenced research premises throughout the 1990s. This is not to say that empirical research was absent or unimportant. The impact of electronic technologies on individual communication practices and social structure has been explored for decades, most well represented by scholars like Marshall McLuhan (1964), Harold Innis (1964), James Carey (1989), and Neil Postman (1986, 1993). Throughout the 1980s, significant empirical and theoretical research examined the impact of computers and information

technology on the practices and structures of work. Sociological accounts (e.g., Turkle, 1984) studied important intersections of technology, self, and society. Crucial to the point is that many exciting but exaggerated texts appeared in the early 1990s, both in trade and academic presses, which fueled further speculative research and led to the publication of accounts that had more novel appeal than careful scholarship in an era of exciting new technological developments. As this field of inquiry evolves, it is vital to examine with a critical lens the foundations upon which current theoretical premises may be built.

3. A similar categorization of critical junctures was developed by the author for a keynote address at a Nordic conference on Ethics and Internet research and has been used subsequently in related publications (Markham, 2003a, 2003b).

4. The material in this section is being written concurrently for a chapter in an edited collection (Markham, 2003c).

5. *The Information Society*, for example, hosted a special issue in 1996 on the ethics of Internet research. The Association of Internet Researchers released a comprehensive report of various stances, comparative guidelines, and an extensive list of resources (2002); a conference panel yielded a set of articles which lay out various perspectives in a special issue of *Ethics and Information Technology* (2002); the first Nordic conference and graduate seminar on ethics and Internet research yielded the edited volume *Applied Ethics in Internet Research*, containing keynote addresses and case studies by Scandinavian students (Thorseth, 2003); and an edited volume by Johns, Chen, and Hall, (2003) entitled *Online Social Research* offers various perspectives and cases. Many other sources discuss both general and specific issues related to Internet research and ethics. All of these resources offer both novice and experienced researchers valuable philosophical, practical, and legal information.

## ◪ REFERENCES

Abram, D. (1997). *The spell of the sensuous*. New York: Vintage Books.

Ackerman, D. (1995). *A natural history of the senses*. New York: Vintage Books.

AOIR Ethics Working Committee. (2002). *Ethical decision-making and Internet research: Recommendations from the AOIR ethics working committee*. Retrieved January 2004 from www.aoir.org/reports/ethics.pdf

Association of Internet Researchers. (2002). Ethical decision making and Internet research. Retrieved January 15, 2004 from http://www.aoir.org/reports/ethics.pdf

Bakhtin, M. (1981). *The dialogic imagination: Four essays*. Edited by Michael Holquist. Trans. C. Emerson and M. Holquist. Austin: University of Texas Press.

Baym, N. (2000). *Tune in, log on: Soaps, fandom, and online community*. Thousand Oaks, CA: Sage.

Baym, N., Zhang, Y. B., & Lin, M. (October 2002). The internet in college social life. Paper presented at the annual conference of the Association of Internet Researchers.

Bell, D., & Kennedy, B. M. (Eds.). (2000). *The Cybercultures reader*. New York: Routledge.

Benedikt, M. (1991). *Cyberspace: First steps*. Cambridge: MIT Press.

Blumer, H. (1969). *Symbolic interactionism*. Engelwood Cliffs, NJ: Prentice-Hall.

Bromseth, J. (2002). Public Places . . . Private Activities? In A. Morrison, (Ed.), *Researching ICTs in context* (pp. 44–72). Oslo: Intermedia Report 3/2002. Oslo: Unipub forlag. Retrieved December 1, 2002, from http://www.intermedia.uio.no/publikasjoner/rapport_3/

Bromseth, J. (2003). Ethical and methodological challenges in research on net-mediated communication. In M. Thorseth, (Ed.), *Applied ethics in internet research* (pp. 67–85). Trondheim, Norway: NTNU University Press.

Buber, M. (1958). *I and Thou* (2nd ed., R. G. Smith, Trans.). New York: Scribner.

Carey, J. (1989). *Communication as culture: Essays on media and society.* Boston: Unwin Hyman.

Carter, S. L. (1996). *Integrity.* New York: Harper Perennial.

Christians, C. (2000). Ethics and politics in qualitative research. In N. K. Denzin & Y. S. Lincoln (Eds.), *Handbook of qualitative research* (2nd ed., pp. 133–155). Thousand Oaks, CA: Sage.

Clifford, J., & Marcus, G. (1986). *Writing culture: The poetics and politics of ethnography.* Berkeley: University of California Press.

Denzin, N. K. (1997). *Interpretive ethnography: Ethnographic practices for the 21st century.* Thousand Oaks, CA: Sage.

Denzin, N. K. (2003). Prologue: Online environments and interpretive social research. In M. Johns, S. L. Chen, & J. Hall (Eds.), *Online social research: Methods, issues, and ethics* (pp. 1–12). New York: Peter Lang.

Dery, M. (1994). *Flame wars: Discourses in cyberspace.* Chapel Hill, NC: Duke University Press.

Dibbell, J. (1996). A rape in Cyberspace; or how an evil clown, a Haitian trickster spirit, two wizards, and a cast of dozens turned a database into a society. In P. Ludlow (Ed.), *High noon on the electronic frontier: Conceptual issues in Cyberspace* (pp. 375–396). Cambridge: MIT Press.

Eichhorn, K. (2001). Sites unseen: Ethnographic research in a textual community. *International Journal of Qualitative Studies in Education, 14*(4), 565–578.

Ess, C. (2003). Beyond contemptus mundi and Cartesian dualism. In M. Thorseth (Ed.), *Applied ethics in internet research.* Trondheim, Norway: NTNU University Press.

*Ethics and Information Technology, 4*(3). (2002). Special issue on Internet research ethics.

Fine, M. (1994). Working the hyphens: Reinventing self and other in qualitative research. In N. K. Denzin & Y. S. Lincoln (Eds.), *Handbook of qualitative research* (pp. 70–82). Thousand Oaks, CA: Sage.

Fine, M., Weis, L., Weseen, S., & Wong, L. (2000). For whom? Qualitative research, representations, and social responsibilities. In N. K. Denzin & Y. S. Lincoln (Eds.), *Handbook of qualitative research* (2nd ed., pp. 107–131). Thousand Oaks, CA: Sage.

Gajjala, R. (July 2002). An interrupted postcolonial/ feminist cyberethnography: Complicity and resistance in the "Cyberfield." *Feminist Media Studies, 2*(2), 177–193.

Gergen, K. (1991). *The saturated self. Dilemmas of identity in contemporary life.* New York: Basic Books.

Gibson, W. (1984). *Neuromancer.* New York: Ace Books.

Goffman, E. (1959). *The presentation of self in everyday life.* New York: Anchor Press.

Haraway, D. (1991). *Simians, cyborgs, and women: The reinvention of nature.* New York: Routledge.

Herring, S. (1993). Gender and democracy in computer-mediated communication. *Electronic Journal of Communication/La Revue Electronique de Communication, 3*(2), 1–17.

Herring, C. S. (2004). Slouching toward the ordinary: Current trends in computer-mediated communication. *New Media and Society, 6*(1), 26–36.

Hine, C. (2000). *Virtual ethnography.* London: Sage.

Innis, H. (1964). *The bias of communication.* Toronto, Canada: University of Toronto Press.

Johns, M. D., Chen, S. L. S., & Hall, G. J. (Eds.). (2003). *Online social research: Methods, issues, and ethics.* New York: Peter Lang.

Johnson, C. (2003). *Social interaction and meaning construction among community websites.* Unpublished Master of Arts thesis. University of Illinois at Chicago.

Jones, S. G. (1995b). Understanding community in the information age. In S. G. Jones (Ed.), *Cybersociety: Computer-mediated communication and community* (pp. 10–35). Thousand Oaks, CA: Sage.

Jones, S. G. (Ed.). (1999). *Doing Internet research: Critical issues and methods for examining the net.* Thousand Oaks, CA: Sage.

Katz, J., & Aakhus, M. (Eds.). (2002). *Perpetual contact: Mobile communication, private talk, public performance.* Cambridge, UK: Cambridge University Press.

Keeps, C. J. (1993). Knocking on heaven's door: Leibbniz, Baudrillard and virtual reality. *Ejournal, 3,* Retrieved December, 1996 via anonymous ftp: EJOURNAL@albany.bitnet.

Keisler, S. (1997). *Culture of the Internet.* Mahwah, NJ: Lawrence Erlbaum.

Kendall, L. (1998). Meaning and identity in "Cyberspace": The performance of gender, class and race online. *Symbolic Interaction, 21*(2), 129–153.

Kendall, L. (2002). *Hanging out in the virtual pub: Masculinities and relationships online.* Berkeley: University of California Press.

Kolko, B. E. (2000). Erasing @race: Going White in the (Inter)Face. In B. E. Kolko, L. Nakamura, & G. B. Rodman (Eds.) *Race in Cyberspace.* (pp. 117–131). New York: Routledge.

Kolko, B. E. (2002). Personal conversation. October. Maastricht, The Netherlands.

Kolko, B. E., Nakamura, L., & Rodman, G. B. (Eds.). (2000). *Race in Cyberspace.* New York: Routledge.

Kramarae, C. (1995). A backstage critique of virtual reality. In S. G. Jones (Ed.). *Cybersociety: Computer-mediated communication and community,* (pp. 36–56). Thousand Oaks, CA: Sage.

Laing, R. D. (1969). *Self and others.* New York: Pantheon.

Lakoff, G., & Johnson, M. (1981). *Metaphors we live by.* Chicago: University of Chicago Press.

Ludlow, P. (1996). (Ed.). *High noon on the electronic frontier.* Cambridge: MIT Press.

Lupton, D. (1995). The embodied computer/user. In M. Featherstone & R. Burrows (Eds.), *Cyberspace/Cyberbodies/Cyberpunk* (pp. 97–112). Thousand Oaks, CA: Sage.

MacKinnon, R. C. (1995). Searching for the Leviathan in usenet. In S. G. Jones (Ed.), *Cybersociety: Computer-mediated communication and community* (pp. 112–137). Thousand Oaks, CA: Sage.

MacKinnon, R. C. (1998). The social construction of rape in Cyberspace. In F. Sudweeks, S. Rafaeli, & M. McLaughlin (Eds.), *Network and netplay: Virtual groups on the Internet.* Menlo Park, CA: AAAI Press. [cited from the online/ascii version. Retrieved March 1997 from http://www.actlab.utexas.edu/~spartan/texts/rape.html]

Mann, C. (June 1, 2002). *Generating data online: Ethical concerns and challenges for the C21 researcher.* Keynote address delivered at Making Common Ground: A Nordic conference on Internet research ethics. Trondheim, Norway.

Mann, C. (2003). Generating data online: Ethical concerns and challenges for the C21 researcher. In M. Thorseth (Ed.), *Applied ethics in internet research* (pp. 31–50). Trondheim, Norway: NTNU University Press.

Mann, C., & Stewart, F. (2000). *Internet communication and qualitative research: A handbook for researching online.* London: Sage.

Markham, A. (1998). *Life online: Researching real experience in virtual space*. Walnut Creek, CA: AltaMira.

Markham, A. (2003a). Representation in online ethnographies. In M. Johns, S. L. Chen, & J. Hall (Eds.), *Online social research: Methods, issues, and ethics* (pp. 141–156). New York: Peter Lang.

Markham, A. (2003b). Critical junctures and ethical choices in internet ethnography. In M. Thorseth (Ed.), *Applied ethics in internet research* (pp. 51–63). Trondheim, Norway: NTNU University Press.

Markham, A. (2004a). The internet as research context. In C. Seale, J. Gubrium, G. Giampietro, & D. Silverman (Eds.), *Qualitative research practice*. London: Sage.

Markham, A. (2004b). Internet as a tool for qualitative research. In D. Silverman (Ed.), *Qualitative research: Theory, method, and practice* (pp. 95–123). London: Sage.

McLuhan, M. (1964). *Understanding media: The extensions of man*. New York: New American Library.

Miller, D., & Slater, D. (2000). *The Internet: An ethnographic approach*. New York: New York University Press.

Nakamura, L. (1995). Race in/for Cyberspace: Identity tourism and racial passing on the Internet. *Works and Days, 13*(1–2), 181–193.

Nakamura, L. (2003). Untitled conference presentation at National Communication Association annual meetings. November 19, Miami, Florida.

Orgad, S. (2002, October 14). *Continuities between the offline and the online*. Paper presented at the conference of the Association of Internet Researchers, Maastricht, The Netherlands, October 13–16.

Poster, M. (1998). Virtual ethnicity: Tribal identity in an age of global communications. In S. G. Jones (Ed.), *Cybersociety 2.0* (pp. 184–211). Thousand Oaks, CA: Sage.

Postman, N. (1986). *Amusing ourselves to death: Public discourse in the age of show business*. New York: Viking Press.

Postman, N. (1993). *Technopoly: The surrender of culture to technology*. New York: Vintage Books.

Reid, E. (1995). Virtual worlds: Culture and imagination. In S. G. Jones (Ed.), *Cybersociety: Computer-mediated communication and community* (pp. 164–183). Thousand Oaks, CA: Sage.

Rheingold, H. (1991). *Virtual reality*. New York: Touchstone.

Rheingold, H. (1993). *The virtual community: Homesteading on the electronic frontier*. Reading, MA: Addison-Wesley.

Rheingold, H. (2002). *Smart mobs: The next social revolution*. New York: Basic Books.

Rommetveit, R. (1980). On "meanings" of acts and what is meant and made known by what is said in a pluralistic social world. In M. Brenner (Ed.), *The structure of action* (pp. 108–149). Oxford: Basil Blackwell.

Ryen, A. (June 1, 2002). Paper presented at Making Common Ground: A Nordic conference on Internet research ethics. Trondheim, Norway.

Senft, T., & Horn, S. (1996). Special issue: Sexuality and Cyberspace: Performing the Digital Body. *Women & Performance: A Journal of Feminist Theory, 17*.

Shane, M. J. (2001). Virtual work teams: An ethnographic analysis. Unpublished dissertation, Fielding Institute, California.

Sondheim, A. (Ed.). (1996). *Being online: Net subjectivity*. New York: Lusitania Press.

Sproull, L., & Kiesler, S. (1991). *Connections: New ways of working in the networked environment.* Cambridge: MIT Press.

Stone, R. A. (1996). *The war of desire and technology at the close of the mechanical age.* Cambridge: MIT Press.

Sveningsson, M. (2001). *Creating a sense of community: Experiences from a Swedish web chat.* Doctoral dissertation. The TEMA Institute, Department of Communication Studies, Linköping, Sweden.

Thomas, J. (2003). Reexamining the ethics of internet research: Facing the challenge of overzealous oversight. In M. Johns, S. L. Chen, & G. J. Hall (Eds.), *Online social research: Methods, issues, and ethics* (pp. 187–201). New York: Peter Lang.

Thorseth, M. (Ed.). (2003). *Applied ethics in Internet research.* Trondheim, Norway: NTNU University Press.

Turkle, S. (1984). *Second Self: Computers and the human spirit.* New York: Simon & Schuster.

Turkle, S. (1995). *Life on the screen: identity in the age of the Internet.* New York: Simon & Schuster.

Vanderpool, H. Y. (Ed.). (1996). *The ethics of research involving human subjects: Facing the 21st century.* Frederick, MD: University Publishing Group.

Walther, J. (2002). Research ethics in Internet-enabled research: Human subjects issues and methodological myopia. *Ethics and Information Technology, 4*(3), Retrieved March 15, 2004, from http://www.nyu.edu/projects/nissenbaum/ethics_walther.html.

Waskul, D., Douglass, M., & Edgley, C. (2000). Cybersex: Outercourse and the enselfment of the body. *Symbolic Interaction, 25 (4)*, 375–397.

Witmer, D. F., & Katzman, S. L. (1998). Smile when you say that: Graphic accents as gender markers in computer-mediated communication. In S. Rafaeli, F. Sudweeks, & M. L. McLaughlin (Eds.), *Network and netplay: Virtual groups on the Internet.* Boston: AAAI/MIT Press.

Woolley, B. (1992). *Virtual worlds: A journey in hype and hyperreality.* Oxford: Blackwell, Press.

Wright, R. (1994). "Life on the Internet: Democracy's salvation or cultural fragmentation?" *Utne Reader,* Jan/Feb: 101–107.

# 9

# ANALYTIC PERSPECTIVES

## Paul Atkinson and Sara Delamont

I n this chapter, we examine a number of related themes under the aegis of analysis.
The analysis of data derived from qualitative research strategies is a potentially vast
field. It is not our intention to generate a comprehensive review of the history of
analysis (Lincoln & Denzin, 2003) or of all its current manifestations (Hardy & Bryman,
2004). There are entire books that go some way in that direction, and virtually no textbook or handbook achieves complete coverage. Rather, through a selective review, we
highlight what we think are some key issues confronting the research community. We do
not, therefore, offer a prescriptive view on how data should be analyzed. Textbooks on
methods themselves are the appropriate place for such practical guidance (e.g., Coffey &
Atkinson, 1996; Silverman, 1997, 2004). Rather, we survey the methodological terrain
selectively as we perceive it.

The extraordinary diffusion of qualitative research among the social and cultural
disciplines is a welcome development, and it is one to which we have made modest
contributions (Atkinson, Coffey, & Delamont, 2003; Delamont, 2002; Hammersley &
Atkinson, 1995). We are personally and professionally committed to disseminating further qualitative research methods and the published work that derives from them. On
the other hand, the very proliferation of qualitative research brings in its train some
potential problems. The conduct of qualitative work has become fragmented. During
an era of hyperspecialization in the academy and beyond, qualitative research has been
subject to the same forces. The range of specialties and emphases can be gauged by
inspecting, by way of example, the contents of recent and current edited collections
(Denzin & Lincoln, 1994, 2001; Gubrium & Holstein, 2002b; Seale, Silverman,
Gubrium, & Gobo, 2004; Silverman, 2004). As qualitative research has become increasingly professionalized and increasingly subject to explicit codification and reflection, it
seems to have become increasingly fragmented.

In the section that follows, we review that process of fragmentation, identify some of its contours and consequences, and suggest some more positive ways of thinking about the proper relations between different methods. In particular, we affirm the rather unfashionable position that there are kinds of social activity and representation that have their indigenous modes of organization. Language and discourse, narratives, visual styles, and semiotic and cultural codes are culturally relative and arbitrary, but they nevertheless display orderliness that is relatively stable and predictable, observable, and describable. Although strongly determinist forms of structuralism or semiotics might not prove to be tenable, that is no excuse for abandoning altogether disciplined attention to such intrinsic ordering principles. Qualitative research needs to remain faithful to that indigenous organization.

We then turn our attention to a different but related issue, that is, the fragmentation of justifications for qualitative analysis and the interpretation of the social world. We contrast a centripetal tendency, a tradition that has tended toward a convergence or consensus within the field (especially in sociology), with a centrifugal tendency that has celebrated and promoted diversity among analytic strategies. The former represents a canonical tradition within the intellectual field, whereas the latter represents a more radical and sometimes transgressive mode. Recent accounts of the history of qualitative research and its practices, with which our own views diverge, tend to locate these differences within a developmental framework, tracing an intellectual history for qualitative research away from a positivist stance toward carnivalesque postmodern diversity (e.g., Lincoln & Denzin, 1994, 2001). Although we recognize that such accounts are partially correct in describing some changes in the most visible thinking, we differ in how best to capture the underlying differences (Atkinson, Coffey, & Delamont, 1999, 2001, 2003). We recapitulate and explore some of these issues briefly. Our perspective is not, however, based on a rearguard appeal to earlier versions of ethnographic or qualitative research and a return to the earlier certainties associated with the "classics" of methodological literature (cf. Atkinson et al., 2003). Our critical stance is, therefore, very different from that articulated by commentators such as Brewer (2002), who seemed to assert a rather vulgar form of realist analysis in distancing himself from postmodernist analytic strategies. Our critical stance also differs from those that embrace and endorse the claims of postmodernism.

We go on to discuss another major axis of contestation within the qualitative tradition and its current manifestations. We suggest that there is a major line of cleavage that separates disciplines or subdisciplines and individual researchers from one another, although it is not always apparent to the main protagonists in the field. We suggest that this reflects differing emphases on experience and action. During recent years, a good deal of qualitative research has been justified, analyzed, and represented in terms of social actors' experiences of their own social worlds, that is, of changes over the life courses of biographical phenomena and disruptions such as mental and physical ill health (Ellis & Flaherty, 1992). In a parallel way, qualitative research has sometimes been transmuted from the biographical to the autobiographical and autoethnographic

(Bochner & Ellis, 2001; Ellis, 2004; Reed-Danahay, 1997, 2001). We do not think, however, that this is derived from a self-evident reason for conducting qualitative research. The purpose of such research is not always to understand the world from the actor's or informant's own perspective or to gain access to his or her personal private realms of experience and feeling (Behar, 1996; Fernandez & Huber, 2001; Radstone, 2000). A great deal of the foundational work in ethnography and other qualitative research was concerned with the analysis of collective social action, that is, how members of society accomplish joint activity through language and other practical activities as well as how they align their activities through shared cultural resources. From this latter perspective, even motives, emotions, intentions, and the like are matters of collective action, expressed through the codes of shared idioms. These distinctions need to be made visible so that the analysis of ethnographic and other data does not become confused (Atkinson et al., 2003; Gubrium & Holstein, 2002a, 2002b).

We then consider another related but distinct issue, that is, the aestheticization of analysis and representation. As some analysts and commentators have moved toward various postmodernist positions, they have sought to free qualitative analysis from the conventions of academic textual writing (Ellis & Bochner, 1996; Goodall, 2000). We thoroughly endorse the principle of critical reflection on the conventions through which social worlds and social actions are reconstructed. Just as we recommend paying attention to the conventional orders of culture and action, we also recommend paying attention to the conventions of textual production and reception. But we warn against the wholesale acceptance of aesthetic criteria in the reconstruction of social life. In many contexts, there is a danger of collapsing the various forms of social action into one aesthetic mode—that is, implicitly revalorizing the authorial voice of the social scientist—and of transforming socially shared and culturally shaped phenomena into the subject matter of an undifferentiated but esoteric literary genre. (For examples of work that we believe exemplify this trend, see Clough, 1998; Richardson, 1997, 2002.)

Finally, we consider the implications of our remarks for social critique. We suggest that an engaged social science should indeed remain faithful to the intrinsic order of social life. We need—more than ever before—principled, systematic, and disciplined ways of accounting *for* the social world and *to* the social world. We need to be able to produce accounts of the social that can recognize the conventions of: media representations, of fashion and consumer culture, of political and everyday discourse, of scientific knowledge, of cinematic and other visual codings. Accounts that reduce the social world to a domain of experience cannot generate faithful, let alone critical, analyses of culture and action.

▣ ANALYTIC FRAGMENTATION

We have no quarrel with attempts to define and practice appropriate strategies for the analysis of particular kinds of data. Indeed, we want to insist on the proper disciplined approach to any and every type of data. In addition, we want data to be analyzed and not just reproduced and celebrated (as sometimes happens with life histories and visual materials). Our main message, however, is that the forms of data and analysis reflect the forms of culture and social action. For instance, we collect and analyze personal narratives and life histories because they are a collection of types or forms—spoken and written—through which various kinds of social activity are accomplished. They are themselves forms of social action in which identities, biographies, and various other kinds of work get done (Ochs & Capps, 2002; O'Dell, 2001; Patterson, 2002). Thus, we accord importance to narratives and narrative analysis because they address important kinds of social action (Atkinson, 1997; Bauman, 1986; Riessman, 2002). In the same spirit, we should pay serious attention to visual data insofar as culture and action have significant visual aspects that cannot be expressed and analyzed except by reference to visual materials. This is by no means equivalent to the assumption that ethnographic film or video constitutes an especially privileged approach to sociological or anthropological understanding (Ball & Smith, 2001; Banks & Morphy, 1997; Pink, 2001, 2004). The same can be said of other analytic approaches. Documentary analysis is significant insofar as a given social setting is self-documenting and important social actions are performed in that setting (Prior, 2003; Scott, 1990). Texts deserve attention because of their socially organized and conventional properties and because of the uses they are put to in their production, circulation, and consumption. The same is true of other material goods, artifacts, technologies, and so forth (Tilley, 1991, 1999, 2001). The analysis of dramaturgy, likewise, is important insofar as social actors and collectivities engage in significant performative activities (Denzin, 2003; Dyck & Archetti, 2003; Gray & Sinding, 2002; Hughes-Freeland, 1998; Tulloch, 1999). But it should not be treated as a privileged way in which to approach all of social life.

We believe, therefore, that it is important to avoid reductionist views that treat one type of data or one approach to analysis as being the prime source of social and cultural interpretation. We should not, in other words, seek to render social life in terms of just one analytic strategy or just one cultural form. The forms of analysis should reflect the forms of social life, their diversity should mirror the diversity of cultural forms, and their significance should be in accordance with their social and cultural functions.

We identify these different analytic approaches not merely to celebrate diversity, that is, not to propose a vulgar version of "triangulation" through methodological pluralism and synthesis (Denzin, 1970; Janesick, 1994). Quite the reverse—we want to assert the importance of rendering the different facets of culture and social action and of reflecting their respective forms. We want, therefore, to affirm that aspects of culture and the mundane organization of social life have their intrinsic formal properties and that the analysis of social life should respect and explore those forms. In so doing, we react against some analytic tendencies that have undervalued anything that smacks of formal analysis. Such formalism seems to fly in the face of the most fashionable appeals to postmodernism. Yet discourse, narratives, performances, encounters, rhetoric, and poetics all have their intrinsic indigenous modes of organization. So too do visual, textual, material, and other cultural embodiments. It is not necessary to endorse a narrowly structuralist analytic perspective or endorse unduly restrictive analyses to recognize the formal properties of talk, the codes of cultural representation, the semiotic structures of visual materials, or the common properties of narratives and documents of life.

It is necessary, therefore, for ethnographers and other analysts of social life to pay attention to the analytic imperatives of such socially shared codes, conventions, and structures. The forms of social and cultural life call for equivalent analyses. These methodological principles give us a way of addressing some fundamental methodological precepts in a disciplined way. Herbert Blumer enunciated the principle that research should be "faithful" to the phenomena under investigation (Blumer, 1954; Hammersley, 1989). In its most general form, this methodological precept seems to beg all the important questions, seeming to imply that one can know the phenomena prior to their investigation. A naïvely naturalist interpretation is clearly inappropriate. Our formulation retrieves for Blumer's principle a more methodologically precise formulation—a more restricted but more fruitful approach. It implies that fidelity to the phenomena means paying attention to the forms and media through which social actions, events, and representations are enacted, encoded, or embodied. It also gives a particular rendering of the notion of "thick description" (Denzin, 1994; Geertz, 1973, 1983). Our approach can be extended to a commentary on versions of "grounded theory" and cognate strategies such as "analytic induction" (Atkinson et al., 2003; Znaniecki, 1934). Again, there are multiple versions of grounded theory, and they have been thoroughly documented (Charmaz & Mitchell, 2001; Glaser, 1978, 1992; Glaser & Strauss, 1967; Strauss & Corbin, 1998). We do not, incidentally, advocate that all ethnographies should deploy every conceivable analytic procedure and examine every possible data type in the interests of a spurious kind of comprehensiveness or "holism." On the other hand, our insistence on attention to the forms of culture and social action gives particular force to notions such as holism. In our version of research methodology, this can refer not to the doomed attempt to document "everything" but rather to a principled respect for the multiplicity of cultural forms. Thus, holistic analysis would refer to *preserving* those forms that are indigenous to the culture in question rather than collapsing them into an undifferentiated plenum.

In the following sections, we elaborate on these general remarks. Before doing so, we outline a number of key analytic areas that demonstrate the force of our general argument. These are among the analytic strategies that can and should contribute to the systematic analysis of social settings, action, and organization.

## ▣ ANALYTIC STRATEGIES

### Narratives and Life Histories

We should not collect and document personal narratives because we believe them to have a privileged or special quality (Atkinson, 1997; Atkinson & Silverman, 1997;

Conle, 2003; Cortazzi, 1993, 2001). Narrative is not a unique mode of organizing or reporting experience. In addition, narrative is an important genre of spoken action and representation in everyday life and in many specialized contexts (Czarniawska, 1997, 1998; Riessman, 1993, 2002). We should, therefore, be studying narrative insofar as it is a particular feature of a given cultural milieu (e.g., Caplan, 1997; Cortazzi, 1991; Gardner, 2002; Lara, 1998; Myerhoff, 1978; Voysey, 1975). Furthermore, narratives are not independent of cultural conventions and shared formats (Holstein, 2000). They are not uniquely biographical or autobiographical materials, and they certainly do not convey unmediated private "experience." Likewise, they do not convey "memory" as a psychological phenomenon. Experiences, memories, emotions, and other apparently personal or private states are constructed and enacted through culturally shared narrative types, formats, and genres (Humphrey, Miller, & Zdravomyslova, 2003; Olney, 1998; Plummer, 1995, 2000, 2001; Tota, 2001; Wagner-Pacifici, 1996). They are related to story types more generally (Fine, 2001). There are affinities with other kinds of stories—of history, mythology, the mass media, and so forth. We need, therefore, to *analyze* narratives and life materials so as to treat them as instances of social action, that is, as speech acts or events with common properties, recurrent structures, cultural conventions, and recognizable genres. Therefore, we treat them as social phenomena like any others. Indeed, we need to treat narratives as performative acts (May, 2001) and treat them as forms of social action like any others.

## Visual Data

The collection and analysis of visual materials tends, unfortunately, to be treated as the preserve of a specialist domain. The production of ethnographic film has a long history, although it has often been oddly divorced from the mainstream textual practices of the ethnographic monograph (Ball & Smith, 1992, 2001; Banks & Morphy, 1997). The use of photography for ethnographic purposes has also been relegated to a somewhat specialist subfield when it has not been relegated to mere illustration of the written monograph (Loizos, 1993). During recent years, the development of small digital camcorders and the development of digital photography have created an enormous range of possibilities for ethnographers in the field. Consequently, visual anthropology and sociology should not be treated as separate genres or specialties. There are many aspects of culture that are intrinsically visual. Many cultural domains and artifacts can be grasped only through their visual representations and the structured properties of their visual codes (Ball & Smith, 2001).

There are many social phenomena that can and should be analyzed in terms of their appearances and performances that may be captured in visual terms. These are not, however, separable from the social settings in which such phenomena are generated and interpreted. They should not be explored purely as "visual" topics; rather, they should be explored as integral to a wide variety of ethnographic projects. Visual phenomena—the mundane as well as the self-consciously aesthetic—have their intrinsic modes of organization (Crouch & Lübbren, 2003). One does not need to endorse the most determinist versions of semiotics or structuralism to recognize that visual culture embodies conventions and codes of representation. There are culturally determined aesthetic and formal principles, and there are conventional forms of representation and expression.

Attention to visual culture also implies serious attention to the ethnoaesthetics of the producers, mediators, and consumers of visual materials. We need to not only "read" the visual but also understand ethnographically how it is read by members of the social world or culture in question (Grimshaw, 2001). In general terms, there has been insufficient attention to the aesthetic codes and judgments deployed by members of a given culture (Attfield, 2000). We know about specialized domains of aesthetic work such as the visual arts. We also know something about the aesthetics of everyday taste in clothes and fashion (Valis, 2003). In addition, there is research relat ing to the decoration and consumption of domestic spaces and objects (Henderson, 1998; Julier, 2000; Miller, 1987; Painter, 2002). In other contexts, there are studies of the visual cultures of advertising and other media of representation (Frosh, 2003). However, there are still many cultural domains in which local aesthetic criteria are important, but their analysis remains poorly integrated within the general ethnographic tradition; for instance, see DeNora (2000, 2003) on music in everyday life as a topic for ethnographic investigation (cf. Bennett & Dawe, 2001; Whiteley, Bennett, & Hawkins, 2004).

## Discourse and Spoken Action

The collection and analysis of spoken materials is one domain where overspecialization is a danger. The development of discourse analysis and conversation analysis has been one of the most egregiously successful domains of qualitative research. Its disciplinary bases have been varied, including linguistics, sociology, and psychology. The emergence of conversation analysis from the work of Harvey Sacks and other ethnomethodologists has been a remarkable contribution to the disciplined empirical study of social order and social action (Atkinson & Heritage, 1984; Moerman, 1988; Sacks, 1992). In the past, there has been a distinct tendency for these approaches to spoken language to become narrowly restricted specialties. Conversation analysis has, in particular, been unduly bounded and self-referential in some cases. There is no need to restrict our analysis of social worlds exclusively to those phenomena that are susceptible to recording for conversation—or discourse—analysis. We need, in contrast, to ensure that the analysis of spoken language remains firmly embedded in studies of organizational context, processes of socialization, routines of work, personal transformation, people processing, and so forth. During recent years, fortunately, the analysis of spoken discourse has engaged more explicitly and systematically with more generic issues of sociological research (e.g., Atkinson, 1995; Sarangi & Roberts, 1999; Silverman, 1987). Spoken language has its own intrinsic forms of organization. Indeed, it demonstrates a densely structured organization at every level, including the most finely grained. It is important, however, that discourse analysis, conversation analysis, discursive psychology, and the like not be treated as analytic ends in their own right and not be intellectually divorced from other aspects of ethnographic inquiry. The expert knowledge required should not be regarded as a specialty in its own right and independent of wider sociological or anthropological competence. The conventions of language use need to be analyzed, therefore, in relation to more general issues of identity, the interaction order, moral work, and the organization of social encounters. In addition, it is important for analysts of spoken action to remain sensitive to wider issues of social analysis and critique and for practitioners of more general qualitative analysis to engage with and use the methods and findings of discourse and conversation analysis. Key discussions that identify the relationships between discourse/conversation analysis and central issues of social research include the accounts by Potter (1996, 2003), Hepburn and Potter (2004), and Potter and Wetherell (1987).

## Material Assemblages and Technologies

The study of material goods and artifacts, technology, and other physical aspects of material culture deserves systematic attention in many ethnographic contexts (Tilley, 1991, 1999), but is too often relegated to specialized esoteric studies or to highly specific topics. The latter include studies of technology and inventions, of very particular kinds of physical display such as museums and art galleries, and of highly restricted kinds of artifacts such as religious, ritual, and artistic objects. But the detailed investigation of objects, assemblages, and inventions demands a place in the general ethnographic study of social and cultural forms (Appadurai, 1986; Bijker, 1995; Macdonald, 2002; Macdonald & Fyfe, 1996; Pinch & Trocco, 2002; Rabinow, 1996; Sandburg, 2003; Saunders, 2003).

It is vital that the study of physical objects, memorials, and technologies be thoroughly incorporated into more general field studies of work organizations, informal settings, cultural production, domestic settings, and so forth (Tilley, 2001). Artifacts and technologies are themselves understood, used, and interpreted by everyday social actors. They are used to document and record the past—and indeed to construct the past—and there is much to be learned from the local situated "ethnoarchaeology" of the material past (Dicks, 2000; Edwards, 2001; Gosden & Knowles, 2001). This includes the "monumental past" of places and their ethnohistories (cf. Herzfeld, 1991; Sciama, 2003; Yalouri, 2001). Issues of practical utility and aesthetic value intersect. Ideas of authenticity may be brought to bear on artifacts and assemblages (Forty & Kuchler, 1999; Handler & Gable, 1997). They may be used to display and warrant individual and collective identities; for instance, the "collection" (whether personal or national) is expressive of taste, identity, commitment, and enthusiasm (Miller, 2001b; Painter, 2002; Quinn, 2002). The material goods of fashion and conspicuous consumption are likewise expressive of status and aspirations. The archaeology of the present, as it were, needs to be integrated with the ethnographic imagination and to enrich the ethnographic eye (cf. Attfield, 2000). Much contemporary ethnographic fieldwork is oddly lacking in material content and physical goods, whereas informants' "voices" are transcribed from an apparent physical void. Field research needs to pay systematic attention to the physical embodiments of cultural values and codings.

More generally, this leads to a consideration of material culture. The material embodiment of culture and the cultural connotations of things have become prominent in recent cultural anthropological analyses (English-Lueck, 2002; Finn, 2001; Lury, 1996). Recent examples have included examinations of: home computers (Lally, 2002), mobile communications (Katz & Aakhus, 2002), photographs (Frosh, 2003), cars (Miller, 2001a), and memorabilia (Kwint, Breward, & Aynsley, 1999). These accounts transcend and transform the mundane material world into domains of signification. We do not need to subscribe to unduly strict and rigid formalisms to recognize that such phenomena can be analyzed in terms of their semiotic codes and conventions.

## Places and Spaces

Most ethnographic reportage seems oddly lacking in physical location. Many sociological and anthropological accounts, for instance, have but sketchy descriptions of the built environment within which social events and encounters take place. The treatment of space is too often restricted to aspects of human geography, urban studies, and architecture (Darby, 2000). It also needs to be integrated within more general ethnographic accounts. But ethnoarchitecture is—as we know from some anthropological accounts—significant in defining the spaces and styles of everyday living (Dodds & Taverner, 2001). Built spaces provide symbolic boundaries as well as physical boundaries (Borden, 2002; Butler, 2003; Crowley & Reid, 2002). They physically enshrine collective memories as well as more personal biographical and emotional work (Bender & Winer, 2001). Homes are endowed with emotional and cultural value through the expression of taste and cultural capital, the celebration of historical authenticity, or the observance of modern minimalism (Jackson, Lowe, Miller, & Mort, 2000). Public spaces also embody tacit cultural assumptions—about the classification and processing of people and things, about commercial and professional transactions, about political processes and citizenship (Benjamin, 1999; Möller & Pehkonen, 2003). The ethnographic exploration of places and spaces includes the commercial transformation of them through tourism and heritage work, the transmutation of downtown areas and waterfronts, the recreation of industrial pasts into leisure and entertainment, and the construction of replicas and spaces for "experience" (Dicks, 2000).

These brief and partial observations are not intended to map out a comprehensive view of the current research literatures or of the general possibilities that they open up for ethnographic and other qualitative social research. More important, these observations are not intended to be a list of actual or potential domains of specialization. On the contrary, the thrust of our argument so far is that these various aspects of culture and the specialized coteries of researchers who document them should not exist in mutual isolation. The goal of ethnographic accounts of everyday life, particularly cultural and organizational milieux, should be to use such analytic perspectives and to analyze such materials in constructing multilayered accounts of the social world.

These observations are not intended to be a comprehensive listing of all relevant domains and strategies of inquiry. On the contrary, our remarks have been highly selective. We have deliberately offered some remarks on a few key fields of research to illustrate and develop our more general argument concerning the treatment of qualitative data in the analysis of social organization and action, social identities and biographies, social contexts and institutions.

## ◨ THE ORDERING OF THE SOCIAL WORLD

It would be easy to misrepresent our remarks. We are not simply suggesting a promiscuous series of analytic perspectives and strategies. We are not advocating simply putting data types and analytic types together in the interests of an ill-defined holism. The holistic ideal has, from time to time, been proposed as the goal of ethnographic and other qualitative research, although few social scientists nowadays would recognize the existence of phenomena such as "communities" that can be described holistically anyway. Such an ideal implies a degree of temporal, spatial, and cultural closure that is a chimera. We do recommend systematic attention to these data types and analytic perspectives because they reflect certain principles of intrinsic organization.

It is not altogether fashionable to invoke notions such as intrinsic organization in the analysis of social life (cf. Atkinson & Delamont, 2004). During the era of poststructuralism and postmodernism, there is widespread rejection of anything that suggests "structure" or stable patterning in social and cultural forms. We believe, on the other hand, that we should recognize that forms can be identified and that they can serve as the basis of an analytic approach to qualitative social and cultural data. Moreover, an approach such as this gives us principled ways of understanding data of different sorts as reflections of the codes of social order. It also gives us ways of reconciling a number of tensions within the current treatment of qualitative research.

It is not necessary to invoke completely determinate and invariant structures so as to identify indigenous principles of order in particular forms of social action. The most obvious starting point—and it is one where there is no room for dispute—lies in the organization of spoken discourse. Discourse analysis and conversation analysis are virtually interchangeable from this perspective, and the disciplinary differences between them are insignificant for our purposes. It is not necessary to recapitulate their major findings here. But the general principles need reaffirmation. From the current vantage point, it is perhaps hard to reconstruct the recentness of any attention to spoken discourse as an object of analysis (as opposed to hypothetical texts or written materials) and of any attention to utterances in their natural context (as opposed to decontextualized individual sentences). The recognition that there can be *order* beyond the syntax of the individual sentence or beyond the single utterance is a relatively recent one. It follows, to a considerable extent, the technology of permanent recording that has permitted the close scrutiny of such phenomena, transforming spoken discourse into an object of inquiry and transforming its features into a topic of sociological, psychological, and linguistic inquiry.

The emergence of discourse analysis has transformed our collective appreciation of the interaction order in ways foreshadowed by Goffman's pioneering remarks and the no less original observations by Sacks (Goffman, 1981; Sacks, 1992; Silverman, 1998). It establishes the fundamental and pervasive principles of order, not least at the micro level of organization. Order in this sense displays itself through a remarkable array of socially shared devices, the operation of which produces and reproduces orderly conduct. The distinctive character of these devices is that they are used locally and recursively to generate strings of ordered interactions. The participants do not need to "know" the overall structure of the encounter to generate it in a predictable and stable way. They do not even need to be aware of the conventions they are using. Similar considerations apply to orderly conduct apart from spoken language. The recursive application of simple rules, in a practical way, generates orderly activity. To generate "structures" such as queues and turn-taking systems, for instance, each participant needs only to apply a simple chaining rule (i.e., "next participant follows the previous actor") and to know his or her relative position for the system to be self-replicating. Again, no actor needs to know the sequence of a complete queue for it to work smoothly, provided that each actor applies the same basic rule.

It is in this sense, therefore, that spoken and unspoken actions can display intrinsic orders that are in some sense independent of the actors' consciousness or intentions. In a similar vein, we can detect the interaction of physical and spoken actions. The capacity we now have to capture and inspect videotapes of human actions and processes of interaction already allows us to identify stable patterns of gesture in a way that was unavailable to earlier generations of observers. To this point, the social sciences have been relatively slow to fully explore the opportunities opened up by new digital technologies. We do know, however, that we can identify recurrent and interactionally functional patterns of movement and repertoires of gesture at a level of delicacy that only such permanent recordings render possible. As we have suggested, many of these analytic opportunities are dependent on contemporary recording technology. The important thing, however, is not the technology per se but rather the opportunity to pay close and systematic analytic attention to the *structures* of action. We can identify what Goffman (1983) referred to as an "interaction order" that displays ordering features that are relatively independent of the individual social actors who bring them into being. We know that social actors notice when the interaction order breaks down and that they share devices that repair mistakes and restore orderly functioning. But they do so as matters of preconscious action. Order is achieved and repaired through the application of recipes of action in a serial fashion. Complex structures and extended chains of action can be generated in a stable and smooth fashion through the local application of simple generative rules applied in a stepwise fashion.

We can identify recurrent ordering principles at a level of organization even greater than turn-by-turn discourse. The close analysis of narratives and similar spoken performances shows them to have recurrent structures. There have been various successful attempts to describe large-scale ordering principles for narrative events. Labov's pioneering work is one key example. Labov's groundbreaking work on language in society was innovative in various ways, with his work on spoken narratives being one example (Labov, 1972). Labov documented a number of basic structural elements that were part of the "grammar" of personal stories and accounts. Although not all of the structural elements were absolutely necessary for the production of a competent narrative, they recognizably generated stories that are sequentially coherent, deliver the story content competently, and are suitably "pointed" to make the story intelligible to speaker and hearer alike (Labov, 1972). We do not need to regard these as "deep structures," or as exerting mysterious powers over social actors, to acknowledge the recurrent patterning of narratives. A similar vein of analysis has been undertaken by Hymes (1996). Hymes's treatment, perhaps less well known than that of Labov, is more subtly grounded in an appreciation of *ethnopoetics,* that is, the culturally specific conventions of aesthetics and rhetoric that inform the competent performance and reception of oral performances. Hymes demonstrated principles that create distinctive internal structures within narratives and other oral performances. From his treatment of the materials, it appears that it is not necessary to reorder actors' own words into "poetic" reconstructions rather than to uncover the ethnopoetic structures and aesthetic principles that are indigenous to many narratives and other accounts.

Forms and functions of narratives and accounts are also identifiable from many analyses of respondents' accounting devices. Among these are the rhetorical repertoires or registers employed by natural scientists to express and reconcile recurrent features of scientific work. Gilbert and Mulkay (1984) demonstrated that natural scientists deploy alternating repertoires to account for scientific discoveries. Scientists proffer explanations that reflect the contingencies of personal and local characteristics while simultaneously attributing scientific discovery to the inexorable and impersonal revelation of nature. They reconcile any discursive or cognitive discrepancies by appealing to the mediating device that "the truth will out" in any event (Gilbert & Mulkay, 1984). A similar analysis of experts' accounts can be found in a subsequent analysis of the rhetorical work of health economists, whereas Atkinson and his colleagues have developed a similar analysis of a research group's accounts of its own scientific breakthrough (Atkinson, Batchelor, & Parsons, 1998). Accounting devices or registers are relatively stable features of these and similar accounts.

In a similar fashion, we have a large number of analyses of professionals' accounts of their work, including the formulation of phenomena such as "cases" and "findings." Occupations such as medicine and social work have narratives and accounts included in their stock-in-trade (Atkinson, 1995; Hunter, 1991; Pithouse, 1987). Their practitioners' routine work is constructed through various kinds of spoken performance. Practitioners persuade one another concerning diagnoses and assessments through the construction of cases that are, in turn, dependent on narrative structures; they use rhetorical devices to invoke evidence in support of their arguments. These are characterized by recurrent rhetorical features of their professional talk. They use characteristic devices to encode issues of evidence, competence, and responsibility in the course of collegial talk. In a very similar vein, we can identify rhetorical features of legal discourse through which cases are constructed, evidence is assembled and presented, or judgments are justified. Again, the major issue here lies not in the local details of particular settings or occupational groups but rather in the presence of stable regular features of spoken actions that can be identified. They can, in turn, be examined in terms of the sort of *work* that they perform. In other words, analytic payoff resides not only in identifying the patterns, structures, and conventions that generate such activity but also in analyzing their moral and practical implications.

We can extend such analytic perspectives beyond the individual narrative. There are systems of *genre*. There are culturally defined and socially shared types of story formats. The existence of such generic types means that we should not regard narrative accounts as reflections of private and individual experiences. Although narratives and biographical accounts may be felt and expressed as if they were highly personal, they are constructed and received in terms of cultural idioms and formats. This is demonstrated well in Plummer's (1995) analysis of sexual stories. Although accounts of coming out or of being a rape victim might be thought of as extremely private— and indeed in one sense they are—Plummer's analysis showed that they are couched in terms of shared forms or genres. Culturally defined formats can be identified in many contexts of spoken and written performance. They prescribe the shape and content of many descriptions and accounts. Many of the forms with which we are entirely familiar, to the point of taking them for granted, are highly conventional—or even arbitrary—cultural impositions. The analyses of documentary types such as the scientific report demonstrate that there are historical and culturally prescribed conventions through which the "plain facts" of nature and its exploration are conveyed. The work of authors such as Myers (1990) is testimony to the significance of the genre of the scientific report.

If it is fairly self-evident that discourse, descriptions, and narratives display indigenous principles of structure and order, we do not need to restrict such analyses to language. The general principles of semiotics can be applied to cultural systems of signification. Hence, visual and material data can be examined in terms of their intrinsic orders. The systems of fashion and clothing, for example, are not exhaustively defined in semiotic terms, but one can readily identify the basic structuring principles of such systems. The alternating and contrasting structuring principles that define the fashion system in recent Euro-American culture include the binary contrasts short/long, close/loose, structured/unstructured, full/narrow, colored/neutral, and plain/patterned. Although individual designers can develop their distinctive idiolects from within such systems, overall the semiotic principles help to define a "look" that is shared among many individual designers and houses in defining the distinctive style of a given season. In a similar vein, the "private" domain of fetishistic fantasy and pleasure is defined in terms of culturally defined, arbitrary features (e.g., leather, rubber, high heels, boots) that are themselves derivatives of and transform from the general system of clothing (Barthes, 1983; Hodkinson, 2002; Manning, 2001; Storr, 2003; Troy, 2002).

Visual styles of many sorts display basic semiotic principles. The visual "languages" of advertising, for instance, use recurrent coding principles that are grounded in representations of gender relations, sexual fantasy, exotic settings, domestic settings, and so forth, with the precise selection and combination of semiotic elements reflecting the product being advertised and the genre of advertisement itself. Goffman's (1979) analysis of gender relations in advertisements in print media is but one example of how advertising forms can be "decoded" from a sociological perspective. In a similar vein, one can identify semiotic principles of style and space in representations of the domestic sphere and its ideals. In the multiplicity of lifestyle magazines and television programs, statements about actual or desired status and identity can be constructed from color schemes, furnishings, and fittings. Styles can be identified through assemblages of materials and objects, for example, defining art nouveau, Bauhaus, art deco, or modernism. Such aesthetic principles may inhabit places of work as well as domestic environments. The visual and material language of the built environment is also susceptible to semiotic analysis. The use of space within and around buildings, the structures of buildings themselves, and the interior layouts of buildings simultaneously reflect the assemblage of cultural forms as well as the individual or corporate taste of the client and the aesthetic style of the architect.

Our general point here should not be lost in the various types and examples to which we have alluded. We are not trying to produce a comprehensive enumeration of all the cultural phenomena that can be analyzed. Rather, we are suggesting that whatever else these artifacts and activities might be, they display various arrays of structuring and semiotic principles. From the built environment, through domestic spaces, to individual self-presentations, biographies, narratives, and conversations, all of these social phenomena can be understood in terms of their intrinsic principles of structure and order. The collection of qualitative data certainly should not be confined to spoken materials, whether they are naturally occurring spoken interaction data or transcribed interview data. There are multiple media of inscription in which culture is enacted, and social action takes place through multiple embodiments.

▣ CLASSIC PRINCIPLES

A systematic ethnography needs to take account of the intrinsic orderings through which social worlds are produced and reproduced. It is not necessary for any one ethnographic study to encompass systems of discourse, narrative, material culture, aesthetics, and performance to satisfy some notional criterion of completeness or adequacy. On the other hand, we should not ignore such structuring principles. There is no long-term benefit to the overall project of social research if styles of data collection and analysis remain fragmented. We certainly need some people to work on specialized technologies and techniques—digital visualization, discourse structures, semiotic structures, and the like—but those analytic domains must not flourish only in mutual isolation. We do not want to see the social world represented as if it consisted only of transcribed talk, spoken narratives, visual artifacts, or material goods.

We have already referred to Blumer's (1954) recommendation that research should be "faithful to the phenomena." In various ways, adherence to that injunction can prove to be problematic. It is hard to know what should count as phenomena in the first place, and it seems dangerous to assume that they have an essence independent of the methods used to construe them. Clearly, perfect correspondence to an independently identifiable realm of social objects and actions is impossible. We cannot aspire to perfect or comprehend fidelity or to capture all of the variations to be found among and between types of social actions and actors. But the upshot of our argument is that ethnographers should certainly be faithful to the *forms* of social phenomena. We should be attentive to the indigenous systems of action and representation. We should not think of ignoring the systems of, say, ethnoaesthetics more than we think of mangling the local language(s) of our chosen research setting. Fidelity to the social worlds in which we work requires a systematic analysis of the principles of order they display. At least to that extent, then, we can retain a sense of fidelity and representation that is firmly rooted in social forms and also retains a notion of rigor.

This is, moreover, a productive way of approaching some key implications of "thick description" (Geertz, 1973). Geertz's (1973) use of the term, derived from Gilbert Ryle's philosophy of mind, has been susceptible to many readings. The most vulgar of uses do little or no justice to Geertz's own inspiration. Thick description is too often used to convey the sense that ethnographic accounts are densely constructed with graphic and detailed cultural descriptions. Although this may be the case, it does not really capture the specific analytic force of Geertz's idea, which is clearly intended to capture the degree to which cultural matters are overdetermined in the sense that there are multiple codings that generate meaning. There are, Geertz stressed, multiple perspectives or interpretive frameworks, that is, multiple motivational frames that inform social events and actions. Our own insistence on the intrinsic forms of culture and action gives a particular force to the notions of thick description. From our point of view, whatever else it might mean or be taken to mean, it should include analytic attention to the multiple codings and structuring principles through which social life is enacted and represented.

In these two senses, therefore, we can bring into close conjunction Blumer's precept and Geertz's insight. Both can find analytic force in the ethnographic analysis that is faithful to the contours of culture and the structures of action. We are mindful at this point to invoke yet a third idea derived from classic accounts of ethnographic analysis, that is, the notion of "triangulation" (Denzin, 1970). Like the first pair of terms we invoked, triangulation has been subject to multiple renderings and misrepresentations. Here, we do not wish to suppress or supersede all other connotations of triangulation, the fruitfulness of which lies partly in the multiplicity of inspirations that researchers can draw from it. Although it is not fruitful to assume, as in oversimplified versions, that research methods or data types can be aggregated to generate a more rounded or complete picture of a social world than would be generated by a single method alone, it might be productive to approach it in a way that is more congruent with our own approach: that is, to recognize that there can be a mode of triangulation derived from an explicit recognition of multiple social orders and principles of structuring. Triangulation thought of in this way has a very specific, if restricted, subset of meanings within the overall analytic strategy. Again, it recognizes the multiplicity and simultaneity of cultural frames of reference—spoken, performed, semiotic, material, and so forth—through which social events and institutions are possible. Consequently, a triangulated account depends not only on an opportunistic combination of methods and sources but also on a principled array of methodological strategies that reflect the indigenous principles of order and action.

Finally, our own approach here gives us some productive ways of recuperating significant aspects of "grounded theory" (Charmaz & Mitchell, 2001; Glaser & Strauss, 1967; Strauss & Corbin, 1998). We have already referred to the contested nature of this idea, or package of ideas, and we do not need to recapitulate the various definitions and applications of grounded theory. We simply reaffirm that grounded theory does not refer to some special order of theorizing per se. Rather, it seeks to capture some general principles of analysis, describing heuristic strategies that apply to any social inquiry independent of the particular kinds of data: indeed, it applies to the exploratory analysis of quantitative data as much as it does to qualitative inquiry. The idea derives directly from the pragmatist roots of interactionism. It captures the *abductive* logic through which analysts explore the social or natural world through practical engagements with it, derive working models and provisional understandings, and use such emergent ideas to guide further empirical explorations. It represents a compromise between the arid philosophy of purely deductive logic (which cannot account for the derivation of fruitful theories and hypotheses in the first place and admits of no place for *experience in the process of discovery*) and purely inductive logic (which never transcends the collection and aggregation of observations in generating generalizations). To a considerable extent, therefore, there is little to choose in practice between grounded theory and *analytic induction* as summary accounts of the practical work of social exploration and the derivation of ideas. Both formulations capture the need for systematic interactions between data and ideas as well as the emergent properties of research design and data analysis, which are in constant dialogue. Both formulations also emphasize the processual and iterative nature of the research process.

Too often, however, grounded theory is construed as a justification for the inductive retrospective inspection of volumes of field data, as if the research strategy were based on the accumulation of cases and the introspective derivation of categories—often through an inductive procedure of data "coding." Some of the descriptions of grounded theory by its own advocates have inadvertently contributed to this impression. But if we take seriously some of the things we have already outlined and claimed, we can discern some possible strategies that suggest principled relationships between data and analysis in a grounded theory manner. In other words, we recognize that culture and action are ordered. Consequently, the work of data collection is not devoted to the accumulation of isolated cases or fragmentary materials, and analysis is not just a matter of sorting and classifying those materials.

Finally, in considering our classic principles, we can sum up several of our themes so far with reference to Schutz's (1973) discussion of first- and second-order constructs. In his development of *verstehen* sociological principles beyond Dilthey or Weber through social phenomenology, Schutz suggested that analytic forms, such as ideal types, are not the sole preserve of the sociological observer. Everyday social actors are engaged in practical interpretations of their own social worlds. They use first-order constructs such as the method of practical reasoning that uses *typifications*. Sociological analysis, therefore, involves a (second-order) meta-analysis of the first-order, everyday analyses of practical social actors. In the same way, everyday social life displays principles of order that the analyst explicates and systematizes. The everyday actor has an implicit grasp of ordering rules and conventions, and it is the task of the analyst to explicate such tacit knowledge (cf. Maso, 2001).

We believe, therefore, that the social world displays various indigenous principles of organization. There are multiple ordering principles—discursive, spatial, semiotic, narrative, and so forth—to which the analysis of qualitative data needs to be attentive. The social analyst develops second-order models of these indigenous codes, conventions, and orders. There should, therefore, be principled relations between the first-order and second-order constructs. There should also be systematic relations between the different second-order analyses and models. Although this formulation might seem to be unduly formalistic, we believe it to be a salutary corrective to the unduly experiential perspectives currently brought to bear on qualitative data analysis. In the following section, we turn our attention to a parallel set of analytic preoccupations concerned with representation and aesthetics.

## ▣ REPRESENTATION AND AESTHETICS

To this point, we have referred exclusively to the contours of culture, the semiotics of indigenous systems of representation, and the structures of social action. We now turn briefly to the analytic work of writing and other modes of ethnographic representation. We do not recapitulate the history of this particular domain, nor do we review all of the contributions that have been made to it. That work has been done elsewhere. Here, we note that there has been a marked tendency among the more innovative ethnographers to experiment with the textual conventions of ethnographic reportage (Faubion, 2001). The use of nontraditional literary forms or performance techniques has been well documented, and there is a growing corpus of published materials in those forms. Such experiments are usually represented as having radical connotations, and they are among the characteristics of ethnography associated with postmodernist ideas and with the most recent "moments" of Lincoln and Denzin's (1994, 2001) developmental model of qualitative research (for a critique of this particular formulation, see Delamont, Coffey, & Atkinson, 2000).

There is no doubt at all that writing ethnography is an important aspect of ethnographic analysis. The process of analysis stretches far beyond the mere manipulation of data and even of the work of grounded theorizing, thick description, and the like. It resides in the reconstruction of a given social world or some key features of it. Such reconstructions are rendered persuasive through the textual and other devices deployed by ethnographers in putting together the texts, films, and the like that constitute "the ethnography." In response to various interventions, all scholars recognize that this process is not innocent. There is no transparent medium through which a social world can be represented. Language is not a transparent medium. The textual conventions to which we have become accustomed are just that—conventions. Photography, film, and video are not merely passive recording media; rather, they actively shape our reception of social and cultural phenomena.

In the pursuit of the experimental turn in ethnographic representation, however, we believe that there have been exaggerated and extravagant moves. In bracketing and transgressing the conventions of realist representations and the textual formats of scientific writing, networks of authors have chosen to assimilate sociological representation to literary forms such as poetry and fiction. In this there lies a danger. The representation of social phenomena through poetry, for instance, inscribes some major assumptions (rarely explicated in the course of this ethnographic genre). First, the focus of attention is shifted radically from the culture and actions of social actors toward the representational work of ethnographers themselves. In sharp contrast to analyses of culture that decenter the "authors," much experimental writing places individual authors firmly—and sometimes exclusively—center stage. Literary work such as poetry here does not necessarily create the "open" or "messy" texts that some critics had sought. Rather, they create closure by creating a new basis for authorial privilege.

Moreover, the ability to construct plausible, let alone meritorious, poetry or autobiographical writing appears to rest on personal authorial qualities. The social world is aestheticized in the process. What counts as a good ethnographic account is, therefore, in danger of resting primarily on aesthetic criteria.

Moreover, the assimilation of cultural and social phenomena to first-person-dominated texts, whether prose or poetry, can do violence to the phenomena themselves. We have already alluded to Blumer's (1954) aphorism concerning fidelity to the phenomena, and we invoke it once more here. We do not think that we are in any possible sense of the term *faithful* to the phenomena if we recast them into forms that derive from quite other cultural domains. We risk losing the intrinsic aesthetic, and other formal characteristics of the original meanings, events, and actions. We have already referred to the principle of ethnopoetics in recognizing that there are indigenous canons of rhetoric and construction in cultural performances. Analysts distort or obliterate the cultures they seek to account for if they translate everything into their own culture-bound aesthetics. First-person autobiographical writing and experientially derived poetry do not enjoy universal value. They are, if anything, among the more culturally specific and limited of expressive forms. There is little or no warrant for elevating them to being the preferred vehicle for cross-cultural or culturally sensitive social research.

Similar reservations can be entertained concerning performance ethnography in general. It is now permissible in some academic contexts to use our ethnographic data and the insights gleaned from ethnographic fieldwork to create various types of performative and aesthetic texts or artifacts. Denzin's (2003) recent volume is a key exemplar and discussion of this perspective. Mienczakowski (2001) also provided an overview of performed ethnography and ethnodrama. We do not seek to detract from these approaches in general except perhaps to suggest that performance ethnographers might engage more fully and systematically with the now wide-ranging ethnographic study of performance (Atkinson, 2004). We do, however, wish to assert something more in keeping with the general thrust of this chapter, namely that we should be very careful indeed of imposing "our" performative and aesthetic criteria and competences in the representation of settings, cultures, and actors while neglecting the indigenous local forms of performance through which culture, organization, and action are actually maintained in everyday life.

## Social Action, Social Organization

In framing our argument as such, we are clearly stressing one particular array of emphases and preferences. We do so partly to redress what we see as a misleading tendency within many contemporary versions of qualitative research. We believe that too much emphasis is currently placed on the identification and documentation of social actors' *experiences* or *perceptions* at the expense of *social action* and *social organization* (cf. Silverman, 2004).

In part, we recapitulate arguments to which we have contributed elsewhere, and here we seek to generalize them further. We stress that among the goals of ethnographic research is to analyze *social action, social order,* and *social organization* as well as to analyze the forms and contents of *culture.* We need to pay serious and systematic attention to the recurrent phenomena of anthropology, sociology, and cognate disciplines such as discursive psychology, linguistics, and semiotics. This means that ethnographic and other qualitative research is much more than the sympathetic description and reportage of informants' experiences. We have argued elsewhere to the effect that qualitative research needs to transcend the culturally pervasive influence of the interview and what Atkinson and Silverman (1997) called the "interview society." We do not subscribe to the view that qualitative research is justified primarily by representing social affairs from the point of view of individual social actors or even from the perspectives of social aggregates.

This does not imply a return to the old methodological contestation between the merits of observation and those of interviewing—between what people *do* and what people *say* (Atkinson et al., 2003). The reverse is true. Instead, we stress that what people say is itself a form of action. We need to analyze social actors' accounts or narratives as types of speech acts. Likewise, we need to recognize that even such "experiences" as memories or emotions are not merely psychological states but also are performed social enactments (cf. Tota, 2001; Wagner-Pacifici, 1996). Moreover, in line with Mills (1940), we need to see motives as socially shared, culturally defined frames of justification or rationalization (Atkinson & Coffey, 2002). So, social action includes the work of representation. Likewise, social action includes the use and circulation of other modes of representation such as material goods and cultural artifacts (Vinck, 2003).

It follows, therefore, that we are recommending a particular approach to the analysis of social life under the aegis of ethnographic or qualitative research. We believe that there is a need for the reevaluation of analytic strategies that avoid the kind of fragmented reductionism to which we referred at the beginning of this chapter. We do not believe that it is productive for analysts to represent the social world primarily or exclusively through the lens of just one analytic strategy or data type. The different types of qualitative research—discourse analysis, visual analysis, narrative analysis, and the like—are not paradigms or disciplines in their own right; rather, they are analytic strategies that reflect and respect the intrinsic complexity of social organization, the forms of social action, and the conventions of social representation. This is not just a matter of juxtaposing different "methods," and it is not just an appeal to rather vague notions of "context" or "holistic" ethnography; rather, it means paying attention to the *systemic* relations among the interaction order, orders of talk, representational orders, and organized properties of material culture. In this way, our analytic perspectives can and should reaffirm certain kinds of rigor, some of which we believe have been lost to view in recent methodological writing. We stress, therefore, the disciplined approach to technical issues such as discourse analysis, narrative analysis, and semiotic analysis. We seek *principled* relationships between the various contributory disciplines and subdisciplines. The analysis of social phenomena is not well served by the kind of fragmentation that equates types of data (e.g., spoken, visual, textual, material) with disciplines or specialties working in relative isolation.

## ▣ REFERENCES

Appadurai, A. (Ed.). (1986). *The social lives of things.* Cambridge, UK: Cambridge University Press.

Atkinson, J. M., & Heritage, J. (Eds.). (1984). *The structures of social action: Studies in conversation analysis.* Cambridge, UK: Cambridge University Press.

Atkinson, P. A. (1995). *Medical talk and medical work: The liturgy of the clinic.* London: Sage.

Atkinson, P. A. (1997). Narrative turn or blind alley? *Qualitative Health Research, 7,* 325–344.

Atkinson, P. A. (2004). Performing ethnography and the ethnography of performance. *British Journal of Sociology of Education, 25,* 107–114.

Atkinson, P. A., Batchelor, C., & Parsons, E. (1998). Trajectories of collaboration and competition in a medical discovery. *Science, Technology, & Human Values, 23,* 259–284.

Atkinson, P. A., & Coffey, A. (2002). Revisiting the relationship between participant observation and interviewing. In J. F. Gubrium & J. A. Holstein (Eds.), *Handbook of interview research: Context and method* (pp. 801–814). Thousand Oaks, CA: Sage.

Atkinson, P. A., Coffey, A., & Delamont, S. (1999). Ethnography: Post, past, and present. *Journal of Contemporary Ethnography, 28,* 460–471.

Atkinson, P. A., Coffey, A., & Delamont, S. (2001). A debate about our canon. *Qualitative Research, 1,* 2–22.

Atkinson, P. A., Coffey, A., & Delamont, S. (2003). *Key themes in qualitative research.* Walnut Creek, CA: AltaMira.

Atkinson, P. A., & Delamont, S. (2004). Analysis and postmodernism. In M. Hardy & A. Bryman (Eds.), *Handbook of analysis* (pp. 667–681). London: Sage.

Atkinson, P. A., & Silverman, D. (1997). Kundera's *Immortality:* The interview society and the invention of the self. *Qualitative Inquiry, 3,* 304–325.

Attfield, J. (2000). *Wild things: The material culture of everyday life.* Oxford, UK: Berg.

Ball, M., & Smith, G. (1992). *Analyzing visual data.* Newbury Park, CA: Sage.

Ball, M., & Smith, G. (2001). Technologies of realism? Ethnographic uses of photography and film. In P. Atkinson, A. Coffey, S. Delamont, J. Lofland, & L. Lofland (Eds.), *Handbook of ethnography* (pp. 302–319). London: Sage.

Banks, M., & Morphy, H. (Eds.). (1997). *Rethinking visual anthropology.* New Haven, CT: Yale University Press.

Barthes, R. (1983). *The fashion system.* New York: Hill & Wang.

Bauman, R. (1986). *Story, performance, and event: Contextual studies of oral narrative.* Cambridge, UK: Cambridge University Press.

Behar, R. (1996). *The vulnerable observer: Anthropology that breaks your heart.* Boston: Beacon.

Bender, B., & Winer, M. (Eds.). (2001). *Contested landscapes: Movement, exile, and place.* Oxford, UK: Berg.

Benjamin, W. (1999). *The Arcades Project* (H. Eiland & K. McLaughlin, Trans.). Cambridge, MA: Harvard University Press.

Bennett, A., & Dawe, K. (Eds.). (2001). *Guitar cultures.* Oxford, UK: Berg.

Bijker, W. (1995). *Of bicycles, Bakelites, and bulbs: Toward a theory of sociotechnical change.* Cambridge: MIT Press.

Blumer, H. (1954). What is wrong with social theory? *American Sociological Review, 19,* 3–10.

Bochner, A. R., & Ellis, C. (Eds.). (2001). *Ethnographically speaking: Autoethnography, literature, and aesthetics.* Walnut Creek, CA: AltaMira.

Borden, I. (2002). *Skateboarding, space, and the city: Architecture and the body.* Oxford, UK: Berg.

Brewer, J. (2002). *Ethnography.* Buckingham, UK: Open University Press.

Butler, T. (2003). *London calling: The middle classes and the remaking of inner London.* Oxford, UK: Berg.

Caplan, P. (1997). *African voices, African lives.* London: Routledge.

Charmaz, K., & Mitchell, R. (2001). Grounded theory and ethnography. In P. Atkinson, A. J. Coffey, S. Delamont, J. Lofland, & L. Lofland (Eds.), *Handbook of ethnography* (pp. 160–173). London: Sage.

Clough, P. T. (1998). *The end(s) of ethnography: From realism to social criticism* (2nd ed.). New York: Peter Lang.

Coffey, A. J., & Atkinson, P. A. (1996). *Making sense of qualitative data: Complementary strategies.* Thousand Oaks, CA: Sage.

Conle, C. (2003). An anatomy of narrative curricula. *Educational Researcher, 32*(3), 3–15.

Cortazzi, M. (1991). *Primary teaching: How it is—A narrative analysis.* London: David Fulton.

Cortazzi, M. (1993). *Narrative analysis.* London: Falmer.

Cortazzi, M. (2001). Narrative analysis. In P. Atkinson, A. Coffey, S. Delamont, J. Lofland, & L. Lofland (Eds.), *Handbook of ethnography* (pp. 384–393). London: Sage.

Crouch, D., & Lübbren, N. (Eds.). (2003). *Visual culture and tourism.* Oxford, UK: Berg.

Crowley, D., & Reid, S. E. (Eds.). (2002). *Socialist spaces: Sites of everyday life in the Eastern Bloc.* Oxford, UK: Berg.

Czarniawska, B. (1997). *Narrating the organization.* Chicago: University of Chicago Press.

Czarniawska, B. (1998). *A narrative approach to organization studies.* Thousand Oaks, CA: Sage.

Darby, W. J. (2000). *Landscape and identity: Geographies of nation and class in England.* Oxford, UK: Berg.

Delamont, S. (2002). *Fieldwork in educational settings* (2nd ed.). London: Falmer.

Delamont, S., Coffey, A., & Atkinson, P. (2000). The twilight years? Educational ethnography and the five moments model. *Qualitative Studies in Education, 13,* 223–238.

DeNora, T. (2000). *Music in everyday life.* Cambridge, UK: Cambridge University Press.

DeNora, T. (2003). *After Adorno: Rethinking music sociology.* Cambridge, UK: Cambridge University Press.

Denzin, N. K. (1970). *The research act.* Chicago: Aldine.

Denzin, N. K. (1994). The art and politics of interpretation. In N. K. Denzin & Y. S. Lincoln (Eds.), *Handbook of qualitative research* (pp. 500–515). Thousand Oaks, CA: Sage.

Denzin, N. K. (2003). *Performance ethnography: Critical pedagogy and the politics of culture.* Thousand Oaks, CA: Sage.

Denzin, N. K., & Lincoln, Y. S. (Eds.). (1994). *Handbook of qualitative research.* Thousand Oaks, CA: Sage.

Denzin, N. K., & Lincoln, Y. S. (Eds.). (2001). *Handbook of qualitative research* (2nd ed.). Thousand Oaks, CA: Sage.

Dicks, B. (2000). *Heritage, place, and community.* Cardiff, UK: University of Wales Press.

Dodds, G., & Taverner, R. (2001). *Body and building: Essays on the changing relations of body and architecture.* Cambridge: MIT Press.

Dyck, N., & Archetti, E. P. (Eds.). (2003). *Sport, dance, and embodied identities.* Oxford, UK: Berg.

Edwards, E. (2001). *Raw histories: Photographs, anthropology, and museums.* Oxford, UK: Berg.

Ellis, C. (2004). *The ethnographic I: A methodological novel about autoethnography.* Walnut Creek, CA: AltaMira.

Ellis, C., & Bochner, A. (Eds.). (1996). *Composing ethnography.* Walnut Creek, CA: AltaMira.

Ellis, C., & Flaherty, M. G. (Eds.). (1992). *Investigating subjectivity: Research on lived experience.* Newbury Park, CA: Sage.

English-Lueck, J. A. (2002). *Cultures @ Silicon Valley.* Stanford, CA: Stanford University Press.

Faubion, J. D. (2001). Currents of cultural fieldwork. In P. Atkinson, A. Coffey, S. Delamont, J. Lofland, & L. Lofland (Eds.), *Handbook of ethnography* (pp. 39–59). London: Sage.

Fernandez, J. W., & Huber, M. T. (Eds.). (2001). *Irony in action: Anthropology, practice, and the moral imagination.* Chicago: University of Chicago Press.

Fine, G. A. (2001). *Difficult reputations: Collective memories of the evil, inept, and controversial.* Chicago: University of Chicago Press.

Finn, C. A. (2001). *Artifacts: An archaeologist's year in Silicon Valley.* Cambridge: MIT Press.

Forty, A., & Kuchler, S. (Eds.). (1999). *The art of forgetting.* Oxford, UK: Berg.

Frosh, P. (2003). *The image factory: Consumer culture, photography, and the visual content industry.* Oxford, UK: Berg.

Gardner, K. (2002). *Age, narrative, and migration: The life course and life histories of Bengali elders in London.* Oxford, UK: Berg.

Geertz, C. (1973). *The interpretation of cultures.* New York: Basic Books.

Geertz, C. (1983). *Local knowledge: Further essays in interpretive anthropology.* New York: Basic Books.

Gilbert, N., & Mulkay, M. (1984). *Opening Pandora's box.* Cambridge, UK: Cambridge University Press.

Glaser, B. (1978). *Theoretical sensitivity.* Mill Valley, CA: Sociology Press.

Glaser, B. (1992). *Emergence versus forcing.* Mill Valley, CA: Sociology Press.

Glaser, B., & Strauss, A. L. (1967). *The discovery of grounded theory.* Chicago: Aldine.

Goffman, E. (1979). *Gender advertisements.* New York: Harper & Row.

Goffman, E. (1981). *Forms of talk.* Philadelphia: University of Pennsylvania Press.

Goffman, E. (1983). The interaction order. *American Sociological Review, 48,* 1–17.

Goodall, H. L. (2000). *Writing the new ethnography.* Walnut Creek, CA: AltaMira.

Gosden, C., & Knowles, C. (Eds.). (2001). *Collecting colonialism: Material culture and colonial change.* Oxford, UK: Berg.

Gray, R., & Sinding, C. (2002). *Standing ovation: Performing social science research about cancer.* Walnut Creek, CA: AltaMira.

Grimshaw, A. (2001). *The ethnographer's eye: Ways of seeing in modern anthropology.* Cambridge, UK: Cambridge University Press.

Gubrium, J. F., & Holstein, J. A. (2002a). From the individual interview to the interview society. In J. F. Gubrium & J. A. Holstein (Eds.), *Handbook of interview research: Context and method* (pp. 3–32). Thousand Oaks, CA: Sage.

Gubrium, J. F., & Holstein, J. A. (Eds.). (2002b). *Handbook of interview research: Context and method.* Thousand Oaks, CA: Sage.

Hammersley, M. (1989). *The dilemma of qualitative method: Herbert Blumer and the Chicago tradition.* London: Routledge.

Hammersley, M., & Atkinson, P. A. (1995). *Ethnography: Principles in practice* (2nd ed.). London: Routledge.

Handler, R., & Gable, E. (1997). *The new history in an old museum: Creating the past at Colonial Williamsburg.* Durham, NC: Duke University Press.

Hardy, M., & Bryman, A. (Eds.). (2004). *Handbook of analysis.* London: Sage.

Henderson, K. (1998). *On line and on paper: Visual representations, visual culture, and computer graphics in design engineering.* Cambridge: MIT Press.

Hepburn, A., & Potter, J. (2004). Discourse analytic practice. In C. Seale, G. Gobo, F. F. Gubrium, & D. Silverman (Eds.), *Qualitative research practice* (pp. 180–196). London: Sage.

Herzfeld, M. (1991). *A place in history: Social and monumental time in a Cretan town.* Princeton, NJ: Princeton University Press.

Hodkinson, P. (2002). *Goth: Identity, style, and subculture.* Oxford, UK: Berg.

Holstein, J. A. (2000). *The self we live by: Narrative identity in a postmodern world.* New York: Oxford University Press.

Hughes-Freeland, F. (1998). *Ritual, performance, media.* London: Routledge.

Humphrey, R., Miller, R., & Zdravomyslova, E. (Eds.). (2003). *Biographical research in Eastern Europe: Altered lives and broken biographies.* Aldershot, UK: Ashgate.

Hunter, K. M. (1991). *Doctors' stories: The narrative structure of medical knowledge.* Princeton, NJ: Princeton University Press.

Hymes, D. (1996). *Ethnography, linguistics, narrative inequality.* London: Taylor & Francis.

Jackson, P., Lowe, M., Miller, D., & Mort, F. (Eds.). (2000). *Commercial cultures: Economies, practices, spaces.* Oxford, UK: Berg.

Janesick, V. J. (1994). The dance of qualitative research design: Metaphor, methodolatry, and meaning. In N. K. Denzin & Y. S. Lincoln (Eds.), *Handbook of qualitative research* (pp. 209–219). Thousand Oaks, CA: Sage.

Julier, G. (2000). *The culture of design.* London: Sage.

Katz, J. E., & Aakhus, M. (Eds.). (2002). *Perpetual contact: Mobile communication, private talk, public performance.* Cambridge, UK: Cambridge University Press.

Kwint, M., Breward, C., & Aynsley, J. (Eds.). (1999). *Material memories.* Oxford, UK: Berg.

Labov, W. (1972). *Language in the inner city.* Philadelphia: University of Pennsylvania Press.

Lally, E. (2002). *At home with computers.* Oxford, UK: Berg.

Lara, M. P. (1998). *Moral textures: Feminist narratives in the public sphere.* Cambridge, UK: Polity.

Lincoln, Y. S., & Denzin, N. K. (1994). The fifth moment. In N. K. Denzin & Y. S. Lincoln (Eds.), *Handbook of qualitative research* (pp. 575–586). Thousand Oaks, CA: Sage.

Lincoln, Y. S., & Denzin, N. K. (2001). The seventh moment: Out of the past. In N. K. Denzin & Y. S. Lincoln (Eds.), *Handbook of qualitative research* (2nd ed., pp. 1047–1065). Thousand Oaks, CA: Sage.

Lincoln, Y. S., & Denzin, N. K. (Eds.). (2003). *Turning points in qualitative research: Tying knots in the handkerchief.* Walnut Creek, CA: AltaMira.

Loizos, P. (1993). *Innovation in ethnographic film.* Manchester, UK: Manchester University Press.

Lury, C. (1996). *Consumer culture.* Cambridge, UK: Polity.

Macdonald, S. (2002). *Behind the scenes at the science museum.* Oxford, UK: Berg.

Macdonald, S., & Fyfe, G. (Eds.). (1996). *Theorising museums.* Oxford, UK: Blackwell.

Manning, P. K. (2001). Semiotics, semantics, and ethnography. In P. Atkinson, A. Coffey, S. Delamont, J. Lofland, & L. Lofland (Eds.), *Handbook of ethnography* (pp. 145–159). London: Sage.

Maso, I. (2001). Phenomenology and ethnography. In P. Atkinson, A. Coffey, S. Delamont, J. Lofland, & L. Lofland (Eds.), *Handbook of ethnography* (pp. 136–144). London: Sage.

May, R. A. B. (2001). *Talking at Trena's: Everyday conversations at an African American tavern.* New York: New York University Press.

Mienczakowski, J. (2001) Ethnodrama: Performed research—Limitations and potential. In P. Atkinson, A. Coffey, S. Delamont, J. Lofland, & L. Lofland (Eds.), *Handbook of ethnography* (pp. 468–476). London: Sage.

Miller, D. (1987). *Material culture and mass communication.* Oxford, UK: Basil Blackwell.

Miller, D. (Ed.). (2001a). *Car cultures.* Oxford, UK: Berg.

Miller, D. (Ed.). (2001b). *Home possessions: Material culture behind closed doors.* Oxford, UK: Berg.

Mills, C. W. (1940). Situated actions and vocabularies of motive. *American Sociological Review, 5,* 439–452.

Moerman, M. (1988). *Talking culture: Ethnography and conversation analysis.* Philadelphia: University of Pennsylvania Press.

Möller, F., & Pehkonen, S. (Eds.). (2003). *Encountering the North: Cultural geography, international relations, and northern landscapes.* Aldershot, UK: Ashgate.

Myerhoff, B. (1978). *Number our days.* New York: Simon & Schuster.

Myers, G. (1990). *Writing biology: Texts in the construction of scientific knowledge.* Madison: University of Wisconsin Press.

Ochs, E., & Capps, L. (2002). *Living narrative: Creating lives in everyday storytelling.* Cambridge, MA: Harvard University Press.

O'Dell, D. (2001). *Sites of southern memory: The autobiographies of Katherine Du Pre Lumpkin, Lillian Smith, and Pauli Murray.* Charlottesville: University Press of Virginia.

Olney, J. (Ed.). (1998). *Autobiography: Essays theoretical and critical.* Princeton, NJ: Princeton University Press.

Painter, C. (Ed.). (2002). *Contemporary art and the home.* Oxford, UK: Berg.

Patterson, W. (2002). *Strategic narrative: New perspectives on the power of personal and cultural stories.* Lanham, MD: Lexington Books.

Pinch, T., & Trocco, F. (2002). *Analog days: The invention and impact of the Moog synthesizer.* Cambridge, MA: Harvard University Press.

Pink, S. (2001). *Doing visual ethnography.* London: Sage.

Pink, S. (2004). Visual methods. In C. Seale, D. Silverman, J. F. Gubrium, & G. Gobo (Eds.), *Qualitative research practice* (pp. 391–406). London: Sage.

Pithouse, A. (1987). *Social work: The social organization of an invisible trade.* Aldershot, UK: Avebury.

Plummer, K. (1995). *Telling sexual stories.* London: Routledge.

Plummer, K. (2000). *Documents of life 2: An invitation to a critical humanism.* London: Sage.

Plummer, K. (2001). The call of life stories in ethnographic research. In P. Atkinson, A. Coffey, S. Delamont, J. Lofland, & L. Lofland (Eds.), *Handbook of ethnography* (pp. 395–406). London: Sage.

Potter, J. (1996). *Representing reality: Discourse, rhetoric, and social construction.* London: Sage.

Potter, J. (2003). Discourse analysis and discursive psychology. In P. M. Camic, J. E. Rhodes, & L. Yardley (Eds.), *Qualitative research in psychology: Expanding perspectives in methodology and design* (pp. 73–94). Washington, DC: American Psychological Association.

Potter, J., & Wetherell, M. (1987). *Discourse and social psychology: Beyond attitudes and behaviour.* London: Sage.

Prior, L. (2003). *Using documents in social research.* London: Sage.

Quinn, B. (2002). *Techno fashion.* Oxford, UK: Berg.

Rabinow, P. (1996). *Making PCR: A story of biotechnology.* Chicago: University of Chicago Press.

Radstone, S. (2000). *Memory and methodology.* Oxford, UK: Berg.

Reed-Danahay, D. (Ed.). (1997). *Auto/Ethnography: Rewriting the self and the social.* Oxford, UK: Berg.

Reed-Danahay, D. (2001). Autobiography, intimacy, and ethnography. In P. Atkinson, A. Coffey, S. Delamont, J. Lofland, & L. Lofland (Eds.), *Handbook of ethnography* (pp. 407–425). London: Sage.

Richardson, L. (1997). *Fields of play: Constructing an academic life.* New Brunswick, NJ: Rutgers University Press.

Richardson, L. (2002). Poetic representation of interviews. In J. F. Gubrium & J. A. Holstein (Eds.), *Handbook of interview research* (pp. 877–891). Thousand Oaks, CA: Sage.

Riessman, C. K. (1993). *Narrative analysis.* Newbury Park, CA: Sage.

Riessman, C. K. (2002). Analysis of personal narratives. In J. F. Gubrium & J. A. Holstein (Eds.), *Handbook of interview research: Context and method* (pp. 695–710). Thousand Oaks, CA: Sage.

Sacks, H. (1992). *Lectures on conversation* (G. Jefferson, Ed., 2 vols.). Oxford, UK: Blackwell.

Sandburg, M. B. (2003). *Living pictures, missing persons: Mannequins, museums, and modernity.* Princeton, NJ: Princeton University Press.

Sarangi, S., & Roberts, C. (Eds.). (1999). *Talk, work, and institutional orders: Discourse in medical, mediation, and management settings.* Berlin, Germany: Mouton de Gruyter.

Saunders, N. J. (2003). *Trench art: Materialities and memories of war.* Oxford, UK: Berg.

Schutz, A. (1973). *The problem of social reality: Collected papers* (Vol. 1, M. Natanson, Ed.). The Hague, Netherlands: Martinus Nijhoff.

Sciama, L. D. (2003). *A Venetian island: Environment, history, and change in Burano.* Oxford, UK: Barghahn.

Scott, J. (1990). *A matter of record.* Cambridge, UK: Polity.

Seale, C., Silverman, D., Gubrium, J. F., & Gobo, G. (Eds.). (2004). *Qualitative research practice.* London: Sage.

Silverman, D. (1987). *Communication and medical practice: Social relations in the clinic.* London: Sage.

Silverman, D. (Ed.). (1997). *Qualitative research: Theory, method, and practice.* London: Sage.

Silverman, D. (1998). *Harvey Sacks: Social science and conversation analysis.* Cambridge, UK: Polity.

Silverman, D. (Ed.). (2004). *Qualitative research: Theory, method, and practice* (2nd ed.). London: Sage.

Storr, M. (2003). *Latex and lingerie: Shopping for pleasure at Ann Summers parties.* Oxford, UK: Berg.

Strauss, A. L., & Corbin, J. A. (1998). *Basics of qualitative research: Theory, procedures, and techniques* (2nd ed.). Thousand Oaks, CA: Sage.

Tilley, C. (1991). *Material culture and the text: The art of ambiguity.* London: Routledge.

Tilley, C. (1999). *Metaphor and material culture.* Oxford, UK: Blackwell.

Tilley, C. (2001). Ethnography and material culture. In P. Atkinson, A. Coffey, S. Delamont, J. Lofland, & L. Lofland (Eds.), *Handbook of ethnography* (pp. 258–272). London: Sage.

Tota, A. L. (Ed.). (2001). *La Memoria Contesta: Studi Sulla Communicazione Sociale del Passato.* Milan, Italy: Angeli.

Troy, N. J. (2002). *Couture culture: A study in modern art and fashion.* Cambridge, UK: Cambridge University Press.

Tulloch, J. (1999). *Performing culture: Stories of expertise and the everyday.* London: Sage.

Valis, N. (2003). *The culture of Cursilería: Bad taste, kitsch, and class in modern Spain.* Durham, NC: Duke University Press.

Vinck, D. (Ed.). (2003). *Everyday engineering: An ethnography of design and innovation.* Cambridge: MIT Press.

Voysey, M. (1975). *A constant burden.* London: Routledge & Kegan Paul.

Wagner-Pacifici, R. (1996). Memories in the making: The shapes of things that went. *Qualitative Sociology, 19,* 301–321.

Whiteley, S., Bennett, A., & Hawkins, S. (Eds.). (2004). *Music, space, and place: Popular music and cultural identity.* Aldershot, UK: Ashgate.

Yalouri, E. (2001). *The Acropolis: Global fame, local claim.* Oxford, UK: Berg.

Znaniecki, F. (1934). *The method of sociology.* New York: Farrar & Rinehart.

# 10

# FOUCAULT'S METHODOLOGIES

## Archaeology and Genealogy

James Joseph Scheurich and Kathryn Bell McKenzie

his chapter is not a true or accurate representation of Foucault's work.[1] No such representation exists or is possible, in our view. There are, consequently, many other possible readings of Foucault's work that are just as defensible as this one. Indeed, this reading, like Foucault's *savoir* (defined and discussed later), is messy, ruptured, often erroneous, broken, discontinuous, originless, fabricated, even a falsification. In other words, as Magritte wrote on his painting of a pipe, "this is not a pipe" (Foucault, 1973b); this is not Foucault.

Moreover, what we intended to accomplish here in our early conceptualizations of this project and what actually emerged are significantly different. Indeed, we might question ourselves as we think our critics will question us, and just as Foucault did at the end of his "Introduction" to *The Archaeology of Knowledge* (1969/1972).[2] We might say,

"Aren't you sure of what you're saying? Are you going to change yet again, shift your position according to the questions that are put to you, and say that the objections are not really directed at the place from which you are speaking? Are you going to declare yet again that you have never been what you have been reproached with being? Are you already preparing the way out that will enable you in your next book to spring up somewhere else and declare as you're now doing: no, no, I'm not where you are lying in wait for me, but over here, laughing at you?" (p. 17, quotes in original)

Although our only laughter is about our own pretensions, what we intended when we started this project was to try to show how archaeology and genealogy might be used as critical "qualitative" (defined broadly) methodologies. We also wanted to illustrate briefly how each of these methods might be applied to education issues, as this is our discipline. Finally, we also envisioned a critical survey of the uses and abuses of Foucault's work in education.

However, some of this happened and much did not. For us, what changed what we did here was our review of Foucault's *oeuvre* (just the books and the order in which they were published) from the "beginning" through his genealogical work (we never thought we would cover what many consider the last phase of his work, the "care of self" or ethics period) and our review of articles and books in education that use Foucault's ideas in a central way. Neither of us had read through Foucault's work in such a systematic, focused, concentrated way, nor had we systematically surveyed the applications of Foucault in education. It was these systematic surveys, then, and the effects they had on our own understandings of Foucault and his use by education scholars that changed what we were doing in this chapter. For example, one change that emerged was our decision to discuss briefly the importance of Georges Canguilhem, arguably Foucault's most influential mentor. It almost seemed to us that to education scholars and, even more broadly, to scholars across the social sciences, Foucault and his ideas had emerged full grown from the forehead of Zeus. Consequently, we decided to provide a subsection within the "Archaeology" section that briefly discusses Foucault's view of Canguilhem and the latter's role in the French intellectual and philosophical context.

The rest of this essay, then, is divided into four parts. First, we discuss Foucault's archaeological method, which includes the Canguilhem discussion. Second, we discuss a particularly important essay, "Nietzsche, Genealogy, History" (Foucault, 1977, in *Language, Counter-Memory, Practice: Selected Essays and Interviews*) that was first published *after* his last archaeological work and *before* his first genealogical work, which we see as thematically bridging between or connecting the two methodologies. Third, we present his genealogical method. While our discussions of his archaeology or genealogy is not comprehensive enough so that a reader could assume that she or he is ready to use either of Foucault's methods after only reading this chapter, we do believe that what we have written was done in a way to help those who are not familiar with Foucault take some beginning steps toward using archaeology and genealogy. We also hope, though, that our coverage of the two is provocative of further reflections for those more experienced in their uses of Foucault's methods.

We accomplish our discussion of his archaeological method by addressing two archaeological concepts in some depth, *savoir* and *connaissance*, and then allude to what the other key archaeological concepts are. To present his genealogies, we discuss in some depth one of them, *Discipline and Punish* (Foucault, 1975/1979). However, in this work, he deploys so many provocative, useful critical tools that we can cover only some of them, let alone cover all of the other critical tools he adds with his second genealogy, *The History of Sexuality*, Volume 1: *An Introduction* (1976/1980a).[3] For the latter, however, we do point out some particularly excellent sections.

Fourth, our conclusion includes a brief overview of what we think some of the critical goals of both his archaeologies and his genealogies were. We summarize some of the points about archaeology and genealogy that we make. We enthusiastically praise a new collection of Foucault's work. We also provide some brief critical remarks on the uses—and abuses—of Foucault in education in particular and in the social sciences in general, although we do not provide a comprehensive or detailed review of this material. (We do try to provide a somewhat comprehensive list of such work in education in our bibliography along with some books on Foucault from outside of education that we think are either useful or influential; indeed, our bibliography is intended to be a resource for those interested in Foucault.) In general, we might forewarn by saying we are somewhat grumpy and surly, dissatisfied, about how Foucault has most frequently been read and used to date in education and the social sciences. In addition, our conclusion contains—and this was a surprise even to us—some substantive critique that we have of Foucault's work that we did not have when we started this chapter. In other words, by the end of our read of all of his books, we arrived at a critique of Foucault that we did not have when we began this read. We expect this critique will upset some advocates of Foucault and will gratify some critics. Our only defense is that we did not intend or desire this critique, although to be intellectually honest, we felt we needed to include it.

Our assumption, at this point, is that by the end of this essay we will leave a jangle, bangle, and tangle among some experienced Foucaultians, but hopefully some useful beginnings to those who have not yet tried on Foucault. Maybe, though, just maybe, some of the former will appreciate and find provocative our efforts to "think" Foucault both comprehensively *and* critically. Maybe we are all coming to a point, even among those of us who have been enthusiastic advocates of Foucault, at which it is possible to consider his work in a more balanced way, that is, without defensiveness. Perhaps. Perhaps not.

## ▣ ARCHAEOLOGY

Many scholars who survey the entire *oeuvre* of Foucault have discerned three sequential phases or periods—archaeology, genealogy, and the care of the self—that represent, it is thought, significant shifts in his philosophical thought, although some would add to this list Foucault's focus on governmentality.[4] Nonetheless, of the three periods, genealogy is the one that has captured the most attention of scholars to date, although one of us (Scheurich, 1997, pp. 94–118, "Policy Archaeology" chapter) has found archaeology useful, and recently Lather (2004) has written about "positivities," a key concept in archaeology. Care of the self, the last of the three periods, has generally received the least attention, although St. Pierre (2004) has recently found it to be fertile territory for her meditations on "the subject and freedom."[5]

Our intent here, however, because this is a chapter in a book on methodology, is to focus on archaeology and genealogy, which could be broadly construed as "qualitative" methods, as Foucault always used texts as his data or, what he sometimes called, the archive. It is not that we think Foucault's care of the self period or focus is unimportant. Nor do we think someone like St. Pierre could not creatively interpret the latter period as a methodology. Our aim is simpler than that. We want to provide a kind of beginner's introduction to the two Foucaultian methodologies that have received the most attention among U.S. scholars and that those interested in Foucault's perspective might use as a starting place of further exploration. What we cannot provide, though, due to space limitations, is some sort of "complete" course on how to use either methodology so that on finishing this essay, someone could move directly to applying either one. There is simply not sufficient space for accomplishing this for even one of Foucault's methods.

## Canguilhem

As we suggested in our introduction to this chapter, it is our judgment that there is a general lack of understanding of the philosophical context and influences within which Foucault worked in France. A good example of the latter is a lack of knowledge about Georges Canguilhem, arguably Foucault's main intellectual mentor and teacher. In general, our view is that Canguilhem's influence on Foucault, especially Canguilhem's influence on Foucault's archaeologies, is unacknowledged, underestimated, or even unknown. Indeed, even among philosophers who know Foucault deeply and use him well, there is much more fascination with Foucault and his relationships with Kant, Nietzsche, and Heidegger (see, e.g., the work of poststructuralist philosophers such as Elizabeth Grosz in *Volatile Bodies* [1994]). In response, we briefly discuss Canguilhem's influence on Foucault and Foucault's own view of Canguilhem's role in French philosophy with the hope that this will spur others to read more deeply into Foucault and his social and intellectual context. However, we are aware that our Canguilhem is but another author function[6] and that the relationship among Foucault, his mentor, and their social, historical, and intellectual "context" is complex, contradictory, and ambiguous.

One excellent example of Foucault's own discussion of Canguilhem and his influences, particularly as a historian of the sciences, is available in *Aesthetics, Method, and Epistemology* (1994a) and is called "Life Experience and Science," which originally appeared in a French-language journal but was modified to appear as Foucault's introduction to the 1989 English translation of Canguilhem's *The Normal and the Pathological* (p. 465). As Foucault says, there has been less awareness "of the significance and impact of a work like that of Georges Canguilhem, extending as it has over the past twenty or thirty years" (p. 465). Foucault also says that when "the sociology of the French intellectual milieus" is considered for "those strange years, the sixties," nearly all French philosophers "were affected directly or indirectly by the teaching or books of Canguilhem" (p. 465), which were primarily focused on critiquing overly rationalistic views of the history of the sciences in a much more thoughtful and complex way than Kuhn ever did in *The Structure of Scientific Revolutions* (1962).[7] Indeed, Foucault suggests that without Canguilhem, the French Marxists like Bourdieu, Castel, Passeron, and Lacan, would have less meaning for us (pp. 465–466)—a hefty claim on Foucault's part. In addition, Foucault suggests that Canguilhem (and others) played the same role in France that the Frankfurt School played elsewhere (p. 469)—another strong claim. Thus, both of these claims indicate how significant Foucault thinks Canguilhem's intellectual role was for him and others in France.

Foucault (1994a) argues that both Canguilhem and the Frankfurt School were raising "the same kind of questions" (p. 469), that is,

> questions that must be addressed to a rationality [the rationality of science] that aspires to be universal while developing within contingency, [a rationality] that asserts its unity and yet proceeds only through partial modifications, [a rationality[8]] that validates itself by its own supremacy but that cannot be dissociated in its history from the inertias, the dullness, or the coercions that subjugate it. In the history of the sciences in France, as in German Critical Theory, what is to be examined, basically, is a reason [a rationality] whose structural autonomy carries the history of dogmatisms and despotisms along with it—a reason [rationality], therefore, that has a liberating effect only provided it manages to liberate itself. (p. 469)

For those who know of Foucault's archaeologies and his genealogies, these are central themes, and he is saying here that these themes come directly from the work of Canguilhem.

Foucault (1994a) suggests that in taking up these questions, Canguilhem "did not just broaden the field of the history of the sciences; he reshaped the discipline itself on a number of essential points" (p. 470). To accomplish this, Foucault relates that Canguilhem "first took up the theme of 'discontinuity'" (p. 470), a theme that many who use Foucault in education and the social sciences think came from Foucault himself. Second, Canguilhem developed the idea that "whoever says 'history of discourse' is also saying recursive method . . . in the sense in which successive transformations of this truthful discourse constantly produce reworkings in their own history" (p. 472). In other words, science or universal reason, contrary to the typical or dominant portrayal of these, has constantly, in a recursive fashion, rewritten its own story, although leaving that rewriting unmentioned (which is another idea that many think came from Foucault himself). Third, Canguilhem places the "sciences of life back into [the] historico-epistemological perspective, [thus bringing] to light a certain number of essential traits that make their development [i.e., the development of the sciences of life] different from that of the other sciences and present historians [of the sciences and, thus, of reason] with specific problems" (p. 475) because all sciences are, in the dominant portrayal, supposed to be unified or the same.

And fourth, Foucault (1994a) said that Canguilhem raised "in a peculiar way, the philosophical question of knowledge" (p. 474). That is, at the center of this philosophical question of the nature of the knowledge of science and universal reason,

> one finds that of error. For, at the most basic level of life, the processes of coding and decoding give way to a chance occurrence [such as the random play of genes] that, before becoming a disease, a deficiency, or a monstrosity, is something like a disturbance in the informative system, something like a "mistake" . . . [and] that "error" [or mistake] constitutes not a neglect or a delay of the promised fulfillment [of life] but the dimension peculiar to the life of human beings and indispensable to the duration of the species. (p. 476)

That is, Canguilhem and Foucault are raising to a philosophical level their contention that, at the physical level of life itself, there is random error that is integral to life itself, a point that is intended, as are the other points previously noted, to undermine the dominant portrayal of science and reason.[9] As Foucault (1994a), then, suggests at the end of this chapter, in recognition of the importance of his mentor's work, especially for Foucault's own work, "Should not the whole theory of the subject be reformulated, seeing that knowledge, rather than opening onto the truth of the world, is deeply rooted in the 'errors' of life?"[10] Thus, once it is understood that it was Canguilhem who developed these four "essential points," it is obvious from whom Foucault himself drew some of his richest intellectual resources, especially for his archaeological method. Consequently, in our view, those who use Foucault throughout the social sciences need to increase their understandings of the French intellectual context in which Foucault thought and wrote and of Canguilhem in particular (see, e.g., Canguilhem, 1988, 1989).

## The Archaeological Method

The first point that is important to understand about Foucault's archaeological method is that it is *not* directly related to the academic discipline of archaeology, that is, the study of past cultures. It is not even particularly useful to be reminded of the iconic picture of the archaeologist using a brush to uncover old bones or artifacts embedded in dirt. As Foucault (1969/1972) says on this subject in *The Archaeology of Knowledge,* his archaeology "does not relate analysis to geological excavation" (p. 131). In fact, we would recommend that you begin to understand Foucault's archaeology by assuming that his archeology has only the faintest allusion to the academic discipline of archaeology. It is not that there are not connections between the two; it is just that thinking of the academic discipline as a lens through which one might understand the shape and meaning of Foucault's archaeology will generally get in your way.

A second point is that there is simply not enough space here to describe archaeology in a comprehensive way. Foucault's archaeology is a complex set of concepts, including *savoir, connaissance,* positivity, enunciations, statements, archive, discursive formation, enunciative regularities, correlative spaces, enveloping theory, level, limit, periodization, division, event, discontinuity, and discursive practices. In addition, there is no book that we know of—and it would certainly take a book-length piece— that completely and thoroughly lays out how to use this method, although Foucault's "Introduction" in *The Archaeology of Knowledge,* which follows three of his archaeologies, is a good synopsis of what he is after with archaeology.[11] Consequently, the only way you can begin to understand archaeology is to study carefully and thoroughly Foucault's own uses and discussions of archaeology in his three archaeologies— *Madness and Civilization* (1961/1988), *The Birth of the Clinic* (1963/1994b), and *The Order of Things* (1966/ 1973a)—and in his reflexive discussion of archaeology as a method, *The Archaeology of Knowledge* (1969/1972). We would especially suggest— and this applies to reading all of Foucault—that getting an in-depth understanding of Foucault requires close, careful, and repeated readings. Indeed, in our view, reading most education or social science texts, even many of the most abstract theorists, is simple and easy compared with reading the density and complexity of Foucault's work, some of which is a function of his writing style, our lack of knowledge of the French philosophy context, our inexperience in reading philosophy of any kind, the depth at which he worked, and the complexity that he was trying to address, much of which is counter to both dominant thought and critical thought. Obviously, though, we think the time and effort needed is worth it. We want to repeat, however, that a substantive use of Foucault's archaeology, in particular, means developing an in-depth understanding of the complex interrelated set of the concepts listed previously.

Two of the more commonly cited of this set of concepts are *savoir* and *connaissance.* In an interview (Foucault, 1994a) that appeared in French in 1966, after the publication of *Madness and Civilization, The Birth of the Clinic,* and *The Order of Things* but before that of *The Archaeology of Knowledge,* Foucault discussed how he defined archaeology:

> By "archaeology," I would like to designate not exactly a discipline but a domain of research, which would be the following: in a society, different bodies of learning, philosophical ideas, everyday opinions, but also institutions, commercial practices and police activities, mores— all refer to a certain implicit knowledge [*savoir*] special to this society. This knowledge is profoundly different from the [formal] bodies of learning [*des connaissances*] that one can find in scientific books, philosophical theories, and religious justifications, but it [*savoir*] is what makes possible at a given moment the appearance of a theory, an opinion, a practice. (p. 261)

Thus, understanding these two arenas of knowledge, *savoir* and *connaissance,* is fundamental to understanding archaeology. *Savoir* includes formal knowledge such as "philosophical ideas" but also "institutions, commercial practices, and police activity,"[12] whereas *connaissance* includes only formal bodies of knowledge such as "scientific books, philosophical theories, and religious justifications." Similarly, Gutting (1989) suggests, "By *connaissance* he [Foucault] means . . . any particular body of knowledge such as nuclear physics, evolutionary biology, or Freudian psychoanalysis" (p. 251). In contrast, *savior,* Gutting continues, "refers to the [broad] discursive conditions that are necessary for the development of *connaissance*" (p. 251).

Foucault provides an example of the difference between these two concepts in the sixth chapter of *The Archaeology of Knowledge* (1969/1972). He says,

> The linch-pin of *Madness and Civilization* was the appearance at the beginning of the nineteenth century of a psychiatric discipline. This discipline had neither the same content, nor the same internal organization, nor the same place in medicine, nor the same practical function, nor the same methods as the traditional chapter on "diseases of the head" or "nervous diseases" to be found in eighteenth century medical treaties. (p. 179)

With this section, Foucault is comparing the psychiatric discipline that emerged at the beginning of the 1800s to the "diseases of the head" and "nervous diseases" of the 1700s because diseases of the head and nervous diseases during the 18th century were the closest comparison to the psychiatric discipline during the 19th century.[13] Foucault (1969/1972) continues,

> But on examining this new discipline, we discovered two things: what made it [i.e., the emerging discipline of psychiatry] possible at the time it appeared, what brought about this great change [i.e., changes from 18th-century diseases of the head to 19th-century psychiatry] in the economy of concepts, analyses, and demonstrations was a whole set of relations between [sic] hospitalization, internment, the conditions and procedures of social exclusion, the rules of jurisprudence, the norms of industrial labor and bourgeois morality, in short a whole group of relations that characterized for this discursive practice [i.e., psychiatry] the formation of its statements. (p. 179)

What made it possible, then, for psychiatry to appear as a formal discipline, as a *connaissance,* was a set of changes in concepts, practices, procedures, institutions, and norms, that is, a change in the much broader *savoir.* As Foucault (1969/1972) further elaborates,

> But this [discursive] practice is not only manifested in a discipline [i.e., psychiatry] possessing a scientific status and scientific pretensions [*connaissance* or psychiatry as a formal discipline]; it is also found in the operation in legal texts, in literature, in philosophy, in political decisions, and in the statements made and the opinions expressed in daily life [*savoir*]. (p. 179)

Thus, whereas the history of psychiatry is typically written solely in terms of psychiatry as a formal discipline, "possessing a scientific status and scientific pretensions," Foucault is arguing that this is inadequate. To better understand the history of psychiatry as a formal academic discipline, it is also necessary to study a much broader array that includes relations among "hospitalization, internment, the conditions and procedures of social exclusion, the rules of jurisprudence, the norms of industrial labor and bourgeois morality" as well as legal texts, literature, philosophy, political decisions, and the statements and opinions of daily life.

For Foucault (1994a), then, archaeology is focused on the study of *savoir,* which is "the condition of possibility[14] of [formal] knowledge [*connaissance*]" (p. 262) for the purpose of showing that psychiatry or other formal disciplines do not simply emerge out of the historical trajectory of those disciplines when that history is restricted solely to the formal discipline as a formal discipline. Instead, a history of a formal discipline must address both *connaissance,* the formal statements of a discipline, and *savoir,* the much broader and less rational array of practices, policies, procedures, institutions, politics, everyday life, and so on. However, Foucault's larger point is that, rather than the traditional view that formal knowledges (*connaissance*), such as psychiatry and economics, have their own formal rational trajectory of emergence, formal knowledges emerge more "irrationally" or not rationally from *savoir,* which includes not just the formal and rational but also the much broader "irrationality" of politics, institutional practices, popular opinions, and so on. In other words, formal knowledges emerge, substantially, from a broad array of complex irrational sources or conditions, and this more complex, messier, more ambiguous "condition[s] of possibility" undermines the modernist rational "story" or "meta-narrative" of formal knowledges.[15]

Accordingly, after understanding the meanings of *connaissance and savoir* and the fact that archaeology is the study of *savoir* as the "condition[s] of possibility" of *connaissance,* it is necessary to return to the larger context of Foucault's archaeological work. With archaeology, Foucault is drawing on the work of Canguilhem, whose work he compared to that of the Frankfurt School. And for both the Frankfurt School and Canguilhem, the nature of reason—"a rationality that aspires to be universal" (Foucault, 1994a, p. 469)—in modernity is their macro text. Furthermore, Foucault is suggesting that the myth or master narrative of modernist reason, when examined carefully, is not just logical and rational but also complex, contradictory, and problematic and that it has embedded within it instances of what we might call "unreason."[16] For example, Foucault says that this modernist reason "validates itself by its own supremacy but that cannot be dissociated in its history from the inertias, the dullness, or the coercions that subjugate it" (p. 469) and that it "is a reason whose structural autonomy carries the history of dogmatisms and despotisms along with it" (p. 469). Thus, according to Foucault, reason (i.e., formal knowledges), as it is typically portrayed within modernity, is not what it is made out to be; that is, the "archaeological" history of reason includes inertias, dullness, coercions, dogmatisms, and despotisms.

What Foucault is attempting, then, with his various archaeologies is to examine specific cases, particular examples, as in *Madness and Civilization, The Birth of the Clinic,* and *The Order of Things* (the human sciences), of the work of reason. And in carrying out these studies of specific cases of the work of reason, he has come to two insights. One is that the history of reason in these specific cases is "not wholly and entirely that of its progressive refinement, its continuously increasing rationality" (Foucault, 1969/1972, p. 4)[17]; that is, reason in these cases does not become progressively more refined, more rational, better, or more true. For example, in the psychiatry example cited previously, Foucault argues that there was no smooth, unbroken trajectory of psychiatry from the 1700s to the 1800s. Instead, he argues, during the 1700s, there was "the traditional chapter on 'diseases of the head' or 'nervous diseases' to be found in eighteenth century medical treatises," and then, at the beginning of the 1800s, there was the emergence of the "psychiatric discipline" (p. 179). However, and this is one of Foucault's key points about reason, the second did not emerge, rationally or logically, out of the first; the two—diseases of the head and nervous diseases, on the one hand, and the discipline of psychiatry, on the other—were separate and different, and the first did not lead logically and progressively to the second. There is, thus, a "discontinuity (threshold, rupture, break, mutation, transformation)" (p. 2) between the two, which again means that reason is not nearly as rational as it has been portrayed within the metanarrative of modernity. Thus, rather than just critiquing this master narrative, in his archaeologies, Foucault is doing the hard work of providing research-based examples that the master narrative is wrong.

Foucault's second point is that disciplines, formal knowledges, or *connaissances* cannot be studied and understood in just their own formal terms. Rather, a *connaissance* emerges out of *savoir*, which includes formal knowledge, such as academic books, but also institutions, laws, processes and procedures, common opinions, norms, rules, morality, commercial practices, and so on. Thus, to understand a particular discipline means that not only must the formal treatises of that discipline be studied, but so too must the *savoir*, this much broader, more complex context that includes, say, institutions and commercial practices "on the same plane" as the formal aspects of the discipline. As a result, reason loses much of its elite exaltedness, its purity, its high status, its very rationality.

However, problematizing modernity's reason is not Foucault's only focus in his archaeologies. His "twin" focus is modernity's subject (Foucault, 1969/1972, p. 12). As he says,

> Making historical analysis the discourse of the continuous [e.g., portraying formal knowledge, *connaissance*, as emerging through a rational, logical, continuous trajectory] and making human consciousness [i.e., the human subject or subjectivity] the *original* subject of *all* historical development and *all* action are the two sides of the same system of thought [i.e., modernity]. (p. 12, emphases added)

Thus, Foucault is arguing that the idea that "man" or the human subject is creating human history and creating, most importantly, formal knowledge (*connaissance*) in a logical, rational, continuous manner is but the ideology of modernity. This ideology, then, becomes a lens through which historians, philosophers, economists, linguists, social scientists, and so on fashion or construct a "picture" or representation of "reality" that is logical and rational and that has the human subject as its main actor or at its privileged center. In addition, this central actor is contradictorily both the doer and the object of the doing, the researcher and the researched. To Foucault, then, this modernist ideology and its resultant representation of "reality" in works of history, philosophy, economy, psychiatry, language, and so on can be undermined by using his archaeological methodology to show that formal knowledges emerge from *savoir*, which is not logical or rational, and that this process of emergence does not have a guiding or agentic subject at its center (i.e., archaeology decenters the modernist subject). For example, near the end of his "Introduction" to *The Archaeology of Knowledge* (Foucault, 1969/ 1972)—again, the last of his archaeological works—he says that the aim of archaeology is "to define a method of historical analysis *freed* from the anthropological [i.e., human subject-centered] theme" and "a method purged of all anthropologism" (p. 16, emphasis added)—a method of historical analyses freed from "man" as its center.

However, despite Foucault's (1969/1972) view that problematizing reason and the agentic subject are "two sides of the same system of thought" (p. 12), for the most part, those who have used Foucault have been more interested in his undermining of modernist reason than in his undermining of the privileged or centered subject. Indeed, some feminists and critical theorists[18] have rejected Foucault because, in their view, he destroys the agency of the subject, whereas others have appropriated parts of Foucault, such as his problematization of reason, while rejecting his decentering of the subject (e.g., Hartsock, 1998). However, other feminists, such as Butler (1993), have agreed with Foucault that the "two sides" are two parts of the "same system of thought." We agree, though, with Butler that the two cannot be separated, that it is not possible to appropriate the one from Foucault while rejecting the other. Indeed, we would argue that taking one side while rejecting the other indicates a fundamental misunderstanding of Foucault, similar to the general lack of understanding of Foucault's intellectual dependency on the work of Canguilhem and to the general lack of understanding of archaeology as a method. Indeed, we would strongly suggest that to appropriate Foucault's critique of reason without simultaneously appropriating his antihumanism is simply wrong. Foucault's critique of reason cannot stand without his antihumanism; as he says, they are "two sides of the same system of thought" (p. 12).

Our advice, then, for those interested in pursuing archaeology—and we would urge this pursuit as we think that archaeology is generally underused and underappreciated— is this: Do not just "cherry pick" a concept here and a concept there and assume that you are doing archaeology or that you are using Foucault appropriately. To learn how to do archaeology, we would suggest reading all of the archaeologies in the order they were published. The first three are actual applications of archaeology, and the fourth, *The Archaeology of Knowledge* (1969/1972), is Foucault's reflexive effort to describe the methodology retrospectively. However, it is important to understand that, as Foucault says of *The Archaeology of Knowledge,* "This work is not an exact description of what can be read in *Madness and Civilization, Naissance de la clinique* [*The Birth of the Clinic*], or *The Order of Things.* It is different on many points. It also includes a number of corrections and internal criticisms" (p. 16). Despite these corrections and criticisms, *The Archaeology of Knowledge* is his best, and final, description of archaeology as a method. Unfortunately, we know of no book, or even article-length work (we doubt an article-length effort would be sufficient), that attempts to actually explain how to use archaeology as a method. There are, though, some works that, at least partially, focus on or critique archaeology, including Gutting's *Michel Foucault's Archaeology of Scientific Reason* (1989). Books like these are helpful, but reading Foucault's four archaeological texts carefully and thoroughly is by far the best approach.

## ▣ CONNECTING ARCHAEOLOGY AND GENEALOGY

Is genealogy the successor to archaeology? Is genealogy the further development of archaeology? Is genealogy superior to archaeology? Did Foucault decide that archaeology did not work, was flawed, so he moved on to genealogy, which he considered to be better? Are the two "methodologies" widely different, clearly separate, or are they closely connected, part of the same larger project? Answers to these questions are multiple and divergent among Foucault scholars, both critics and advocates. Our sense is that the dominant, but certainly not the only, conclusion among U.S. scholars of the social sciences, and more specifically among U.S. scholars of education, is that genealogy is superior to archaeology. Partially validating this conclusion is the fact that there are many more instances of these scholars claiming to do genealogies than there are of those claiming to do archaeologies. However, basing our perspective on that of Foucault, we would have to disagree with this conclusion.

In the first of Foucault's "Two Lectures" (1980, *Power/Knowledge*), which was given on January 7, 1976, and which is *after* Foucault had written his four archaeologies and *after* he had written his two genealogies (*Discipline and Punish* and *The History of Sexuality,* Volume 1: *An Introduction*), he says,

> If we were to characterize it in two terms, then "archaeology" would be the appropriate methodology of this analysis of local discursivities, and "genealogy" would be the tactics whereby, on the basis of the descriptions of these local discursivities, the subjected knowledges which were thus released would be brought into play. (p. 85)

Also, in an interview just prior to his death on June 25, 1984, in Paris,[19] Foucault hopes that other scholars will continue to use both archaeology and genealogy, as he continues to consider both of them equally useful. Most tellingly, though, is what Foucault says in *The History of Sexuality,* Volume 2: *The Use of Pleasure* (1984/1990), which was published the year he died. Three times in this "Introduction" (on pages 4–5, 5–6, and 11–12), Foucault divides his work into three "axes" (p. 4) or arenas of analyses; he also labels these three "theoretical shifts" that he had to make to study "the games of truth" (p. 6). The first is "the analysis of discursive practices [that] made it possible to trace the formation of disciplines (*saviors*)" (p. 4), that is, archaeology. The second is "the analysis of power relations and their technologies" (p. 4), that is, genealogy. And the third is "the modes according to which individuals are given to recognize themselves as . . . subjects" (p. 5) or "the games of truth in the relationship of self with self and the forming of oneself as a subject" (p. 6), that is, the care of the self work. Then, at the end of this section, he calls these three the "archaeological dimension," the "genealogical dimension," and the "practices of the self," respectively (pp. 11–12).[20]

Unquestionably, then, Foucault himself does not see archaeology as less than genealogy or as superseded by it. Instead, throughout his work, he sees both archaeology and genealogy as continuing to be important and valid. Where, then, does this conclusion that genealogy is a correction of archaeology come from for U.S. scholars? We would suggest that it comes mainly from Dreyfus and Rabinow in their highly influential *Michel Foucault: Beyond Structuralism and Hermeneutics,* first published in 1983 when U.S. scholars were just beginning to read Foucault.[21] As a result, these two scholars, from early on, have been enormously influential in introducing both Foucault and his work to U.S. scholars; indeed, it could be said that they have been virtually canonical in their interpretations, at least for the U.S. audience. For example, that they think genealogy is the superior successor to archaeology is evident in their "Introduction" to their book. They say that they "will argue at length [about 40% of the book] that the project of *Archaeology* founder[ed]" (p. xxiv, emphasis in original) and that Foucault abandoned it (p. xxvi). They also say, at the end of their analysis of archaeology, that their "detailed study of the new archaeological method has revealed . . . that it suffers from several internal strains" (p. 90). In response, then, to the failure of archaeology, they assert that Foucault, based on "his reading of Nietzsche" (p. xxvii), developed genealogy, which Dreyfus and Rabinow claim is "his most original contribution" (p. xxvii). However, although Foucault never directly corrected them (as far as we can find), possibly because Dreyfus and Rabinow were leading the charge in touting Foucault and his work to a large U.S. audience, Foucault persisted throughout his life in maintaining the equal value and validity of archaeology and genealogy. Thus, siding with Foucault, along with others such as Mahon (1992), we think that both of his methodologies—archaeology and genealogy—should continue to be seen as equally useful and valuable.

To further illustrate this point and to draw increased attention to what we think is a critically important essay, we now discuss "Nietzsche, Genealogy, History" (Foucault, 1977, 1994a), which we would suggest can be seen as a bridge between Foucault's archaeological period and his genealogical one. Although "Nietzsche, Genealogy, History" was published in English in 1977 in *Language, Counter-Memory, Practice:*

*Selected Essays and Interviews,* it was actually first published in French in 1971 after Foucault finished publishing his four archaeologies but before he published his two genealogies. However, it is now available, in a better version in our view,[22] in *Aesthetics, Method, and Epistemology,* Volume 2 (1998), and one of the improvements in this latter version is that it better connects this essay to his archaeological work, especially in the use of two key archaeological terms, *savoir* and *connaissance.* In this essay, Foucault provides his first description of his genealogical method, but throughout the essay he clearly maintains the connection of his second method, genealogy, to his first one, archaeology.

In "Nietzsche, Genealogy, History" (Foucault, 1994a), although his language is often literary and poetic, playing off of specific quotes and issues in Nietzsche's own works, particularly *The Genealogy of Morals,* Foucault makes four strong claims as to what a genealogist does (although it would be easy to argue that there are five, six, seven, or more such claims throughout the piece). One claim, drawn directly from Nietzsche, is that the genealogist "challenge[s] the pursuit of the origin" (p. 371). For Foucault and Nietzsche, "the pursuit of the origin" is the pursuit, largely in philosophy, history, and the social sciences, of the beginning of some phenomena or categories such as "values, morality, asceticism, and knowledge" (p. 373). Foucault says that this pursuit is "an attempt to capture the exact essence of things, their purest possibilities, and their . . . original identity" (p. 371). Instead, by refusing "metaphysics" and by listening to "history," the genealogist finds that "there is 'something altogether different' behind things: not a timeless and essential secret but the secret that they [things] have no essence, or that their essence was fabricated in a piecemeal fashion from alien forms" (p. 371). Foucault also says, "What is found at the historical beginning of things is not inviolable identity of their origin, it is the dissension of other things. It is disparity" (pp. 371–372). It is the "vicissitudes of history" (p. 373). For example, he says that by

> examining the history of reason, he [the genealogist] learns that it [reason] was born . . . from chance; [that] devotion to truth and the precision of scientific methods arose from the passion of scholars, their reciprocal hatred, their fanatical and unending discussions, and their spirit of competition—the personal conflicts that slowly forged the weapons of reason. (p. 371)

Thus, the target of Foucault's critique, his genealogy, much like with this archaeological work, is the foundational assumptions of Western modernity. In this case, his critical focus is on modernity's teleological assumption that history moves upward or forward from some origin. In contrast, he argues that the genealogist finds that there are no such origins and that origins are often fabricated. What the genealogist finds, instead, as she or he explores origins is randomness, piecemeal fabrications, dissension, disparity, passion, hatred, competition, "details and accidents" (Foucault, 1998, p. 373), "petty malice" (p. 373), "the minute deviations—or conversely, the complete reversals—the errors, the false appraisals, and the faulty calculations" (p. 374) (similar to *savoir*) mixed together with devotion to truth, precise methods, scientific discussions, and so on (similar to *connaissance*). In other words, Foucault is not denying that reason is a part of this history, but it is only one player amid a much broader cast in the dramaturgy of modernity.

A second focus of the genealogist, one that becomes much more important in later works although not a large one in this essay, is the body. Foucault (1998) says, "The body is the inscribed surface of events (traced by language and dissolved by ideas), the locus of a dissociated Self (adopting the illusion of a substantial unity), and a volume in perpetual disintegration" (p. 375). He, then, indicates that "genealogy is . . . thus situated within the articulation of the body and history. Its take is to expose a body totally imprinted by history" (pp. 375–376). This last sentence is key; the "take" of genealogy is "to expose a body totally imprinted by history." However, these few remarks are the extent of Foucault's effort to connect genealogy to the body in this essay, but he returns to this particular focus in subsequent scholarship. For example, in *Discipline and Punish,* Foucault (1975/1979) says,

> The body is also directly involved in the political field; power relations have an immediate hold upon it; they invest it, mark it, train it, torture it, force it to carry out tasks, to perform ceremonies, to emit signs. This political investment of the body is bound up, in accordance with complex reciprocal relations, with its economic use; it is largely as a force of production that the body is invested with relations of power and domination; but, on the other hand, its constitution as labour power is possible only if it is caught up in a system of subjection (in which need is also a political instrument system meticulously prepared, calculated, and used); the body becomes a useful force only if it is both a productive body and subjected body. (pp. 25–26)

This focus on the body has inspired numerous philosophers, especially feminists such as Elizabeth Grosz and Nancy Fraser, who assert that the body has been left out of philosophy. For example, Grosz (1994) says in *Volatile Bodies: Toward a Corporeal Feminism* that she intends to "explore the work of theorists of corporeal instruction, primarily Nietzsche, Foucault, and Deleuze and Guattari," because each "explores the position of the body as a site of the subject's social production" (p. xiii).

A third claim that Foucault (1998) makes for the genealogist is a focus on describing "the various systems of subjection" (p. 376) and "the endlessly repeated play of dominations" (p. 377). For example, he says that "the domination of certain men over others leads to the differentiation of values" and that "class domination generates the idea of liberty" (p. 377). He also says that domination

> establishes marks of its power and engraves memories on things and even within bodies. It makes itself accountable for debts and gives rise to the universe of rules, which is by no means designed to temper violence, but rather to satisfy it. (p. 377)

Foucault is arguing here that the modernist rationale for debts, rules, laws, and the current social, economic, governmental, and legal arrangements diverts critical attention from its domination and subjection effects. For example, he says that the law is a calculated and relentless pleasure, delight in promised blood, which permits the perpetual instigation of new dominations and the staging of meticulously repeated scenes of violence. The desire for peace, the serenity of compromise, and the tacit acceptance of the law, far from representing a major moral conversion or a utilitarian calculation that gave rise to the law, are but its result and, in point of fact, its perversion. (p. 378)

Foucault follows this with a direct quote from Nietzsche's *Genealogy of Morals:* "guilt, conscience, and duty had their threshold of emergence in the right to secure obligations and their inception, like that of any major event on earth, saturated in blood" (p. 378). Foucault then concludes that

humanity does not gradually progress from combat to combat until it arrives at universal reciprocity, where the rule of law finally replaces warfare; humanity installs each of its violences in a system of rules and thus proceeds from domination to domination. (p. 378)

Foucault thus contends that the rationales that support modernity as humane and as becoming more so are false and that, instead, modernity is but a new installation of domination and violence as a "system of rules." For example, schools, the prison system, commerce, and so on are installations of domination and violence masquerading as systems of rules, and it is the work of the genealogist to describe and reveal this domination and violence.

The final focus of the genealogist that we take from this essay is drawn from what Foucault calls "effective history." Foucault's (1998) critique of traditional history or the "history of historians" (p. 380) is what he calls "effective history." This critique is "without [the] constants" of traditional history. Foucault argues,

The traditional devices for constructing a comprehensive view of history and for retracing the past as a patient and continuous development must be systematically dismantled. Necessarily, we must dismiss those tendencies which encourage the consoling play of recognitions. Knowledge [*savoir*], even under the banner of history, does not depend on "rediscovery of ourselves." (p. 380, brackets and emphasis in original)

Once again, the now familiar targets of Foucault's critique are the same foundational assumptions of modernity. The regime of traditional history is one that constructs "a comprehensive view of history," retraces "the past as a patient and continuous development," "encourages the consoling play of recognitions," dissolves "the singular event into an ideal continuity" (Foucault, 1998, p. 380), asserts that history is controlled by "destiny or regulative mechanisms" (p. 381), and "confirm[s] our belief that the present rests upon profound intentions and immutable necessities" (p. 381).

In response to this regime,

History becomes "effective" to the degree that it introduces discontinuity into our very being—as it divides our emotions, dramatizes our instincts, multiplies our body, and sets it against itself. Effective history leaves nothing around the self, deprives the self of the reassuring stability of life and nature, and it will not permit itself to be transported by a voiceless obstinacy toward a millennial ending. It will uproot its traditional foundations and relentlessly disrupt its pretended continuity. (Foucault, 1998, p. 380)

Also, "'Effective' history differs from the history of historians in being without constants" (p. 380):

"Effective" history . . . deals with events in terms of their most unique characteristics; there most acute manifestations. An [historical] event, consequently, is not a decision, a treaty, a reign, or a battle, but the reversal of relationship of forces, the usurpation of power, the appropriation of vocabulary turned against those who had once used it, a domination that grows feeble, poisons itself, grows slack. (pp. 380–381)

This "effective" historical sense "confirms our existence among countless lost events, without a landmark or a point of reference" (Foucault, 1998, p. 381). Finally, it is an "affirmation of a perspectival knowledge [*savoir*]," as traditional "historians take unusual pains to erase the elements in their work which reveal their grounding in a particular time and place" (p. 382). In a sense, then, Foucault is making an argument that traditional (modernist) history is an effort to console ourselves with the assumptions that there is unity, continuity, teleology, meaning, destiny, and so on built into history itself, a view that makes us feel safe or that would make "history" our safe harbor. In critique of the latter modernist and humanist view, Foucault argues that this aspect of traditional history is predominantly dependent on a metaphysics (p. 381), a kind of modernist psychosis or spell, that hides the fact that history is "the luck of the battle," the "randomness of events," "a profusion of entangled events," "a 'host of errors and phantasms' [a quote from Nietzsche]," and "countless lost events" (p. 381).

The work, then, of the genealogist in this bridging essay between archaeology and genealogy is fourfold. The genealogist is to critique the pursuit of origins by showing they are fabrications, to show that the body is "imprinted by history" (Foucault, 1998, p. 376), to describe "systems of subjection" (p. 376) and "the endlessly repeated play of dominations" (p. 377), and to do what Foucault calls "effective history." We now turn, after this explication of this bridging essay, to his two genealogies, which did immediately follow his "Nietzsche, Genealogy, History" (Foucault, 1977/1994a) bridging essay. To accomplish this, we discuss his extensive comments on genealogy in the first of his two genealogies, *Discipline and Punish* (1975/1979), and then end the "Genealogy" section with some brief comments on his second and last genealogy, *The History of Sexuality*, Volume 1: *An Introduction* (1976/1980a).

## Genealogy

*Discipline and Punish* first appeared in French in 1975, was translated into English by Alan Sheridan in 1977, and finally was published by Vintage Books in 1979, which is the version we are using. Although there is much in this book that is provocative and uncomfortable reading, such as Foucault's well-researched descriptions of torture used by the French penal system prior to the contemporary period,[23] we focus here primarily on what Foucault has to say about *doing* genealogy. As with his archaeologies, another of the many similarities between his archaeological work and his genealogical work,[24] Foucault is comparing one period with another period. For example, he says that during the second period, "in Europe and in the United States, the entire economy of punishment was redistributed. [There was] a new theory of law and crime, a new moral or political justification, old laws were abolished, old customs died out" (Foucault, 1975/1979, p. 7). "By the end of the eighteenth and the beginning of the nineteenth century" (p. 8), the old penal style was dying out.

During this new period, then, "punishment has become an economy of suspended rights. . . . As a result a . . . whole army of technicians took over from the executioner, the immediate anatomist of pain: warders, doctors, chaplains, psychiatrists, psychologists, educationalists" (Foucault, 1975/ 1979, p. 11). And the consequence of this change seemingly was a "reduction in the penal severity," "a phenomenon with which legal historians are well acquainted" (p. 16)—"less cruelty, less pain, more kindness, more respect, more 'humanity'" (p. 16). However, not surprisingly, Foucault is going to critique "the new tactics of power" (p. 23) of this liberal progressive view of less cruelty and pain. For example, he is going to argue that the penal system had become "a strange scientifico–juridical complex," the focus of which is now the soul rather than the body (p. 19), which, to some extent, Foucault considers a more oppressive focus than that of the old penal regime. He is also going to argue that the ultimate target of this complex "is not simply a judgment of guilt. . . . It bears within it an assessment of normality and a technical prescription for a possible normalization" (pp. 20–21), which applies throughout society rather than just to criminals. In other words, to Foucault, one effect of the new penal regime is not to punish the criminal but rather to normalize the larger population in terms of correct behavior.

Foucault (1975/1979), then, says that *Discipline and Punish* "is intended as a correlative history of the modern soul and of a new power to judge; a genealogy of the present scientifico–legal complex from which the power to punish derives its bases, justifications, and rules" (p. 23). "But from what point can such a history of the modern soul on trial be written?" (p. 23). First, he answers that this cannot be written

> by studying only the general social forms, as Durkheim did, [because] one runs the risk of positing as the principle of greater leniency in punishment processes of individualization that are rather one of the effects of the new tactics of power, among which can be included the new penal mechanisms. (p. 23)

In other words, focusing on the "greater leniency in punishment" in this new penal regime, as if that were a causal principle of the new regime, would be a mistake; instead, this "greater leniency" should be seen as an "effect" of "the new tactics of power."

Immediately thereafter, Foucault (1975/1979) lays out "four general rules" for his genealogical study. Although these four rules are focused specifically on this particular study, they highlight well several areas of possible work for the genealogist. What we do here, then, is present each of the rules, discuss its implications for the genealogist, and briefly speculate as to how it might be applied to some facet of public education. The following is his first rule:

> Do not concentrate the study of the punitive mechanisms on their "repressive" effects alone, on their "punishment" aspects alone, but situate them in a whole series of their possible *positive* effects, even if these seem marginal at first sight. As a consequence, regard punishment as a complex social function. (p. 23, emphasis added)

Foucault wants us to look beyond the obvious "'repressive' effects" of punishment to examine "a whole series of their possible *positive* effects." By positive, though, he does not mean an effect that we might like or approve of; he means something produced rather than something repressed or excluded. For example, as mentioned previously, one "positive" or produced effect of the new penal regime is the normalization of appropriate behavior among the general population. Indeed, one of Foucault's favorite genealogical maneuvers is to focus not just on the negative or repressive effects of power but also on the positive or productive effects of power. To Foucault, power does not just exclude or repress; power also produces. However, he is not saying that the repressive effects of power should be ignored by the genealogist; rather, he is arguing that the genealogist should regard "punishment as a complex *social* function" (emphasis added) that includes both the repressive and the productive. For instance, school discipline programs do not just punish (repress) certain student behaviors among a small group of students; they also, and perhaps more importantly, produce a normalization (a "positive" effect) of correct behavior among the rest of the students. Thus, to Foucault, these discipline programs could be said to be both negative (repressive) effects and positive (productive) effects.

Foucault's (1975/1979) second rule is to "analyze punitive methods not simply as consequences of legislation or as indicators of social structures, but as techniques possessing their own specificity in the more general field of other ways of exercising power. Regard punishment as a political tactic" (p. 23). Thus, how social acts or policies get analyzed or thought about is critical to the genealogist. However, the norm of the mainstream social sciences is to see actions that are related to the government as the result of legislative policymakers or other governmental actors, that is, a function of social actors or agents. In contrast, the norm of critical theorists and other structuralists is to see governmental actions as a function of the social structures. Foucault, though, wants us to turn our thinking in a different direction. He wants us—and this is a persistent point he made throughout his career—to see specific acts, procedures, or processes, such as "punitive methods" and school discipline programs, as having a kind of a quasi-independent standing or importance, a "specificity," within "the more general field of other ways of exercising power." They are not just actions of individual agents, and they are not merely functions of something more important and larger, some social structure; these methods or programs need to be looked at by the genealogist as having their own specificity or independent standing. Moreover, by "ways of exercising power," Foucault does not usually mean the power exercised by an intentional actor, although his view encompasses that; instead, he usually means that a procedure or process multiplies across a social field because of a complex set or collection of reasons or causes that are not entirely intentional or rational. Thus, these governmental acts, procedures, or processes are not only or simply a function of legislation or social structures; instead, to the genealogist, they are ways that power multiplies, without some agentic agent consciously accomplishing this, across a social field. For instance, the new emphasis on student-centered classrooms[25] should not be analyzed only as a new and better approach emerging from progressive educational theorists or only as a function of social structures; instead, it should also be analyzed as a practice of power that has emerged and circulates more broadly in society and as a practice of power that is, in many ways, actually more oppressive than teacher-centered classrooms. The reason why Foucault might offer that the new student-centered classrooms are more oppressive is because the work of this new tactic of power is to imprint the souls of the children rather than just their behaviors, as the old teacher-centered classrooms did.

The third rule, and a critically important one to those of us in the social sciences, is as follows:

> Instead of treating the history of penal law and the history of the human sciences as two separate series whose overlapping appears to have had on one [penal law] or the other [the history of the human sciences], or perhaps on both, a disturbing or useful effect, according to one's point of view, see whether there is not some common matrix or whether they do not both derive from a single process of "epistemologico–juridical" formation; in short, make the technology of power the very principle both of the humanization of the penal system and of the knowledge of man. (Foucault, 1975/1979, p. 23)

Thus, the history of penal law, the public educational system, or nursing should not be examined just as a separate, albeit sometimes overlapping, series running parallel to the history of the social sciences but should also be examined as emerging from "some common matrix" or as deriving from a single "process of epistemologico–[fill in the blank with a juridical, educational, or medical] formation." Again, as with the second rule, the principal focus of the genealogist should be on the technologies of power and the ways that the same technology of power spreads across and is enacted both within particular systems, such as those of prisons, schools, or hospitals, and in the social sciences. Thus, technologies of power, arising out of a "common matrix" or a "'epistomologico–[fill in the blank]' formation," may multiply across both particular systems and social sciences in general, and this multiplication is likely to be both intentional and unintended, both rational and not rational. For example, we might find that contemporary public education—its practices, procedures, and policies—and the history of education scholarship, its research, and its theories have emerged from the same "common matrix" or the same epistemologico–educational formation. Although this seems to be a less radical assertion than Foucault's similar assertion about penal systems, it is important to understand that he does not simply mean that both contemporary public education and education scholarship share the same general assumptions about schools or education; instead, he means that there is a more primary matrix or formation that is not necessarily intentionally or rationally created, and that is not necessarily education oriented, out of which both are emerging. For example, perhaps, on genealogical investigation, both the new movement emphasizing student-oriented classrooms and the growth of qualitative research methodologies arise out of the same "pastoral" matrix or formation (e.g., see Foucault's use of the concept of the pastoral in *The History of Sexuality*, Volume 1: *An Introduction* [1976/1980a]).

Foucault's (1975/1979) fourth rule is as follows:

> Try to discover whether this entry of the soul on to the scene of penal justice, and with it the insertion in legal practice of a whole corpus of "scientific" knowledge, is not the effect of a transformation of the way in which the body itself is invested by power relations.
>
> In short, try to study the metamorphosis of punitive methods on the basis of a political technology of the body in which might be read a common history of power relations and object relations. Thus, by an analysis of penal leniency as a technique of power, one might understand both how man, the soul, [and] the normal or abnormal individual have come to duplicate crime as objects of penal intervention and in what way a specific mode of subjection was able to give birth to man as an object of knowledge for a discourse with a "scientific" status. (p. 24)

By his use of the word "soul," Foucault means that the focus of the new penal system is "not only on what they [the criminals] *do* but also on what they *are, will be, may be*" (p. 18, emphases added); that is, the new focus is not on their behavior but rather on their being or their selves. The new penal perspective has "taken to judging something other than crimes, namely, the 'soul' of the criminal" (p. 19). Then, this new focus on the "soul" of the criminal is combined with a new "corpus of 'scientific' knowledge," *both* of which are the "effect of a transformation of the way in which the body itself is invested by power relations." It is, as Foucault says, "a political technology of the body." Thus, what is generally seen as more humane and more liberal (i.e., "penal leniency"), in this case, is argued by Foucault to be but "a new technique of power," one in which "the body itself is invested by power relations." And he indicates that he sees this change as another example of the modernist social construction of "man [or the subject] as an object of knowledge for a discourse with 'scientific' status."[26] An example of this in education might be a consideration of "site-based management," "distributive leadership," and "community of learners," all of which are generally seen as more humane or more democratic approaches to school leadership or governance, as new "techniques of power" that are not just endemic to education but also part of a larger formation, the effect of which might be seen as a worse oppression at the level of the soul. In other words, these new techniques of power in education focus on controlling or managing the "soul" of educators rather than just their behaviors, which, to Foucault, is much more oppressive than techniques of power that seek to control only behaviors.

Although we find these four rules to be a particularly rich source for understanding the work of the Foucaultian genealogist, they certainly do not exhaust *Discipline and Punish* in terms of what the work of a genealogist is. For example, we find the entire last section of the same chapter that contains the four rules (Foucault, 1975/1979, pp. 16–31) to be a particularly exciting discussion of genealogy. We also have a strong appreciation for (a) the "The Composition of Forces" section (pp. 162–169) in the chapter, titled "Docile Bodies," which includes some direct statements about education; (b) the entire chapter titled "The Means of Correct Training," which includes sections on "Hierarchical Observation," "Normalizing Judgments," and "The Examination" as well as some direct comments on education; and (c) the last chapter, "The Carceral," which is another particularly rich and provocative section in *Discipline and Punish*. In contrast, we are not as enamored as many are with the chapter on "Panopticism," as we find it to be one of his more simplistic, more totalized, and more poorly developed concepts. Our point, though, is that this first genealogy is literally a panoply of critical tools and ideas that can be used to do Foucaultian genealogies.

Foucault's (1976/1980a) second and last genealogy was *The History of Sexuality, Volume 1: An Introduction*. What we do here, given space limitations, is provide just some brief comments and offer some suggestions about reading this volume. Provocatively, and one of the main reasons why we have used more space discussing *Discipline and Punish*, is that the *History of Sexuality* includes little direct discussion of genealogy as a method, whereas *Discipline and Punish* includes considerable discussion of the genealogical method. Indeed, through a systematic search of the text,[27] we found that in his second genealogy, he uses the word "genealogy" only five times (four times in the Introduction and once on p. 171).[28] Nonetheless, in general, in our view, *History of Sexuality* is the better genealogy of the two, more confident, smoother, better worked out, as if he had more deeply integrated the methodology of genealogy by the time he did this second one. It is as if he had worked out his genealogical method in *Discipline and Punish*, whereas in *History of Sexuality* he was applying what he had already worked out. In addition, we particularly recommend "Part Four: The Deployment of Sexuality" section. In many ways, this is the mature Foucault at his best. The writing is excellent, the organization is clear, and, the insights are powerful.[29] It is in this section that Foucault provides some extended discussion of how he thought of power differently, what he calls an "analytics" of power (p. 82), as not just negative and repressive but also positive. Even more specifically, we recommend the "Objective" subsection (pp. 81–91) and his discussion at the beginning of the "Method" subsection of "Part Four" (pp. 92–97). Indeed, we would suggest that one of Foucault's greatest contributions to intellectual thought has been his reconceptualization of power, and a good discussion of this reconceptualization is abundantly available in *History of Sexuality*. Finally, however, what generally distinguishes his second method, genealogy, from his first one, archaeology, in our view, is that his archaeological method is dependent on a highly structured, highly interrelated set of constructs, all of which need to be deployed together to actually do an archaeology, whereas his genealogical method is more like a set of critical tools that can be used in any sort of grouping. And it is this difference, we believe, that is one of the chief reasons why the latter is much more appealing to scholars.[30]

## ▣ CONCLUSION

Overall, it could be argued that Foucault's archaeological and genealogical work was mainly a critique of the modernist view of the human sciences and of "man" as simultaneously both the human scientist and the object of the human sciences. Then, in his conduct of any particular critique, whether archaeological or genealogical, he almost always takes up one "period" (although his "periods" often do not parallel those of mainstream history) prior to the one (the second period) he will critique and describes this first period to lay the basis for his description and critique of the subsequent period. However, his description of one period, his description of the change from one to the next, and his description of the second period move far beyond the territory typically covered in conventional history. For example, see our comparison of *connaissance* and *savoir* earlier, where *connaissance* covers the conventional territory, whereas *savoir*, which is what Foucault is focused on with both his archaeologies and his genealogies, is much broader, even including social phenomena that seem to have little direct connection to the particular *connaissance*. His point here is that the conventional or traditional view of the formal academic social sciences is but one part of an "effective history" and that when the *savoir* is considered, it becomes much more obvious that the human sciences are much less rational, much more ambiguous, much messier, much more filled with random error, and more driven by the petty jealousies and competitions of social scientists than is conventionally assumed. Thus, if you understand the difference between *connaissance* and *savoir*, and if you understand the fact that Foucault focused mostly on *savoir* as the territory of the archaeologist or the genealogist, you understand a significant piece of what Foucault was up to with his critiques.

A second point he makes with these "period" comparisons is that, contrary to the self-story of modernity that the more recent is more humane, the "modernist" period is actually, when critiqued with an archaeology or a genealogy, worse, more oppressive, more demeaning. For example, whereas the prior penal system tortured bodies, the target of the subsequent one was the soul, not what people do but rather what they are. Thus, Foucault stands as a major critic of Western modernity, particularly calling into question a wide array of "progressive" assumptions that modernity is considerably better, more humane, and more rational than that which came before modernity.

A third focus for Foucault is to decenter "man" as the primary subject of modernity. To Foucault, modernity constructed man, the subject, the agent running the world. It was modernity that fashioned the whole of human life as constructed around and for man, the central subject, the central agentic actor. It was modernity that wrote a history of the progressive rational rise of the human sciences guided by and for man, the central subject. In contrast, Foucault suggests a different and effective history of the human sciences. Based on his critical examination of historical documents, he suggests that, although rationality is part of Western history, there is much, much more that is not rational and that is not guided by any central actor. Indeed, in both his archaeologies and his genealogies, history is not predominantly created by a subject, particularly a logical rational subject who has "his" hands on the guiding wheel of history. Instead, history is created by a complex array of processes, dispersions, procedures, accidents, hatreds, policies, desires, dominations, unintended or uncontrolled circulations of techniques of power, commercial practices, mores, analyses and demonstrations, the norms of industrial labor and bourgeois morality, the endlessly repeated play of dominations, literature, political decisions, discontinuities, opinions expressed in daily life, the fanatical and unending discussions of scholars, randomness, dissensions, petty malice, precise scientific methods, subjected bodies, and faulty calculations, to name but just a few—and man, the subject, is not running this show called history. In addition, he repeatedly points out the contradiction within modernity of simultaneously having man as both the subject and object of history. However, given the dominance of our modernist romanticized view of ourselves as the center of our lives and our society and, given our deep ontological and epistemological attachment to this romanticized view, it is usually ignored or critiqued by scholars while they appropriate other aspects of Foucault's critique of modernity. This, to us, is a serious mistake. His critique of modernity and his critique of the agentic subject at the center are deeply intertwined; thus, separating the two violates Foucault's perspective at the most basic level of his thought.

There are other lesser abuses, and some erroneous readings, of Foucault that we have tried to address or correct. First, Foucault was, by his own words, enormously influenced by Canguilhem and saw Canguilhem and others as playing a role in French intellectual work similar to that which the Frankfurt School played in German intellectual work. Thus, we suggest that Canguilhem and others, such as Gaston Bachelard, should receive increased attention, as themes that Foucault draws from Canguilhem continue through his genealogies. Second, the amount of time and energy that Foucault gave to archaeology was much larger than that which he gave to genealogy. Thus, we suggest that much more attention be given to archaeology. Indeed, there is no legitimate doubt that Foucault continued throughout his life to highly value it as a method, despite what others concluded. Third, again by his own words, genealogy was not seen by Foucault as being superseded by or superior to archaeology. Thus, in comparing the two methods, more attention needs to be given to how Foucault saw the relationship of the two. Fourth, archaeology and genealogy are much less different than is often assumed, and this also could use more attention. Fifth, it was, in our opinion, Dreyfus and Rabinow who were largely responsible for what we see as a distorted view of the relationship of archaeology and genealogy in the United States. Thus, we suggest more problematization of this contention. And sixth, in any considerations of the two methods, the essay on "Nietzsche, Genealogy, History" should receive increased attention, as it is a good bridge that directly connects the two methods.

In this conclusion, we also want to strongly recommend a relatively new collection of Foucault's work. The entire set is called *Essential Works of Foucault, 1954–1984*, and Paul Rabinow is the series editor.[31] The first volume is *Ethics, Subjectivity, and Truth* (1994/1997) and was edited by Rabinow. The second volume is *Aesthetics, Method, and Epistemology* (1994a) and was edited by Faubion. The third volume is *Power* (1994c), and it too was edited by Faubion. In this set, when the English translations provided in it are compared with alternative ones, we consistently find that the translations in this set are superior. In addition, this set thematically groups parts of Foucault's books with some of his articles and interviews. We would suggest that, especially for beginners, this set is an excellent place to start reading Foucault, as it makes Foucault more accessible.

Undeniably, though, whichever books, articles, and interviews are considered, Foucault has left us with an impressive body of work and new methodologies and with a host of powerful analytic concepts, some of which we have tried to introduce to a broader range of readers. We want to end, then, with two more statements. The first is a very brief summary of our take on the use of Foucault in education scholarship. Unfortunately, we do not have space to comment in any detail on the use of Foucault in the social sciences generally or in education, our field, specifically. Indeed, commenting on the uses of Foucault across the social sciences in the United States alone is already probably too large for anything less than a book. Even just the use of Foucault as a primary focus by education scholars, as can be seen in one part of our bibliography, is rather large. However, after reviewing the scholarship in education using Foucault as the main theoretical resource, our conclusion is that a very high percentage of this work engages Foucault's work at only a fairly superficial level.

Probably the most popular use, or abuse, is to cherry pick one concept, such as "panopticon" or "disciplinary society," and then use that one concept within a more traditional critical framework, even though there are epistemological contradictions between Foucault and most U.S. critical theory.[32] In general, we would say this cherry picking is a mistake, as typically the single concept, in its Foucaultian meaning, does not really integrate with the rest of the assumptions in the article or book. Our point is that Foucault's concepts are but aspects of a general epistemological position that needs to be engaged with as a whole. Another similar error that we found in the uses of Foucault's work by U.S. education scholars, as well as by many social scientists, is to adopt his critique of modernity while ignoring his simultaneous critique of subjectivity itself. We are uncomfortable saying this because we sound like we are policing Foucault, but we think that it is simply undeniable that there is a tremendous amount of fairly superficial and ill-informed use of Foucault; in fact, we concluded that many have used his work without ever reading carefully through several volumes of it. Of course, the line between substantive engagements of Foucault and superficial ones can never be securely drawn. Thus, we are decidedly not arguing that we know and can define the canonical Foucault, but we would suggest that a supple use, or even an adequate use, of Foucault requires more than one close reading of any one book, article, or interview. Instead, we would suggest close readings of several books, along with articles and interviews, before trying to use or apply his work. When U.S. scholars do not engage in this kind of in-depth study of Foucault, we would remind them that their ignorance is fairly transparent to those who do study and use Foucault in a more substantive way.

Our second final point is what surprised us the most with our systematic review of Foucault's books. Also, we should say that we were reluctant to make this point, but we decided that we had to for us to maintain the integrity of our recent rereading of all of Foucault's major works in the order that he published them. Before we did this review, we were strong advocates of Foucault's work and not too receptive to the many critiques of his work, as we saw most of them as conscious or unconscious defenses of the foundational assumptions of modernity. What emerged, though, for us is a new openness to one of the main critiques that has been made of Foucault's work. That is, there have been numerous complaints that in Foucault's consideration of the truth regimes of social life, such as those of prisons, the clinic, and sexuality, Foucault's descriptions of these regimes make them relentlessly oppressive, perhaps even totalized, with no way "out" (see, e.g., Hartsock, 1998). Clearly, we cannot go into a lengthy discussion of this critique, nor do we want to debate it at this point. What we can do, however, is strongly suggest that other advocates and persistent users of Foucault need to more openly and more carefully consider this critique. In other words, we would suggest that our experienced Foucault scholars need to engage this critique in a more balanced way and recognize that there is some "validity" to it.

After recently rereading straight through all of his books in the order that he published them, we were truly struck, unexpectedly struck, with how unrelenting Foucault is in his critique of the social forms in which we live. We began to understand what others have concluded about his totalizations of these social forms. We began, for example, to understand where others have concluded that, in his descriptions of penal institutions or the social sciences, there appears to be "no exit." His critique and the described oppression are powerfully unrelenting and do appear to approach a totalization. It is almost as if he has discovered that, for example, the new penal regime is not just a 6-sided cube of oppression and control but also a 500-sided cube and that, in brilliantly describing all of these sides, he leaves us with no recourse, no path for resistance or emancipation. What simultaneously reinforces this is the fact that in his major works, he rarely offers any alternative for resistance or emancipation from the oppression he so thoroughly describes. (See, e.g., Grosz, 1994, who uses Foucault extensively but is simultaneously critical of how unrelenting his lack of alternative spaces and possibilities is; in fact, for us, Grosz exemplifies a balanced, in-depth use of Foucault that is both critical and appreciative.) Thus, for example, while Foucault provides an insightful characterization of the complexity of a discipline or regime, virtually every aspect, every facet, of the new complexity that Foucault describes becomes a critical moment for Foucault so that while he is opening up new perspectives on specific truth regimes, he is also foreclosing, through his totalized critique, the possibility that these new frontiers might become new possibilities or imaginaries.

Of course, we realize that the words "resistance" and "emancipation" are humanist ones arising out of modernity; thus, an advocate for Foucault might say that Foucault's unwillingness to offer any such alternative is simply his maintenance of a consistently anti-humanist-, anti-subject-centered epistemology. However, as Fraser (1989) pointed out some time ago, what is often ignored with Foucault is that much of his language, such as "systems of subjection" (Foucault, 1975/1979, p. 376) and "the endlessly repeated play of dominations" (p. 377), is itself language that is modernist and humanist and that the power Foucault's critiques have for us is a function of our immersion in and attachment to this modernist, humanist language. We would, thus, point out that what we have here is another modernist binary. Accordingly, whereas Foucault powerfully appropriates one side of this binary (e.g., subjection and domination), he largely avoids the other (e.g., resistance and emancipation). This, as Derrida[33] has pointed out so well with his deconstructive methodology, does not mean that the other side of the binary, variously labeled resistance or emancipation, is not equally in play.

Thus, again, we want to suggest that scholars who are advocates of Foucault take this critique more seriously and approach Foucault more the way that Grosz (1994) generally does. However, we are not saying that Foucault never addresses some "positive" change possibilities. We are saying, though, that in all of the archaeologies he overwhelmingly does not and that in *Discipline and Punish* (1975/1979) he largely does not. Also, for the most part in *The History of Sexuality, Volume 1: An Introduction* (1976/1980a) he does not, although in this latter work he does begin to talk about countering "the grips of power" with the "rallying point" being "bodies and pleasures" (p. 157). In *The History of Sexuality,* Volume 1, near the end, for example, he says,

> We must not think that by saying yes to sex, one says no to power; on the contrary, one tracks along the course laid out by the general deployment of sexuality [when one says yes to sex]. It is the agency of sex that we must break away from if we aim—through a tactical reversal of the various mechanisms of sexuality—to counter the grips of power with the claims of bodies, pleasures, and knowledges, in their multiplicity and their possibility of resistance. The rallying point for the counterattack against the deployment of sexuality ought not to be sex-desire, but bodies and pleasures. (p. 157)

This is clearly an effort by Foucault to begin to explore resistance and a space of possible change, but this is by far the exception. In fact, some might argue that it is with this work that Foucault's interest in working on resistance and change emerges in the care of the self period that is said to follow the two genealogies. In addition, he was an activist, especially around prison issues, and in his interviews he supported activism while resisting critiques of the lack of activism in his books. For example, in an interview published in an Italian journal in 1978, he said (somewhat defensively, we would say), "I don't construct my analyses in order to say, 'This is the way thing are, you are trapped.' I say these things only insofar as I believe it enables us to transform them" (Foucault, 1994c, pp. 295–295).

However, our point here is that through all of the archaeologies and the first genealogy and even most of the second genealogy, while Foucault is opening up new ways to think about our social world, his unrelenting, almost totalized, critique serves to foreclose how to use those new ways of thinking for resistance, for countering "the grips of power," and for developing spaces of valuable change. To us, this should be a major concern because, in our view, his descriptive accounts of the complexities of disciplines, social arenas, and institutions could as well show that within these complexities, there are almost always spaces for resistance, "counterattack," appropriation, and construction, and this is also a point that Grosz (1994) makes. Similarly, Gubrium and Holstein (2000), in the second edition of the *Handbook,* drawing strongly on Foucault, have tried to develop "an interpretive practice [that] works against [the kind of Foucaultian] totalization that views all interpretations as artifacts of particular regimes of power/knowledge" (p. 501). By raising these criticisms of Foucault, though, we are not trying to be definitive, as that would require a more extended, in-depth discussion of the whole range of critiques of Foucault on this issue. Instead, we are more modestly suggesting, based on our recent systematic read of Foucault, that Foucault's advocates, as we ourselves have been, need to take another, more careful, more balanced consideration of this critique of Foucault's work. Or, as Foucault himself said, "The only valid tribute to [anyone's] thought . . . is precisely to use it, to deform it, to make it groan and protest. And if commentators then say that I am being faithful or unfaithful . . . that is of absolutely no interest" (Foucault, 1980b, pp. 53–54).

Nonetheless, even with such reconsiderations, Foucault remains a powerful, innovative intellectual whose work has opened up insightful and provocative avenues of thought, critique, and understanding. Moreover, without a doubt, his work has become enormously influential worldwide. Deleuze (1990/1995), though, said this much more poetically:

> When people follow Foucault, when they're fascinated by him, it's because they're doing something with him, in their own work, in their own independent lives. It's not just a question of [Foucault's] intellectual understanding or agreement, but of intensity, resonance, musical harmony. (p. 86)[34]

Hopefully, our interpretations presented here will add to this influence by helping those who have not yet engaged Foucault to understand where they might begin. We also hope we have been useful and provocative to those who are more experienced friends of Foucault, even if we may have disturbed them a bit with our critical remarks. Whatever the reads of our read, though, we want to *again* and *again* strongly emphasize that our interpretations of Foucault, our comments on the uses and abuses of Foucault in education and the social sciences, our critiques of Foucault and others, and our concluding remarks are not the correct, the best, the authoritative, or the canonical ones. Even if you forget everything else we have written here, do not forget this point. As we said at the beginning of this essay, the comments we offer here are not *true* interpretations of Foucault's work, nor are such interpretations possible in our view. The primary issue to us is how substantive the engagement is, not whether the engagement is the correct one. Thus, whether there is agreement or disagreement with what we have said here, we truly hope that all readers will see this essay as a substantive effort to engage primarily not only with Foucault but also, to a smaller extent, with his users and abusers, his advocates and critics.

## ▣ NOTES

1. Despite the fact that this essay is not a "true" one, we want to thank our reviewers for their suggestions, comments, and criticisms. There is simply no question that this essay was substantively improved due to their responses even when we disagreed with those responses. Those reviewers were Jaber Gubrium, Patti Lather, Bill Black, Elizabeth St. Pierre, Norman Denzin, and Jack Bratich. However, none of them should be held responsible for anything we have written here as we used and abused, agreed and disagreed with, incorporated and ignored their words.

2. The American Psychological Association (APA) style format rule is that the original publication date for a publication in another language precedes the publication date in English, just as we have done it here. However, we wanted to make sure that everyone paid attention to these dates because they are part of a significant point that we are making in this essay.

3. Foucault himself actually calls his archaeologies and genealogies toolboxes: "All my books . . . are little toolboxes, if you will" (Halperin, 1995, p. 52). Thanks to Elizabeth St. Pierre for pointing out this quote.

4. See, for example, Burchell, Gordon, and Miller's *The Foucault Effect: Studies in Governmentality* (1991), Barry, Osborne, and Rose's *Foucault and Political Reason* (1996), and parts of Popkewitz and Brennan's *Foucault's Challenge* (1998).

5. Jaber Gubrium also suggests John Rajchman, Lisa King, and Lee Quimby as doing similar work. We would agree with the Rajchman suggestion, but we are not familiar with the other two. Nonetheless, we think Gubrium knows what he is talking about.

6. See Foucault's "What Is an Author?" in *Language, Counter-Memory, Practice* (1977).

7. In other words, we are suggesting to those enamored of and influenced by Kuhn that they should read the work of Canguilhem because, in our view, Canguilhem's work with the history of sciences is much more impressive, much more substantive, than that of Kuhn.

8. Throughout this essay, when we quote Foucault, we add words or phrases in brackets to help readers follow his meaning. Foucault often writes in long sentences and is often not clear with his referents or words he substitutes for other words. Thus, reading Foucault typically requires paying very close attention to his meaning as a sentence or paragraph progresses. Our added brackets are intended, then, to help readers follow his meaning more easily.

9. It is certainly easy to imagine the good uses to which Lincoln and Guba could have put Canguilhem in their critique of science and reason in 1985 in *Naturalistic Inquiry* (1985).

10. It should not be assumed that Canguilhem was trying to totally undermine the history of the sciences or to destroy the value and importance of reason. He was not. In fact, it is clear that Canguilhem appreciates and values both science and reason. Instead, Canguilhem could be said to be trying to develop an approach to the study of the history of science and the history of reason that was much less hagiographic.

11. However, Gutting's *Michel Foucault's Archaeology of Scientific Reason* (1989) is a useful discussion of archaeology, though we disagree with some of his interpretations of Foucault.

12. It should be noted that for Foucault, practices and institutions, theories and disciplines, all exist at the same level. As he says, "I deal with practices, institutions, and theories on the same plane and according to the same isomorphisms" (Foucault, 1994c, p. 262).

13. Foucault always felt that to understand something, say a discursive formation, he needed another one to which to compare it. Comparison, then, is almost always a key part of his analytic work.

14. Foucault uses "possibility" because the process is not deterministic; that is, it is not deterministically inevitable that a *connaissance* will emerge out of a *savoir*.

15. This point is similar to points made by Canguilhem, as was already discussed.

16. Remember here how Canguilhem had asserted that "error" is an integral part of life at the biological level.

17. In the specific part of *The Archaeology of Knowledge* from which this cite is drawn (p. 4), Foucault (1969/1972) cites Canguilhem. Indeed, as we argued in an earlier section, much of archaeology comes from Foucault's use, interpretation, and transformation of his mentor's work.

18. Habermas would be an example of the latter.

19. Unfortunately, we cannot find this interview at this point, but we know we have read it. Our apologies to our readers. If someone comes across it, she or he should e-mail it so that we can add the citation to any future revisions of this essay.

20. One of the reviewers of this chapter argued that *The History of Sexuality*, Volume 2: *The Use of Pleasure* was clearly a genealogy, but it is our view that Foucault's own words in this text indicate that Volume 2 is not another genealogy. In the "Introduction" to Volume 2, Foucault discusses the genealogy he originally intended to do but then turns away from this. A good discussion of the three periods and Foucault's intentions with each can be found in Davidson (1986).

21. We would also suggest that because of their critique of archaeology, Dreyfus and Rabinow (1983) played a key role in the lack of attention to Canguilhem, as they mention him only once throughout *Beyond Structuralism and Hermeneutics*.

22. The reason why this more recent version is better, in our view, is that it clearly distinguishes knowledge as *connaissance* and knowledge as *savoir*, both of which we have discussed as key concepts of Foucault's archaeology.

23. It is hard not to conclude that Foucault actually either enjoyed writing about the torture or enjoyed shocking readers or both, given the extended detail in his descriptions.

24. Obviously, one of the points we are trying to make here is that there is less of a break between archaeology and genealogy than is commonly assumed.

25. Foucault would likely call the new focus on student-centered classrooms one of the effects of a "pastoral" approach.

26. This point is a good example of a concern that started with Canguilhem and continues from Foucault's archaeologies into his genealogies.

27. Amazon.com now allows anyone to do two-word or phrase searches of an entire book of any book that is contained in this system. It is a marvelous system, but any single person can do this only twice a month without buying the book.

28. One odd little note is that although Foucault's convention is to compare two periods in his various analyses, in *History of Sexuality* he compares three.

29. Contrary to what many assume, Foucault is exceedingly logical in his written presentations. He constantly divides an arena of focus into numbered parts and then proceeds to define those parts in an orderly fashion. Indeed, at this point, we have begun to wonder why there is all of this commentary as to how Foucault writes in some disrupted "postmodern" fashion. We find, after our lengthy review of his work, that he writes in a fairly conventional way for complex intellectual work. Actually, other than learning to think differently, which is really the hardest task in reading Foucault, what is required is to carefully follow the meaning in his long complex sentences, as it is sometimes difficult to follow to what he is referring. In other words, it takes a close reading to follow his meaning, but there is little that is "disrupted" in his texts, in our view.

30. One of our reviewers argued that the larger problem with the archaeological methodology is that very few areas of social life lend themselves to the kind of complex discursive structures that Foucault addresses in his archaeologies. We would clearly disagree. We would suggest that before Foucault's archaeological analyses, few would have seen the complex *savoir*-based discursive patterns that Foucault identified in *Madness and Civilization* (1961/1988), *The Birth of the Clinic* (1963/1994b), and *The Order of Things* (1966/1973a). For instance, we think education could definitely be a fertile arena for archaeological analyses.

31. There is a new comprehensive set of all of Foucault's work that has been published in French, called *Dits et Ecrits*. It is two volumes, *Dits et Ecrits, tome 1, 1954–1975* (2001a, 1,700 pages) and *Dits et Ecrits, tome 2, 1976–1988* (2001b, 1,976 pages). We certainly hope that some group will provide an English translation of the entire set.

32. There is no doubt that Foucault is part of a critical tradition in Western philosophy, but he had fundamental arguments with that part of the critical tradition that has been labeled Marxist, neo-Marxist, or critical theory.

33. As Foucault scholars well know, Derrida was strongly critical of Foucault's work.

34. Thanks to Elizabeth St. Pierre for this delightful quote.


◨  BIBLIOGRAPHY

## Foucault Books

(This is an attempt to list all of Foucault's major books, but it is not intended to be comprehensive of all of Foucault's work in English. In addition, these are the books that we own and have studied.)

Foucault, M. (1972). *The archaeology of knowledge and the discourse on language* (A. M. Sheridan Smith, Trans.). New York: Pantheon Books. (Original work published 1969)

Foucault, M. (1973a). *The order of things: An archaeology of the human sciences.* New York: Vintage Books. (Original work published 1966)

Foucault, M. (1973b). *This is not a pipe* (J. Harkness, Trans.). Berkeley: University of California Press.

Foucault, M. (1977). *Language, counter-memory, practice: Selected essays and interviews by Michel Foucault* (D. F. Bouchard, Ed.; D. F. Bouchard & S. Simon, Trans.). Ithaca, NY: Cornell University Press.

Foucault, M. (1979). *Discipline and punish: The birth of the prison* (A. Sheridan, Trans.). New York: Vintage Books. (Original work published 1975)

Foucault, M. (1980a). *The history of sexuality,* Vol. 1: *An introduction* (R. Hurley, Trans.). New York: Vintage Books. (Original work published 1976)

Foucault, M. (1980b). *Power/Knowledge: Selected interviews and other writings, 1972–1977* (C. Gordon, Ed.; C. Gordon, L. Marshall, J. Mepham, & K. Soper, Trans.). New York: Pantheon Books.

Foucault, M. (1986). *The history of sexuality,* Vol. 3: *Care of the self* (R. Hurley, Trans.). New York: Pantheon Books. (Original work published 1984)

Foucault, M. (1988). *Madness and civilization: A history of insanity in the age of reason* (R. Howard, Trans.). New York: Vintage Books. (Original work published 1961)

Foucault, M. (1989). *Foucault live: Interviews, 1966–84* (S. Lotringer, Ed.; J. Johnston, Trans.). New York: Semiotext(e).

Foucault, M. (1990). *The history of sexuality,* Vol. 2: *The use of pleasure* (R. Hurley, Trans.). New York: Pantheon Books. (Original work published 1984)

Foucault, M. (1994a). *Aesthetics, method, and epistemology* (J. D. Faubion, Ed.; R. Hurley & others, Trans.). New York: New Press.

Foucault, M. (1994b). *The birth of the clinic: An archaeology of medical perception* (A. M. Sheridan-Smith, Trans.). New York: Vintage Books. (Original work published 1963)

Foucault, M. (1994c). *Power* (J. D. Faubion, Ed.; R. Hurley & others, Trans.). New York: New Press.

Foucault, M. (1997). *Ethics, subjectivity, and truth* (Vol. 1; P. Rabinow, Ed.; R. Hurley & others, Trans.). New York: New Press. (Original work published 1994)

Foucault, M. (1998). *Aesthetics, method, and epistemology* (Vol. 2; J. D. Faubion, Ed.; R. Hurley and others, Trans.). New York: New Press.

Foucault, M. (2001a). *Dits et Ecrits, tome 1, 1954–1975.* Paris: Gallimard.

Foucault, M. (2001b). *Dits et Ecrits, tome 2, 1976–1988.* Paris: Gallimard.

Foucault, M. (2001c). *Fearless speech* (J. Pearson, Ed.). Los Angeles: Semiotext(e).

Foucault, M. (2003). *"Society must be defended": Lectures at the Collège de France, 1975–1976* (M. Bertaini & A. Fontana, Eds.; D. Macey, Trans.). New York: Picador.

Rabinow, P. (Ed.). (1984). *Foucault reader.* New York: Pantheon Books.

## Foucault-Oriented Education Books

(This list is meant to be comprehensive of *all* books in education that apply Foucault to education as their primary purpose. It does not include books that just use Foucault among many others; it includes only those that we could find that explicitly take Foucault as their main theoretical frame.)

Baker, B., & Heyning, K. (Eds.). (2004). *Dangerous coagulations? The uses of Foucault in the study of education.* New York: Peter Lang.

Ball, S. (Ed.). (1990). *Foucault and education: Disciplines and knowledge.* London: Routledge.

Ball, S., & Tamboukou, M. (2003). *Dangerous encounters: Genealogy and ethnography.* New York: Peter Lang.

Marshall, J. D. (1996). *Michel Foucault: Personal autonomy and education.* Dordrecht, Netherlands: Kluwer Academic.

Peters, M. (1996). *Poststructuralism, politics, and education.* Westport, CT: Bergin & Garvey.

Popkewitz, T. S., & Brennan, M. (1998). *Foucault's challenge: Discourse, knowledge, and power in education.* New York: Columbia University, Teachers College Press.

Scheurich, J. J. (1997). *Research method in the postmodern.* London: Falmer.

Tamboukou, M., & Ball, S. J. (2003). Genealogy and ethnography: Fruitful encounters or dangerous liaisons? In M. Tamboukou & S. J. Ball (Eds.), *Dangerous encounters: Genealogy and ethnography* (pp. 1–36). New York: Peter Lang.

## General Foucault Books

(These are books on Foucault's work that we have found to be helpful and/or influential, but it is not meant to be a comprehensive list of all books in English on Foucault. These are books that we own and have studied.)

Armstrong, T. J. (Trans.). (1992). *Michel Foucault: Philosopher.* New York: Routledge.

Barker, P. (1998). *Michel Foucault: An introduction.* Edinburgh, UK: Edinburgh University Press.

Barry, A., Osborne, T., & Rose, N. (Eds.). (1996). *Foucault and political reason: Liberalism, neoliberalism, and the rationalities of government.* Chicago: University of Chicago Press.

Bernauer, J., & Rasmussen, D. (Eds.). (1991). *The final Foucault.* Cambridge: MIT Press. (Includes a biographical chronology of Foucault interspersed with some quotes from Foucault as he remembers different times in his life)

Best, S., & Kellner, D. (1991). *Postmodern theory: Critical interrogations.* New York: Guilford.

Burchell, G., Gordon, C., & Miller, P. (1991). *The Foucault effect: Studies in governmentality.* Chicago: University of Chicago Press.

Butler, J. (1993). *Bodies that matter: On the discursive limits of "sex."* New York: Routledge.

Canguilhem, G. (1988). *Ideology and rationality in the history of the life sciences.* Cambridge: MIT Press.

Canguilhem, G. (1989). *The normal and the pathological.* New York: Zone Books.

Caputo, J., & Yount, M. (1993). *Foucault and the critique of institutions.* University Park: Pennsylvania State University Press.

Davidson, A. I. (1986). Archaeology, genealogy, ethics. In D. Couzens Hoy (Ed.), *Foucault: A critical reader* (pp. 221–234). Oxford, UK: Basil Blackwell.

Deleuze, G. (1995). *Negotiations: 1972–1990* (M. Joughin, Trans.). New York: Columbia University Press. (Original work published 1990)

Dreyfus, H. L., & Rabinow, P. (1983). *Michel Foucault: Beyond structuralism and hermeneutics* (2nd ed.). Chicago: University of Chicago Press.

Eribon, D. (1991). *Michel Foucault* (B. Wing, Trans.). Cambridge, MA: Harvard University Press.

Fraser, N. (1989). *Unruly practices: Power, discourse, and gender in contemporary social theory.* Minneapolis: University of Minnesota Press.

Grosz, E. (1994). *Volatile bodies: Toward a corporeal feminism.* Bloomington: Indiana University Press.

Gubrium, J. F., & Holstein, J. A. (2000). Analyzing interpretive practice. In N. K. Denzin & Y. S. Lincoln (Eds.), *Handbook of qualitative research* (2nd ed., pp. 487–508). Thousand Oaks, CA: Sage.

Gutting, G. (1989). *Michel Foucault's archaeology of scientific reason.* Cambridge, UK: Cambridge University Press.

Gutting, G. (Ed.). (1994). *The Cambridge companion to Foucault.* Cambridge, UK: Cambridge University Press.

Halperin, D. M. (1995). *Saint Foucault: Towards a gay hagiography.* New York: Oxford University Press.

Han, B. (2002). *Foucault's critical project: Between the transcendental and the historical.* Stanford, CA: Stanford University Press.

Hartsock, N. C. M. (1998). *The feminist standpoint revisited and other essays.* Boulder, CO: Westview.

Hoy, D. C. (Ed.). (1986). *Foucault: A critical reader.* Oxford, UK: Basil Blackwell.

Jones, C., & Porter, R. (1994). *Reassessing Foucault: Power, medicine, and the body.* London: Routledge.

Kendall, G., & Wickham, G. (1999). *Using Foucault's methods.* Thousand Oaks, CA: Sage.

Kuhn. T. (1962). *The structure of scientific revolutions.* Chicago: University of Chicago Press.

Lather, P. (2004). Foucauldian "in discipline" as a sort of policy application. In B. Baker & K. Hayning (Eds.), *Dangerous coagulations? The uses of Foucault in the study of education* (pp. 281–306). New York: Peter Lang.

Lincoln, Y. S., & Guba, E. G. (1985). *Naturalistic inquiry.* Beverly Hills, CA: Sage.

Mahon, M. (1992). *Foucault's Nietzschean genealogy: Truth, power, and the subject.* Albany: State University of New York Press.

McHoul, A., & Grace, W. (1993). *A Foucault primer: Discourse, power, and the subject.* New York: New York University Press.

Merquior, J. G. (1985). *Foucault.* Berkeley: University of California Press.

Miller, J. (1993). *The passion of Michel Foucault.* New York: Simon & Schuster.

Nilson, H. (1998). *Michel Foucault and the games of truth* (R. Clark, Trans.). New York: St. Martin's.

Poster, M. (1987). *Foucault, Marxism, and history: Mode of production versus mode of information.* Cambridge, UK: Polity.

Rajchman, J. (1985). *Michel Foucault: The freedom of philosophy.* New York: Columbia University Press.

Rouse, J. (1987). *Knowledge and power: Toward a political philosophy of science.* Ithaca, NY: Cornell University Press.

Sawicki, J. (1991). *Disciplining Foucault: Feminism, power, and the body.* New York: Routledge.

Shumany, D. R. (1989). *Michel Foucault.* Charlottesville: University Press of Virginia.

Stoler, A. L. (2000). *Race and the education of desire: Foucault's* History of Sexuality *and the colonial order of things.* Durham, NC: Duke University Press.

St. Pierre, E. A. (2004). Care of the self: The subject and freedom. In B. Baker & K. E. Heyning (Eds.), *Dangerous coagulations? The uses of Foucault in the study of education* (pp. 325–358). New York: Peter Lang.

Visker, R. (1995). *Michel Foucault: Genealogy as critique* (C. Turner, Trans.). London: Verso.

Opfer, V. D. (2001). Charter schools and the panoptic effect of accountability. *Education and Urban Society, 33,* 201–215.

Peters, M. (2000). Writing the self: Wittgenstein, confession, and pedagogy. *Journal of Philosophy of Education, 34,* 353–368.

Pignatelli, F. (1993). What can I do? Foucault on freedom and the question of teacher agency. *Educational Theory, 43,* 411–432.

Pignatelli, F. (2002). Mapping the terrain of a Foucauldian ethics: A response to the surveillance of schooling. *Studies in Philosophy and Education, 21,* 157–180.

Popkewitz, T. S. (1997). The production of reason and power: Curriculum history and intellectual traditions. *Journal of Curriculum Studies, 29,* 131–164.

Popkewitz, T. S., & Brennan, M. (1997). Restructuring of social and political theory in education: Foucault and a social epistemology of school practices. *Educational Theory, 47,* 287–313.

Raddon, A. (2002). Mothers in the academy: Positioned and positioning within discourses of the "successful academic" and the "good mother." *Studies in Higher Education, 27,* 387–403.

Roth, W-M. (2002). Reading graphs: Contributions to an integrative concept of literacy. *Journal of Curriculum Studies, 34,* 1–24.

Ryan, J. (1991). Observing and normalizing: Foucault, discipline, and inequality in schooling. *Journal of Educational Thought, 25*(2), 104–119.

Schubert, D. J. (1995). From a politics of transgression toward an ethics of reflexivity. *American Behavioral Scientist, 38,* 1003–1018.

Seals, G. (1998). Objectively yours, Michael Foucault. *Educational Theory, 48,* 59–68.

Selden, S. (2000). Eugenics and the social construction of merit, race, and disability. *Journal of Curriculum Studies, 32,* 235–252.

Selwyn, N. (2000). The national grid for learning: Panacea or panopticon? *British Journal of Sociology of Education, 21,* 243–255.

Slaughter, S. (1997). Class, race, and gender and the construction of post-secondary curricula in the United States: Social movement, professionalization, and political economic theories of curricular change. *Journal of Curriculum Studies, 29,* 1–30.

Spears, R., & Lea, M. (1994). Panacea or panopticon? *Communication Research, 21,* 427–459.

St. Pierre, E. S. (2002). "Science" rejects postmodernism. *Educational Researcher, 31*(8), 25–27.

Stygall, G. (1994). Resisting privilege: Basic writing and Foucault's author function. *College Composition and Communication, 45,* 320–341.

Styslinger, M. E. (2000). Relations of power and drama in education: The teacher and Foucault. *Journal of Educational Thought, 34,* 183–199.

Walshaw, M. (2001). A Foucauldian gaze on gender research: What do you do when confronted with the tunnel at the end of the light? *Journal for Research on Mathematics Education, 32,* 471–492.

Willis, A. I. (2002). Literacy at Calhoun Colored School 1892–1945. *Reading Research Quarterly, 37*(1), 8–44.

Zembylas, M. (2002). "Structures of fooling" in curriculum and teaching: Theorizing the emotional rules. *Educational Theory, 52,* 187–208.

## Additional Reading

Didion, J. (2003, January 16). Fixed opinions, or the hinge of history. *The New York Review of Books,* pp. 54–59.

# 11

# ANALYZING TALK AND TEXT

Anssi Peräkylä

There are two much used but distinctively different types of empirical materials in qualitative research: interviews and naturally occurring materials. Interviews consist of accounts given to the researcher about the issues in which he or she is interested. The topic of the research is not the interview itself but rather the issues discussed in the interview. In this sense, research that uses naturally occurring empirical material is different; in this type of research, the empirical materials themselves (e.g., the tape-recordings of mundane interactions, the written texts) constitute specimens of the topic of the research. Consequently, the researcher is in more direct touch with the very object that he or she is investigating.

Most qualitative research probably is based on interviews. There are good reasons for this. By using interviews, the researcher can reach areas of reality that would otherwise remain inaccessible such as people's subjective experiences and attitudes. The interview is also a very convenient way of overcoming distances both in space and in time; past events or faraway experiences can be studied by interviewing people who took part in them.

In other instances, it is possible to reach the object of research directly using naturally occurring empirical materials (Silverman, 2001). If the researcher is interested in, say, strategies used by journalists in interviewing politicians (cf. Clayman & Heritage, 2002a), it might be advisable to tape-record broadcast interviews rather than to ask journalists to tell about their work. Or, if the researcher wants to study the historical evolution of medical conceptions regarding death and dying, it might be advisable to study medical textbooks rather than to ask doctors to tell what they know about these concepts.

The contrast between interviews and naturally occurring materials should not, however, be exaggerated (cf. Potter, 2004; Speer, 2002). There are types of research materials that are between these two pure types. For example, in *informal interviews that are part of ethnographic fieldwork,* and in *focus groups,* people describe their practices and ideas to the researcher in circumstances that are much closer to "naturally occurring" than are the circumstances in ordinary research interviews. Moreover, even "ordinary" interviews can be, and have been, analyzed as specimens of interaction and reasoning practices rather than as representations of facts or ideas outside the interview situation. As Speer (2002) recently put it, "The status of pieces of data as natural or not depends largely on what the researcher intends to 'do' with them" (p. 513). Wetherell and Potter (1992), for example, analyzed the ways in which interviewees use different linguistic and cultural resources in constructing their relation to racial and racist discourses. On the other hand, as Silverman (2001) put it, no data—not even tape recordings—are "untouched by the researcher's hands" (p. 159; see also Speer, 2002, p. 516); the researcher's activity is needed, for example, in obtaining informed consent from the participants. The difference between researcher-instigated data and naturally occurring data should, therefore, be understood as a continuum rather than as a dichotomy.

This chapter focuses on one end of this continuum. It presents some methods that can be used in analyzing and interpreting tape-recorded interactions and written texts, which probably are the types of data that come closest to the idea of "naturally occurring."

## ▣ Analyzing Texts

### Uses of Texts and Variety of Methods of Text Analysis

As Smith (1974, 1990) and Atkinson and Coffey (1997) pointed out, much of social life in modern society is mediated by written texts of different kinds. For example, modern health care would not be possible without patient records; the legal system would not be possible without laws and other juridical texts; professional training would not be possible without manuals and professional journals; and leisure would not be possible without newspapers, magazines, and advertisements. Texts of this kind have provided an abundance of material for qualitative researchers.

In many cases, qualitative researchers who use written texts as their materials do not try to follow any predefined protocol in executing their analysis. By reading and rereading their empirical materials, they try to pin down their key themes and, thereby, to draw a picture of the presuppositions and meanings that constitute the cultural world of which the textual material is a specimen. An example of this kind of informal approach is Seale's (1998) small but elegant case study on a booklet based on a broadcast interview with the British playwright Dennis Potter (pp. 127–131). The interviewee was terminally ill at the time of the interview. Seale showed how the interview conveys a particular conception of death and dying, characterized by intensive awareness of the imminent death and special creativity arising from it.

An informal approach may, in many cases, be the best choice as a method in research focusing on written texts. Especially in research designs where the qualitative text analysis is not at the core of the research but instead is in a subsidiary or complementary role, no more sophisticated text analytical methods may be needed. That indeed was the case in Seale's (1998) study, in which the qualitative text analysis complemented a larger study drawing mostly on interview and questionnaire materials as well as on theoretical work. In projects that use solely texts as empirical materials, however, the use of different kinds of analytical procedures may be considered.

There are indeed many methods of text analysis from which the researcher can choose. The degree to which they involve predefined sets of procedures varies; some of them do to a great extent, whereas in others the emphasis is more on theoretical presuppositions concerning the cultural and social worlds to which the texts belong. Moreover, some of these methods can be used in the research of both written and spoken discourse, whereas others are exclusively fitted to written texts. In what follows, I briefly mention a few text analytical methods and then discuss two a bit more thoroughly.

*Semiotics* is a broad field of study concerned with signs and their use. Many tools of text analysis have arisen from this field. The most prominent of them may be *semiotic narrative analysis*. The Russian ethnologist Propp (1968) and the French sociologist Greimas (1966) developed schemes for the analysis of narrative structures. Initially their schemes were developed in fairy tales, but later on they were applied to many other kinds of texts. For example, by using Greimas's scheme, primordial structural relations (e.g., subject vs. object, sender vs. receiver, helper vs. opponent) can be distilled from the texts. Törrönen (2000, 2003) used and developed further Greimasian concepts in analyzing newspaper editorials addressing alcohol policy, showing how these texts mobilize structural relations so as to encourage readers to take action to achieve particular political goals.

The term *discourse analysis* (DA) may refer, depending on context, to many different approaches of investigation of written texts (and of spoken discourse as well). In the context of linguistics, DA usually refers to research that aims at uncovering the features of text that maintain coherence in units larger than the sentence (Brown & Yule, 1983). In social psychology, DA (or *discursive psychology*, as it has been called more recently) involves research in which the language use (both written and spoken) underpinning mental realities, such as cognition and emotion, is investigated. Here, the key theoretical presupposition is that mental realities do not reside "inside" individual humans but rather are constructed linguistically (Edwards, 1997; Potter & Wetherell, 1987). *Critical discourse analysis* (CDA), developed by Fairclough (1989, 1995), constitutes yet another kind of discourse analytical approach in which some key concerns of linguistic and critical social research merge. Critical discourse analysts are interested in the ways in which texts of different kinds reproduce power and inequalities in society. Tainio's (1999) study on the language of self-help communication guidebooks for married couples is one example of a CDA study. Tainio showed, for example, how in these texts the woman is expected to change for the communication problems to be solved, whereas the man is treated as immutable.

*Historical discourse analysis* (HDA) constitutes yet another form of DA, and that is an approach I introduce a bit more thoroughly through a research example.

## Historical Discourse Analysis: Armstrong's Work as an Example

Many scholars working with written texts have drawn insights and inspiration from the work of Michel Foucault. (For examples of his own studies, see Foucault, 1973, 1977, 1978. For examples of accessible accounts of his theories and methods, see Kendall & Wickham, 1999; McHoul & Grace, 1993.) Foucault did not propose a definite set of methods for the analysis of texts; hence, the ways of analyzing and interpreting texts of scholars inspired by him vary. For all of them, however, a primary concern is, as Potter (2004) aptly put it, how a set of "statements" comes to constitute objects and subjects. The constitution of subjects and objects is explored in historical context—or, in Foucault's terms, through *archeology* and *genealogy*.

David Armstrong's work is a good example of the Foucaultian, or historical, approach in text analysis. In a string of studies (Armstrong, 1983, 1987, 1993, 1998, 2002; Gothill & Armstrong, 1999), he investigated medical textbooks and journal articles, showing how objects such as bodies, illnesses, and death, as well as subjects such as doctors, patients, and nurses, have been constituted in these texts during the past two centuries. Armstrong's approach is radically constructionistic; he argued that these objects and subjects—in the sense that we know them now—did not exist before they were constructed through textual and other practices. For example, it has always been the case that some people die at a very early age, but according to Armstrong (1986), "infant mortality" as a discrete social object came into being around 1875. Only after that did the Registrar-General's annual reports (in Britain) orient to such a fact.

Let us examine briefly Armstrong's (1993) article on "public health spaces" so as to understand his Foucaultian way of analyzing and interpreting texts. Basically, Armstrong was concerned about hygienic rules. Using textual material derived from medical and hygienic textbooks and instructions, Armstrong showed how the rules defining the difference between the dangerous and the safe, or between the pure and the dirty, have changed during the past two centuries. In and through examining the rules and their change, Armstrong explored evolution of the spaces in which individual identity is located.

Armstrong (1993) identified four phases, or "regimes," in the development of hygienic rules. During the *quarantine* phase (from the late Middle Ages until the first half of the 19th century), the dividing line between pure and dirty demarcated different geographic spaces. Ships carrying diseases, or towns and villages where infectious diseases were found, were separated from "clean" localities. During the *sanitary science* phase (ca. 1850–1900), the key boundary separated the human body (clean) and the substances outside the body such as (contaminated) air and water. During the *interpersonal hygiene* phase (early to mid-20th century), the dividing line went between individual bodies so as to prevent the spread of contagious diseases from one body to another. Finally, during the *new public health* phase, the danger arose from the incursion of the activities of human bodies into nature in the form of pollution of the environment. Armstrong pointed out that each hygienic regime incorporated practices of the formation of human identity. For example, the shift from quarantine to sanitary science involved dissection of the mass and recognition "of separable and calculable individuality" (p. 405), interpersonal hygiene constructed individual differences, and new public health outlined a reflective subject. Through his analysis, Armstrong also entered into discussion with sociological and anthropological writings of Durkheim (1948) and Douglas (1966), giving historical specification to their concepts and reformulating some of their assumptions regarding the social significance of the boundaries between the sacred and the profane or between the pure and the dirty.

Armstrong's results are impressive. How did he do it? How did he analyze his texts? He recently gave an illuminating account of his method (Armstrong, 2002, chap. 17). Independent of, but still in line with, his own account, I now point out a few things that appear as central in the context of the *Handbook*. In a technical sense, Armstrong's way of analyzing texts is not very different from what was referred to earlier as "the informal approach." He focused on the "propositional content" (not the linguistic forms) of the texts, trying to pin down the assumptions and presuppositions that the texts incorporated. But there were at least three additional features. First, Armstrong was very sensitive about the time of the publication of the texts. A key aspect of his analysis was showing at which time each new hygienic regime arose, and he argued that quite exact times could be documented through an historical survey of texts. Second, Armstrong's analysis was informed by theory. Along with the Foucaultian concerns, Douglas's (1966) arguments presented in her modern classic *Purity and Danger* offered him a standpoint. For Douglas, the separation between the pure and the dangerous objects was the key issue. Third, for Armstrong (as for all Foucaultians), texts and *practices* are inseparable. The medical and hygienic texts that he read had a strong instructive component in them; they not only were establishing boundaries between "ideal" objects but also served as (and Armstrong read them as) guidelines for actual social practices where these boundaries were maintained.

Armstrong's historical and Foucaultian way of analyzing and interpreting texts offers one compact alternative for qualitative text analysis. We now turn to a quite different way of reading texts in qualitative research, that is, *membership categorization analysis* (MCA).

## Membership Categorization Analysis

Whereas Armstrong's Foucaultian analysis was concerned with the propositional content and not the formal properties of texts, MCA can be said to focus more on the latter. However, MCA is not about grammatical forms but rather about the normative and cognitive forms concerning social relations that are involved in the production and understanding of texts. To put it another way, Armstrong's Foucaultian approach is concerned about the assumptions that underlie *what* is said (and what is not said) in the text, whereas MCA is concerned about *the descriptive apparatus* that makes it possible to say whatever is said.

Before we start to examine MCA, I want to remind the reader about the wide range of applications that this approach has. In addition to the analysis of written texts, it can be used in the analysis of interviews (e.g., Baker, 1997) and in the analysis of naturally occurring talk (e.g., Cuff, 1994). In the following, however, I focus on the text analytical applications.

The idea of membership categorization came from the American sociologist Sacks (1974b, 1992). *Description* was a key analytical question for Sacks; he was concerned about the conditions of description, that is, what makes it possible for us to produce and understand descriptions of people and their activities. As Silverman (2001) aptly put it, Sacks was concerned about "the apparatus through which members' descriptions are properly produced" (p. 139). This interest led Sacks to examine categorization.

People are usually referred to by using categories. The point of departure for MCA is recognition of the fact that at any event, a person may be referred to by using many alternative categories. As the author of this chapter, I may also be referred to as a man, as a middle-aged person, as a Finn, as a sociologist, as a professor, as the father of two children, as a husband, and so forth. MCA is about the selection of categories such as these and about the conditions and consequences of this selection.

Sacks's (1974b) famous example is the beginning of a story written by a child: *The baby cried. The mommy picked it up.* There are two key categories in this story: "baby" and "mommy." Why are these categories used, and what is achieved by them? If the mommy happened to be a biologist by profession, why would the story not go like this: *The baby cried. The scientist picked it up* (Jayyusi, 1991, p. 238)? Why do we hear the story being about a baby and *its* mother and not just about any baby and any mother? MCA provides answers to questions such as these and offers a toolkit for analyzing various kinds of texts.

Sacks (1992) noted that categories form sets, that is, collections of categories that go together. Family is one such collection, and "baby," "mother," and "father" are some categories of it. "Stage of life" is another collection; it consists of categories such as "baby," "toddler," "child," and "adult." Now, "baby" could in principle be heard as belonging to both collections, but in the preceding little story we hear it as belonging to the "family" collection. This is because in hearing (or reading) descriptions where two or more categories are used, we orient to a rule according to which we hear them as being from the same collection if they indeed can be heard in that way. Therefore, in this case we hear "baby" and "mommy" being from the device "family" (p. 247).

Categories also go together with *activities*. Sacks used the term "category-bound activities" in referring to activities that members of a culture take to be "typical" of a category (or some categories) of people. "Crying" is a category-bound activity of a baby, just as "picking a (crying) baby up" is a category-bound activity of a mother. In a similar fashion, "lecturing" is a category-bound activity of a professor. Activities such as these can be normative; it is appropriate for the baby to cry and for the mother to pick it up, but it is not appropriate for an adult to cry (like a baby) or for a mother to fail to pick a crying baby up. *Standardized relational pairs* consist of two categories where incumbents of the categories have standardized rights and obligations in relation to each other, with "mother and baby" clearly being one pair, just as "husband and wife" and "doctor and patient" are common pairs. Moreover, the receivers of descriptions can and do infer from actions to categories and vice versa. By knowing actions, we infer the categories of the agents; by knowing categories of agents, we infer what they do.

Even on the basis of these fragments of Sacks's ideas (for more thorough accounts, see Hester & Eglin, 1997; Silverman, 1998), the reader may get an impression of the potential that this account offers for the analysis of texts. Sacks's ideas are resources for the analysis of texts as sites for the production and reproduction of social, moral, and political orders. Merely by bearing in mind that there is always more than one category available for the description of a given person, the analyst always asks "Why this categorization now?"

Let us examine a brief example of MCA. Eglin and Hester (1999) gave a thoughtful account of the local newspaper coverage of a tragic event, namely the killing of 13 female students and a data processing worker by a gunman at the Ecole Polytechnique in Montreal in December 1989. Their aim was to show how a "deviant act" was constructed by members of culture. They did this by identifying the categorical resources that were drawn on in the newspaper coverage.

Eglin and Hester (1999) showed how the description of the tragic event was entirely dependent on the resources or the "apparatus" of categorization. The headlines of the first news about the event implicated an initial pair of categories employed in describing the event, namely "offender" and "victims," which Eglin and Hester (p. 200) considered to be a special kind of a standardized relational pair. In the body of the news, these categories got transformed (e.g., "offender" got transformed into "murder suspect") and new categories, such as "police," "witnesses," "relatives," and "friends" of the victims, entered the scene. As Eglin and Hester put it,

> These categories and category pairs . . . provide, then, some of the procedural resources that news writer and news reader may use to produce and recognize, respectively, the relevance of the variety of actors and actions that appeared in the text of the articles. (p. 202)

Categories are not, however, neutral resources of description. Eglin and Hester (1999) went on to analyze how the use of categorical resources made possible an *embedded commentary,* or *assessment,* of the events. They distinguished among several different "stories" in the news coverage, with each being based on particular operations with categories. For example, *the horror story* arose from the *disjuncture* between the membership categories made relevant by *the setting* and those made relevant by *the event.* On a university campus, the setting made relevant categories such as "student," "teacher," and "staff member." The horror story involved the transformation of these category identities into those of "offender," "victims," "witnesses," and so forth. This disjuncture was encapsulated in reports such as the following: *I was doing a presentation in front of the class, and suddenly a guy came in with what I think was a semi-automatic rifle* (Canadian Press, 1989, cited in Eglin & Hester, 1999, p. 204). Another kind of commentary was involved in the *story of the tragedy.* This story drew on two categorical resources: *the stage of life* device and what Sacks (1974b) called the *R-collection,* that is, the collection of standardized relational pairs relevant for a search for help. In terms of the stage of life, the victims were young people who had their futures ahead of them: *Fourteen young women [are] brutally mowed down in the beauty of their youth when everything seemed to assure them of a brilliant future* (Malarek, 1989, cited in Eglin & Hester, 1999, p. 205). With respect to the R-collection, the tragedy arose from the loss experienced by the incumbents of the categorical "pair parts"—parents, brothers/ sisters, and friends. Yet another commentary involved *the story about the killing of women.* The victims were women who were purposefully chosen by the gunman on the basis of their gender, and the categories "man" and "woman" ran through much of the news coverage. In subsequent articles, the massacre was linked with broader issues of male violence against women and with gender relations in general.

Because all description draws on categorization, it is obvious that MCA has wide applicability in the analysis of texts. The analysis of categorization gives the researcher access to the cultural worlds and moral orders on which the texts hinge. Importantly, however, categorization analysis is not *only* about specific cultures or moralities. In developing his concepts, Sacks was not primarily concerned about the "contents" of the categorizations; rather, he was concerned about the ways in which we use them (Atkinson, 1978, p. 194). Therefore, at the end of the day, membership categorization analysis invites the qualitative researcher to explore the conditions of action of description in itself.

◙ ANALYZING TALK

Face-to-face social interaction (or other live interaction mediated by phones and other technological media) is the most immediate and the most frequently experienced social reality. The heart of our social and personal being lies in the immediate contact with other humans. Even though ethnographic observation of face-to-face social interaction has been done successfully by sociologists and social psychologists, video and audio recordings are what provide the richest possible data for the study of talk and interaction today. Such recordings have been analyzed using the same methods that were discussed previously in the context of interpretation of written texts. CDA, MCA, and even Foucaultian DA have all of their applications in researching transcripts based on video and/or audio recordings. However, as Goffman (1983) pointed out, to be fully appreciated, the face-to-face social interaction also requires its own specific methods. The interplay of utterances and actions in live social interaction involves a complex organization that cannot be found in written texts. *Conversation analysis* (CA) is presented as a method specialized for analyzing that organization.

## Origins of Conversation Analysis

CA is a method for investigating the structure and process of social interaction between humans. As their empirical materials, CA studies use video and/or audio recordings made from naturally occurring interactions. As their results, these studies offer qualitative (and sometimes quantitative) descriptions of interactional structures (e.g., turn taking, relations between adjacent utterances) and practices (e.g., telling and receiving news, making assessments).

CA was started by Sacks and his coworkers, especially Emanuel Schegloff and Gail Jefferson, at the University of California during the 1960s. At the time of its birth, CA was something quite different from the rest of social science. The predominant way of investigating human social interaction was quantitative, based on coding and counting distinct, theoretically defined actions (see especially Bales, 1950). Goffman (e.g., 1955) and Garfinkel (1967) had challenged this way of understanding interaction with their studies that focused on the moral and inferential underpinnings of social interaction. Drawing part of his inspiration from them, Sacks started to study qualitatively the real-time sequential ordering of actions—the rules, patterns, and structures in the relations between consecutive actions (Silverman, 1998). Schegloff (1992a) argued that Sacks made a radical shift in the perspective of social scientific inquiry into social interaction; instead of treating social interaction as a screen on which other processes (Balesian categories or moral and inferential processes) were projected, Sacks started to study the very structures of the interaction itself (p. xviii).

## Basic Theoretical Assumptions

In the first place, CA is not a theoretical enterprise but rather a very concretely empirical one. Conversation analysts make video and/or audio recordings of naturally occurring interactions, and they transcribe these recordings using a detailed notation system (see appendix). They search, in the recordings and transcripts, for recurrent distinct interactive practices that then become their research topics. These practices can involve, for example, specific sequences (e.g., news delivery [Maynard, 2003]) or specific ways of designing utterances (e.g., "oh"-prefaced answers to questions [Heritage, 1998]). Then, through careful listening, comparison of instances, and exploration of the context of them, conversation analysts describe in detail the properties and tasks that the practices have.

However, through empirical studies—in an "inductive" way—a body of theoretical knowledge about the organization of conversation has been accumulated. The actual "techniques" in doing CA can be understood and appreciated only against the backdrop of these basic theoretical assumptions of CA. In what follows, I try to sketch some of the basic assumptions concerning the organization of conversation that arise from these studies. There are perhaps three most fundamental assumptions of this kind (cf. Heritage, 1984, chap. 8; Hutchby & Wooffitt, 1998), namely that (a) talk is action, (b) action is structurally organized, and (c) talk creates and maintains intersubjective reality.

*Talk is action.* As in some other philosophical and social scientific approaches, in CA talk is understood first and foremost as a vehicle of human action (Schegloff, 1991). The capacity of language to convey ideas is seen as being derived from this more fundamental task. In accomplishing actions, talk is seamlessly intertwined with (other) corporeal means of action such as gaze and gesture (Goodwin, 1981). Some CA studies have as their topics the organization of actions that are recognizable as distinct actions even from a vernacular point of view. Thus, conversation analysts have studied, for example, openings (Schegloff, 1968) and closings (Schegloff & Sacks, 1973) of conversations, assessments and ways in which the recipients agree or disagree with them (Goodwin & Goodwin, 1992; Pomerantz, 1984), storytelling (Mandelbaum, 1992; Sachs, 1974a), complaints (Drew & Holt, 1988), telling and receiving news (Maynard, 2003), and laughter (Haakana, 2001; Jefferson, 1984). Many CA studies have as their topic actions that are typical in some institutional environment. Examples include diagnosis (Heath, 1992; Maynard, 1991, 1992; Peräkylä, 1998, 2002; ten Have, 1995) and physical examination (Heritage & Stivers, 1999) in medical consultations, questioning and answering practices in cross-examinations (Drew, 1992), ways of managing disagreements in news interviews (Greatbatch, 1992), and advice giving in a number of different environments (Heritage & Sefi, 1992; Silverman, 1997; Vehviläinen, 2001). Finally, many important CA studies focus on fundamental aspects of conversational organization that make any action possible. These include turn taking (Sacks, Schegloff, & Jefferson, 1974), repair (Schegloff, Jefferson, & Sacks, 1977; Schegloff, 1992c), and the general ways in which sequences of action are built (Schegloff, 1995).

*Action is structurally organized.* In the CA view, the practical actions that comprise the heart of social life are thoroughly structured and organized. In pursuing their goals, the actors have to orient themselves to rules and structures that only make their actions possible. These rules and structures concern mostly the relations between actions. Single acts are parts of larger, structurally organized entities. These entities may be called "sequences" (Schegloff, 1995).

The most basic and the most important sequence is called the "adjacency pair" (Schegloff & Sacks, 1973). It is a sequence of two actions in which the first action ("first pair part"), performed by one interactant, invites a particular type of second action ("second pair part") to be performed by another interactant. Typical examples of adjacency pairs include question–answer, greeting–greeting, request–grant/refusal, and invitation–acceptance/declination. The relation between the first and second pair parts is strict and normative; if the second pair part does not come forth, the first speaker can, for example, repeat the first action or seek explanations for the fact that the second action is missing (Atkinson & Drew, 1979, pp. 52–57; Merritt, 1976, p. 329).

Adjacency pairs often serve as a core around which even larger sequences are built (Schegloff, 1995). So, a *preexpansion* can precede an adjacency pair, for example, in cases where the speaker first asks about the other's plans for the evening and only thereafter (if it turns out that the other is not otherwise engaged) issues an invitation. An *insert expansion* involves actions that occur between the first and second pair parts and makes possible the production of the latter, for example, in cases where the speaker requests specification of an offer or a request before responding to it. Finally, in *postexpansion,* the speakers produce actions that somehow follow from the basic adjacency pair, with the simplest example being "okay" or "thank you" to close a sequence of a question and an answer or of a request and a grant (Schegloff, 1995).

*Talk creates and maintains the intersubjective reality.* CA has sometimes been criticized for neglecting the "meaning" of talk at the expense of the "form" of talk (cf. Alexander, 1988, p. 243; Taylor & Cameron, 1987, pp. 99–107). This is, however, a misunderstanding, perhaps arising from the impression created by technical exactness of CA studies. Closer reading of CA studies reveals that in such studies, talk and interaction are examined as a site where intersubjective understanding about the participants' intentions is created and maintained (Heritage & Atkinson, 1984, p. 11) As such, CA gives access to the construction of meaning in real time. But it is important to notice that the conversation analytical "gaze" focuses exclusively on meanings and understandings that are made public through conversational action and that it remains "agnostic" regarding people's intrapsychological experience (Heritage, 1984).

The most fundamental level of intersubjective understanding—which in fact constitutes the basis for any other type of intersubjective understanding—concerns *the understanding of the preceding turn displayed by the current speaker.* Just like any turn of talk that is produced in the context shaped by the previous turn, it also displays its speaker's understanding of that previous turn (Atkinson & Drew, 1979, p. 48). Thus, in simple cases, when producing a turn of talk that is hearable as an answer, the speaker also shows that he or she understood the preceding turn as a question. Sometimes these choices can be crucial for the unfolding of the interaction and the social relation of its participants, for example, in cases where a turn of talk is potentially hearable in two ways (e.g., as an announcement or a request, as an informing or a complaint) and the recipient makes the choice in the next turn. In case the first speaker considers the understanding concerning his talk to be incorrect or problematic, as displayed in the second speaker's utterance, the first speaker has an opportunity to correct this understanding in the "third position" (Schegloff, 1992c), for example, by saying "I didn't mean to criticize you; I just meant to tell you about the problem."

Another important level of intersubjective understanding concerns the *context* of the talk. This is particularly salient in institutional interaction, that is, in interaction that takes place to accomplish some institutionally ascribed tasks of the participants (e.g., psychotherapy, medical consultations, news interviews) (Drew & Heritage, 1992). The participants' understanding of the institutional context of their talk is documented in their actions. As Schegloff (1991, 1992b) and Drew and Heritage (1992) pointed out, if the "institutional context" is relevant for interaction, it can be observed in the details of the participants' actions—in their ways of giving and receiving information, asking and answering questions, presenting arguments, and so forth. CA research that focuses on institutional interactions explores the exact ways in which the performers of different institutional tasks shape their actions to achieve their goals.

## Research Example

After these rather abstract considerations, let us consider a concrete example of CA research. In my own work on AIDS counseling (Peräkylä, 1995), one of the topics was a practice called "circular questioning" in therapeutic theory. The clients in these sessions were HIV-positive patients and their family members or other significant others. In circular questions, the counselor asked one client to describe the thoughts or experiences of another person; for example, the counselor might ask the mother of an HIV-positive patient to describe what her (copresent) son's greatest concern is. In my analysis, I showed how such questioning involves a powerful practice to incite the clients to talk about matters that they otherwise would be reluctant to discuss. In circular questions, it was not only the counselors who encouraged the clients to talk about their fears and worries. A local interactional context where the clients encouraged each other to talk was built.

One type of evidence for this "function" of the circular questions comes from the structure of such questioning sequences. Without exception, each circular question was followed by the person whose experience was described ("the owner of the experience") himself or herself giving an account of the experience in question. Often the counselor asked the "owner's" view directly after hearing the coparticipant's version, and sometimes the owner volunteered his or her view. In both cases, the pattern of questioning made the owner of the experience speak about his or her fears and worries. In what follows, Extract 1 provides an example of such a sequence. The participants are an HIV-positive patient (P), his boyfriend (BF), and the counselor (C). Arrows 1 to 4 stand for the initiation of key utterances: 1 for the counselor's circular question, 2 for the boyfriend's answer, 3 for the follow-up question to the owner of the experience, and 4 for his response. Here, as in many other cases that I analyzed, the circular question leads the owner of the experience to disclose his deep worries (see especially lines 45–61). For transcription symbols, see the appendix.

*Extract 1* (AIDS Counselling *[Peräkylä, 1995, p. 110]*):

```
01 C:(1)    →   What are some of things that you think E:dward might
02              have to do.=He says he doesn't know where to go
03              from here maybe: and awaiting results and things.
04              (0.6)
05 C:           What d'you think's worrying him.
06              (0.4)
07 BF:(2)   →   Uh::m hhhhhh I think it's just fear of the unknow:n.
08 P:           Mm[:
09 C:              [Oka:y.
10 BF:             [At- at the present ti:me. (0.2) Uh:m (.) once:
11              he's (0.5) got a better understanding of (0.2) what
12              could happen
13 C:           Mm:
14 BF:          uh:m how .hh this will progre:ss then: I think (.)
15              things will be a little more [settled in his
16 C:                                         [Mm
17 BF:          =own mi:nd.
18 C:           Mm:
19              (.)
20 P:           Mm[:
21 C:(3)    →      [E:dward (.) from what you know:: (0.5) wha- what-
22              what do you think could happen. (0.8) I mean we're
23              talking hypothetically [now because I know
24 P:                                  [Mm:: (well)-
25 C:           =no [more than you do about your actual state of=
26 P:               [uh::
27 C:           =health except that we do. know,-
28 P:           =uh
29 C:           .hhh you're carrying the virus::, (0.6) as far as-
30              (0.3) the- that first test is concerned.
31 P:           Umh
32              (1.4)
33 P:(4)    →   (Well I feel) I see like two different extremes.=I
34              see [that I can just- (0.8) carry on (in an)
35 C:               [umh
36 P:           incubation state:, [for many years [and (up)
37 C:                              [umh            [umh
38 P:           .hhhh you know just being very careful about (it)
39              [sexually:.
40 C:           [uhm:
41              (0.4)
42 P:           [and: er (0.3) can go on with a normal life.
43 C:           [umh
```

*(Continued)*

(Continued)

```
44 C:        umh
45 P:        And then I get my greatest fears: that- (0.2) you
46           know just when I've get my life go:ing: you know a
47           good job=
48 C:        =um:h=
49 P:        things going very well,
50 C:        uhm::
51           (0.3)
52 P:        that (I [::) er: : (0.2) my immunity will collapse,
53 C:             [umh
54 C:        um[h
55 P:          [you know: (and I will) become very ill:: (0.2)
56           >quickly?<
57           (1.0)
58 P:        .hhh[hh an]d lose control of th- the situation,
59 C:           [um::h]
60 C:        umh:
61 P:        That's my greatest fear actually.
```

The frequent sequence structure in circular questioning posed a kind of a puzzle for the researcher: Why do the owners of the experience always give their authoritative versions after their experience has been described by somebody else, often even without the counselor asking for it? By examining the minute aspects of the recordings, I started to grasp how the owners' special status vis-à-vis these descriptions, and thereby the relevance of their eventual utterance, was collaboratively and consistently built up in these sequences. *Response tokens* and *postural orientation* were among the means of this buildup.

Response tokens are little particles through which the receivers of an utterance can "receipt" what they have heard and, among other things, indicate that they have no need to ask for clarification or to initiate any other kind of repair, thereby "passing back" the turn of talk to the initial speaker (Schegloff, 1982; Sorjonen, 2001). Usually in question–answer sequences, response tokens would be produced by the questioners. However, in circular questions, the owners of the experience regularly produced response tokens when their significant others were describing the owners' minds and circumstances. As such, the owners indicated their special involvement in the matters that were discussed. That was also the case in Extract 1; in lines 8 and 20, P responded to BF's answer to C's questions with "Mm:"s. He showed his ownership of the matters that were spoken about, thereby also building up the relevance of his own description of them.

The same orientation was shown by the participants through their body posture. The clients who answered the circular question regularly shifted their gaze to the owner at the beginning of the answer, and only toward the end of it did they gaze at the counselor (to whom the answer is given). This organization of gaze contributes to the relevancy of the owner's utterance where he or she eventually describes his or her concerns. A segment from Extract 1 (see below) shows this pattern:

At the beginning of his answer, BF was not oriented to the questioner (the counselor); rather, he was oriented to the person whose mind he was describing (P). Likewise, P was gazing at BF; thus, they are in a mutual gaze contact. BF, the speaker, turned his gaze to the counselor at the end of the first sentence of his answer, and shortly after that P withdrew his gaze from the speaker and also turned to the counselor. Through these actions, P's special status vis-à-vis the things spoken about was collaboratively recognized.

The analysis of circular questioning led me to conclude that in this way of asking questions, a special context was created for the clients' talk about sensitive issues. Unlike "direct" questions, circular questions mobilize *the clients* in the work of eliciting and encouraging each other's talk. CA as a method for analyzing talk made it possible to examine this elicitation in detail.

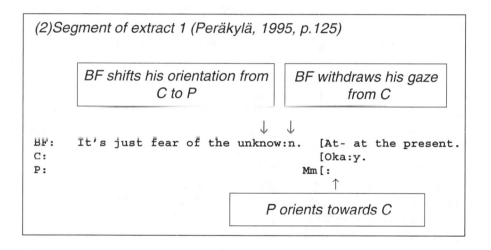

**(2)Segment of extract 1 (Peräkylä, 1995, p.125)**

> BF shifts his orientation from C to P

> BF withdraws his gaze from C

> ↓ ↓

> BF: It's just fear of the unknow:n. [At- at the present.
> C:                                  [Oka:y.
> P:                              Mm [:
>                                    ↑

> P orients towards C

**Figure 11.1**

## ⊡ CONCLUSION

It is a special concern of the third edition of these volumes based on the *Handbook* to be explicit politically, that is, to advance a democratic project committed to social justice. To conclude this chapter, therefore, I compare some of the methods discussed in terms of their relation to issues of *power* and *social change*. I focus on the three methods discussed most thoroughly: HDA, MCA, and CA.

The HDA exemplified in the chapter by Armstrong's work is most directly a method for investigating social change. Armstrong showed us the evolvement of hygienic regimes. At the same time, his analysis of texts was about power—about the discourses and practices through which the boundary between pure and dirty had been established and, in relation to that, through which human identities had been formed. Armstrong, like all Foucaultians, treated power here as a productive force—as something that calls realities into being rather than suppresses them.

The potential of MCA in dealing with questions pertaining to power and social change is well shown in a key text by Sacks (1992), "'Hotrodders' as a Revolutionary Category" (pp. 169–174; see also Sacks, 1979). There are at least two relevant aspects of categorization involved here. The more obvious one is the linkage between categorization and racial and other prejudice. By identifying the actors who have committed crimes or other "evils" by racial or other categories, we can create a link between *all* members of the category and the evil that was done by an individual. Thus, categorization, which is an inherent property of language and thought, is a central resource for racism. However, as Silverman (1998) pointed out, the categorical references can also be used in "benign" ways, for example, in invoking and maintaining institutional identities such as "doctor" (p. 18). The other relevant aspect to categorization is more subtle. Sacks (1992) argued that categories can be *owned, resisted,* and *enforced* (p. 172). Following his examples, young persons may be categorized as "teenagers." In (contemporary Western) society, this category is owned by those who are not teenagers, that is, those who are called "adults." It is adults who enforce and administer this categorization. Those who are categorized as "teenagers" can, however, resist this categorization by constructing their own categorizations and by deciding themselves to whom it will be applied. In Sacks's environment, one such categorization was "hotrodders"; it was a category set up by young people themselves, the incumbency of which they controlled. So far as the "others" (e.g., adults) adopted this new categorization, the revolution in categorization was successful. As a whole, Sacks's examples showed how categorization is a field of changing power relations. Analyzing texts using MCA offers one way in which to analyze them.

The relation of CA to questions of power and social change is more complex. CA that focuses on generic practices and structures of mundane everyday talk might seem irrelevant in terms of power and social change. Billig (1998) argued that this irrelevance may, in fact, imply politically conservative choices. Even in researching institutional interaction, the fact that conversation analysts often focus on small details of video-or audio-recorded talk might seem to render their studies impotent for the analysis of social relations and processes *not* incorporated in talk (cf. Hak, 1999).

From the CA point of view, two responses can be given to these criticisms. First, the significance of orderly organization of face-to-face (or other "live") interaction for *all* social life needs to be restated. No "larger scale" social institutions could operate without the substratum of the interaction order. It is largely through questions, answers, assessments, accusations, accounts, interpretations, and the like that these institutions operate. Hence, even when not focusing on hot social and political issues that we read about in the newspapers, CA is providing knowledge about the basic organizations of social life that make these issues, as well as their possible solutions and the debate about them, possible in the first place.

There is, however, also CA research that is more directly relevant for political and social concerns. For example, many CA studies have contributed to our understanding of the ways in which specific interactional practices contribute to the maintenance or change of the *gender system*. Work by West (1979) and Zimmerman (Zimmerman & West, 1975) on male–female interruptions is widely cited. More recently, Kitzinger (2000) explored the implications of preference organization for the politics of rape prevention and turn-taking organization for the practices of "coming out" as gay or lesbian. In a somewhat more linguistic CA study, Tainio (2002) explored how syntactical and semantic properties of utterances are used in the construction of heterosexual identities in elderly couples' talk. Studies such as these (for a fresh overview, see McIlvenny, 2002) also amply demonstrate the *critical* potential of CA. Yet a different CA study on social change was offered in Clayman and Heritage's (2002b) work on question design in U.S. presidential press conferences. By combining qualitative and quantitative techniques, they showed how the relative proportions of different types of journalist questions, exhibiting different degrees of "adversarialness," have changed over time. As such, they explored the historical change in the U.S. presidential institution and media.

The "dissection" of practices of talk may, therefore, lead to insights that may have some political significance. As a final note, consider again the analysis of circular questioning briefly presented in the preceding section. I sought to show how the recurrent structure of the questioning sequence, as well as the use of discourse particles and the postural orientation, contributed to a context where the patients and their significant others were *incited to speak* about their fears and worries. Now, as scholars working with the methods of historical text analysis have shown (Armstrong, 1984; Arney & Bergen, 1984), a clinic that incites patients to talk about their experience is a relatively new development that evolved during the latter half of the 20th century. Prior to that, Western medicine was not concerned about patients' subjective experience and focused on the body only. AIDS was arguably an illness that was more penetrated by this new medical gaze than was any other illness previously (Peräkylä, 1995, p. 340). Therefore, in observing the skillful practices through which AIDS counselors encourage their clients to talk about their subjective experiences, we were also observing the operation of an institution, involving power relations and bodies of knowledge, at a particular moment in its historical development.

In analyzing AIDS counseling, the results of historical text analysis provided a context for the understanding of the significance of the results of CA. Here, different methods of analyzing and interpreting talk and text complemented each other. This does not mean, however, that these methods could or should merge; the research object and the procedures of analysis in CA and HDA remain different. So, rather than combining different methods (which might be what, e.g., Wetherell, 1998, would propose), we should perhaps let each method do its job in its own way and on its own field and then, only at the end of that, let their results cross-illuminate each other.

# APPENDIX

## ▣ TRANSCRIPTION SYMBOLS IN CA

| | |
|---|---|
| [ | Starting point of overlapping speech. |
| ] | End point of overlapping speech |
| (2.4) | Silence measured in seconds |
| (.) | Pause of less than 0.2 seconds |
| ↑ | Upward shift in pitch |
| ↓ | Downward shift in pitch |
| word | Emphasis |
| wo:rd | Prolongation of sound |
| °word° | Section of talk produced in lower volume than the surrounding talk |
| WORD | Section of talk produced in higher volume than the surrounding talk |
| w#ord# | Creaky voice |
| £word£ | Smile voice |
| wo(h)rd | Laugh particle inserted within a word |
| wo- | Cut off in the middle of a word |
| word< | Abruptly completed word |
| >word< | Section of talk uttered in a quicker pace than the surrounding talk |
| <word> | Section of talk uttered in a slower pace than the surround talk |
| (word) | Section of talk that is difficult to hear but is likely as transcribed |
| ( ) | Inaudible word |
| .hhh | Inhalation |
| hhh | Exhalation |
| . | Falling intonation at the end of an utterance |
| ? | Rising intonation at the end of an utterance |
| , | Flat intonation at the end of an utterance |
| word.=word | "Rush through" without the normal gap into a new utterance |
| ((word)) | Transcriber's comments |

Source: Adapted from Drew and Heritage (Eds.). (1992). *Talk at work: Interaction in institutional settings.* Cambridge, UK: Cambridge University Press.

## ▣ REFERENCES

Alexander, J. (1988). *Action and its environments: Toward a new synthesis.* New York: Columbia University Press.

Armstrong, D. (1983). *Political anatomy of the body: Medical knowledge in Britain in the twentieth century.* Cambridge, UK: Cambridge University Press.

Armstrong, D. (1984). The patient's view. *Social Science and Medicine, 18,* 734–744.

Armstrong, D. (1986). The invention of infant mortality. *Sociology of Health and Illness, 8,* 211–232.

Armstrong, D. (1987). Silence and truth in death and dying. *Social Science and Medicine, 19,* 651–657.

Armstrong, D. (1993). Public health spaces and the fabrication of identity. *Sociology, 27,* 393–410.

Armstrong, D. (1998). Decline of the hospital: Reconstructing institutional dangers. *Sociology of Health and Illness, 20,* 445–447.

Armstrong, D. (2002). *A new history of identity: A sociology of medical knowledge.* Basingstoke, UK: Palgrave.

Arney, W., & Bergen, B. (1984). *Medicine and the management of living.* Chicago: University of Chicago Press.

Atkinson, J. M. (1978). *Discovering suicide: Studies in the social organization of sudden death.* London: Macmillan.

Atkinson, J. M., & Drew, P. (1979). *Order in court: The organization of verbal interaction in judicial settings.* London: Macmilllan.

Atkinson, P., & Coffey, A. (1997). Analysing documentary realities. In D. Silverman (Ed.), *Qualitative research: Theory, method, and practice* (pp. 45–62). London: Sage.

Baker, C. (1997). Membership categorization and interview accounts. In D. Silverman (Ed.), *Qualitative research: Theory, method, and practice* (pp. 130–143). London: Sage.

Bales, R. F. (1950). *Interaction process analysis: A method for the study of small groups.* Reading, MA: Addison-Wesley.

Billig, M. (1998). Whose terms? Whose ordinariness? Rhetoric and ideology in conversation analysis. *Discourse & Society, 10,* 543–558.

Brown, G., & Yule, G. (1983). *Discourse analysis.* Cambridge, UK: Cambridge University Press.

Canadian Press. (1989, December 7). *The Globe and Mail.*

Clayman, S., & Heritage, J. (2002a). *The news interview: Journalists and public figures on the air.* Cambridge, UK: Cambridge University Press.

Clayman, S., & Heritage, J. (2002b). Questioning presidents: Journalistic deference and adversarialness in the press conferences of Eisenhower and Reagan. *Journal of Communication, 52,* 749–775.

Cuff, E. C. (1994). *Problems of versions in everyday situations.* Lanham, MD: University Press of America.

Douglas, M. (1966). *Purity and danger.* London: Routledge & Kegan Paul.

Drew, P. (1992). Contested evidence in courtroom cross-examination: The case of a trial for rape. In P. Drew & J. Heritage (Eds.), *Talk at work: Interaction in institutional settings* (pp. 470–520). Cambridge, UK: Cambridge University Press.

Drew, P., & Heritage, J. (1992). Analyzing talk at work: An introduction. In P. Drew & J. Heritage (Eds.), *Talk at work: Interaction in institutional settings* (pp. 3–65). Cambridge, UK: Cambridge University Press.

Drew, P., & Holt, E. (1988). Complainable matters: The use of idiomatic expression in making complaints. *Social Problems, 35,* 398–417.

Durkheim, E. (1948). *Elementary forms of religious life.* Glencoe, IL: Free Press.

Edwards, D. (1997). *Discourse and cognition.* London: Sage.

Eglin, P., & Hester, S. (1999). Moral order and the Montreal massacre: A story of membership categorization analysis. In P. L. Jalbert (Ed.), *Media studies: Ethnomethodological approaches* (pp. 195–230). Lanham, MD: University Press of America.

Fairclough, N. (1989). *Language and power.* London: Longman.

Fairclough, N. (1995). *Media discourse.* London: Edward Arnold.

Foucault, M. (1973). *The birth of the clinic: An archaeology of medical perception.* New York: Pantheon.

Foucault, M. (1977). *Discipline and punish: The birth of the prison.* London: Allen Lane.

Foucault, M. (1978). *The history of sexuality,* Vol. 1: *An introduction.* New York: Pantheon.

Garfinkel, H. (1967). *Studies in ethnomethodology.* Englewood Cliffs, NJ: Prentice Hall.

Goffman, E. (1955). On face work. *Psychiatry, 18,* 213–231.

Goffman, E. (1983). The interaction order. *American Sociological Review, 48,* 1–17.

Goodwin, C. (1981). *Conversational organization: Interaction between speakers and hearers.* New York: Academic Press.

Goodwin, C., & Goodwin, M. H. (1992). Assessments and the construction of context. In A. Duranti & C. Goodwin (Eds.), *Rethinking context: Language as interactive phenomenon* (pp. 147–190). Cambridge, UK: Cambridge University Press.

Gotthill, M., & Armstrong, D. (1999). Dr. No-Body: The construction of the doctor as an embodied subject in British general practice 1955–97. *Sociology of Health and Illness, 21*(1), 1–12.

Greatbatch, D. (1992). On the management of disagreement between news interviewees. In P. Drew & J. Heritage (Eds.), *Talk at work: Interaction in institutional settings* (pp. 268–302). Cambridge, UK: Cambridge University Press.

Greimas, A. J. (1966). *Semantique Structurale.* Paris: Larousse.

Haakana, M. (2001). Laughter as a patient's resource: Dealing with delicate aspects of medical interaction. *Text, 21,* 187–219.

Hak, T. (1999). "Text" and "con-text": Talk bias in studies of health care work. In S. Sarangi & C. Roberts (Eds.), *Talk, work, and institutional order* (pp. 427–452). Berlin, Germany: Mouton de Gruyter.

Heath, C. (1992). The delivery and reception of diagnosis in the general-practice consultation. In P. Drew & J. Heritage (Eds.), *Talk at work: Interaction in institutional settings* (pp. 235–267). Cambridge, UK: Cambridge University Press.

Heritage, J. (1984). *Garfinkel and ethnomethodology.* Cambridge, UK: Polity.

Heritage, J. (1998). Oh-prefaced responses to inquiry. *Language in Society, 27,* 291–334.

Heritage, J., & Atkinson, J. M. (1984). Introduction. In J. M. Atkinson & J. Heritage (Eds.), *Structures of social action* (pp. 1–15). Cambridge, UK: Cambridge University Press.

Heritage, J., & Sefi, S. (1992). Dilemmas of advice: Aspects of the delivery and reception of advice in interactions between health visitors and first time mothers. In P. Drew &

J. Heritage (Eds.), *Talk at work: Interaction in institutional settings* (pp. 359–417). Cambridge, UK: Cambridge University Press.

Heritage, J., & Stivers, T. (1999). Online commentary in acute medical visits: A method for shaping patient expectations. *Social Science and Medicine, 49,* 1501–1517.

Hester, S., & Eglin, P. (Eds.). (1997). *Culture in action.* Lanham, MD: University Press of America.

Hutchby, I., & Wooffitt, R. (1998). *Conversation analysis: Principles, practices, and applications.* Cambridge, UK: Polity.

Jayyusi, L. (1991). Values and moral judgement: Communicative praxis as moral order. In G. Button (Ed.), *Ethnomethodology and the human sciences* (pp. 227–251). Cambridge, UK: Cambridge University Press.

Jefferson, G. (1984). On the organization of laughter in talk about troubles. In J. M. Atkinson & J. Heritage (Eds.), *Structures of social action* (pp. 346–369). Cambridge, UK: Cambridge University Press.

Kendall, G., & Wickham, G. (1999). *Using Foucault's methods.* London: Sage.

Kitzinger, C. (2000). Doing feminist conversation analysis. *Feminism & Psychology, 10,* 163–193.

Malarek, V. (1989, December 12). *The Globe and Mail.*

Mandelbaum, J. (1992). Assigning responsibility in conversational storytelling: The interactional construction of reality. *Text, 13,* 247–266.

Maynard, D. W. (1991). Interaction and asymmetry in clinical discourse. *American Journal of Sociology, 97,* 448–495.

Maynard, D. W. (1992). On clinicians co-implicating recipients' perspective in the delivery of diagnostic news. In P. Drew & J. Heritage (Eds.), *Talk at work: Interaction in institutional settings* (pp. 331–358). Cambridge, UK: Cambridge University Press.

Maynard, D. W. (2003). *Bad news, good news: Conversational order in everyday talk and clinical settings.* Chicago: University of Chicago Press.

McHoul, A. W., & Grace, A. (1993). *A Foucault primer: Discourse, power, and the subject.* Melbourne, Australia: Melbourne University Press.

McIlvenny, P. (2002). *Talking gender and sex.* Amsterdam, Netherlands: John Benjamins.

Merritt, M. (1976). On questions following questions (in service encounters). *Language in Society, 5,* 315–357.

Peräkylä, A. (1995). *AIDS counselling; Institutional interaction and clinical practice.* Cambridge, UK: Cambridge University Press.

Peräkylä, A. (1998). Authority and accountability: The delivery of diagnosis in primary health care. *Social Psychology Quarterly, 61,* 301–320.

Peräkylä, A. (2002). Agency and authority: Extended responses to diagnostic statements in primary care encounters. *Research on Language and Social Interaction, 35,* 219–247.

Pomerantz, A. (1984). Agreeing and disagreeing with assessments: Some features of preferred/dispreferred turn shapes. In J. M. Atkinson & J. Heritage (Eds.), *Structures of social action: Studies in conversation analysis* (pp. 67–101). Cambridge, UK: Cambridge University Press.

Potter, J. (2004). Discourse analysis as a way of analysing naturally occurring talk. In D. Silverman (Ed.), *Qualitative research: Theory, method, and practice* (2nd ed., pp. 200–201). London: Sage.

Potter, J., & Wetherell, M. (1987) *Discourse and social psychology: Beyond attitudes and behaviour.* London: Sage.

Propp, V. I. (1968). *Morphology of the folk tale* (rev. ed., L. A. Wagner, Ed.). Austin: University of Texas Press.

Sacks, H. (1974a). An analysis of the course of a joke's telling in conversation. In R. Bauman & J. Sherzer (Eds.), *Explorations in the ethnography of speaking* (pp. 337–353). Cambridge, UK: Cambridge University Press.

Sacks, H. (1974b). On the analysability of stories by children. In R. Turner (Ed.), *Ethnomethodology* (pp. 216–232). Harmondsworth, UK: Penguin.

Sacks, H. (1979). Hotrodder: A revolutionary category. In G. Psathas (Ed.), *Everyday language: Studies in ethnomethodology* (pp. 7–14). New York: Irvington.

Sacks, H. (1992). *Lectures on conversation* (Vol. 1, G. Jefferson, Ed., with an introduction by E. Schegloff). Oxford, UK: Basil Blackwell.

Sacks, H., Schegloff, E., & Jefferson, G. (1974). A simplest systematics for the organization of turn-taking for conversation. *Language, 50,* 696–735.

Schegloff, E. A. (1968). Sequencing in conversational openings. *American Anthropologist, 70,* 1075–1095.

Schegloff, E. A. (1982). Discourse as an interactional achievement: Some uses of "uh huh" and other things that come between sentences. In D. Tannen (Ed.), *Georgetown University Round Table on Languages and Linguistics 1981* (pp. 71–93). Washington, DC: Georgetown University Press.

Schegloff, E. A. (1991). Reflection on talk and social structure. In D. Boden & D. Zimmerman (Eds.), *Talk and social structure* (pp. 44–70). Cambridge, UK: Polity.

Schegloff, E. A. (1992a). Introduction. In G. Jefferson (Ed.), *Harvey Sacks: Lectures on conversation,* Vol. 1: *Fall 1964–Spring 1968.* Oxford, UK: Blackwell.

Schegloff, E. A. (1992b). On talk and its institutional occasion. In P. Drew & J. Heritage (Eds.), *Talk at work: Interaction in institutional settings* (pp. 101–134). Cambridge, UK: Cambridge University Press.

Schegloff, E. A. (1992c). Repair after next turn: The last structurally provided defense of intersubjectivity in conversation. *American Journal of Sociology, 98,* 1295–1345.

Schegloff, E. A. (1995). *Sequence organization* [mimeo]. Los Angeles: University of California, Los Angeles, Department of Sociology.

Schegloff, E. A., Jefferson, G., & Sacks, H. (1977). The preference for self-correction in the organization of repair in conversation. *Language, 53,* 361–382.

Schegloff, E. A., & Sacks, H. (1973). Opening up closings. *Semiotica, 8,* 289–327.

Seale, C. (1998). *Constructing death: The sociology of dying and bereavement.* Cambridge, UK: Cambridge University Press.

Silverman, D. (1997). *Discourses of counselling.* London: Sage.

Silverman, D. (1998). *Harvey Sacks: Social science and conversation analysis.* Cambridge, UK: Polity.

Silverman, D. (2001). *Interpreting qualitative data: Methods for analyzing talk, text, and interaction* (2nd ed.). London: Sage.

Smith, D. (1974). The social construction of documentary reality. *Sociological Inquiry, 44,* 257–268.

Smith, D. (1990). *The conceptual practices of power.* Toronto: University of Toronto Press.

Sorjonen, M-L. (2001). *Responding in conversation: A study of response particles in Finnish.* Amsterdam, Netherlands: John Benjamins.

Speer, S. (2002). "Natural" and "contrived" data: A sustainable distinction, *Discourse Studies, 4,* 511–525.

Tainio, L. (1999). Opaskirjojen kieli ikkunana suomalaiseen parisuhteeseen. *Naistutkimus, 12*(1), 2–26.

Tainio, L. (2002). Negotiating gender identities and sexual agency in elderly couples' talk. In P. McIlvenny (Ed.), *Talking gender and sexuality* (pp. 181–206). Amsterdam, Netherlands: John Benjamins.

Taylor, T. J., & Cameron, D. (1987). *Analyzing conversation: Rules and units in the structure of talk.* Oxford, UK: Pergamon.

ten Have, P. (1995). Disposal negotiations in general practice consultations. In A. Firth (Ed.), *The discourse of negotiation: Studies of language in the workplace* (pp. 319–344). Oxford, UK: Pergamon.

Törrönen, J. (2000). The passionate text: The pending narrative as a macrostructure of persuasion. *Social Semiotics, 10*(1), 81–98.

Törrönen, J. (2003). The Finnish press's political position on alcohol between 1993 and 2000. *Addiction, 98,* 281–290.

Vehviläinen, S. (2001). Evaluative advice in educational counseling: The use of disagreement in the "stepwise entry" to advice. *Research on Language and Social Interaction, 34,* 371–398.

West, C. (1979). Against our will: Male interruption of females in cross-sex conversation. *Annals of the New York Academy of Science, 327,* 81–97.

Wetherell, M. (1998). Positioning and interpretative repertoires: Conversation analysis and post-structuralism in dialogue. *Discourse & Society, 9,* 387–412.

Wetherell, M., & Potter, J. (1992). *Mapping the language of racism: Discourse and the legitimation of exploitation.* London: Harvester.

Zimmerman, D. H., & West, C. (1975). Sex roles, interruptions, and silences in conversation. In B. Thorne & N. Henley (Eds.), *Language and sex: Difference and dominance* (pp. 105–129). Rowley, MA: Newbury House.

# 12

# FOCUS GROUPS

## *Strategic Articulations of Pedagogy, Politics, and Inquiry*

### George Kamberelis and Greg Dimitriadis

O ur goal in this chapter is primarily conceptual and transdisciplinary as we explore the complex and multifaceted phenomena of focus group research. At the broadest possible level, focus groups are collective conversations or group interviews. They can be small or large, directed or nondirected. As Table 12.1 indicates, focus groups have been used for a wide range of purposes over the past century or so. The U.S. military (e.g., Merton, 1987), multinational corporations, Marxist revolutionaries (e.g., Freire), literacy activists (e.g., Kozol, 1985), and three waves of radical feminist scholar-activists, among others, all have used focus groups to help advance their concerns and causes. These different uses of focus groups have overlapped in both distinct and disjunctive ways, and all have been strategic articulations of pedagogy, politics, and inquiry.

Given our primary goal in this chapter, we discuss only occasionally and in passing procedural and practical issues related to selecting focus group members, facilitating focus group discussion, and analyzing focus group transcripts. There are many texts available for readers who are looking for this kind of treatment (e.g., Bloor, Frankland, Thomas, & Robson, 2001; Krueger, 1994; Morgan, 1998; Schensul, LeCompte, Nastatsi, & Borgatti, 1999). Instead, we both explore and attempt to move beyond historical and theoretical treatments of focus groups as "instruments" of qualitative research. More specifically, we try to show how focus groups, independent of their intended purposes, are nearly always complex and multivalent articulations of instructional, political, and

**Table 12.1.**     Discursive Formations and the Deployment of Focus Groups Over Time

| Discursive Formation | Pre–World War II | 1950–1980 | 1980–2000 | 2000– |
|---|---|---|---|---|
| Military intelligence | X | | | |
| Market research | X | X | X | X |
| Emancipatory pedagogy | | X | X | X |
| First-wave feminism | X | | | |
| Second-wave feminism | | X | X | |
| Third-wave feminism | | | X | X |

empirical practices and effects. As such, focus groups offer unique insights into the possibilities of or for critical inquiry as a deliberative, dialogic, and democratic practice that is always already engaged in and with real-world problems and asymmetries in the distribution of economic and social capital (Bourdieu & Wacquant, 1992).

We begin with a very basic insight. Focus groups are little more than quasi-formal or formal instances of many of the kinds of everyday speech acts that are the part and parcel of unmarked social life—conversations, group discussions, negotiations, and the like (Bakhtin, 1986). Although their appropriation for the strategic purposes of teaching, challenging hegemonies, and conducting research makes sense, the kinds of interactions and purposes that constitute focus groups were there all along. Taking such an approach allows us to expand and challenge the conscribed parameters of focus group work within qualitative inquiry. Thus, we highlight here three overlapping domains in which focus groups have proliferated: pedagogy, politics, and qualitative research practice. Or, perhaps these terms represent the three primary and overlapping functions of focus groups rather than the three separate domains in which such groups typically operate. We suggest this alternative distinction because all three functions may be (and often are) present when focus groups are enacted in any domain.

Through our analyses of converging and diverging methods and uses of focus groups in these three domains or functions, we conclude that focus groups are unique and important formations of collective inquiry where theory, research, pedagogy, and politics converge. As such, they provide us with important insights and strategies for better understanding and working through the practices and effects signaled by the "seventh moment" of qualitative inquiry (Lincoln & Denzin, 2000) with its emphasis on praxis, methodological syncretism, dialogic relations in the field, the production of polyvocal texts, and the cultivation of sacredness in our daily lives.

In writing this chapter, we are also working out a broader project within which to read the history of qualitative inquiry against the grain (Kamberelis & Dimitriadis, 2005). Here, we focus on methodological practices in general, and on focus groups in particular, with an eye toward revisioning their histories in ways that will open them to new and creative uses. As Lincoln and Denzin (2000) suggested, qualitative researchers no longer have recourse to the kinds of linear histories that have so typically (if tacitly) informed mostly "procedural" discussions of research methods. Instead, we find ourselves always already enmeshed within complex and transversing social-material spaces where we must act as *bricoleurs*, using whatever we find at hand to create whatever effects we believe are possible and desirable. So, if researchers in the seventh moment have an approach at all, it must be something like what Foucault (1984) called a genealogical approach. Basically, a genealogical approach attempts to understand how any "subject" (e.g., a person, a social formation, a social movement, an institution) has been constituted out of particular intersections of forces and systems of forces. A genealogy maps the complex, contingent, and (often) contradictory ways in which these forces and systems of force came together to produce the formation in a particular way. Importantly, because of the complexity and contingency involved, the production of such formations cannot be predicted with any accuracy but can readily be "read" after the fact. Also important here is the fact that genealogies are not histories of causes but rather histories of effects, and their value lies not so much in what they tell us about the past as in what they enable us to do. From the perspective of genealogy,

> history becomes "effective" to the degree that it introduces discontinuity into our very being—as it divides our emotions, dramatizes our instincts, multiplies our body and sets it against itself. "Effective" history deprives the self of the reassuring stability of life and nature, and it will not permit itself to be transported by a voiceless obstinacy toward a millennial ending. It will uproot its traditional foundations and relentlessly disrupt its pretended continuity. This is because knowledge is not made for understanding; it is made for cutting. (Foulcault, 1984, p. 88)

In this spirit, we place three histories or genealogies of focus group activity in dialogue with each other: dialogic focus groups as critical pedagogical practice, focus groups as political practice, and focus groups as research practice. These three histories represent three different ways of thinking about the nature and functions of focus groups. We think that this dialogic juxtaposition begins to decenter the more popularly available treatments of focus groups within qualitative inquiry—suggesting new contexts, uses, and potentials—and begins to disclose the "effectivity" that affords the "cutting" that Foucault regarded as so important.

## ▣ DIALOGIC FOCUS GROUPS AS CRITICAL PEDAGOGICAL PRACTICE

In this section, we highlight how focus groups have been important pedagogical sites or instruments in the work of Paulo Freire in Brazil and Jonathan Kozol in New York.

Through analyses of these exemplars, we show how collective critical literacy practices were used to address local politics and concerns about social justice. Among other things, we foreground the ways in which Freire and Kozol worked *with* people and not *on* them, thereby modeling an important praxis disposition for contemporary educators and qualitative researchers (e.g., Barbour & Kitzinger, 1999). As we show in what follows, Freire and Kozol used focus groups in ways that were very different from those used by people for propaganda and market research. The latter used focus groups to "extract" information from participants, that is, to figure out how to manipulate them more effectively. In contrast, Freire and Kozol used focus groups for imagining and enacting the emancipatory political possibilities of collective work, that is, as useful tools for accomplishing seventh moment imperatives.

Freire's (1970/1993) most famous book, *Pedagogy of the Oppressed,* can be read as equal parts social theory, philosophy, and pedagogical method. His claims about education are foundational, rooted both in his devout Christian beliefs and also in his Marxism. Throughout *Pedagogy of the Oppressed,* Freire argued that the goal of education is to begin to name the world and to recognize that we all are "subjects" of our own lives and narratives, not "objects" in the stories of others. We must acknowledge the ways in which we, as humans, are fundamentally charged with producing and transforming reality together. Those who do not acknowledge this, or those who want to control and oppress, are committing a kind of epistemic "violence":

> To surmount the situation of oppression, people must first critically recognize its causes, so that through transforming action they can create a new situation, one that makes possible the pursuit of a fuller humanity. But the struggle to be more fully human has already begun in the authentic struggle to transform the situation. (Foulcault, 1984, p. 29)

Freire often referred to these situations as "limit situations," that is, situations that people cannot imagine themselves beyond. Limit situations naturalize people's sense of oppression, giving it a kind of obviousness and immutability.

To help people imagine lives beyond these "limit situations," Freire spent long periods of time in communities trying to understand community members' interests, investments, and concerns so as to elicit comprehensive sets of "generative words." These words were used as starting points for literacy learning, and literacy learning was deployed in the service of social and political activism. More specifically, generative words were paired with pictures that represented them and then were interrogated by people in the community for both what they revealed and what they concealed with respect to the circulation of multiple forms of capital. Freire encouraged the people both to explore how the meanings and effects of these words functioned in their lives and to conduct research on how their meanings and effects did function, or could function, in a variety of ways in different social and political contexts. The primary goals of these activities were to help people feel in control of their words and to be able to use them to exercise power over the material and ideological conditions of their own lives.

Thus, Freire's literacy programs were designed not so much to teach functional literacy as to raise people's critical consciousness (or *conscientization*) and to encourage them to engage in "praxis" or critical reflection inextricably linked to political action in the real world. Freire underscored the fact that praxis is never easy and always involves power struggles—often violent ones.

As this description of Freire's pedagogies for the oppressed suggests, he believed that humans live both "in" the world and "with" the world and, thus, can be active participants in making history. In fact, he argued that a fundamental possibility of the human condition is to be able to change the material, economic, and spiritual conditions of life itself through *conscientization* and praxis. He posited human agency, then, as situated or embodied freedom—a kind of limited but quite powerful agency that makes it possible to change oneself and one's situation for the better. To enact such agency, he argued, people need to emerge from their unconscious engagements with the world, reflect on them, and work to change them. Viewed in this way, the enactment of freedom is an "unfinalizable" process. In constantly transforming their engagements in and with the world, people are simultaneously shaping the conditions of their lives and are constantly recreating themselves.

Freire's insistence that the unending process of emancipation must be a collective effort is far from trivial. Central to this process is a faith in the power of dialogue. Importantly, for Freire, dialogue is defined as collective reflection or action. He believed that dialogue, fellowship, and solidarity are essential to human liberation and transformation:

> We can legitimately say that in the process of oppression, someone oppresses someone else; we cannot legitimately say that in the process of revolution, someone liberates someone else, nor yet that that someone liberates himself, but rather that men in communion liberate each other. (Freire, 1970/1993, p. 103)

Within Freirean pedagogies, the development and use of generative words and phrases and the cultivation of *conscientization* are enacted in the context of locally situated "study circles" (or focus groups). The goal for the educator or facilitator within these study circles is to engage with people in their lived realities, producing and transforming them. Again, for Freire (1970/1993), pedagogical activity is always already grounded in larger philosophical and social projects concerned with how people might "narrate" their own lives more effectively:

> The starting point for organizing the program content of education or political action must be the present, existential, concrete situation, reflecting the aspirations of the people. Utilizing certain basic contradictions, we must pose the existential, concrete, present situation to the people as a problem which challenges them and requires a response—not just at the intellectual level, but [also] at the level of action. . . . The task of the dialogical teacher in an interdisciplinary team working on the thematic universe revealed by [the team's] investigation is

to "re-present" that universe to the people from whom she or he first received it—and "re-present" it not as a lecture, but as a problem. (pp. 76–90)

To illustrate this kind of problem-posing education rooted in people's lived realities and contradictions, Freire discussed a research program designed around the question of alcoholism. Because alcoholism was a serious problem in the city, a researcher showed an assembled group a photograph of a drunken man walking past three other men talking on the corner. The group responded, in effect, by saying that the drunken man was a hard worker—the only hard worker in the photograph—and that he was probably worried about his low wages and having to support his family. In the group members' words, "He is a decent worker and a souse like us" (Freire, 1970/ 1993, p. 99). The men in the study circle seemed to recognize themselves in this man, noting that he was a "souse" and situating his drinking in a politicized context. In this situation, alcoholism was "read" as a response to oppression and exploitation. The goal was to "decode" images and language in ways that eventually led to questioning and transforming the material and social conditions of existence. Freire offered other examples as well, including showing people different (and contradictory) news stories covering the same event. In each case, the goal was to help people understand the contradictions they live and to use these understandings to change their worlds.

Freire's pedagogical framework could not be readily contained within traditional educational contexts where the historical weight of the "banking model" imposed powerful and pervasive constraints. His work inspired a wide range of important social movements within education, and the activities of these movements have provided yet more models for how intensive group activity—the kinds realized in focus groups—can be imagined and enacted in innovative ways to produce "effective histories" within which knowledge is made not for understanding but rather for cutting (Foucault, 1984, p. 88). Freire exerted a particularly strong influence on the work of critical pedagogues such as Henry Giroux, Peter McLaren, and Jonathan Kozol, all of whom helped to reimagine Freire's work within a U.S. context.

Freire's work has been influential outside the field of education as well. Augusto Boal, for example, developed the "theater of the oppressed," which is grounded in the liberation impulses of Freire, and used theater to blur the line between the actors on-stage and the audience off-stage. The theater of the oppressed is a public, improvisational, and highly interactive form of theater with strong transformative and pedagogical impulses and potentials (Casali, 2002). In addition, Freire profoundly influenced the participatory action research (PAR) movement led by Orlando Fals Borda, among others. Here, researchers work with subordinated populations around the world to solve unique local problems with local funds of knowledge. The PAR movement is profoundly Freirean in its impulses (Fals Borda, 1985).

Freire was an especially powerful influence on several educationally oriented social movements in the United States. Kozol, perhaps best known for his groundbreaking book *Savage Inequalities* (1991), drew on Freire's emancipatory work to research and write another book, *Illiterate America*. In this book, Kozol (1985) wrote, "Paulo Freire's work among the people of northeast Brazil during the early 1960s is one instance of a government campaign which takes its energies from the illiterates themselves" (p. 95). Like Freire, Kozol grounded his own literacy programs in New York City in the actual lives of the people with whom he worked to create dialogic collectives with horizontal leadership:

> There is a tremendous difference between knocking on a door to tell somebody of a program that has been devised already and which they are given the choice, at most, to join or else ignore—and, on the other hand, to ask them to assist in the creation of that plan. . . . Some of the best ideas that I have heard have come out of discussions held within the neighbor-hoods themselves. People, moreover, are far more likely to participate in something which they or their neighbors have been invited to assist in planning—and something in which ideas they have offered have been more than "heard" but given application. (p. 106)

In practice, Kozol advocated working in study circles or focus groups in much the same way as did Freire—as key pedagogical instruments or sites:

> I have come to be convinced that groups of six or seven learners and one literacy worker represent an ideal unit of instruction for this plan. The presence of a circle of [a] half-dozen friends or neighbors helps to generate a sense of common cause and to arouse a sense of optimistic ferment that is seldom present in the one-to-one encounter. (p. 108)

Groups with such a composition allow for the emergence of dynamics that open up pos-sibilities for constructing effective histories. They also function as spawning grounds for the emergence of locally situated and effective leadership:

> Learning in groups, people at length will generate group leaders; because these leaders will emerge out of their ranks, they will remain susceptible to criticism and correction. At the same time, because of their point of origin and their proximity to pain, they may be in an ideal position to discover and encourage others. (p. 109)

Taking his cues from Freire, Kozol also advocated the elicitation and use of genera-tive words or phrases that are likely to lead to discussion, reflection, *conscientization*, and praxis. Extending the work of Freire, he argued that for both pedagogical and polit-ical reasons, these generative words or phrases should necessarily be complex because more complex words provide more access to the common phoneme–grapheme rela-tions in any particular natural language (e.g., Spanish, English) and, thus, facilitate "reading the word" (Freire, 1970/1993). More complex words also have richer meaning potentials than do simpler words, and their precise meanings vary more as a function of their specific contexts and purposes of use, thereby facilitating "reading the world"

(Freire, 1970/1993) in more critical ways. Collective discussions of complex words or phrases typically result in "unpacking" their structures, meaning potentials, and various "effectivities" within and across different social and political contexts. Kozol noted,

> The word "revolutionary," for example, might appear to be the paradigm of active language in a literacy struggle that is rooted in the anguish of impoverished people. Here is a single adjective which dominates the public dialogue of hope and fear, are all five vowels of the English language, four of the more common consonants, the difficult suffix "tion" which is used in several dozen common words, as well as the occasional vowel *y*. (Kozol, 1985, p. 136)

The lexical and syntactic complexity embodied in this word facilitates literacy learning or reading the word. The word also has an extraordinary surplus of meanings, and its meanings vary tremendously both within and across the different contexts in which it is commonly used. This complexity facilitates reading the world. For example, in lieu of its emancipatory political connotations, the word "revolutionary" is often diluted and domesticated in all kinds of ways, for example, the phrase "a revolutionary new detergent" or, more recently, "revolutionary technology." This word has also been used by the political right to "name" particular groups as dangerous and to strike fear in the hearts of patriotic (and even not so patriotic) citizens. Furthermore, the word has been appropriated by resistance and counterresistance groups as an emblematic indicator of their collective identities and to motivate and legitimate their struggles.

Kozol also noted the importance of *space* as a dimension of the decentering activity that occurs in relation to the pedagogically oriented study circles (or focus groups). These study circles seldom take place in "official" spaces such as public schools and other public institutions. Instead, they take place in church basements, people's apartments, recreation centers, and so forth. Like generative words and phrases, these spaces mark intellectual workers as committed to working with and within marginalized communities for the purpose of helping these communities to take over responsibility for their own struggles and their own existences. These spaces also become emblematic indicators of or for the collective identities of the communities themselves, and they create the kind of overdetermined solidarity that seems to be necessary for producing effective histories with forward momentum.

## Summary

Dialogic focus groups have always been central to the kinds of radical pedagogies that have been advocated and fought for by intellectual workers such as Freire and Kozol. Organized around "generative" words and phrases, and usually located within unofficial spaces, focus groups become sites of or for collective struggle and social transformation. As problem-posing formations, they operate locally to identify, interrogate, and change specific lived contradictions that have been rendered invisible by hegemonic power/knowledge regimes. Their operation also functions to reroute the circulation of power within hegemonic struggles and even to redefine what power is and how it works. Perhaps most important for our purposes here, the impulses that motivate focus groups in pedagogical domains or for pedagogical functions have important implications for imagining and using focus groups as resources for constructing "effective histories" within qualitative research endeavors in the "seventh moment." (We return to this issue in the final section of the chapter.)

Importantly, these histories are largely situated and context dependent. For Freire and Kozol, as well as for Giroux and McLaren, one could not predict a priori what might be involved in emancipating political and educative agendas. Whereas both Freire and Kozol shared progressive roots and impulses, the next movement we explore more explicitly placed focus groups at the center of an explicitly defined political agenda—feminism.

## FOCUS GROUPS AS POLITICAL PRACTICE: FEMINIST CONSCIOUSNESS-RAISING GROUPS AS EXEMPLARS

In this section, we offer descriptions and interpretations of focus groups in the service of radical political work designed within social justice agendas. In particular, we focus on how consciousness-raising groups (CRGs) of second- and third-wave feminism have been deployed to mobilize empowerment agendas and to enact social change. This work provides important insights relevant for reimagining the possibilities of focus group activity within qualitative research endeavors. Whereas the primary goal of Freire and Kozol was to use literacy (albeit broadly defined) to mobilize oppressed groups to work against their oppression through praxis, the primary goal of the CRGs of second- and third-wave feminism was to build "theory" from the lived experiences of women that could contribute to their emancipation.

In our discussion of CRGs, we draw heavily on Esther Madriz's retrospective analyses of second-wave feminist work as well as on her own third-wave empirical work. In both of these endeavors, Madriz focused on political (and politicized) uses of focus groups within qualitative inquiry. As Madriz (2000) demonstrated, there is a long history of deploying focus groups in consciousness-raising activities and of promoting social justice agendas within feminist and womanist traditions. Importantly, as a form of collective testimony, focus group participation has often been empowering for women, especially women of color (p. 843). There are several reasons why this is the case. Focus groups decenter the authority of the researcher, providing women with safe spaces to talk about their own lives and struggles. These groups also allow women to connect with each other collectively, share their own experiences, and "reclaim their humanity" in a nurturing context (p. 843). Madriz noted that women themselves often take over these groups, reconceptualizing them in fundamental ways and with simple yet far-reaching political and practical consequences. In this regard, Madriz argued,

> Focus groups can be an important element in the advancement of an agenda of social justice for women, because they can serve to expose and validate women's everyday experiences

of subjugation and their individual and collective survival and resistance strategies.... Group interviews are particularly suited for uncovering women's daily experience through collective stories and resistance narratives that are filled with cultural symbols, words, signs, and ideological representations that reflect different dimensions of power and domination that frame women's quotidian experiences. (pp. 836–839)

As such, these groups constitute spaces for generating collective "testimonies," and these testimonies help both individual women and groups of women to find or produce their own unique and powerful "voices."

As Madriz and others have noted, focus groups have multiple histories within feminist lines of thought and action. Soon after slavery ended, for example, churchwomen and teachers gathered to organize political work in the South (e.g., Gilkes, 1994). Similarly, turn-of-the-century "book clubs" were key sites for intellectual nourishment and political work (e.g., Gere, 1997). Mexican women have always gathered in kitchens and at family gatherings to commiserate and work together to better their lives (e.g., Behar, 1993; Dill, 1994). And in 1927, Chinese women working in the San Francisco garment industry held focus group discussions to organize against their exploitation, eventually leading to a successful strike (e.g., Espiritu, 1997). Although we do not unpack these and other complex histories in this chapter, we do offer general accounts of the nature and function of focus groups within second- and third-wave feminism in the United States. These accounts pivot on the examination of several key, original, manifesto-like texts generated within the movement that we offer as synecdoches of the contributions of a much richer, more complex, contradictory, and intellectually and politically "effective" set of histories.

Perhaps the most striking realization that emerges from examining some of the original texts of second-wave feminism is the explicitly self-conscious ways in which women used focus groups as "research" to build "theory" about their everyday experiences and to deploy theory to enact political change. Interestingly but not surprisingly, this praxis-oriented work was dismissed by male radicals at the time as little more than "gossip" in the context of "coffee klatches." Ironically, this dismissal mirrors the ways in which qualitative inquiry is periodically dismissed for being "soft," "subjective," or "nonscientific." Nevertheless, second-wave feminists persisted in building theory from the "standpoint" of women's lived experiences and eventually became a powerful social force in the struggle for equal rights.

In response to claims that feminist theory was nonscientific, Sarachild (1978) argued,

The decision to emphasize our own feelings and experiences as women and to test all generalizations and reading we did by our own experiences was actually the scientific method of research. We were in effect repeating the 17th century challenge of science to scholasticism: "study nature, not books," and put all theories to the test of living practice and action. (p. 145)

Sarachild continued, noting that the goal of CRGs was not simply for women to share atomized experiences, to express themselves, or to confess before the groups:

> The idea of consciousness-raising was never to end generalizations. It was to produce truer ones. The idea was to take our own feelings and experience more seriously than any theories which did not satisfactorily clarify them, and to devise new theories which did reflect the actual experience and necessities of women. (p. 148)

In other words, a primary imperative of these groups was to use power in productive ways (e.g., Foucault, 1977, 1980), that is, to experiment with and intervene in reality itself (Deleuze & Guattari, 1987). This imperative went beyond representation toward reinvention. Attending to the current realities of women was a means toward the end of remapping those realities and connecting them to strategic political interests.

Despite this poststructural imperative, these discussions were often peppered with the language of "truth" and "science," making them seem decidedly postpositivist by today's standards. In many respects, this is not surprising because these women were working out of an essentialist, foundationalist perspective and also needed to inflect their arguments in ways that would allow them to be heard within a social and political climate that was unquestionably Euro-American, male-dominated, and heterosexist. Yet they also seemed to realize that building political agendas around women's experiences is an inexhaustible and unfinalizable activity. In this regard, Sarachild (1978) contrasted "consciousness-raising groups" with "study groups" and "rap groups." She referred to CRGs as "revolutionary" and to the latter two kinds of groups as products of "left liberalism error" and "right liberalism error," respectively (p. 150). These contrasts are fascinating for many reasons. In a discussion with a Freirean sub-text, she noted that the errors introduced by both the right liberalism and the left liberalism did not really investigate things. Instead, they began with a priori conclusions and then attempted to justify them with dogma or some semblance of empiricism. More specifically, she saw left-leaning study groups as dogmatists and saw right-leaning groups as post hoc empiricist. In contrast, she saw evolutionary CRGs as rooted in "investigation and discovery" and saw their political agendas as radical. Importantly, Sarachild was playing with the polysemic and heteroglossic meanings of "root" and "radical" here. She noted, "We were interested in getting to the roots of problems in society. You might say we wanted to pull up weeds in the garden by their roots, not just pick off the leaves at the top to make things look good momentarily" (p. 144). So, although these CRGs were intensely personal, the personal was always deployed in the service of larger theoretical and political agendas.

In many respects, the CRGs of second-wave feminism helped set the agenda for a whole generation of feminist activism. As Eisenstein (1984) noted, these groups helped to bring personal issues in women's lives to the forefront of political discourse. Issues such as abortion, incest, sexual molestation, and domestic and physical abuse emerged from these groups as pressing social issues around which public policy and legislation had to be enacted. Importantly, these issues had previously been considered to be too personal and too intensely idiosyncratic to be taken seriously by men at the time, whether they were scholars, political activists, politicians, or the like. By finding out which issues were most pressing in women's lives, CRGs were able to advance what had previously been considered individual, psychological, and private matters to the agendas of local collectives and eventually to social and political agendas at regional and national levels.

Like the work of Freire and Kozol, most focus group work within second-wave feminist qualitative inquiry has recognized the constitutive power of *space* and *place*. Groups are typically held in familiar settings such as kitchens, church basements, senior citizens' dining or living rooms, and women's shelters. Madriz (2000) noted, "Using participants' familiar spaces further diffuses the power of the researcher, decreasing the possibilities of 'otherization'" (p. 841).

In addition to the second-wave feminist work that was primarily theoretical and political, there was a large body of work that was quite practical, focusing largely on how to conduct CRGs. In other words, discourses on method were part and parcel of the movement. Not surprisingly, these discourses nearly always displayed a praxis orientation—the articulation of theory and practice for social and political change. Moreover, careful attention was paid to issues of power, especially with respect to micropolitical power relations that seemed to represent *internal* threats to the potential for second-wave feminists to produce effective histories. The ideal composition of CRGs, for example, was heavily debated. How homogeneous or heterogeneous should they be? How large should the groups be to be maximally effective? How centralized or decentralized should group leadership be? Should the groups be "single-sexed," with sympathetic men doing other kinds of work in other contexts?

Much thought and effort were also devoted to developing "manuals" for women who wanted to develop and maintain CRGs from the ground up. The Cape Cod Women's Liberation Movement (1972), for example, distributed a pamphlet that advised the following:

I. You might start by discussing something everyone has read, to get over the initial awkwardness.

II. Try talking about what each woman imagines feminism to be. Or what each expects—hopes and/or fears—to get out of the group.

III. Personal histories can be shared, what each woman does, her living situation, how long she has been interested, and how each found out about the group.

IV. Each woman can briefly describe her background. We all have childhoods: they influenced us but are less threatening to discuss than recent events.

V. Whatever we start with, one simple method is to "go around the room." Each woman talks in turn. That way no one is passed over. It is vitally important that every woman speak.

VI. After the first meeting, you might want to choose topics in advance. Some groups do; some do not. You might proceed by "going around" and seeing what people need to discuss that evening. You might discuss some external event that relates to women.

This pamphlet also discussed several obstacles and ways of overcoming them such as what to do when some women dominate the group or threaten each other and how to protect each other's privacy. The overall goals of pamphlets and flyers such as this were to build theory from the women's lived experiences and to articulate this theory with contemporary political agendas in ways that would promote equal rights for women under the law.

Like many collective efforts, the CRGs of second-wave feminism had some limitations. As Eisenstein (1984) noted, for example, these groups often operated under the constraints of what she called "false universalism." In other words, these groups often purported to speak for all women in unproblematic ways as if the experiences of white middle-class women were universal. This limitation is common among most social movements where members tend to be "alike" in many ways and where collective identities need to be overdetermined to amass any political weight. In the case of second-wave feminism, a primary goal was "to enable the participants to deemphasize their differences and to focus on the experiences they had in common. The generalizations, of course, only describe the experiences of those women who participated. By and large, these were college-educated white women" (p. 133).

These universalist tendencies alienated many women of color who saw feminism as a "middle-class white thing." As Madriz (2000) emphasized, however, many of the insights and strategies generated within the CRGs of second-wave feminism could be easily adapted to be relevant to the desires, needs, and hopes of women of color and other multiply marginalized groups of women. Indeed, if we map the trajectory from second-wave to third-wave feminism, we see both continuities and discontinuities.

The next generation of feminist scholars and researchers did indeed build on and extend the agendas of second-wave feminism while also stressing the differences within and between "groups" of women. The standpoint positions of African American, Latina, and gay women, for example, all became pronounced during this time period. Working within the movement(s) of third-wave feminism, Madriz (1997) used focus groups in powerful ways, some of which are evidenced in her book, *Nothing Bad Happens to Good Girls.* In this book, Madriz discussed the many ways in which the fear of crime works to produce an insidious form of social control over women's lives. Fear of crime produces certain ideas about what women "should" and "should not" do in public to protect themselves, enabling debilitating ideas about what constitutes "good girls" versus "bad girls" and severely constraining the range of everyday practices available to women.

With respect to research methods, Madriz called attention to the fact that most research findings on women's fear of crime had previously been generated from large survey studies of both men and women. This approach, she argued, severely limits the range of thought and experience that participants are willing to share and, thus, leads to unnecessarily partial and inaccurate accounts of the phenomenon. In other words, it is hard to get people—women in particular—to talk about sensitive topics, such as their own fears of assault or rape, in uninhibited and honest ways in the context of oral or written surveys completed alone or in relation to a single social scientist interviewer. This general problem is further complicated by differences in power relations between researchers and research participants that are a function of age, social class, occupation, language proficiency, race, and so forth.

To work against the various alienating forces that seem inherent in survey research and to collect richer and more voluminous accounts of experience with greater verisimilitude, Madriz used focus groups, noting that these groups provided a context where women could support each other in discussing their experiences of crime as well as their fears and concerns about crime. Indeed, these groups do mitigate against the intimidation, fear, and suspicion with which many women approach the one-on-one interview. In the words of one of Madriz's (1997) participants, "When I am alone with an interviewer, I feel intimidated, scared. And if they call me over the telephone, I never answer their questions. How do I know what they really want or who they are?" (p. 165). In contrast, focus groups afford women much safer and more supportive contexts within which they may explore their lived experiences and the consequences of these experiences with other women who will understand what they are saying intellectually, emotionally, and viscerally.

This idea of safe and supportive spaces ushers in another important dimension of focus group work within third-wave feminist research, namely the importance of constituting groups in ways that mitigate against alienation, create solidarity, and enhance community building. To achieve such ends, Madriz emphasized the importance of creating homogeneous groups in terms of race, class, age, specific life experiences, and so forth—all of which are hallmarks of third-wave feminism.

Both in her own work and in her efforts to be a spokesperson for third-wave feminist approaches to qualitative inquiry, Madriz (1997) outlined a set of attitudes and practices that built on and extended the work of the second wave. Among other things, she acknowledged a long history of feminist approaches to qualitative work grounded within a long history of "no name" feminist and womanist practices—"exchanges with mothers, sisters, neighbors, friends" (p. 166). She also revisioned focus groups as vehicles for collective testimony, which offer affordances that help women to get beyond the social isolation that has historically characterized their lives (p. 166). These affordances clearly grew out of the initiatives and imperatives of second-wave CRGs already discussed, but they extended the CRGs as well. In particular, Madriz argued that the nonessentialist, social constructionist, and (often) postcolonial nature of third-wave feminist research projects accounts more fully for the extraordinary variability that often exists between and among women's experiences depending on social positioning with respect to race, class, region, age, sexual orientation, and so forth. Third-wave feminist researchers, thus, refracted and multiplied the standpoints from which testimonies might flow and voices might be produced. Although researchers such as Madriz held onto the postpositivist ideal of building theory from lived experiences, they also pushed for theory that accounted more fully for the local, complex, and nuanced nature of lived experiences that are always already constructed within power relations produced at the intersections of multiple social categories.

In the end, a primary goal of focus group activity within third-wave feminist research is not to offer prescriptive conclusions but rather to highlight the productive potentials (both oppressive and emancipatory) of particular social contexts (with their historically produced and durable power relations) within which such prescriptions typically unfold. In this regard, the work of Madriz is a synecdoche for third-wave feminist work more broadly conceived, particularly by women of color such as Dorinne Kondo, Smadar Lavie, Ruth Behar, Aiwa Ong, and Lila Abu-Lughod.

## Summary

The nature and functions of CRGs within second- and third-wave feminism offer many important insights into the potential of focus groups to function in the service of the key imperatives of "seventh moment" qualitative inquiry. Building on Madriz's political reading of focus groups, and more specifically on the constructs of "testimony" and "voice," we highlight some of these possibilities here.

One key function of focus groups within feminist work has been to elicit and validate collective testimonies and group resistance narratives. These testimonies and narratives have been used by women—and could be used by any subjugated group—"to unveil specific and little-researched aspects of women's daily existences, their feelings, attitudes, hopes, and dreams" (Madriz, 2000, p. 836). Another key emphasis of focus groups within feminist and womanist traditions has been the discovery or production of voice. Because focus groups often result in the sharing of similar stories of everyday experiences of struggle, rage, and the like, they often end up validating individual voices that had previously been constructed within and through mainstream discourses as idiosyncratic, selfish, and even evil. Because focus groups foreground and exploit the power of testimony and voice, they can become sites for the overdetermination of collective identity as strategic political practice. This overdetermination creates a critical mass of visible solidarity that seems to be a necessary first step toward social and political change.

A major concern of feminist researchers has been the moral dilemmas inherent in interviewing and the researcher's role in these dilemmas. Focus groups mitigate against these dilemmas by creating multiple lines of communication that help to create "safe spaces" for dialogue in the company of others who have had similar life experiences and who are struggling with similar issues. In relation to this point, focus groups can allow for unique forms of access to the "natural" interaction that can occur between and among participants. Because focus groups privilege "horizontal interaction" over "vertical interaction," they are also constituted as social spaces that tend to decrease the influence of the researcher in controlling the topics and flow of interaction. Among other things, this horizontality increases the potential for rearticulating power dynamics within focus group interactions in ways that can lead to the collection of especially rich information (i.e., high-quality data) that will eventually result in accounts that are replete with "thick description" and rich in verisimilitude.

Focus groups within feminist and womanist traditions have also mitigated against the Western tendency to separate thinking and feeling, thereby opening up possibilities for reimagining knowledge as distributed, relational, embodied, and sensuous. Viewing knowledge in this light brings into view the complexities and contradictions that are always a part of fieldwork. It also illuminates the relations between power and knowledge and, thus, insists that qualitative research is always already political—implicated in social critique and social change.

Either out of necessity or for strategic purposes, feminist work has always taken into account the constitutive power of *space*. To further work against asymmetrical power relations and the processes of "othering," focus group meetings are nearly always held in safe spaces where women feel comfortable, important, and validated. This is a particularly important consideration when working with women who have much to lose from their participation, for example, undocumented immigrants and so-called deviant youths.

Finally, the break from second-wave to third-wave feminism called into question the monolithic treatment of difference under the sign of "woman" that characterized much of second-wave thinking and also highlighted the importance of creating focus groups that are relatively homogeneous in terms of life histories, perceived needs, desire, race, social class, region, age, and so forth because such groups are more likely to achieve the kind of solidarity and collective identity that are necessary for producing "effective histories." Although coalition building across such relatively homogeneous groups of women may be important in some instances, focused intellectual and political work is often most successful when it is enacted by people with similar needs, desires, struggles, and investments.

Together, the various insights and practices of CRGs within feminist work have been invaluable in propelling us toward the seventh moment and in helping us to imagine and enact (a) a commitment to morally sound, praxis-oriented research; (b) the strategic use of eclectic constellations of theories, methods, and research strategies; (c) the cultivation of dialogic relationships in the field; (d) the production of polyvocal nonrepresentational texts; and (e) the conduct of mindful inquiry attuned to what is sacred in and about life and text.

## ▣ FOCUS GROUPS AS RESEARCH PRACTICE

Interest in focus groups in the social sciences has ebbed and flowed over the course of the past 60 years or so. In many respects, the first really visible use of focus groups for conducting social science research may be traced back to the work of Paul Lazarsfeld and Robert Merton. Their focus group approach emerged in 1941 as the pair embarked on a government-sponsored project to assess media effects on attitudes toward America's involvement in World War II. As part of their research at the Columbia University Office of Radio Research, Lazarsfeld and Merton recruited groups of people to listen and respond to radio programs designed to boost morale for the war effort (Merton, 1987, p. 552). Originally, the researchers asked participants to push buttons to indicate their positive or negative responses to the radio programs. Because the data yielded from this work could help them to answer "what" questions but not "why" questions about participants' choices, the researchers used focus groups as forums for getting participants to explain why they responded in the ways they did. Importantly, Lazarsfeld and Merton's use of focus groups as a qualitative research strategy was always secondary (and less legitimate) than the various quantitative methods of data collection and analysis the researchers deployed. They used focus groups in exploratory ways to generate new questions that could be used to develop new quantitative strategies or simply to complement or annotate the more quantitative findings of their research. Lunt (1996) observed that Merton saw "the role of the focus groups as identifying the salient dimensions of complex social stimuli as [a] precursor to further quantitative tests" (p. 81). Two dimensions of Lazarsfeld and Merton's research efforts constitute part of the legacy of using focus groups within qualitative research: (a) capturing people's responses in real space and time in the context of face-to-face interactions and (b) strategically "focusing" interview prompts based on themes that are generated in these face-to-face interactions and that are considered particularly important to the researchers.

In philosophy of science terms, the early use of focus groups as resources for conducting research was quite conservative in nature. This is not at all surprising given that the work of Lazarsfeld and Merton was funded by the military and included "interviewing groups of soldiers in Army camps about their responses to specific training films and so-called morale films" (Merton, 1987, p. 554). Their research also included studies of why people made war bond pledges. The goal of much of this work was to better understand people's beliefs and decision-making processes so as to develop increasingly effective forms of propaganda.

The kind of focus group research conducted by scholars such as Lazarsfeld and Merton all but disappeared within the field of sociology during the middle part of the 20th century, only to reemerge in the early 1980s, particularly around "audience analysis" work (Morley, 1980). When it did reemerge, it was no longer wed to—or used in the service of—predominantly quantitative-oriented research, a fact that Merton (1987) bemoaned:

> I gather that much of the focus-group research today as a growing type of market research does not involve this composite of both qualitative and quantitative inquiry. One gains the impression that focus-group research is being mercilessly misused as quick-and-easy

claims for the validity of the research [that] are not subjected to further quantitative tests. . . . For us, qualitative focused group interviews were taken as sources of new ideas and new hypothes[es], not as demonstrated findings with regard to the extent and distribution of the provisionally identified qualitative patterns of response. (pp. 557–558)

Criticisms such as these notwithstanding, audience analysis research was decidedly interpretive. Its primary goal was to understand the complexities involved in how people understood and interpreted media texts; its methods were nearly exclusively qualitative. In contrast to Lazarsfeld and Merton's work, which focused on expressed content, audience analysis researchers focused on group dynamics themselves, believing that the meanings constructed within groups of viewers were largely socially constructed.

Janice Radway, for example, used focus groups to great effect in her pioneering research on the reading practices of romance novel enthusiasts that resulted in her book, *Reading the Romance*. Radway's (1991) research took place in and around a local bookstore, and her participants included the store owner and a group of 42 women who frequented the store and were regular romance readers. Radway developed a mixed-method research design that included text analysis and focus group interviews. Assisted by the store owner ("Dot"), Radway was able to tap into the activity dynamics of the existing networks of women who were avid romance novel readers. These women depended heavily on the store owner for advice about the latest novels, and they interacted with each other as well. Radway simply "formalized" some of these ongoing social activities to generate a systematic and rich store of information about the social circumstances, specific reading practices, attitudes, reading preferences, and multiple and contradictory functions of romance reading among the women she studied. In this regard, only days after meeting Dot for the first time, Radway "conducted two four-hour discussion sessions with a total of 16 of Dot's most regular customers" (p. 47). Radway's involvement with romance novels and romance readers further intensified as the study progressed. She read all of the books that her participants were reading. She talked with many of the participants informally whenever she saw them at the bookstore. She took her cues about what books to read and what issues to focus discussions on from Dot and the other participants.

Radway (1991) noted, among other things, the importance of group dynamics in how different romance novels were interpreted and used. She also underscored the importance of belonging to a reading group in mitigating the stigma often associated with the practice of reading romance novels. Through their collective involvement, Dot and her customers (i.e., Radway's participants) created a kind of solidarity with political potential. Radway used her knowledge of the political potential of collective activity strategically in her research:

Because I knew beforehand that many women are afraid to admit their preference for romantic novels for fear of being scorned as illiterate or immoral, I suspected that the strength of numbers might make my informants less reluctant about discussing their obsession. (p. 252)

Finally, the ways in which Radway positioned herself within the reading groups were crucial. She noted, for example, that when she gently encouraged participants and backgrounded her own involvement, "the conversation flowed more naturally as the participants disagreed among themselves, contradicted one another, and delightedly discovered that they still agreed about many things" (p. 48).

All of the strategies that Radway deployed helped to mobilize the collective energy of the group and to generate kinds and amounts of data that are often difficult, if not impossible, to generate through individual interviews and even observations. In addition, these strategies—and participation in the focus groups themselves—helped to build a stronger and more effective collective with at least local political teeth. In this regard, Radway (1991) noted that the women used romance reading for two primary purposes: *combative* and *compensatory*. Each purpose is political in its own way, and each became understood more fully by the women in the context of their conversations and focus group discussions:

> It is *combative* in the sense that it enables them to refuse the other-directed social role prescribed for them within the institution of marriage. In picking up a book, as they have so eloquently told us, they are refusing temporarily their famil[ies'] otherwise constant demand that they attend to the wants of others even as they act deliberately to do something for their own private pleasure. Their activity is *compensatory*, then, in that it permits them to focus on themselves and to carve out a solitary space within an arena where their self-interest is usually identified with the interests of others and where they are defined as a public resource to be mined at will by the family. (p. 211)

These two political functions were clearly in tension at the end of *Reading the Romance*, and how this tension might work itself out over time was left unresolved. However, Radway concluded her book with a hopeful call for praxis: "It is absolutely essential that we who are committed to social change learn not to overlook this minimal but nonetheless legitimate form of protest . . . and to learn how best to encourage it and bring it to fruition" (p. 222).

If the work of Radway began to outline the political, ethical, and praxis potential of focus groups within qualitative inquiry, the work of Patti Lather has pushed the "limit conditions" of focus groups about as far as has the work of anyone in the field of qualitative research today, especially with respect to how focus groups can bring post-foundational possibilities for research "into the clearing" (Heidegger, 1975). In their book *Troubling the Angels*, for example, Lather and Smithies (1997) explored the lives, experiences, and narratives of 25 women living with HIV/AIDS. *Troubling the Angels* is a book filled with overlapping and contradictory voices that grew out of 5 years of focus group interviews conducted in the context of "support groups" in five major cities in Ohio:

> In the autumn of 1992, we met with one of the support groups to explore what questions we should use in the interviews. The women attending this meeting were spilling over with

excitement and ideas; their talk became a dialogue of issues and feelings and insights. Group process was producing a form and level of collaboration that could not be remotely duplicated in one-on-one interviews, so the decision was made to maintain the group format for most of the data collection. (p. xix)

Lather and Smithies also met and talked with these women at birthday parties and holiday get-togethers, hospital rooms and funerals, baby showers and picnics. The participation frameworks for interaction changed constantly across the project. Smithies, for example, noted that group dynamics were quite unpredictable and that the women often became upset or annoyed with each other (p. 194).

Although much of this book is devoted to troubling the waters of ethnographic representation, the lived experience of conducting fieldwork primarily through focus groups also troubles the waters of research practice. In this regard, Lather and Smithies integrated sociological, political, historical, therapeutic, political, and pedagogical practices and discourses in their work with the women they studied. In Lather's (2001) "postbook," for example, she claimed to have looked constantly for "the breaks and jagged edges of methodological practices from which we might draw useful knowledge for shaping present practices of a feminist ethnography in excess of our codes but, still, always already: forces already active in the present" (pp. 200–201). She continued,

> The task becomes to throw ourselves against the stubborn materiality of others, willing to risk loss, relishing the power of others to constrain our interpretive "will to know," saving us from the narcissism and its melancholy through the very positivities that cannot be exhausted by us, the otherness that always exceeds us. . . . Ethnography becomes a kind of self-wounding laboratory for discovering the rules by which truth is produced. Attempting to be accountable to complexity, thinking the limit becomes the task, and much opens up in terms of ways to proceed for those who know both too much and too little. (pp. 202–203)

In this regard, Lather elaborated on times when her experiences with the HIV/AIDS-afflicted women or their stories brought her to tears. She realized, in working with these women, that she had to negotiate her own relationship to loss. She wondered whether and how she could ever do it, and she sometimes doubted whether she could even go on with the project. In the most real sense, Lather came to realize the ways in which knowledge is always already embodied—bodily, viscerally, and materially— and the consequences that such a realization has for fieldwork and writing.

One of the most interesting sections of Lather and Smithies's (1997) book, for our purposes in this chapter, is one where the researchers cultivated a "methodology of getting lost":

> At some level, the book is about getting lost across the various layers and registers, about not finding one's way into making a sense that maps easily onto our usual ways of making sense. Here we all get lost: the women, the researchers, the readers, [and] the angels, in order to open up present frames of knowing to the possibilities of thinking differently. (p. 52)

Although these reflections refer to the book itself rather than to the process of conducting the research that led to the writing of the book, in the sense that the reflections index the political and ethical dimensions of all practices and all knowledge, they apply equally well to working with research participants in the field. For example, Lather and Smithies refused to position themselves as grand theorists and to interpret or explain the women's lives to them. Instead, they granted

> weight to lived experience and practical consciousness by situating both researcher and researched as bearers of knowledge while simultaneously attending to the "price" we pay for speaking out of discourses of truth, forms of rationality, effects of knowledge, and relations of power. (Lather, 2001, p. 215)

Through their tactical positioning, Lather and Smithies challenged the researcher's right to know and interpret the experiences of others while, at the same time, interrupting and getting in the way of their participants' attempts to narrate their lives through a kind of innocent ethnographic realism of voices speaking for themselves that included, among other things, the construction of AIDS as the work of God's will. In this regard, Lather and Smithies acknowledged their impositions and admitted that a different kind of book—a book that may, for example, be sold at Kmart—might have pleased their participants more. But such a book would not have served the researchers' own desires and goals to problematize the practice of qualitative inquiry. In the end, the book had to "please" both researchers and research participants—if only in partial and not completely satisfying ways.

These various relational and rhetorical tactics bring to light the very complicated and sometimes troubling micropolitics that are part and parcel of research practice in the "seventh moment," whether or not we are willing to "see" these micropolitics and enact them in our own work. The work of Lather and Smithies constantly reminds us that there are no easy separations between the researcher and the researched and that research itself is always already relational, political, and ethical work. There is no privileged place from which to experience and report on experiences objectively—only positions in dialogue. The key point here is that, more than most other research of which we are aware, the work of Lather and Smithies offers us ways in which to think about research that transcends and transforms the potentials of using focus groups for revisioning epistemology, interrogating the relative purchase of both lived experience and theory, reimagining ethics within research practice, and enacting fieldwork in ways that are more attuned to its sacred dimensions. This is difficult and dangerous work indeed:

> The danger is to steal knowledge from others, particularly those who have little else, and to use it for the interests of power. This is so even when the intended goal is to extend the reach of the very counter-knowledge [on which] the [work] is based, the stories entrusted to those "who enter [such alliances] from the side of privilege" (Fiske, 1996, p. 211) in order to transform the ubiquitous injustices of history into a readable place. (Lather, 2001, p. 221)

## Summary

As we have demonstrated, focus groups have been used as instruments of qualitative inquiry within several distinct epistemological moments—Merton's positivism, second-wave critical feminism, and poststructural feminism. And although focus groups have always been a critical part of qualitative research practice, their use seems to be expanding (e.g., Bloor et al., 2001; Fontana & Frey, 2000; Morgan, 2000). Among other things, the use of focus groups has allowed scholars to move away from the dyad of the clinical interview and to explore group characteristics and dynamics as relevant constitutive forces in the construction of meaning and the practice of social life. Focus groups have also allowed researchers to explore the nature and effects of ongoing social discourse in ways that are not possible through individual interviews or observations. Individual interviews strip away the critical interactional dynamics that constitute much of social practice and collective meaning making. Observations are a bit of a "crap shoot" in terms of capturing the focused activity in which researchers may be interested. In contrast to observations, focus groups can be used strategically to cultivate new kinds of interactional dynamics and, thus, access to new kinds of information.

For example, as Radway (1991) and Lather and Smithies (1997) showed, focus groups can be used strategically to inhibit the authority of researchers and to allow participants to "take over" and "own" the interview space. Focus groups are also invaluable for promoting among participants synergy that often leads to the unearthing of information that is seldom easy to reach in individual memory. Focus groups also facilitate the exploration of collective memories and shared stocks of knowledge that might seem trivial and unimportant to individuals but that come to the fore as crucial when like-minded groups begin to revel in the everyday. In addition, as was demonstrated especially in the work of Radway (1991) and Lather and Smithies (1997), focus groups can become sites for local political work. Finally, and perhaps most important, the work of Lather and Smithies brings to light the fact that focus groups are rife with multiple affordances for conducting "seventh moment" qualitative inquiry that will help it move through (and perhaps beyond) the triple crisis of representation, legitimation, and praxis that has haunted qualitative work for the past two decades. In this regard, focus groups can lead to the kinds of "breakdowns" that Lather (2001) described and that Heidegger (1927/1962) argued are essential to genuine understanding. They can also serve as constant reminders that researchers should cultivate productive relations among description, interpretation, and explanation in their work. And perhaps most important, the dialogic possibilities afforded by focus groups help researchers to work against premature consolidation of their understandings and explanations, thereby signaling the limits of reflexivity and the importance of intellectual/empirical modesty as forms of ethics and praxis. Such modesty allows us to engage in "doubled practices" where we listen to the attempts of others as they make sense of their lives. It also allows us to resist the seductive qualities of "too easy" constructs such as "voice" as we trouble experience itself, which is always already constituted within one "grand narrative" or another (Lather, 2001, p. 218). In the end, the strategic development of focus group activity for conducting qualitative inquiry foregrounds the possibility that focus groups can be key democratic spaces during an age when such spaces are becoming increasingly eclipsed and atomized (Giroux, 2001; Henaff & Strong, 2001).

## ◨ A CRITICAL SUMMARY OF FOCUS GROUPS IN RESEARCH PRACTICE

Focus group research is a key site or activity where pedagogy, politics, and interpretive inquiry intersect and interanimate each other. On a practical level, focus groups are efficient in the sense that they generate large quantities of material from relatively large numbers of people in a relatively short time. In addition, because of their synergistic potentials, focus groups often produce data that are seldom produced through individual interviewing and observation and that result in especially powerful interpretive insights. In particular, the synergy and dynamism generated within homogeneous collectives often reveal unarticulated norms and normative assumptions. They also take the interpretive process beyond the bounds of individual memory and expression to mine the historically sedimented collective memories and desires. This is one of the reasons why focus group work has been so well suited to the kinds of "problem-posing" and "problem-solving" pedagogies highlighted by Freire and Kozol. "Real-world" problems cannot be solved by individuals alone; instead, they require rich and complex funds of communal knowledge and practice.

In addition to enhancing the kinds and amounts of empirical material yielded from qualitative studies, focus groups foreground the importance not only of content, but also of expression, because they capitalize on the richness and complexity of group dynamics. Acting somewhat like magnifying glasses, focus groups induce social interactions akin to those that occur in everyday life but with greater focus. Focus groups, to a greater extent than observations and individual interviews, afford researchers access to the kinds of social interactional dynamics that produce particular memories, positions, ideologies, practices, and desires among specific groups of people.

As "staged conversations," focus groups are especially useful to researchers who want to conduct various kinds of discourse analyses such as those that we discussed earlier in relation to audience analysis. Focus groups allow researchers to see the complex ways in which people position themselves in relation to each other as they process questions, issues, and topics in focused ways. These dynamics themselves become relevant "units of analysis" for study.

In addition to inducing simulations of naturally occurring talk and social interaction, focus groups function to decenter the role of the researcher. As such, focus groups can facilitate the democratization of the research process, providing participants with more ownership over it, promoting more dialogic interactions and the joint construction of more polyvocal texts. These social facts were brought to light by the feminist work conducted by Madriz, Radway, and Lather and Smithies that we discussed earlier.

Focus groups, while functioning as sites for consolidating collective identities and enacting political work, also allow for the proliferation of multiple meanings and perspectives as well as for interactions between and among them. Because focus groups put multiple perspectives "on the table," they help researchers and research participants alike to realize that both the interpretations of individuals and the norms and rules of groups are inherently situated, provisional, contingent, unstable, and changeable. In this regard, focus groups help us to move toward constructing a "methodology of getting lost" and toward enacting "doubled practices" (Lather, 2001), which seem to be necessary first steps toward conducting "seventh moment" qualitative research.

▣  RETROSPECT AND PROSPECT: FOCUS GROUPS AS STRATEGIC
   ARTICULATIONS OF PEDAGOGY, POLITICS, AND INQUIRY

We conclude with some conceptual musings on focus group methodology as negotiated accomplishment and performative pedagogy rooted in local activism. Focus groups, we maintain, are sites where pedagogy, politics, and interpretive methodology converge, providing a way in which to think about new horizons in qualitative inquiry as praxis-oriented and ethically grounded relational work.

Importantly, opening up focus groups to genealogical analysis allows us to decenter our understanding of this method and to imagine and enact new uses and functions. Indeed, if linear or procedural methodological narratives have buttressed positivist and postpositivist approaches to research, the search for different origins makes us realize that there are no such safe spaces. If nothing else, Foucault's notion of genealogy makes us responsible for the discourses we inhabit and for the histories we evoke. Broadening the range of focus group "referents" allows us to think through contemporary research praxis in more expansive ways.

But there are no ready-made answers here. Ethics and responsibility must guide such a discussion, one that wholly implicates researchers every step of the way. This includes the ways in which researchers are positioned within and against the groups with which they work. To echo Fine (1994), researchers today must "work the hyphen" in their different roles (e.g., participant-observer) and responsibilities, always acknowledging the roles we inhabit, including what they allow and what they deny. Indeed, according to Fine, researchers must actively work against "othering" in fieldwork (i.e., objectively creating neatly bounded subjects on which to report) while also resisting self-reflexivity or navel gazing (i.e., the danger of looking inward as a way of avoiding the ethical responsibility of acting in the world). Fine challenged us to avoid what Haraway (1991) called the "god-tricks" of "relativism" and "totalization." As Haraway wrote, "Relativism is the perfect twin of totalization in the ideologies of objectivity; both deny the stakes in location, embodiment, and partial perspective" (p. 191). Location, embodiment, and partial perspective are critical to the project of fieldwork, according to Fine.

More recently, Fine and Weis (1998) extended these concerns to explicitly address the complexities of political activism and policymaking. They argued, for example, that we must try to "meld *writing about* and *working with*" politically invested actors in more compelling and constitutive ways (p. 277, emphases in original). Ultimately, Fine, Weis, Wessen, and Wong (2000) demanded that we "think through the power, obligations, and responsibilities of social research" on multiple levels, accounting for multiple social contexts and concerns (p. 108). Self-reflexivity means increasing kinds of responsibility for such questions in social contexts that are always difficult to prefigure. As Fine and Weis (1998) argued,

> our obligation is to come clean "at the hyphen," meaning that we interrogate in our writings who *we* are as we co-produce the narratives we presume to "collect." . . . As part of this discussion, we want, here, to try to explain how we, *as researchers,* work *with* communities to capture and build upon community and social movements. (pp. 277–278, emphasis in original)

This means expanding the range of roles that we play as researchers, field-workers, and authors to include political activism and policymaking—roles that do not always map easily onto each other. There are, in short, no safe spaces for qualitative researchers today. The notion of an objective and neutral qualitative inquiry has been decentered, leaving researchers with, to echo Bakhtin (1993), no alibis for their effectivity in the field. In the absence of foundational claims and clear splits between researchers and research participants, what is left is an uncertain landscape that asks us—no, demands us—to work with our participants to help make their situations better than they were when we found them. "The moral imperative of such work cannot be ignored," Lincoln and Denzin (2000) argued. They added, "We face a choice . . . of declaring ourselves committed to detachment or solidarity with the human community" (p. 1062).

Echoing Gramsci, we conclude that the "we" enabled by focus groups has "no guarantees." With no guarantees, focus groups must operate according to a "hermeneutics of vulnerability" (Clifford, 1988). Clifford developed the construct of a hermeneutics of vulnerability to discuss the constitutive effects of relationships between researchers and research participants on research practice and research findings. A hermeneutics of vulnerability foregrounds the ruptures of fieldwork, the multiple and contradictory positionings of all participants, the imperfect control of researchers, and the partial and perspectival nature of all knowledge. Among the primary tactics for achieving a hermeneutics of vulnerability, according to Clifford, is the tactic of self-reflexivity, which may be understood in at least two senses. In the first sense, self-reflexivity involves making transparent the rhetorical and poetic work of researchers in representing the objects of their studies. In the second (and, we think, more important) sense, self-reflexivity refers to the efforts of researchers and research participants to engage in acts of self-defamiliarization in relation to each other.

In this regard, Probyn (1993) discussed how the fieldwork experience can engender a virtual transformation of the identities of both researchers and research participants even as they are paradoxically engaged in the practice of consolidating them. This is important theoretically because it allows for the possibility of constructing a mutual ground between researchers and research participants even while recognizing that the ground is unstable and fragile. Self-reflexivity in this second sense is also important because it encourages reflection on interpretive research as the dual practice of knowledge gathering and self-transformation through self-reflection and mutual reflection with the other. Finally, as Lather (2001) showed, even self-reflexivity has serious limits with respect to working against the triple crisis of representation, legitimation, and praxis. Indeterminacies always remain. And allowing ourselves to dwell in (and perhaps even celebrate) these indeterminacies might be the best way of traveling down the roads of qualitative research practice and theory building at this particular historical juncture. Again, opening up to the unfinalizable complexity and heterogeneity of "others" within focus group interactions is at least one way of traveling down these roads.

## ▣ REFERENCES

Bakhtin, M. M. (1986). *Speech genres and other late essays* (V. W. McGee, Trans.). Austin: University of Texas Press.

Bakhtin, M. M. (1993). *Toward a philosophy of the act* (V. Liapunov, Trans.). Austin: University of Texas Press.

Barbour, R., & Kitzinger, J. (1999). *Developing focus group research.* Thousand Oaks, CA: Sage.

Behar, R. (1993). *Translated woman: Crossing the border with Esperanza's story.* Boston: Beacon.

Bloor, M., Frankland, J., Thomas, M., & Robson, K. (2001). *Focus groups in social research.* Thousand Oaks, CA: Sage.

Bourdieu, P., & Wacquant, L. J. D. (1992). *An invitation to reflexive sociology.* Chicago: University of Chicago Press.

Cape Cod Women's Liberation Movement. (1972). *Getting together: How to start a consciousness raising group.* [Online.] Retrieved March 10, 2003, from http://research.umbc.edu/~koren man/wmst/crguide2.html

Casali, A. (2002). The application of Paulo Freire's legacy in the Brazilian educational context. *Taboo, 6*(2), 9–16.

Clifford, J. (1988). *The predicament of culture.* Cambridge, MA: Harvard University Press.

Deleuze, G., & Guattari, F. (1987). *A thousand plateaus: Capitalism and schizophrenia* (B. Massumi, Trans.). Minneapolis: University of Minnesota Press.

Dill, B. T. (1994). Fictive kin, paper sons, and compadrazgo: Women of color and the struggle for family survival. In M. B. Zinn & B. T. Dill (Eds.), *Women of color in U.S. society* (pp. 149–169). Philadelphia: Temple University Press.

Eisenstein, H. (1984). *Contemporary feminist thought.* New York: Macmillan.

Espiritu, Y. L. (1997). *Asian women and men: Labor, laws, and love.* Thousand Oaks, CA: Sage.

Fals Borda, O. (Ed.). (1985). *The challenge of social change.* Beverly Hills, CA: Sage.

Fine, M. (1994). Working the hyphen: Reinventing self and other in qualitative research. In N. K. Denzin & Y. S. Lincoln (Eds.), *Handbook of qualitative research* (pp. 70–82). Thousand Oaks, CA: Sage.

Fine, M., & Weis, L. (1998). *The unknown city: Lives of poor and working-class young adults.* Boston: Beacon.

Fine, M., Weis, L., Wessen, S., & Wong, L. (2000). For whom? Qualitative research, representations, and social responsibilities. In N. K. Denzin & Y. S. Lincoln (Eds.), *Handbook of qualitative research* (2nd ed., pp. 107–131). Thousand Oaks, CA: Sage.

Fiske, J. (1996). Black bodies of knowledge: Notes on an effective history. *Cultural Critique, 33,* 185–212.

Fontana, A., & Frey, J. (2000). The interview: From structured questions to negotiated text. In N. K. Denzin & Y. S. Lincoln (Eds.), *Handbook of qualitative research* (2nd ed., pp. 645–672). Thousand Oaks, CA: Sage.

Foucault, M. (1977). *Discipline and punish: The birth of the prison* (A. Sheridan, Trans.). New York: Vintage.

Foucault, M. (1980). *Power/Knowledge: Selected interviews and other writings, 1972–1977* (C. Gordon, L. Marhall, J. Mepham, & K. Soper, Trans.). New York: Pantheon.

Foucault, M. (1984). Nietzsche, genealogy, history. In P. Rabinow (Ed.), *The Foucault reader* (pp. 76–100). New York: Pantheon Books.

Freire, P. (1993). *Pedagogy of the oppressed.* New York: Continuum (Original work published 1970).

Gere, A. R. (1997). *Writing groups: History, theory, and implications.* Carbondale: Southern Illinois University Press.

Gilkes, C. T. (1994). "If it wasn't for the women . ": African American women, community work, and social change. In M. B. Zinn & B. T. Dill (Eds.), *Women of color in U.S. society* (pp. 229–246), Philadelphia: Temple University Press.

Giroux, H. (2001). *Public spaces, private lives: Beyond the culture of cynicism.* Lanham, MD: Rowman & Littlefield.

Haraway, D. (1991). *Simians, cyborgs, and women.* London: Routledge.

Heidegger, M. (1962). *Being and time* (J. Macquarrie & E. Robinson, Trans.). San Francisco: Harper. (Original work published 1927)

Heidegger, M. (1975). *Poetry, language, and thought* (A. Hofstadter, Trans.). New York: Perennial.

Henaff, M., & Strong, T. (2001). *Public space and democracy.* Minneapolis: University of Minnesota Press.

Kamberelis, G., & Dimitriadis, G. (2005). On *qualitative inquiry.* New York: Columbia University, Teachers College Press.

Kozol, J. (1985). *Illiterate America.* New York: Random House.

Kozol, J. (1991). *Savage inequalities: Children in America's schools.* New York: Harper Perennial.

Krueger, R. A. (1994). *Focus groups: A practical guide for applied research* (2nd ed.). Thousand Oaks, CA: Sage.

Lather, P. (2001). Postbook: Working the ruins of feminist ethnography. *Signs: Journal of Women in Culture and Society, 27*(1), 199–227.

Lather, P., & Smithies, C. (1997). *Troubling the angels: Women living with HIV/AIDS.* Boulder, CO: Westview.

Lincoln, Y. S., & Denzin, N. K. (2000). The seventh moment: Out of the past. In N. K. Denzin & Y. S. Lincoln (Eds.), *Handbook of qualitative research* (2nd ed., pp. 1047–1065). Thousand Oaks, CA: Sage.

Lunt, P. (1996). Rethinking focus groups in media and communications research. *Journal of Communication, 46*(2), 79–98.

Madriz, E. (1997). *Nothing bad happens to good girls: Fear of crime in women's lives.* Berkeley: University of California Press.

Madriz, E. (2000). Focus groups in feminist research. In N. K. Denzin & Y. S. Lincoln (Eds.), *Handbook of qualitative research* (2nd ed., pp. 835–850). Thousand Oaks, CA: Sage.

Merton, R. (1987). The focused group interview and focus groups: Continuities and discontinuities. *Public Opinion Quarterly, 51,* 550–566.

Morgan, D. L. (1998). *The focus group guidebook.* Thousand Oaks, CA: Sage.

Morgan, D. L. (2000). Focus group interviewing. In J. Gubrium & J. Holstein (Eds.), *Handbook of interview research: Context and method* (pp. 141–160). Thousand Oaks, CA: Sage.

Morley, D. (1980). *The "nationwide" audience.* London: British Film Institute.

Probyn, E. (1993). *Sexing the self: Gendered positions in cultural studies.* New York: Routledge.

Radway, J. (1991). *Reading the romance: Women, patriarchy, and popular literature.* Chapel Hill: University of North Carolina Press.

Sarachild, K. (1978). Consciousness-raising: A radical weapon. In Redstockings of the Women's Liberation Movement (Eds.), *Feminist revolution* (pp. 144–150). New York: Random House.

Schensul, J. J., LeCompte, M. D., Nastatsi, B. K., & Borgatti, S. P. (1999). *Enhanced ethnographic methods: Audiovisual techniques, focused group interviews, and elicitation techniques.* Walnut Creek, CA: AltaMira.

# Part II

# THE ART AND PRACTICES OF INTERPRETATION, EVALUATION, AND REPRESENTATION

I n conventional terms, Part II signals the terminal phase of qualitative inquiry. The researcher or evaluator now assesses, analyzes, and interprets the empirical materials that have been collected. This process, conventionally conceived, implements a set of analytic procedures that produce interpretations, which are then integrated into a theory or put forward as a set of policy recommendations. The resulting interpretations are assessed in terms of a set of criteria, from the positivist or postpositivist tradition, including validity, reliability, and objectivity. Those interpretations that stand up to scrutiny are put forward as the findings of the research.

The contributors to this Part explore the art, practices, and politics of interpretation, evaluation, and representation. In so doing, they return to the themes of Part I (Volume 1)—that is, asking *how the discourses of qualitative research can be used to help create and imagine a free democratic society.* In returning to this question, it is understood that the processes of analysis, evaluation, and interpretation are neither terminal nor mechanical. They are like a dance, to invoke the metaphor used by Valerie Janesick. This dance is informed at every step of the way by a commitment to this civic agenda. The processes that define the practices of interpretation and representation are always ongoing, emergent, unpredictable, and unfinished. They are always embedded in an ongoing historical and political context. As argued throughout this volume, in the United States, neoconservative discourse in the educational arena (e.g., No Child Left Behind, National Research Council) privileges experimental criteria in the funding, implementation, and evaluation of scientific inquiry. Many of the authors in this volume observe that this creates a chilling climate for qualitative inquiry. We begin by assessing a number of criteria that have been traditionally (as well as recently) used to judge the adequacy of qualitative research. These criteria flow from the major paradigms now operating in this field.

## ▣ RELATIVISM, CRITERIA, AND POLITICS

John Smith and Phil Hodkinson (Chapter 13, this volume) remind us that we live in an age of relativism. In the social sciences today, there is no longer a God's-eye view that guarantees absolute methodological certainty; to assert such is to court embarrassment. Indeed, as Guba and Lincoln discuss in detail in Volume 1, Chapter 8 (Part II), there is considerable debate over what constitutes good interpretation in qualitative research. Nonetheless, there seems to be an emerging consensus that all inquiry reflects the standpoint of the inquirer, that all observation is theory laden, and that there is no possibility of theory-free knowledge. We can no longer think of ourselves as neutral spectators of the social world.

Consequently, as Smith and Hodkinson observe, until quite recently few spoke in terms of foundational epistemologies and ontological realism. Before the assault of methodological conservativism, relativists would calmly assert that no method is a neutral tool of inquiry, hence the notion of procedural objectivity could not be sustained. Anti-foundationalists thought that the days of naïve realism and naïve positivism were over. In their place stand critical and historical realism and various versions of relativism. The criteria for evaluating research had become relative, moral, and political.

However, events during the past 5 years, including governmental attempts to mandate research criteria in the United States and the United Kingdom, have disturbed this situation. Power and politics now play a major part in discussions of criteria.

Extending Smith and Hodkinson, there are three basic positions on the issue of evaluative criteria: foundational, quasi-foundational, and nonfoundational. There are still those who think in terms of a *foundational* epistemology. They would apply the same criteria to qualitative research as are employed in quantitative inquiry, contending that there is nothing special about qualitative research that demands a special set of evaluative criteria. As indicated in our introduction to Part II, the positivist and postpositivist paradigms apply four standard criteria to disciplined inquiry: internal validity, external validity, reliability, and objectivity. The use of these criteria, or their variants, is consistent with the foundational position.

In contrast, *quasi-foundationalists* approach the criteria issue from the standpoint of a non-naïve, neo-, or subtle realism. They contend that the discussion of criteria must take place within the context of an ontological neorealism and a constructivist epistemology. They believe in a real world that is independent of our fallible knowledge of it. Their constructivism commits them to the position that there can be no theory-free knowledge. Proponents of the quasi-foundational position argue that a set of criteria unique to qualitative research needs to be developed. Hammersley (1992, p. 64; 1995, p. 18; see also Wolcott, 1999, p. 194) is a leading proponent of this position. He wants to maintain the correspondence theory of truth while suggesting that researchers assess a study in terms of its ability to (a) generate generic/formal theory, (b) be empirically grounded and scientifically credible, (c) produce findings that can be generalized or transferred to other settings, and (d) be internally reflexive in terms of taking account of the effects of the researcher and the research strategy on the findings that have been produced.

Hammersley reduces his criteria to three essential terms: plausibility (is the claim plausible?), credibility (is the claim based on credible evidence?), and relevance (what is the claim's relevance for knowledge about the world?). Of course, these terms require social judgments. They cannot be assessed in terms of any set of external or foundational criteria. Their meanings are arrived at through consensus and discussion in the scientific community. Within Hammersley's model, there is no satisfactory method for resolving this issue of how to evaluate an empirical claim.

For the *nonfoundationalists,* relativism is not an issue. They accept the argument that there is no theory-free knowledge. Relativism or uncertainty is the inevitable consequence of the fact that, as humans, we have finite knowledge of ourselves and the world in which we live. Nonfoundationalists contend that the injunction to pursue knowledge cannot be given epistemologically; rather, the injunction is moral and political. Accordingly, the criteria for evaluating qualitative work are also moral and fitted to the pragmatic, ethical, and political contingencies of concrete situations. Good or bad inquiry in any given context is assessed in terms of criteria such as those outlined by Greenwood and Levin (Volume 1, Chapter 2), Fine and Weis (Volume 1, Chapter 3), Smith (Volume 1, Chapter 4), Bishop (Volume 1, Chapter 5), and Christians (Volume 1, Chapter 6) in Volume 1, Part I; Guba and Lincoln (Volume 1, Chapter 8 in Part II); Kemmis and McTaggart (Volume 2, Chapter 10); and Angrosino (Chapter 5, this volume). These are the criteria that flow from a feminist, communitarian moral ethic of empowerment, community, and moral solidarity. Returning to Christians (Volume 1, Chapter 6), this moral ethic calls for research rooted in the concepts of care, shared governance, neighborliness, love, and kindness. Furthermore, this work should provide the foundations for social criticism and social action.

In an ideal world, the anti- or nonfoundational narrative would be uncontested. But today in the United States and the United Kingdom, as Smith and Hodkinson observe, opponents are embracing "more crudely empiricist procedures, even the experimental or quasi-experimental procedures common to the natural sciences." There is a concerted effort by governmental regimes to reform research. This is disconcerting, all the more so when social scientists collaborate in the project. Dark days are ahead of us.

## ▣ EMANCIPATORY DISCOURSES AND THE ETHICS AND POLITICS OF INTERPRETATION

Norman Denzin's (Chapter 14, this volume) contribution invites indigenous and nonindigenous qualitative researchers to take up an emancipatory discourse, connecting indigenous epistemologies and theories of decolonization with critical pedagogy, and a global decolonizing discourse. Advocating the use of critical personal narratives, Denzin encourages the development of a postcolonial indigenous participatory theater focused on racism, inequality, memory, and cultural loss.

## ▣ WRITING: A METHOD OF INQUIRY

Writers interpret as they write, so writing is a form of inquiry, a way of making sense of the world. Laurel Richardson and Elizabeth Adams St. Pierre (Chapter 15, this volume) explore new writing and interpretive styles that follow from the narrative literary turn in the social sciences. They call these different forms of writing CAP (creative analytical processes) ethnography. Their chapter is divided into three parts. Part 1, authored by Richardson, explores these forms. In Part 2, St. Pierre provides an analysis of how writing as a method of inquiry coheres with the development of ethical selves. In Part 3, Richardson provides some writing practices and exercises for the qualitative writer.

New forms include autoethnography, fiction stories, poetry, drama, performance texts, polyvocal texts, readers' theater, responsive readings, aphorisms, comedy and satire, visual presentations, conversation, layered accounts, writing stories, and mixed genres. Richardson discusses in detail one class of experimental genre that she calls evocative representations. Work in this genre includes narratives of the self, writing stories, ethnographic fictional representations, poetic representation, ethnographic drama, and mixed genres.

The crystal is a central image in Richardson's text, and she contrasts it with the triangle. Traditional postpositivist research has relied on triangulation, including the use of multiple methods, as a method of validation. The model implies a fixed point of reference that can be triangulated. Richardson illustrates the crystallization process with excerpts from her recent book with Ernest Lockridge.

Mixed genre texts do not triangulate. The central imag;e is the crystal, which "combines symmetry and substance with an infinite variety of shapes, substances, transmutations, . . . and angles of approach." Crystals are prisms that reflect and refract, creating ever-changing images and pictures of reality. Crystallization deconstructs the traditional idea of validity, for now there can be no single or triangulated truth.

Richardson offers five criteria for evaluating CAP ethnography: substantive contribution, aesthetic merit, reflexivity, impactfulness, and ability to evoke lived experience. She concludes with a list of writing practices—ways of using writing as a method of knowing.

St. Pierre troubles conventional understandings of ethics. Drawing on Derrida and Deleuze, she places ethics under deconstruction: "What happens when we cannot apply the rules?" We must not be unworthy of what happens to us. We struggle to be worthy, to be willing to be worthy.

## ▣   ANTHROPOLOGICAL POETICS

Anthropologists have been writing experimental, literary, and poetic ethnographic texts for at least 40 years. In this part, three different forms of poetics are represented. Ivan Brady (Chapter 16, this volume) writes poetically about method, about a way of getting to know places by their effects on our personal experience. He invokes the environmental poets, offering a prolegomena to a poetics of place.

Using the literary poetic form, Brady enacts a moral aesthetic, an aesthetic that allows him to say new things about place, space, wild spaces, beings, self, nature, identity, meaning, and life on this threatened planet. In so doing, he pushes the boundaries of artful discourse. Thus are the boundaries between the humanities and the human sciences blurred. In this blurring, our moral sensibilities are enlivened. We are able to imagine new ways of being ourselves in this bewilderingly complex world called the present.

## ▣   CULTURAL POESIS

In a chapter that defies description, Kate Stewart (Chapter 17, this volume) offers a piece of imaginative writing grounded in the poetics of ordinary things. She gives us provocations, glimpses out of the corner of the eye, a montage, a fractured text, cultural poesis during times of violence, chaos and loss in U.S. public culture, a roller-coaster ride through somebody's dreamland, ordinary life somewhere, games, eating in, walking the dog, shopping, raking the yard, political posters in the front yard, a plastic Jesus, a shrine, yellow ribbons, surging bodies, the train screaming out a warning, nothing adding up to anything except some of us starting to lose hope yesterday.

## ▣   INVESTIGATIVE POETICS

Stephen Hartnett and Jeremy Engels (Chapter 18, this volume) offer a poetics of witnessing, an aria in time of war. In so doing, they respond to the call of Ralph Waldo Emerson, who demanded that a poet should strive toward becoming "the knower, the doer, and the sayer." Building on Emerson, they advocate an investigative poetics, a "combination of serious scholarship, passionate activism, and experimental representation."

Hartnett and Engels write to offer a poetry that problematizes politics, that bears witness to the ways in which social structures are embodied in lived experience, a poetic that functions as a genealogical critique of power. Their essay unfolds in four movements, going from the political poetry of Carolyn Forché and Edward Sanders to a discussion of social justice discourse in the humanities. They then criticize the movement known as ethnopoetics, concluding with a positive discussion of the political poetics of John Dos Passos, Carolyn Forché, and Peter Dale Scott.

## ◼ QUALITATIVE EVALUATION AND CHANGING SOCIAL POLICY

Program evaluation, of course, is a major site of qualitative research. (Earlier *Handbook* chapters by Greenwood & Levin [Volume 1, Chapter 2] in Part I and by Stake [Volume 2, Chapter 3], Kemmis & McTaggart [Volume 2, Chapter 10], and Miller & Crabtree [Volume 2, Chapter 11] established this fact.) Evaluators are interpreters. Their texts tell stories. These stories are inherently moral and political. Starting in 1965 and moving to the present, House (Chapter 19, this volume) offers a sobering historical analysis of qualitative evaluation and changing social policy. He observes that the field has moved from faddish experimental and quantitative evaluation studies (1960s), to small-scale qualitative studies, to meta-analyses and program theory. A move from a model of value-free inquiry to committed social justice projects, and back again, is also part of this history. During the 1980s, evaluation moved away from "quantitative methods and value-free studies toward multiple methodologies and qualitative studies focused on stakeholders, social justice issues, and participatory techniques."

Neoconservatives viewed such work as too permissive and argued against it. Since September 11, 2001, a neoconservative fundamentalism has taken hold of federal policy—from foreign affairs, to domestic affairs, to evaluation itself. President George W. Bush's neofundamentalism has taken the form of methodological fundamentalism in the field of evaluation. As argued previously, federal agencies that sponsor evaluation have "aggressively pushed the concept of 'evidence-based' progress, policies, and programs."

The core of this belief is the argument that research and evaluation must be scientific, that is, based on randomized experimental designs. This method of inquiry is written into federal legislation! The Bush educational policy thus implements four concepts: accountability, options for parents, local control, and evidence-based instruction.

The use of the medical model of evidence-based inquiry is predicated on the belief that education is a field of fads; the failure of our schools reflects this. In contrast, medicine, with its randomized field trials, has made significant progress in improving human health. Education should do the same. Of course, many of the fads in education have been inspired by conservatives—vouchers, charter schools, accountability through test scores. Medicine's progress can be attributed to breakthroughs in allied fields, not randomized trials.

And so the field comes full circle. We are back to the experimental models of the 1960s. Do we have the courage to stand up to this conservative assault?

## ▣ CONCLUSIONS

The chapters in Part II affirm our position that qualitative research has come of age. Multiple discourses now surround topics that during earlier historical moments were contained within the broad grasp ways of the positivist and postpositivist epistemologies. There are now many in which to write, read, assess, evaluate, and apply qualitative research texts. Even so, there are pressures to turn back the clock. This complex field invites reflexive appraisal, hence the topic of Volume 1, Part III—the future of qualitative research.

## ▣ REFERENCES

Hammersley, M. (1992). *What's wrong with ethnography?* London: Routledge.
Hammersley, M. (1995). *The politics of social research.* London: Sage.
Wolcott, H. F. (1999). *Ethnography: A way of seeing.* Walnut Creek, CA: AltaMira.

# 13

# RELATIVISM, CRITERIA, AND POLITICS

John K. Smith and Phil Hodkinson

I n a chapter that one of the authors (John Smith) wrote with Deborah Deemer on criteria for judging social and educational research for the second edition of the *Handbook,* the issue of power and criteria was briefly mentioned. Smith and Deemer (2000) said that they were not so naïve as to claim that power, and by extension (but unmentioned) politics, could ever be eliminated from judgments about the quality of research as these judgments are played out in a social context. Citing Hazelrigg (1989), they added that there was no point in embracing some sort of a romanticized "intellectualized flight from power" (Smith & Deemer, 2000, p. 202). In fact, although they did not say so, they certainly could have added that there is nothing wrong with politics and the exercise of power per se in this instance or in other instances. The central issue has been, and remains, about how the political process operates, how power is exercised, and what goals those participating in the process desire.

Because of certain events over the past few years, including governmental attempts to mandate research criteria in both the United States and the United Kingdom, it is clear that the relationship of power, politics, and criteria must be discussed at much greater length. In this chapter, we elaborate on these issues.

The starting point for our discussion is a reiteration of the main conclusion that Smith and Deemer (2000) reached in the second edition of the *Handbook:* We have come to the end of our attempts to secure an epistemological foundation for our knowledge and must acknowledge that we are in the era of relativism.

We pursue this reiteration in two parts. First, we discuss the well-known and frequently argued point that individual researchers cannot step outside their own social and historical standpoints. Because there is no possibility of theory-free observation and knowledge, the subject–object dualism of empiricism is untenable and the claim to objectivity is a chimera. Second, we discuss the condition that the conduct of research, and especially the judgments about its worth, represents social activities. In the absence of an epistemological foundation, which is essential to any claim that criteria can be neutral and objective, decisions about what the criteria for research are or should be, as well as decisions about how criteria are put into practice, result from complex social interactions. And, as with all such social interactions, individuals and groups work to further their own interests, both legitimately and (occasionally) illegitimately, although it must be added that judgments about what is legitimate versus illegitimate are themselves socially determined at any given time and place. These conditions make the process of determining research criteria and how they are to be applied unavoidably contestable and, hence, political.

Following this revisiting, we then briefly note two common responses to the demise of empiricism and the end of the pretense to objectivity, define relativism, and discuss what the latter means for the issue of criteria. Finally, we examine the role that politics plays, both generally and in the specific U.S. and U.K. contexts at the time when this chapter was being written, in the making of judgments about the quality of social and educational research. This examination, in particular, focuses on the political pressures that are being brought to bear in the attempt to reestablish or reassert that the broadly empiricist understandings about research and criteria are the only understandings that can, or should, be accepted. We find in play here both a politics of avoidance of the compelling arguments advanced against empiricism by relativist researchers and a politics directed at marginalizing the messengers.

Two basic definitions are needed before we begin. First, we define politics in a conventional sense as the process of allocating scarce resources. Any desired resource that is not totally abundant—be it money, social prestige, recognition, research grants, or whatever—must be divided up through a political process with some people getting more and others getting less of whatever is desired. Judgments about research quality and what counts as research are central to the allocation of such scarce resources for researchers. It is here that the political dimensions of research activity are most significant. Power is the ability of individuals or groups to realize their will even if others are opposed. If one knows the distribution of access to power in a group, an organization, or a society, one can understand the distribution of scarce resources and vice versa.

## ▣ CRITERIA AS METHOD

The point of research as traditionally, and thus conventionally, understood has long been thought of as a matter of discovering the truth. Within the empiricist epistemological perspective that has dominated our understanding of research, truth is defined as the accurate representation of an independently existing reality. The accumulation of knowledge is thereby considered to be the accumulation of accurate representations of what is (independently) outside of us. The paradigmatic example of what also is called the spectator theory of knowledge, with the accompanying definition of truth in corresponding terms, involves the cat and the mat. If one says the cat is on the mat and, in fact, we observe that the cat is actually on the mat, then words correspond to reality and the truth has been spoken.

The central problem with this empiricist perspective on inquiry is that of making good on this idea of correspondence. Making good in this context means somehow connecting that which empiricism separated—the knowing subject from the object of knowing—and doing so in such a way that the activities of the former would not distort the reality of the latter. The solution of choice to cash in this correspondence theory, as has long been noted in our social and educational research textbooks, is a methodical one. The point is quite straightforward: If the proper procedures are applied, the subjectivities (e.g., opinions, ideologies) of the knowing subject would be constrained and the knower could thereby gain an accurate and objective depiction of reality. Those researchers who adhered to method would thereby possess, in contrast to all others, what one might call the well-polished Cartesian mirror of the mind. Kerlinger (1979) put it bluntly:

> The procedures of science are objective—not the scientists. Scientists, like all men and women, are opinionated, dogmatic, [and] ideological. . . . That is the very reason for insisting on procedural objectivity: to get the whole business outside of ourselves. (p. 264)

Method is thereby *the* crucial factor in any judgment made about the quality of research.

Over the course of the past half century, empiricism as a theory of knowledge with the claims of objectivity, neutrality, and so forth has come on hard times; as a result, the methodical solution to the problem of criteria has been very seriously undermined. Philosophers of science, and especially philosophers of social science, have noted numerous intractable problems associated with this methodical solution to reconnect what empiricism had separated—the dualism of the knowing subject and the object of knowing. Because this territory has been covered with frequency (for a brief recounting of this history, see Smith, 1989), we need to mention only a few key points.

Within Anglo-American philosophical circles, a good case can be made that Hanson and Kuhn were central among those who brought the subject–object dualism issue to the forefront. At the core of Hanson's (1958) arguments was the now seemingly obvious point that "the theory, hypothesis, framework, or background held by an investigator can strongly influence what is observed" (p. 7). A few years later, Kuhn (1962) followed up on this line of reasoning with his talk about incommensurable paradigms, paradigm shifts, the fact that all knowledge is framework dependent, and so forth. By the mid- to late 1980s, the work of numerous other people left little doubt that the claim that theory-free knowledge and observation is possible and is intellectually untenable (e.g., see Bernstein, 1983; Gadamer, 1995; Goodman, 1978; Nagel, 1986; Putnam, 1981; Taylor, 1971).

The arguments made by these philosophers combined with another series of arguments that focused directly on the claim that method itself was neutral or that it could be the repository of procedural objectivity. The fact that such a claim could not be sustained is the central message that can be taken from the work of Cherryholmes (1988), Giddens (1976), Hesse (1980), MacKenzie (1981), Smith (1985), and others. The result of all this intellectual ferment was the elaboration of a number of points of great consequence for any discussion of criteria, namely that there is no possibility of theory-free observation and knowledge, the claim of the duality of subject and object cannot be made good, no special epistemic privilege can be attached to any particular method or set of methods, and we cannot have the kind of access to an external extralinguistic referent that would allow us to claim the discovery of truth in accurate representation or correspondence terms.

Based on these points, the only conclusion that can be reached is that we no longer can talk in terms of a foundational epistemology and a direct contact with reality. There is no possibility of the objective stance or view—often called the "God's eye" point of view—and all we can have are "the various points of view of actual persons reflecting various interests and purposes that their descriptions and theories subserve" (Putnam, 1981, p. 50). With the demise of empiricism and the methodical stance on criteria, social and educational research must be seen for what it has always been—a practical and moral activity, not an epistemological one. And because we have no epistemological foundation for our practical and moral activities, any discussion of criteria must come to terms with, in one form or another, the issue of relativism.

## ▣ RESPONSES

Over the recent past, there have been at least two general responses, with the usual numerous variations on theme, to those who have argued that epistemological foundationalism is over and that the criteria for judging research cannot be "fixed" but rather are the product of time- and place-contingent social processes. In the first instance, some people have advanced various lines of argument that can be labeled, albeit loosely, as neorealist (e.g., see Bhaskar, 1979; Hammersley, 1990; Manicas, 1987; Manicas & Secord, 1983; Phillips & Burbules, 2000; Pring, 2000; see also Popper, 1959, 1972, arguably the intellectual precursor of all neorealists). Second, other people recently have attempted to reassert empiricism and criteria as method (e.g., so far as educational research is concerned, see Oakley, 2000; Shavelson & Towne, 2002; Slavin, 2002; Tooley & Darby, 1998).

Other than a brief summary, we do not discuss or critique the neorealist and reassertive positions and their respective approaches to criteria. In the past, we have written such "attempt to persuade" or "conversion" pieces, as we now have come to call them, and these are readily available to interested readers (Garratt & Hodkinson, 1998; Hodkinson, 1998, 2004; Hodkinson & Smith, 2004; Smith, 1993). Although we think that the philosophical exchanges we have engaged in have been intriguing and are important to keep a conversion going, conversion by way of persuasive argument seems to occur rather rarely. Thus, in this chapter, we forgo such attempts and only summarize briefly the previously noted positions, with very limited comments, and then elaborate on our take on relativism, criteria, and politics.

There is little question that non-naïve realists or neorealists have made numerous sophisticated attempts to address the issue of criteria. These neorealist responses share in common a commitment to an ontological realism, on the one side, and a constructivist epistemology, on the other. The former means that these neorealists are committed to the proposition that there is a real world out there independent of our interest in or knowledge of that world. The latter announces their commitment to the idea that we can never know for sure whether we have depicted that reality as it really is. Although the line of argument varies, these non-naïve realists or neorealists "assert a belief in a real world independent of our knowledge while also making it clear that our knowledge of this metacognitive world is quite fallible" (Leary, 1984, p. 918).

Given these dual commitments, the neorealists then argue that criteria that are not strictly contingent on time and place can be developed. Hammersley (1990), for example, attempted to elaborate criteria to hold off the contingent nature of judgment or, put differently, to prevent a slide into what is, for him, the void of relativism. His criteria of choice, or the two key elements necessary for judging the validity of a study, are what he called plausibility and credibility. In the former instance, to say that a claim is plausible is to say that it is "likely to be true given our existing knowledge" (p. 61). He argued that some claims are so plausible that we can immediately accept them at face value, whereas other claims require the presentation of evidence. In the latter case, a judgment about credibility must be undertaken "given the nature of the phenomena concerned, the circumstances of the research" (p. 61), and so forth. And, as with plausibility, when a claim lacks face credibility, evidence is required. However, Hammersley further recognized that the particular evidence presented by a researcher in support of the plausibility and credibility of a study must itself be assessed for its own plausibility and credibility. And, as he continued, "we may require further evidence to support that evidence, which we shall judge in terms of plausibility and credibility" (p. 62).

For us, Hammersley's (1990) argument became deeply entangled in an infinite regress—if not a hermeneutic circle. It is at this point where it was necessary for him to call on his neorealism to do some work—in particular, the work of making contact with reality in such a way as to blunt this infinite regress or get one out of the hermeneutic circle of interpretation. Or, put differently, it was time for him to call on his version of realism to prevent the relativism that would seem to lie at the end of it all. This was not the case, however, and any notions about correspondence and realism, no matter how subtle, played no role of consequence for the balance of Hammersley's discussion. His arguments ultimately ended up at the only place they could go—with a discussion of the norms that *should* govern discourse among members of a scientific community as they attempt to make judgments about plausibility and credibility. These are norms because they refer to what "should be" and thereby yield to no final or foundational answers that are contestable and inevitably influenced by political processes.

A similar situation can be pointed out with reference to the work of Manicas and Secord (1983) and the well-known idea of warranted assertability. Their version of neorealism led them to note that "knowledge is a social and historical product" (p. 401), there is "no preinterpreted 'given,' and the test of truth cannot be 'correspondence.' Epistemologically, there can be nothing known to which our ideas (sentences, theories) can correspond" (p. 401). Based on these points, Manicas and Secord then addressed the issue of how to connect experiences, which are always—and can only—be culturally and historically mediated, with reality independent from experience. Their response was the negative assertion that although there is no theory-free observation, this "does not eliminate the possibility of objectivity, construed here as warranted assertability" (p. 410). For us, this placed them in the same situation as was faced by Hammersley (1990) because the warrants that one brings to judgments are themselves socially and historically conditioned—as are the warrants that warrant the warrants, and so forth. Again, they were caught in a hermeneutic circle or an infinite regress and were unable to offer a way in which to access an external referent that would allow them out of the former or to stop the latter.

A second line of response, recently asserted with vigor in both the United States and the United Kingdom, holds that social and educational inquiry should strongly embrace more crudely empiricist procedures, even the experimental or quasi-experimental procedures common to the natural sciences. In the United States, this position has been most widely advanced by the report from the National Research Council Committee (Shavelson & Towne, 2002). This report was supported by a contract between the National Research Council and the U.S. Department of Education's National Educational Research Policy and Priorities Board. In the United Kingdom, a similar but less harshly experimental position has been advanced with the critiques of the quality of British educational research at the hands of Tooley with Darby (1998) and Hillage, Pearson, Anderson, and Tamkin (1998). The former report was commissioned by the Office for Standards in Education (OFSTED), the government-established national inspection agency for schools, whereas the latter report was sponsored by the government department directly responsible for education.

In Chapter 3 of the Shavelson and Towne (2002) report, the principles of scientific inquiry were set forth. These guiding principles for educational research, not surprisingly, are very much like those that have been central to standard, empiricist-inspired, introductory research texts. The terms of discourse, for example, are those of replicate, generalize, random assignment, and so forth. In Chapter 5 of the report, the committee fleshed out these principles with a discussion of the designs for conducing scientific educational research. What they referred to as "more rigorous studies" are those that are of an experimental nature with well-defined hypotheses and so forth in place before data collection and analysis. At this point, it is clear that the methods or procedures employed by researchers are the crucial factor in any judgment of their research as good or bad.

Placed between these two chapters in the Shavelson and Towne (2002) report was one in which they addressed some of the unique features of educational inquiry—and, again by extension, social inquiry—that they argued set this inquiry apart from other fields of inquiry. They noted factors such as human volition, the central role of ethics that limits control group possibilities, rapid changes in educational programs, and so forth. These and other conditions mean that educational and social researchers are not able to exercise the same degree of control over their subject matter as are, for example, physical scientists. The committee's response to this diminution of control was to say that educational and social researchers must "pay close attention to context" when pursuing and interpreting the results of their research. Exactly what they meant by paying close attention to context was not clearly discussed. What is clear, and what is most important, is that they did not include the researcher as part of the context. This position runs counter to the now generally accepted idea that we, even as researchers, cannot undertake theory-free observation and produce theory-free knowledge.

Finally, Shavelson and Towne's (2002) comments about qualitative research and the relationship of qualitative and quantitative approaches to inquiry are difficult to interpret in that there appeared to be some ambiguity present. They declared, with citations but without argument, that the two approaches are "epistemologically quite similar" and that "we do not distinguish between them as being different forms of inquiry" (p. 19). That said, they also noted that "sharp distinctions between qualitative and qualitative inquiry have divided the field" (p. 19). This comment was followed by a concern that "the current trend of schools of education to favor qualitative methods, often at the expense of quantitative methods, has invited criticism" (p. 19). This statement was not supported by citations, and the nature of the criticism was not mentioned. Not surprisingly, one is then left to wonder about what the problem is here. If both approaches are similar and we cannot distinguish between them, then what is the reason for the concern and criticism?

In Chapter 5 of Shavelson and Towne's (2002) report, however, their take on the position of qualitative inquiry relative to quantitative inquiry could be noted more clearly. They stated that all scientific studies must begin with clear questions that can be researched empirically. They added,

> More rigorous studies will begin with more precise statements of the underlying theory driving the inquiry and will generally have a well-specified hypothesis before [the] data collection and testing phase is begun. Studies that do not start with clear conceptual

frameworks and hypotheses may still be scientific, although they are obviously at a more rudimentary level and will generally require follow-up study to contribute significantly to scientific knowledge. (p. 101)

Because qualitative studies are more loosely defined before data gathering begins, they are more rudimentary than quantitative studies—the lack of epistemological distinction between them notwithstanding—and are primarily valuable for generating hypotheses for studies that are more rigorous. (As an aside, we must note that this may have taken us "full circle," so to speak. See Abel's [1948] comments about how interpretive inquiry is valuable for generating hypotheses to be turned over to real researchers for rigorous testing with their empiricist or scientific methods.)

The position taken by Shavelson and Towne (2002) is paralleled in the discussions of research quality in the United Kingdom, as advanced by Tooley and Darby (1998) and Hillage and colleagues (1998). Tooley and Darby's approach was to analyze the quality of educational research articles that appeared in four high-status U.K. academic journals. They declared that the overall standard of inquiry was far too low and their sponsor concluded that "much [educational research] that is published is, on this analysis, at best no more than an irrelevance or distraction" (p. 1). They found two main problems with a significant portion of educational research. First, there was the issue of the increasing prominence of qualitative research. About this greater increase, they stated, "The key problem lies in the subjectivity of qualitative research" (p. 43) because of the lack, most particularly, of triangulation. In addition, they were very critical of the large amount of research—overwhelmingly of a qualitative approach—that uses broad sociological theorizing and/or focuses on the lives of disadvantaged people and groups in society. Thus, Tooley and Darby chose as an example of particular strident criticism an article by Sparkes (1994) in which he argued that the oppressions faced by a lesbian physical education teacher were a social issue rather than an individual one.

Hillage and colleagues (1998), following Tooley and Darby (1998), also took an approach similar to that of Shavelson and Towne (2002). Hillage and colleagues stated that not enough educational research was of sufficient quality and relevance to serve the needs of practitioners and policymakers. The essence of their critique was that educational research in the United Kingdom was too small scale, was not cumulative, was too often of low standard, and (most interesting) was biased toward qualitative case studies. The solution was obvious: What was needed was more large-scale, cumulative research based on a scientific approach—in other words, an increase in quantitative research and/or research using mixed methods.

Although there are certainly many variations among them, in the end, Shavelson and Towne (2002), Tooley and Darby (1998), and Hillage and colleagues (1998) broadly shared three things. First, they all wrote reports sponsored or funded by government educational agencies that had decided to get into the business of sponsoring certain criteria for judging research in a way that has no precedent of which we are aware. Second, as they defined high-quality research, they all reiterated—to one degree or another—Kerlinger's (1979) approach and embraced a continuation of the so thoroughly undermined empiricist or spectator theory of knowledge and favored the definition of criteria as a certain set of methods. Finally, they all expressed a great deal of ambiguity, at least in what they wrote, about the value or standing of qualitative inquiry when compared with the supposedly more rigorous, methodologically driven approaches to research. This led all of them to conclude that whereas qualitative researchers can be part of the educational research club, they cannot be rigorous members.

## ▣ RELATIVISM

For us, as critics of these responses to the demise of empiricism and the realization that adherence to method will not lead to theory-free knowledge and so forth, the idea is to move past the epistemological project, to change our metaphors and imageries of research from those of discovery and finding to those of constructing and making, and to accept that relativism is our inescapable condition as finite humans. However, to make such statements and employ the term *relativism* is deeply problematic for many people. Even the mention of relativism provokes strongly negative intellectual and emotional reactions.

For many writers, "relativism" is equated with some illogical and irrational abyss where every claim to knowledge has equal validity and credibility with every other claim. They argue that such a position is not only nonsensical but also dangerous in that it can lead only to a form of research anarchy and, for that matter, cultural anarchy. But to say that relativism means "anything goes" is nonsense for one simple reason: No one believes that all things are equal, and no one could lead his or her life guided by that belief. We all have preferences for some things over other things, and we make choices accordingly. This process of preferring some things to other things and making judgments accordingly has been going on since time immemorial and will continue for as far as can be seen into the future. Put differently, it is impossible to imagine a human life without judgment and discriminations. Taylor (1989) expressed the situation as follows: "To know who you are is to be oriented in moral space, a space in which questions arise about what is good or bad, what is worth doing and what not, what has meaning and importance for you and what is trivial and secondary" (p. 28). To not make judgments is to lose sight of one's orientation in such a moral space, that is, to lose one's grounding as a human.

We must also briefly address another long-standing canard, namely that relativism is self-refuting. The argument is well known: To say that all things are relative is to make a nonrelative or absolute statement and thereby to contradict oneself and so forth. Both Rorty (1985) and Gadamer (1995) addressed this issue of self-refuting. The latter agreed that relativism is self-refuting but then maintained that to make this point is to make a point of no interest because it "does not express any superior insight of value" (p. 334). Rorty (1985), on the other hand, argued that it is a mistake to think of relativism as a theory of knowledge to compete with other theories of knowledge. He dispensed with the self-refuting issue by stating that because his type of pragmatist is not interested in advancing any "epistemology, a fortiori, he does not have a relativist one" (p. 6).

We agree with these perspectives and hold that relativism, as we understand the condition, is not a theory of knowledge and advances no pretense that we can escape our finite—or time- and place-constrained—condition of being in the world. Taking a page from Godel's idea of incompleteness (Hofstadter, 1979), this situation is only what we should expect from any human (i.e., socially and historically influenced) construction. As such, relativism stands for nothing more or less than recognition of our human finitude. It is not something to be transcended; rather, it is merely something with which we, as finite beings, must learn to live.

Schwandt (1996) summarized this nonfoundational situation quite succinctly:

> We must learn to live with uncertainty, with the absence of final vindications, without the hope of solutions in the form of epistemological guarantees. Contingency, fallibilism, dialogue, and deliberation mark our way of being in the world. But these ontological conditions are not equivalent to eternal ambiguity, the lack of commitment, [and] the inability to act in the face of uncertainty. (p. 59)

As such, our problem as inquirers is that of how to make and defend judgments when there can be no appeal to foundations, to methods, or to something outside of the time- and place-constrained social processes of knowledge construction. This immediately engages us in complex social processes with obvious political implications.

## ◼ CRITERIA

The end of the epistemological project, the shift in metaphors from discovery to constructing, and the realization that social and educational inquiry is a practical and moral affair all mean that criteria must be thought of not as abstract standards but rather as socially constructed lists of characteristics. As we approach judgment in any given case, we have in mind a list of characteristics that we use to judge the quality of that production. This is not a well-defined and precisely specified list; to the contrary, this list of characteristics is always open-ended, in part unarticulated, and always subject to constant interpretation and reinterpretation. Moreover, the items on the list can never be the distillation of some abstracted epistemology, as has been attempted in the case of empiricism and method as criteria. Our lists are inevitably rooted in our standpoints and are elaborated through social interactions—or, in Gadamer's (1995) terms, they must evolve out of and reflect our "effective history [or histories]" (pp. 301–302).

The lists that we bring to judgment are open-ended in that we have the capacity to add items to and subtract items from the lists. The limits for recasting our lists derive not primarily from theoretical labor but rather from the practical use to which the lists are put as well as from the social, cultural, and historical contexts in which they are used. The limits on modification are worked and reworked within the context of actual practices or applications. Also, any lists that we bring to judgment are only partly articulated and only partly rational. Some items can be more or less specified, whereas others seem to resist such specification. Polanyi's (1962) concern about tacit knowledge applies very well in this case. We make what Beckett and Hager (2002) termed "embodied judgments" about research quality and value, that is, judgments that are practical and emotional as well as discursively considered. When we make judgments, we generally can specify some of the reasons, but other things seem to be out there—what might be called a surplus of meaning that seems to stand just beyond our grasp, just beyond our ability to completely specify or articulate. This does not mean that we should not, and do not, attempt to bring this surplus to fuller artic- ulation; it only means that this can never be done completely.

Furthermore, the lists that people think characterize good versus bad research studies are often contested, overlap one another, and partly contradict one another (Garratt & Hodkinson, 1998). Any list can be challenged, changed, and/or modified not primarily through abstracted discussions of the items themselves but rather in application to actual inquiries. For example, something "new" is presented to us. This was the case with qualitative inquiry in the recent past. Qualitative work did not fit well with the empiricist list of methodical characteristics (e.g., sampling, null hypotheses) that were the basis for distinguishing good research studies from bad research studies. To accept qualitative inquiry meant that one had to reformulate one's list of characteristics and replace the exemplars that are always called on in the never- ending process of making judgments. However, the key here is "accept" because people may choose, as many have done, to preserve and reassert the existing list of character- istics that distinguish the good from the bad and thereby reject the "new" as something that does not even qualify to be considered as research. This, of course, is a com- ment that has been, and is still, offered up about qualitative research.

## ▣ MAKING JUDGMENTS ABOUT RESEARCH

The various conditions noted in the previous section, in that they constrain all human activity—including social and educational research and thus judgments about the quality of such research—mean that politics and power are part of that complex process by which we sort out the good from the bad and the indifferent. The hope that method would allow us to make judgments about the quality of research "untainted" by our opinions, emotions, and self-interests has been a false hope. Politics and power are part of the process of judgment and always have been. At times, of course, when there is a more general agreement among researchers about how research is conceptualized and how the activity should be conducted, the politics and power aspects of judgment do not reveal themselves to any great extent. At other times, such as when there are challenges to conventional empiricist forms of inquiry as has recently been the case with qualitative research—especially when such inquiry draws on postmodernist understandings, philosophical hermeneutics, and so forth—political and power factors are much more obvious at both a micro level (i.e., within the research profession) and a macro level (i.e., a situation where outside elements, such as government officials, enter into the process). However, we must immediately note that the line between micro and macro is often very blurry indeed.

In a groundbreaking study of the school as an organization, Hoyle (1982, 1986) coined the phrase "micropolitics," an idea later expanded by Ball (1987). Hoyle (1982) described micropolitics as including "those strategies by which individuals and groups in organizational contexts seek to use their resources of power and influence to further their interests" (p. 88). One way of understanding issues of research judgment is as a micropolitical process, even if the context is wider and more complex than that of a particular organization. Hodkinson (2004) argued that educational research can be seen as a field in the sense described by Bourdieu (e.g., Bourdieu & Wacquant, 1992). That is, academics strive for distinction in that field, using whatever capital (resources) they have at their disposal. One of the major activities in such a field is that people work to support, preserve, or strengthen those rules (or lists of characteristics) that they approve of or are in their interests and/or to change the rules (or lists) in a direction that favors their interests.

This drive to promote self-interest is not the only motivation for people. The politics of research judgment is driven by deeply held and sincere beliefs about what determines research quality and the role that research should play, for example, in relation to policy and practice. That is, people may defend method as the criterion for judgment because they truly believe that methodically driven inquiry or the application of the "scientific method" is the best way in which to solve educational and social problems, to help educate children, to bring greater equity to society, and so forth. But then, this is also the case for those who critique methodically driven inquiry and insist that we must change our metaphors. However, this does not render the process any less political. Such beliefs strengthen the resolve to assert particular approaches, that is, to win the political struggles over allocation of resources. The careers and self-interests of those concerned are intimately locked into those processes and struggles.

In short, academics strive explicitly and implicitly to influence those criteria (or lists of characteristics) that determine research quality as well as to perform well against them. In Hoyle's (1982, 1986) terms, academics are micropolitical. Aspects of these rules are codified and written. Those who fund research have criteria against which bids will be judged, and journals have criteria against which submitted articles can be evaluated. However, such written codes take us only so far. Many of the rules of academic research are uncodified, having developed through custom and practice, as we have already argued. Part of the micropolitics lies is the selection and use of codes, contexts, and informal practices that best fit with the interests of a researcher or a group of researchers. Academics are, both as laypeople and as researchers, finite beings living during the era of relativism.

Although we strongly suspect that none of this is news to those who, over the years, have had research articles published and rejected, it will help to illustrate the pervasive presence of micropolitical activity with two brief examples. The first example concerns the allocation of scarce publication space in a high-status journal, the *Educational Researcher (ER)*, and the refreshing—but all too rare—musings of an editor about the decision-making process. A few years ago, Donmoyer (1996) talked about his "gate-keeping" role as editor of *ER* during a time of what many called "paradigm proliferation." Donmoyer did an excellent job of noting that he, as a gatekeeper, could not "widen the gates [he] monitors; [he] simply gets to decide which sorts of people can walk through them" (p. 20). He also went on to note that although different approaches to inquiry might be incommensurable, he agreed with Bernstein (1983) that this did not mean they were necessarily logically incompatible. That said, Donmoyer (1996) then acknowledged that when one moves away from the conceptual to the actual practice of publishing some papers and rejecting others, and when one is in the "realm of action . . . where resources are often scarce and hard choices consequently have to be made, a sort of pragmatic incommensurability will inevitably come into play" (p. 20).

It is precisely at this point of scarcity and hard choices, in light of philosophical differences and disputes concerning the nature of inquiry, that power and politics become very visible as part of the quality judgment process. This does not mean that the process is necessarily venal or somehow tainted, although it certainly can be and can often be judged as such—depending, of course, on how "venal" and "tainted" are defined. All we wish to convey here is that this is the way things are because we all are, at least in part, political beings with a desire to advance our respective self-interests.

Our second example illustrates the current interest in reasserting empiricism as the philosophical basis for social and educational inquiry and, in so doing, blurs the line between macro and micro. For reasons that will be made clear later, the U.K. government's Department for Education and Employment, now the Department for Education and Skills (DfES), funded the Evidence for Policy and Practice Information and Coordinating Centre (EPPI Centre) for 5 years beginning in 2000. The remit was to support groups of researchers and others in carrying out systematic reviews of existing research findings. It was based on earlier systematic review work in medical research under what has become known as the "Cochrane Collaboration." The founder of the EPPI Centre, Ann Oakley, is a determined advocate of scientific research and the primacy of the controlled experiment (Oakley, 2000, 2003). Within the center's approach, a systematic review must meet various criteria:

means of specifying a particular answerable research question; criteria about what kinds of studies . . . will be included in, and excluded from, the domain of literature to be surveyed; making explicit, justifiable decisions about the methodological quality of studies regarded as generating reliable findings; . . . [and] has involved input from research users at all stages in the review process. (Oakley, 2003, p. 24)

The first two of the criteria demonstrate unashamedly empiricist underpinnings. The research question comes first and stands apart from and prior to the research that is to be surveyed in the review, and the quality of any research to be considered is determined by the methods used by the researchers and how clearly they are described. Also of note is the fact that although user involvement in the review process is specified, prior academic knowledge of the field to be surveyed is not. This implies that the review process is seen as a technical operation that does not require sophisticated research understanding.

As Oakley (2000, 2003) described them, the EPPI processes appear to be designed to maximize objectivity and minimize subjectivity. Part of that objectivity is the claim that "the basic principle behind EPPI Centre reviews is transparency of methods, which allows replication and updating" (Gough & Elbourne, 2002, p. 229). The reality is less clear-cut. Each EPPI group has to determine its own chosen set of criteria— clearly a social and micropolitical process. In a training event for these procedures attended by a colleague in June 2003, David Gough, deputy director of the EPPI Centre, stressed the fact that during all stages of the process, skilled interpretation was necessary. Groups would need to debate what their review questions were, what criteria should be applied, and how those criteria were to be applied in respect of individual research papers. In a group exercise, the significance of this sort of judgment making became apparent. Within one group, some participants claimed that qualitative case study research did not contain any empirical data and, therefore, always should be excluded. Others disagreed. Toward the end of this session, Gough shared a list of criteria for judging qualitative research. This is not an official EPPI list, but he claimed that it was a list with which no one will disagree:

an explicit account of theoretical framework and/or inclusion of literature review; clearly stated aims and objectives; a clear description of context; a clear description of sample; a clear description of fieldwork methods including systematic data collection; an analysis of data by more than one researcher; and sufficient original data to mediate between evidence and interpretation.

This list is actually deeply controversial, and many high-quality research papers would be rejected if all of these criteria were seriously enforced. For example, the list sits very uncomfortably with Wolcott's (1999) claim that ethnography is research with no method—or, at least, often lacks what Gough termed "systematic data collection" or "a clear sample." It is "a way of seeing," and any aims may be general rather than specific. Becker's (1971) seminal work on becoming a marijuana user would have failed on several of these criteria, as would Wolcott's (2002) own work on the "sneaky kid." The implication that two (or more) poor interpretations are better than one good one is common but is logically bizarre. More seriously, what does "clear" mean in this context, and at what point does, for example, a description of the sample become clear as opposed to unclear? The suspicion is that clear stands for the very precise—exactly how many interviews were conducted with how many people of what categories and so forth. There is also no recognition in this list that in a short journal article, meeting every one of these criteria fully might leave little space to actually present any findings.

Far from being scientific, transparent, and replicable, every aspect of the EPPI procedures is shot through with subjective judgment making, and there is a micropolitical purpose to the work. Oakley and her colleagues are strongly promoting one approach to research and judgment-making processes about research, as Oakley's (2000) book makes clear. In so doing, life for researchers in the field who do not agree is being made much more difficult. The potential seriousness of this situation was apparent in a conversation between one of the authors (Hodkinson) and the director of a research program of which he is a part. The director stressed the need to ensure that books reporting the research contain full accounts of the method, including "the precise dates of the fieldwork," lest the books be excluded by some future EPPI groups, whose criteria are not yet even known. The sorts of nonempiricist ways of judging qualitative research described by Sparkes (2002) are so far off the agenda as to be denied existence. The fact that the EPPI Centre is funded by the U.K. government illustrates the link between the micropolitics of judgment and the more recently obvious macropolitics of research judgment.

## ▣ MACRO-LEVEL POLITICS

The most interesting turn of events regarding criteria for judging inquiry has involved political moves at what we have defined as the macro level. By this, we mean that concerns over the issue of criteria are no longer the virtually exclusive province of researchers themselves. In both the United States and the United Kingdom, there have been moves to governmentally establish, if not impose, certain criteria not only to judge the quality of research but also to distinguish what qualifies as research and what does not.

In the United States, the most significant move has been the 2002 legislative reauthorization of the Elementary and Secondary School Act of 1965 known as No Child Left Behind (NCLB). In the United Kingdom, there have been a number of governmental moves to influence or even establish criteria for judging the quality of inquiry. Among the more important of these are the just-discussed funding by the DfES of the EPPI Centre and the government-funded and -led National Educational Research

Forum (NERF). In both countries, the idea has been to set out the kinds of things that researchers must do to have a quality study and then restrict research funding to those researchers who follow the rules or the prescribed methods.

In the NCLB legislation, the criteria for judging the quality of research studies are elaborated in the definition of what is called scientifically based research. The standards or criteria (i.e., list of characteristics in our language) are that the study be systematic and empirical, involve rigorous data analysis (i.e., statistical analysis), employ reliable and valid data collection procedures (e.g., repeated measures), possess a strong research design (i.e., experimental or quasi-experimental), allow for the possibility of replication, and invoke expert scrutiny of results.

These elements, not surprisingly, have been translated into a hierarchy of approaches. The randomized control group approach is referred to as the "gold standard" for research. Quasi-experimental designs are second in order in the hierarchy and are referred to as the "silver standard." Correlational studies, descriptive studies, case studies, and the like are further down the list. The question, of course, is where qualitative inquiry fits into the picture. Because it does not meet the standards as noted in the legislation, so far as NCLB is concerned, qualitative inquiry is not research—or, if it is accepted as research, it must be thought of as quite rudimentary indeed.

Why this elimination of qualitative research from the status of scientific? At one level, it is very likely the case that many people, including researchers, believe philosophically or for epistemological reasons that qualitative inquiry is not "real" research. This is a feeling that has been maintained by many empiricist-oriented researchers since the 1980s, when qualitative inquiry began to gain increasing attention. For them, qualitative approaches have been, at worst, a useless distraction or, at best, a way of generating possible research questions for much more "rigorous" scientific investigations with control groups, statistical analysis, and so forth.

Be this as it may, we suspect that there is a major reason for this desire to impose criteria by way of governmental intervention that pushes qualitative inquiry to the sidelines of acceptable inquiry. This reason centers on what we refer to as the subversive nature—with regard to empiricism—of qualitative inquiry. There is a great deal to be gained by social and educational researchers in terms of social prestige and economic advantage by claiming to be scientists, on par with natural scientists, and convincing others to honor this claim. The problem is that much of qualitative inquiry was nurtured by philosophical arguments that undermined the claims, and even the hopes, that a science of the social was possible (on our inability to find law-like generalizations and why this is important, see Smith, 1993; on the systematic unpredictability of human affairs and the like, see Cziko, 1989, and MacIntyre, 1984). And, of course, it must be noted that if there is no science of the social, there can be no scientists of the social. It bears repeating; there is a great deal at stake here for many people.

In a very similar sense, when qualitative inquiry was subversive of the supposedly scientific approach to inquiry, it also was subversive of the claims to neutrality and objectivity—that comfortable image of the researcher as a "neutral broker" of information for policymakers. Many versions of qualitative inquiry offered the challenge that research must have a direct ameliorative intent and effect. In an echo of Marx, many people—although not necessarily being Marxists—have argued that research is not just about studying the world but also about changing it. As such, qualitative inquiry is very often driven by social purpose to improve the lives of marginalized and oppressed peoples. This is why qualitative research is often driven by perspectives that go under labels such as postcolonialist, feminist, gay/lesbian, and disablist. We suspect that for many conventional researchers, and certainly for many officials in the government, this idea of research as direct social engagement poses an unacceptable situation and must be controlled.

Finally, a speculative comment about what NCLB might mean for the American Educational Research Association (AERA) and why Shavelson and Towne (2002) discussed qualitative inquiry with such ambiguity (as noted previously) is in order. A significant number of AERA members now think of themselves as qualitative researchers. Certainly, some would accept methodical constraints and act accordingly, even though obeying methods is unlikely to gain them significant respect from the scientific types. Others, however, have adopted an ameliorative agenda and are doing readers' theater, autoethnographies, postmodernist approaches, artistic approaches, and so forth. Because the nonmethodical are considered not to be doing research at all, and the methodically oriented qualitative researchers—their adherence to method notwithstanding—are considered not to be doing really rigorous research, does this mean that the AERA should divide itself into the research members, the sort of research members, and the nonresearch members? Or, perhaps, should people go their own different ways and form different associations? We suspect that the thought of this is unacceptable, maybe not to those who wrote the NCLB definition of research but possibly to Shavelson and Towne (2002) and the members of the National Research Council Committee. We can think of no other explanation for their wavering comments about the status of qualitative research—yes it is research, no it really isn't research, maybe it is sort of research, and so forth. Maybe the report itself is a political document; any beliefs the authors may have really had about the status of qualitative research aside, they had to temper those beliefs in the face of the fact that there are a whole lot of qualitative educational researchers around. The politics of criteria is inescapable.

In the United Kingdom in the year 2000, the then secretary of state for education argued that the research community had to do much more to meet the needs of policymakers and practitioners (Blunkett, 2000). This statement was followed by a raft of government-led and -supported initiatives to ensure that this happened. The funding of Oakley's EPPI Centre was described earlier. Others included the establishment of the government-funded and -led NERF, whose role was to coordinate and direct educational research efforts, bringing together all major research funders, major journal editors, and key users of research. Membership in this group is by invitation, and during its early days a simplistic empiricist stance, if not a positivist one, was adopted. It was originally suggested that the NERF would draw up "agreed criteria" that would be universally used by all funders and journals to ensure that only high-quality educational research survived (NERF, 2000). The NERF later backed off, in the face of arguments that such an approach would undermine academic freedom. The NERF was paralleled and predated by a major new research program, the Teaching and Learning Research Programme (TLRP). Although it was administered by an independent government-funded agency, the Economic and Social Research Council (ESRC), funding came from other government sources. The remit was to produce high-quality scientific educational research that would lead directly to improvements in teaching and learning. Projects were to be relatively large, with few under £300,000 and several over £800,000. Mixed qualitative and quantitative methods were to be preferred over qualitative research alone. Money was also to be devoted to research capacity building, but initially for experimental and quantitative educational research. More recently, this program has widened its approaches but still retains a broadly empiricist rationale.

This concerted and government-driven movement to reform research in ways that make it more "rigorous" and more useful to policymakers does not apply only to education. In the U.K./English government structure (we need to specify England because recent partial devolution means that practices in Scotland, Wales, and Northern Ireland are becoming increasingly different), major departments, such as the DfES, are separate fiefdoms. Since the Labour Party came to power in 1996, there has been significant growth of more centralized control through the Cabinet Office, which answers directly to the prime minister. In 2003, the Cabinet Office published a major report on the criteria that should be used to judge the worth of qualitative research (Spencer, Ritchie, Lewis, & Dillon, 2003).

The ostensible purpose of this report is to aid policymakers and others in judging the quality of government-funded and -sponsored evaluation reports, which contained mainly or partly qualitative data. However, the size and form of the report suggest wider unarticulated motives. The report sets out what is claimed to be "a comprehensive and systematic review of the research literature relating to standards in qualitative research" (Spencer et al., 2003, p. 6). Through this approach and other approaches, including "a review of existing frameworks for reviewing quality in qualitative research" (p. 17), the authors produced their own framework. This is, they claimed, suitable for judging "qualitative research more generally [than just evaluations]" (p. 17), especially research that uses "interviews, focus groups, observation, and documentary analysis" (p. 19). The resulting framework consists of 18 "appraisal questions," each of which is accompanied by a series of "quality indicators." These items are "recurrently cited as markers of quality in the literature, in pre-existing frameworks, and in the interviews [with some researchers and policymakers] conducted for this study" (p. 19). According to the authors, these questions entail interpretation in their use; not all will apply in every circumstance, and additional questions will sometimes be needed. Above all, the authors claimed that because their framework is not "procedural," it is not subject to previous criticisms of predetermined and universal sets of research criteria, which we discussed earlier in the chapter.

Thus, despite disclaimers, the framework is being set up as something approaching a definitive tool that pulls together the accumulated wisdom of the current times. Therefore, it becomes the touchstone against which other frameworks and most, if not all, qualitative research outputs can be judged. This view is reinforced when we examine those types of qualitative research that Spencer and colleagues (2003) claimed are not covered. In addition to research not using interviews, focus groups, observations, or documentary analysis, other research that is "out of scope" includes a set of extreme alternatives to which few researchers, if any, could sign up. There is space here for only a couple of examples: "An external reality exists independently of human constructors and is accessible directly or exactly . . . OR there is no (shared) reality, only alternative individual human constructions" (p. 50). Also out of scope are studies where either "it is possible to produce accurate accounts which one knows with certainty correspond directly with reality OR . . . there are no privileged accounts, only alternative understandings" (p. 50). The force of these sorts of supposed qualification is that nearly all reasonable research perspectives are easily included. In these ways, what starts as an attempt to help policymakers use their own evaluations ends up as a government-sponsored framework to judge nearly all qualitative research.

This all-encompassing and flexible framework has clear epistemological underpinnings that were never critically acknowledged by Spencer and colleagues (2003). The report claimed, "For the purposes of this framework, the quality of the qualitative research that generates the evidence . . . is seen as lying at the heart of any assessment [of an evaluation output]" (p. 16); method is the prime determinant of truth. Thus, to identify the extent to which a research report contributes to knowledge, it is not necessary to know much about the substantive area to which the contribution is made. Rather, it is more important to check whether there is a literature review, whether the research design was "set in the context of existing knowledge/understanding" (p. 22), whether there is a "credible/clear discussion of how findings have contributed to knowledge and understanding [and] findings [are] presented or conceptualized in a way that offer[s] new insights" (p. 22), and whether there is "discussion of limitations of evidence and what remains unknown/unclear" (p. 22).

This approach was presented as uncontroversial despite detailed, if superficial, attention to the paradigm debates in the report. Furthermore, there is something very odd about this approach when it is set alongside the exclusionary categories described previously. From the neorealist perspective of Spencer and colleagues (2003), what does it mean to claim that research based on what they called "naïve realism" or "radical constructivism" is "out of scope"? This implies that issues of ontology and epistemology are matters of personal belief (relativist in our terms) and that the beliefs and values of either the researcher or the research reader should determine the criteria that are applied. Unsurprisingly, the implications of such a stance are not acknowledged or addressed because the political and rhetorical purpose of these "out of scope" exclusions is to legitimize the universality of the framework despite explicit claims that this is not the case.

Other than raising further and ongoing debates, it is the political context and purpose of the report that makes this logical paradox significant. This framework is explicitly and implicitly intended as a means of judging the worth of qualitative research, with clear and obvious implications for the allocation of scarce research resources—both the cultural capital of esteem and recognition and the economic capital of future research contract success. In effect, through this report, the government was striving once more to establish universal criteria for the control of social and educational research that the NERF set as its early goal before backing off in response to charges that it was curtailing academic freedom. The detailed and complex articulation of a wide range of literature, the tone of self-evident reasonableness, and the arguments that are advanced to demonstrate the credibility and applicability of this framework will nullify any such simplistic response this time around. If a few of us are foolish enough to adopt one of the extreme positions that are "out of scope," we are free to do so, and the framework acknowledges our existence outside its frame. Of course, those of us who do so should not expect either funding or esteem to follow. If this framework infiltrates indirect forms of U.K. government research funding, such as the award of ESRC research contracts or the evaluation of outputs used in the Research Assessment Exercise, political control over research will become nearly universal.

Taken collectively, these initiatives amount to a deliberate and powerful U.K. government intervention into the conduct and nature of educational research, ostensibly to improve its quality and make it more relevant to policymakers and policy implementers. As these initiatives changed the educational research map of the United Kingdom, researchers themselves became engaged in a high-stakes political process. Some celebrated the new climate and worked hard to reinforce and strengthen it while no doubt looking for opportunities to further their own work and careers. Others worked to oppose and resist the changes, trying to preserve spaces for alternative research approaches, including the sorts of work that they wanted to do. Still others worked to play the new regime by describing research in ways that might attract TLRP funding but without subscribing to its original hardline philosophy.

## ▣ INTERESTING TIMES

We close with two comments about the increasingly evident political nature of research and criteria. First, we have argued that the major macropolitical interventions of both the U.S. and U.K. governments into social and educational research are framed around softer or harder versions of empiricism and neorealism. This link, of course, is not coincidental. There are strong relations between governments' desires to predict and control complex social and economic processes and the well-known role that prediction and control of phenomena and processes plays within empiricism. Put differently, current approaches are dominated by what Habermas (1972) termed "technical interests" and are also part of the much wider social and political growth of an audit society (Power, 1997) or an audit culture (Strathern, 1997, 2000). The audit culture is dominated by attempts to measure the success and value of everything. Thus, in both the United States and the United Kingdom, education establishments are increasingly judged comparatively against measures such as the retention of students, the proportions of students who complete the courses, the levels of eventual qualification that students attain, and standardized test scores. In this context, it is hardly surprising that there are strong government pressures for similar measured and supposedly objective performance criteria for research. It is this audit culture, and its nearly universal assumptions of measured value, that lies behind Shavelson and Towne's (2002) report in the United States and the Cabinet Office's report (Spencer et al., 2003) in the United Kingdom. In this audit climate, the view that research judgment is a matter of embodied interpretation, and that lists of criteria are fluid and changing, is alien self-indulgence at best.

As Habermas (1972) argued, this link among empiricism, positivism, and government interests is more than just technical. Such technical approaches deflect attention away from deeper issues of value and purpose. They make radical critiques much more difficult to mount and, as we have seen, render largely invisible partisan approaches to research under the politically useful pretence that judgments are about objective quality only. As Bourdieu (1998) wrote, empiricism and positivism are tools of the powerful:

> The dominants, technocrats, and epistemocrats of the right or the left are hand in glove with reason and the universal: one makes one's way through universes in which more and more technical, rational justifications will be necessary in order to dominate and in which the dominated can and must also use reason to defend themselves against domination, because the dominants must increasingly invoke reason, and science, to exert their domination. (p. 90)

Second, we think that governmental intervention into the politics of criteria is an announcement that the "culture wars" have come to educational and social research. Since the 1960s, more strongly in the United States and less so in the United Kingdom, there have been ongoing battles over the shape of our societies and cultures. These disputes over issues have ranged from abortion, to gay/lesbian marriages, to the content of history and sociology and other courses in our schools, to the content of television shows. It seems that it was only a matter of time until these types of divisions would become a prominent part of our judgments about acceptable versus unacceptable social and educational research. And just as the social discourse has become more strident, so might the discussions of research quality in the future. Of course, we can only wait and see.

For us, the conclusion to all of this is very clear. There is no point in pretending that power and politics, at both the micro level and the macro level, are not a part of the process by which we make judgments about the quality of research. We live in the era of relativism, and there can be no time- and place-independent criteria for judgment—that is, criteria that are "untainted" by our various opinions, ideologies, emotions, and self-interests. Power and politics are with us, and the only issues are how power is used and how the political process is played out. And of course, the answers will not be found in epistemology; instead, they will be found in our reasoning as finite practical and moral beings.

## ▣ REFERENCES

Abel, T. (1948). The operation called *verstehen*. *American Journal of Sociology, 54,* 211–218.

Ball, S. J. (1987). *The micro-politics of the school.* London: Methuen.

Becker, H. S. (1971). Becoming a marijuana user. In B. R. Cosin, I. R. Dale, G. M. Esland, & D. M. Swift (Eds.), *School and society: A sociological reader* (pp. 141–147). London: Routledge & Kegan Paul.

Beckett, D., & Hager, P. (2002). *Life, work, and learning: Practice in postmodernity.* London: Routledge.

Bernstein, R. (1983). *Beyond objectivism and relativism.* Philadelphia: University of Pennsylvania Press.

Bhaskar, R. (1979). *The possibility of naturalism.* Atlantic Highlands, NJ: Humanities Press.

Blunkett, D. (2000, February). *Influence or irrelevance: Can social science improve government?* Secretary of State's Economic and Social Research Council lecture speech, London.

Bourdieu, P. (1998). *Practical reason.* Cambridge, UK: Polity.

Bourdieu, P., & Wacquant, L. J. D. (1992). *An invitation to reflexive sociology.* Cambridge, UK: Polity.

Cherryholmes, C. (1988). *Power and criticism.* New York: Columbia University, Teachers College Press.

Cziko, G. (1989). Unpredictability and indeterminism in human behavior: Arguments and implications for educational research. *Educational Researcher, 18*(3), 17–25.

Donmoyer, R. (1996). Educational research in an era of paradigm proliferation: What's a journal editor to do? *Educational Researcher, 25*(2), 19–25.

Gadamer, H-G. (1995). *Truth and method* (2nd rev. ed., J. Weinsheimer & D. G. Marshall, Trans.). New York: Crossroad.

Garratt, D., & Hodkinson, P. (1998). Can there be criteria for selecting research criteria? A hermeneutical analysis of an inescapable dilemma, *Qualitative Inquiry, 4,* 515–539.

Giddens, A. (1976). *New rules of sociological method: A positive critique of interpretive sociologies.* London: Hutchinson.

Goodman, N. (1978). *Ways of worldmaking*. Indianapolis, IN: Hackett.

Gough, D., & Elbourne, D. (2002). Systematic research synthesis to inform policy, practice, and democratic debate. *Social Policy and Society, 1,* 225–236.

Habermas, J. (1972). *Knowledge and human interests* (2nd ed.). London: Heinemann.

Hammersley, M. (1990). *Reading ethnographic research: A critical guide*. London: Longman.

Hanson, N. (1958). *Patterns of discovery*. Cambridge, UK: Cambridge University Press.

Hazelrigg, L. (1989). *Claims of knowledge*. Tallahassee: Florida State University Press.

Hesse, M. (1980). *Revolutions and reconstructions in the philosophy of science*. Brighton, UK: Harvester.

Hillage, J., Pearson, R., Anderson, A., & Tamkin, P. (1998). *Excellence in schools*. London: Institute for Employment Studies.

Hodkinson, P. (1998, August). Naïveté and bias in educational research: The Tooley Report. *Research Intelligence*, pp. 16–17.

Hodkinson, P. (2004). Research as a form of work: Expertise, community, and methodological objectivity. *British Educational Research Journal, 30*(1), 9–26.

Hodkinson, P., & Smith, J. K. (2004). The relationship between research, policy, and practice. In R. Pring & G. Thomas (Eds.), *Evidence-based practice* (pp. 150–163). Buckingham, UK: Open University Press.

Hofstadter, D. (1979). *Gödel, Escher, Bach: An eternal golden braid*. New York: Basic Books.

Hoyle, E. (1982). Micropolitics of educational organizations. *Educational Management and Administration, 10,* 87–98.

Hoyle, E. (1986). *The politics of school management*. London: Hodder & Stoughton.

Kerlinger, F. (1979). *Behavioral research*. New York: Holt, Rinehart & Winston.

Kuhn, T. S. (1962). *The structure of scientific revolutions*. Chicago: University of Chicago Press.

Leary, D. (1984). Philosophy, psychology, and reality. *American Psychologist, 39,* 917–919.

MacIntyre, A. (1984). *After virtue* (2nd ed.). Notre Dame, IN. University of Notre Dame Press.

MacKenzie, D. (1981). *Statistics in Great Britain: 1885–1930*. Edinburgh, UK: Edinburgh University Press.

Manicas, P. (1987). *A history and philosophy of the social sciences*. Oxford, UK: Basil Blackwell.

Manicas, P., & Secord, P. (1983). Implications for psychology of the new philosophy of science. *American Psychologist, 39,* 399–413.

Nagel, T. (1986). *The view from nowhere*. New York: Oxford University Press.

National Educational Research Forum. (2000). *Research and development in education: A national strategy consultation paper*. Nottingham, UK: Author.

Oakley, A. (2000). *Experiments in knowing: Gender and method in the social sciences*. London: Polity.

Oakley, A. (2003). Research evidence, knowledge management, and educational practice: Early lessons from a systematic approach. *London Review of Education, 1*(1), 21–33.

Phillips, D. C., & Burbules, N. C. (2000). *Postpositivism and educational research*. Lanham, MD: Rowman & Littlefield.

Polanyi, M. (1962). *Personal knowledge*. Chicago: University of Chicago Press.

Popper, K. (1959). *The logic of scientific discovery*. London: Hutchinson.

Popper, K. (1972). *Objective knowledge*. Oxford, UK: Clarendon.

Power, M. (1997). *The audit society: Rituals of verification*. Oxford, UK: Oxford University Press.

Pring, R. (2000). *Philosophy of educational research*. London: Continuum.

Putman, H. (1981). *Reason, truth, and history.* Cambridge, UK: Cambridge University Press.

Rorty, R. (1985). Solidarity or objectivity? In J. Rajchman & C. West (Eds.), *Post-analytic philosophy* (pp. 3–19). New York: Columbia University Press.

Schwandt, T. (1996). Farewell to criteriology. *Qualitative Inquiry, 2,* 58–72.

Shavelson, R., & Towne, L. (2002). *Scientific research in education.* Washington, DC: National Academy Press.

Slavin, R. (2002). Evidence-based policies: Transforming educational practice and research. *Educational Researcher, 31*(7), 15–21.

Smith, J. K. (1985). Social reality as mind-dependent versus mind-independent and the interpretation of test validity. *Journal of Research and Development in Education, 1,* 1–9.

Smith, J. K. (1989). *The nature of social and educational inquiry: Empiricism versus interpretation.* Norwood, NJ: Ablex.

Smith, J. K. (1993). *After the demise of empiricism: The problem of judging social and educational inquiry.* Norwood, NJ: Ablex.

Smith, J. K., & Deemer, D. K. (2000). The problem of criteria in the age of relativism. In N. K. Denzin & Y. S. Lincoln (Eds.), *Handbook of qualitative research* (2nd ed., pp. 877–896). Thousand Oaks, CA: Sage.

Sparkes, A. C. (1994). Self, silence, and invisibility as a beginning teacher: A live history of lesbian experience. *British Journal of Sociology of Education, 15*(1), 93–118.

Sparkes, A. C. (2002). *Telling tales in sport and physical activity: A qualitative journey.* Leeds, UK: Human Kinetics.

Spencer, L., Ritchie, J., Lewis, J., & Dillon, L. (2003). *Quality in qualitative evaluation: A framework for assessing research evidence.* London: Cabinet Office.

Strathern, M. (1997). "Improving ratings": Audit in the British university system. *European Review, 5,* 305–321.

Strathern, M. (2000). The tyranny of transparency. *British Educational Research Journal, 26,* 309–321.

Taylor, C. (1971). Interpretation and the sciences of man. *Review of Metaphysics, 25,* 3–51.

Taylor, C. (1989). *Sources of the self.* Cambridge, UK: Cambridge University Press.

Tooley, J., with Darby, D. (1998). *Education research: An OFSTED critique.* London: OFSTED.

Wolcott, H. (1999). *Ethnography: A way of seeing.* Walnut Creek, CA: AltaMira.

Wolcott, H. (2002). *Sneaky Kid and its aftermath: Ethics and intimacy in fieldwork.* Walnut Creek, CA: AltaMira.

# 14

# EMANCIPATORY DISCOURSES AND THE ETHICS AND POLITICS OF INTERPRETATION

Norman K. Denzin

From the vantage point of the colonized, a position from which I write, and choose to privilege, the term "research" is inextricably linked to European imperialism and colonialism. The word itself, "research," is probably one of the dirtiest words in the indigenous world's vocabulary. (Smith, 1999, p. 1)

A story grows from the inside out and the inside of Navajoland is something I know little of. But I do know myself if I begin traveling with an awareness of my own ignorance, trusting my instincts, I can look for my own stories embedded in the landscapes I travel through. . . .

I am not suggesting we emulate Native Peoples—in this case, the Navajo. We can't. We are not Navajo. Besides their traditional stories don't work for us. It's like drinking another man's medicine. Their stories hold meaning for us only as examples. They can teach us what is possible. We must create and find our own stories, our own myths. (Williams, 1984, pp. 3, 5)

This chapter, in the form of a manifesto, invites indigenous and nonindigenous qualitative researchers to think through the implications of a practical, progressive politics of performative inquiry, an emancipatory discourse connecting indigenous epistemologies (Rains, Archibald, & Deyhle, 2000, p. 338) and theories of decolonization and the postcolonial (Soto, 2004, p. ix; Swadener & Mutua, 2004, p. 255) with critical pedagogy, with new ways of reading, writing, and performing

culture in the first decade of a new century (Kincheloe & McLaren, 2000, p. 285).[1]
I believe the performance-based human disciplines can contribute to radical social
change, to economic justice, to a utopian cultural politics that extends localized critical (race) theory and the principles of a radical democracy to all aspects of decolonizing, indigenous societies (Giroux, 2000a, pp. x, 25; Kaomea, 2004, p. 31; L. T. Smith,
2000, p. 228; Swadener & Mutua, 2004, p. 257).

I advocate change that "envisions a democracy founded in a social justice that is 'not
yet'" (Weems, 2002, p. 3). I believe that nonindigenous interpretive scholars should be
part of this project (see Denzin, 2004a, 2004b, in press). How this endeavor is implemented in specific indigenous contexts should be determined by the indigenous peoples
involved. I also believe that this initiative should be part of a larger conversation—
namely, the global decolonizing discourse connected to the works of anticolonialist
scholars, including those of First Nations, Native American, Alaskan, Australian
Aboriginal, New Zealand Māori, and Native Hawaiian heritage (see Smith, Volume 1,
Chapter 4; Bishop, Volume 1, Chapter 5; see also Mutua & Swadener, 2004; Smith, 1999).[2]

A postcolonial, indigenous participatory theater is central to this discourse (Balme &
Carstensen, 2001; Greenwood, 2001).[3] Contemporary indigenous playwrights and performers revisit and make a mockery of 19th-century racist practices. They interrogate and
turn the tables on blackface minstrelsy and the global colonial theater that reproduced
racist politics through specific cross-race and cross-gender performances. They show how
these performances used whiteface and blackface in the construction of colonial models of
whiteness, blackness, gender, and national identity (Kondo, 2000, p. 83; Gilbert, 2003).

Indigenous theater nurtures a critical transnational yet historically specific critical
race consciousness. It uses indigenous performance as means of political representation (Magowan, 2000, p. 311). Through the reflexive use of historical restagings, masquerade, ventriloquism, and doubly inverted performances involving male and female
impersonators, this subversive theater undermines colonial racial representations
(Bean, 2001, pp. 187–188). It incorporates traditional indigenous and nonindigenous
cultural texts into frameworks that disrupt colonial models of race relations. This theater takes up key diasporic concerns, including those of memory, cultural loss, disori-
entation, violence, and exploitation (Balme & Carstensen, 2001, p. 45). This is a utopian
theater that addresses issues of equity, healing, and social justice.[4]

▣ ▣ ▣

Consider the following:

- In her play *House Arrest* (2003), Anna Deavere Smith offers "an epic view of slavery, sexual
  misconduct, and the American presidency. Twelve actors, some in blackface, play across
  lines of race, age, and gender to 'become' Bill Clinton, Thomas Jefferson, Sally
  Hemings . . . and a vast array of historical and contemporary figures" (Kondo, 2000, p. 81).

- In Native Canadian Daniel David Moses's play *Almighty Voice and His Wife* (1992), Native performers, wearing whiteface minstrel masks, mock such historical figures as Wild Bill Cody, Sitting Bull, and young Indian maidens called Sweet Sioux (Gilbert, 2003, p. 692).
- In Sydney, Australia, Aboriginal theater groups perform statements of their indigenous rights, demanding that politicians participate in these performance events "as co-producers of meaning rather than as tacit consumers" (Magowan, 2000, pp. 317–318).

Thus do indigenous performances function as strategies of critique and empowerment.

◻ ◻ ◻

The "Decade of the World's Indigenous Peoples" (1994–2004; Henderson, 2000, p. 168) has ended. Nonindigenous scholars have yet to learn from it, to learn that it is time to dismantle, deconstruct, and decolonize Western epistemologies from within, to learn that research does not have to be a dirty word, to learn that research is always already both moral and political.

Shaped by the sociological imagination (Mills, 1959), building on George Herbert Mead's (1938) discursive, performative model of the act, critical qualitative research imagines and explores the multiple ways in which performance can be understood, including as imitation, or *mimesis*; as construction, or *poiesis;* and as motion or movement, or *kinesis* (Conquergood, 1998, p. 31). The researcher-as-performer moves from a view of performance as imitation, or dramaturgical staging (Goffman, 1959), to an emphasis on performance as liminality and construction (McLaren, 1999), then to a view of performance as struggle, as intervention, as breaking and remaking, as kinesis, as a sociopolitical act (Conquergood, 1998, p. 32.)

Viewed as struggles and interventions, performances and performance events become transgressive achievements, political accomplishments that break through "sedimented meanings and normative traditions" (Conquergood, 1998, p. 32). It is this performative model of emancipatory decolonized indigenous research that I develop here (Garoian, 1999; Gilbert, 2003; Kondo, 2000; Madison, 1999). Drawing on Garoian (1999), Du Bois (1926), Gilbert (2003), Madison (1998), Magowan (2000), and Smith (2003), this model enacts a utopian performative politics of resistance (see below). Extending indigenous initiatives, this model is committed to a form of revolutionary political theater that performs pedagogies of dissent for the new millennium (McLaren, 1997b).

◻ ◻ ◻

My argument in this chapter unfolds in several parts. Drawing throughout from an ongoing performance text, I begin with a set of obstacles that confront the nonindigenous critical theorist. I then briefly discuss race, the call to performance, and the history of indigenous theater. I next address a group of concepts and the arguments associated with them; these include the concepts of indigenous epistemology, pedagogy, discourses of resistance, politics as performance, and counternarratives as critical inquiry. I briefly discuss a variety of indigenous pedagogies as well as the concept of indigenous research as localized critical theory. I elaborate variations within the personal narrative approach to decolonized inquiry, extending Richardson's (2000) model of "creative analytic practices," or CAP ethnography (p. 929). Then, after outlining a politics of resistance, I conclude the chapter with a discussion of indigenous models of power, truth, ethics, and social justice.

In the spirit of Du Bois, Dewey, Mead, Blumer, hooks, and West, I intend to create a dialogue between indigenous and nonindigenous members of the qualitative research community. I want to move our discourse more fully into the spaces of a global yet localized progressive, performative pragmatism. I want to extend those political impulses within the feminist pragmatist tradition that imagine a radical, democratic utopia. Following Du Bois, hooks, and West, I see these impulses as constantly interrogating the relevance of pragmatism and critical theory for race relations and inequality in the global neoliberal capitalist state.

## ▣ OBSTACLES CONFRONTING THE NONINDIGENOUS CRITICAL THEORIST

In proposing a conversation between indigenous and nonindigenous scholars, I am mindful of several difficulties. First, scholars must resist the legacy of the Western colonizing other. As Smith (1999) observes of the Western colonizers, "They came, they saw, they named, they claimed" (p. 80). As agents of colonial power, Western scientists discovered, extracted, appropriated, commodified, and distributed knowledge about the indigenous other. Many indigenous critics contend that these practices have placed control over research in the hands of Western scholars. This means, for example, that Māori are excluded from discussions concerning who has control over the initiation of research about Māori, the methodologies used, the evaluations and assessments made, the resulting representations, and the distribution of the newly defined knowledge (see Bishop, Volume 1, Chapter 5). The decolonization project challenges research practices that perpetuate Western power by misrepresenting and essentializing indigenous persons, often denying them voice or identity.

A second difficulty is that critical, interpretive performance theory and critical race theory will not work within indigenous settings without modification. The criticisms of Graham Smith (2000), Linda Tuhiwai Smith (1999, 2000), Bishop (1994, 1998), Battiste (2000a, 2000b), Churchill (1996), Cook-Lynn (1998), and others make this very clear. Critical theory's criteria for self-determination and empowerment perpetuate neocolonial sentiments while turning the indigenous person into an essentialized "other" who is spoken for (Bishop, Volume 1, Chapter 5). The categories of race, gender, and racialized identities cannot be turned into frozen, essential terms, nor is racial identity a free-floating signifier (Grande, 2000, p. 348). Critical theory must be localized, grounded in the specific meanings, traditions, customs, and community relations that operate in each indigenous setting. Localized critical theory can work if the goals of critique, resistance, struggle, and emancipation are not treated as if they have "universal characteristics that are independent of history, context, and agency" (L. T. Smith, 2000, p. 229).

A third difficulty lies in the pressing need for scholars to decolonize and deconstruct those structures within the Western academy that privilege Western knowledge systems and their epistemologies (Mutua & Swadener, 2004, p. 10; Semali & Kincheloe, 1999). Indigenous knowledge systems are too frequently made into objects of study, treated as if they were instances of quaint folk theory held by the members of primitive cultures. The decolonizing project reverses this equation, making Western systems of knowledge the object of inquiry.

A fourth difficulty is that the nonindigenous scholar must carefully and cautiously articulate the spaces between decolonizing research practices and indigenous communities (to paraphrase Smith's comments in Volume 1, Chapter 4). These spaces are fraught with uncertainty. Neoliberal and neoconservative political economies turn knowledge about indigenous peoples into a commodity. Conflicts exist between competing epistemological and ethical frameworks, including in the area of institutional regulations concerning human subject research. Currently, research is regulated by positivist epistemologies. Indigenous scholars and intellectuals are pressed to produce technical knowledge that conforms to Western standards of truth and validity. Conflicts over who initiates and who benefits from such research are especially problematic. Scholars must develop culturally responsive research practices that locate power within indigenous communities, so that these communities determine and define what constitutes acceptable research. Such work encourages self-determination and empowerment (see Bishop, Volume 1, Chapter 5).

In arguing for a dialogue between critical and indigenous theorists, I must acknowledge my position as an outsider to the indigenous colonized experience. I write as a privileged Westerner. At the same time, however, I seek to be an "allied other" (Kaomea, 2004, p. 32; Mutua & Swadener, 2004, p. 4), a fellow traveler of sorts, an antipositivist, an insider who wishes to deconstruct the Western academy and its positivist epistemologies from within. I endorse a critical epistemology that contests notions of objectivity and neutrality. I believe that all inquiry is moral and political. I value autoethnographic, insider, participatory, collaborative methodologies (Fine et al., 2003). These are narrative, performative methodologies, research practices that are reflexively consequential, ethical, critical, respectful, and humble. These practices require that scholars live with the consequences of their research actions (Smith, 1999, pp. 137–139).

▣ ▣ ▣

In proposing a dialogue between indigenous and nonindigenous qualitative researchers, in positioning myself as an "allied other," I am mindful of Terry Tempest Williams's cautious advice about borrowing stories and narratives from indigenous peoples. In her autoethnography *Pieces of White Shell: A Journey to Navajoland* (1984), she praises the wisdom of Navajo storytellers and the stories they tell (pp. 3–4). But she also warns her nonindigenous readers: We cannot emulate Native peoples. "We are not Navajo . . . their traditional stories don't work for us. . . . Their stories hold meaning for us only as examples. They can teach us what is possible. We must create and find our own stories" (p. 5).

As a nonindigenous scholar seeking a dialogue with indigenous scholars, I must construct stories that are embedded in the landscapes I travel through. These will be dialogical counternarratives, stories of resistance, of struggle, of hope, stories that create spaces for multicultural conversations, stories embedded in the critical democratic imagination. I briefly sample below from *Searching for Yellowstone* (Denzin, in press), a work in progress.

▣ ▣ ▣

*Searching for Yellowstone* consists of a series of coperformance texts and plays, each with multiple speaking parts. Drawing on verbatim theater, I quote from interviews, letters, books, and other documents written by historical and contemporary figures; in some cases, I present material that was originally written as prose in the format of poetry. "Indians in the Park" (excerpted below) is a four-act play of sorts. It can be performed on a simple set, around a seminar table, or on a stage in front of an audience. Overhead, a series of images should be projected on a full-size screen. To one side, a large roving spotlight, the "Camera Eye," should stand, with its light moving from speaker to speaker, returning always to the narrator.[5] More than 35 individuals speak or are quoted, some more than once. Audience members are asked to participate in the performance by assuming speaking parts.

▣ ▣ ▣

## ▣ Prologue

"Indians in the Park" (Denzin, 2004a) enacts a critical cultural politics concerning the representations of Native Americans and their historical presence in Yellowstone National Park. Beginning with the sting of childhood memory (Ulmer, 1989, pp. 209, 211), I follow Ulmer's (1989) and Benjamin's (1983–1984, p. 24) advice concerning history; that is, to write history means to quote history, and to quote history means to rip the historical object out of its context. In so doing,

I expose the contradictions, cracks, and seams in official ideology. The intent is to rediscover the past as a series of scenes, inventions, emotions, images, and stories (Benjamin, 1969, p. 257; Ulmer, 1989, p. 112). In bringing the past into the auto-biographical present, I insert myself into the past and create the conditions for rewriting and hence reexperiencing it.

The history at hand is the history of Native Americans in two cultural and symbolic landscapes, mid-central Iowa in the 1940s and 1950s and Yellowstone National Park in the 1870s. I read Yellowstone, America's first national park, metaphorically. In and across the discourses that historically define the park are deeply entrenched meanings concerning nature, culture, violence, gender, wilderness, parks, whites, and Native Americans (see Schullery, 1997).

I situate these voices and discourses in my own biography. The place of Native Americans in the collective white imagination is almost entirely a matter of racist myth, shifting meanings of the color line, the "Veil of Color" (Du Bois, 1903/1989, pp. xxxi, 2–3), theatricality, and minstrelsy (Spindel, 2000).

▣ ▣ ▣

For example:

## Author's Aside to Audience:

As a child I lived inside this white imaginary. I played a dress-up game called "cowboys and Indians." I watched *Red Rider and Little Beaver* and *The Lone Ranger* on Saturday-morning television. On Saturday nights my grandfather took me to see western movies—*Shane, Stagecoach, Broken Arrow, The Searchers*—at the Strand Theater in Iowa City, Iowa. (see Denzin, 2003, p. 175)

▣ ▣ ▣

In challenging the cultural representations of Native Americans, I follow Hall (1996a) and Smith (1997), who argue that it is not enough to replace negative representations with positive representations.[6] The positive-negative debate essentializes racial identity and denies its "dynamic relation to constructions of class, gender, sexuality [and] region" (Smith, 1997, p. 4). It takes two parties to do racial minstrelsy. Stereotypes of whiteness are tangled up in racial myth, in minstrel shows that replay the Wild West, leading whites to look like cowboys and Native Americans to look like Indians (Dorst, 1999). I employ this critical race theory and critical pedagogy to confront Yellowstone National Park and its histories.

Here are some excerpts from "Indians in the Park":

▣ ▣ ▣

## Second Author's Aside to Audience:

I wanted to be a cowboy when I grew up. So did Mark, my brother. On Saturday mornings, while Grandma made hot doughnuts for us in the new deep-fat fryer in her big country kitchen, we watched "cowboy and Indian" television shows: *The Lone Ranger, Red Rider and Little Beaver, The Roy Rogers Show, Hopalong Cassidy.* Mark and I had cowboy outfits— wide-brimmed hats, leather vests, chaps, and spurs, along with toy pistols and holsters. Grandpa bought us a horse. I have a photograph of Mark and me in our cowboy outfits on the back of swaybacked Sonny, who was deaf in his right ear. We'd ride Sonny around and around the corral, waving at Grandpa and Grandma. When I was in fourth grade, I was Squanto in the Thanksgiving play about the pilgrims. My skin was painted brown.

## ◙ Aᴄᴛ 1

## Scene 1: Sacagawea and Other Myths

*Newsreel 1*

**Voice 1: Horton:**

*Keeping the Legacy Alive*

Two hundred years ago the Corps of Discovery, led by captains Meriwether Lewis and William Clark, struck out from the Falls of Ohio, near Louisville, Kentucky, to explore the newly acquired territory of the Louisiana Purchase. Their 8,000-mile trek took them through perilous, forbidding country by canoe, horseback, and foot. Lewis, the party's scientist, and Clark, its surveyor, mapped geological features and fixed the longitudes and latitudes of the rivers and plains. Lewis described or preserved specimens of some 178 plants and 122 animals—the majority as-yet unknown to science. . . .

> None of this, of course,
>
> would have been possible
>
> without the aid and assistance
>
> of the Native Americans they met
>
> [nearly 50 tribes in all]
>
> along the way.
>
> Their Shoshone guide,
>
> Sacagawea, a 15-year-old girl,
>
> proved indispensable. (Horton, 2003, p. 90)

◙ ◙ ◙

**Voice 2:**    **Skeptic:** This is revisionist white history!

▣ ▣ ▣

**Voice 3:**    **Slaughter:**
Sacagawea is elusive,
fictive,
mythic
and real.
She is the Indian princess
required by myths
of discovery and conquest. (Slaughter, 2003, p. 86)

▣ ▣ ▣

**Voice 4:**    **Spindel:**
If we do a census of the population in our collective imagination,
imaginary Indians are one of the largest demographic groups.
They dance, they drum; they go on the warpath;
they are always young men who wear trailing feather bonnets.
Symbolic servants, they serve as mascots,
metaphors. We rely on these images to anchor us
to the land and verify our account of
our own past. But these Indians exist only
in our imaginations. (Spindel, 2000, p. 8)

▣ ▣ ▣

## Scene 2: Park Performances

*The Camera Eye (2)*

**Narrator:**    Staged performances based on lore and myth from Hollywood westerns
and Wild West shows represent and connect Indians with war bonnets,
horses, western landscapes, parks, wilderness, tourism, nature, and danger
(see Spindel, 2000, p. 8). These representations simultaneously place Native

Americans within and outside white culture, hence the phrase "Indians in the park." Parks are safe places, sites carved out of the wilderness, and other spaces where whites go to view and experience nature and the natural world. Indians are not part of this cultural landscape. The "natural world" they inhabit is outside the park. It is a wild, violent, and uncivilized world.

▣ ▣ ▣

"Remembering to Forget" is a second coperformance text. It continues my interrogation of the cultural politics surrounding the Lewis and Clark expedition of 1804–1806. It is also fractured, revisionist, personal history, an attempt at a personal mythology that contests the rhetorical uses of nature, discovery, and science for political, patriotic purposes. This play is woven in, through, and around memories of blankets, families, Native Americans, illness, and Lewis and Clark in the greater Yellowstone region. The following excerpt is from Act 1, Scenes 1 and 2.

## ▣  ACT 1

### Scene 1: Getting Started

*Course Announcement, Yellowstone Association Institute, Summer 2003*

"Along the Yellowstone River with Lewis & Clark"

July 25–27, Limit 19

*Location:* Mammoth Hot Springs/Three Forks, and Dillon, Montana; Credit Pending; Instructor: Jim Garry, M.S.

$180 (member's fee $170)

> In the summer of 1805, Lewis and Clark passed
> through the Yellowstone region en route to the
> Pacific Ocean. They came up the Missouri River from the Great Falls and
> camped in the Three Forks area before
> following the Jefferson River west to the headwaters of the Missouri system at
> Lemhi Pass.
>      Almost 200 years later, we will walk in their
> footsteps, see what they saw, read their journals, and
> speculate on what they would think of this country today. We'll journey to Three
> Forks and from there to Dillon and Lemhi Pass where we will look at some of
> the impacts on the country since the days of Lewis and Clark.

(pause)

It was something like the Lewis and Clark [traveling] Medicine Show. (Ronda, 1984, p. 18; see also Ambrose, 1996, p. 157)

(pause)

But the park did not exist in 1805. What kind of history is this?

(pause)

Our image of [history] is indissolubly bound up with the image of redemption. (Benjamin, 1969, p. 256)

## Scene 2: Canadian Blankets

**Voice 2:**  **Narrator (to audience, explaining project):** On July 5, 1955, my father returned to our little house on Third Street in Indianola, Iowa, from a fishing trip in Ontario, Canada. Mother greeted him at the door. Slightly drunk, Dad handed her a Hudson's Bay wool blanket as a present and promptly left for the office. I still have that blanket. In this family we value such blankets and exchange them as gifts. This exchange system gives me a somewhat indirect historical connection to Lewis and Clark, Canada, Hudson's Bay Company blankets, the fur trade, 19th-century British and French traders, and Native Americans. This connection takes me right into the myths about Yellowstone Park, Lewis and Clark, the Corps of Discovery, and Sacagawea. Lewis and Clark, it appears, also traded blankets for goodwill on their expedition. But this was a tainted exchange, for in many instances these blankets were carriers of smallpox. Likewise, the blanket my father gave to my mother was embedded within a disease exchange system, in this case alcoholism. Although Dad's alcoholism was not full-blown in 1955, it would become so within 2 years of his return from that fishing trip.

▣  ▣  ▣

Read together, the above excerpts model a form of writing that moves back and forth between personal and official history. Using the language of the colonizer, they quote history back to itself, refusing to treat Lewis and Clark and the past as if they are things that can be fixed in time, as performances that can be unproblematically staged in the present. Indeed, the historical reenactment of Lewis and Clark's expedition is endowed with special powers. It stands outside time. Performers benevolently re-create the past, performing and remembering it "the way it really was" (Benjamin, 1969, p. 257).

There is great danger in such historical masquerades. The past is frozen in time. Particular versions of whiteness and white history are performed. The sins of the past are ignored, and a peaceful bond is forged between the imagined past and the present.

In this nostalgic space, the benign pastness of Lewis and Clark's expedition comes alive. Their historic journey of conquest is celebrated. A territorial and cultural politic is signified. The white community owns this land, this river, this park, this place, these meanings. The white community and its city fathers have the right to re-create on this land, and in these cultural spaces, their version of the past, their version of how these two men helped win the West for Thomas Jefferson and White America (Williams, 1997). In such a utopian scenario, redemption for the handful of sins committed by the explorers is sought and easily achieved (see Grossman, 2003, pp. 2–5). Indeed, redemption gives way to celebration, to a displacement, a shift from conquest to ecoenvironmentalism, to nature, the joy of floating the Yellowstone or the Missouri River under the banner of Lewis and Clark.

## ▣ RACE, INDIGENOUS OTHERS, AND THE CALL TO PERFORMANCE

Many qualitative researchers and interpretive ethnographers are in the seventh moment, performing culture as they write it, understanding that the dividing line between performativity (doing) and performance (done) has disappeared (Conquergood, 1998, p. 25). But even as this disappearance occurs, matters of racial injustice remain. The indigenous other is a racialized other.

On this W. E. B. Du Bois (1901/1978), reminds us that "the problem of the twenty-first century, on a global scale, will be the problem of the color line" (p. 281) and that "modern democracy cannot succeed unless peoples of different races and religions are also integrated into the democratic whole" (p. 288). This integration cannot be imposed by one culture or nation on another; it must come from within the cultures involved.

Du Bois addressed race from a performance standpoint. He understood that "from the arrival of the first African slaves on American soil . . . the definitions and meanings of blackness have been intricately linked to issues of theater and performance" (Elam, 2001, p. 4).[7] In his manifesto for an all-black, indigenous theater, Du Bois (1926) imagined a site for pedagogical performances that articulate positive black "social and cultural agency" (Elam, 2001, p. 6). His radical theater (Du Bois, 1926, p. 134), like that of Anna Deavere Smith (2003), is a political theater about blacks, written by blacks, for blacks, performed by blacks in local theaters. Radical indigenous theater is a weapon for fighting racism and white privilege. Gilbert (2003) elaborates on this topic, showing how indigenous whiteface performances unsettle fixed racial categories based on skin color: "Such acts . . . remind us of the historical role played by theatre in negotiating suppressed fears and fantasies of colonizing nations" (p. 680).

### A Brief History of Indigenous Theater

Lhamon (1998) traces the origins of blackface minstrelsy in the United States to the early 1800s and marketplace transactions in New York City. By the 1840s, white performers in blackface where using blackness as a way to represent the color of nonwhite persons, including African Americans, Asian Americans, and Native Americans (Bean, 2001, p. 173). According to Bean (2001), the "first black minstrels . . . existed as early as 1850" (p. 177), and within a short time African American male and female impersonators where engaged in satiric, subversive performances that were critical of white stereotypes of blacks (p. 187). Ellison (1964) observes that such black performers were tricksters, playing a joke on the white audience, laughing at the audience among themselves, understanding that blackface was a "counterfeiting of the black American's identity" (p. 53). Thus by the mid-19th century a subversive theater was born within the racist institution of minstrelsy.

Gilbert (2003) describes blackface minstrelsy as the "symptomatic nineteenth-century stage form for an era of territorial expansion, not just in the United States but also in other settler colonies with growing non-indigenous populations" (p. 683). From the 1850s forward, minstrelsy had a transnational presence in the performances of touring groups that performed in Australia, New Zealand, Canada, the United States, Britain, Germany, France, Italy, India, Jamaica, Nigeria, and South Africa. The American minstrel show traveled to the popular stage in the Canadian West, where its subject matter included narratives about runaway slaves and Native Canadians (Gilbert, 2003, p. 683). When William Cody's Wild West show toured Europe, it offered audiences a Far East section called the "Dream of the Orient" (Reddin, 1999, p. 158). In every geographic location where the minstrel show appeared, it validated racism and imperialism.

At the same time, indigenous performance companies were contributing to a counterdiscourse that embodied the critical race consciousness identified by Ellison (1964). Indians playing Indians for whites and blacks playing blacks for whites were engaged in reflexive, doubly inverted performances that mocked and ridiculed white racist stereotypes. In this way, indigenous theater criticizes the racial masquerade behind blackface. In such performances the performativity of race is revealed. The indigenous performer in whiteface (or blackface) peels back, as in pentimento, the colors and shades of whiteness, showing that "white is a color that exists only because some of us get told we're black or yellow or Indians" (Gilbert, 2003, p. 689).

Using a ventriloquized discourse, the whiteface performer forces spectators to confront themselves "mirrored/parodied in the whiteface minstrel mask" (Gilbert, 2003, p. 693). Native Canadian whiteface performers in Daniel David Moses's play *Almighty Voice and His Wife* (1992) deploy ventriloquism to turn the tables on whites. In the stand-up section of the play, just before the finale, the Interlocutor, dressed in top hat and tails along with white gloves and studded white boots taunts the audience:

You're that redskin! You're that wagon burner! That feather head, Chief Bullshit. No, Chief Shitting Bull! Oh, no, no. Bloodthirsty savage. Yes, you're primitive, uncivilized, a cantankerous cannibal. Unruly redman, you lack human intelligence! Stupidly stoic, sick, demented, foaming at the maws! Weirdly mad and dangerous, alcoholic, diseased, dirty, filthy, stinking, ill fated degenerate race, vanishing, dying lazy, mortifying. (pp. 94–95; quoted in Gilbert, 2003, p. 693)

Through double coding, race and gender exchanges, and the deployment of minstrel tropes, Moses has Indians criticizing Indians playing Indians. In this way, Gilbert (2003) observes, Moses "critiques hegemonically defined Indian stereotypes" (p. 692) even as he reflexively stages a grotesque spectacle of "Native performers enacting their own objectification" (p. 693).

Such performances function as genealogies. As Gilbert (2003) notes, they document the "historical dissemination of particular performance practices across space and time" (p. 696). By manipulating the tropes of minstrelsy, indigenous performers use whiteface and blackface to critique specific colonial practices. Thus Aboriginal Australians in whiteface performances protest the colonial habit of poisoning Aborigines with flour, just as Moses uses Indians in whiteface in his reenactment of the massacre at Wounded Knee (Gilbert, 2003, p. 696). In these ways, Gilbert argues, whiteface "is continually subjected to processes of citation and appropriation that triangulate white, black, and indigenous performance traditions in complex ways" (p. 696). Indigenous theater thus exposes whiteness in its ordinary and extreme forms. Made visible as a repressive sign of violent racial domination, whiteness "is forced to show its colors" (p. 698).

▣   ▣   ▣

Some African American authors, such as bell hooks, have elaborated the need for a black political performance aesthetic. Writing about her childhood, hooks (1990) has described how she and her sisters learned about race in America by watching

the Ed Sullivan show on Sunday nights. . . . seeing on that show the great Louis Armstrong, Daddy, who was usually silent, would talk about the music, the way Armstrong was being treated, and the political implications of his appearance. . . . responding to televised cultural production, black people could express rage about racism. . . . unfortunately . . . black folks were not engaged in writing a body of critical cultural analysis. (pp. 3–4)

▣   ▣   ▣

## ▣ INDIGENOUS VOICES, CRITICAL PEDAGOGY, AND EPISTEMOLOGIES OF RESISTANCE

Several scholars, such as Sandoval (2000), Collins (1998), Mutua and Swadener (2004), and Bishop (Volume 1, Chapter 5), have observed that we are in the midst of what Lopez (1998) calls "a large-scale social movement of anticolonialist discourse" (p. 226). This movement is evident in the emergence and proliferation of indigenous epistemologies and methodologies (Sandoval, 2000), including the arguments of African American, Chicana/o, Latina/o, Native American, First Nations, Native Hawaiian, and Māori scholars. These epistemologies are forms of critical pedagogy; that is, they embody a critical politics of representation that is embedded in the rituals of indigenous communities. Always already political, they are relentlessly critical of transnational capitalism and its destructive presence in the indigenous world (see Kincheloe & McLaren, 2000).

## Epistemologies of Resistance

Indigenous pedagogies are grounded in an oppositional consciousness that resists "neocolonizing postmodern global formations" (Sandoval, 2000, pp. 1–2). These pedagogies fold theory, epistemology, methodology, and praxis into strategies of resistance that are unique to each indigenous community. Thus the oppositional consciousness of Kaupapa Māori research is both like and unlike black feminist epistemology (Collins, 1991, 1998), Chicana feminisms (Anzaldúa, 1987; Moraga, 1993), "red pedagogy" (Grande, 2000; Harjo & Bird, 1997), and Hawaiian epistemology (Meyer, 2003). Common to all is a commitment to indigenism, to an indigenist outlook, that assigns the highest priority to the rights of indigenous peoples, to the traditions, bodies of knowledge, and values that have "evolved over many thousands of years by native peoples the world over" (Churchill, 1996, p. 509).

Indigenist pedagogies are informed, in varying and contested ways, by decolonizing, revolutionary, and socialist feminisms. Such feminisms, in turn, address issues of social justice, equal rights, and nationalisms of "every racial, ethnic, gender, sex, class, religion, or loyalist type" (Sandoval, 2000, p. 7). Underlying each indigenist formation is a commitment to moral praxis, to issues of self-determination, empowerment, healing, love, community solidarity, respect for the earth, and respect for elders.

Indigenists resist the positivist and postpositivist methodologies of Western science because nonindigenous scholars too frequently use these formations to validate colonizing knowledge about indigenous peoples. Indigenists deploy, instead, interpretive strategies and skills that fit the needs, languages, and traditions of their respective indigenous communities. These strategies emphasize personal performance narratives and *testimonios*.

### A Māori Pedagogy

Māori scholar Russell Bishop (1994, 1998) presents a collaborative, participatory epistemological model of Kaupapa Māori research, which is characterized by the absence of a need to be in control and by a desire to be connected to and part of a moral community in which a primary goal is the compassionate understanding of another's moral position (see also Bishop, Volume 1, Chapter 5; Heshusius, 1994). The Māori indigenist researcher wants to participate in a collaborative, altruistic relationship in which, as Bishop (1998) puts it, nothing "is desired for the self" (p. 207). The research is evaluated against participant-driven criteria based in the cultural values and practices that circulate in Māori culture, including metaphors that stress self-determination, the sacredness of relationships, embodied understanding, and the priority of community over self. Researchers are led to develop new storylines and criteria of evaluation that reflect these understandings. These participant-driven criteria function as resources for resistance against positivist and neoconservative desires to "establish and maintain control of the criteria for evaluating Māori experience" (p. 212).

Sandoval (2000) observes that indigenists enact an ethically democratizing stance that is committed to "equalizing power differentials between humans" (p. 114). The goal "is to consolidate and extend . . . manifestos of liberation in order to better identify and specify a mode of emancipation that is effective within first world decolonizing global conditions during the twenty-first century" (p. 2).

### Treaties as Pedagogy

Indigenist pedagogies confront and work through government treaties, ideological formations, historical documents, and broken promises that connect indigenist groups and their fates to the capitalist colonizers. For example, as Churchill (1996) notes, during the "first 90-odd years of its existence the United States entered into and ratified more than 370 separate treaties . . . [and] has . . . defaulted on its responsibilities under every single treaty obligation it ever incurred with regard to Indians" (pp. 516–517; see also Stirling, 1965). The aboriginal rights of First Nations tribes in Canada were not recognized in law until the Constitution Act of 1982 (Henderson, 2000, p. 165). In New Zealand, Māori debate the Treaty of Waitangi, which was signed between Māori chiefs and the British Crown in 1840. This treaty was defined as a charter for power sharing between Māori and *pakeha*, or white settlers, but in reality it subjugated Māori to the *pakeha* nation-state (Smith, 1999, p. 57; see also Bishop, Volume 1, Chapter 5).

Linda Smith (2000) observes that Māori attempts "to engage in the activities of the state through the mechanisms of the Treaty of Waitangi have won some space . . . [but] this space is severely limited . . . as it has had to be wrestled not only from the state, but also from the community of positivist scientists whose regard for Māori is not sympathetic (p. 232). What is "now referred to as 'Kaupapa Māori research'" (p. 224) is an attempt to find a space and set of practices that honors Māori culture, convinces Māori people of the value of research for Māori, and shows the *pakeha* (white) research community the need for greater Māori involvement in research. Kaupapa Māori research is culturally safe and relevant, and it involves the mentorship of Māori (p. 228).

### A Red Pedagogy

Native American indigenous scholars thicken the argument by articulating a spoken indigenous epistemology "developed over *thousands* of years of *sustained* living on this Land" (Rains et al., 2000, p. 337). An American Indian or "red" pedagogy

(Grande, 2000) criticizes simplistic readings of race, ethnicity, and identity. This pedagogy privileges personal identity performance narratives—that is, stories and poetry that emphasize self-determination and indigenous theory (Brayboy, 2000). Grande (2000) describes the four characteristics of a red pedagogy: (a) politically, it maintains "a quest for sovereignty, and the dismantling of global capitalism"; (b) epistemologically, it privileges indigenous knowledge; (c) the earth is its "spiritual center"; (d) socioculturally, it is grounded in "tribal and traditional ways of ways of life" (p. 355). The performance of such rituals validates traditional ways of life. The performance embodies the ritual. It is the ritual. In this sense the performance becomes a form of public pedagogy. It uses the aesthetic to foreground cultural meanings and to teach these meanings to performers and audience members alike.

### A Hawaiian Pedagogy

Manulani Aluli Meyer's (2003) discussion of Hawaiian epistemology complements the above description of a red pedagogy. As Meyer notes, a Hawaiian pedagogy resists colonial systems of knowing and educating; and it fights for an authentic Hawaiian identity (p. 192). It defines epistemology culturally; that is, it asserts that there are specific Hawaiian ways of knowing and being in the world (p. 187). According to Meyer, seven themes shape this epistemology: spirituality, physical space, the cultural nature of the senses, relational knowing, practical knowing, language as being, and the unity of mind and body (p. 193).

This framework stresses the place of morality in knowledge production. Culture restores culture. Culture is sacred. Culture is performed. Spirituality is basic to culture. It is sensuous and embodied, involving all the senses—taste, sight, smell, hearing, and touch. Knowledge is experienced and expressed in sensuous terms, in stories and critical personal narratives that focus on the importance of practice and repetition (p. 185). Knowledge is relational. The self knows itself through the other. Knowing the other and the self locates the person in a relational context. This involves harmony, balance, being generous, being responsible, being a good listener, and being kind.

## Decolonizing the Academy

As I have argued above, critical indigenist pedagogies contest the complicity of the modern university with neocolonial forces (Battiste, 2000a). They encourage and empower indigenous peoples to make colonizers confront and be accountable for the traumas of colonization. In rethinking and radically transforming the colonizing encounter, these pedagogies imagine postcolonial societies that honor difference and promote healing. Indigenist pedagogies attempt to rebuild nations and their peoples through the use of restorative indigenous ecologies. These native ecologies celebrate survival, remembering, sharing, gendering, new forms of naming, networking, protecting, and democratizing daily life (Battiste, 2000b; Smith, 1999, pp. 142–162).

Theory, method, and epistemology are aligned in this project, anchored in the moral philosophies that are taken for granted in indigenous cultures and language communities (L. T. Smith, 2000, p. 225). This worldview endorses pedagogies of emancipation and empowerment, pedagogies that encourage struggles for autonomy, cultural well-being, cooperation, and collective responsibility. Such pedagogies demand that indigenous groups own the research process. They speak the truth "to people about the reality of their lives" (Collins, 1998, p. 198), equip them with the tools they need to resist oppression, and move them to struggle, to search for justice (Collins, 1998, pp. 198–199).

## Indigenous Research as Localized Critical Theory

In their commitments, indigenous epistemologies overlap with critical theory. Indeed, Linda Smith (2000) connects her version of indigenous inquiry, Kaupapa Māori research, with critical theory and cultural studies, suggesting, with Graham Smith (2000), that Kaupapa Māori research is a "local theoretical position that is the modality through which the emancipatory goal of critical theory, in a specific historical, political and social context is practised" (L. T. Smith, 2000, p. 229; see also Bishop, Volume 1, Chapter 5). However, critical theory fits well with the Māori worldview, which asserts that Māori are connected to the universe and their place in it through the principle of *whakapapa*. This principle tells Māori that they are the seeds or direct descendants of the heavens. Through this principle, Māori trace their heritage to the very beginning of time (L. T. Smith, 2000, pp. 234–235).

*Whakapapa* turns the universe into a moral space where all things great and small are interconnected, including science and research. Smith (2000, p. 239) argues that this and related beliefs lead the Māori to ask eight questions about any research project, including those projects guided by critical theory:

1. What research do we want done?

2. Whom is it for?

3. What difference will it make?

4. Who will carry it out?

5. How do we want the research done?

6. How will we know it is worthwhile?

7. Who will own the research?

8. Who will benefit?

These questions are addressed to Māori and non-Māori alike. For research to be acceptable, each question must be answered in the affirmative; that is, Māori must conduct, own, and benefit from any research that is done on or for them.

These eight questions serve to interpret critical theory through a moral lens, through key Māori principles, including *whakapapa*. They shape the moral space that aligns Kaupapa Māori research with critical theory. Thus both formations are situated within the antipositivist debate. Both rest on antifoundational epistemologies. Each privileges performative issues of gender, race, class, equity, and social justice. Each develops its own understandings of community, critique, resistance, struggle, and emancipation (L. T. Smith, 2000, p. 228). Each understands that the outcome of a struggle can never be predicted in advance, that struggle is always local and contingent. It is never final (L. T. Smith, 2000, p. 229).

As Linda Smith (2000) observes, by localizing discourses of resistance, and by connecting these discourses to performance ethnography and critical pedagogy, Kaupapa Māori research enacts what critical theory "actually offers to oppressed, marginalized and silenced groups . . . [that is,] through emancipation groups such as the Māori would take greater control of their own lives and humanity" (p. 229). This requires that indigenous groups "take hold of the project of emancipation and attempt to make it a reality on their own terms" (p. 229). This means that inquiry is always political and moral, grounded in principles centered on autonomy, home, family, and kinship, on a collective community vision that requires that research not be a "purchased product . . . owned by the state" (p. 231).

Localized critical indigenous theory encourages indigenists to confront key challenges connected to the meanings of science, community, and democracy. Graham Smith (2000, pp. 212–215) and Linda Smith (2000) outlines these challenges, asking that indigenists do the following:

1. Be proactive; they should name the world for themselves. (Further, "being Māori is an essential criterion for carrying out Kaupapa Māori research"; L. T. Smith, 2000, pp. 229–230.)

2. Craft their own version of science, including how science and scientific understandings will be used in their world.

3. Develop a participatory model of democracy that goes beyond the "Westminister 'one person, one vote, majority rule'" (G. Smith, 2000, p. 212).

4. Use theory proactively, as an agent of change, but act in ways that are accountable to the indigenous community and not just the academy.

5. Resist new forms of colonization, such as the North American Free Trade Agreement, while contesting neocolonial efforts to commodify indigenous knowledge.

By proactively framing participatory views of science, democracy, and community, indigenous peoples take control of their own fates. They refuse to be sidetracked into always responding to nonindigenous others' attempts to define their life situations (G. Smith, 2000, p. 210).

## Pedagogies of Hope and Liberation

Linda Smith (1999, pp. 142–162) outlines some 25 different indigenous projects that have been developed in response to the continuing pressures of colonialism and colonization, including projects that create, name, restore, democratize, reclaim, protect, remember, and celebrate lost histories and cultural practices.[8] These indigenous projects embody a pedagogy of hope and freedom. They turn the pedagogies of oppression and colonization into pedagogies of liberation. They are not purely utopian, for they map concrete performances that can lead to positive social transformations. They embody ways of resisting the process of colonization.

Smith's moral agenda privileges four interpretive research processes. The first is *decolonization,* which reclaims indigenous cultural practices and reworks these practices at the political, social, spiritual, and psychological levels. *Healing,* the second process, also involves restorative physical, spiritual, psychological, and social practices. The third process, *transformation,* focuses on changes that move back and forth from the psychological level to the social, political, economic, and collective levels. *Mobilization*, at the local, national, regional, and global levels, is the fourth basic process. It speaks to collective efforts to change Māori society.

These four interdependent processes encompass issues of cultural survival and collective self-determination. In every instance they work to decolonize Western methods and forms of inquiry and to empower indigenous peoples. These are the states of "being through which indigenous communities are moving" (Smith, 1999, p. 116). These states involve spiritual and social practices. They are pedagogies of healing and hope, pedagogies of recovery, material practices that benefit indigenous peoples both materially and spiritually.

## ▣ CRITICAL PERSONAL NARRATIVE AS COUNTERNARRATIVE

The move to performance has been accompanied by a shift in the meanings of ethnography and ethnographic writing. As Richardson (2000) observes, the narrative genres connected to ethnographic writing have "been blurred, enlarged, altered to include poetry [and] drama" (p. 929). She uses the term *creative analytic practice* (CAP) to describe these many different reflexive performance narrative forms, which include not only performance autoethnography but also short stories, conversations, fiction, personal narratives, creative nonfiction, photographic essays, personal essays, personal narratives of the self, writing-stories, self-stories, fragmented and layered texts, critical autobiographies, memoirs, personal histories, cultural criticism writings, co-constructed performance narratives, and performance writings that blur the edges between text, representation, and criticism.

Critical personal narratives are counternarratives, testimonies, autoethnographies, performance texts, stories, and accounts that disrupt and disturb discourse by exposing the complexities and contradictions that exist under official history (Mutua & Swadener, 2004). The critical personal narrative is a central genre of contemporary decolonizing writing. As a creative analytic practice, it is used to criticize "prevailing structures and relationships of power and inequity in a relational context" (Mutua & Swadener, 2004, p. 16).

Counternarratives such as those presented in Guantánamo: "Honor Bound to Defend Freedom," "Indians in the Park," and "Remembering to Forget" explore the "intersections of gender and voice, border crossing, dual consciousness, multiple identities, and selfhood in a . . . post-colonial and postmodern world" (Mutua & Swadener, 2004, p. 16). The testimonio is another form of counternarrative. One of the purposes of the testimonio is to raise political consciousness by bearing witness to social injustices experienced at the group level (Mutua & Swadener, 2004, p. 18). Linda Smith (1999) begins her discussion of the testimonio with these lines from Menchú (1984): "My name is Rigoberta Menchú, I am twenty three years old, and this is my testimony" (p. 1). The testimonio presents oral evidence to an audience, often in the form of a monologue. As Smith describes it, the indigenous testimonio is "a way of talking about an extremely painful event or series of events." The testimonio can be constructed as "a monologue and as a public performance" (p. 144).

Critics have contended that Menchú made up her story; they have concluded that it is not the truth because it cannot be verified through scientific methodology (Cook-Lynn, 2001, p. 203; see also Beverley, 2000). But, as Cook-Lynn (2001, p. 34) observes, respectfully, testimonio should be read as remembering and honoring the past, not as factual truthfulness. Further, Cook-Lynn notes, Menchú was appealing to nonindigenous audiences to respect the treaties of the past so that Indigenous and nonindigenous peoples might build new and harmonious relationships based on mutual respect and cooperation. Menchú's critics have ignored the ethical tenets and utopian impulses behind her story (pp. 34–35).

The struggle of colonized indigenous peoples to tell their own stories is at stake in criticisms of the testimonio. Those who reject these stories because they do not exhibit so-called factual truthfulness are denying indigenous voices their rightful place in this political discourse (Cook-Lynn, 2001, p. 203).

The contemporary neocolonial world stages existential crises grounded in issues of race and gender. Following Turner (1986, p. 34), the performance ethnographer enters these existential spaces, writing and performing personal narratives that make racial prejudice and oppression visible. Focusing on racial epiphanies, the writer imposes a utopian narrative on the text, imagining how situations of racial conflict and strife could be different. The utopian counternarrative offers hope, showing others how to engage in actions that decolonize, heal, and transform. In this way, critical personal narratives extend Linda Smith's project.

Poet and social activist Mary Weems (2002, p. xx) reads the sign below as she crosses the state line between Indiana and Illinois:

**"The People of Illinois Welcome You"**

comes right after the LYNCH ROAD sign

and the LYNCH ROAD sign comes right after

I see a thin road strung with the bodies

of black men like burned out lights

their backs twisting in the wind,

the road littered with try out ropes,

gleaned chicken parts, and cloth napkins

soiled wiping the lips of the audience.

I know roads don't hang,

but the welcome sandwiched between

the word like bread

cuts off my air

and I pull to the side of the road

loosen my collar

and search for bones.

Narratives such as Weems's embrace the critical democratic storytelling imagination. They are hopeful of peaceful, nonviolent change, understanding that hope, like freedom, is "an ontological need" (Freire, 1992/1999, p. 8). Hopeful stories are grounded in struggles and interventions that enact the sacred values of love, care, community, trust, and well-being (Freire, 1992/1999, p. 9). Hopeful stories confront and interrogate cynicism, the belief that change is not possible.

The critical democratic storytelling imagination is pedagogical. As a form of instruction, it helps persons think critically, historically, and sociologically. It exposes the pedagogies of oppression that produce injustice (see Freire, 2001, p. 54). It contributes to reflective ethical self-consciousness. It gives people a language and a set of pedagogical practices that turn oppression into freedom, despair into hope, hatred into love, doubt into trust. This ethical self-consciousness shapes a critical racial self-awareness that contributes to utopian dreams of racial equality and racial justice.

## ▣ PERFORMANCE, PEDAGOGY, AND POLITICS

Clearly, the current historical moment requires morally informed performance- and arts-based disciplines that will help indigenous and nonindigenous peoples recover meaning in the face of senseless, brutal violence, violence that produces voiceless screams of terror and insanity. Globally, cynicism and despair rein. Never have we had a greater need for a militant utopianism to help us imagine a world free of conflict, oppression, terror, and death. We need oppositional performance disciplines that will show us how to create radical utopian spaces within our public institutions.

"Performance-sensitive ways of knowing" (Conquergood, 1998, p. 26) contribute to an epistemological and political pluralism that challenges existing ways of knowing and representing the world. Such formations are more inclusionary and better suited than other ways for thinking about postcolonial or "subaltern" cultural practices (Conquergood, 1998, p. 26). Performance approaches to knowing insist on immediacy and involvement. They consist of partial, plural, incomplete, and contingent understandings, not analytic distance or detachment, the hallmarks of positivist paradigms (Conquergood, 1998, p. 26; Pelias, 1999, pp. ix, xi).

The interpretive methods, democratic politics, and feminist communitarian ethics of performance (auto)ethnography offer progressives a series of tools for countering reactionary political discourse. At stake is an "insurgent cultural politics" (Giroux, 2000a, p. 127; see also Giroux, 2000b) that challenges neofascist state apparatuses.[9] This cultural politics encourages a critical race consciousness that flourishes within the free and open spaces of a "vibrant democratic public culture and society" (Giroux, 2000a, p. 127).

Within the spaces of this new performative cultural politics, a radical democratic imagination redefines the concept of civic participation and public citizenship.[10] Struggle, resistance, and dialogue are key features of its pedagogy. The rights of democratic citizenship are extended to all segments of public and private life, from the political to the economic, from the cultural to the personal. This pedagogy seeks to regulate market and economic relations in the name of social justice and environmental causes. A genuine democracy requires hope, dissent, and criticism.

These ideals embrace a democratic-socialist-feminist agenda. This agenda queers straight heterosexual democracy (Butler, 1997). It asserts capitalism's fundamental incompatibility with democracy while thinking its way into a model of critical citizenship that attempts to unthink whiteness and the cultural logics of white supremacy (McLaren, 1997a, 1997b, 1998a, 1998b, 1999, 2001; Roediger, 2002; West, 1993). It seeks a revolutionary multiculturalism that is grounded in relentless resistance to the structures of neoliberalism. It critiques the ways in which the media are used to manufacture consent (Chomsky, 1996). It sets as its goal transformations of global capital, so that individuals may begin to "truly live as liberated subjects of history" (McLaren, 1997b, p. 290).

## A Moral Crisis

Indigenous discourse thickens the argument, for the central tensions in the world today go beyond the crises in capitalism and neoliberalism's version of democracy. The central crisis, as defined by Native Canadian, Native Hawaiian, Māori, and American Indian pedagogy, is spiritual, "rooted in the increasingly virulent relationship between human beings and the rest of nature" (Grande, 2000, p. 354). Linda Smith (1999), discusses the concept of spirituality within Māori discourse, giving added meaning to the crisis at hand:

> The essence of a person has a genealogy which could be traced back to an earth parent. . . . A human person does not stand alone, but shares with other animate . . . beings relationships based on a shared "essence" of life . . . [including] the significance of place, of land, of landscape, of other things in the universe. . . . Concepts of spirituality which Christianity attempted to destroy, and then to appropriate, and then to claim, are critical sites of resistance for indigenous peoples. The value, attitudes, concepts and language embedded in beliefs about spirituality represent . . . the clearest contrast and mark of difference between indigenous peoples and the West. It is one of the few parts of ourselves which the West cannot decipher, cannot understand and cannot control . . . yet. (p. 74)

A respectful performance pedagogy honors these views of spirituality. It works to construct a vision of the person and the environment that is compatible with these principles. This pedagogy demands a politics of hope, of loving, of caring nonviolence grounded in inclusive moral and spiritual terms.

## Performance (Auto)Ethnography as a Pedagogy of Freedom

Within this framework, to extend Freire (1998) and elaborate Glass (2001, p. 17), performance autoethnography contributes to a conception of education and democracy as pedagogies of freedom. Dialogic performances enacting a performance-centered ethic provide materials for critical reflection on radical democratic educational practices. In so doing, performance ethnography enacts a theory of selfhood and being. This is an ethical, relational, and moral theory. The purpose of "the particular type of relationality we call research ought to be enhancing . . . moral agency" (Christians, 2002, p. 409; see also Lincoln, 1995, p. 287), moral discernment, critical consciousness, and a radical politics of resistance.

Indeed, performance ethnography enters the service of freedom by showing how, in concrete situations, persons produce history and culture, "even as history and culture produce them" (Glass, 2001, p. 17). Performance texts provide the grounds for liberation practice by opening up concrete situations that are being transformed through acts of resistance. In this way, performance ethnography advances the causes of liberation.

## ▣ CRITICAL PERFORMANCE PEDAGOGY

A commitment to critical performance pedagogy and critical race theory gives the human disciplines a valuable lever for militant utopian cultural criticism. In his book

*Impure Acts,* Henry Giroux (2000a) calls for a practical, performative view of pedagogy, politics, and cultural studies. He seeks an interdisciplinary project that would enable theorists and educators to form a progressive alliance "connected to a broader notion of cultural politics designed to further racial, economic, and political democracy" (p. 128).

Such a project engages a militant utopianism, a provisional Marxism without guarantees, a cultural studies that is anticipatory, interventionist, and provisional. It does not back away from the contemporary world in its multiple global versions, including the West, the Third World, the moral, political, and geographic spaces occupied by First Nations and Fourth World persons, persons in marginal or liminal positions (Ladson-Billings, 2000, p. 263). Rather, it strategically engages this world in those liminal spaces where lives are bent and changed by the repressive structures of the new conservatism. This project pays particular attention to the dramatic increases around the world in domestic violence, rape, child abuse, hate crimes, and violence directed toward persons of color (Comaroff & Comaroff, 2001, pp. 1–2).

## Critical Race Theory and Participatory, Performance Action Inquiry

Extending critical legal theory, critical race theory theorizes life in these liminal spaces, offering "pragmatic strategies for material and social transformation" (Ladson-Billings, 2000, p. 264). Critical race theory assumes that racism and white supremacy are the norms in U.S. society. Critical race scholars use performative, storytelling autoethnographic methods to uncover the ways in which racism operates in daily life. Critical race theory challenges those neoliberals who argue that civil rights have been attained for persons of color. It also criticizes those who argue that the civil rights crusade is a long, slow struggle (Ladson-Billings, 2000, p. 264). Critical race theorists argue that the problem of racism requires radical social change and that neoliberalism and liberalism lack the mechanisms and imaginations to achieve such change (Ladson-Billings, 2000, p. 264). Critical race theorists contend that whites have been the main beneficiaries of civil rights legislation.

Strategically, critical race theory examines the ways in which race is performed, including the cultural logics and performative acts that inscribe and create whiteness and nonwhiteness (McLaren, 1997b, p. 278; Roediger, 2002, p. 17). In an age of globalization and diasporic, postnational identities, the color line should no longer be an issue, but, sadly, it is (McLaren, 1997b, p. 278).

Drawing on the complex traditions embedded in participatory action research (Fine et al., 2003; Kemmis & McTaggart, 2000), critical performance pedagogy implements a commitment to participation and performance *with,* not *for,* community members. Amplifying the work of Fine et al. (2003, pp. 176–177), this project builds on local knowledge and experience developed at the bottom of social hierarchies. Following Linda Smith's (1999) lead, participatory, performance work honors and respects local knowledge, customs, and practices and incorporates those values and beliefs into participatory, performance action inquiry (Fine et al., 2003, p. 176).

Work in this participatory, activist performance tradition gives back to the community, "creating a legacy of inquiry, a process of change, and material resources to enable transformations in social practices" (Fine et al., 2003, p. 177). Through performance and participation, scholars develop a "participatory mode of consciousness" (Bishop, 1998, p. 208) that folds them into the moral accountability structures of the group.

## ▣ CULTURAL POLITICS AND AN INDIGENOUS RESEARCH ETHIC

Nonindigenous scholars have much to learn from indigenous scholars about how radical democratic practices can be made to work. As I have indicated above, scholars such as Graham Smith, Linda Smith, and Russell Bishop are committed to a set of moral and pedagogical imperatives and, as Smith (1999) notes, "to acts of reclaiming, reformulating, and reconstituting indigenous cultures and languages . . . to the struggle to become self-determining" (p. 142). These acts lead to a research program that is devoted to the pursuit of social justice. In turn, a specific approach to inquiry is required. In his discussion of a Māori approach to creating knowledge, Bishop (1998) observes that researchers in Kaupapa Māori contexts are

> repositioned in such a way as to no longer need to seek to *give voice to others,* to *empower* others, to *emancipate* others, to refer to others as *subjugated* voices, but rather to listen and participate . . . in a process that facilitates the development in people of a sense of themselves as agentic and of having an authoritative voice. . . . An indigenous Kaupapa Māori approach to research . . . challenges colonial and neo-colonial discourses that inscribe "otherness." (pp. 207–208)

This participatory mode of knowing privileges sharing, subjectivity, personal knowledge, and the specialized knowledges of oppressed groups. It uses concrete experience as a criterion against which to measure meaning and truth. It encourages a participatory mode of consciousness (Bishop, 1998, p. 205), asking that the researcher give the group a gift as a way of honoring the group's sacred spaces. If the group picks up the gift, the group members and the researcher can create a shared reciprocal relationship (Bishop, 1998, p. 207). This relationship is built on understandings about Māori beliefs and cultural practices.

In turn, the research is evaluated against Māori-based criteria. As in Freire's revolutionary pedagogy, West's prophetic pragmatism, and Collins's Afrocentric feminist moral ethic, dialogue is valued as a method for assessing knowledge claims in Māori culture. The Māori moral position also privileges storytelling, listening, voice, and personal performance narratives (Collins, 1991, pp. 208–212). This moral pedagogy rests on an ethic of care, love, and personal accountability that honors individual uniqueness and emotionality in dialogue (Collins, 1991, pp. 215–217). This is a performative, pedagogical ethic, grounded in the ritual, sacred spaces of family, community, and everyday moral life (Bishop, 1998, p. 203). It is not imposed by some external bureaucratic agency.

This view of knowing parallels the commitment within certain forms of red peda- gogy to the performative as a way of being, a way of knowing, and a way of expressing moral ties to the community (Grande, 2000, p. 356; Graveline, 2000, p. 361). Fyre Jean Graveline (2000, p. 263), a Metis woman, speaks:

As Metis woman, scholar, activist, teacher, healer

I enact First Voice as pedagogy and
methodology

Observing my own lived experience as an Educator
 Sharing meanings with Others . . .

My Voice is Heard
 in concert with Students and Community Participants . . .

I asked: What pedagogical practices
 Enacted through my Model-In-Use
  contribute to what kinds of transformational learning?
   For whom?

## Moral Codes and the Performative as a Site of Resistance

Because it expresses and embodies moral ties to the community, the performative view of meaning serves to legitimate indigenous worldviews. Meaning and resistance are embodied in the act of performance itself. The performative is political, the site of resistance. At this critical level, the performative provides the context for resistance to neoliberal and neoconservative attacks on the legitimacy of the worldview in question. The performative is where the soul of the culture resides. The performative haunts the liminal spaces of the culture. In their sacred and secular performances, the members of the culture honor one another and the culture itself.

In attacking the performative, critics attack the culture.[11] Smith (1999) states the issue clearly: "The struggle for the validity of indigenous knowledges may no longer be over the *recognition* that indigenous people have ways of knowing the world which are unique, but over proving the authenticity of, and control over, our own forms of knowledge" (p. 104).

Scholars need a new set of moral and ethical research protocols. Fitted to the indige- nous (and nonindigenous) perspective, these are moral matters. They are shaped by the feminist, communitarian principles of sharing, reciprocity, relationality, community, and neighborliness (Lincoln, 1995, p. 287). They embody a dialogic ethic of love and faith grounded in compassion (Bracci & Christians, 2002, p. 13; West, 1993). Accordingly, the purpose of research is not the production of new knowledge per se. Rather, the purposes are pedagogical, political, moral, and ethical, involving the enhancement of moral agency, the production of moral discernment, a commitment to praxis, justice, an ethic of resistance, and a performative pedagogy that resists oppression (Christians, 2002, p. 409).

A code embodying these principles interrupts the practice of positivist research, resists the idea that research is something that white men do to indigenous peoples. Further, unlike the institutional review board model of Western inquiry, which is not content driven, an indigenous code is anchored in a particular culture and that culture's way of life; it connects its moral model to a set of political and ethical actions that will increase well-being in the indigenous culture. The code refuses to turn indigenous peoples into subjects who are the natural objects of white inquiry (Smith, 1999, p. 118). It rejects the Western utilitarian model of the individual as someone who has rights distinct from the rights of the larger group, "for example the right of an individual to give his or her own knowledge, or the right to give informed consent" (Smith, 1999, p. 118)—rights that are not recognized in Māori culture. As Smith (1999) observes, "Community and indigenous rights or views in this area are generally not . . . respected" (p. 118).

Research ethics for scholars working with the members of Māori and other indigenous communities "extend far beyond issues of individual consent and confidentiality" (L. T. Smith, 2000, p. 241). These ethics are not "prescribed in codes of conduct for researchers but tend to be prescribed for Māori researchers in cultural terms," advising researchers to show respect for the Māori by exhibiting a willingness to listen, to be humble, to be cautious, to avoid flaunting knowledge, and to avoid trampling over the *mana* of people (L. T. Smith, 2000, p. 242).

## Turning the Tables on the Colonizers

Here at the end it is possible to imagine scenarios that turn the tables on the colonizer. It is possible to imagine, for example, research practices that really do respect the rights of human subjects, protocols for obtaining subjects' informed consent that truly inform and do not deceive, and research projects that not only do no harm but in fact benefit human communities.

Here I borrow from indigenous scholar Robert Williams (1997, pp. 62–67), who takes us back to Lewis and Clark and asks us to imagine another version, or telling, of the Lewis and Clark myth. Williams turns Jefferson back on himself, arguing that it is possible to use the Lewis and Clark narratives as an occasion for reimagining the human rights of indigenous peoples. Williams argues that indigenous peoples should take up Jefferson's theory of democracy and claim, as whites did, their natural, inalienable rights to self-recognition, self-governance, survival, autonomy, life, liberty, the pursuit of happiness, and sovereign authority over their own lands.

Similarly, the celebrations of Lewis and Clark's expedition that took place in 2003–2004 can be turned into political performances, transgressive events. In this form of historical theater, Lewis and Clark would be pushed aside, ignored. In their place, performers would enact a utopian disruptive theater, reclaiming and celebrating the inalienable rights of Native Americans to own and control their own history. These performance texts would be occasions for indigenous peoples to write their way into the journals, to offer their stories and narratives about the effects of Lewis and Clark on their ancestors and on themselves. Like the writings of William Least Heat-Moon (1999), these tellings would recover buried history, moments, representations, ancient pictographs that write across "all of us—red, white, mixed" (p. 217). This theater would advance the project of indigenous decolonization (Williams, 1997, p. 62). These performance events would represent Lewis and Clark as colonizers whose "undaunted courage" will no longer be recognized, honored, or celebrated.

## ▣ CONCLUSION

The ethical and moral models of Russell Bishop, Graham Smith, and Linda Smith call into question the more generic, utilitarian, biomedical Western model of ethical inquiry (see Christians, 2000, 2002; Bracci & Christians, 2002). They outline a radical ethical path for the future that transcends the institutional review board model, which focuses almost exclusively on the problems associated with betrayal, deception, and harm. They call for a collaborative social science research model that makes the researcher responsible not to a removed discipline (or institution) but to those studied. This model stresses personal accountability, caring, the value of individual expressiveness, the capacity for empathy, and the sharing of emotionality (Collins, 1991, p. 216). This model implements collaborative, participatory, performative inquiry. It forcefully aligns the ethics of research with a politics of the oppressed, with a politics of resistance, hope, and freedom.

This model directs scholars to take up moral projects that respect and reclaim indigenous cultural practices. Such work produces spiritual, social, and psychological healing, which in turn leads to multiple forms of transformation at the personal and social levels. These transformations shape the processes of mobilization and collective action, and the resulting actions help persons realize a radical politics of possibility. This politics enacts emancipatory discourses and critical pedagogies that honor human differences and draw inspiration from the struggles of indigenous peoples. In listening to indigenous storytellers, we learn new ways of being moral and political in the social world. Thus *research* ceases to be a dirty word.

## ▣ NOTES

1. This chapter extends some of the arguments I present in my book *Performance Ethnography* (Denzin, 2003, pp. 1–23, 242–262). A performative cultural studies enacts a critical, cultural pedagogy. It does so by using dialogue, performative writing, and the staging and performance of texts involving audience members. Regarding the terms *decolonization* and *the postcolonial*, which I use here, it should be noted that decolonizing research is not necessarily post-colonial research. Decolonization is a process that critically engages, at all levels, imperialism, colonialism, and postcoloniality. Decolonizing research implements indigenous epistemologies and critical interpretive practices that are shaped by indigenous research agendas (Smith, 1999, p. 20). In this chapter, I draw on the work of Shohat (1992), Hall (1996b), Dimitriadis and McCarthy (2001), and Swadener and Mutua (2004) in troubling the concept of "post-colonial"—with Hall, I ask, When was the colonial ever post? In its hyphenated form, the term *post-colonial* functions as a temporal marker, implying linearity and chronology. With Swadener and Mutua, I prefer the form *postcolonial*, which implies a constant, complex, intertwined back-and-forth relationship between past and present. In this sense there is no postcolonial, there are only endless variations on neocolonial formations (Soto, 2004, p. ix). Regarding the term *critical pedagogy:* As Kincheloe and McLaren (2000) note, cultural production functions as "a form of education, as it generates knowledge, shapes values, and constructs identity. . . . By using the term *cultural pedagogy,* we are specifically referring to the ways particular cultural agents produce particular hegemonic ways of seeing" (p. 285; see also McLaren, 1998a, p. 441). Critical pedagogy attempts to disrupt and deconstruct these cultural practices performatively in the name of a "more just, democratic, and egalitarian society" (Kincheloe & McLaren, 2000, p. 285; but see Lather, 1998).

2. See also Ashcroft, Griffiths, and Tiffin (2002); Battiste (2000a, 2000b); Balme and Christopher (2001); Beverley (2000); Bishop (1994, 1998); Churchill (1996); Cook-Lynn (1998); Cruikshank (1990); Ellsworth (1989); Gilbert (2003); Greenwood (2001); Harjo and Bird (1997); Kondo (2000); Magowan (2000); Marker (2003); Menchú (1984, 1998); Pratt (2001); G. Smith (2000); L. T. Smith (2000); and C. W.-I.-T.-R. Smith (2000).

3. This theater often uses verbatim accounts of injustices and acts of violence encountered in daily life. Mienczakowski (1995, 2001) provides a history of "verbatim theater" and discusses extensions of this approach that use oral history, participant observation, and the methods of ethnodrama (see also Chessman, 1971). One contemporary use of verbatim theater is the play *Guantánamo: "Honor Bound to Defend Freedom,"* created by Victoria Brittain, a former journalist, and Gillian Slovo, a novelist. This play addresses the plight of British citizens imprisoned at the U.S. naval base at Guantánamo Bay, Cuba, in the period since the September 11, 2001, terrorist attacks on the United States. According to Alan Riding (2004), writing for the *New York Times,* the "power of 'Guantánamo' is that it is not really a play but a re-enactment of views expressed in interviews, letters, news conferences and speeches by various players in the post-Sept. 11 Iraq war drama, from British Muslim detainees to lawyers, from Mr. Rumsfeld to Jack Straw, Britain's foreign secretary." Riding notes that Nicolas Kent, the play's director, believes that "political theater works here [in England] because the British have an innate sense of justice. 'When we do stories about injustice,' he said, 'there is a groundswell of sympathy . . . people are furious that there isn't due process.' . . . 'With Islamophobia growing around the world today,' he said, 'I wanted to show that we, too, think there is an injustice'" (p. B2).

4. At another level, indigenous participatory theater extends the project connected to Third World popular theater—that is, political theater "used by oppressed Third World people

to achieve justice and development for themselves" (Etherton, 1988, p. 991), The International Popular Theatre Alliance, organized in the 1980s, uses existing forms of cultural expression to fashion improvised dramatic productions that analyze situations of poverty and oppression. This grassroots approach uses agitprop and sloganizing theater pieces (pieces designed to foment political action) to stimulate collective awareness and collective action at the local level. This form of theater has been popular in Latin America, in Africa, in parts of Asia, in India, and among Native populations in the Americas (Etherton, 1988, p. 992).

5. The *Camera Eye* and *Newsreel* are Dos Passos's (1937) terms (and methods) for incorporating current events and newsworthy items into a text.

6. The positive-negative debate often neglects indigenous discourses, presupposes consensus where there may be none, shuts down nuanced debate, and ignores the performative features of racial identity (Smith, 1997, pp. 3–4).

7. For Du Bois, race and racism were social constructions. Performances, minstrelsy, blackface are powerful performance devices that produce and reproduce the color line. Du Bois believed that African Americans need performance spaces where they can control how race is constructed. Consequently, as Elam (2001, pp. 5–6) observes, African American theater and performance have been central sites for the interrogation of race and the color line (see also Elam & Krasner, 2001). As Elam notes, "The inherent 'constructedness' of performance and the malleability of the devices of the theater serve to reinforce the theory that blackness . . . and race . . . are hybrid, fluid concepts" (pp. 4–5). Stuart Hall (1996a, p. 473) is correct in his observation that persons of color have never been successful in escaping the politics and theaters of (racial) representation.

8. Other projects involve a focus on testimonies, new forms of storytelling, and returning to, as well as reframing and regendering, key cultural debates.

9. I define fascism as a conservative, extreme right-wing political, economic, and sociolegal state formation characterized by authoritarian forms of government, extreme nationalism, manufactured consent at key levels of public opinion, racism, a large military-industrial complex, foreign aggressiveness, anticommunism, state-supported corporate capitalism, state-sponsored violence, extreme restrictions on individual freedom, and tendencies toward an "Orwellian condition of perpetual war . . . [and] a national security state in which intelligence agencies and the military replace publicly elected officials in deciding national priorities" (Rorty, 2002, p. 13).

10. Here there are obvious political connections to Guy Debord's (1970) situationist project.

11. Smith (1999, p. 99) presents 10 performative ways to be colonized, 10 ways in which science, technology, and Western institutions place indigenous peoples—indeed, any group of human beings—their languages, cultures, and environments, at risk. These ways include the Human Genome Diversity Project as well as scientific efforts to reconstruct previously extinct indigenous peoples and projects that deny global citizenship to indigenous peoples while commodifying, patenting, and selling indigenous cultural traditions and rituals.

▣ REFERENCES

Ambrose, S. (1996). *Undaunted courage: Meriwether Lewis, Thomas Jefferson, and the opening of the American West.* New York: Simon & Schuster.

Anzaldúa, G. (1987). *Borderlands/la frontera: The new mestiza.* San Francisco: Aunt Lute.

Ashcroft, B., Griffiths, G., & Tiffin, H. (2002). *The empire writes back: Theory and practice in post-colonial literature* (2nd ed.). New York: Routledge.

Balme, C., & Carstensen, A. (2001). Home fires: Creating a Pacific theatre in the diaspora. *Theatre Research International, 26,* 35–46.

Battiste, M. (2000a). Introduction: Unfolding the lessons of colonization. In M. Battiste (Ed.), *Reclaiming indigenous voice and vision* (pp. xvi–xxx). Vancouver: University of British Columbia Press.

Battiste, M. (2000b). Maintaining aboriginal identity: Language and culture in modern society. In M. Battiste (Ed.), *Reclaiming indigenous voice and vision* (pp. 192–208). Vancouver: University of British Columbia Press.

Bean, A. (2001). Black minstrelsy and double inversion, circa 1890. In H. J. Elam, Jr., & D. Krasner (Eds.), *African American performance and theater history: A critical reader* (pp. 171–191). New York: Oxford University Press.

Benjamin, W. (1969). *Illuminations* (H. Zohn, Trans.). New York: Harcourt, Brace & World.

Benjamin, W. (1983–1984). Theoretics of knowledge: Theory of progress. *Philosophical Forum, 15* (1–2), 1–40.

Beverley, J. (2000). *Testimonio,* subalternity, and narrative authority. In N. K. Denzin & Y. S. Lincoln (Eds.), *Handbook of qualitative research* (2nd ed., pp. 555–565). Thousand Oaks, CA: Sage.

Bishop, R. (1994). Initiating empowering research. *New Zealand Journal of Educational Studies, 29,* 175–188.

Bishop, R. (1998). Freeing ourselves from neo-colonial domination in research: A Māori approach to creating knowledge. *International Journal of Qualitative Studies in Education, 11,* 199–219.

Bracci, S. L., & Christians, C. G. (2002). Editors' introduction. In S. L. Bracci & C. G. Christians (Eds.), *Moral engagement in public life: Theorists for contemporary ethics* (pp. 1–15). New York: Peter Lang.

Brayboy, B. M. (2000). The Indian and the researcher: Tales from the field. *International Journal of Qualitative Studies in Education, 13,* 415–426.

Butler, J. (1997). *Excitable speech: A politics of the performative.* New York: Routledge.

Chessman, P. (1971). Production casebook. *New Theatre Quarterly, 1,* 1–6.

Chomsky, N. (1996). *Class warfare: Interviews with David Barasamian.* Monroe, ME: Common Courage.

Christians, C. G. (2000). Ethics and politics in qualitative research. In N. K. Denzin & Y. S. Lincoln (Eds.), *Handbook of qualitative research* (2nd ed., pp. 133–155). Thousand Oaks, CA: Sage.

Christians, C. G. (2002). Introduction. In Ethical issues and qualitative research [Special issue]. *Qualitative Inquiry, 8,* 407–410.

Churchill, W. (1996). I am an indigenist: Notes on the ideology of the Fourth World. In W. Churchill, *From a native son: Selected essays in indigenism, 1985–1995* (pp. 509–546). Boston: South End.

Collins, P. H. (1991). *Black feminist thought: Knowledge, consciousness, and the politics of empowerment.* New York: Routledge, Chapman & Hall.

Collins, P. H. (1998). *Fighting words: Black women and the search for justice.* Minneapolis: University of Minnesota Press.

Comaroff, J., & Comaroff, J. L. (2001). Millennial capitalism: First thoughts on a second coming. In J. Comaroff & J. L. Comaroff (Eds.), *Millennial capitalism and the culture of neoliberalism* (pp. 1–56). Durham, NC: Duke University Press.

Conquergood, D. (1998). Beyond the text: Toward a performative cultural politics. In S. J. Dailey (Ed.), *The future of performance studies: Visions and revisions* (pp. 25–36). Washington, DC: National Communication Association.

Cook-Lynn, E. (1998). American Indian intellectualism and the new Indian story. In D. A. Mihesuah (Ed.), *Natives and academics: Researching and writing about American Indians* (pp. 111–138). Lincoln: University of Nebraska Press.

Cook-Lynn, E. (2001). *Anti-Indianism in modern America: A voice from Tatekeya's earth.* Urbana: University of Illinois Press.

Cruikshank, J. (in collaboration with Sidney, A., Smith, K., & Ned, A.). (1990). *Life lived like a story: Life stories of three Yukon Native elders.* Lincoln: University of Nebraska Press.

Debord, G. (1970). *Society of the spectacle.* Detroit: Black & Red.

Denzin, N. K. (2003). *Performance ethnography: Critical pedagogy and the politics of culture.* Thousand Oaks, CA: Sage.

Denzin, N. K. (2004a). Indians in the park. *Qualitative Research, 4*(3).

Denzin, N. K. (2004b). Remembering to forget: Lewis and Clark and Native Americans in Yellowstone. *Communication and Critical/Cultural Studies, 1,* 219–249.

Denzin, N. K. (in press). *Searching for Yellowstone.* London: Sage.

Dimitriadis, G., & McCarthy, C. (2001). *Reading and teaching the postcolonial: From Baldwin to Basquiat and beyond.* New York: Teachers College Press.

Dorst, J. D. (1999). *Looking west.* Philadelphia: University of Pennsylvania Press.

Dos Passos, J. (1937). *U.S.A.: I. The 42nd parallel; II. Nineteen nineteen; III. The big money.* New York: Modern Library.

Du Bois, W. E. B. (1926, July). Krigwa Players Little Negro Theatre: The story of a little theatre movement. *Crisis,* pp. 134–136.

Du Bois, W. E. B. (1978). The problem of the twentieth century is the problem of the color line. In W. E. B. Du Bois, *On sociology and the black community* (D. S. Green & E. Driver, Eds.) (pp. 281–289). Chicago: University of Chicago Press. (Original work published 1901)

Du Bois, W. E. B. (1989). *The souls of black folk.* New York: Bantam. (Original work published 1903)

Elam, H. J., Jr. (2001). The device of race: An introduction. In H. J. Elam, Jr., & D. Krasner (Eds.), *African American performance and theater history: A critical reader* (pp. 3–16). New York: Oxford University Press.

Elam, H. J., Jr., & Krasner, D. (Eds.). (2001). *African American performance and theater history: A critical reader.* New York: Oxford University Press.

Ellison, R. (1964). Change the joke and slip the yoke. In R. Ellison, *Shadow and act* (pp. 45–59). New York: Random House.

Ellsworth, E. (1989). Why doesn't this feel empowering? Working through the repressive myths of critical methodology. *Harvard Education Review, 59,* 297–324.

Etherton, M. (1988). Third World popular theatre. In M. Banham (Ed.), *The Cambridge guide to theatre* (pp. 991–992). Cambridge: Cambridge University Press.

Fine, M., Roberts, R., Torre, M., Upegui, D., Bowen, I., Boudin, K., et al. (2003). Participatory action research: From within and beyond prison bars. In P. M. Camic, J. E. Rhodes, & L. Yardley (Eds.), *Qualitative research in psychology: Expanding perspectives in methodology and design* (pp. 173–198). Washington, DC: American Psychological Association.

Freire, P. (1998). *Pedagogy of freedom: Ethics, democracy, and civic courage* (P. Clarke, Trans.). Boulder, CO: Rowman & Littlefield.

Freire, P. (1999). *Pedagogy of hope: Reliving* Pedagogy of the oppressed. New York: Continuum. (Original work published 1992)

Freire, P. (2001). *Pedagogy of the oppressed* (30th anniversary ed.). New York: Continuum.

Garoian, C. R. (1999). *Performing pedagogy: Toward an art of politics.* Albany: State University of New York Press.

Gilbert, H. (2003). Black and white and re(a)d all over again: Indigenous minstrelsy in contemporary Canadian and Australian theatre. *Theatre Journal, 55,* 679–698.

Giroux, H. (2000a). *Impure acts: The practical politics of cultural studies.* New York: Routledge.

Giroux, H. (2000b). *Stealing innocence: Corporate culture's war on children.* New York: Palgrave.

Glass, R. D. (2001). On Paulo Freire's philosophy of praxis and the foundations of liberation education. *Educational Researcher, 30*(2), 15–25.

Goffman, E. (1959). *The presentation of self in everyday life.* New York: Doubleday.

Grande, S. (2000). American Indian identity and intellectualism: The quest for a new red pedagogy. *International Journal of Qualitative Studies in Education, 13,* 343–360.

Graveline, F. J. (2000). Circle as methodology: Enacting an aboriginal paradigm. *International Journal of Qualitative Studies in Education, 13,* 361–370.

Greenwood, J. (2001). Within a third space. *Research in Drama Education, 6,* 193–205.

Grossman, E. (2003). *Adventuring along the Lewis and Clark trail.* San Francisco: Sierra Club.

Hall, S. (1996a). What is this "black" in black popular culture? In D. Morley & K.-H. Chen (Eds.), *Stuart Hall: Critical dialogues in cultural studies* (pp. 465–475). London: Routledge.

Hall, S. (1996b). When was "the post-colonial"? Thinking at the limit. In I. Chambers & L. Curt (Eds.), *The post-colonial question: Common skies, divided horizons* (pp. 242–260). London: Routledge.

Harjo, J., & Bird, G. (1997). Introduction. In J. Harjo & G. Bird (Eds.), *Reinventing the enemy's language: Contemporary Native women's writings of North America* (pp. 19–31). New York: W. W. Norton.

Henderson, J. (S.) Y. (2000). Postcolonial ledger drawing: Legal reform. In M. Battiste (Ed.), *Reclaiming indigenous voice and vision* (pp. 161–171). Vancouver: University of British Columbia Press.

Heshusius, L. (1994). Freeing ourselves from objectivity: Managing subjectivity or turning toward a participatory mode of consciousness. *Educational Researcher, 23*(3), 15–22.

hooks, b. (1990). *Yearning: Race, gender, and cultural politics.* Boston: South End.

Horton, S. (2003, March). Keeping their legacy alive. *Audubon Magazine,* pp. 90–93.

Kaomea, J. (2004). Dilemmas of an indigenous academic: A native Hawaiian story. In K. Mutua & B. B. Swadener (Eds.), *Decolonizing research in cross-cultural contexts: Critical personal narratives* (pp. 27–44). Albany: State University of New York Press.

Kemmis, S., & McTaggart, R. (2000). Participatory action research. In N. K. Denzin & Y. S. Lincoln (Eds.), *Handbook of qualitative research* (2nd ed., pp. 567–605). Thousand Oaks, CA: Sage.

Kincheloe, J. L., & McLaren, P. (2000). Rethinking critical theory and qualitative research. In N. K. Denzin & Y. S. Lincoln (Eds.), *Handbook of qualitative research* (2nd ed., pp. 279–313). Thousand Oaks, CA: Sage.

Kondo, D. (2000). (Re)visions of race: Contemporary race theory and the cultural politics of racial crossover in documentary theatre. *Theatre Journal, 52,* 81–107.

Ladson-Billings, G. (2000). Racialized discourses and ethnic epistemologies. In N. K. Denzin & Y. S. Lincoln (Eds.), *Handbook of qualitative research* (2nd ed., pp. 257–277). Thousand Oaks, CA: Sage.

Lather, P. (1998). Critical pedagogy and its complicities: A praxis of stuck places. *Educational Theory, 48,* 487–497.

Least Heat-Moon, W. (1999). *River horse: A voyage across America.* Boston: Houghton Mifflin.

Lhamon, W. T., Jr. (1998). *Raising Cain: Blackface performance from Jim Crow to hip hop.* Cambridge, MA: Harvard University Press.

Lincoln, Y. S. (1995). Emerging criteria for quality in qualitative and interpretive inquiry. *Qualitative Inquiry, 1,* 275–289.

Lopez, G. R. (1998). Reflections on epistemology and standpoint theories: A response to "A Māori approach to creating knowledge." *International Journal of Qualitative Studies in Education, 11,* 225–231.

Madison, D. S. (1998). Performances, personal narratives, and the politics of possibility. In S. J. Dailey (Ed.), *The future of performance studies: Visions and revisions* (pp. 276–286). Washington, DC: National Communication Association.

Madison, D. S. (1999). Performing theory/embodied writing. *Text and Performance Quarterly, 19,* 107–124.

Magowan, F. (2000). Dancing with a difference: Reconfiguring the poetic politics of Aboriginal ritual as national spectacle. *Australian Journal of Anthropology, 11,* 308–321.

Marker, M. (2003). Indigenous voice, community, and epistemic violence: The ethnographer's "interests" and what "interests" the ethnographer. *International Journal of Qualitative Studies in Education, 16,* 361–375.

McLaren, P. (1997a). The ethnographer as postmodern flaneur: Critical reflexivity and posthybridity as narrative engagement. In W. G. Tierney & Y. S. Lincoln (Eds.), *Representation and the text: Re-framing the narrative voice* (pp. 143–177). Albany: State University of New York Press.

McLaren, P. (1997b). *Revolutionary multiculturalism: Pedagogies of dissent for the new millennium.* Boulder, CO: Westview.

McLaren, P. (1998a). Revolutionary pedagogy in post-revolutionary times: Rethinking the political economy of critical education. *Educational Theory, 48,* 431–462.

McLaren, P. (1998b). Whiteness is .... The struggle for postcolonial hybridity. In J. L. Kincheloe, S. Steinberg, N. Rodriguez, & R. Chennault (Eds.), *White reign: Deploying whiteness in America* (pp. 63–75). New York: St. Martin's.

McLaren, P. (1999). *Schooling as a ritual performance: Toward a political economy of educational symbols and gestures* (3rd ed.). Lanham, MD: Rowman & Littlefield.

McLaren, P. (2001). Che Guevara, Paulo Freire, and the politics of hope: Reclaiming critical pedagogy. *Cultural Studies↔Critical Methodologies, 1,* 108–131.

Mead, G. H. (1938). *The philosophy of the act.* Chicago: University of Chicago Press.

Menchú, R. (1984). *I, Rigoberta Menchú: An Indian woman in Guatemala* (E. Burgos-Debray, Ed.; A. Wright, Trans.). London: Verso.

Menchú, R. (1998). *Crossing borders* (A. Wright, Trans.). London: Verso.

Meyer, M. A. (2003). *Ho'oulu: Our time of becoming; Hawaiian epistemology and early writings.* Honolulu: 'Ai Pohaku Press Native Books.

Mienczakowski, J. (1995). The theater of ethnography: The reconstruction of ethnography into theater with emancipatory potential. *Qualitative Inquiry, 1,* 360–375.

Mienczakowski, J. (2001). Ethnodrama: Performed research—limitations and potential. In P. Atkinson, A. Coffey, S. Delamont, J. Lofland, & L. H. Lofland (Eds.), *Handbook of ethnography* (pp. 468–476). London: Sage.

Mills, C. W. (1959). *The sociological imagination.* New York: Oxford University Press.

Moraga, C. (1993). *The last generation: Prose and poetry.* Boston: South End.

Moses, D. D. (1992). *Almighty Voice and his wife.* Stratford, ON: Williams-Wallace.

Mutua, K., & Swadener, B. B. (2004). Introduction. In K. Mutua & B. B. Swadener (Eds.), *Decolonizing research in cross-cultural contexts: Critical personal narratives* (pp. 1–23). Albany: State University of New York Press.

Pelias, R. J. (1999). *Writing performance: Poeticizing the researcher's body.* Carbondale: Southern Illinois University Press.

Pratt, M. L. (2001). *I, Rigoberta Menchú* and the "culture wars." In A. Arias (Ed.), *The Rigoberta Menchú controversy* (pp. 29–48). Minneapolis: University of Minnesota Press.

Rains, F. V., Archibald, J. A., & Deyhle, D. (2000). Through our eyes and in our own words: The voices of indigenous scholars. *International Journal of Qualitative Studies in Education, 13,* 337–342.

Reddin, P. (1999). *Wild West shows.* Urbana: University of Illinois Press.

Richardson, L. (2000). Writing: A method of inquiry. In N. K. Denzin & Y. S. Lincoln (Eds.), *Handbook of qualitative research* (2nd ed., pp. 923–948). Thousand Oaks, CA: Sage.

Riding, A. (2004, June 15). On a London stage, a hearing for Guantánamo detainees. *New York Times,* p. B2.

Roediger, D. (2002). *Colored white: Transcending the racial past.* Berkeley: University of California Press.

Ronda, J. P. (1984). *Lewis and Clark among the Indians.* Lincoln: University of Nebraska Press.

Rorty, R. (2002, October 21). Fighting terrorism with democracy. *The Nation, 275,* 11–14.

Sandoval, C. (2000). *Methodology of the oppressed.* Minneapolis: University of Minnesota Press.

Schullery, P. (1997). *Searching for Yellowstone: Ecology and wonder in the last wilderness.* Boston: Houghton Mifflin.

Semali, L. M., & Kincheloe, J. L. (1999). Introduction: What is indigenous knowledge and why should we study it? In L. M. Semali & J. L. Kincheloe (Eds.), *What is indigenous knowledge? Voices from the academy* (pp. 3–57). New York: Falmer.

Shohat, E. (1992). Notes on the post colonial. *Social Forces, 31/32,* 99–111.

Slaughter, T. P. (2003). *Exploring Lewis and Clark: Reflections on men and wilderness.* New York: Knopf.

Smith, A. D. (2003). *House arrest and Piano.* New York: Anchor.

Smith, C. W.-I.-T.-R. (2000). Straying beyond the boundaries of belief: Māori epistemologies inside the curriculum. *Educational Philosophy and Theory, 32,* 43–51.

Smith, G. (2000). Protecting and respecting indigenous knowledge. In M. Battiste (Ed.), *Reclaiming indigenous voice and vision* (pp. 209–224). Vancouver: University of British Columbia Press.

Smith, L. T. (1999). *Decolonizing methodologies: Research and indigenous peoples.* Dunedin, New Zealand: University of Otago Press.

Smith, L. T. (2000). Kaupapa Māori research. In M. Battiste (Ed.), *Reclaiming indigenous voice and vision* (pp. 225–247). Vancouver: University of British Columbia Press.

Smith, V. (1997). Introduction. In V. Smith (Ed.), *Representing blackness: Issues in film and video* (pp. 1–12). New Brunswick, NJ: Rutgers University Press.

Soto, L. D. (2004). Foreword: Decolonizing research in cross-cultural contexts: Issues of voice and power. In K. Mutua & B. B. Swadener (Eds.), *Decolonizing research in cross-cultural contexts: Critical personal narratives* (pp. ix–xi). Albany: State University of New York Press.

Spindel, C. (2000). *Dancing at halftime: Sports and the controversy over American Indian mascots.* New York: New York University Press.

Stirling, E. W. (1965). The Indian reservation system of the Northern Plains. In M. S. Kennedy (Ed.), *The red man's West* (pp. 300–312). New York: Hastings House.

Swadener, B. B., & Mutua, K. (2004). Afterword. In K. Mutua & B. B. Swadener (Eds.), *Decolonizing research in cross-cultural contexts: Critical personal narratives* (pp. 255–260). Albany: State University of New York Press.

Turner, V. M. (1986). Dewey, Dilthey, and drama: An essay in the anthropology of experience. In V. M. Turner & E. M. Bruner (Eds.), *The anthropology of experience* (pp. 33–44). Urbana: University of Illinois Press.

Ulmer, G. L. (1989). *Teletheory: Grammatology in the age of video.* New York: Routledge.

Weems, M. (2002). *I speak from the wound that is my mouth.* New York: Peter Lang.

West, C. (1993). *Keeping the faith: Philosophy and race in America.* New York: Routledge.

Williams, R. A., Jr. (1997). Thomas Jefferson: Indigenous American storyteller. In J. P. Ronda (Ed.), *Thomas Jefferson and the changing West: From conquest to conservation* (pp. 43–74). Albuquerque: University of New Mexico Press.

Williams, T. T. (1984). *Pieces of white shell: A journey to Navajoland.* Albuquerque: University of New Mexico Press.

# 15

# WRITING

## A Method of Inquiry

### Laurel Richardson and Elizabeth Adams St. Pierre

T he world of ethnography has expanded in ways that were unimaginable a decade ago, when this chapter was first written for the first edition of the *Handbook*. Qualitative researchers in a variety of disciplines—medicine, law, education, the social sciences, and the humanities—have since found *writing as a method of inquiry* to be a viable way in which to learn about themselves and their research topic. The literature is vast and varied.

In light of these developments, this chapter's revision is organized into three parts. In Part 1, Laurel Richardson discusses (a) the contexts of social scientific writing both historically and contemporaneously, (b) the creative analytical practice ethnography genre, and (c) the direction her work has taken during the past decade, including "writing stories" and collaborations across the humanities/social sciences divide. In Part 2, Elizabeth St. Pierre provides an analysis of how writing as a method of inquiry coheres with the development of ethical selves engaged in social action and social reform. In Part 3, Richardson provides some writing practices/exercises for the qualitative writer.

Just as the chapter reflects our own processes and preferences, we hope that your writing will do the same. The more different voices are honored within our qualitative community, the stronger—and more interesting—that community will be.

▣ PART 1: QUALITATIVE WRITING

Laurel Richardson

A decade ago, in the first edition of the *Handbook,* I confessed that for years I had yawned my way through numerous supposedly exemplary qualitative studies. Countless numbers of texts had I abandoned half read, half scanned. I would order a new book with great anticipation—the topic was one I was interested in, the author was someone I wanted to read—only to find the text boring. In "coming out" to colleagues and students about my secret displeasure with much of qualitative writing, I found a community of like-minded discontents. Undergraduates, graduates, and colleagues alike said that they found much of qualitative writing to be—yes—boring.

We had a serious problem; research topics were riveting and research valuable, but qualitative books were underread. Unlike quantitative work that can carry its meaning in its tables and summaries, qualitative work carries its meaning in its entire text. Just as a piece of literature is not equivalent to its "plot summary," qualitative research is not contained in its abstract. Qualitative research has to be read, not scanned; its meaning is in the reading. It seemed foolish at best, and narcissistic and wholly self-absorbed at worst, to spend months or years doing research that ended up not being read and not making a difference to anything but the author's career. Was there some way in which to create texts that were vital and made a difference? I latched onto the idea of *writing as a method of inquiry.*

I had been taught, as perhaps you were as well, not to write until I knew what I wanted to say, that is, until my points were organized and outlined. But I did not like writing that way. I felt constrained and bored. When I thought about those writing instructions, I realized that they cohered with mechanistic scientism and quantitative research. I recognized that those writing instructions were themselves a sociohistorical invention of our 19th-century foreparents. Foisting those instructions on qualitative researchers created serious problems; they undercut writing as a dynamic creative process, they undermined the confidence of beginning qualitative researchers because their experience of research was inconsistent with the writing model, and they contributed to the flotilla of qualitative writing that was simply not interesting to read because writers wrote in the homogenized voice of "science."

Qualitative researchers commonly speak of the importance of the individual researcher's skills and aptitudes. The researcher—rather than the survey, the questionnaire, or the census tape—is the "instrument." The more honed the researcher, the better the possibility of excellent research. Students are taught to be open—to observe, listen, question, and participate. But in the past, they were not being taught to nurture their writing voices. During the past decade, however, rather than suppressing their voices, qualitative writers have been honing their writing skills. Learning to write in new ways does not take away one's traditional writing skills any more than learning a second language reduces one fluidity in one's first language. Rather, all kinds of qualitative writing have flourished.

## Writing in Contexts

Language is a constitutive force, creating a particular view of reality and of the Self. Producing "things" always involves value—what to produce, what to name the productions, and what the relationship between the producers and the named things will be. Writing things is no exception. No textual staging is ever innocent (including this one). Styles of writing are neither fixed nor neutral but rather reflect the historically shifting domination of particular schools or paradigms. Social scientific writing, like all other forms of writing, is a sociohistorical construction and, therefore, is mutable.

Since the 17th century, the world of writing has been divided into two separate kinds: literary and scientific. Literature, from the 17th century onward, was associated with fiction, rhetoric, and subjectivity, whereas science was associated with fact, "plain language," and objectivity (Clifford & Marcus, 1986, p. 5). During the 18th century, the Marquis de Condorcet introduced the term "social science." Condorcet (as cited in Levine, 1985) contended that "knowledge of the truth" would be "easy," and that error would be "almost impossible," if one adopted precise language about moral and social issues (p. 6). By the 19th century, literature and science stood as two separate domains. Literature was aligned with "art" and "culture"; it contained the values of "taste, aesthetics, ethics, humanity, and morality" (Clifford & Marcus, 1986, p. 6) as well as the rights to metaphorical and ambiguous language. Given to science was the belief that its words were objective, precise, unambiguous, noncontextual, and nonmetaphorical.

As the 20th century unfolded, the relationships between social scientific writing and literary writing grew in complexity. The presumed solid demarcations between "fact" and "fiction" and between "true" and "imagined" were blurred. The blurring was most hotly debated around writing for the public, that is, journalism. Dubbed by Thomas Wolfe as the "new journalism," writers consciously blurred the boundaries between fact and fiction and consciously made themselves the centers of their stories (for an excellent extended discussion of the new journalism, see Denzin, 1997, chap. 5). By the 1970s, "crossovers" between writing forms spawned the naming of oxymoronic genres— "creative nonfiction," "faction," "ethnographic fiction," the "nonfiction novel," and "true fiction." By 1980, the novelist E. L. Doctorow (as cited in Fishkin, 1985) would assert, "There is no longer any such things as fiction or nonfiction, there is only narrative" (p. 7).

Despite the actual blurring of genre, and despite our contemporary understanding that all writing is narrative writing, I would contend that there is still one major difference that separates fiction writing from science writing. The difference is not whether the text really is fiction or nonfiction; rather, the difference is the claim that the author makes for the text. Declaring that one's work is fiction is a different rhetorical move than is declaring that one's work is social science. The two genres bring in different audiences and have different impacts on publics and politics—and on how one's "truth claims" are to be evaluated. These differences should not be overlooked or minimized.

We are fortunate, now, to be working in a postmodernist climate, a time when a multitude of approaches to knowing and telling exist side by side. The core of postmodernism is the doubt that any method or theory, any discourse or genre, or any tradition or novelty has a universal and general claim as the "right" or privileged form of authoritative knowledge. Postmodernism suspects all truth claims of masking and serving particular interests in local, cultural, and political struggles. But conventional methods of knowing and telling are not automatically rejected as false or archaic. Rather, those standard methods are opened to inquiry, new methods are introduced, and then they also are subject to critique.

The postmodernist context of doubt, then, distrusts all methods equally. No method has a privileged status. But a postmodernist position does allow us to know "something" without claiming to know everything. Having a partial, local, and historical knowledge is still knowing. In some ways, "knowing" is easier, however, because postmodernism recognizes the situational limitations of the knower. Qualitative writers are off the hook, so to speak. They do not have to try to play God, writing as disembodied omniscient narrators claiming universal and atemporal general knowledge. They can eschew the questionable metanarrative of scientific objectivity and still have plenty to say as situated speakers, subjectivities engaged in knowing/telling about the world as they perceive it.

A particular kind of postmodernist thinking that I have found to be especially helpful is poststructuralism (for application of the perspective in a research setting, see Davies, 1994). Poststructuralism links language, subjectivity, social organization, and power. The centerpiece is language. Language does not "reflect" social reality but rather produces meaning and creates social reality. Different languages and different discourses within a given language divide up the world and give it meaning in ways that are not reducible to one another. Language is how social organization and power are defined and contested and the place where one's sense of self—one's subjectivity— is constructed. Understanding language as competing discourses—competing ways of giving meaning and of organizing the world—makes language a site of exploration and struggle.

Language is not the result of one's individuality; rather, language constructs one's subjectivity in ways that are historically and locally specific. What something means to individuals is dependent on the discourses available to them. For example, being hit by one's spouse is experienced differently depending on whether it is thought of as being within the discourse of "normal marriage," "husband's rights," or "wife battering." If a woman sees male violence as normal or a husband's right, she is unlikely to see it as wife battering, which is an illegitimate use of power that should not be tolerated. Similarly, when a man is exposed to the discourse of "childhood sexual abuse," he may recategorize and remember his own traumatic childhood experiences. Experience and memory are, thus, open to contradictory interpretations governed by social interests and prevailing discourses. The individual is both the site and subject of these discursive struggles for identity and for remaking memory. Because the individual is subject to multiple and competing discourses in many realms, one's subjectivity is shifting and contradictory—not stable, fixed, and rigid.

Poststructuralism, thus, points to the continual cocreation of the self and social science; they are known through each other. Knowing the self and knowing about the subject are intertwined, partial, historical local knowledges. Poststructuralism, then, permits—even invites or incites—us to reflect on our method and to explore new ways of knowing.

Specifically, poststructuralism suggests two important ideas to qualitative writers. First, it directs us to understand ourselves reflexively as persons writing from particular positions at specific times. Second, it frees us from trying to write a single text in which everything is said at once to everyone. Nurturing our own voices releases the censorious hold of "science writing" on our consciousness as well as the arrogance it fosters in our psyche; writing is validated as a method of knowing.

## CAP Ethnography

In the wake of postmodernist—including poststructuralist, feminist, queer, and critical race theory—critiques of traditional qualitative writing practices, the sacrosanctity of social science writing conventions has been challenged. The ethnographic genre has been blurred, enlarged, and altered with researchers writing in different formats for a variety of audiences. These ethnographies are like each other, however, in that they are produced through creative analytical practices. I call them "CAP [creative analytical processes] ethnographies."[1] This label can include new work, future work, or older work—wherever the author has moved outside conventional social scientific writing. CAP ethnographies are not alternative or experimental; they are, in and of themselves, valid and desirable representations of the social. In the foreseeable future, these ethnographies may indeed be the most desirable representations because they invite people in and open spaces for thinking about the social that elude us now.

The practices that produce CAP ethnography are both creative and analytical. Any dinosaurian beliefs that "creative" and "analytical" are contradictory and incompatible modes are standing in the path of a meteor; they are doomed for extinction. Witness the evolution, proliferation, and diversity of new ethnographic "species"—autoethnography, fiction, poetry, drama, readers' theater, writing stories, aphorisms, layered texts, conversations, epistles, polyvocal texts, comedy, satire, allegory, visual texts, hypertexts, museum displays, choreographed findings, and performance pieces, to name some of the categories that are discussed in the pages of the *Handbook*. These new "species" of qualitative writing adapt to the kind of political/social world we inhabit—a world of uncertainty. With many outlets for presentation and publication, CAP ethnographies herald a paradigm shift (Ellis & Bochner, 1996).

CAP ethnography displays the writing process and the writing product as deeply intertwined; both are privileged. The product cannot be separated from the producer, the mode of production, or the method of knowing. Because both traditional ethnographies and CAP ethnographies are being produced within the broader postmodernist climate of "doubt," readers (and reviewers) want and deserve to know how the researchers claim to know. How do the authors position the selves as knowers and tellers? These issues engage intertwined problems of subjectivity, authority, authorship, reflexivity, and process, on the one hand, and of representational form, on the other.

Postmodernism claims that writing is always partial, local, and situational and that our selves are always present no matter how hard we try to suppress them—but only partially present because in our writing we repress parts of our selves as well. Working from that premise frees us to write material in a variety of ways—to tell and retell. There is no such thing as "getting it right," only "getting it" differently contoured and nuanced. When using creative analytical practices, ethnographers learn about the topics and about themselves that which was unknowable and unimaginable using conventional analytical procedures, metaphors, and writing formats.

In traditionally staged research, we valorize "triangulation." (For a discussion of triangulation as method, see Denzin, 1978. For an application, see Statham, Richardson, & Cook, 1991.) In triangulation, a researcher deploys different methods—interviews, census data, documents, and the like—to "validate" findings. These methods, however, carry the same domain assumptions, including the assumption that there is a "fixed point" or an "object" that can be triangulated. But in CAP ethnographies, researchers draw from literary, artistic, and scientific genres, often breaking the boundaries of those genres as well. In what I think of as a postmodernist deconstruction of triangulation, CAP text recognizes that there are far more than "three sides" by which to approach the world. We do not triangulate; we crystallize.

I propose that the central imaginary for "validity" for postmodernist texts is not the triangle—a rigid, fixed, two-dimensional object. Rather, the central imaginary is the crystal, which combines symmetry and substance with an infinite variety of shapes, substances, transmutations, multidimensionalities, and angles of approach. Crystals grow, change, and are altered, but they are not amorphous. Crystals are prisms that reflect externalities and refract within themselves, creating different colors, patterns, and arrays casting off in different directions. What we see depends on our angle of repose—not triangulation but rather crystallization. In CAP texts, we have moved from plane geometry to light theory, where light can be both waves and particles.

*Travels With Ernest: Crossing the Literary/Sociological Divide* (Richardson & Lockridge, 2004) is a recent example of crystallization practices. *Travels With Ernest* is built on geographical travels (e.g., Russia, Ireland, Beirut, Copenhagen, Russia, Sedona, St. Petersburg Beach) that I shared with my husband Ernest Lockridge, who is a novelist and professor of English. We experienced the same sites but refracted them through different professional eyes, gender, sensibilities, biographies, spiritual and emotional longings. After we each independently wrote a narrative account—a personal essay—inspired by the travel, we read each other's account and engaged in wide-ranging (taped/transcribed) conversations across disciplinary lines about writing, ethics, authorship, collaboration, witnessing, fact/fiction, audiences, relationships, and the intersection of observation and imagination. The travels, thus, are physical, emotional, and intellectual.

The collaborative process modeled in *Travels With Ernest* honors each voice as separate and distinct, explores the boundaries of observation and imagination, witnessing and retelling, memory and memorializing, and it confirms the value of crystallization. I remain a sociologist; he remains a novelist. Neither of us gives up our core visions. In the process of our collaboration, however, we discovered many things about ourselves— about our relationships to each other, our families, our work, and our writing—that we would not have discovered if we were not collaborating. For example, we discovered that we wanted the last piece in the book to break the book's writing format—to model other possibilities. We constructed from our conversation (and its multiple interruptions) a movie script set in our own Great American Kitchen. We especially like that the collaborative method we displayed in our text is one that is open to everyone; indeed, it is strategic writing through which established hierarchies between the researcher and the researched, between the student and the teacher, can be breached.

Crystallization, without losing structure, deconstructs the traditional idea of "validity"; we feel how there is no single truth, and we see how texts validate themselves. Crystallization provides us with a deepened, complex, and thoroughly partial understanding of the topic. Paradoxically, we know more and doubt what we know. Ingeniously, we know there is always more to know.

### Evaluating CAP Ethnographies

Because the epistemological foundations of CAP ethnography differ from those of traditional social science, the conceptual apparatus by which CAP ethnographies can be evaluated differ. Although we are freer to present our texts in a variety of forms to diverse audiences, we have different constraints arising from self-consciousness about claims to authorship, authority, truth, validity, and reliability. Self-reflexivity brings to consciousness some of the complex political/ideological agendas hidden in our writing. Truth claims are less easily validated now; desires to speak "for" others are suspect. The greater freedom to experiment with textual form, however, does not guarantee a better product. The opportunities for writing worthy texts—books and articles that are "good reads"—are multiple, exciting, and demanding. But the work is harder and the guarantees are fewer. There is a lot more for us to think about.

One major issue is that of criteria. How does one judge an ethnographic work—new or traditional? Traditional ethnographers of good will have legitimate concerns about how their students' work will be evaluated if they choose to write CAP ethnography.

I have no definitive answers to ease their concerns, but I do have some ideas and preferences.

I see the ethnographic project as humanly situated, always filtered through human eyes and human perceptions, and bearing both the limitations and the strengths of human feelings. Scientific superstructure is always resting on the foundation of human activity, belief, and understandings. I emphasize ethnography as constructed through *research practices*. Research practices are concerned with enlarged understanding. Science offers some research practices—literature, creative arts, memory work (Davies et al., 1997), introspection (Ellis, 1991), and dialogical (Ellis, 2004). Researchers have many practices from which to choose and ought not be constrained by habits of somebody else's mind.

I believe in holding CAP ethnography to high and difficult standards; mere novelty does not suffice. Here are four of the criteria I use when reviewing papers or monographs submitted for social scientific publication:

1. *Substantive contribution.* Does this piece contribute to our *understanding* of social life? Does the writer demonstrate a deeply grounded (if embedded) social scientific perspective? Does this piece seem "true"—a credible account of a cultural, social, individual, or communal sense of the "real"? (For some suggestions on accomplishing this, see Part 3 of this chapter.)

2. *Aesthetic merit.* Rather than reducing standards, another standard is added. Does this piece succeed aesthetically? Does the use of creative analytical practices open up the text and invite interpretive responses? Is the text artistically shaped, satisfying, complex, and not boring?

3. *Reflexivity.* How has the author's subjectivity been both a producer and a product of this text? Is there adequate self-awareness and self-exposure for the reader to make judgments about the point of view? Does the author hold himself or herself accountable to the standards of knowing and telling of the people he or she has studied?

4. *Impact.* Does this piece affect me emotionally or intellectually? Does it generate new questions or move me to write? Does it move me to try new research practices or move me to action?

These are four of my criteria. Science is one lens, and creative arts is another. We see more deeply using two lenses. I want to look through both lenses to see a "social science art form"—a radically interpretive form of representation.

I am not alone in this desire. I have found that students from diverse social backgrounds and marginalized cultures are attracted to seeing the social world through two lenses. Many of these students find CAP ethnography beckoning and join the qualitative community. The more this happens, the more everyone will profit. The implications of race and gender would be stressed, not because it would be "politically correct" but rather because race and gender *are axes* through which symbolic and actual worlds have been constructed. Members of nondominant worlds know that and could insist that this knowledge be honored (cf. Margolis & Romero, 1998). The blurring of the humanities and the social sciences would be welcomed, not because it is "trendy" but rather because the blurring coheres more truly with the life sense and learning style of so many. This new qualitative community could, through its theory, analytical practices, and diverse membership, reach beyond academia and teach all of us about social injustice and methods for alleviating it. What qualitative researcher interested in social life would not feel enriched by membership in such a culturally diverse and inviting community? Writing becomes more diverse and author centered, less boring, and humbler. These are propitious opportunities. Some even speak of their work as spiritual.

## Writing Stories and Personal Narratives

The ethnographic life is not separable from the Self. Who we are and what we can be—what we can study, how we can write about that which we study—are tied to how a knowledge system disciplines itself and its members and to its methods for claiming authority over both the subject matter and its members.

We have inherited some ethnographic rules that are arbitrary, narrow, exclusionary, distorting, and alienating. Our task is to find concrete practices through which we can construct ourselves as ethical subjects engaged in ethical ethnography—inspiring to read and to write.

Some of these practices include working within theoretical schemata (e.g., sociology of knowledge, feminism, critical race theory, constructivism, poststructuralism) that challenge grounds of authority, writing on topics that matter both personally and collectively, experiencing *jouissance*, experimenting with different writing formats and audiences simultaneously, locating oneself in multiple discourses and communities, developing critical literacy, finding ways in which to write/present/teach that are less hierarchal and univocal, revealing institutional secrets, using positions of authority to increase diversity both in academic appointments and in journal publications, engaging in self-reflexivity, giving in to synchronicity, asking for what one wants, not flinching from where the writing takes one emotionally or spiritually, and honoring the embodiedness and spatiality of one's labors.

This last practice—honoring the location of the self—encourages us to construct what I call "writing stories." These are narratives that situate one's own writing in other parts of one's life such as disciplinary constraints, academic debates, departmental politics, social movements, community structures, research interests, familial ties, and personal history. They offer critical reflexivity about the writing self in different contexts as a valuable creative analytical practice. They evoke new questions about the self and the subject; remind us that our work is grounded, contextual, and rhizomatic; and demystify the research/writing process and help others to do the same.

They can evoke deeper parts of the self, heal wounds, enhance the sense of self—or even alter one's sense of identity.

In *Fields of Play: Constructing an Academic Life* (Richardson, 1997), I make extensive use of writing stories to contextualize 10 years of my sociological work, creating a text that is more congruent with poststructural understandings of the situated nature of knowledge. Putting my papers and essays in the chronological order in which they were conceptualized, I sorted them into two piles: "keeper" and "reject." When I reread my first keeper—a presidential address to the North Central Sociological Association— memories of being patronized, marginalized, and punished by my department chair and dean reemerged. I stayed with those memories and wrote a writing story about the disjunction between my departmental life and my disciplinary reputation. Writing the story was not emotionally easy; in the writing, I was reliving horrific experiences, but writing the story released the anger and pain. Many academics who read that story recognize it as congruent with their experiences—their untold stories.

I worked chronologically through the keeper pile, rereading and then writing the writing story evoked by the rereading—different facets, different contexts. Some stories required checking my journals and files, but most did not. Some stories were painful and took an interminable length of time to write, but writing them loosened their shadow hold on me. Other stories were joyful and reminded me of the good fortunes I have in friends, colleagues, and family.

Writing stories sensitize us to the potential consequences of all of our writing by bringing home—inside our homes and workplaces— the ethics of representation. Writing stories are not about people and cultures "out there"—ethnographic subjects (or objects). Rather, they are about ourselves—our workspaces, disciplines, friends, and family. What can we say and with what consequences? Writing stories bring the danger and poignancy or ethnographic representation "up close and personal."

Each writing story offers its writer an opportunity for making a situated and pragmatic ethical decision about whether and where to publish the story. For the most part, I have found no ethical problem in publishing stories that reflect the abuses of power; I consider the damage done by the abusers far greater than any discomfort my stories might cause them. In contrast, I feel constraint in publishing about my immediate family members. I check materials with them. In the case of more distant family members, I change their names and identifying characteristics. I will not publish some of my recent writing because doing so would seriously "disturb the family peace." I set that writing away for the time being, hoping that I will find a way to publish it in the future.

In one section of *Fields of Play* (Richardson, 1997), I tell two interwoven stories of "writing illegitimacy." One story is my poetic representation of an interview with Louisa May, an unwed mother, and the other is the research story—how I wrote that poem along with its dissemination, reception, and consequences for me. There are multiple illegitimacies in the stories—a child out of wedlock, poetic representation as research "findings," a feminine voice in the social sciences, ethnographic research on ethnographers and dramatic representation of that research, emotional presence of the writer, and unbridled work *jouissance*.

I had thought that the research story was complete, not necessarily the only story that could be told but one that reflected fairly, honestly, and sincerely what my research experiences had been. I still believe that. But missing from the research story, I came to realize, were the personal biographical experiences that led me to author such a story.

The idea of "illegitimacy," I have come to acknowledge, has had a compelling hold on me. In my research journal, I wrote, "My career in the social sciences might be viewed as one long adventure into illegitimacies." I asked myself why I was drawn to constructing "texts of illegitimacy," including the text of my academic life. What is this struggle I have with the academy—being in it and against it at the same time? How is my story like and unlike the stories of others who are struggling to make sense of themselves, to retrieve their suppressed selves, to act ethically?

Refracting "illegitimacy" through allusions, glimpses, and extended views, I came to write a personal essay, "Vespers," the final essay in *Fields of Play* (Richardson, 1997). "Vespers" located my academic life in childhood experiences and memories; it deepened my knowledge of my self and has resonated with others' experiences in academia. In turn, the writing of "Vespers," has refracted again, giving me desire, strength, and enough self-knowledge to narrativize other memories and experiences, to give myself agency, and to construct myself anew for better or for worse.

Writing stories and personal narratives have increasingly become the structures through which I make sense of my world, locating my particular biographical experiences in larger historical and sociological contexts. Using writing as a method of discovery in conjunction with my understanding of feminist rereadings of Deleuzian thought, I have altered my primary writing question from "how to write during the crisis of representation" to "how to document becoming."

Like Zeno's arrow, I will never reach a destination (destiny?). But unlike Zeno, instead of focusing on the endpoint of a journey that never ends, I focus on how the arrowsmiths made the arrow, its place in the quiver, and the quiver's placement—displacement, replacement—in the world. I look at the promises of progressive ideologies and personal experiences as ruins to be excavated, as folds to unfold, as paths through academic miasma. I am convinced that in the story (or stories) of becoming, we have a good chance of deconstructing the underlying academic ideology—that *being* a something (e.g., a successful professor, an awesome theorist, a disciplinarian maven, a covergirl feminist) is better than *becoming*. For me, now, discovering the intricate interweavings of class, race, gender, education, religion, and other diversities that shaped me early on into the kind of sociologist I did become is a practical way of refracting the worlds—academic and other—in which I live. None of us knows his or her final destination, but all of us can know about the shape makers of our lives that we can choose to confront, embrace, or ignore.

I am not certain how others will document their becoming, but I have chosen structures that suit my disposition, theoretical orientation, and writing life. I am "growing myself up" by refracting my life through a sociological lens, fully engaging C. Wright Mills's "sociology"—the intersection of the biographical and the historical. I am discovering that my concerns for social justice across race, class, religion, gender, and ethnicity derive from these early childhood experiences. These have solidified my next writing questions. How can I make my writing matter? How can I write to help speed into this world a democratic project of social justice?

I do not have catchy or simple answers. I know that when I move deeply into my writing, both my compassion for others and my actions on their behalf increase. My writing moves me into an independent space where I see more clearly the interrelationships between and among peoples worldwide. Perhaps other writers have similar experiences. Perhaps thinking deeply and writing about one's own life has led, or will lead, them to actions that decrease the inequities between and among people and peoples and that decrease the violence.

## ▣ PART 2: WRITING AS A METHOD OF NOMADIC INQUIRY

### Elizabeth Adams St. Pierre

My writing about writing as a method of inquiry in this doubled text appears after Laurel Richardson's for good reason; it is an effect of Richardson's work in the sense that it is a trajectory, a "line of flight" (Deleuze & Parnet, 1977/1987, p. 125), that maps what can happen if one takes seriously her charge to think of writing as a *method* of qualitative inquiry. I read a very early draft of this chapter, titled "Writing: A Method of Discovery," in 1992 in a sociology class that Richardson taught on postmodern research and writing. I had been trained years earlier, as an English major, to think of expository writing as a tracing of thought already thought, as a transparent reflection of the known and the real—writing as representation, as repetition. I still use that strategy for certain purposes and certain audiences even though I now chiefly use writing to disrupt the known and the real—writing as *simulation* (Baudrillard, 1981/1988), as "subversive repetition" (Butler, 1990, p. 32).

Thinking Richardson and Deleuze together, I have called my work in academia "nomadic inquiry" (St. Pierre, 1997a, 1997c), and a great part of that inquiry is accomplished in the writing because, for me, writing *is* thinking, writing *is* analysis, writing *is* indeed a seductive and tangled *method* of discovery. Many writers in the humanities have known this all along, but Richardson has brought this understanding to qualitative inquiry in the social sciences. In so doing, she has deconstructed the concept *method,* putting this ordinary category of qualitative inquiry *sous rature,* or under erasure (Spivak, 1974, p. xiv), and thereby opened it up to different meanings.

This concept certainly needs to be troubled. Two decades ago, Barthes (1984/1986) wrote, "Method becomes a Law," but the "will-to-method is ultimately sterile, everything has been put into the method, nothing remains for the writing" (p. 318). Thus, he said, "it is necessary, at a certain moment, to turn against Method, or at least to regard it without any founding privilege" (p. 319). In other words, it is important to interrogate whatever limits we have imposed on the concept method lest we diminish its possibilities in knowledge production.

This is one of postmodernism's lessons—that foundations are contingent (Butler, 1992). In fact, every foundational concept of conventional, interpretive qualitative inquiry, including method, is contingent, and postmodernists have deconstructed many of them, including data (St. Pierre, 1997b), validity (Lather, 1993; Scheurich, 1993), interviewing (Scheurich, 1995), the field (St. Pierre, 1997c), experience (Scott, 1991), voice (Finke, 1993; Jackson, 2003; Lather, 2000), reflexivity (Pillow, 2003), narrative (Nespor & Barylske, 1991), and even ethnography (Britzman, 1995; Visweswaran, 1994). This is not to say that postmodern qualitative researchers reject these concepts and others that have been defined in a certain way by interpretivism; rather, researchers have examined their effects on people and knowledge production during decades of research and have reinscribed them in different ways that, of course, must also be interrogated. Nor do postmodern qualitative researchers necessarily reject the words themselves; that is, they continue to use, for example, the words *method* and *data*. As Spivak (1974) cautioned, we are obliged to work with the "resources of the old language, the language we already possess and which possesses us. To make a new word is to run the risk of forgetting the problem or believing it solved" (p. xv). So, we use old concepts but ask them to do different work. Interestingly, it is the inability of language to close off meaning into concept that prompts postmodern qualitative researchers to critique the presumed coherency of the structure of conventional, interpretive qualitative inquiry. For some of us, the acknowledgment that that structure is, and always has been, contingent is good news indeed.

## Language and Meaning

Richardson gestured toward the work of language earlier in this chapter, but here I describe in more detail the tenuous relation between language and *meaning* in order to ground my later discussion of postrepresentation in a postinterpretive world. We know that much deconstructive work has been done in the human sciences since the "linguistic turn" (Rorty, 1967), the "postmodern turn" (Hassan, 1987), the "crisis of legitimation" (Habermas, 1973/1975), and the "crisis of representation" (Marcus & Fischer, 1986), all of which employ a "consciousness of a language which does not forget itself" (Barthes, 1984/1986, p. 319) or, as Trinh (1989) put it, a consciousness that understands "language as language" (p. 17). Nearly four decades ago, Foucault (1966/1970) wrote that "language is not what it is because it has a meaning" (p. 35), and Derrida (1967/1974) theorized *différance*, which teaches us that meaning cannot be fixed in language but is always deferred. As Spivak (1974) explained, "word and thing or thought never in fact become one" (p. xvi), so language cannot serve as a transparent medium that mirrors, "represents," and contains the world.

The ideas that meaning is not a "portable property" (Spivak, 1974, p. lvii) and that language cannot simply transport meaning from one person to another play havoc with the Husserlian proposition that there is a layer of prelinguistic meaning (pure meaning, pure signified) that language can express. In this respect, postmodern discourses differ from "the interpretive sciences [that] proceed from the assumption that there is a deep truth which is both known and hidden. It is the job of interpretation to bring this truth to discourse" (Dreyfus & Rabinow, 1982, p. 180). These discourses also play havoc with the belief that noise-free rational communication (Habermas, 1981/1984, 1981/1987)—some kind of transparent dialogue that can lead to consensus—is possible, or even desirable, since consensus often erases difference. Further, Derrida's statement (as cited in Spivak, 1974) that "the thing itself always escapes" (p. lxix) throws into radical doubt (and, some would say, makes irrelevant) the hermeneutic assumption that we can, in fact, answer the ontological question "What is . . . ?"—the question that grounds much interpretive work.

But postmodernists, after the linguistic turn, suspect that interpretation is not the discovery of meaning in the world but rather the "introduction of meaning" (Spivak, 1974, p. xxiii). If this is so, we can no longer treat words as if they are deeply and essentially *meaningful* or the experiences they attempt to represent as "brute fact or simple reality" (Scott, 1991, p. 26). In this case, the interpreter has to assume the burden of meaning-making, which is no longer a neutral activity of expression that simply matches word to world. Foucault (1967/1998) wrote that "interpretation does not clarify a matter to be interpreted, which offers itself passively; it can only seize, and violently, an already-present interpretation, which it must overthrow, upset, shatter with the blows of a hammer" (p. 275). However, despite the dangers of the hermeneutic rage for meaning, we interpret incessantly, perhaps because of our "human inability to tolerate undescribed chaos" (Spivak, 1974, p. xxiii). In this regard, Foucault (as cited in Dreyfus & Rabinow, 1982) suggested that we are "condemned to meaning" (p. 88). But Derrida (1972/1981) had another take on meaning and suggested, "To risk meaning nothing is to start to play, and first to enter into the play of *différance* which prevents any word, any concept, any major enunciation from coming to summarize and to govern . . . differences" (p. 14). Derrida (1967/1974) called this deconstructive work *writing under erasure*, "letting go of each concept at the very moment that I needed to use it" (p. xviii). The implications for qualitative inquiry of imagining writing as a letting go of meaning even meaning proliferates rather than a search for and containment of meaning are both compelling and profound.

Clearly, postmodern qualitative researchers can no longer think of inquiry simply as a task of making meaning—comprehending, understanding, getting to the bottom of the phenomenon under investigation. As I mentioned earlier, this does not mean they reject meaning but rather that they put meaning in its place. They shift the focus from questions such as "What does this or that mean?" to questions such as those posed by Scott (1988): "How do meanings change? How have some meanings emerged as normative and others been eclipsed or disappeared? What do these processes reveal about how power is constituted and operates?" (p. 35). Bové (1990) offered additional questions, and I suggest that we can substitute any object of knowledge (e.g., marriage, subjectivity, race) for the word "discourse" in the following: "How does discourse function? Where is it to be found? How does it get produced and regulated? What are its social effects? How does it exist?" (p. 54).

And since Richardson and I especially love writing, we have asked ourselves these questions about writing and have posed another that we find provocative: *What else might writing do except mean?* Deleuze and Guattari (1980/1987) offered some help here when they suggested, "writing has nothing to do with signifying. It has to do with surveying, mapping, even realms that are yet to come" (pp. 4–5). In this sense, writing becomes a "field of play" (Richardson, 1997) in which we might loosen the hold of received meaning that limits our work and our lives and investigate "to what extent the exercise of thinking one's own history can free thought from what it thinks silently and to allow it to think otherwise" (Foucault, as cited in Racevskis, 1987, p. 22). In this way, the linguistic turn and the postmodern critique of interpretivism open up the concept writing and enable us to use it as a *method of inquiry,* a condition of possibility for "producing different knowledge and producing knowledge differently" (St. Pierre, 1997b, p. 175).

## Writing Under Erasure: A Politics and Ethics of Difficulty

So what might the work of *writing as inquiry* be in postmodern qualitative research? What might writing under erasure look like, and how, in turn, might such writing rewrite inquiry itself? My own experiences in this regard have emerged from a long-term postmodern qualitative research project that has been both an interview study with 36 older white southern women who live in my hometown and an ethnography of the small rural community in which they live (St. Pierre, 1995). It is important to note that this study was not designed to do interpretive work—to answer the questions "who are these women?" and "what do they mean?" I never presumed I could know or understand the women—uncover their authentic voices and essential natures and then represent them in rich thick description. Rather, my task was twofold: (1) to use postmodernism to study subjectivity by using Foucault's (1984/1985, 1985/1986) ethical analysis, care of the self, to investigate the "arts of existence" or "practices of the self" the women have used during their long lives in the construction of their subjectivities and (2) to use postmodernism to study conventional qualitative research methodology, which I believe is generally both positivist and interpretive.

Also, since I call myself a writer—thanks to Richardson (it took a sociologist to teach this English teacher writing)—I determined early in the study to use writing as a method of inquiry in at least these two senses: (1) I would think of writing as a *method of data collection* along with, for example, interviewing and observation and (2) I would think of writing as *a method of data analysis* along with, for example, the traditional—and what I think of as structural (and positivist)—activities of analytic induction; constant comparison; coding, sorting, and categorizing data; and so forth. It should be clear at this point that the coherence of the positivist and/or interpretivist concept method has already been breached by investing it with these different and multiple meanings and, henceforth, efforts to maintain its unity may be futile. (Indeed, I hope others will follow my lead and imagine other uses for writing as a method of inquiry.) Further, these two methods are not discrete as I have made them out to be. Making such a distinction is to stay within the confines of the structure of conventional qualitative inquiry in which we often separate data collection from data analysis. Nevertheless, I retain the distinction temporarily for the purpose of elucidation.

In my study, I used writing as a method of data collection by gathering together, by collecting—*in the writing*—all sorts of data I had never read about in interpretive qualitative textbooks, some of which I have called *dream data, sensual data, emotional data, response data* (St. Pierre, 1997b), and *memory data* (St. Pierre, 1995). Such data might include, for example, a pesky dream about an unsatisfying interview, the sharp angle of the southern sun to which my body happily turned, my sorrow when I read the slender obituary of one of my participants, my mother's disturbing comment that I had gotten something wrong, and very real "memor[ies] of the future" (Deleuze, 1986/1988, p. 107), a mournful time bereft of these women and others of their generation. These data were neither in my interview transcripts nor in my fieldnotes where data are supposed to be, for how can one textualize everything one thinks and senses in the course of a study? But they were always already in my mind and body, and they cropped up unexpectedly and fittingly in my writing—fugitive, fleeting data that were excessive and out-of-category. My point here is that these data might have escaped entirely if I had not *written;* they were collected only *in the writing.*

I used writing as a method of data analysis by using writing to think; that is, I wrote my way into particular spaces I could not have occupied by sorting data with a computer program or by analytic induction. This was rhizomatic work (Deleuze & Guattari, 1980/1987) in which I made accidental and fortuitous connections I could not foresee or control. My point here is that I did not limit data analysis to conventional practices of coding data and then sorting it into categories that I then grouped into themes that became section headings in an outline that organized and governed my writing in advance of writing. *Thought happened in the writing.* As I wrote, I watched word after word appear on the computer screen—ideas, theories, I had not thought before I wrote them. Sometimes I wrote something so marvelous it startled me. *I doubt I could have thought such a thought by thinking alone.*

And it is thinking of writing in this way that breaks down the distinction in conventional qualitative inquiry between data collection and data analysis—one more assault to the structure. Both happen at once. As data are collected in the writing—as the researcher thinks/writes about her Latin teacher's instruction that one should thrive in adversity; about a mink shawl draped elegantly on aging, upright shoulders; about the sweet, salty taste of tiny country ham biscuits; about all the other things in her life that seem unrelated to her research project but are absolutely unleashed within it—she produces the strange and wonderful transitions from word to word, sentence to sentence, thought to unthought. Data collection and data analysis cannot be separated when writing is a method of inquiry. And positivist concepts, such as audit trails and data saturation, become absurd and then irrelevant in postmodern qualitative inquiry in which writing is a field of play where anything can happen—and does.

There is much to think about here as conventional qualitative inquiry comes undone—in this case, as writing deconstructs the concept *method,* proliferating its meaning and thereby collapsing the structure that relied on its unity. But how does one "write it up" after the linguistic turn? Postmodern qualitative researchers have been courageous and inventive in this work, and Richardson identified and described this writing both as "experimental writing" (Richardson, 1994) and as "CAP ethnography" (Richardson, 2000). Of course, there is no model for this work since each researcher and each study requires different writing. I can, however, briefly tell a small writing story about my own adventures with *postrepresentation.*

As I said earlier, in my study with the older women of my hometown, I set out to study subjectivity and qualitative inquiry using poststructural analyses, so my charge was to critique both the presumed unified structure of an autonomous, conscious, knowing woman who could be delivered to the reader in rich, thick description as well as the presumed rational, coherent structure of conventional qualitative inquiry that could guarantee true knowledge about the women. Never having read a postmodern qualitative textbook, I initially tried to force—to no avail—postmodern methodology into the grid of interpretive/positivist qualitative inquiry. When the lack of fit became apparent and then absurd, I began to deconstruct that structure to make room for difference.

At the same time, I began to assume a writerly reticence to describe or represent my participants and thereby encourage some kind of sentimental identification. After all, it was subjectivity, not the women, that was the object of my inquiry. I became wary of the not-so-innocent assumption of interpretivism that the women should be drilled and mined for knowledge ("Who are they?" "What do they mean?") and then represented. This did not seem to be the kind of ethical relation these women who had taught me how to be a woman required of me. I am reminded here of a comment by Anthony Lane, the film critic for *The New Yorker,* who suggested that instead of asking whether David Lynch's film, *Mulholland Drive,* makes sense ("What does it mean?"), viewers should ask what Laurence Olivier once demanded of Dustin Hoffman ("Is it safe?") (Lane, 2001). In interpretive research, we believe representation is possible, if perhaps unsafe, but we do it anyway with many anxious disclaimers. In postmodern research, we believe it isn't possible *or* safe, and so we shift the focus entirely, in my case, away from the women to subjectivity. We increasingly distrust the "old promise of representation" (Britzman, 1995, p. 234) and, with Pillow (2003), question a science whose goal is representation.

In my own work, I have developed a certain writerly incompetence and under-achievement and am unable to write a text that "runs to meet the reader" (Sommer, 1994, p. 530), a comfort text (Lather & Smithies, 1997) that gratifies the interpretive entitlement to know the women. Rather than being an "epistemological dead end" (Sommer, 1994, p. 532) (the women as objects that can be known), the women are a line of flight that take me elsewhere (the women as provocateurs). This is not to deny the importance of the women or to say that they are not in my texts since they are everywhere, but I gesture toward them in oblique ways in my writing by relating, for example, one of our vexing conversations that burgeoned into splendid and productive confusion about subjectivity or by relating an aporia about methodology they insist I think. And when someone asks for a story about the women, I give them a good one, and if they ask for another, I say, "Go find your own older women and talk with them. They have stories to tell that will change your life."

Nevertheless, I long to write about these older women who are dying, dying, dying and fear I will someday, but only after wrestling with that postrepresentational question: *What else might writing do except mean?* That writing will involve a *politics and ethics of difficulty* that, on the one hand, can only be accomplished if I write but, on the other, cannot be accomplished on the basis of anything I already know about writing. There are no rules for postrepresentational writing; there's nowhere to turn for authorizing comfort.

What has postmodernism done to qualitative inquiry? I agree with Richardson's (1994) response to this question: "I do not know, but I do know that we cannot go back to where we were" (p. 524). Or, as Deleuze and Parnet (1977/1987) put it, "It might be thought that nothing has changed and nevertheless everything has changed" (p. 127). At this point, I return to the criteria that Richardson has set for postmodern ethnographic texts. Can the kind of writing I have gestured toward here—writing under erasure—exhibit a substantive contribution, aesthetic merit, reflexivity, impact, and reflect lived experience? I believe it can. But even more importantly, writing as a method of inquiry carries us "across our thresholds, toward a destination which is unknown, not foreseeable, not preexistent" (Deleuze & Parnet, 1977/1987, p. 25), perhaps toward the spectacular promise of what Derrida (1993/1994) called the "democracy *to come*" (p. 64), a promise those who work for social justice cannot not want. I think about this democracy often since it promises the possibility of different relations—relations more generous than those I live among, fertile relations in which people thrive.

The paradox, however, is that this democracy will never "present itself in the form of full presence" (Derrida, 1993/1994, p. 65) but nonetheless demands that we prepare ourselves for its arrival. Derrida (1993/1994) explained that it turns on the idea that we must offer "hospitality without reserve" to an "alterity that cannot be anticipated" from whom we ask nothing in return (p. 65). Thus, the setting-to-work of deconstruction in the democracy-to-come is grounded in our relations with the Other. In postmodern qualitative inquiry, the possibilities for just and ethical encounters with alterity occur not only in the field of human activity but also in the field of the text, in our writing. In these overlapping spaces, we prepare ourselves for a democracy that has no model, for a postjuridical justice that is always contingent on the case at hand and must be effaced even as it is produced. Settling into a transcendental justice and truth, some deep meaning we think will save us, may announce a lack of courage to think and live beyond our necessary fictions.

Ethics under deconstruction then, is ungrounded, it is "what happens when we cannot apply the rules" (Keenan, 1997, p. 1). This ethics of difficulty hinges on a tangled responsibility to the Other "that is not a moment of security or of cognitive certainty. Quite the contrary: the only responsibility worthy of the name comes with the withdrawal of rules or the knowledge on which we might rely to make our decisions for us." The event of ethics occurs when we have "no grounds, no alibis, no elsewhere to which we might refer the instance of our decisions." In this sense, *we will always be unprepared to be ethical.* Moreover, the removal of foundations and originary meaning, which were always already fictions, simply leaves everything as it is but without those markers of certainty we counted on to see us intact through a text of responsibility. So, how do we go on from here? How do we get on with our work and our lives?

Deleuze (1969/1990) suggested that the events in our lives—and in this essay, I'm thinking specifically of all those relations with the Other that qualitative inquiry enables—tempt us to be their equal by asking for our "best and most perfect. Either ethics makes no sense at all, or this is what it means and has nothing else to say: *not to be unworthy of what happens to us*" (pp. 148–149). The event, then, calls us to be worthy at the instant of decision, when what happens is all there is—*when meaning will always come too late to rescue us.* At the edge of the abyss, we step without reserve toward the Other. This is deconstruction at its finest and, I believe, the condition of Derrida's democracy-to-come. This democracy calls for a renewed "belief in the world" (Deleuze, 1990/1995, p. 176) that, I hope, will enable relations less impoverished than the ones we have thus far imagined and lived. As I said earlier, the setting-to-work of deconstruction is already being accomplished by postmodern qualitative researchers in all the fields of play in which they work.

As for me, I struggle every day not to be unworthy of the older women of my hometown who keep on teaching me ethics. It may seem that I am not writing about them in this essay, but I assure you they are speaking to you in every word you read. Brooding and writing about our desire for their presence (meaning) in this text and others I might write occupies much of my energy, yet I trust writing and know that one morning I will awaken and write toward these women in a way I cannot yet imagine. I trust you will do the same, that you will use writing as a method of inquiry to move into your own impossibility, where anything might happen—and will.

▣  PART 3: WRITING PRACTICES

Laurel Richardson

*Writing, the creative effort, should come first—at least for some part of every day of your life. It is a wonderful blessing if you will use it. You will become happier, more enlightened, alive, impassioned, light-hearted, and generous to everybody else. Even your health will improve. Colds will disappear and all the other ailments of discouragement and boredom.*

—Brenda Ueland, If You Want to Write

In what follows, I suggest some ways of using writing as a method of knowing. I have chosen exercises that have been productive for students because they demystify writing, nurture the researcher's voice, and serve the processes of discovery about the self, the world, and issues of social justice. I wish that I could guarantee them to bring good health as well.

## Metaphor

Using old worn-out metaphors, although easy and comfortable, invites stodginess and stiffness after a while. The stiffer you get, the less flexible you are. Your ideas get ignored. If your writing is clichéd, you will not "stretch your own imagination" (Ouch! Hear the cliché of pointing out the cliché!) and you will bore people.

1.  In traditional social scientific writing, the metaphor for theory is that it is a "building" (e.g., structure, foundation, construction, deconstruction, framework, grand) (see the wonderful book by Lakoff & Johnson, 1980). Consider a different metaphor such as "theory as a tapestry," "theory as an illness," "theory as story," or "theory as social action." Write a paragraph about "theory" using your metaphor. Do you "see" differently and "feel" differently about theorizing using an unusual metaphor? Do you want your theory to map differently onto the social world? Do you want your theory to affect the world?

2.  Look at one of your papers and highlight your metaphors and images. What are you saying through metaphors that you did not realize you were saying? What are you reinscribing? Do you want to do so? Can you find different metaphors that change how you "see" ("feel") the material and your relationship to it? Are your mixed metaphors pointing to confusion in yourself or to social science's glossing over of ideas? How do your metaphors both reinscribe and resist social inequities?

## Writing Formats

1. Choose a journal article that exemplifies the mainstream writing conventions of your discipline. How is the argument staged? Who is the presumed audience? How does the article inscribe ideology? How does the author claim "authority" over the material? Where is the author? Where are "you" in the article? Who are the subjects and objects of research?

2. Choose a paper that you have written for a class or published and that you think is pretty good. How did you follow the norms of your discipline? Were you conscious of doing so? What parts did the professor/reviewer laud? Did you elide over some difficult areas through vagueness, jargon, a call to authorities, science writing norms, and/or other rhetorical devices? What voices did you exclude in your writing? Who is the audience? Where are the subjects in the paper or article? Where are you? How do you feel about the paper or article now? How do you feel about your process of constructing it?

## Creative Analytical Writing Practices

1. Join or start a writing group. This could be a writing support group, a creative writing group, a poetry group, a dissertation group, a memoir group, or the like (on dissertation and article writing, see Becker, 1986; Fox, 1985; Richardson, 1990; Wolcott, 1990).

2. Work through a creative writing guidebook (for some excellent guides, see Goldberg, 1986; Hills, 1987; Ueland, 1938/1987; Weinstein, 1993).

3. Enroll in a creative writing workshop or class. These experiences are valuable for both beginning and experienced researchers.

4. Use "writing up" fieldnotes as an opportunity to expand your writing vocabulary, habits of thought, and attentiveness to your senses and to use as a bulwark against the censorious voice of science. Where better to develop your sense of Self—your voice—than in the process of doing your research? What better place to experiment with point of view—seeing the world from different persons' perspectives—than in your fieldnotes. Keep a journal. Write writing stories, that is, research stories.

5. Write a writing autobiography. This would be the story of how you learned to write, the dicta of English classes (topic sentences? outlines? the five-paragraph essay?), the dicta of social science professors, how and where you write now, your idiosyncratic "writing needs," your feelings about writing and about the writing process, and/or your resistance to "value-free" writing. (This is an exercise used by Arthur Bochner.)

6. If you wish to experiment with evocative writing, a good place to begin is by transforming your fieldnotes into drama. See what ethnographic rules you are using (e.g., fidelity to the speech of the participants, fidelity in the order of the speakers and events) and what literary ones you are invoking (e.g., limiting how long a speaker

speaks, keeping the "plot" moving along, developing character through actions). Writing dramatic presentations accentuates ethical considerations. If you doubt that, contrast writing up an ethnographic event as a "typical" event with writing it as a play, with you and your hosts cast in roles that will be performed before others. Who has ownership of spoken words? How is authorship attributed? What if people do not like how they are characterized? Are courtesy norms being violated? Experiment here with both oral and written versions of your drama.

7. Experiment with transforming an in-depth interview into a poetic representation. Try using only the words, rhythms, figures of speech, breath points, pauses, syntax, and diction of the speaker. Where are you in the poem? What do you know about the interviewee and about yourself that you did not know before you wrote the poem? What poetic devices have you sacrificed in the name of science?

8. Write a "layered text" (cf. Ronai, 1995; Lather & Smithies, 1997). The layered text is a strategy for putting yourself into your text and putting your text into the literatures and traditions of social science. Here is one possibility. First, write a short narrative of the self about some event that is especially meaningful to you. Step back and look at the narrative from your disciplinary perspective. Then insert into the narrative— beginning, midsections, end, or wherever—relevant analytical statements or references using a different typescript, alternative page placement, or a split page or marking the text in other ways. The layering can be a multiple one, with different ways of marking different theoretical levels, different theories, different speakers, and so forth. (This is an exercise used by Carolyn Ellis.)

9. Try some other strategy for writing new ethnography for social scientific publications. Try the "seamless" text in which previous literature, theory, and methods are placed in textually meaningful ways rather than in disjunctive sections (for an excellent example, see Bochner, 1997). Try the "sandwich" text in which traditional social science themes are the "white bread" around the "filling" (Ellis & Bochner, 1996), or try an "epilogue" explicating the theoretical analytical work of the creative text (cf. Eisner, as cited in Saks, 1996).

10. Consider a fieldwork setting. Consider the various subject positions you have or have had within it. For example, in a store you might be a sales clerk, a customer, a manager, a feminist, a capitalist, a parent, or a child. Write about the setting (or an event in the setting) from several different subject positions. What do you "know" from the different positions? Next, let the different points of view dialogue with each other. What do you discover through these dialogues? What do you learn about social inequities?

11. Write your "data" in three different ways—for example, as a narrative account, a poetic representation, and readers' theater. What do you know in each rendition that you did not know in the other renditions? How do the different renditions enrich each other?

12. Write a narrative of the self from your point of view (e.g., something that happened in your family or in your seminar). Then, interview another participant (e.g., a family member or seminar member) and have that participant tell you his or her story of the event. See yourself as part of *the participant's* story in the same way as he or she is part of your story. How do you rewrite your story from the participant's point of view? (This is an exercise used by Ellis.)

13. Collaborative writing is a way in which to see beyond one's own naturalisms of style and attitude. This is an exercise that I have used in my teaching, but it would be appropriate for a writing group as well. Each member writes a story of his or her life. For example, it could be a feminist story, a success story, a quest story, a cultural story, a professional socialization story, a realist tale, a confessional tale, or a discrimination story. Stories are photocopied for the group. The group is then broken into subgroups (I prefer groups of three). Each subgroup collaborates on writing a new story—the collective story of its members. The collaboration can take any form—drama, poetry, fiction, narrative of the selves, realism, and so forth. The collaboration is shared with the entire group. Each member then writes about his or her feelings about the collaboration and what happened to his or her story—and life—in the process.

14. Consider a part of your life outside of or before academia with which you have deeply resonated. Use that resonance as a "working metaphor" for understanding and reporting your research. Students have created excellent reports and moored themselves through the unexpected lens (e.g., choreography, principles of flower arrangement, art composition, sportscasting). Those resonances nurture a more integrated life.

15. Different forms of writing are appropriate for different audiences and different occasions. Experiment with writing the same piece of research for an academic audience, a trade audience, the popular press, policymakers, research hosts, and so forth (Richardson, 1990). This is an especially powerful exercise for dissertation students who might want to share their results in a "user-friendly" way with their fellow students.

16. Write writing stories (Richardson, 1997). These are reflexive accounts of how you happened to write the pieces you wrote. The writing stories can be about disciplinary politics, departmental events, friendship networks, collegial ties, family, and/or personal biographical experiences. What these writing stories do is situate your work in contexts, tying what can be a lonely and seemingly separative task to the ebbs and flows of your life and your self. Writing these stories reminds us of the continual cocreation of the self and social science.

> *Willing is doing something you know already—there is no new imaginative understanding in it. And presently your soul gets frightfully sterile and dry because you are so quick, snappy, and efficient about doing one thing after*

*another that you have no time for your own ideas to come in and develop and gently shine.*

—Brenda Ueland, *If You Want to Write*

## ▣ NOTE

1. The CAP acronym resonates with "cap" from the Latin for "head," *caput*. Because the head is both mind and body, its metaphorical use breaks down the mind–body duality. The products, although mediated throughout the body, cannot manifest without "headwork." In addition, "cap," both as a noun (product) and as a verb (process), has multiple common and idiomatic meanings and associations, some of which refract the playfulness of the genre—a rounded head covering or a special head covering indicating occupation or membership in a particular group, the top of a building or fungus, a small explosive charge, any of several sizes of writing paper, putting the final touches on, lying on top of, surpassing or outdoing. And then, there are the other associated words from the Latin root, such as capillary and capital(ism), that humble and contextualize the labor.

## ▣ REFERENCES

Barthes, R. (1986). *The rustle of language* (R. Howard, Trans.). Berkeley: University of California Press. (Original work published 1984)

Baudrillard, J. (1988). Simulacra and simulations. In M. Poster (Ed.), *Jean Baudrillard: Selected writings* (P. Foss, P. Patton, & P. Beitchman, Trans., pp. 166–184). Stanford, CA: Stanford University Press. (Original work published 1981)

Becker, H. S. (1986). *Writing for social scientists: How to finish your thesis, book, or article.* Chicago: University of Chicago Press.

Bochner, A. (1997). It's about time: Narrative and the divided Self. *Qualitative Inquiry, 3,* 418–438.

Bové, P. A. (1990) Discourse. In F. Lentricchia & T. McLaughlin (Eds.), *Critical terms for literary study* (pp. 50–65). Chicago: University of Chicago Press.

Britzman, D. P. (1995). "The question of belief": Writing poststructural ethnography. *International Journal of Qualitative Studies in Education, 8*(3), 229–238.

Butler, J. (1990). *Gender trouble: Feminism and the subversion of identity.* New York. Routledge.

Butler, J. (1992). Contingent foundations: Feminism and the question of "postmodernism." In J. Butler & J. W. Scott (Eds.), *Feminists theorize the political* (pp. 3–21). New York: Routledge.

Clifford, J., & Marcus, G. E. (Eds.). (1986). *Writing culture: The poetics and politics of ethnography.* Berkeley: University of California Press.

Davies, B. (1994). *Poststructuralist theory and classroom practice.* Geelong, Australia: Deakin University Press.

Davies, B., Dormer, S., Honan, E., McAllister, N., O'Reilly, R., Rocco, S., & Walker, A. (1997). Ruptures in the skin of silence: A collective biography. *Hecate: A Woman's Interdisciplinary Journal, 23*(1), 62–79.

Deleuze, G. (1988). *Foucault* (S. Hand, Trans.). Minneapolis: University of Minnesota Press. (Original work published 1986)

Deleuze, G. (1990). *The logic of sense* (C. V. Boundas, Ed.; M. Lester, Trans.). New York: Columbia University Press. (Original work published 1969)

Deleuze, G. (1995). *Negotiations: 1972–1990* (M. Joughin, Trans.). New York: Columbia University Press. (Original work published 1990)

Deleuze, G., & Guattari, F. (1987). Introduction: Rhizome. In *A thousand plateaus: Capitalism and schizophrenia* (B. Massumi, Trans., pp. 3–25). Minneapolis: University of Minnesota Press. (Original work published 1980)

Deleuze, G., & Parnet, C. (1987). Many politics. In *Dialogues* (H. Tomlinson & B. Habberjam, Trans.). New York: Columbia University Press. (Original work published 1977)

Denzin, N. K. (1978). *The research act.* New York: McGraw–Hill.

Denzin, N. K. (1997). *Interpretive ethnography: Ethnographic practices for the 21st century.* Thousand Oaks, CA: Sage.

Derrida, J. (1974). *Of grammatology* (G. C. Spivak, Trans.). Baltimore, MD: Johns Hopkins University Press. (Original work published 1967)

Derrida, J. (1981). *Positions* (A. Bass, Trans.). Chicago: University of Chicago Press. (Original work published 1972)

Derrida, J. (1994*). Specters of Marx: The state of the debt, the work of mourning, and the new international* (P. Kamuf, Trans.). New York: Routledge. (Original work published 1993)

Dreyfus, H. L., & Rabinow, P. (1982*). Michel Foucault: Beyond structuralism and hermeneutics* (2nd ed.). Chicago: University of Chicago Press.

Ellis, C. (1991). Sociological introspection and emotional experience. *Symbolic Interaction, 14,* 23–50.

Ellis, C. (2004). *The ethnographic "I": A methodological novel about autoethnography.* Walnut Creek, CA: AltaMira.

Ellis, C., & Bochner, A. P. (Eds.). (1996). *Composing ethnography: Alternative forms of qualitative writing.* Walnut Creek, CA: AltaMira.

Finke, L. A. (1993). Knowledge as bait: Feminism, voice, and the pedagogical unconscious. *College English, 55*(1), 7–27.

Fishkin, S. F. (1985). *From fact to fiction: Journalism and imaginative writing in America.* Baltimore, MD: Johns Hopkins University Press.

Foucault, M. (1970). *The order of things: An archaeology of the human sciences.* New York: Vintage Books. (Original work published 1966)

Foucault, M. (1985). *The history of sexuality,* Vol. 2: *The use of pleasure* (R. Hurley, Trans.). New York: Vintage Books. (Original work published 1984)

Foucault, M. (1986). *The history of sexuality,* Vol. 3: *The care of the self* (R. Hurley, Trans.). New York: Vintage Books. (Original work published 1985)

Foucault, M. (1998). Nietzsche, Freud, Marx. In J. D. Faubion (Ed.), *Aesthetics, method, and epistemology* (J. Anderson & G. Hentzi, Trans., pp. 269–278). New York: New Press. (Original work published 1967)

Fox, M. F. (Ed.). (1985). *Scholarly writing and publishing: Issues, problems, and solutions.* Boulder, CO: Westview.

Goldberg, N. (1986). *Writing down the bones: Freeing the writer within.* Boston: Shambala.

Habermas, J. (1975). *Legitimation crisis* (T. McCarthy, Trans.). Boston: Beacon. (Original work published 1973)

Habermas, J. (1984). *The theory of communicative action,* Vol. 1: *Reason and the rationalization of society* (T. McCarthy, Trans.). Boston: Beacon. (Original work published 1981)

Habermas, J. (1987). *The theory of communicative action,* Vol. 2: *Lifeworld and system: A critique of functionalist reason* (T. McCarthy, Trans.). Boston: Beacon. (Original work published 1981)

Hassan, I. (1987). *The postmodern turn: Essays in postmodern theory and culture.* Columbus: Ohio State University Press.

Hills, R. (1987). *Writing in general and the short story in particular.* Boston: Houghton Mifflin.

Jackson, A. (2003). Rhizovocality. *International Journal of Qualitative Studies in Education, 16,* 693–710.

Keenan, T. (1997). *Fables of responsibility: Aberrations and predicaments in ethics and politics.* Stanford, CA: Stanford University Press.

Lakoff, G., & Johnson, M. (1980). *Metaphors we live by.* Chicago: University of Chicago Press.

Lane, A. (2001, October 8). Road trips. *The New Yorker,* p. 8.

Lather, P. (1993). Fertile obsession: Validity after poststructuralism. *Sociological Quarterly, 34,* 673–693.

Lather, P. (2000). Against empathy, voice, and authenticity. *Women, Gender, and Research, 4,* 16–25.

Lather, P., & Smithies, C. (1997). *Troubling the angels: Women living with HIV/AIDS.* Boulder, CO: Westview.

Levine, D. H. (1985). *The flight from ambiguity: Essays in social and cultural theory.* Chicago: University of Chicago Press.

Marcus, G. E., & Fischer, M. M. J. (1986). A crisis of representation in the social sciences. In G. E. Marcus & M. M. J. Fischer (Eds.), *Anthropology as cultural critique: An experimental moment in the human sciences* (pp. 7–16). Chicago: University of Chicago Press.

Margolis, E., & Romero, M. (1998). The department is very male, very white, very old, and very conservative: The functioning of the hidden curriculum in graduate sociology departments. *Harvard Educational Review, 68,* 1–32.

Nespor, J., & Barylske, J. (1991). Narrative discourse and teacher knowledge. *American Educational Research Journal, 28,* 805–823.

Pillow, W. S. (2003). Confession, catharsis, or cure? Rethinking the uses of reflexivity as methodological power in qualitative research. *International Journal of Qualitative Studies in Education, 16*(2), 175–196.

Racevskis, K. (1987). Michel Foucault, Rameau's nephew, and the question of identity. In J. Bernauer & D. Rasmussen (Eds.), *The final Foucault* (pp. 21– 33). Cambridge: MIT Press.

Richardson, L. (1990). *Writing strategies: Reaching diverse audiences.* Newbury Park, CA: Sage.

Richardson, L. (1994). Writing: A method of inquiry. In N. K. Denzin & Y. S. Lincoln (Eds.), *Handbook of qualitative research* (pp. 516–529). Thousand Oaks, CA: Sage.

Richardson, L. (1997). *Fields of play: Constructing an academic life.* New Brunswick, NJ: Rutgers University Press.

Richardson, L. (2000). Writing: A method of inquiry. In N. K. Denzin & Y. S. Lincoln (Eds.), *Handbook of qualitative research* (2nd ed., pp. 923–948). Thousand Oaks, CA: Sage.

Richardson, L., & Lockridge, E. (2004). *Travels with Ernest: Crossing the literary/sociological divide.* Walnut Creek, CA: AltaMira.

Ronai, C. (1995). Multiple reflections of child sexual abuse: An argument for a layered account. *Journal of Contemporary Ethnography, 23,* 395–426.

Rorty, R. (1967). *The linguistic turn: Essays in philosophical method*. Chicago: University of Chicago Press.

Saks, A. L. (1996). Viewpoints: Should novels count as dissertations in education? *Research in the Teaching of English, 30*, 403–427.

Scheurich, J. J. (1993). The masks of validity: A deconstructive investigation. *International Journal of Qualitative Studies in Education, 9*(11), 49–60.

Scheurich, J. J. (1995). A postmodernist critique of research interviewing. *International Journal of Qualitative Studies in Education, 8*(3), 239–252.

Scott, J. W. (1988). Deconstructing equality-versus-difference: Or, the uses of poststructuralist theory for feminism. *Feminist Studies, 14*(1), 33–50.

Scott, J. W. (1991). The evidence of experience. *Critical Inquiry, 17*, 773–797.

Sommer, D. (1994). Resistant texts and incompetent readers. *Poetics Today, 15*, 523–551.

Spivak, G. C. (1974). Translator's preface. In J. Derrida, *Of grammatology* (G. C. Spivak, Trans., pp. ix–xc). Baltimore, MD: Johns Hopkins University Press.

Statham, A., Richardson, L., & Cook, J. A. (1991). *Gender and university teaching: A negotiated difference*. Albany: State University of New York Press.

St. Pierre, E. A. (1995). *Arts of existence: The construction of subjectivity in older, white southern women*. Unpublished doctoral dissertation, Ohio State University, Columbus, OH.

St. Pierre, E. A. (1997a). Circling the text: Nomadic writing practices. *Qualitative Inquiry, 3*, 403–417.

St. Pierre, E. A. (1997b). Methodology in the fold and the irruption of transgressive data. *International Journal of Qualitative Studies in Education, 10*(2), 175–189.

St. Pierre, E. A. (1997c). Nomadic inquiry in the smooth spaces of the field: A preface. *International Journal of Qualitative Studies in Education, 10*(3), 363–383.

Trinh, M. T. (1989). *Women, native, other: Writing postcoloniality and feminism*. Bloomington: Indiana University Press.

Ueland, B. (1987). *If you want to write: A book about art, independence, and spirit*. St. Paul, MN: Graywolf Press. (Original work published 1938)

Visweswaran, K. (1994). *Fictions of feminist ethnography*. Minneapolis: University of Minnesota Press.

Weinstein, D. (1993). *Writing for your life: A guide and companion to the inner worlds*. New York: HarperCollins.

Wolcott, H. F. (1990). *Writing up qualitative research*. Newbury Park, CA: Sage.

# 16

# POETICS FOR A PLANET

## Discourse on Some Problems of Being-in-Place

Ivan Brady

We are dwellers, we are namers, we are lovers, we make homes and search for our histories. And when we look for the history of our sensibilities, . . . it is to . . . the stable element, the land itself, that we must look for continuity.

—Seamus Heaney,
"The Sense of Place"

The great function of poetry is to give us back the situations of our dreams.

—Gaston Bachelard,
*The Poetics of Space*

**Author's Note.** I thank Yvonna Lincoln, Norman K. Denzin, John F. Sherry, Jr., Stephen Saraydar, Tracy Lewis, and Sara Varhus for their generous comments on earlier drafts of this chapter. I am also grateful to Beth Messana and Crystal Knowland for technical support along the way.

*A poetics must return to a way of dreaming works and the declarations that accompany them, of conceiving their possibility, and of working for their reality.*

—Fernand Hallyn,
*The Poetic Structure of the World*

*Stonehenge, Wessex Chalklands, July 21, 1997*

### A Gift of the Journey

*Magical megaliths. Stonehenge. Sun mask. Druid dance.*
*The hand brushes the obelisk—mossy green and grey,*
*cold for a summer's day—dragging fingertips across*
*the texture. Braille for a pulse? We want to touch*
*the mystery of this place, even as the mind's eye squints*

*for a glimpse of deeper meanings, sequestered in time*
*and cultural distance, some of which seem to be murmured*
*in the eclipse of stones at dusk and dawn. But the magic*
*does not reside in the stones themselves. It is embedded in*
*the reading, the immersion of self in place, and the puzzle*

*of the circle that only gets more puzzling when spotted*
*by the eye of the sun. Like the morning dew, this Druid*
*magic is tied to a clock of nature. It emerges from nowhere*
*and disappears just as mysteriously with the heat of midday*
*—or too much inspection. Poets who would see this clearly*

*must chase the beams gently, introspectively, as they refract*
*on the traces of magicians and astronomers who have danced*
*through the bosom of these stones in patterns and rhythms*
*we hope are coded within us all. The experience steps us*
*into another reality and with all the power of ritual turns*

*day to dream, taking us out of ourselves for a while to show*
*us something about ourselves—about how we have been*
*and where we think we used to be—a kind of mythopoeic*
*archaeology. The best poets still know how to do it. Magic,*
*it seems, is a gift of the journey.*

This is a poem I wrote about method (Brady, 2003b, p. 34). It suggests that one can get to know places marked as culturally distant through careful reflections on current experiences, that is, introspectively and imaginatively, relative to whatever hard facts or remnants may appear to lie at hand. That is how landscapes become semiotically rich, historical, and perhaps even sacred. They are projections of self, of each of us— all of us—now and before. But interpreting such investments from previous inhabitants is extraordinarily difficult, if for no other reason than the fact that even with widely shared constructs about the meaning of this place or that in any society, individual interpretations can vary widely. The same place can mean different things to different people in intensity of social and emotional commitment, if not in more dramatically different terms, even when they engage it on the same culturally standardized premises (e.g., when Americans visit the Grand Canyon or some other richly defined sacred national retreat). A sense of place, especially sacred space, shows all the volatility and variations of ritual inferences for these reasons (Brady, 1999). Moreover, as an interpreter from another cultural epoch, excavating that information in some semblance of its original form from an otherwise mute landscape cannot be done without a code or guide, living or otherwise, to the semiotic investments of those who have passed that way before and perhaps are no longer represented there (cf. Lame Deer & Erdoes, 1972, pp. 96–107). And even then, interpretations of artifact use or texts slide into the soup of polyvalence and multivocality and themselves become creative rejuvenations of performances tied through time to a sea of shifting landscapes—to the intertextualities of life that we study as ethnographers. For these and other reasons, places such as Stonehenge and the great petroglyph areas of the American Southwest are steeped in mystery, compelling and interesting in the shadows of their kinships to us but puzzles that are nonetheless ripe for wide-ranging interpretations.

That said, we must wonder what exactly environmentally concerned critics, such as poet Gary Snyder, nature writer Barry Lopez, mountain climber Jack Turner, and art historian Simon Schama, have in mind when they exhort us to relearn respect for the land we inhabit and to renew our ties to places both sacred and less exalted as a countermeasure to the thoughtless destruction of modern life.[1] I think that what they want us to know is a kind of history that includes, but reaches far beyond, what we can learn from the archaeologies and histories one finds in museums today (which are themselves, of course, specialized interpretations in their own right).[2] These caring citizens share a quest for personal knowledge, for self-conscious information about being-in-place, and for participation that can catch us in the act of complacency about who we are, where we have been, and where we are going and thereby might change our thinking about the meaning of life in the landscapes of our respective pasts and presents. What they seek is, in that sense, more poetic than scientific. They are committed more to methods of immersion and self-conscious saturation than to those of clinical distancing as forms of learning. Each approach in the extreme begs comparisons of peoples and their changing environmental circumstances, and each for those reasons is appropriate for pursuing the overall problem at hand, but the various approaches do so on vastly different terms of evidence and reporting. Our critics find common ground in the middle—respect for facts, as they can be determined more or less objectively, that is mixed with the first-person powers of poetic interpretation and representation (not just poetry). The overall effort loops into the area of educated imagination, that is, thoughtfulness focused on what is reasonable and possible in solving puzzles. On that score, poetics and science share common ground. Inference, speculation, and metaphor play an important role in both cases.[3] The result, in this case, is approximately what I have referred to elsewhere as "artful science."[4] It shows up here as prolegomena to a poetics of place pushed through the following five organizing questions. What are we supposed to learn from such environmental inquiries? What are the sources of information? What are the obstacles in and prospects for doing so? What can we hope to gain? How shall we tell the story?

What follows is an attempt to answer these questions and, in the process, outline a poetics of place with a conscience.[5] It is rooted in our propensities to make sense of material and imaginative experiences through projections of being-in-the-world and the use of our culturally appropriated bodies—our sensuous–intellectual apparatuses—as the primary instruments for doing so. It draws on landscapes variously described as "home," "wild," and "sacred," where the sensuous is conspicuously brought to the fore through most forms of participation (sites where emotional content often dominates conscious interpretations). It pursues knowledge mostly ignored or formally discounted by the extremes of logical positivism. It advocates as a complement (not as a replacement) *a kind of knowing and reporting* that (a) promotes phenomenology as a philosophy that puts the observer (the seeker, the knower) upfront in the equation of interpreting and representing experience; (b) pushes interpretive anthropology back into the loop of sensual experience, a body-centered position that includes a consideration of but transcends the sweeping metaphor that everything (e.g., people, landscapes) can and should be rendered as texts to be interpreted; (c) finds some continuity in the structures and orientations of body-groundedness and myth despite important limitations posed by language itself and by epistemic interference between the present and our preliterate past; and (d) gives poets special cachet through their offering forms of knowing and saying (robust metaphors and more) that can engage the senses and visions of being-in-place in ways that both exceed and complement more conventional strategies in anthropology and history. In deference to the critics named and the need for advocacy in the social sciences, all of this is tied to considerations of who we think we are, where we have been, and where we might go from here with the idea of reclaiming respect for the land and its inhabitants, human and otherwise, past and present.

## ▣ OPPORTUNITY: BEING THERE

*I travel your length, like a river / I travel your body, like a forest, / Like a mountain path that ends at a cliff / I travel along the edge of your thoughts, / and my shadow falls from your white forehead, / my shadow shatters, and I gather the pieces / and go on with no body, groping my way.*

—Octavio Paz, *Piedra de Sol*[6]

"Ways of dividing up space vary enormously in intricacy and sophistication, as do techniques of judging size and distance," Yi-Fu (1979, p. 34) tells us, and if we look for fundamental principles of spatial organization in all cultures, we find them in two kinds of facts: "the posture and structure of the human body, and the relations (whether close or distant) between human beings" (p. 34). We organize the space we occupy through intimate experiences with these two things to make it serve our social and physical needs.[7] That deeply evolved sense of place is strong and is linked to (among other things) natality, kinship, and mortality—to sacred and personal space, spiritual help, travel, the seasons, and the calendar (cf. Geertz, 1996, p. 259). Personal space itself is a collecting center for experience and identity construction, as an individual and as a member of groups, and is a center for *re*collection that can be variously hoarded and shared with others through storytelling about life as lived (Brady, 2003b, pp. xiv–xv). Movement in these fields creates histories and also puts an emphasis on the present. Thoughts about past landscapes are necessarily grounded in contemporary processes of mind and knowledge about being-in-place, so the cleavage between now and what we think "used to be" cannot just give itself to us freely sans interpretation. Historical knowledge of any kind involves a culturally constructed, cognitively filtered, and reciprocal process, an apprehension and a *re*presentation of place to mind and back again, revolving and evolving in its constructions.[8] It is a mixed conscious and unconscious process, received much like the patterns of puzzlements that we take to task in the circle of stones and, therefore, subject to a variety of selective perception biases and omissions, if not simply paving the high road to inventing the truth that we *need* to find, the conclusions that comfort and support us no matter what the evidence by other calculations.[9] Context is the key to it. Knowing the context of words, behaviors, and artifacts is practically everything for determining meaning. Whatever Stonehenge or other historical landscapes used to be, the larger point is that they can be known in meaningful elaborations only as they are grounded by perceptions in the moments of our current existence.[10] There is no way to bypass that process. That is the sine qua non of a poetics of place, of being-in-place, and it starts in the ultimate home—the embodied self.

Is there some common ground that can be apprehended through the trowels, brushes, and screens of the senses that will give us a realistic impression of life in ancient places and thereby address the concerns of our environmental critics? We are one species, one subspecies in biological form, embodied more or less the same every-where, and as conscious beings we need to know (or think we know) where we are before we are able to choose definitive courses of action. The comparative framework provided by that posture gives us access to other humans through sympathy and empathy, that is, by tapping into "fellow feeling" with speculation and imagination at work, both of which are essential parts of the interpretive equation. Both can also be souped up in special ways by being on-site, in-place—by "being there" (cf. Geertz 1983)—anywhere. That by itself does not guarantee anything specific in terms of knowledge of culture or place. Getting *there* takes existing knowledge from which one can update or launch a new perspective, thereby invoking a boatload of biases and related selective constructions of mind about exactly *where* one is, "home" or not, and so on. But the processes of projecting a physical and cultured self on the places and moments at hand and making sense of them through an educated imagination—no matter how fantastic (we can learn things only in terms of what we already know)—are fundamental to human thought and, thus, to conditions of being-in-place. They provide a context for analogies between things present and past. Guided tours of historical and ancient places rely precisely on such in-person emulations to add realism (literally realization, an internalizing process) to the experience (see also Coles, 1979; Saraydar, 1976; Saraydar & Shimada, 1973). They also generally provide specific scripts or guidebooks to fill in historical details. That combination of "being and seeing" writ large situates itself in what we can call the *sensuous–intellectual con-tinuum,* the biocultural grounding that we all bring to consciousness of being-in-place through our bodies and that, because of its integrated and systemic nature, can be represented in a common frame of reference (Blackburn, 1971). That is what makes us tick and know that we are ticking as sentient beings, as movers and makers of metaphors in place—the baseline of being and seeing and sharing it with others.[11]

By using this model and relying especially on the comparative strengths of engag-ing in "parallel enterprises" as humans,[12] it follows that we can tap into the sensuous–intellectual continuum as we know and experience it, heighten consciousness of our own culturally constructed screens of beliefs and behaviors (with and without scripts of expert testimony), and draw reasonable conclusions about how we are now as beings *in* and *of* place and perhaps what it *might* have been like to have occupied and left our marks on particular landscapes before us.

## ▣ GETTING THERE: THE ONTOGENY OF SPACE AND PLACE

> *Man is nowhere anyway/Because nowhere is here/And I am here to testify.*
>
> —Jack Kerouac, *Mexico City Blues*[13]

"*Getting* there" complements "*being* there" as an important concept in ethnography and must be maintained in any attempt to create a poetics of place. Approaching literature as an existentialist, and thereby leapfrogging any narrowly textual or ethnographic forms of analysis in favor of an anthropology of experience, poet/ethnographer Michael Jackson puts a premium on the meaning in journeying rather than on the stacked-up facts that an ethnographer is likely to report after having reached and researched a destination. Jackson (1995) argues that "the authenticity of ethnographic knowledge depends on the ethnographer recounting in detail the events and encounters that are the grounds on which the very possibility of this knowledge rests" (p. 163). Getting to that point cognitively is seldom discussed in any ethnographic context. But that is where a phenomenological account of being-in-place must begin. Let me start with myself, going and being nowhere in particular (something on the order of my current employment), just negotiating my own existence in space and place.[14]

For me, *space* is transparent, ethereal, abstract, a vacuum cornered in the mind's eye abstractly as empty geometry. It is a cognitive and culturally defined container of sorts into which concrete and meaningful things can occur or be put. *Place,* in my comfortable view, is a filled space, tangible, concrete, habitable, traversable, or defined specifically against such interests as those unavailable for human occupation (e.g., mountain peaks). It is the geography of earth, mind, body, and lived experience, the semiotically enriched site of events human and otherwise. It is where whatever happens in my experience does happen. My experience also leads me to believe that all people make something special of their engagements with the properties of place, including drawing boundaries of time, space, consciousness, and memory of being in it to orient and define themselves (see also Basso, 1996a, 1996b; Feld, 1982; Feld & Basso, 1996; Low & Lawrence-Zúñiga, 2003; Yi-Fu, 1979). They make life-in-place meaningful and push it way beyond shelter making and survival (Danesi & Perron, 1999, p. 137). They turn it into signifying systems, render it in signs and images of themselves, apprehend it through metaphors and imagery of their own making—their languages, cultures, and histories—and use it to govern relations among families, native and stranger, own and other, things near and far, things past and future, and the everyday realities of being in particular places. They mark it with their embraces and alienations of kinship in a composite world, their horizons and trails of history, and the eschatologies of their fears. They find it in the high peaks of their hearts and minds and externalize the imprints of both in the physical world by accident and by design while exploring, claiming, residing, nurturing, repelling, depositing, building, storying, and sometimes even erasing the paths of their lives. For these reasons, as soon as we start identifying features of landscape (peopled or not) and marking off boundaries (actual or implied), we situate ourselves in particular concepts of place—in something approximating, by structure and category, the worldviews and histories of the cultures whose members "make sense" of these experiences—ours and those of others.

Nevertheless, thinking about space as a container for place can be misleading for analytic purposes (cf. Hirsch & O'Hanlon, 1995; Low & Lawrence-Zúñiga, 2003), especially when one projects that sequence on the ontogeny of place in individual experience (cf. Thompson, 1989, p. 127)—the essence of a phenomenological stance.[15] The conceptual relationship between space and place is transitional and metonymic, but not necessarily unidirectional in our emerging consciousness. The connection of bringing place to consciousness creates the illusion that its meaning is a function of the landscape itself, something external and discovered, shaped beyond us. But as Schama (1995) says, "Before it can ever be a repose for the senses, landscape is the work of the mind. Its scenery is built up as much from state of memory as from layers of rock" (pp. 6–7). A sense of being-in-place is given to us cognitively at some deep level, but it is also appropriated by culture and rendered meaningful in a variety of ways. It is a manufactured concept, a pan-human construct that anchors our sense of meaningful location—our *position in* space relative to other specific people or things (including social distance between persons or objects)—and it comes to mind only as our *re*presentational capacity makes the world appear twice: "once as a recalcitrant external reality and again as a malleable inner actuality" (Brann, 1991, p. 7).[16] Places in this way are turned into cultural products, and our experiences of them, as Casey (1996) argues persuasively, are "never precultural or presocial" (p. 17). From a phenomenological perspective, the ontogeny is such that we emerge consciously *in* an occupied place and abstract the concept of space from that. In a phenomenological account, place is prior to space. It is *where* being-in-the-world happens.[17] The *how* of it includes concrete immediacy in perception: Lowe (1982) says, "Before anything else, it is for me a real, pretheoretical world, wherein I undertake everyday living. This is my primary reality" (p. 170).[18] Moreover, Casey (1996) continues, even though a phenomenological approach has "its own prejudicial commitments and ethnocentric stances," its commitment to concrete description honors the experiences of its practitioners. That connects both the anthropological field-worker and the indigenes in place: "Both have no choice but to begin with experience. As Kant insisted, 'there can be no doubt that all our knowledge begins with experience'" (p. 16; see also Csordas, 1994).[19]

▣ IMAGINATION: PRIMARY TRANSPORT

> *I think I have told you, but if I have not, you must have understood, that a man who has a vision is not able to use the power of it until after he has performed the vision on earth for the people to see.*
>
> —Black Elk, *Black Elk Speaks*[20]

We can add poets to the list of those conjoined by a phenomenological perspective (Heidegger, 1971) and use that thought to invite a deeper investigation of the role of imagination and creativity in constructing a poetics of place. Because places function as grounds for our projections of self and culture and a history of both—one private, the other public, all of it personal—and because we convert our place experiences into the "idioms" (the language and images) of the world as we know it, believe it, see it, and ordinarily argue it, the content may include what noninitiates see as mythical impossibilities (including landscapes peopled by spirits, etc.).[21] That interiorizing and largely unconscious process is often taken for granted or conflated with the significance that people assign to what they see as the dominant or "definitive" contents of particular landscapes. These are specific constructs for mentally centering and filing one kind of experience or another, including the circumscriptions of turf traveled on foot or touched only in our imaginations. Thus, place is defined by what we see in terms of landscape features through projections of self and culture and, therefore, by fantasy and wish fulfillment and other trappings of consciousness in the identity of the perceivers. For these same reasons, Thompson (1989) sees history as

> an imaginary landscape—a tableau of battles for some, a mural of scientific discoveries and technological inventions for others; and for those who avert their eyes from horizons of mystery or hallways of propaganda, there still remains an internal cinema of unconsciously edited perceptions in which self is the *figure* and nature the *ground*. (p. 127)

In fact, he suggests that "consciousness itself, as either a Buddhist heap (*skandha*) or a scientific narrative, is a landscape, for one cannot know without a world" (p. 127). Life in this sense is a constant process of negotiating landscapes (internal and external), and interpretation is as necessary to the process as is breathing, no matter how bizarre or fantastic it may seem from the outside looking in.

These creative dimensions, flexibilities, and transitive minglings of process pose a variety of analytic problems and beg the question of how we will tell the stories of places that structure our lives.[22] The concept of place cannot in any absolute way be separated from its contents—from the meanings assigned to its location and the activities or features marked in association with it. It cannot be seen as a "thing in itself." That would require an unobtainable absolute or clinical view beyond the cultural constructions of human consciousness (and that is why both logical positivism and, ultimately, hermeneutic "bracketing" fail here). But we can get closer to the essence of the concept of place—to the concrete and the sublime and largely ineffable qualities of it as a stabilizing, orienting framework for action—by looking for common denominators in the diversity of the meanings assigned to it by ourselves and others. Whatever they are, they ultimately form a comparative context with a personal sense of home at the center.

## ▣ UNIVERSAL PLACE: HOME AND HEARTH

> *He had no use for sensual gratification, unless that gratification consisted of pure, incorporeal odors. He had no use for creature comforts either and would have been quite content to set up camp on bare stone.*
>
> —Patrick Suskind, *Perfume*[23]

"Like a mirror," Snyder (1990) writes, "a place can hold anything, on any scale" (p. 25). Everyone knows that it holds a sense of "home" at its roots.[24] We all have homes, and in some ways none of us has the same one. Individual perceptions and experiences vary to the point where even family experiences shared in the same geographic location, in a common dwelling, and in the same hearth from childhood to old age do not produce clones. There are always individual versions of the experience. We mark them with personal names and related claims, and we spend time pooling them more or less in our stories and related interactions with others as a way of constructing the social reality of events that define home for all. Home is, in this sense, a place held in common by experience but unpackable in its semiotic particulars as a single version for each person involved. It is never "a seamless whole, a single story. Our imaginations set free in us other selves that seldom see the light. We lead several lives in the course of one" (Jackson, 1995, p. 161).

Despite sometimes radical differences in cultural content, in this ego-centered and relativistic way our homes are the essence of our being-in-place and our becomings in life. Even at their weakest and most fragmented moments, they are grounded in bodily experiences as emotionally loaded and semiotically coded memories, either positive or negative, and they all have a networking or centrifugal quality attached to them. These bundles of thoughts and emotions fan out as meaningful expectations about how life is or ought to be in relations with others, intersecting with the hearths and homes in surrounding neighborhoods and regions and ultimately linking up with the natal centers, the fetal and fatal places, the ancestral turfs of the rest of the world. Various physical and cultural processes make that a shifting landscape, including natural disasters, the aggrandizements and failures of colonial expansions and conquering economies, the fortunes and misfortunes of war, and the furrows of migration plowed by things such as homesteading, job seeking, refugee evacuations, and the influential cultural ship jumpers—the beachcombers of life—crossing into the frontiers of strangers and making homes there. Although certain adaptations must be made in new places (including the option of "going home"), on some scale migrants always carry their homes with them in the form of the languages, cultures, and traditions that defined their natal places (Jackson, 1995; Marshall, 2004). There is security in the transportable nest of knowledge that we call culture—the histories and desires embedded in knowing how to make and provision a hearth, in deciding who should share it and the wedding bed, and in determining where all of it literally might be placed.[25]

One good bet nowadays is that most people will not place a long-term hearth in what they consider to be a wilderness area. Doing so through the orientations and transport of modern culture puts many elements of the environment at risk, including one's own body—especially for the uninitiated. That would also constitute yet another episode in—a continuation of powerful forces already set in motion by—colonization and urbanization. But these concerns can also be very misleading. Wilderness has always been fundamental to human experience. For hundreds of thousands of years, nature has been more than a place to visit. Snyder (1990) says that it *is* home, a territory with more *and* less familiar places. Some "are more difficult and remote, but all are *known* and even named" (p. 7).[26] Nonetheless, some places in our modern experiences remain decidedly "wild," beyond the pale of what most of us would consider comfortable and secure habitation. What urbanites see as wilderness today helps to define the centering concept of home place in the breach, that is, by conceptualizing what is plainly *not* home—and that can foster two dramatically different consequences. One is to relegate such areas to a netherland of mind, out of sight and out of concern, thereby letting the strip-and-sweep policies of economic development take their tolls on these places unnoticed. Such culture runs its course, economies are stimulated, hearths get provisioned by the substantially employed, the rich get richer, ancestral places get erased at exponential rates, and no one except the developers, the politicians, the people exploited on the margins, and a few odd ethnographers seem to care. The other consequence is to recognize wilderness as foundational to our history of being-in-place in the long run as humans, let alone what is arguably a key to the future of the planet itself. This reaction shows up as an attempt to cherish and preserve what remains as wilderness, to learn from it some of the things we used to know about sustaining ourselves in body and spirit, and that in turn makes every such experience a candidate for creating sacred space. Mindful of the foundations of body and home, let me consider each of the categories of wild and sacred landscapes in more detail and then talk about their relationships and how we story them in ways that matter.

▣ WILD PLACES AND THE ASSEMBLY OF ALL BEINGS

*The rain comes over the hills, / like fluttering birds it comes. / I stand in my brother's tears / happy as the running stream. / Ho! Brother. / Tread upon the wide plains. / Lonely rugged mountains rule the land.*

—Archie Weller, "The Hunter"[27]

"Wild" places, such as home turf and sacred spaces, are sites where emotional content often dominates interpretations. If you say that you are going to live "in the wild" or "go wild" or just be "wild at parties," no one ever thinks that you are about to be placid and contemplative. Internally, we are in fact rooted in whatever was and is wild by our biology—by our "creatureliness." As a conscious motivation, aiming to "be wild" is a commitment of an embodied self to irregular and emotionally stimulating conditions. Externally, wild is a condition of landscape that modern Westerners might contemplate in fantasy or engage in person as adventurers, explorers, or castaways, among other marginal categories of being. The point is that being of the flesh and working in and with wild things in wild areas is a source of special identity for most of us, a marker of unusual boundaries. When *wild* becomes a *where*, it generally transforms into *wilderness*, a condition of wild landscape, a place where meaning abounds. It is, therefore, ripe picking for poets and artisans of all types, for all who would love its riches and lament its losses. It forms another "architectonic" link to the peoples and processes that are fundamental to a poetics of place.[28] But *where* is it? Gone? Seldom near? Far away and gasping for breath under the crush of a global economy? Or, is it somehow all of the above yet always with us? Snyder (1990) has some answers.

A Western sense of the "wild" is a place where "nature" rules—a place marked by ancient and eternal activities, untamed animals, uncultivated plants, and "an ordering of impermanence," if not "unruliness, disorder, and violence" (Snyder, 1990, p. 5). Although wilderness cannot be seen in any way other than through the screens of culture, it is commonly thought of as an environment that is culturally unbuilt, ungoverned, unscarred, or otherwise unmodified by humans. Encountering it always gets our attention in special ways. *Where* we find it is important. It is not confined to isolated mountains, deserts, or forests. Snyder (1990) reminds us that "a ghost wilderness hovers around the entire planet; the millions of tiny seeds of the original vegetation are hiding in the mud on the foot of an Arctic tern, in the dry desert sands, or in the wind" (p. 14). He suggests that it may, in fact, return at some point, although not in "as fine a world as the one that was glistening in the early morning of the Holocene" (p. 14). Wildness, on the other hand, is now and has always been everywhere with its "ineradicable populations of fungi, moss, mold, yeast, and such that surround and inhabit us. Deer mice on the back porch, deer bounding across the freeway, pigeons in the park, spiders in the corners" (p. 14). Urbanites live constantly in a sublimated or ignored wildness in this sense (bug and vermin exterminators take care of the rest), and although it can be a source of both reverence and wonder for the people who case its margins, enter it, and dwell in it for any length of time, the wilderness where wildness dominates is often consciously displaced, moved to its own outback in the geography of our minds until it shows up in a television travelogue or the vicarious thrill of adventure novels or Arctic explorer accounts-turned-coffee table displays.[29] The wilderness that most people know is "a charade of areas, zones, and management plans that is driving the real wild into oblivion" (J. Turner, 1996, p. 23). It is a nice place to visit through the glass of an automobile in the national parks of Nairobi or Yellowstone or in the few brave steps from the paved roads that roll through these areas like carpets for the conquering kings.[30] Few would want to live there. The farmers of these margins get a little closer to the culturally untamed, but only on the other sides of their fences. More than anyone, their job for thousands of years has been to erase the wilderness, homestead its meadows, tame its grasses, and replace its original animals with liveries and livestock. But all of the farmers in the world cannot hold a candle to the environmental corruptions and erasures of the great urban developers. Our wild landscapes have changed as wildernesses have disappeared.

Snyder (1990) asks us to stand up and be counted on this both intellectually and ecologically:

Wilderness is a place where the wild potential is fully expressed, a diversity of living and nonliving beings flourishing according to their own sorts of order. In ecology we speak of "wild system." When an ecosystem is fully functioning, all members are present at the assembly. To speak of wilderness is to speak of wholeness. Human beings came out of that wholeness, and to consider the possibility of reactivating membership in the Assembly of All Beings is in no way regressive. (p. 12)

But we have to ask how that can be done. How will we know when it *is* being done? Where is the map for being-in-place this way? Some of the answers lie in history. Others lie in the politics and sensitivities of the moment. The only sure way of putting them together is to increase one's awareness of and participation in the landscapes of lived experience.[31] Moreover, raising the stakes on both our being-in-place and having been there, Lopez (1990b) asserts,

A sense of place must include, at the very least, knowledge of what is inviolate about the relationship between a people and the place they occupy, and certainly, too, how the destruction of this relationship, or the failure to attend to it, wounds people. Living in North America and trying to develop a philosophy of place—a recognition of the spiritual and psychological dimensions of geography—inevitably brings us back to our beginnings here, to the Spanish incursion. (p. 41)

It brings us back to the history of a place whose home crossings have uprooted practically everything indigenous and wild and have pushed it around in a movable tragedy of cross-cultural casualties and increasingly fluid disconnections from the land itself. That marks a dramatic change from what was once kindled and supplicated in the worldviews of many people, including Native Americans (see, e.g., Deloria, 1993), to something profane and dangerous. Setting overromanticized views of noble savages and pristine nature aside, one can discover that both kinds of circumstances— supportive and accommodating or dangerous to one's well-being—can hold value as "sacred" at one level or another. Only corruption kills the prospect altogether.

## ◨ SACRED SPACES AND MYTH

*There is a place of great importance to me on a pine-skirted plateau in Utah's Uinta Mountains. Elk and deer weave trails of meaning through the trees and into the escape of cliffs and heavy timber; coyotes plant scat, gorged with hair and bone, among sagebrush and juniper. The place resounds with voices of birds and small mammals, and a thousand smells of the wilderness. To me, this place is cleanly holy. I cannot explain why; I only know that for twenty years it has filled me with awe and yearning, and solitude and peace. It is a space of great sacredness, seldom visited, always appreciated.*

—Richard Poulsen, *The Pure Experience of Order*[32]

Perhaps no other experiential domain shows the "made" or implied impositions of culture on geography more than places held to be sacred by the beholders (Brady, 2004). They are precious by definition. On the positive and more conventional side of that, the combination of cultural values and memory applied to such places can produce a poetics of reverie and respect, of awe and mystery, if not specific rituals designed to commemorate and renew such experiences.[33] But we know that the same places can be experienced very differently (the "parallax factor"). Unlike stepping in the puddles on a clay road after a rain, one can step in some sacred space as an outsider and never feel the change.[34] As Nelson (1983) observes quite correctly,

> Reality is not the world as it is perceived directly by the senses; reality is the world as it is perceived by the mind through the medium of the senses. . . . [It] is what we have learned to see through our own traditions, and they do not always line up as equivalents from one culture to the next. The interactions between Koyukon people and nature illustrate this clearly, for theirs is a world in which nature moves with power and humans are bound to a special system of environmental morality. (p. 239)[35]

Such space is easily trammeled by the uninitiated, by the claims of interlopers—the mini-colonials that ethnocentrism makes of us—who see all before them as an unfolding of their own turf. Access to the initiates' codes can save us from this error, that is, at least remind us that natural landscapes are everywhere more than physiography. They are, first and foremost, repositories of meaning that, not counting our own impositions of view and minus an artifact or two to flag other human presence, are most likely to remain invisible without a living guide.[36]

Investing the experiences of smell, taste, touch, sight, and hearing in a landscape whose features endear themselves to us or frighten us is a way of appropriating meaningful contexts in which to exist; to act in pleasure and remembrance; to meditate, marvel, and mystery over; to *re*assure; to *re*issue; to *re*member as a *re*consideration of life circumstances in plans for the future, for the next step, perhaps for the rest of our lives and the emplotments of our deaths. Such projections can make sacred space in our mind's eye and the behaviors steered by it; they create places for communion, ecstatic immersion, or other forms of poetic inspiration, on the one hand, and places for piaculum, supplication out of fear and anxiety (Yi-Fu, 1979), literally places to be avoided except under the most carefully calculated circumstances (e.g., rituals of sacrifice), on the other.[37] But the separation of these forms is not always clear because of cross-cultural misunderstandings and the knowledge that opposite interpretations can occupy the same geographic location (Brady, 2003b, pp. 93–100; Fernandez, 2003). There is also always much that appears "in between." Sacred places can stand alone as territory marked in the minds of those who know of them vicariously or in person. But when engaged in person and recognized as such, they inevitably beg questions of boundaries (where the sacred "ends" and something more secular begins) and thereby form an avenue to liminality, that is, to spiritual or imaginary places and conditions of being not only between particular people and their geography but also in the alignments of persons and spirits in a community that ostensibly shares such views.[38] These are "neither here nor there" spaces that become a crossing ground for senses of self and cultures, individuals and gods, powerful landscapes and access to the sublime, among other possibilities. That does not make them any less stimulating to the imagination or diminish the need to know how we, as intruders or observers, might or might not fit into them. On the contrary, once discovered, culturally defined environmental borders are even more likely to be conspicuous and puzzling if for no other reason than the semiotic diversity of their stimulations and expressions.[39]

▣ OPAQUE FACILITATOR: THE NATIVE MYTH-MIND

*The leaves on the trees, the grasses on the hills and in the valleys, the waters in the creeks and in the rivers and the lakes, the four-legged and the two-legged and the wings of the air—all danced together to the music of the stallion's song.*

—Black Elk, *Black Elk Speaks*[40]

All other things being equal, language communicates the mental being and moods corresponding to it in the communicator. "In the psychotopographic universe, language is also subject to transformation, and its disintegration from a vehicle for recognizable human communication into something 'other'—both divine and demonic—also signals the shift in the transcendental world of merged subject and object" (Nelson, 1996, p. 106). That makes the story context or form of communicating voice paramount to its meaning, and it includes stories about place, some of which are focused on places that are both wild *and* sacred. Among the gatherers and hunters of the world, these are sites that are rich with meaning and power and that have multiple uses (e.g., menstrual seclusion, graveyards, ritual initiations) and realities tied to them. They are the stuff of legends tied to human and more-than-human landscapes, and the memories of them "are very long" (Snyder, 1990, pp. 81–82).[41] One reason for "the profound association between storytelling and the more-than-human terrain" in tribal societies, as Abram (1996) suggests, is that it "resides in the encompassing, enveloping wholeness of a story in relation to the characters that act and move within it" (p. 163). Indeed, because "we are situated in the land in much the same way that characters are situated in a story," the members of a deeply oral culture may experience this relation "as something more than mere analogy; along with the other animals, the stones, the trees, and the clouds, we ourselves are characters within a huge story that is visibly unfolding all around us, participants within the vast imagination or dreaming of the world" (p. 163)—and that is, at best, a shifting landscape, a moving target, but not totally beyond the scope of reclamations.[42]

From his travels in Australia, Snyder (1990) offers the following "as one example of the many ways [in which] landscape, myth, and information were braided together in preliterate societies":

We were traveling by truck over dirt tract west from Alice Springs in the company of a Pintubi elder named Jimmy Tjungurrayi. As we rolled along the dusty road, sitting back in the bed of a pickup, he began to speak very rapidly to me. He was talking about a mountain over there, telling me a story about some wallabies that came to that mountain in the dreamtime and got into some kind of mischief with some lizard girls. He had hardly finished that and he started in on another story about another hill over here and another story over there. I couldn't keep up. I realized after about half an hour of this that these were tales to be told while *walking*, and that I was experiencing a speeded-up version of what might be told over several days of foot travel. Mr. Tjungurrayi felt graciously compelled to share a body of lore with me by virtue of the simple fact that I was there.

So remember a time when you journeyed on foot over hundreds of miles, walking fast and often traveling at night, traveling night-long and napping in the acacia shade during the day, and these stories were told to you as you went. In your travels with an older person, you were given a map you could memorize, full of lore and song and also practical information. Off by yourself, you could sing those songs to bring yourself back. And you could maybe travel to a place that you'd never been, steering only by the songs you had learned. (pp. 82–83)

Even this little snippet about sacred space illustrates nicely the principle that existential interpretations situated in worldviews give place a temporal dimension and also reflect both the predicaments and the solutions to them posed by changing environmental circumstances.[43] Focusing in particular on Native American materials, Leonard and McClure (2004) see such stories as important

because in them the mythic breaks through into our present world, embodying the very kinds of boundary crossing that are so central to all mythological thinking. *Such stories give us a chance to see, to feel, the present of mythic truth in the midst of our perceptions of contemporary reality.* Whether they are the repositories of national or ethnic identity or the site of supernatural revelation or visitation, whether they are actual places where we can stand and hear the echoes of long-ago battles or imaginary places shaped by the requirements of mythic vision, sacred places serve to teach and remind us of who we are and how we ought to behave in our day-to-day lives. . . . Sacred places, especially in the various senses that Native Americans use the term, call out to us to *become* "down to earth," to remember and honor and revitalize our essential connections to the earth and the natural world, to the sacred all around us. They invite us to associate the spiritual with such natural material phenomena as mountains, rivers, lakes, trees, and caves. The study of stories about sacred places might just allow us to see such opposed binaries as past versus present, realistic versus mythological, or spiritual versus material as not so mutually exclusive. (p. 320, emphasis added)[44]

Certain places within the mutually owned territory of old cultures, Snyder (1990) says, are loaded with "numinous life and spirit." They are "perceived to be of high spiritual density because of plant or animal habitat intensities, or associations with legend, or connections with human totemic ancestry, or because of some geomorphological anomaly, or some combination of qualities" (p. 93). They are cultural and spiritual "gates through which one can—it would be said—more easily be touched by a larger-than-human, larger-than-personal, view" (p. 93; see also Deloria, 1993; Munn, 2003). Such sites offer a glimpse of the internal workings of belief and behaviors that put cultural histories into ecologies of place, some of which might be seen as "spiritual game management" (Snyder, 1990, p. 87). They also show us that storytelling is much more than amusement. It is fundamental to human life—especially (it seems) in myth, where one can change the content and bend the structure to achieve common understanding of perennial problems. Indeed, Verene (1976) finds that "human understanding must always have at its center the notion of the myth. In its movement toward the recollecting of origin, it discovers always again the myth, the original power of image-making or mimesis, the science of which, as Vico says, is the first that must be learned" (p. 34).

Within limits of coherence of the whole, consistency of theme, and related structural concerns, myths are a flexible and highly generalizable form of storytelling about the past in personal terms. They are linked to the now and then through one Gordian knot or another in terms aimed specifically at stirring up something poetic in the audience.[45] Poetry itself is tied to the context of the immediate and the immanent, to the processes of "being there" and sensual saturation, and to the art of the possible and not necessarily the actual, in or out of what might seem to be an obvious historical or mythological context (Brady, 2003b). Like myth, poetry addresses the long run by allowing for diverse particulars in accounting for events of the moment in forms that tap into the larger continuities and commonalities of being human. Access to some of this material is guaranteed through studies of oral poetry, for much of that is tied directly to the timekeepings and implications of ritual and myth, to stories of origins and the peoplings of landscapes through events and discoveries over time as conceptualized by the tellers—and perhaps defended in what is viewed from other perspectives as a mix of fantasy and reality (Tedlock, 1983, p. 55). In this way, myths provide a complicated source of information on worldviews and associated behaviors that pervades both history (with its mix of literate and preliterate participants) and prehistory (with its exclusively preliterate participants) and thereby helps to frame meaning and action in our lives today.[46]

Schama (1995), in his provocatively aesthetic and historical *Landscape and Memory*, argues that to put that to work in environmental review and renewal, "what we need are new 'creation myths' to repair the damage done by our recklessly mechanical abuse of nature and to restore the balance between man and the rest of the organisms with which he shares the planet" (p. 13; see also Kozinets & Sherry, 2004; Leonard & McClure, 2004, p. 324; Richardson, 1975; Saraydar, 1986; Sherry & Kozinets, 2004).[47] Wondering whether or not this is a cure for what ails us is not "to deny the seriousness of our ecological predicament, nor to dismiss the urgency with which it needs repair and redress" (Schama, 1995, p. 14), but we have to ask about the old ones in the process:

> For notwithstanding the assumption, commonly asserted in these texts, that Western culture has evolved by sloughing off its nature myths, they have, in fact, never gone away. For

if, as we have seen, our entire landscape tradition is the product of shared culture, it is by the same token a tradition built from a rich deposit of myths, memories, and obsessions. The cults which we are told to seek in other native cultures—of the primitive forest, of the river of life, of the sacred mountain—are in fact alive and well and all about us *if we only know where to look for them.* (p. 14, emphasis added)[48]

On the premise that "strength is often hidden beneath the commonplace," Schama's study is "constructed as an excavation below our conventional sight-level to recover the veins of myth and memory that lie beneath the surface" (p. 14). It is an archaeology of knowledge, another architectonic connection to a poetics of place that supplements and gives new instructions to the more parochial endeavors of academic archaeology and history. It is a deeply poetized effort that may coach us into finding something of our internal but dusty guidebooks in the places set aside as wilderness in our cultural traditions and in portrayals of those and other landscapes in writing, painting, and photography, both past and present. It is "a way of looking, of rediscovering what we already have, but which somehow eludes our recognition and our appreciation. Instead of being yet another explanation of what we have lost, it is an exploration of what we may yet find" (p. 14).[49]

Snyder and others share the hope in this. The native myth-mind—first encountered by Europeans in North America by Cabeza de Vaca, last known fully by the Native American Ishi—is "not dead and gone. It is perennially within us, dormant as a hard-shelled seed, awaiting the fire or flood that awakes it again" (Snyder, 1990, p. 13; cf. Saraydar, 1986). This thinking again raises the issue of both myth-time and history in relation to landscape. "We are all capable of extraordinary transformations. In myth and story, these changes are animal-to-human, human-to-animal, animal-to-animal, or even farther leaps" (Snyder, 1990, p. 20) to other shared forms of being-in-place,[50] including the dreams we have had about such things and the oral and graphic representations we have left behind in the winding and sometimes broken trails of being human over the long haul. "The essential nature" of being in any part of this equation, Snyder asserts with optimism, "remains clear and steady through these changes" (p. 20). That does not guarantee access to the particulars of our pasts, of course, but it does put us in a perpetual and comparative present of sorts. We cannot lose sight of ourselves even if we try, and yet even when we look closely, we find fuzzy boundaries, much to learn, and much that is known at some level but difficult to express.

## ◧ INTANGIBLE OBSTACLES: BEYOND WORDS

*What moves on this archaic force / Was wild and welling at the source.*

—N. Scott Momaday, *The Way to Rainy Mountain*[51]

Myth and history are two related ways in which we have kept records of being around as conscious beings-in-place for many thousands of years.[52] But despite a track record of sameness in narrative form, especially written form, there is nothing in the rulebook that precludes innovation in the presentation of either (Brady, 2004). The pervasiveness of myth in all aspects of our lives shows that not to be a new idea in itself, and history in its most conventional sense, spliced into myth-time as a form of accounting since the advent of writing and the genre building of modern academies, can also be a poem (Brady, 2003b; Dening, 1995, 1998a). Getting at the larger goals of environmental reform staked out here might benefit by building on the kinds of narrative and artistic diversity in Schama's (1995) compilation, not only by taking a new look at some older ways of telling the story of being- in-place but also by carefully inspecting what exactly is conveyed by such storying by asking about the larger perceptual context.

Reading within and between the lines of Schama's inspiring work suggests quite readily that some of what we seek in a poetics of place, both ancient and modern, lies beyond words. Language gathers at the root of all storytelling, including myth, but as Jackson (1995) says, it does not exhaust its content or its possibilities. Experience covers everything. Words do not.[53] Consciousness itself is mediated through language, and image and everything that we know emerges in one form or another from experiences of landscape and story. "Such a conception of fieldwork implies a conception of writing" (p. 113) and of language as constitutive of reality, but it does not restrict the inquiry to it even as it puts considerable emphasis on "the creative and ethical domains of human social existence" (Jackson, 1982, p. 2). The oral storyteller and the writer share the task of revealing "people to themselves and to their possibilities" (p. 2).[54] Furthermore, during this modern age,

> one must have recourse to art and literature if one is to keep alive a sense of what hard science, with its passion for definitive concepts and systematic knowledge, often forgoes or forgets. The painter who dispenses with framing in order to reunite the field of artistic vision with the space of the world, or the composer who breaks down the boundaries between what is deemed music and noise . . . find a natural ally in the philosopher who, aware that concepts never cover the fullness of human experience, sees that task of description as more compelling than that of explanation [including descriptions of being-in-place]. (Jackson, 1995, pp. 4–5)[55]

Nonetheless, posing a conundrum of sorts, it is through the conveyance forms and content of language and story that we must enter an *analysis* of places and the events that unfold in them. Like the oral performances that house myths in some embrace of the long-run and second-tier translations of them by experts with their own cultural and textual biases, we need to learn how to interpret the places and events of others and relate them to our own sensuous–intellectual experiences with the best possible representations, that is, in a manner true to what we know, think, and *can* say with reasonable persuasion. But the sources of that information and the language we need to use to understand and communicate it are not always easily obtained—if they are obtained at all.

## ▣ LIMITED OPPORTUNITY: ORAL POETRY AND MYTH

> *[Secret Road:] There are trees, crags, gorges, rivers, precipitous places of precipitous land, various places of precipitous land, various precipitous places, gorges, various gorges. It is a place of wild animals, a place of wild beasts, full of wild beasts. It is a place where one is put to death by stealth; a place where one is put to death in the jaws of the wild beasts of the land of the dead.*

> —Bernardino de Sahagún, "Aztec Definitions"[56]

What is lost from, or created and added to, discourse when it is moved from one person to the next in the same culture pool? Across cultural and linguistic boundaries? It is important to remember the dialogic character of such communications and to keep in mind Bakhtin's wisdom that language never moves through uncluttered space. It is heteroglossic and mutually constructive in all utterances—all contexts of development, reception, and discovery (Holquist, 1981, p. xx; 1990, p. 69). Combined with what can be learned from history, archaeology, and on-site experiences (however changed over time), we can bolster our sense of past landscapes by studying the legends and tales, the myths and meanings, as we discover them through oral and written texts and the performances and translations of each. They all are, at one level or another, functions of language, and in the quest to understand the nature of being-in-place, language and storytelling are essential but also, in some ways, are inadequate to the task.

In some of his pioneering work on Native American narratives, Hymes (1987) points out that ethnopoetics necessarily starts with language (p. 80), that "it is first of all a matter of taking seriously the ways in which narrators select and group words" (p. 41), and that the stories of Native American oral discourse "are to be heard, or seen, in lines, and thus are a form of poetry" (p. 49; see also Kroeber, 1983; Swann, 1983; Tedlock, 1972, 1983; Zolbrod, 1983). This is fairly recent and profound thinking that runs against the grain of Western ethnocentrisms concerning what does and does not count as poetry. As Zolbrod (1983) says, it has taken a while for scholars to recognize that there is a substantial Native American poetic tradition once misperceived as little more than "casual tale-telling" that is conspicuously poetic to those who know how to recognize its "implicit semantic and rhetorical patterns" and who understand that performance and setting have "a bearing on the utterance of a storyteller not evident in ordinary prose" or in "the printed medium conventionally employed by most translators" (p. 227).[57]

This is empowering knowledge. Tedlock (1983) argues that treating oral narratives as dramatic poetry clearly promises many analytic . . . [and] aesthetic rewards. The apparent flatness of many past translations is not a reflection but a distortion of the originals, caused by the dictation process, the notion that content and form are independent, a pervasive deafness to oral qualities, and a fixed notion of the boundary between poetry and prose. Present conditions, which combine new recording techniques with a growing sensitivity to verbal art as performed "event" rather than as fixed "object" on the page, promise the removal of previous difficulties. (pp. 54–55)

Moreover, taking advantage of the poetic dimension in every act of speech or writing (which is "related but not identical to its linguistic dimension") and recognizing that all people in the world "continuously produce, reproduce, and revise their own cultures in dialogues among themselves," with or without ethnographers present, as an act of being human, language's dialogical potential can be used "to balance each representation with an alternative representation, producing poetry that is built on a process of translation rather than made to resist translation" (Tedlock, 1999, p. 155). But projecting the most modern of mentalities—reading as an avenue to interpretation—as a facile metaphor on all that we wish to understand (e.g., "reading" oral performances and landscapes) can be an obstacle in the study of both oral *and* written traditions, that is, a problem in translating Native American and comparable oral presentations firsthand and also in deciphering the written translations we get from others before us (see, e.g., Finnegan, 1992; Hymes, 1987; Kroeber, 1983; Saraydar, 1986; Swann & Krupat, 1987; Tedlock, 1983, 1993, 1999). Times have changed, and our sensibilities have changed along with them.

◙ PERCEPTUAL OBSTACLES: EPISTEMIC INTERFERENCE

> At first there is just one line, horizontal / A second appears / It's already closer / Soon one notices lines everywhere / They draw rapidly together / Too late one realizes that / There is no escape.
>
> —Walter Helmut Fritz,
> "Fesselung [Entrapment]"[58]

Texts are an important avenue to the discovery of place in its diverse purchases and appearances everywhere, but using them as evidence for anything is problematic, in part because of the creativities inherent in text construction and reception that change with contexts of interpretation (as we all know and as the history of hermeneutics and interpretive social science in general shows) and in part because of diversity in textual form, performance, and appreciation (cf. Finnegan, 1992, p. xii; Lansing, 1985). Oral or written, they are bound to be multivocal and polyvalent at one level or another and are, therefore, always subject to context-sensitive interpretations that we ourselves impose and that cannot always be determined for the original authors in the case of *re*presentations or *re*readings. That makes original meanings elusive (cf. Barthes, 1972, 1977; Brady, 1991b; Herzfeld, 2004, p. 39), but it does not preclude the construction of reasonable or agreeable interpretations between author and reader, speaker and hearer, for communication would then be impossible (Brady, 2003b, p. xxiv). Only the immaculate reception gets foiled in the process, and we do have some empirical data to help us steer and contextualize the problem rationally. But using oral or written texts as an avenue of access to really old things and behaviors is doubly complicated for other reasons as well, not least because we are separated from any possible dialogue with the original authors and from aboriginal conceptions of life in place by fundamental changes in perceptions of the world—by what we can cull from Foucault (1972) as *epistemic interference* in the gaps between prehistory and now, mostly because of the profound changes in our perceptions of ourselves, our products, and our landscapes insinuated through the invention of alphabetic literacy and compounded by the mass production of texts by way of the printing press (Abram, 1996; Lowe, 1982). Our views of the nature of the world and our embodied place in it have changed accordingly.[59]

The rise of alphabetic literacy and its dissemination through printing technology have had a profound effect on what Lowe (1982) calls the "hierarchy of the senses" and, thus, on the way in which we register and store information as humans. One sea change (among others) in this put a special premium on seeing over hearing in the field of perception and provided a means for separating knowledge from speech. Lacking written records, speech in an oral culture fulfills many functions that tend to be compartmentalized in chirographic and typographic cultures. Speech is communication in the latter, and knowledge is primarily preserved by writing. In an oral culture, however, "speech has to fulfill both functions of preserving knowledge as well as of communication, for only in the act of speaking can its knowledge be preserved" (p. 3).[60] Oral cultures have "an 'artisan' form of communication" where "stories arise from the rhythms of a preindustrial order: a world with time to listen, a language that is communal and founded on shared perceptions of reality, a respect for wisdom born of the accrued experience of generations, and a sense of life as still organized around the cycles of nature" (Wolf, 1982, p. 108; see also Feld, 1996). This knowledge is reinforced through personal experiences and is shared through tellings in oral performances— some ancient, some contemporary. Some with obvious continuity through both. In that connection it is important to recognize that the "residues from the earlier type persist to affect the later one" (Lowe, 1982, p. 2). It follows that aboriginal storytelling "is an art intrinsically at odds with a culture organized around writing and the dissemination of 'information'" (Wolf, 1982, p. 108), and so it is problematic as a source of ancient anything. By replacing or in other ways influencing folk and oral traditions, written culture undermines our ability to interpret them. The apparent "naturalness" of "seeing" or "reading" knowledge, as opposed to making the more direct connection between oral productions and aural registers, makes all interpretations of preliterate communications subject to deep-seated biases by modern interpreters.

The mix of ancient and modern shows up in contemporary studies of oral narratives and is played out in a synchronic version of epistemic interference that we can call *epistemic pooling*. The pooling part refers to the inevitable mix of diachronic continuities and traces from different traditions that show up at any given moment in history. The principle and context of the problem are encapsulated in Finnegan's (1992) observation that in folklore studies there is now "a deepening understanding of the *interaction* of oral and written forms as a regular and surprising process across a multi-dimensional continuum, rather than as something which involves bridging some deep divide" (p. xiii, emphasis added; see also Ong, 1967; Rothenberg, 1985, p. xxiii). That is precisely the scenario encountered today by ethnographers, linguists, and folklorists who seek secrets of the past from their contemporaries in other cultures, most pointedly for our purposes here, in the study of oral narratives and poetries as a measure of aboriginal forms of thought and behavior in ancient landscapes.[61] Despite some identifiable presence and separations of those forms in such contexts, the epistemic conditions of current "tribal" tellers are as mixed as anyone else's. They are modern people as well, and so they are influenced by the thoughts and premises of literacy at one level or another in text and performance (cf. Bauman, 1992; Finnegan, 1992; Finnegan & Orbell, 1995; Sammons & Sherzer, 2000). Nonetheless, with new sensitivities to the long-run obstacles that separate us, regardless of how subject to muddling they are today, we need to be optimistic. The very fact that there *is* continuity with things ancient in the oral narratives and poetries of some surviving tribal traditions (see, e.g., Perrin, 1987, p. 154) ought to spark our attention and motivate us to refine our methods for studying them. That would help us to get over the hump of what we already know, namely that oral narratives and poetry add an important source to our quest for reclaiming a sense of being in ancient places.[62]

These are some of the particulars that give motion and distinction to individuals and whole societies. They include fundamental differences that must be taken into account in any attempt to reconcile the separations and connections of language, story, and performance within and between communities, including ethnographers and their informants caught up in the mutually constructing and slippery ventriloquisms (as Dennis Tedlock would say) of speaking for others. That is equally true of attempts to reconcile the separations, and perhaps the traces of continuity, between modern written texts and the aboriginally unwritten (i.e., oral) accounts of being-in-place before the advent of writing (see, e.g., Layton, 1997). It also raises the stakes on the study of sacred space in aboriginal contexts—residual or lasting and reformed in our modern day or not—to something on the order of landscape poetics, to the study of poetries of place on both sides of the cultural fences that divide them. There is no guaranteed method to conquer it all. Meanings can be slippery, fugitive, irreducibly plural things—trains departed from the station leaving only warm tracks behind for us to touch and speculate on (Barthes, 1972, 1977, 1982; Brady, 1991b, pp. 10–11; 2003b, pp. xiii–xiv). But ethnopoetic research to date shows plainly that self-awareness and sensitivity to the impositions of cultural biases—the cultural "truths" that we take for granted, see as "natural" if we are aware of them at all, or favor in some guise as the "truth we need to find" to validate our identities—are "ground zero" for even starting such projects.[63] Knowing about them advances the prospect of *resituating* ourselves in myth-time and the history of place through texts and associated images. Like Snyder's Australian experience, that journey will also run the horizon of the old and the new. It will be history as we see it and live it, and so as we create it, with all of the interpretive problems outlined so far, but with the distinct advantage of locating the experience in a realistic site—the body itself, using language geared to sensuous–intellectual grounding and set analytically in an anthropology of ourselves.

## ▣ ROOT FACILITATOR: POETICS AT HOME

> To understand the fashion of any life, one must know the land it is lived in and the procession of the year.
>
> —Mary Austin, *The Land of Little Rain*[64]

Cull out the poets from among the bards and other performers of life as lived, put them on the peaks of what they consider to be their own lives and lands (Suiter, 2002), and they will likely share the experience with you as an epiphany of landscape—a dance with the sublime, the ancient, the foundational, the deeply personal poetry of themselves as beings-in-place (Bachelard, 1964, pp. 214–215).[65] Ask them how they know so much, and they will tell you that it is a matter of being-in-place for the long run, of internalizing its smells, sounds, and images—its flow of events and articulations of people and things. It is a matter of building an *embodied* history, they will say, and sometimes of launching that history through trips in the wider world and then "coming home."

We all have been somewhere beyond the homestead and its heather, and we know that returns can have a profound effect on views of the original experiences (Brady, 2003b). For one thing, nothing remains exactly the same. As Merwin (1997) says, "When I come back I find / a place that was never there" (p. 121). Times, places, and people change right under our noses. But triggered by sensuously doused memories, recombing the local landscape with a head full of new experiences (and absences) can yield a deeply contextualized poetic that both reinforces and redefines one's place *in* place, that is, by reworking the margins of self and other, native and stranger, old and new, even as the experience unfolds.[66] Conceptually *re*registering something as simple as place names in this context—for example, by virtue of their marrying "the legendary and the local" (or, say, in the case of Gettysburg, the legendary and the national)—can move the trekkers to special sentiments and symbolism of thought and action. The process is informed by both "being there" and "going there," by a then and a now, and by what we know from encounters with other cultures, including the academic and aesthetic works (e.g., painted, chanted, written) of other places, as pooled and compared with existing knowledge of our own (Agee & Evans, 1960; Brady, 2003b; Heaney, 1980b; Kerouac, 1958, 1959, 1960; Williams, 1973, pp. 1–12).[67]

All of these things "interanimate" in the mind's eye (Heaney, 1980b, p. 148), and they are the kinds of things that the poetic-minded Williams (1973) says can be "summoned and celebrated by the power of poetry" (p. 17). But the mental associations are not unfettered archaic recoveries. Nowadays they are sure to be a mix of the kinds of knowledge learned at home, on one's own through personal experience, and through the social entrainments of formal education (Heaney, 1980b, p. 131). Global networking and vast increases in access to public education, according to Heaney (1980b), ensure that in Ireland, for example, people are no longer innocent and that once local parishes now cast a wider net in the world:

> Yet those primary laws of our nature are still operative. We are dwellers, we are namers, we are lovers, we make homes and search for our histories. . . .When we look for the history of our sensibilities, I am convinced . . . that it is to . . . the stable element, the land itself, that we must look for continuity. (pp. 148–149)

And in the weave of personal emotion, myth, and symbol that Yeats once spun so effectively in Irish consciousness of self and place, so too do some of the new poets "weave their individual feelings round places they and we know, in a speech that they and we share; and in a world where the sacral vision of place is almost completely eradicated they offer in their art what Michael Longley has called 'the sacraments we invent for ourselves'" (p. 148). Their work shows that home and sacred go hand in hand as much for the sake of grounded identity—literally for locating a culturally defined self—as for the conservation and defense of an historical sanctuary of collected selves, a community, a plural being-in-place, a gathering of individuals with both shared and redefinable "roots" in matters sacred and profane.[68] Poetry latches on to that and *re*presents for us places that matter plus something as dear as the self to cherish as part of them, as something interanimated and nuanced with the rest of life and the landscapes of its expression.

Perhaps it is also true that a planet of poets so embodied and emplaced would be much less likely to trammel the very source of its own existence; to cut off the milk, the honey, the aesthetic and ecological sustenance of its forests and waterholes, its peaks and valleys; to shatter the web of life that ties coral reef to caribou, owl and finch to prairie grass, buffalo to ground squirrel, and the winds of Sahara and stratosphere to the quality of life in Chicago, Honolulu, and Madrid. Removal from the thick of it by cultural amnesia or ignorance, ideological preference, or insulated physical means does not give this experience. Personal immersion does. It does not guarantee as a process love or admiration or even acceptance of what is encountered. It does force the issue of participation.[69] The trick is to do it and to share the experience in ways that matter, perhaps on the order of Yeats, who had, as Heaney (1980b) remarks, a dual purpose: (a) "to restore a body of old legends and folk beliefs that would bind the people of the Irish place to the body of their world" and (b) "to supplement this restored sense of historical place with a new set of associations that would accrue when a modern Irish literature, rooted in its own region and using its own speech, would enter the imaginations of his countrymen" (p. 135). For that nourishment, I think, we will be well served by turning to the poets of place, Irish or not, American and Australian aborigines included, and find some way of hearing them that both represents them accurately in translation and resonates with our deepest being.

## ▣ HEAVY LIFTING: POETS AT WORK

*I think white people are so afraid of the world they created that they don't want to see, feel, smell, or hear it.*

—John (Fire) Lame Deer,
*Lame Deer: Seeker of Visions*[70]

To meet the goals of conscience in a poetics of place, to move people to action in environmental reform, we need to get beyond considerations of strictly conventional representations and into something richer, more robust, and more tuned to the wider domains of body-centered experience as an avenue to (among other things) the sublime, to epiphanies of place, at home and elsewhere. And if we succeed to some degree in our reclamations and rehearsals of such experiences through these means, we have to ask not only about the kinds of information mustered in the process but, once again, also about who should tell the story and on what terms (cf. Levenson, 2004; Weinstein, 1990; White, 2004). It cannot be the usual social science sources. They prefer language that has the life of uncommon metaphors and personal participation squeezed out of it. Theirs is a language of mortification, that is, of dead metaphors and dried-up facts applied through distanced, or what are supposed to be clinical, observations (cf. Graves, 1948, pp. 223–224). Poets take a different tack. We all are to some degree defined by where we are, where we have been, and where we think we are going. Our *selves* are insinuated in place culturally, historically, linguistically, and so forth through the usual channels of socialization, enculturation, and individual life experiences. But we are also insinuated in place sensually, as sentient beings, and poetry marks sensual space more consistently than does any other form of representation (Brady, 2004).[71] Although poetry cannot (and will not try to) free itself completely from the inevitable screens and biases of alphabetic literacy, it uses metaphor as a tool for discovering and positing the relations among things, and a poetic immersion of self in the experience of a much-traveled and culturally marked ancient place has a better chance of getting at a realistic account of such experiences primarily because of its devotion to sensuous particulars. Poets are potentially expert *re*presenters who offer comparative experiences in a commonly held domain—that of the body itself— and the ultimate aim of poetic expression is to touch the universal through the particular, to evoke and enter into discourse about the sublime, to move the discourse to what defines us all—what we share as humans.[72]

This argument may apply to any finely wrought figurative language, whether verse or prose, that is, to *poesis* in general (Hallyn, 1990). Joseph Conrad's powerful prose may have the same effect as, or an even more exalted effect than, finely crafted verse by inspiring its audience with the kind of self-consciousness of being that can change lives (cf. Cushing, 1970; Hinsley, 1999). As verse or prose, the content of poetic representations exceeds the literal: "All poetic language is language strenuously composed beyond the requirements of information and therefore striking, perhaps most striking, when most apparently 'transparent'" (Vendler, 1985, p. 59). The "surplus" beyond the literal is inference and argument by analogy and allegory, among many other possible tropic combinations and prospects (cf. White, 1978). In its most creative form, poetry, surplus meaning is a protest against the constraints of the ordinary rules of inquiry: "When a rhyme surprises and extends the fixed relations between words, that in itself protests against necessity. When language does more than enough, as it does in all achieved poetry, it opts for the conditions of overlife and rebels at limit" (Heaney, 1995, p. 158). More than simple mimesis, poesis is a process of "being" and "doing" in variable contexts, a dynamic and reflexive process of construction and selection.[73] Because its reception depends markedly on the experiences, preferences, and related biases of the receiver (e.g., reader, hearer), trying to legislate the one correct interpretation is futile; no aesthetic experience can be so governed (Brady, 2003b, p. xvii).[74] Like myth, one has to know how to interpret these creations. To do that successfully, following Jackson (1995), one has to know something about how and under what circumstances they were produced.

What I am proposing is much more than a change in writing style. More than selective editing is required to get from here to there in a poetics of place. We cannot revisit foundational human experiences in the wildernesses of our pasts simply by writing up knowledge in the present tense, much as one might do in trying to make a film in the ethnographic present, that is, by erasing traces of modern occupation through selective visions and contrived replications. Poetry offers a difference in forms of knowing as well as representing,[75] and as Howes (1990) sees it,

No amount of experimenting with one's writing style is going to make up for the deficiency of failing to experiment with one's perceptions or "sensory ratio" first. To understand a culture is to "make sense" of it, . . . [and that] involves more than a "rejection of visualism" . . . or exchanging an ear for an eye. Making sense involves, minimally, learning how to *be of two sensoria* at once and reflecting upon how the interplay of the senses in another culture's perceptual system both converges and diverges from their interplay in one's own [culture]. (p. 69)

What distinguishes the best of this writing—thoughtful prose, not poetry (see, e.g., Ohnuki-Tierney, 1981; Seeger, 1975, 1981; Stoller & Olkes, 1986, 1987)—"is the extent to which expositions on odors, sounds, and tastes are treated as intrinsic to the ethnographic message rather than extraneous. . . . To analyze these expositions [exclusively] as textual markers of having 'been there' . . . would be to miss their point" (Howes, 1990, p. 69; see also Stoller, 1987, 2004).[76] Moreover, the emotional truths of such experiences are perhaps best communicated emotionally (Sherry & Schouten, 2002, p. 219), and that is an open invitation to poetic bodies everywhere (Joy & Sherry, 2003). They all are equipped to make the case for how they are at any given time, with or without lines of words that by some estimations glow in the dark with eloquence.[77]

Poetry immerses itself and revels in these sensual features (cf. Brady, 2003b, 2004; Carpenter, 1980; Classen, 1993). In so doing, it favors the analytic perspectives embodied in phenomenology and an anthropology of experience. All three perspectives attempt to represent a "natural" and self-conscious emerging in the world, a matter that begins with experiences of space and place and in some ways reaches beyond language itself as a form of knowing.[78] Each puts the observer upfront in the equation of interpreting and representing experience, starting with an upright and horizontal sentient being, present and accounting for itself. But each has its intellectual and methodological limitations as well. None offers perfect vision. Aside from its own ultimate puzzles (*aporias*) on time and being-in-place, among other considerations, a phenomenological approach has the problem of "tacit knowledge" as a fuzzy but strategic edge that is difficult to know or at least to put into words (Polanyi & Prosch, 1975). It does not deal with the unconscious in any accessible way (Joy & Sherry, 2003, p. 279; Lakoff & Johnson, 1999). The anthropology of experience finds words as subsets, imperfect and selective renderings of the larger realm of what can be known from being alive and awake as a sentient being, and so must find some way in which to account for these experiences. Poets want to stretch the limits of language, to wring everything possible out of words and metaphoric processes, ultimately to reach beyond the shortcomings of language in the landscapes of literature, speech, the sublime, and the ineffable and then pass on the whole bundle to all who will listen. They want work, as Heaney (1995) remarks about Dylan Thomas's early poetry, where "the back of the throat and the back of the mind" (p. 141) answer and support each other. That is both the promise and the genius of poetry. It might not always apply or be accepted as intended, for any of several reasons.[79] But the aim and the prospects of putting a finger on "that great unity which is neither here nor beyond" (p. 141), of creating interpretations that "still make a catch in the breath and establish a positively bodily hold upon the reader" when "the wheel of total recognition has been turned" (p. 70), of engaging "the mechanical gears of a metre" that also takes hold "on the sprockets of our creatureliness" (p. 70), and in so many other ways of "recovering a past" or "prefiguring a future" (pp. 8–9), are always there. They are funded by imagination, by a need to articulate with the physical and social environments that surround us, and by an opportunity to communicate about what matters to us as we see it in the experiences of life as lived.[80]

From that robust ground, tracking the sensual and imaginative qualities of experience through the emotionally open and rich language forms of poetry may create desire (one hopes) in the listener or reader to experience the same things in person, that is, in body. Getting to some authentic emulation or understanding of being in ancient landscapes in that context is in part a job for ethnographically informed translators and in part a job for the poets of all cultures; this is not an ethnically proprietary thing (Hymes, 1987). We cannot get there through any procedure that starts by attempting to throw out the single most important elements—the saturations of individual lives as lived, the biases of being personal, interpretive, alive, and awake on a planet that can, in the imaginaries of some, also be inhabited by ghosts of the past and fantasies of the future (cf. Heidegger, 1977, p. 333). That is the stuff of ordinary reality, and it is in terms of such things that we act first as cultured beings. By virtue of its secondary extractions, its focus on stasis (linear "snapshots" of events) rather than kinesis (the simultaneity of immersion or "ongoing film") and other distancing techniques, hard science cannot ever capture these realities.[81] But neither is just writing poetry enough. Internalizing poesis as experience by immersing in its subjects is what matters most for depth of understanding, and that must be followed by an attempt to make it as carefully coached and exact a statement (including fantasy) of lived experience as we can.[82] If the "great function of poetry is to give us back the situations of our dreams" (Bachelard, 1964, p. 15), the great demand of ethnographic poetics is that we render those experiences as clearly and accurately as possible through our sense of being-in-place and the guidance of histories—our own and those of others— that appear to contextualize the material best (Hartnett & Engels, Chapter 18, this volume; on the same problem in science, cf. Hallyn, 1990). Such analyses can teach us things that are not available in any other way (Brady, 2003b, 2004).[83] Among many other possibilities, they can show us mystery and beauty and the need for being in them as we pass through the landscapes of our lives, and that in itself may motivate us to care about repairs where we see breaches in our rights and opportunities to continue.[84] Poetry, in one very important sense of the term, literally puts it all in place.

## ▣  REPRISE: ROOTS AND FUTURES

[Then:] *The word was born / in the blood, / it grew in the dark body, pulsing, / and took flight with the lips and mouth.*

—Pablo Neruda, "The Word"[85]

[Next:] *Long enough in the desert a man like other animals can learn to smell water. Can learn, at least, the smell of things associated with water— the unique and heartening odor of the cottonwood tree, for example, which in the canyonlands is the tree of life.*

—Edward Abbey, *Desert Solitaire*[86]

We are trainable, inventive, adaptable, and corporeal beings capable of making new and renewed associations among things and thoughts. With that in mind, and in the interest of breaking free as much as possible from the forces and forms of modern life that have ravaged the earth and its ancient creatures, if we have pumped up the appetite for "a kind of experience deep enough to change our selves, our form of life" (J. Turner, 1996, p. 104), and if we also realize in the process that "our ecological crisis is not, at the roots, caused by industrialization, capitalism, and technology, but by a particular form of the human self" (p. 104), then self-renewal and reform are the applied agenda at hand. We have asked how to do that and found it to be problematic. What is the instrument? How do we *re*imagine, *re*claim, and *re*surrect some semblance of participation in the changing environmental circumstances of the past and apply it to the present? Creating and sustaining a passion for place requires both primary and vicarious experience and language suitable for conveying the results realistically, that is, as they are conceptualized and felt and can be explored creatively by the participants through immersions in subject and place. Clinical abstractions tend to defeat that project, or at least they work in the wrong directions. But none of it comes to mind and body unfettered, beyond culture, personal bias, or predilections for certain kinds of interpretations against others.

The critics say that one path to a fair clearing in this, of doing something that counts in the Assembly of All Beings, is new myths, new applications of old myths, and thereby a renewed appreciation of continuities with the poetries and sacred spaces of yesterday. We need to *re*engage the study of myth and legend as embodied in landscapes and modern tellings (see especially Abram, 1996; Basso, 1996a, 1996b; Feld & Basso, 1996; Crapanzano, 2004). To reopen our eyes to the cross-cultural and ecological collisions of modern life, to "reveal the richness, antiquity, and complexity of our landscape tradition" as a way of showing the high cost of doing nothing (Schama, 1995, p. 14), we need to move from our own conceptions of a "natural" reading of cultural values and landscapes—our own blind ethnocentrisms—to something larger and more comparative, enlightening, and pragmatic through careful research and carefully reasoned imagination. Each of these efforts is a constructive and transferable source of identity. Each can tell us important things about how we are and where we have been and can thereby mark an important sense of where we are going from here as humans. But each also has its lacunae, its shortcomings, and its impossibilities, and given that the action of *re*visiting and *re*imagining circumstances *creates* original material, and thus another source of distortion in the effort to recontextualize the past through the present, the bottom line has to be not simply a study of texts and artifacts but rather a critical exercise in the larger and more inclusive realm of an anthropology of experience. To enfranchise that, we need to return consciously to the sensuous (Abram, 1996), to the body as instrument of all we can do and know, and to history and practice with all we can learn about embodiment as sentient beings in the world. Developing an unromanticized but keenly felt sense of being-in-place—of the constructive powers of getting there versus being there along with the knowledge that the basic instrument in the process is our emotionally loaded and culturally coded physical selves—is fundamental to the effort.[87] The inner and outer landscapes of our bodies are the locations where these things take place. What happens to people under these circumstances is sensuous–intellectual experience, a point of negotiation in the landscapes of life (some of which shows up in worldviews, rituals, etc.), and defines our existence, especially when things go wrong as they have for us today in the "slow-motion explosions" (Snyder, 1990, pp. 4–5) of expanding urban frontiers.

At the heart of these concerns is a primary sense of home and the structures of our very survival. Bass (2000) declares with insight that "the more fragmented the world becomes, the more critical it is that we try and hold the weave of it together, and the more clearly we will notice that which is still full and whole" (p. 73; see also Deloria, 1993; Snyder, 1978). Added to the inevitable conflict of human interests and the natural world, that may be sufficient reason to renew our inquiries among aboriginal cultures "concerning the nature of time and space and other (invented) dichotomies; the relationship between hope and the exercise of will; the role of dreams and myths in human life; and the therapeutic aspects of long term intimacy with a landscape" (Lopez, 1986, pp. 368–369). We need to reclaim a sense of sacred space, both as personal enlightenment and in a more applied sense as an avenue to deeper understandings of place that will support commitments to social and environmental security for future generations. To earn constructive influence in the Assembly of All Beings, we need to immerse ourselves in it and be informed by it. We need to know and *reevaluate* the transformations of place and space embedded in the landscapes of history—private and public, national and colonial—including the destruction of meaning in the land by translating encounters with other creatures and cultures into the signs of empire. We need to know the secrets sleeping both in the land and in ourselves, the experiences of being-in-place that once made the wilderness sacred to all who would pass that way or dwell there in shared dominion. We need to rediscover the sacred in the wild and the wilderness in ourselves realistically, but with all the passion of a commitment to survival in an untamed land. We need to *rekindle* our relationship with the wilderness by putting it in the kind of caring custody that we assign to our own ancestries and the offspring who gather at the hearth. We need to be a civilization that recognizes lessons learned from the wild as training for an "etiquette of freedom," as Snyder (1990, p. 24) says, that "can live fully and creatively together with wildness"

(p. 6), and the New World is where we must start growing it. Such commitments can launch the opportunity for developing new sacred space, for resurrecting old myths, and for creating new myths on which to hang our survival in the long run, but only if we find some powerful way of communicating the experiences.

Meaningful life presumes a vital existence in the first place, and as we know and I have said in triplicate here, for humans that is accomplished not only by knowing and doing but also by sharing the knowledge. *Telling* the story of place means *teaching* it as well, and Gruenewald (2003) has some very specific thoughts on that matter as applied to formal education. He argues that although culture and place are deeply intertwined, our educational system obscures that relationship by distracting our attention from, and our responses to, the actual contexts of our existences in place (p. 621). We can join our children in the equation of solving some of these problems by giving them firsthand experiences in different places—some wild, some not so wild, but all differentiated by comparisons of the overbuilt urban areas and the never-built few remaining wild areas of the planet. They must be able to distinguish between human social environments and natural environments and, in the process, to recognize that we are biological beings embedded in and embodied by both. Filtered through the social constructions of community talk and marked (one hopes) with some exalted feelings, such experiences may lead them to affinities with the planet otherwise long diminished by a frustrating and destructive search for fulfillment in a scheme of endless wants with limited means. Perhaps it will lead to a taming of the wild in their minds by recognizing and accepting it for what it is—wild, our past, our future, the place that more than any other shows us what we are and are not, where we have been and must be—perhaps by recognizing that the wilderness is ultimately our home, the baseline of the place we call our planet. Better that than building it into oblivion. Better that than squeezing its margins into creature habitats smaller than Japanese hotel rooms, skinning it for its pelts, or corralling it for rodeos, circuses, and zoos of all kinds. Perhaps this montage of old tragedies and new hopes will lead to the consciousness and rituals needed to create the myths of the future, including a philosophy of place less destructive of ecosystem, self, and the long run of humanity. History has shown us that soaking the land with cultural values means investing it with the power to change it and ourselves.[88] However idealistic and improbable that is in a world beset and distracted by the harsh realities of terrorism and murder endorsed by instructions from imaginary gods, that is power that we can reclaim and use for social and ecological justice in the Assembly of All Beings, humans and non-humans alike.[89]

The concept of being-in-place embraces all of this, and a poetic underpinning helps to reveal the process of putting that concept to work in various forms. Poetry can educate and move us into awe, mystery, the sublime, and related realizations by "stirring things up in us." It thrives on empathy and emulation and draws us into the sensuous–intellectual anchor for all knowing—that which comes from lived experience, where words are a subset of what is known and poetic expression is an attempt to render such experiences in texts and performances in a manner that often enlists the art of the possible more directly than it does the facts of the actual. While invested in radically different traditions of knowing, including an essential association with the multilayered metaphorics of myth (see, e.g., Barthes, 1972; Dundes, 1984; Graves, 1948; Meletinsky, 1998, p. 153; Schama, 1995; Snyder, 1978; Thompson, 1989), poetry can also yield accurate and detailed information on being and doing and thereby can supplement even more directly the conventional methods and knowledge products of archaeology and history. But a poetic stance (poetry and more) always starts with the truth of raw experience, with life as lived and seen from the inside, from the role of the participant, not from some disembodied tortured analytic imposed from the outside on the premise that our sentient selves get in the way of discovery. By being inherently comparative, a poetic perspective also addresses anthropology's first principle. It moves us to draw comparisons from our own immersions in life in relation to those of others, as separated from them perhaps by the cultural differences of age, gender, generation, personal characteristics, and favored gods—by the gaps that have always separated "own" from "other" in the landscapes of cultures whose home territories touch but do not match. It begs comparisons between being now and being then, between being one and being other, between being here and being there, and it thereby situates itself in our experience as fundamental to knowing other people, their histories, and the environmental complications of being-in-place today.[90] It gives us knowable contexts for constructing more or less satisfying meanings about the nature of the world and our place in it. In that respect, it enters the concerns of art and science with the opportunity to inform in both. The problem in each domain is to learn how to listen, especially when the poesis is not drawn from our own cultural wells.

The particulars of preliterate experiences in wild and sacred space are more or less lost to us as modern peoples through the displacements and reorientations of language and the concomitant separation of knowledge and thought that has come with writing, the cultural erasures and amalgamations of colonialism, and the appetites of mindless urbanization. But the important lessons of being a long-run creature in and of place are not. They are just too often obscured by the pace and rapacious confusions of modern life. A conscientious effort to develop a poetics of place, with careful attention paid to the sensuous and intellectual components of our existence that are laced into our own and other cultural traditions, and to the possibilities of both *re*immmersing and *re*inventing ourselves in the process, might bring us as close as we ever can be to the peaks of our human ancestry. Coupled with a critical use of the archaeologies, histories, and museologies of the day, that may give us our best glimpse of being-in-place in ancient circles of stones, our best claim on the spaces of ancestral voices, longings and desires, catastrophes and dilemmas, joys and defeats, the dreams of old horizons, and the life forms that contextualized all of it prior to the great steerage of alphabetic literacy, the indelible footprints of Columbus on the New World, and the launching of a loop of Western industrialism into outer space that has left no part of the planet untouched by its influence. Careful attention paid to, and a willingness to act in, that context may open the agenda of self-renewal and reform with greater wisdom and less complacency about the circumstances of our lives as lived. As interloper in an anthropology of experience, a poetics of place wants to insinuate itself in this milieu by starting with what makes us the same, the commonalities of sentient beings as seen through the great diversities of our collective meaningful existences. Being action oriented, it strives to know such things in every way possible and to defend them where they promote greater harmony in the Assembly of All Beings. In more ways than one, that is essential ethnography.[91]

◨ ◨ ◨

◨ CODA

*I know that it is unusual to put theory in the same box with passion and commitment in the study of anything (Noam Chomsky to the contrary), and I know that I have romped through a whole industry of specialized interests in as many disciplines on the way to this point. So, a pithy review of the structure of the argument—the landscape of this text, if you will—might be useful in conclusion. Here is what I think I have done. In the interest of developing a conscientious and environmentally concerned poetics of place, including cultivating sources of information on experiences at "home" and in modern and ancient landscapes that might best be described as "wild" and "sacred" (while discounting, for the purposes of this chapter, detailed discussions of the archaeologies and histories housed in museums that are themselves specialized interpretations of related materials), I have emphasized the need for (a) "being there" (on-site, grounded in the sensuous–intellectual continuum of the body itself, imagination, and home experience, a data source that is fundamental to interpreting experience and transfers to ancient contexts mostly by educated analogy); (b) accounting for "getting there" in personal and epistemological terms; (c) studying "tribal" poetries and myths as sources of body-grounded information (albeit complicated) on worldviews and associated behaviors that pervades both history and prehistory and is embedded in oral performances (a source of hard data and, given the paucity of expert native performers, scarce opportunity) and written texts (a source of hard data and plentiful opportunity provided by secondary observers), with the caution that we need to learn how to interpret poetries and mythical thought in those contexts, especially in the light of epistemic problems insinuated in Western perceptions since the development of writing and mass production printing and in the light of certain inadequacies of language itself to convey experience.*

*As models of and for interpreting these materials, I have compared (a) scientific approaches (especially logical positivism with its distancing techniques) and (b) artisan*

*frameworks (with their essential immersion techniques, including nonverbal representa-
tions and poetics) and collected them under the heading of "artful science." I have cultivated
the good fit of phenomenology as a philosophical underpinning for an anthropology of
experience and for poetics as a way of knowing and communicating experiences of being-
in-place. I have also given poetry per se special cachet under this umbrella, both because of
and despite its composition beyond the requirements of basic information and because it is
body grounded and can be a powerful source of communicating at both a sensuous and an
intellectual level. Unlike the prerequisites for scientific discovery and representation, phenomenology, poetics, and an anthropology of experience put the observer upfront in the
interpretive equation as an active participant. Each of these sources has its lacunae and
other shortcomings relative to the other sources. But the composite attention paid to them in
accounts of being-in-place and to culture as something constructed out of the interplay of
the senses, filtered through imagination and the historical shapings that individuals and
groups get from socialization and enculturation in particular traditions and perpetuate
by storytelling, can give the overall effort an authenticity complementary to, but otherwise
unavailable through, more conventional thinking in philosophy, anthropology, history, geography, and the social sciences in general. The end result has important applications in active
research, formal education, and concerns for the quality of life on the planet.*

## ▣ NOTES

1. Geertz (1996) writes that the anthropology of place has a "sort of preludial quality, as
if it marked the beginning of something that will reach far beyond the matters under immediate consideration" and that it "can be brought to bear on the grand complexities that plague
the world" (p. 262). The current argument moves in that direction.

2. I do not wish to slight the academic disciplines of archaeology and history. So, too, for
not reviewing the successes and failures of museology—that complex blend of representational problems in archaeology, history, and performance studies. Museums are an important
area of contest on problems of ethnographic representation, authenticity, and the like (see
especially Karp & Levine, 1991). I cannot burden the current argument with all of these asides.
But I must argue in the same breath that what is presented here is relevant to the practitioners
of those fields, including the politics of their reclamations and presentations, if one accepts the
necessity of putting the observer in the equation of interpretation (e.g., compare the themes of
this work with Allison, Hockey, & Dawson, 1997; Clifford & Marcus, 1986; Clifton, 1990;
Dening, 2004; Gewertz & Errington, 1991; Greenblatt, 1991; Hobsbawm & Ranger, 1983;
Hodder, 1982, 1987, 1989; Marcus, 1998; Metcalf, 2002; Pluciennik, 1999; Pratt, 1992; Wolf,
1992; see also Hartnett & Engels, Chapter 18, this volume). Excising the observer is, for me, an
unacceptable fiction; (and, of course, that begs the whole issue of postmodernism and its various levels of intellectual shootouts and misfires (Brady, 1998; Denzin & Lincoln, 2000, 2002;
Lincoln & Denzin, 2003b). Moreover, I have poets and their fictions in the mix of all of it
(Brady, 2003b). Given Western conventions aimed at protecting science from art and vice
versa, that is guaranteed to be controversial.

3. Roughly speaking, "Metaphor, calling one thing by the name of another, is not a strange poetic event. It is at the heart of language, and the direction of the metaphors is important. The body's influence [sensation and perception] spreads outwards, to features of the environment, and inwards to the mind" (Aitchison, 2000, p. 124; cf. Brady, 1991a, pp. 69–71; Snyder, 1990, p. 16). On body-grounded metaphors and the use of them in science and everyday life, see Brady (2003b, 2004), Brown (2003), Danesi (1999, p. 111), Fernandez (2003), Gibbs (1994), Hallyn (1990), Kövecses (2002), Lakoff and Johnson (1999), Laughlin, McManus, and d'Aquili, (1992), Midgley (2001), Montgomery (1996), and M. Turner (1996).

4. For more on the concept of artful science, see Brady (1991a, 1991b, 2000, 2003a, 2003b, 2004) and Brady and Kumar (2000).

5. What I mean by poetics follows Hallyn (1990) in his study of abduction in science. He does "not use the term poetics in the Aristotelian sense of a system of normative rules, but rather in the sense that one speaks about the poetics of Racine or Baudelaire, namely to designate a collection of choices made at different levels (style, composition, thematics . . .) by an author or a group. On the one hand, these choices lead to operations that inform the concrete work. On the other, they are loaded with meanings that more or less both determine and are determined by the artistic endeavor, for which the work is the result and sign. Ultimately, a study of poetics, in the sense understood here, comes down to what Umberto Eco calls 'the plan for shaping and structuring the work.' It is the program for the execution of a work, informed by presuppositions and exigencies whose traces one can locate, on the one hand, in explicit declarations, and on the other, in the work itself, to the extent that its completed form, with respect to other works, gives witness to the intentions that presided over its production. A poetics must return to a way of dreaming works and the declarations that accompany them, of conceiving their possibility, and of working for their reality" (pp. 14–15).

6. Paz (1981, p. 15). Compare Schama (1995, pp. 367–374).

7. Yi-Fu (1979) says, "The organization of human space is uniquely dependent on sight. Other senses expand and enrich the visual space" (p. 16). Sound "enlarges one's spatial awareness to include areas behind the head that cannot be seen," and it "dramatizes spatial experience. Soundless space feels calm and lifeless despite the visible flow of activity in it, as in watch[ing] events through binoculars or on the television screen with the sound turned off" (p. 16). In his view, "Taste, smell, and touch are capable of exquisite refinement. They discriminate among the wealth of sensations and articulate gustatory, olfactory, and textual worlds," whereas "odors lend character to objects and places, making them distinctive, easier to identify and remember" (p. 10). And he asks, "Can senses other than sight and touch provide a spatially organized world? Is it possible to argue that taste, odor, and even hearing cannot in themselves give us a sense of space?" (p. 10). Fortunately, "The question is largely academic, for most people function with the five senses, and these constantly reinforce each other to provide the intricately ordered and emotionally charged world in which we live" (p. 10). See also Ackerman (1990) and the "sensorium of the blind" described by Kuusisto (1998). The concept of place is also a product of the various cultural experiences, themes, and beliefs about the circumstances and transformations of lives as lived through the senses. But that does not mean that all cultures put the same hierarchical valuations on sensory experience or that they represent the senses in storytelling about life as lived in the same ways (Brady, 2003b, pp. 93–101; Carpenter, 1980; Joy & Sherry, 2003; Mitchell, 1983; Nelson, 1980, 1983).

8. The logic here is the ordinary logic of understanding for humans and their conjectural mentalities. It is both structural and hermeneutic in process (Brady, 1993), but I have conceptualized it as a progressive hermeneutic, as more of a spiral than the classic "hermeneutic circle," to accommodate the accretions and shifts of knowledge that occur through time (see also Brady, 1991b).

9. There is a scholarly danger in that, of course, especially when one seeks the truth of "what actually happened" exclusive of the experiences of being there in body and spirit (Dening, 2004), or vice versa, by thinking that one can rely only on the intuitions of body and tacit knowledge to apprehend the particulars of cultural performance. But we need to accept the fact that multiple reality frameworks can be applied to all experience and then do our best to defend the one we prefer to all others *without* deprecating or dismissing out of hand competing arguments and systems of signification from, say, the tribal world. On allowing "sufficient cognitive 'space' for conflicting ontologies to coexist," see Layton (1997, p. 128).

10. See Brady (in press) and Dening (1974, 1980, 1988, 1995, 1996, 1998a, 1998b, 2004).

11. The semiotics of talk and thought, artifact and architect, testament and text, teacher, trainer, seer, shaman, priest, and dreamer—the meaningful landscapes of "everyman" particularized in individual groups—are precisely the kind of information that is likely to dissipate with the death or disappearance of whole cultures or populations. But alluding at several levels to the kinds of problems identified in a common frame by 18th-century Italian philosopher Giambattista Vico in his *New Science* (Tagliacozzo & Verene, 1976) and to works by various phenomenologists (particularly Merleau-Ponty, 1962), and following an argument made explicit by Howes (1990), we can say that (a) *all* of this—culture itself—is "*constructed* out of the interplay of all the senses" (p. 68; see also Laughlin & D'Aquili, 1974; Laughlin et al., 1992; Stoller, 1987, 1989; Stoller & Olkes, 1986, 1987), (b) it is embedded in a conjectural mentality that is compelled to make sense of changing environmental circumstances (Laughlin & Brady, 1978), and (c) it is filtered through imagination and the historical shapings that individuals and groups get from socialization and enculturation in particular traditions, including language and its body-grounded metaphors. The resulting knowledge is perpetuated largely by stories—oral, written, performed in other ways—in units as small as parables, giving new meanings to perceptions of changing environmental circumstances (M. Turner, 1996). Accounts of being-in-place ultimately must reengage this mix of sensuous–intellectual properties and processes—the broad landscape of human experience that forms a body-centered system—to have any legitimate claim to authenticity.

12. Engaging in parallel universes and common projects as sentient beings makes it possible for us to understand each other (Merrell, 2000, pp. 73–74; on Vico's *fantasia,* thinking through the body, and the age of poetic wisdom, see Verene, 1976; on Quine's principle of charity and related comments, see Brady, 2000). Thinking "through the body and to sense the world as an order of bodies, with meaning not being separable from bodies," is difficult to imagine (Verene, 1976, p. 31; cf. Lowe, 1982), but a critical rereading of Vico's arguments about body-centeredness is nonetheless a reminder that we are all animals—sensuous–intellectual creatures—and that there are some universal responses to things that we all share. The possibilities for understanding the beliefs and experiences of others are grounded both in the common sensory apparatus that we occupy as biological beings and in the comparable modes of thought and action when we respond to the feelings and sensations of environmental stimulation

(Merrell, 2000, p. 73). "The body is, so to speak, in the mind. They are both wild" (Snyder, 1990, p. 16). The same possibilities must also be realized *in an interpretive relation* to other communicative organisms (and things that are believed to be animated, e.g., rocks and trees), that is, through the interactive processes that lead to the social construction of reality through whatever cultural screens (Berger & Luckmann, 1966; see also Zolbrod, 1983, pp. 227–228). Compare Wilmsen (1999): "Separate lives are congruent in experience, no matter how disparate their cultural environments. Once the words are learned, native speakers of different languages begin to recognize each other—thirst thick under an arid sun, identical errors in navigating unknown landscapes, parallel blunderings through sexual awakening—in evoked images of their separate experiences. For it is individuals, not cultures, who meet and re-present their contexts to each other" (p. xi). See also Fletcher (1967, p. 197).

13. Kerouac (1959, p. 106).

14. Because we are creatures in and of place—embedded, embodied, and emplaced—it is difficult to extract a proper concept of place for conversation and instruction (Geertz, 1996). But I do mean to flag the process of being and becoming emplaced as a biological and cultural system that is subject to an inherent creativity of perception and expression and, above all, to inscriptions and transferences between the body and its sociocultural milieu. See Low and Lawrence-Zúñiga (2003), Merleau-Ponty (1962), Miller (1996), and Spiegelberg (1975). To have practical value as a principle, that thought needs to be played out and observed in the everyday world. On mimesis and its complexities, see Taussig (1993). For an exquisite coarticulation of theory and practice in cultural spaces, see Stewart (1996). On living persons and practical problems, see Smith (1997, p. 2).

15. See especially Merleau-Ponty (1962), Spiegelberg (1975), and adaptations of Merleau-Ponty's work in Abram (1996) and Gruenewald (2003). The upshot is that humans enter into a participatory relationship with other phenomena through the multisensory perception of direct experience. On phenomenology and culture, see Csordas (1994), Laughlin and Brady (1978), and Laughlin and colleagues (1992).

16. Thus, meaning is made, not found, and making sense of places is a reciprocal and mutually constructing process, taking shape and acquiring meaning "when the inner realm is projected onto the outer scene" (Brann, 1991, p. 7). Feld (1996) puts it this way: "As place is sensed, senses are placed; as places make sense, senses make place" (quoted in Casey, 1996, p. 19).

17. Ethnographers generally take us to a "location," that is, to a place where *something happens.* Like watching a movie, we seldom have reason to focus on the projector or the serving apparatus. Phenomenology brings the observer's equipment to the fore and makes it part of the equation of meaningful construction and participation. Compare Thompson (1989): "So here I sit, looking at the screen of a Macintosh and in imagination, rolling the screen of history back and forth. Instructed by the natural history of life, I suspect that what I am looking for are not 'events' but thresholds of emergence that are also projections of my own framing of perceptions" (p. 135).

18. Following Lowe (1982), "By 'perception' I do not mean the neurophysiology of perception, or the behavioral psychology of perception, but an immanent description of perception as human experience. . . . Perception as the crucial connection includes the subject as the perceiver, the act of perceiving, and the content of the perceived. The perceiving subject, from an embodied location, approaches the world as a lived, horizontal field. The act of perceiving unites the subject with the perceived. And the content of the perceived, which results from that

act, affects the subject's bearing in the world. Perception is therefore a reflexive, integral whole, involving the perceiver, the act of perceiving, and the content of the perceived" (p. 1). Moreover, according to Feld (1996), "places may come into existence through the experience of bodily sensation, but it is through expression that they reach heightened emotional and aesthetic dimensions of sensual inspiration" (p. 134). Among the Kaluli, "the poetics of place merge with the sensuousness of place as soundscape and with the sensuality of the singing voice" (p. 134).

19. We do not need Kant to tell us how fundamental space and time are to our lives. As Yi-Fu (1979) says, "'Space' and 'place' are familiar words denoting common experiences. . . . Basic components of the lived world; we take them for granted. When we think about them, however, they may assume unexpected meanings and raise questions we had not thought to ask" (p. 3). For some concrete examples, see also Gallagher (1993).

20. Neihardt (1959, p. 173).

21. See the various works by Claude Lévi-Strauss regarding the fantasy factor in all myths (e.g., Lévi-Strauss, 1976). On creativity and imagination in general, see especially Miller (1996). No categories of place have any meaning without imagination. It has a geography of its own— landscapes of fear and comfort where poets of virtual worlds bridge the concrete and the abstract, where the sign and its referent emerge in consciousness as places of soil, rock, sea, air, innumerable critters, and mind (Brady, 2003b). The expression "leap of the imagination" is often heard in discussions of writing, but that may be less of a leap than "a sauntering, a stepping across" into the reality at hand (Bass, 2000, p. 72). See also Caughey (1984), Joy and Sherry (2000), and Wooley (1992). Crapanzano (2004) says, "Like James, the literary critic Jean Starobinski stresses the determining role of the imagination in the perception—the constitution—of reality. 'Insinuated into perception itself, mixed with the operations of memory, opening up around us a horizon of the possible, escorting the project, the hope, the fear, speculations—the imagination is much more than a faculty for evoking images which double the world of our direct perceptions; it is a distancing power thanks to which we represent to ourselves distant objects and we distance ourselves from present realities. Hence, the ambiguity that we discover everywhere; the imagination, because it anticipates and previews, serves action, draws us before the configuration of the realizable before it can be realized.' . . . Not only does the imaginative consciousness allow us to transcend (*depasser*) the immediacy of the present instant in order to grasp a future that is at first indistinct, Starobinski argues, but it enables us to project our 'fables' in a direction that does not have to reckon with the 'evident universe.' It permits fiction, the game, a dream, more or less voluntary error, pure fascination. It lightens our existence by transporting us into the region of the phantasm. In turn it facilitates our 'practical domination over the real' or our breaking ties with it" (p. 174).

22. On art, science, and humanism, see Bruner (1986, pp. 49–50). On extrapolations from laconic representations as simple as a dateline in a poem, see Richardson (1999b, p. 334) and Brady (2003b, p. xiv). We are compelled to interpret such signs and cues about our environment because, in a general sense, our very existence as human creatures depends on it. Place is the anchor of fundamental human experience. But how do we recognize it? "Do we know enough about it to enjoy a fanciful imagining of passage there? If we visit a place at three separate times, is it still the same place? Does the place remember us? The answers are as much a function of landscape evolving as they are of finders finding what they want or need to see— a cultural meaning and orientation problem with historical implications" (Brady, 2003b, p. xv).

23. Suskind (1986, pp. 147–148).

24. As might be expected, the concept of home as a stable place is deeply embedded in our thinking about writing. On language and embodied space, see Jackson (1995, p. 6) and Low and Lawrence-Zúñiga (2003, pp. 6–7). The real work for individuals centered more or less (cf. Stewart, 1996, p. 3, on Appalachia) in what they recognize and perpetuate as a common home and the wider world, is to determine how all of these rooted poolings of life intersect so as to figure out who and by what commonalities of ancestral experience and related cultural claims should be grouped together by category and actual location and who and what, in our estimation, should not. That is the essence of kinship and a classic set of norms for deciding issues of access and trespass, that is, for deciding who and what are to be included or excluded from particular activities at particular times in the places we call home.

25. On a larger scale, one thinks immediately of America in this context given its history as a collecting point for international migration processes and diverse cultural interests. On travel and uprootedness, see Snyder (1990, pp. 23–26). On travel as metaphor, see Jackson (1995, p. 1) and Van den Abeele (1992).

26. Naming a place is a way of taming it, bringing it at least to the control of a mental appropriation in a familiar set of signs—to the level of place punctuated by the hearths and travels of the imagination if not of the physical self. That is the same process applied through colonial appropriations of others; that is, by translating them into our own cultural system of signs, we render them "subordinate," at least by category of existence. On the importance of naming in human experience, see Cheyfitz (1997) and Aitchison (2000, p. 94ff). Schama (1995) notes, "The wilderness, after all, does not locate itself, does not name itself. It was an act of Congress in 1864 that established Yosemite Valley as a place of sacred significance for the nation" (p. 7). See also Momaday (1969, p. 27).

27. Weller (1990, p. 14).

28. More or less following Bakhtin, by "architectonics" I mean the architecture of connections revealed between individuals and their wider environments, parts to whole in changing landscapes, including other people and other points of view, over time (Holquist, 1990, p. 149ff). Sensitive to readings from both sides of the cultural fences that separate us in fieldwork and life in general, and to the mutual constructions of our interactions under those circumstances, a poetics of place must be dialogic in nature. Furthermore, "a dialogic poetics must first of all be able to identify and arrange relations between points of view; it must be adequate to the complex architectonics that shape the viewpoint of the author toward his characters, the characters toward the author, and of all of these toward each other" (p. 162).

29. Speaking of an incident in the foothills of the Rocky Mountains, Smith (1997) recalls a telling moment "in the description of a colleague who had taken her class to the mountains, sat them in a circle, enticing them, in an ecological exercise, to 'breathe this place, to recollect themselves and their relations to . . . reconnect.' Suddenly, the heavy sounds of a cougar circling them can be heard, followed by the instantaneous and terrified evacuation of the place by the recollectors, the breathers, and the reconnectors! Whatever the pedagogy of the place may be, it has little to do with a warm cozy relationship with an imagined nature, and perhaps more to do with the courage to befriend one's own mortality in the midst of the ongoing project of self understanding" (p. 4). The wild inspires us to be practical. It also can be a tough experience (Snyder, 1990, p. 23).

30. Ducking the television travelogues designed to sell products on commercial breaks, the closest we usually can come to wilderness today is to traffic in its remainder in places such as

Yosemite, heavily marked by people—in fact, even created by people in so many important ways, including mapping and marking it as a preserve of sorts (Schama, 1995)—or in the outback stretches of earth where the timid never tread, be it alpine, desert, or swamp (Snyder, 1990, p. 6). Snyder (1990) sees these places as "the shrines saved from all the land that was once known and lived on by the original people, the little bits left as they were, the last little places where intrinsic nature totally wails, blooms, nests, glints away. They make up only 2 percent of the land of the United States" (p. 14).

31. Immersion in the unpaved has special merits for helping the process unfold. "A week in the Amazon, the high Arctic, or the northern side of the Western Himalayas," J. Turner (1996) writes, can show us that "what counts as wildness and wilderness is determined not by the absence of people, but by the relationship between people and place. A place is wild," he says, "when it is self-willed land. Native peoples usually (though definitely not always) 'fit' that order, influencing it but not controlling it, though probably not from a superior set of values but because they lack the technical means. Control increases with civilization, and modern civilization, being largely about control—an ideology of control projected onto the entire world—must control or deny wildness" (pp. 112–113).

32. Poulsen (1982, p. 116).

33. Some sacred spaces, of course, are purely manmade in their physical construction (e.g., the Vietnam memorial in Washington, D.C.), but even these are likely to be landscaped for beauty with a "natural" theme (Osborne, 2001; Véliz, 1996). Others are located in conspicuous landscapes, such as Mount Sinai and Devil's Mountain, none of which is a "sacred" space in its own right. They are interesting in their irregularities or are novel to people who encounter them as necessary interpreters of space. But that very reading is a primary source of significance—a projection of self, culture, and emotion that occurs somewhat ironically through an appropriation of the otherwise unobtainable by wrapping the experiences in metaphor, by acquiring places in image and imagination, and by bringing them near through semiosis and fantasy, if not actual physical presence. In his analysis of Native American sites, Gulliford (2000) identifies nine categories of sacred places: "(1) sites associated with emergence and migration tales; (2) sites of trails and pilgrimage routes; (3) places essential to cultural survival; (4) altars; (5) vision quest sites; (6) ceremonial dance sites; (7) ancestral ruins; (8) petroglyphs and pictographs; and (9) burial or massacre sites" (quoted in Leonard & McClure, 2004, p. 321). Building on that and Vine Deloria's work on Native American sites, Leonard and McClure (2004) identify sacred places on two axes: one that follows "a continuum from historical/actual to imaginary/metaphorical" and one that follows "a continuum from human to divine agency" (p. 325). Deloria gives us four categories "arranged on a scale of 'agency'—entirely human agency at one end versus the agency of 'Higher Powers' at the other" (p. 322). See also Dundes (1984) and Lane (2001).

34. Some sacred sites are deeply personal and private. On places sacred to one person that fail to move another, see Poulsen (1982, pp. 116–117).

35. True to this experience, and illustrative of the power of poetry to address such issues in laconic ways, see the defining principles and irony in Gregor's (2004) smart poem, "Mammals of North America." Despite the importance of hunting in both cultures, nothing could be further removed from the place of mammals in the world of the Koyukon (Brody, 1982; Nelson, 1983).

36. Only the overall story form and perhaps the emotions of shared experiences as sentient beings-in-place, especially in the conspicuous places of whatever we can call "nature" today,

can frame these inferences for us. The rest must come from material representations (cf. Clarkson, 1998; Hodder, 1982, 1987, 1989; Lewin, 1986; Richardson, 1982; Zolbrod, 1987), from written history, or from that wonderful interim point—a living person whose knowledge pool runs a continuum of semiotica from early tribal history to the present. Such guides are rare, of course, if they exist at all in ultimately reliable forms. They all are influenced by literacy and related forms of communication in the modern world, but they can be found in our current landscapes. On teachers of sacred space, see Layton (1997, p. 122) and Snyder (1990, pp. 12, 78). On contemporary horticultural experts in the American Southwest, see Nabhan (1982). See also Behar (1993), Nelson (1980, 1983), Swann (1983), Swann and Krupat (1987), and Tedlock (1972, 1983, 1990, 1993).

37. Note the irony that what are often held to be the most palatable and picturesque landscapes are also sometimes the least habitable (Barthes, 1972, pp. 74–77). With an overview of the relationships of landscapes, aesthetics, and pleasure as they might obtain in the human species, Brown (1991) says, "One of the fundamental assumptions of evolutionary psychology is that matters closely related to our survival and reproduction have a likelihood of engaging our emotions. Thus, although there might be little evidence of a general adaptation for an aesthetic sense, a . . . disparate collection of emotion-producing activities and entities may structure what we consider aesthetic. . . . Orians (1980) has examined such matters as the emotional reactions of explorers to different natural settings, the landscaping and planting of parks, and the criteria that make particular pieces of real estate especially valuable, to show that humans seem to have an innate preference for settings that would have been optimal habitats for our Pleistocene foraging ancestors. We like 'lakes, rivers, cliffs, and savannahs,' settings in which food, water, and protection (as in caves) were in optimal combination. Key elements in Orians's arguments are the emotional nature of the human preferences, and comparisons with habitat selection in other species, where its innate component is less questionable. Here the argument is that we have an innate tendency to prefer, seek out, and construct certain kinds of settings because we feel good in them" (pp. 115–116). On forests and the emergence of poetic wisdom, compare Rubinoff (1976, p. 104).

38. This is especially true in the light of the horrifying events of September 11, 2001, in the United States and the country's subsequent declaration of war on terrorism (Lincoln & Denzin, 2003a). The whole problem can be framed in its fundamentals as one of sacred space and what is or is not allowed to take place in it. On poetries and place and the different imaginaries of country and city, see Williams (1973). On entering an age of human flourishing, see Lincoln and Guba (2000). On the Burning Man Project, see Kozinets and Sherry (2004) and Sherry and Kozinets (2004).

39. They are often represented in the mix of more than one culture, society, and/or physical landscape, the kind of heterogeneous zones we find bisected by the colliding margins of cross-cultural frontiers. They are "borderlands" of the here and the hereafter or are "beaches" as Dening (1980, 1996) liberated the concept from the stereotyped margin of surf and sand. On the U.S.–Mexican border, see also Brady (2003b, pp. 89–90). On Chicano narratives and their literary and cultural borders, see Rosaldo (1989). On Australian aboriginal notions of trespass and "spatial prohibitions as a mode of boundary making," see Munn (2003). On frontiers and the possibilities of passing into myth time, see Snyder (1990, p. 14). On the concept of "regeneration through violence," see Slotkin (1973).

40. Neihardt (1959, p. 35).

41. According to Snyder (1990), "For preagricultural people, the sites considered sacred and given special care were of course wild" (p. 79). He adds, "The idea that 'wild' might also be 'sacred' returned to the Occident only with the Romantic movement" (p. 80).

42. In answering the question of why native cultures in general give so much importance to places, Abram (1996) sees the answer as obvious: "In oral cultures the human eyes and ears have not yet shifted their synaesthetic participation from the animate surroundings to the written word. Particular mountains, canyons, streams, boulder-strewn fields, or groves of trees have not yet lost the expressive potency and dynamism with which they spontaneously present themselves to the senses. A particular place in the land is never, for an oral culture, just a passive or inert setting for the human events that occur there. *It is an active participant in those occurrences* [precisely a poetic posture]. Indeed, by virtue of its underlying and enveloping presence, the place may even be felt to be the source, the primary power that expresses itself through the various events that unfold there" (p. 162). He adds, "It is precisely for this reason that stories are not told without identifying the earthly sites where the events in those stories occur. For the Western Apache, as for other traditionally oral peoples, human events and encounters simply cannot be isolated from the places that engender them. . . . From the Distant Time stories of the Koyukon people, and from the 'agodzaahi tales of the Western Apache, we begin to discern that storytelling is a primary form of human speaking, a mode of discourse that continually weds the human community to the land. Among the Koyukon, the Distant Time stories serve, among other things, to preserve a link between human speech and the spoken utterances of other species, while for the Western Apache, the 'agodzaahi narratives express a deep association between moral behavior and the land and, when heard, are able to effect a lasting kinship between persons and particular places. . . . The telling of stories, like singing and praying, would seem to be an almost ceremonial act, an ancient and necessary mode of speech that tends the earthly rootedness of human language. For narrated events, as Basso reminds us, always happen *somewhere*. And for an oral culture, that locus is never merely incidental to those occurrences. The events belong, as it were, to the place, and to tell the story of those events is to let the place itself speak through the telling" (pp. 162–163). See also Basso (1996a, 1996b), Carpenter (1980), Crapanzano (2004), Feld and Basso (1996), and Nelson (1983).

43. On movements toward symbolic order in modern architecture and the idea that every force evolves a form, compare Poulsen (1982, pp. 118, 123–124). Schama (1995) adds, "And it is just because ancient places are constantly being given the topdressings of modernity (the forest primeval, for example, turning into the 'wilderness park') that the ambiguity of the myths at their core is sometimes hard to make out. It is there, all the same" (pp. 15–16).

44. Apropos of the current thesis, Deloria (1993) calls for "the possibility of new sacred places, underscoring even more the present, ongoing nature of the kinds of interactions between the human and the spiritual realms" (cited in Leonard & McClure, 2004, p. 324).

45. By dwelling on the language associated with primary emotions (and, therefore, the limbic system of the brain), poetry is capable of moving us sensuously and emotionally. Speaking of the power of poetry and prophecy, Leavitt (1997) says, "Much of this power is already implied in the nature of language itself. For the speaking subject, a linguistic element—a phoneme or word or grammatical pattern—not only says what it says, but does so cast in a specific form and carrying specific implications. That is to say, each linguistic element carries with it not only a

semantic load but also both a material presence as a pattern of sound and a cloud of connotations and colorations picked up through the subject's life experience and the elements of our own history of use. In some circumstances, people attend not only to what is being said but equally or primarily to the sound- and meaning-resonances of how it is being said. This 'poetic mode of speech perception'. . . and production defines . . . the poetic function of language; language carries sometimes actualized but always potential punch above and beyond the punch of information conveyed. The effect may be aesthetic, emotional, or physical" (p. 3). On the "thrill" or "physical emotion" that can come from reading, "the undisappointed joy of finding that everything holds up and answers the desire it awakens," compare Heaney (1995, pp. 8–9). Bass (2000) notes that the artist has an "imperative to get as close to a thing as possible, not so much to create metaphors as to uncover them; to peel them way back to their source. For me there is undeniable solace and excitement in moving in as close as possible to things, in art, and in the woods—as close as possible to the source" (p. 73). On emotions and landscapes, see also Brown (1991, pp. 115–116).

46. See Abram (1996), Barthes (1972), Benjamin (1969a), Brady (2003a, 2003b), Crapanzano (2004), Gibbs (1994), Hoffman (1999), and Meletinsky (1998). Bachelard (1964), in his classic text *The Poetics of Space,* notes, "Great images have both a history and a prehistory; they are always a blend of memory and legend, with the result that we never experience an image directly. Indeed, every great image has an unfathomable oneiric depth to which the personal past adds special color" (p. 33). To him, "Primal images, simple engravings are but so many invitations to start imagining again. . . . By living in such images as these, in images that are as stabilizing as these are, we could start a new life, a life that would be our own, that would belong to us in our very depths. . . . And because of this very primitiveness, restored, desired, and experienced through simple images, an album of pictures of huts would constitute a textbook of simple exercises for the phenomenology of the imagination" (p. 33). Schama's (1995) collection of images and texts presents exactly that—an album of experiences that give us the past (albeit recent) as both imaginative history and a history of the imagination. It directs attention to the nature of landscape as myth, and vice versa, on America's frontiers and is, therefore, most instructive for our current purposes and fair ground for contextualizing creations and renewals of sacred space.

47. Finding (or reinventing) new leaders for positive turns on sacred space is consistent with the moral and ethical goals of our environmental critics (see, e.g., Snyder, 1990, p. 78). But in the process we must also ask *whether* we really want to renew these things as sacred in our personal lives and to integrate them uncritically in modern views of what is sacred. The relativity of the concept—what is sacred for you is not necessarily the same for others—has led, as J. Turner (1996, p. 22) reminds us, to one violent confrontation after another throughout history. Moreover, a failure to distinguish between formal and popular religions has bastardized the concept in contemporary America. Turner suggests that Disneyland, national parks, the site of President John F. Kennedy's assassination, and related "pilgrimage sites" are sacred "because of the function of entertainment and tourism in our culture. In a commercial culture, the sacred will have a commercial base. For many people, nothing is more sacred than the Super Bowl" (p. 22). That is not the sense of "sacred" that Snyder has in mind, but whatever the course of action taken, there is huge personal responsibility attached to it, for ourselves and for the collective futures of all who would revisit the savannahs and forests of our beginnings with a sense of respect and preservation rather than rapacious destruction.

48. Consider Schama (1995): "Whether such relationships are, in fact, habitual, at least as habitual as the urge toward domination of nature, said to be the signature of the West, I will leave the reader to judge. Jung evidently believed that the universality of nature myths testified to their psychological indispensability in dealing with interior terrors and cravings. And the anthropologist of religion Mircea Eliade assumed them to have survived, fully operational, in modern, as well as traditional, cultures" (p. 15). Schama marks his own view as "necessarily more historical, and by that token much less confidently universal. Not all cultures embrace nature and landscape myths with equal ardor, and those that do go through periods of greater or less enthusiasm. What the myths of ancient forest mean for one European national tradition may translate into something entirely different in another" (p. 15). Schama has "tried not to let these important differences in space and time be swallowed up in the long history of landscape metaphors sketched in [his] book. But while allowing for these variations, it is clear the inherited landscape myths and memories share two common characteristics: their surprising endurance through the centuries and their power to shape institutions that we still live with. National identity, to take just the most obvious example, would lose much of its ferocious enchantment without the mystique of a particular landscape tradition: its topography mapped, elaborated, and enriched as a homeland" (pp. 15–16).

49. We are reminded in the process that "understanding the past traditions of landscapes can be a source of illumination for the present and the future," and with a lien on that, Schama (1995) says that it can also be a source for redeeming "the hollowness of contemporary life" (p. 17). This is not a promise of passage into Nirvana, an escape from the evils of the present into something constructed out of blind fantasy and a heavily romanticized past that can be regained in the future. Schama is too much of a realist for that. In acknowledging "the ambiguous legacy of nature myths," he points out that we must also "recognize that landscapes will not always be simple 'places of delight'—scenery as sedative, topography so arranged to feast the eye. For those eyes . . . are seldom clarified of the promptings of memory. And the memories are not all of pastoral picnics" (p. 18).

50. Compare Kroeber (1983): "Evidence of . . . interactivity is likely to impress us most in stories, such as those dealing with Coyote. These we find baffling because Coyote can be animal or man at any time and without any seeming consistency. This is a crucial imaginative point. The Indian imagination is not so rigidly tied as our own to given material forms and patterns. For us, to be 'characters' animals have to be anthropomorphized. The Indian imagination recognizes Coyote as both animal and man, or either animal or man, the duality in fact making him 'Coyote' rather than 'just' the exceedingly interesting four-footed predator. The complexity of the Indian imagination is germane to the practical core of the hunting songs we are considering here" (p. 329). See also Bright (1987), Buller (1983), Diamond (1986), Ekkehart and Lomatuway'ma (1984), Haile (1984), Hymes (1987), Lopez (1977, 1986, 1990a), Snyder (1990), and Tedlock and Tedlock (1975). On Abram, Merleau-Ponty, and the phenomenological argument that "places are the ground of direct human experience" and associated assumptions about the interactions of the body with things, including the idea that "all objects or things are 'alive' and capable of entering into a relationship with a human perceiver," see Gruenewald (2003, p. 623).

51. Momaday (1969, p. 6).

52. Consider Yi-Fu (1979): "Three principal types [of space], with large areas of overlap, exist—the mythical, the pragmatic, and the abstract or theoretical. Mythical space is a

conceptual schema, but it is also pragmatic space in the sense that within the schema a large number of practical activities, such as the planting and harvesting of crops, are ordered. A difference between mythical and pragmatic space is that the latter is defined by a more limited set of economic activities. [On "trails to heaven" and "maps of dreams," see also Brody, 1982, pp. 46–47.] The recognition of pragmatic space, such as belts of poor and rich soil, is of course an intellectual achievement. When an ingenious person tries to describe the soil pattern cartographically, by means of symbols, a further move toward the conceptual mode occurs. In the Western world, systems of geometry—that is, highly abstract spaces—have been created out of primal spatial experiences" (pp. 16–17). Leonard and McClure (2004) argue, "Myths which take us to a sacred place where rejuvenation or immortality is possible—whether that place is a garden, a forest, a mountain, a well, lake, stream, fountain, or river—have the effect of transporting us back to the primordial and womblike condition that preceded our quotidian struggles with money, relationships, and the eventual loss of our physical and mental powers" (p. 325). Compare Brown (1991, p. 116).

53.  Snyder (1990) likens language to "some kind of infinitely interfertile family of species spreading or mysteriously declining over time, shamelessly and endlessly hybridizing, changing its own rules as it goes" (p. 7). It is "a mind–body system that coevolved with our needs and nerves. Like imagination and the body, [it] rises unbidden . . . [with] a complexity that eludes our rational intellectual capacities" (p. 9). However, in developing his anthropology of experience, Jackson (1995) makes the cogent observation that experience, unlike language, "covers everything that is the case. This is why words alone can never do justice to experience" (p. 160). "Words are signs, stand-ins, arbitrary and temporary, even as language reflects (and informs) the shifting values of the people whose minds it inhabits and glides through" (Snyder, 1990, p. 8). But "no word is able to contain the moods of a moment" (Jackson, 1995, p. 5). "Life eludes our grasp and remains at large, always fugitive," never captured completely (p. 5). It "outstrips our vocabulary" (p. 5). "Like a forest in which there are clearings. Like a forest through whose canopy sunlight filters and falls" (p. 5). "Theodor Adorno called this the untruth of identity, by which he meant that concepts plunder but never exhaust the wealth of experience. Life cannot be pressed [exclusively] into the service of language. Concepts represent experience at the cost of leaving a lot unsaid. So long as we use concepts to cut up experience, giving value to some things at the expense of others, . . . we gain some purchase on the world, to be sure, but claiming that our concepts contain all that can be usefully said about experience, we close off the possibility of critique. It is only when we cease trying to control the world that we can overcome our fixation on the autarchy of concepts" (p. 5). "An anthropology of experience," Jackson says in that connection, "shares with phenomenology a skepticism toward determinate systems of knowledge. It plays up the indeterminate, ambiguous, and manifold character of lived experience. It demands that we enlarge our field of vision to take into account things central *and* peripheral, focal *and* subsidiary, illuminated *and* penumbral" (p. 160). These are the kinds of things, sometimes esoteric, bundled up by deep cultural contexts that are not easily discovered without access to the granaries of knowledge through the people who have built them. And even then, unable to be the "thing in itself," we will always have to settle for partial truths. On the difficulty of describing the experience of the *duende,* see Lorca (1985).

54.  Richardson (1999b) observes, "To say that we must be in a story is not to say that we have our destiny already engraved in our neurons or awash in our subconscious. On the contrary, our life story continuously unfolds, shifts, changes. . . . Both place and story have to do with where

we are, with location, but the *where* of each is distinct. The poetics of place is preeminently sensory. Smell, sound, touch, and especially sight are attributes of place, which is consequently visual and spatial. On the other hand, words strung together in speech and in writing constitute stories. Narrative, therefore, is verbal and temporal. In place, our dominant mode of relating to one another is through seeing; in written narrative, it is through reading. Interestingly, we use each mode as a metaphor of the other. When we want to emphasize that we're interpreting what we look at, we speak of 'reading the landscape.' Conversely, we exclaim, 'I see!' to convey the insight gained by reading a text" (p. 332). See also Brady (2003b, pp. xiv–xv).

55. Bass (2000) tells the story of how nature writers at a conference, "much to the initial confusion of some of the audience—kept talking about *specifics:* about buffalo, about native medicines, about narwhals, caribou, grizzlies and ravens; about the things they *knew*—and it was not until the second or third day that the audience began to grumble, 'What about the writing?' The panelists looked at one another in confusion. This *was* the writing. The world they inhabited—the so-called natural world of rock and sand and wood and ice—had become so imbued with power by their living deeply within it that the only language they were comfortable with was that of the specific. So deeply and passionately did they inhabit their landscapes—physically, emotionally, and spiritually—that trees became both trees and metaphors; wolves were both wolves *and* symbols; and the lives, the movements of these things, had a logic and pattern that did not transcend art but became art. They were living in their stories. They had stepped across that line, so that everything was story. They believed intensely in the world in which they lived" (pp. 71–72). This is an ancient process so far separated from contemporary writers by the invention and absorption of alphabetic literacy that the participants failed to recognize it until they were called out for their "absence of writing."

56. de Sahagún (1985, pp. 23–24).

57. Consider Tedlock (1983): "The argument that American Indian spoken narratives are better understood (and translated) as dramatic poetry than as an oral equivalent of written prose fiction may be summarized as follows: The content tends toward the fantastic rather than the prosaic, the emotions of the characters are evoked rather than described, there are no patterns of repetition or parallelism ranging from the level of words to that of whole episodes, the narrator's voice shifts constantly in amplitude and tone, and the flow of that voice is paced by pauses that segment its sounds into what I have chosen to call lines. Of all these realities of oral narrative and performance, the plainest and grossest is the sheer alternation of sound and silence; the resultant lines often show an independence from intonation, from syntax, and even from boundaries of plot structure. I understand the fundamental sound-shape of spoken narrative in much the same way that Robert W. Corrigan understood drama when he wrote that "the playwright—and also the translator—cannot really be concerned with 'good prose' or with 'good verse' in the usual sense of those terms. The structure is action, not what is said or how it is said but *'when.'* It is above all the *when,* or what dramatists call 'timing,' that is missing in printed prose" (pp. 55–56).

58. Fritz (unknown date and source), translated by Thomas F. Powell.

59. My thinking on this builds on Foucault's concept of *epistemes* as the totality of relations in knowledge of a given epoch (Dreyfuss & Rabinow, 1983; Foucault, 1970, 1972), which I have in this case applied to the separation of human activities before and after the invention of writing and the subsequent proliferations of it through mass production printing. Abram's (1996) articulate treatment of the distortions posed by studying preliterates through the mentality of

alphabetic literacy is applied directly to considerations of place and translation. Lowe (1982) has an extended delineation of the root of the problem: "Recent scholarship reveals that communications media, hierarchy of sensing, and epistemic order change in time. Hence the perceptual field constituted by them differs from period to period. There is a history of perception [that delimits] the changing content of the known" (p. 2), and it has changed dramatically in the communication pools that have separated human societies before and after the advent of writing and its proliferation through mass production printing.

60. Lowe (1982) says, "Without the support of print, speech in oral culture is assisted by the art of memory. Rhythmic words are organized into formulas and commonplaces, then set to metric patterns. In this way, they can be recalled and recited with great facility. That which can be recited and repeated will be preserved. The metric recitation of rhythmic formulas and commonplaces provides a communicational grid to determine knowledge in oral culture. Only those phenomena which fit existing formulas and commonplaces can be preserved as knowledge. The new and distinctly different will soon be forgotten. Knowledge in oral culture therefore tends to be preservative and unspecialized, its content nonanalytical but formulaic" (p. 3). He adds, "The introduction of written language, whether ideographic or alphabetic, and its preservation in some type of manuscript constituted a chirographic culture. Although it took a long time to accomplish, writing eventually detached knowledge from speech and memory. A written language preserved knowledge after the act of speech and beyond the lapse of memory. One could go over a piece of writing at will, learn it, and criticize it; whereas formerly, in an oral culture, knowledge depended on the performance of the speaker" (p. 3). On the modernization of myth, see Barthes (1972).

61. See Jackson (1995, pp. 156–157). Elsewhere, Jackson (1982) says, "Whenever one retraces one's steps in the imagination, an inevitable transformation occurs. One gives thought to things one did without thinking. One replaces words actually said with a vocabulary of one's own choosing. Face-to-face reality is subverted by a second order—written reality. Life gets rendered as [written] language" (p. 3). In constructing this thesis, Jackson draws "extensively on many studies in the ethnography of speaking" in an effort to "avoid any inadvertent domination of the world of preliterate possibilities by the modes of abstract analysis developed in literate cultures" (p. 3). See also Tedlock (1983): "I am reminded of the Zuni who asked me, 'When I tell these stories do you picture it, or do you just write it down?'" (p. 55). On Geertz and cultures as "texts" to be read, see also Tedlock (1999, p. 161).

62. Anthropologists are generally happy to declare that shamanism (the world's oldest profession) is the root of all performative art—a point made effectively by the ethnopoet Rothenberg (1981; see also Rothenberg & Rothenberg, 1983) and the anthropologist Harner (1990), among others. That links us to the Paleolithic era (ca. 100,000 years ago) and opens up ethnographic inquiry to what we are considering in the current work—an enlarged sense of communal ties through the history of talk, performance, myth, poetry, and being-in-place.

63. For various expressions of the same topic, compare Abram (1996), Abu-Lughod (1988), Basso (1996a, 1996b), Brody (1982), Clifton (1990), Damon (2003), Dundes (1972), Feld (1982), Feld & Basso (1996), Howes (1990), Hymes (1987), Jackson (1982), Kroeber (1983), Lavie (1991), Layton (1997), Metcalf (2002), Munn (2003), Nabhan (1982), Ricoeur (1991), Rothenberg (1972, 1985), Rothenberg & Rothenberg (1983), Swann & Krupat (1987), B. Tedlock (1992), D. Tedlock (1972, 1983, 1993, 1999), Zolbrod (1983, 1987).

64. Austin (1997, p. 61).

65. The concept of the sublime as "tending to inspire awe usually because of elevated quality (as of beauty, nobility, or grandeur) or transcendent excellence" figures into our sentient existence and survival prospects in several ways. Brown (1991) says, "One of the fundamental assumptions of evolutionary psychology is that matters closely related to our survival and reproduction have a likelihood of engaging our emotions. Thus, although there might be little evidence of a general adaptation for an aesthetic sense, a . . . disparate collection of emotion-producing activities and entities may structure what we consider aesthetic" (p. 115), including the experiences of being-in-place. Writing about Burke, Bromwich (1997) says, "Burke's conclusion is that the feelings of the sublime and the beautiful in life, . . . which may also be excited by moments of works in art, are an inseparable condition of existence" (p. 30). They push the edges and the limits of human nature. The theorist's job "is to show how the affective powers of the sublime and beautiful can be causes of mental activity without ideas or images. At the very end, he will offer a possible reason why words above all can affect us like this. The mind has a hunger for belief, and it has a natural tendency toward abstraction. The appeal of the sublime and the beautiful must somehow relate to that hunger and that tendency of the mind. And words, which bear no resemblance to things, which at the height of their influence on the passions leave no image at all, are therefore the leading artificial and natural source of our sympathy with the sublime and beautiful" (p. 32). Compare Denzin (1997) and Diamond (1987). Denzin (1997) points out, "Modernist ethnographers (and poets) stood outside their texts so as to produce a sense of awe or reverence or respect for what is being written about. The writer was missing from the text. The postmodern writer also seeks the sublime, but it is a new sublime—a nostalgic sublime that transgresses Diamond's poetry of pain. The new scribe seeks a sense of respect and awe for the lost writer who experiences what is being written about. What was previously unpresentable (the writer's experiences) is now what is presented. Paradoxically, that which is most sought after remains the most illusive" (p. 215).

66. Yi-Fu (1979) notes, "Place can acquire deep meaning for the adult through the steady accumulation of sentiment over the years. Every piece of heirloom furniture, or even a stain on the wall, tells a story" (p. 33). According to Schama (1995), "To see the ghostly outline of an old landscape beneath the superficial covering of the contemporary is to be made vividly aware of the endurance of core myths. . . . And it is just because ancient places are constantly being given the topdressings of modernity (the forest primeval, for example, turning into the 'wilderness park') that the ambiguity of the myths at their core is sometimes hard to make out. It is there, all the same" (p. 16).

67. Historical trekking can be at once a new and a renewed experience. The "new" information (as word, image, symbol, sensation, etc.) builds on the "old" in that process and has the prospect of resorting it all in still newer terms, including the extensive "mazeway resyntheses" of individuals and groups in revitalization movements (Wallace, 1970). Smith (1997) argues, "The relationship between place and language is perhaps best understood through the experience of breakdown—personal and collective—when one experiences the sense that one's received language, with all of its grammatical enframements and vocabulary tools, is inadequate to express what one is currently realizing to be true about the world" (p. 3).

68. On poets making place an element of their own private mythology as opposed to surrendering obediently to the existing mythology of place, see Heaney (1980b, p. 148). That is a sensuous and intellectual mingling—a tension—of past and present in a nutshell, and therein lies a path to a personal poetics, to a poetry of history and place that speaks to consciousness,

commitment, action, and myth—to a possible "marriage between the geographical country and the country of the mind, whether that country of the mind takes its tone unconsciously from a shared oral inherited culture, or from a consciously savored literary culture, or from both . . . that constitutes the sense of place in its richest possible manifestation" (p. 132). See also Graves (1948:14–15) and, of course, Thoreau's (1854/1995) classic, *Walden.*

69. Poetic experiences also show that immersion in place has its shiftings as well, its contradictions and alienations, and that the alienations of an ethnographer are not restricted to encounters with other cultures (Damon, 2003). Estrangement can happen through the intellectual and aesthetic encounters that one has at home, that is, by freezing moments and interpreting their particulars as both ethnographers and poets must do. On close inspection, everything is strange, and that can be a powerful source of alienation, even from hearth and family (Heaney, 1980b, pp. 137–138). On the other hand, Heaney knows that staying with the comfort and imagination of a summer's day in a strange and rural landscape can bring forth an aesthetic sense of communion with "prehistoric timelessness." These experiences must give way to the imagination, for that is the carpet on which the Muses fly and is the beacon that signals fair landing. The work is subjective, but that should not be a disqualification for anything except mathematics crammed into teaching formulas. Participation and self-conscious interpretation are how we learn about ourselves in place. Nature can be more in our appreciations than can "inanimate stone." It can be "active nature, humanized, and humanizing" (pp. 144–145).

70. Lame Deer and Erdoes (1972, p. 110).

71. For related work in an anthropological vein, see especially the verse and/or prose of Abu-Lughod (1988), Basso (1996a, 1996b), Brady (2003b, 2004), Cahnmann (2000, 2001), Diamond (1982, 1986, 1987), Farella (1993), Feld (1982), Feld and Basso (1996), Flores (1982, 1999), Hartnett (2003), Heaney (1980a, 1987), Hymes (1995, 2001), Jackson (1995), Kusserow (1998, 1999), Lavie (1991), Lewis (2002), Lopez (1991), Maynard (2003), Nowak (2000), Prattis (1985), Richardson (1982, 1998a, 1998b, 1999a, 1999b, 2001), Rosaldo (2003); Rose (1991), Sherry (1997), Simonelli (2001), Snyder (1969, 1974), Stewart (1996), Suiter (2002), Tarn (1991, 2002), B. Tedlock (1992), and D. Tedlock (1990, 1993).

72. Compare Vendler (1985): "In trying to speak for 'all men and women,' the poet risks losing selfhood altogether" (p. 60).

73. Thompson (1989) says, "What frames and defines a world is the act of participating in a context. To take part in something is to take part from an immensity of possibilities" (pp. 129–130). See also Taussig (1993).

74. None of this is to say that poetic texts (including myths) are empty of important or precise information—another blind prejudice of positivistic science (Brady, 1991a, 1991b, 1998, 2000, 2003a, 2003b; Brady & Kumar, 2000)—or to say that creativity in thought and communication enfranchises a free-for-all of interpretation, ungoverned by existing constraints on sensibility, reality, clarity, and possibility (Brady, 2003b, p. xxiv). On the inversions of poetry and myth, compare Barthes (1972, p. 134).

75. Everybody knows that scientific writing differs from poetry in fundamental ways, for example, that scientific writing is more clinical and less given to uncommon metaphors than is poetry. But an important theoretical implication that often goes unappreciated in these discussions is that each form technically plays a different language game; the positivists use language that is supposed to be transparent or invisible, whereas the humanists (and most pointedly the poets) do exactly the opposite by openly displaying their presence as observers

and authors in their works. More than just a difference of "style," each mode of representation thereby has different criteria for deciding on acceptable or satisfactory forms of expression, and the implications of that are enormous. Changing the language of our descriptions, as Wittgenstein (1974) says, also changes the analytic game itself, including changing the premises for research entry points (Brady, 2004).

76. See also Stoller (1987, 2004) and Joy and Sherry (2003). Yi-Fu (1979) says, "The Eskimos' sense of space and place is very different from that of Americans" (p. 5). Compare Carpenter (1980) and Dundes (1972).

77. Not all poetry travels with equal effectiveness across personal and cultural boundaries—but then, what does? On the roles of preferences and form, on critics who enter a world not of their own making, and on the importance of slipping any poem into mind with good effect, see Brady (2000, p. 958). On Western ethnocentrisms, see Zolbrod (1983).

78. On Australian writer David Malouf and being at a loss for words, see Smith (1997, p. 3). J. Turner (1996), after an encounter with a mountain lion, says, "An aura of prehistory marked the night. Undoubtedly people still have experiences with animals like those of ancient epochs, however unintelligible to our modern lives—unintelligible because we no longer know how to describe them. The vocabularies of shamanism, totems, synchronicities, and She are *tongues again made bold by such experiences*—experiences many believe are irretrievably lost. I believe in the experiences, but I do not understand the vocabularies. I perceive this as my own failing. My life is devoid of practices that might link such events and words. And yet the very existence of such experience is moving—beyond words" (p. 47). Moreover, in a discussion of Hemingway, he asks the question: Where is the point "at which myth and nonlinguistic practices would be required to communicate?" (p. 97). On the whiteness of the page and experiential space beyond writing, see Juarroz (1988, cited in Brady, 1991a, p. 341). On the subjected body exceeding itself and becoming "a space of excess in which the physicality of cultural politics (vocality, tactility, touch, resonance) exceeds the rationalized clarity of 'system' and transcendent understanding," see Stewart (1996, p. 130). Rickman (2002–2003) argues, "Nature is not just a linguistic edifice and language is meaningless if it does not refer beyond itself" (p. 31). See also Maslow (1964) and Sherry and Schouten (2002).

79. Poetry loses, however, if it does not conform at some level to the experience of its audience. We must be able to exchange experiences. On separations of private and public voices, see Benjamin (1969b, p. 156) and Wolf (1982, p. 108). On lyric poetry, see Damon (2003) and Tedlock (1999, p. 56). On poetry and the need for historical contexts, see Hartnett and Engels (Chapter 18, this volume). On poetry and the senses, see Stewart (2002). On ways of articulating history and place through poetry and painting, see Brady (2003b).

80. Addressing similar issues, Jackson (1995) says, "I wanted to develop a style of writing which would be consonant with lived experience in all its variety and ambiguity" (p. 4), including consciousness itself as a form of projected and prospective awareness. Consciousness "expresses interrelationships *between* self and other, subject and object, which do not have to be contrived because they are the very precondition of our human situation" (p. 169). Moving in that intellectual zone with an appealing and innovative mixed verse and prose account of his fieldwork in Africa, the poet/ethnographer Wilmsen (1999), knowing little of the local languages as his African journey began, queries himself: "While walking in the debilitating heat, I asked myself how I was going to make my experience intelligible to others" (p. xii). His answer? "It seemed to me that a way to do this lay in exposing the simultaneity of experience in

individual life: recurrences in which earlier occurrences resonate—recognized as memories, expectations, reveries, informing each momentary awareness, shaping each" (pp. xi–xii). Wilmsen continues, "I have tried only to translate the texture of experience without claiming it to be mine alone. . . . I wanted to demonstrate that simultaneity of experience is not an exclusive prerogative of today's world but is a condition of being human. . . . I wanted to find a way to express the historicities of persons in contact—to express the fact that there are no alien cultures, only alienating ways of categorizing diversity" (p. xiv).

81. But consider the notion of "messy texts," that is, "texts that are aware of their own narrative apparatuses, that are sensitive to how reality is social[ly] constructed, and that [understand] that writing is a way of 'framing' reality. Messy texts are many sited, intertextual, always open-ended, and resistant to theoretical holism, but always committed to cultural criticism" (Denzin, 1997, p. 224). According to Denzin (1997), "Ethnopoetics and narratives of the self are messy texts: They always return to the writerly self—a self that spills over into the world being inscribed. This is a writerly self with a particular hubris that is neither insolent nor arrogant. The poetic self is simply willing to put itself on the line to take risks. These risks are predicated on a simple proposition: This writer's personal experiences are worth sharing with others. Messy texts make the writer part of the writing project. These texts, however, are not just subjective accounts of experience; they attempt to reflexively map the multiple discourses that occur in a given social space [see especially Wilmsen, 1999]. Hence, they are always multivoiced. No interpretation is privileged. These texts reject the principles of the realist ethnographic narrative that makes claims to both textual autonomy and epistemological validity" (p. 225). See also Brady (1998, 2000, 2003b, in press) and Marcus (1994).

82. "Theodor Adorno speaks of 'exact fantasy' to describe a genre of writing that is rigorously empirical but, without 'going beyond the circumference' of the empirical, rearranges constellations of experienced facts in ways that render them accessible and readable. It is a method of writing that repudiates the form of lineal and progressive argumentation. It is paratactic. No one element is subordinated to another. Perhaps the term 'exact fiction' best describes such an approach to ethnographic writing" (Jackson, 1995, pp. 163–164). Compare Brady (2003b), Favero (2003), and Metcalf (2002).

83. There are other effects as well. Tedlock (1983) argues, "'Event' orientation, together with an intensified appreciation of fantasy, has already led modern poets to recognize a kinship between their own work and the oral art of tribal peoples. As Jerome Rothenberg points out in *Technicians of the Sacred*, both 'modern' and tribal poets are concerned with oral performance, both escape the confines of Aristotelian rationalism, both transcend the conventional genre boundaries of written literature, and both sometimes make use of stripped-down forms that require maximal interpolation by audiences" (p. 55). These kinds of interests and the focus on poetry and interpretive methods in general in ethnopoetics join up with other forms of experimental texts in making "public what sociologists and anthropologists have long kept hidden: the private feelings, doubts, and dilemmas that confront the field-worker in the field setting" (Denzin, 1997, p. 214). They "humanize the ethnographic disciplines . . . under a postmodern aesthetic assumption concerning the sublime to make what was previously unpresentable part of the presentation itself" (p. 215). They simultaneously break from and continue "the ethnographic tradition of representing experiences of others," rejecting "the search for absolute truth that is suspicious of totalizing theory," breaking down as part of the process "the moral and intellectual distance between reader and writer" (p. 215), and perhaps

helping to close the gap with fresh approaches to what we, as modern peoples, have lost (or buried or in other ways deprioritized) since the advent of writing and the removal from daily contact with the soil and animals of our ancient selves.

84. Compare Lopez (1990b): "If, in a philosophy of place, we examine our love of the land—I do not mean a romantic love, but the love Edward Wilson calls biophilia, love of what is alive, and the physical context in which it lives, which we call 'the hollow' or 'the canebrake' or the 'woody draw' or 'the canyon'—if, in measuring our love, we feel anger, I think we have a further obligation. It is to develop a hard and focused anger at what continues to be done to the land not so that people can survive, but so that a relatively few people can amass wealth" (p. 42).

85. Neruda (1997, p. 213).

86. Abbey (1968, p. 131).

87. Fawning over noble savages or pristine environments and societies only clouds the issue. We need to catch ourselves in the act of oversimplifications and ethnocentric wishes. We need to be cognizant of the fact that, as Hartnett and Engels point out elsewhere in this volume (Chapter 18), the life circumstances of the ancients were "like our own world—wracked with political, economic, and cultural dilemmas."

88. Gruenewald (2003) says, "An expanded framework for analyzing the power of place might include more discussion of Native American and other indigenous traditions, natural history, psychology, anthropology, architecture, sociology, cybernetics, ecological science, and religious studies, as well as all genres of imaginative literature. Once one begins interrogating the power of place as a construct for analysis, one sees that it might be, and increasingly is, applied constructively to any realm of human experience or inquiry. . . . The question is worth asking: Without focused attention to places, what will become of them—and of us?" (p. 646). On poetry in educational research, see also Cahnmann (2003).

89. By writing from their own body-grounded experiences and addressing directly those of others similarly embodied, both personally and conscientiously, poets can dice up what ails us into vivid and believable accounts. That is an empowering and political act, and poets are not strangers to it. On poetry and politics, see Heaney (1995, pp. 1, 7–8), von Hallberg (1987), and Rich (2003). On educational reform and taking "teachers and students beyond the experience and study of places to engage them in the political process that determines what these places are and what they will become," see Gruenewald (2003, pp. 620, 640). See also the pioneering and thoughtful work on "investigative poetry" by Hartnett and Engels (Chapter 18, this volume) and the powerful testament to poetic rendering as a course of social action in Hartnett (2003).

90. See Lopez (1990b, 1998) and Snyder (1985). In *Arctic Dreams,* Lopez (1986) says that the "ethereal and timeless power of the land, that union of what is beautiful with what is terrifying, is insistent. It penetrates all cultures, archaic and modern" (p. 368). And just as we are necessarily situated in the land, "The land gets inside us, and we must decide one way or another what this means, what we will do about it"—accept it as it is, attempt "to achieve congruence with a reality that is already given a . . . reality of 'horror within magnificence, absurdity within intelligibility, suffering within joy,'" as one could argue fits the worldviews of the Inuit, or should we take our profound modern ability to alter the land, that is, "change it into something else" (p. 368)? In one respect, there is no choice at all. "The long pattern of purely biological evolution . . . strongly suggests that a profound collision of human will with immutable aspects of the natural order is inevitable" (p. 368). On place, technology, and representation, see also Sherry (2000).

91. Denzin (1997) knows that "good ethnography always uses language poetically, and good poetry always brings a situation alive in the mind of the reader" (p. 26).

## ▣ References

Abbey, E. (1968). *Desert solitaire: A season in the wilderness.* New York: Ballantine.

Abram, D. (1996). *The spell of the sensuous.* New York: Random House.

Abu-Lughod, L. (1988). *Veiled sentiments: Honor and poetry in a Bedouin society.* Berkeley: University of California Press.

Ackerman, D. (1990). *A natural history of the senses.* New York: Vintage.

Agee, J., & Evans, W. (1960). *Let us now praise famous men.* New York: Ballantine.

Aitchison, J. (2000). *The seeds of speech: Language origin and evolution.* New York: Cambridge University Press.

Allison, J., Hockey, J., & Dawson, A. (Eds.). (1997). *After writing culture: Epistemology and praxis in contemporary anthropology.* New York: Routledge.

Austin, M. (1997). *The land of little rain.* New York: Penguin.

Bachelard, G. (1964). *The poetics of space.* Boston: Beacon.

Barthes, R. (1972). *Mythologies* (A. Lavers, Trans.). New York: Hill & Wang.

Barthes, R. (1977). *Image, music, text* (S. Heath, Trans.). New York: Hill & Wang.

Barthes, R. (1982). *The empire of signs* (R. Howard, Trans.). New York: Hill & Wang.

Bass, N. (2000, Autumn). Why so many native writers? *Orion,* pp. 69–73.

Basso, K. H. (1996a). *Wisdom sits in places: Landscape and language among the Western Apache.* Albuquerque: University of New Mexico Press.

Basso, K. H. (1996b). Wisdom sits in places: Notes on a Western Apache landscape. In S. Feld & K. H. Basso (Eds.), *Senses of place* (pp. 53–90). Santa Fe, NM: School of American Research Press.

Bauman, R. (Ed.). (1992). *Folklore, cultural performances, and popular entertainment: A communications-centered handbook.* New York: Oxford University Press.

Behar, R. (1993). *Translated woman: Crossing the border with Esperanza's story.* Boston: Beacon.

Benjamin, W. (1969a). *Illuminations* (H. Arendt, Ed.). New York: Schocken.

Benjamin, W. (1969b). The storyteller. In H. Arendt (Ed.), *Illuminations* (pp. 83–109). New York: Schocken.

Berger, P. L., & Luckmann, T. (1966). *The sociology of knowledge.* New York: Doubleday.

Blackburn, T. R. (1971). Sensuous–intellectual complementarity in science. *Science, 172,* 1003–1007.

Brady, I. (Ed.). (1991a). *Anthropological poetics.* Savage, MD: Rowman & Littlefield.

Brady, I. (1991b). Harmony and argument: Bringing forth the artful science. In I. Brady (Ed.), *Anthropological poetics* (pp. 3–30). Savage, MD: Rowman & Littlefield.

Brady, I. (1993). Tribal fire and scribal ice. In P. Benson (Ed.), *Anthropology and literature* (pp. 248–278). Urbana: University of Illinois Press.

Brady, I. (1998). Two thousand and what? Anthropological moments and methods for the next century. *American Anthropologist, 100,* 510–516.

Brady, I. (1999). Ritual as cognitive process, performance as history. *Current Anthropology, 40,* 243–248.

Brady, I. (2000). Anthropological poetics. In N. K. Denzin & Y. S. Lincoln (Eds.), *Handbook of qualitative research* (2nd ed., pp. 949–979). Thousand Oaks, CA: Sage.

Brady, I. (2003a). Poetics. In M. Lewis-Beck, A. E. Bryman, & T. F. Liao (Eds.), *The Sage encyclopedia of social science research methods* (pp. 825–827). Thousand Oaks, CA: Sage.

Brady, I. (2003b). *The time at Darwin's Reef: Poetic explorations in anthropology and history.* Walnut Creek, CA: AltaMira.

Brady, I. (2004). In defense of the sensual: Meaning construction in ethnography and poetics. *Qualitative Inquiry, 10,* 622–644.

Brady, I. (in press). Greg Dening's *Islands and Beaches* (or, why some anthropological history is suspected of being literature). In B. V. Lal & D. Munro (Eds.), *Texts and contexts: Essays on the foundational texts of Pacific Islands historiography.* Honolulu: University of Hawaii Press.

Brady, I., & Kumar, A. (2000). Some thoughts on sharing science. *Science Education, 84,* 507–523.

Brann, E. T. (1991). *The world of the imagination: Sum and substance.* Savage, MD: Rowman & Littlefield.

Bright, W. (1987). The natural history of Old Man Coyote. In B. Swann & A. Krupat (Eds.), *Recovering the word: Essays on Native American literature* (pp. 339–387). Berkeley: University of California Press.

Brody, H. (1982). *Maps and dreams.* New York: Pantheon.

Bromwich, D. (1997). The sublime before aesthetics and politics. *Raritan, 16*(4), 30–51.

Brown, D. E. (1991). *Human universals.* New York: McGraw–Hill.

Brown, T. L. (2003). *Making truth: Metaphor in science.* Chicago: University of Illinois Press.

Bruner, J. (1986). *Actual minds, possible worlds.* Cambridge, MA: Harvard University Press.

Buller, G. (1983). Commanche and Coyote, the culture maker. In B. Swann (Ed.), *Smoothing the ground: Essays on Native American literature* (pp. 245–258). Berkeley: University of California Press.

Cahnmann, M. (2000). Driving through North Philly. *Quarterly West, 51,* 98–99.

Cahnmann, M. (2001, November–December). Fathering. *American Poetry Review,* p. 50.

Cahnmann, M. (2003). The craft, practice, and possibility of poetry in educational research. *Educational Researcher, 32*(3), 29–36.

Carpenter, E. (1980). If Wittgenstein had been an Eskimo. *Natural History, 89*(2), 72–76.

Casey, E. S. (1996). How to get from space to place in a relatively short stretch of time. In S. Feld & K. Basso (Eds.), *Senses of place* (pp. 13–52). Santa Fe, NM: School of American Research Press.

Caughey, J. L. (1984). *Imaginary social worlds: A cultural approach.* Lincoln: University of Nebraska Press.

Cheyfitz, E. (1997). *The poetics of imperialism: Translation and colonization from the Tempest to Tarzan.* Philadelphia: University of Pennsylvania Press.

Clarkson, P. B. (1998). Archaeological imaginings: Contextualization of images. In D. S. Whitley (Ed.), *Reader in archaeological theory: Post-processual and cognitive approaches* (pp. 119–130). New York: Routledge.

Classen, C. (1993). *Worlds of sense: Exploring the senses in history across cultures.* New York: Routledge.

Clifford, J., & Marcus, G. (Eds.). (1986). *Writing culture: The poetics and politics of ethnography.* Berkeley: University of California Press.

Clifton, J. A. (Ed.). (1990). *The invented Indian: Cultural fictions and government policies.* New Brunswick, NJ: Transaction.

Coles, J. (1979). *Experimental archaeology.* New York: Academic Press.

Crapanzano, V. (2004). *Imaginative horizons: An essay in literary–philosophical anthropology.* Chicago: University of Chicago Press.

Csordas, T. (1994). *Embodiment and experience: The existential ground of culture and self.* Cambridge, UK: Cambridge University Press.

Cushing, F. H. (1970). *My adventures in Zuni.* Palo Alto, CA: American West.

Damon, M. (2003). Some discourses on/of the divided self: Lyric, ethnography, and loneliness. *Xcp* [Cross-Cultural Poetics], *12,* 31–59.

Danesi, M. (1999). *Sign, thought, and culture.* Toronto: Canadian Scholars' Press.

Danesi, M., & Perron, P. (1999). *Analyzing cultures.* Bloomington: Indiana University Press.

de Sahagún, B. (1985). Aztec definitions. In J. Rothenberg (Ed.), *Technicians of the sacred* (2nd ed., pp. 23–24). Berkeley: University of California Press.

Deloria, V. (1993). *God is red: A native view of religion.* Golden, CO: Fulcrum.

Dening, G. (Ed.). (1974). *The Marquesan journal of Edward Robarts, 1797–1824.* Honolulu: University Press of Hawaii.

Dening, G. (1980). *Islands and beaches: Discourse on a silent land—Marquesas 1774–1880.* Honolulu: University Press of Hawaii.

Dening, G. (1988). *The bounty: An ethnographic history.* Melbourne, Australia: University of Melbourne, Department of History.

Dening, G. (1995). *The death of William Gooch: History's anthropology.* Melbourne, Australia: Melbourne University Press.

Dening, G. (1996). *Performances.* Chicago: University of Chicago Press.

Dening, G. (1998a). *Readings/Writings.* Melbourne, Australia: Melbourne University Press.

Dening, G. (1998b). Writing, rewriting the beach. *Rethinking History, 2*(2), 143–172.

Dening, G. (2004). *Beach crossings: Voyaging across times, cultures, and self.* Melbourne, Australia: Melbourne University Press.

Denzin, N. K. (1997). *Interpretive ethnography: Ethnographic practices for the 21st century.* Thousand Oaks, CA: Sage.

Denzin, N. K., & Lincoln, Y. S. (Eds.). (2000). *Handbook of qualitative research* (2nd ed.). Thousand Oaks, CA: Sage.

Denzin, N. K., & Lincoln, Y. S. (Eds.). (2002). *The qualitative inquiry reader.* Thousand Oaks, CA: Sage.

Diamond, S. (1982). *Totems.* Barrytown, NY: Open Book/Station Hill.

Diamond, S. (1986). *Going west.* Northampton, NY: Hermes House Press.

Diamond, S. (1987). The beautiful and the ugly are one thing, the sublime another: A reflection on culture. *Cultural Anthropology, 2,* 268–271.

Dreyfuss, H. L., & Rabinow, P. (1983). *Michel Foucault: Beyond structuralism and hermeneutics.* Chicago: University of Chicago Press.

Dundes, A. (1972, May). Seeing is believing. *Natural History,* pp. 11–14.

Dundes, A. (1984). *Sacred narrative: Readings in the theory of myth.* Berkeley: University of California Press.

Ekkehart, M., & Lomatuway'ma, M. (1984). *Hopi Coyote tales: Istutuwutsi.* Lincoln: University of Nebraska Press.

Farella, J. (1993). *The wind in a jar.* Albuquerque: University of New Mexico Press.

Favero, P. (2003). Phantasms in a "starry" place: Space and identification in a central New Delhi market. *Cultural Anthropology, 18,* 551–584.

Feld, S. (1982). *Sound and sentiment: Birds, weeping, poetics, and song in Kaluli expression.* Philadelphia: University of Pennsylvania Press.

Feld, S. (1996). Waterfalls of song: An acoustemology of place resounding in Bosavi, Papua New Guinea. In S. Feld & K. H. Basso (Eds.), *Senses of place* (pp. 91–135). Santa Fe, NM: School of American Research.

Feld, S., & Basso, K. H. (Eds.). (1996). *Senses of place.* Santa Fe, NM: School of American Research.

Fernandez, J. (2003). Emergence and convergence in some African sacred places. In S. M. Low & D. Lawrence-Zúñiga (Eds.), *The anthropology of space and place: Locating culture* (pp. 186–203). Oxford, UK: Blackwell.

Finnegan, R. (1992). *Oral poetry: Its nature, significance, and social context.* Bloomington: Indiana University Press.

Finnegan, R., & Orbell, M. (Eds.). (1995). *South Pacific oral traditions.* Bloomington: Indiana University Press.

Fletcher, C. (1967). *The man who walked through time.* New York: Random House.

Flores, T. (1982). Field poetry. *Anthropology and Humanism Quarterly, 7*(1), 16–22.

Flores, T. (1999). *In place.* Geneva, NY: Hobart and William Smith Colleges Press.

Foucault, M. (1970). *The order of things: An archaeology of the human sciences.* New York: Random House.

Foucault, M. (1972). *The archaeology of knowledge.* New York: Pantheon.

Fritz, W. H. (unknown). Fesselung [Entrapment] (T.. F. Powell, Trans.).

Gallagher, W. (1993). *The power of place: How our surroundings shape our thoughts, emotions, and actions.* New York: Harper.

Geertz, C. (1983). *Local knowledge. Further essays in interpretive anthropology.* New York: Basic Books.

Geertz, C. (1996). Afterword. In S. Feld & K. Basso (Eds.), *Senses of place* (pp. 259–262). Santa Fe, NM: School of American Research Press.

Gewertz, D. B., & Errington, F. K. (1991). *Twisted histories, altered contexts: Representing the Chambri in a world system.* New York: Cambridge University Press.

Gibbs, R. W., Jr. (1994). *The poetics of mind: Figurative thought, language, and understanding.* New York: Cambridge University Press.

Graves, R. (1948). *The white goddess: A historical grammar of poetic myth.* New York: Octagon.

Greenblatt, S. (1991). *Marvelous possessions: The wonder of the New World.* Chicago: University of Chicago Press.

Gregor, D. (2004). Mammals of North America [poem]. *Raritan, 23*(3), 20–23.

Gruenewald, D. (2003). Foundations of place: A multidisciplinary framework for place-conscious education. *American Educational Research Journal, 40,* 619–654

Gulliford, A. (2000). *Sacred objects and sacred places: Preserving tribal tradition.* Boulder, CO: University of Colorado Press.

Haile, B. H. (1984). *Navajo Coyote tales: The Curly Tó Aheedlíinii version.* Lincoln: University of Nebraska Press.

Hallyn, F. (1990). *The poetic structure of the world: Copernicus and Kepler.* New York: Zone Books.

Harner, M. (1990). *The way of the shaman.* New York: Harper & Row.

Hartnett, S. J. (2003). *Incarceration nation: Investigative prison poems of hope and terror.* Walnut Creek, CA: AltaMira.

Heaney, S. (1980a). *Poems 1965–1975.* New York: Farrar, Straus, & Giroux.

Heaney, S. (1980b). The sense of place. In S. Heaney (Ed.), *Preoccupations: Selected prose, 1968–1978* (pp. 131–149). London: Faber & Faber.

Heaney, S. (1987). *The Haw lantern.* New York: Farrar, Straus, & Giroux.

Heaney, S. (1995). *The redress of poetry.* New York: Farrar, Straus, & Giroux.

Heidegger, M. (1971). *Poetry as language and thought.* New York: Harper & Row.

Heidegger, M. (1977). Building, dwelling, thinking. In A. Hofstader (Trans.), *Poetry, language, thought* (pp. 145–161). New York: Harper & Row.

Herzfeld, M. (2004). *The body impolitic: Artisans and artifice in the global hierarchy of value.* Chicago: University of Chicago Press.

Hinsley, C. M. (1999). Life on the margins: The ethnographic poetics of Frank Hamilton Cushing. *Journal of the Southwest, 41,* 371–382.

Hirsch, E., & O'Hanlon, M. (Eds.). (1995). *The anthropology of landscape: Perspectives on place and space.* New York: Oxford University Press.

Hobsbawm, E., & Ranger, T. (Eds.). (1983). *The invention of tradition.* New York: Cambridge University Press.

Hodder, I. (1982). *Symbols in action: Ethnoarchaeological studies of material culture.* London: Cambridge University Press.

Hodder, I. (1987). Converging traditions: The search for symbolic meanings in archaeology and geography. In J. M. Wagstaff (Ed.), *Landscape and culture: Geographical and archaeological perspectives* (pp. 134–145). Oxford, UK: Blackwell.

Hodder, I. (Ed.). (1989). *The meaning of things: Material culture and symbolic expression.* London: Unwin Hyman.

Hoffman, C. (1999). *The seven story tower: A mythic journey through space and time.* Cambridge, MA: Perseus.

Holquist, M. (1981). Introduction. In M. M. Bakhtin (Ed.), *The dialogic imagination: Four essays by M. M. Bakhtin* (pp. xv–xxxiv). Austin: University of Texas Press.

Holquist, M. (1990). *Dialogism: Bakhtin and his world.* New York: Routledge.

Howes, D. (1990). Controlling textuality: A call for a return to the senses. *Anthropologica, 32,* 55–74.

Hymes, D. (1987). Anthologies and narrators. In B. Swann & A Krupat (Eds.), *Recovering the word; Essays on Native American literature* (pp. 41–84). Berkeley: University of California Press.

Hymes, D. (1995). Port Orford. *American Anthropologist, 97,* 659–660.

Hymes, D. (2001). Poetry. In A. Duranti (Ed.), *Key terms in language and culture* (pp. 187–189). Oxford, UK: Blackwell.

Jackson, M. (1982). *Allegories of the wilderness: Ethics and ambiguity in Karanko narratives.* Bloomington: Indiana University Press.

Jackson, M. (1995). *At home in the world.* Durham, NC: Duke University Press.

Joy, A., & Sherry, J. F., Jr. (2003). Speaking of art as embodied imagination: A multisensory approach to understanding aesthetic experience. *Journal of Consumer Research, 30,* 259–282.

Juarroz, R. (1988). *Vertical poetry* (W. S. Merwin, Trans.). San Francisco: North Point Press.

Karp, I., & Levine, S. (Eds.). (1991). *Exhibiting cultures: The poetics and politics of museum display.* Washington, DC: Smithsonian Institution Press.

Kerouac, J. (1958). *The Dharma bums.* New York: Penguin.

Kerouac, J. (1959). *Mexico City blues.* New York: Grove.

Kerouac, J. (1960). *Lonesome traveler.* London: Mayflower.

Kövecses, Z. (2002). *Metaphor: A practical introduction.* New York; Oxford University Press.

Kozinets, R. V., & Sherry, J. F., Jr. (2004). Dancing on common ground: Exploring the sacred at Burning Man. In G. St. John (Ed.), *Rave culture and religion* (pp. 287–303). New York: Routledge.

Kroeber, K. (1983). Poem, dream, and the consuming of culture. In B. Swann (Ed.), *Smoothing the ground: Essays on Native American oral literature* (pp. 323–333). Berkeley: University of California Press.

Kusserow, A. (1998). Poems. *Anthropology and Humanism, 23,* 209–210.

Kusserow, A. (1999). American nomads. *Anthropology and Humanism, 24,* 65–70.

Kuusisto, S. (1998). *Planet of the blind: A memoir.* New York: Dial Press.

Lakoff, G., & Johnson, M. (1999). *Philosophy in the flesh: The embodied mind and its challenge to Western thought.* New York: Basic Books.

Lame Deer. J. F., & Erdoes, R. (1972). *Lame Deer: Seeker of visions.* New York: Pocket Books.

Lane, B. C. (2001). Giving voice to place: Three models for understanding American sacred space. *Religion and American Culture, 11*(1), 53–81.

Lansing, J. S. (1985). The aesthetics of the sounding of the text. In J. Rothenberg & D. Rothenberg (Eds.), *Symposium of the whole: A range of discourse toward an ethnopoetics* (pp. 241–257). Berkeley: University of California Press.

Laughlin, C. D., Jr., & d'Aquili, E. G. (Eds.). (1974). *Biogenetic structuralism.* New York: Columbia University Press.

Laughlin, C. D., Jr., & Brady, I. (Eds.). (1978). *Extinction and survival in human populations.* New York: Columbia University Press.

Laughlin, C. D., Jr., McManus, J., & d'Aquili, E. G. (1992). *Brain, symbol, and experience.* New York: Columbia University Press.

Lavie, S. (1991). *The poetics of military occupation: Mzeina allegories of Bedouin identity under Israeli and Egyptian rule.* Berkeley: University of California Press.

Layton, R. (1997). Representing and translating people's place in the landscape of Northern Australia. In J. Allison, J. Hockey, & A. Dawson (Eds.), *After writing culture: Epistemology and praxis in contemporary anthropology* (pp. 122– 143). New York: Routledge.

Leavitt, J. (1997). *Poetry and prophecy: The anthropology of inspiration.* Ann Arbor: University of Michigan Press.

Leonard, S., & McClure, M. (2004). *Myth and knowing: An introduction to world mythology.* New York: McGraw–Hill.

Levenson, J. C. (2004). Writing history in the age of Darwin. *Raritan, 23*(3), 115–148.

Lévi-Strauss, C. (1976). *Structural anthropology* (Vol. 2). New York: Basic Books.

Lewin, R. (1986). Anthropologist argues that language cannot be read in stones. *Science, 233,* 23–24.

Lewis, T. (2002). Five poems in three languages. *Anthropology and Humanism, 27,* 192–198.

Lincoln, Y. S., & Denzin, N. K. (Eds.). (2003a). *9/11 in American culture.* Walnut Creek, CA: AltaMira.

Lincoln, Y. S., & Denzin, N. K. (Eds.). (2003b). *Turning points in qualitative research: Tying knots in a handkerchief.* Walnut Creek, CA: AltaMira.

Lincoln, Y., & Guba, E. (2000). Paradigmatic controversies, contradictions, and emerging confluences. In N. K. Denzin & Y. S. Lincoln (Eds.), *Handbook of qualitative research* (2nd ed., pp. 163–188). Thousand Oaks, CA: Sage.

Lopez, B. (1977). *Giving birth to Thunder, sleeping with his daughter: Coyote builds North America.* New York: Avon.

Lopez, B. (1986). *Arctic dreams: Imagination and desire in a northern landscape.* New York: Bantam Books.

Lopez, B. (1990a). *Crow and weasel.* San Francisco: North Point Press.

Lopez, B. (1990b). *The rediscovery of North America.* New York: Vintage.

Lopez, B. (1991, Autumn). A sense of place. *Old Oregon,* pp. 15–17.

Lopez, B. (1998). *Desert notes/River notes.* New York: Bard.

Lorca, F. G. (1985). The duende. In J. Rothenberg & D. Rothenberg (Eds.), *Symposium of the whole: A range of discourse toward an ethnopoetics* (pp. 43– 51). Berkeley: University of California Press.

Low, S. M., & Lawrence-Zúñiga, D. (Eds.). (2003). *The anthropology of space and place: Locating culture.* Oxford, UK: Blackwell.

Lowe, D. M. (1982). *History of bourgeois perception.* Chicago: University of Chicago Press.

Marcus, G, (1994). What comes (just) after "post"? The case of ethnography. In N. K. Denzin & Y. S. Lincoln (Eds.), *Handbook of qualitative research* (pp. 563–574). Thousand Oaks, CA: Sage.

Marcus, G. (1998). *Ethnography through thick and thin.* Princeton, NJ: Princeton University Press.

Marshall, M. (2004). *Namoluk beyond the reef: The transformation of a Micronesian community.* Boulder, CO: Westview.

Maslow, A. H. (1964). *Religions, values, and peak experiences.* Columbus: Ohio State University Press.

Maynard, K. (2003, February). Thirteen ways of looking at a camel. *Anthropology News,* pp. 8, 11.

Meletinsky, E. M. (1998). *The poetics of myth* (G. Lanoue & A. Sadestsky, Trans.). New York: Routledge.

Merleau-Ponty, M. (1962). *Phenomenology of perception.* London: Routledge & Kegan Paul.

Merrell, F. (2000). *Change through signs of body, mind, and language.* Prospect Heights, IL: Waveland.

Merwin, W. S. (1997). *Flower and hand: Poems 1977–1983.* Port Townsend, WA: Copper Canyon Press.

Metcalf, P. (2002). *They lie, we lie: Getting on with anthropology.* London: Routledge.

Midgley, M. (2001). *Science and poetry.* New York: Routledge.

Miller, A. I. (1996). *Insights of genius: Imagery and creativity in science and art.* New York: Springer-Verlag.

Mitchell, R. G. (1983). *Mountain experience: The psychology and sociology of adventure.* Chicago: University of Chicago Press.

Momaday, N. S. (1969). *The way to Rainy Mountain.* Albuquerque: University of New Mexico Press.

Montgomery, S. L. (1996). *The scientific voice.* New York: Guilford.

Munn, N. D. (2003). Excluded spaces: The figure in the Australian aboriginal landscape. In S. M. Low & D. Lawrence-Zúñiga (Eds.), *The anthropology of space and place: Locating culture* (pp. 92–109). Oxford, UK: Blackwell.

Nabhan, G. P. (1982). *The desert smells like rain: A naturalist in Papago Indian country.* San Francisco: North Point Press.

Neihardt, J. G. (1959). *Black Elk speaks.* New York: Pocket Books.

Nelson, R. K. (1980). *Shadow of the hunter: Stories of Eskimo life.* Chicago: University of Chicago Press.

Nelson, R. K. (1983). *Make prayers to the raven: A Koyukon view of the northern forest.* Chicago: University of Chicago Press.

Nelson, V. (1996). H. P. Lovecraft and the Great Heresies. *Raritan, 15*(3), 92–121.

Neruda, P. (1997). The word. In S. Mitchell (Trans.), *Full woman, fleshly apple, hot moon: Selected poems of Pablo Nerudapp* (pp. 213–217). New York: HarperCollins.

Nowak, M. (2000). *Revenants.* Minneapolis: Coffee House Press.

Ohnuki-Tierney, E. (1981). *Illness and healing among the Sakhalin Ainu.* Cambridge, UK: Cambridge University Press.

Ong, W. (1967). *The presence of the word.* New Haven, CT: Yale University Press.

Orians, G. H. (1980). *Habitat selection: General theory and applications to human behavior.* In J. S. Lockard (Ed.), *The evolution of human social behavior* (pp. 49–66). New York: Elsevier.

Osborne, B. S. (2001). Landscapes, memory, monuments, and commemoration: Putting identity in its place. *Canadian Ethnic Studies, 33,* 39–77.

Paz, O. (1981). *Piedra de Sol/Sunstone* (E. Weinberger, Trans.). New York: New Directions.

Perrin, M. (1987). *The way of the dead Indians: Guajiro myths and symbols* (M. Fineberg, Trans.). Austin: University of Texas Press.

Pluciennik, M. (1999). Archaeological narratives and other ways of telling. *Current Anthropology, 40,* 653–678.

Polanyi, M., & Prosch, H. (1975). *Meaning.* Chicago: University of Chicago Press.

Poulsen, R. C. (1982). *The pure experience of order: Essays on the symbolic in the folk material culture of western America.* Albuquerque: University of New Mexico Press.

Pratt, M. L. (1992). *Imperial eyes: Travel writing and transculturation.* New York: Routledge.

Prattis, I. (Ed.). (1985). *Reflections: The anthropological muse.* Washington, DC: American Anthropological Association.

Rich, A. (2003). *What is found there: Notebooks on poetry and politics.* New York: Norton.

Richardson, M. (1975). Anthropologist: The myth teller. *American Ethnologist, 2,* 517–533.

Richardson, M. (1982). Being-in-the-plaza versus being-in-the-market: Material culture and the construction of social reality. *American Ethnologist, 9,* 421–436.

Richardson, M. (1998a). Poetics in the field and on the page. *Qualitative Inquiry, 4,* 451–462.

Richardson, M. (1998b). The poetics of a resurrection: Re-seeing 30 years of change in a Colombian community and in the anthropological enterprise. *American Anthropologist, 100,* 11–22.

Richardson, M. (1999a). The Anthro in Cali. *Qualitative Inquiry, 5,* 563–565.

Richardson, M. (1999b). Place, narrative, and the writing self: The poetics of being in the Garden of Eden. *Southern Review, 35,* 330–337.

Richardson, M. (2001). The Anthro writes a day. *Qualitative Inquiry, 7,* 54–58.

Rickman, P. (2002–2003/December–January). The poet's metaphysical role. *Philosophy Now,* pp. 30–31.

Ricoeur, P. (1991). *From text to action: Essays in hermenutics II.* Evanston, IL: Northwestern University Press.

Rosaldo, R. (1989). *Culture and truth: The remaking of social analysis.* Boston: Beacon.

Rosaldo, R. (2003). Poems. *Anthropology and Humanism, 28,* 111–113.

Rose, D. (1991). In search of experience: The anthropological poetics of Stanley Diamond. In I. Brady (Ed.), *Anthropological poetics* (pp. 219–233). Savage, MD: Rowman & Littlefield.

Rothenberg, J. (Ed.). (1972). *Shaking the pumpkin: Traditional poetry of the Indian North Americas.* New York: Doubleday.

Rothenberg, J. (1981). *Pre-faces and other writings.* New York: New Directions.

Rothenberg, J. (Ed.). (1985). *Technicians of the sacred: A range of poetries from Africa, America, Asia, Europe, and Oceania* (2nd ed.). Berkeley: University of California Press.

Rothenberg, J., & Rothenberg, D. (Eds.). (1983). *Symposium of the whole: A range of discourse toward an ethnopoetics.* Berkeley: University of California Press.

Rubinoff, L. (1976). Vico and the verification of historical interpretation. In M. M. Tagliacozzo & D. P. Verene (Eds.), *Vico and contemporary thought* (pp. 94–121). New York: Humanities Press.

Sammons, K., & Sherzer, J. (Eds.). (2000). *Translating Latin American verbal art.* Washington, DC: Smithsonian Institution Press.

Saraydar, S. C. (1976). Experimental archaeology: A dynamic approach to reconstructing the past. *Artifacts, 5,* 6–7,10.

Saraydar, S. C. (1986). Are legend days over? *Anthropology and Humanism Quarterly, 11,* 10–14.

Saraydar, S. C., & Shimada, I. (1973). Experimental archaeology: A new outlook. *American Antiquity, 38,* 344–350.

Schama, S. (1995). *Landscape and memory.* New York: Knopf.

Seeger, A. (1975). The meaning of body ornaments. *Ethnology, 14,* 211–224.

Seeger, A. (1981). *Nature and society in Central Brazil: The Suya Indians of Mato Grasso.* Cambridge, MA: Harvard University Press.

Sherry, J. F., Jr. (1997). Trivium Siam. *Consumption, Markets, and Culture, 1*(1), 91–95.

Sherry, J. F., Jr. (2000). Place, technology, and representation. *Journal of Consumer Research, 27,* 273–278.

Sherry, J. F., & Kozinets, R. V. (2004). Sacred iconography in secular space: Altars, alters, and alterity at the Burning Man Project. In C. C. Otnes & T. M. Lowrey (Eds.), *Contemporary consumption rituals: A research anthology* (pp. 291–311). Mahwah, NJ: Lawrence Erlbaum.

Sherry, J. F., Jr., & Schouten, J. (2002). A role for poetry in consumer research. *Journal of Consumer Research, 29,* 218–234.

Simonelli, J. (2001). Conflict zone: Expressions of fieldwork in Chiapas. *Anthropology and Humanism, 26,* 91–100.

Slotkin, R. (1973). *Regeneration through violence: The semantics of social creation and control.* Middletown, CT: Wesleyan University Press.

Smith, D. G. (Ed.). (1997). The geography of theory and the pedagogy of place. *Journal of Curriculum Theorizing, 13*(3), 2–4.

Snyder, G. (1969). *Earth house hold.* New York: New Directions.

Snyder, G. (1974). *Turtle Island.* New York: New Directions.

Snyder, G. (1978). *Myths and texts.* New York: New Directions.

Snyder, G. (1985). Poetry and the primitive: Notes on poetry as an ecological survival technique. In J. Rothenberg & D. Rothenberg (Eds.), *Symposium of the whole: A range of discourse toward an ethnopoetics* (pp. 90–103). Berkeley: University of California Press.

Snyder, G. (1990). *The practice of the wild.* New York: North Point Press.

Spiegelberg, H. (1975). *Doing phenomenology: Essays on and in phenomenology.* The Hague, Netherlands: Martinus Nijhoff.

Stewart, K. (1996). *A space on the side of the road: Cultural poetics in an "other" America.* Princeton, NJ: Princeton University Press.

Stewart, S. (2002). *Poetry and the fate of the senses.* Chicago: University of Chicago Press.

Stoller, P. (1987). *Sensuous scholarship.* Philadelphia: University of Pennsylvania Press.

Stoller, P. (1989). *The taste of ethnographic things: The senses in anthropology.* Philadelphia: University of Pennsylvania Press.

Stoller, P. (2004). Sensuous ethnography, African persuasions, and social knowledge. *Qualitative Inquiry, 10,* 817–835.

Stoller, P., & Olkes, C. (1986). Bad sauce, good ethnography. *Cultural Anthropology, 1,* 336–352.

Stoller, P., & Olkes, C. (1987). *In sorcery's shadow: A memoir of apprenticeship among the Songhay of Niger.* Chicago: University of Chicago Press.

Suiter, J. (2002). *Poets on the peaks: Gary Snyder, Philip Whalen, and Jack Kerouac in the North Cascades.* Washington, DC: Counterpoint.

Suskind, P. (1986). *Perfume: The story of a murderer.* New York: Pocket Books.

Swann, B. (Ed.). (1983). *Smoothing the ground: Essays on Native American oral literature.* Berkeley: University of California Press.

Swann, B., & Krupat, A. (Eds.). (1987). *Recovering the word; Essays on Native American literature.* Berkeley: University of California Press.

Tagliacozzo, M. M., & Verene, D. P. (Eds.). (1976). *Vico and contemporary thought.* New York: Humanities Press.

Tarn, N. (1991). *Views from the Weaving Mountain: Selected essays in poetics and anthropology.* Albuquerque: University of New Mexico Press.

Tarn, N. (2002). *Selected poems: 1950–2000.* Middletown, CT: Wesleyan University Press.

Taussig, M. (1993). *Mimesis and alterity. A particular history of the senses.* New York: Routledge.

Tedlock, B. (1992). *The beautiful and the dangerous: Dialogues with the Zuni Indians.* New York: Penguin.

Tedlock, D. (1972). *Finding the center: Narrative poetry of the Zuni Indians.* New York: Dial Press.

Tedlock, D. (1983). *The spoken word and the work of interpretation.* Philadelphia: University of Pennsylvania Press.

Tedlock, D. (1990). *Days from a dream almanac.* Urbana: University of Illinois Press.

Tedlock, D. (1993). *Breath on the mirror: Mythic voices and visions of the living Maya.* Albuquerque: University of New Mexico Press.

Tedlock, D. (1999). Poetry and ethnography: A dialogical approach. *Anthropology and Humanism, 24,* 155–167.

Tedlock, D., & Tedlock, B. (Eds.). (1975). *Teachings from the American Earth: Indian religion and philosophy.* New York: Liverlight.

Thompson, W. I. (1989). *Imaginary landscape: Making worlds of myth and science.* New York: St. Martin's.

Thoreau, H. D. (1995). *Walden.* Boston: Houghton Mifflin. (Original work published 1854)

Turner, J. (1996). *The abstract wild.* Tucson: University of Arizona Press.

Turner, M. (1996). *The literary mind.* New York: Oxford University Press.

Van den Abeele, G. (1992). *Travel as metaphor: From Montaigne to Rousseau.* Minneapolis: University of Minnesota Press.

Véliz, C. (Ed.). (1996). *Monuments for an age without heroes.* Boston: Boston University Press.

Vendler, H. (1985, November 7). Looking for poetry in America. *New York Review of Books,* pp. 53–60.

Verene, D. P. (1976). Vico's philosophy of imagination. In M. M. Tagliacozzo & D. P. Verene (Eds.), *Vico and contemporary thought* (pp. 20–43). New York: Humanities Press.

von Hallberg, R. (1987). *Politics and poetic value.* Chicago: University of Chicago Press.

Wallace, A. F. C. (1970). Revitalization movements. In A. F. C. Wallace (Ed.), *Culture and personality* (pp. 188–189). New York: Random House.

Weinstein, F. (1990). Who should write history? *SUNY Research, 10*(3), 20–21.

Weller, A. (1990). The hunter. In J. Davis, S. Muecke, M. Narogin, & A. Shoemaker (Eds.), *Paperbark: A collection of black Australian writings* (p. 14). St. Lucia, Australia: University of Queensland Press.

White, H. (1978). *Tropics of discourse: Essays in cultural criticism.* Baltimore, MD: Johns Hopkins University Press.

White, R. (2004). The geography of American empire. *Raritan, 23*(3), 1–19.

Williams, R. (1973). *The country and the city.* New York: Oxford University Press.

Wilmsen, E. N. (1999). *Journeys with flies.* Chicago: University of Chicago Press.

Wittgenstein, L. (1974). *On certainty* (G. E. M. Anscombe & G. H. Von Wright, Eds.). Oxford, UK: Blackwell.

Wolf, B. J. (1982). *Romantic re-vision: Culture and consciousness in nineteenth-century American painting and literature.* Chicago: University of Chicago Press.

Wolf, M. (1992). *A thrice-told tale: Feminism, postmodernism, and ethnographic responsibility.* Stanford, CA: Stanford University Press.

Wooley, N. (1992). *Virtual worlds: A journey in hype and hyperreality.* Cambridge, MA: Blackwell.

Yi-Fu, T. (1979). *Landscapes of fear.* New York: Pantheon.

Zolbrod, P. G. (1983). Poetry and culture: The Navajo example. In B. Swann (Ed.), *Smoothing the ground: Essays on Native American oral literature* (pp. 221–244). Berkeley: University of California Press.

Zolbrod, P. G. (1987). When artifacts speak: What can they tell us? In B. Swann & A. Krupat (Eds.), *Recovering the word: Essays on Native American literature* (pp. 13–40). Berkeley: University of California Press.

# 17

# CULTURAL POESIS

## The Generativity of
## Emergent Things

Kathleen Stewart

W
hat follows is a piece of imaginative writing grounded in an intense attention to the *poesis,* or creativity, of ordinary things. This is an ethnographic
attention, but it is one that is loosened from any certain prefabricated
knowledge of its object. Instead, it tracks a moving object in an effort (a) to somehow
record the state of emergence that animates things cultural and (b) to track some of the
effects of this state of things—the proliferation of everyday practices that arise in the
effort to know what is happening or to be part of it, for instance, or the haunting or exciting presence of traces, remainders, and excesses uncaptured by claimed meanings.

The writing here is committed to speculations, experiments, recognitions, engagements, and curiosity, not to demystification and uncovered truths that snap into place
to support a well-known picture of the world. I ask the reader to read actively—to follow along, read into, imagine, digress, establish independent trajectories and connections, disagree. My own voice is particular and partial, tending in this case to be
a surreal, dream-like description of ordinary spaces and events. The subject I "am" in
the stories I tell is a point of impact meandering through scenes in search of linkages,
surges, and signs of intensity. I suppose that the writing gropes toward embodied
affective experience. Finally, the writing is also a set of provocations in that it tries to
cull attention to moments of legibility and emergence, to moments of impact (instead
of to stable subjects), to models of agency that are far from simple or straightforward,
to the vitality or animus of *cultural poesis* in the jump or surge of affect (rather than

on the plane of finished representations), and to the still life—the moment when things resonate with potential and threat.

In calling this particular arena of things cultural poesis—the creativity or generativity in things cultural—I am thinking of the ways in which this field of emergent things has been written into cultural theory in various ways by Walter Benjamin, Michel Foucault, Mikhail Bakhtin, Roland Barthes, Gilles Deleuze, Raymond Williams, Donna Haraway, Marilyn Strathern, Eve Sedgwick, Michael Taussig, and others. There are Foucault's (1990) theses on the productivity and micropoetics of power, Williams's (1977) attention to emergent structures of feeling, Benjamin's (1999, 2003) theories of allegory (vs. symbol) and his own nomadic tracking of dream worlds still resonant in material things, Bakhtin's (1982, 1984) fundamental theorization and elaboration of the social poetics lodged in language, texts, and social worlds, and Barthes's (1975, 1977, 1981, 1985) intense and sustained insistence on the workings of spaces and pleasures in between, or outside, or somehow in excess of the recognized objects we call texts, experience, meaning, concept, and analysis. Deleuze and Guattari (1987) polemicized the conflict between meaning-based models of culture and models that track actual events, conjunctures, and articulations of forces to see what they do. In the wake of their critique, they outlined a theory of the affective as a state of potential, intensity, and vitality (see also Guattari, 1995). Contemporary feminist theorists, notably Haraway (1997, 2003), Strathern (1991, 1992a, 1992b, 1999), and Sedgwick (1992, 1993, 1997, 2003), have carefully—and with enormous creative energy of their own— worked to theorize the generativity in things cultural and to make room for ways of thinking and writing it, as has Taussig (1986, 1992, 1993, 1997, 1999).

Here, I try to incite curiosity about the vitality and volatility of cultural poesis in contemporary U.S. public culture through a story of ethnographic encounters (see also Stewart, 1996, 2000a, 2000b, 2002a, 2002b, 2003a, 2003b).

## ▣ ORDINARY INTENSITIES: AFFECT, VITALITY, GENERATIVITY

This is a story about public circulations in moments of vital impact. It takes place in the United States during an ongoing present that began some time ago. This is a time and place in which an emergent assemblage made up of a wild mix of things— technologies, sensibilities, flows of power and money, daydreams, institutions, ways of experiencing time and space, battles, dramas, bodily states, and innumerable practices of everyday life—has become actively generative, producing wide-ranging impacts, effects, and forms of knowledge with a life of their own. This is what I mean by cultural poesis.

Here, I offer some random examples of the generativity of all things in a state of cultural emergence. The objects of my story are emergent vitalities and the ordinary practices that instantiate or articulate them, if only partially and fleetingly. Caught, or glimpsed, in their very surge to be realized, these are things that are necessarily fugitive, shifting, opportunistic, polymorphous, indiscriminate, aggressive, dreamy, unsteady, practical, unfinished, and radically particular.

The writing here is one that tries to mimic felt impacts and half-known effects as if the writing were itself a form of life. It follows leads, sidesteps, and delays, and it piles things up, creating layers on layers, in an effort to drag things into view, to follow trajectories in motion, and to scope out the shape and shadows and traces of assemblages that solidify and grow entrenched, perhaps doing real damage or holding real hope, and then dissipate, morph, rot, or give way to something new. It talks to the reader not as a trusted guide carefully laying out the perfect links between theoretical categories and the real world but rather as a subject caught in the powerful tension between what can be known and told and what remains obscure or unspeakable but is nonetheless real. Its thoughts are speculative, and its questions are the most basic. What is going on? What floating influences now travel through public routes of circulation and come to roost in the seemingly private domains of hearts, homes, and dreams? What forces are becoming sensate as forms, styles, desires, and practices? What does it mean to say that particular events and strands of affect generate impacts? How are impacts registered in lines of intensity? How are people quite literally charged up by the sheer surge of things in the making? What does cultural poesis look like?

## ◩ DREAMLAND

The roller-coaster ride of the American dream had come into a sharp-edged focus. Good and bad. Winning and losing. Those were your choices. Anxious and haunted sensibilities tracked unwanted influences and veiled threats in idioms of addiction, trauma, and conspiracy while dreams of transcendence and recluse set afloat reckless hopes of winning or escape. Life was animated in equal parts by possibility and impossibility. We lurched between poles of hope and despair as overwrought dreams flopped to the earth, only to rise up again, inexplicably revitalized, like the monster in a horror movie or the fool who keeps going back for more. Lines of escape were fascinating too—the rocketing fortunes of the rich and famous, the dream of a perfect getaway cottage, the modest success stories of people getting their lives together again. New lifestyles proliferated at the same dizzying pace as did the epidemic of addictions and the self-help shelves at the bookstore.

The political dynamism of this tense mix of dreams and nightmares registered in an everyday life infused with the effort to track and assimilate the possibilities and threats lodged in things. Newly charged forms of the desire to know, to see, and to make a record of what was behind or underneath surfaces and systems formed a network of ordinary practices. Proliferating practices of turning desires and ideals into matter both encoded the everyday effort to master, test, and encounter emergent forces and demarcated a state of being tuned in to the mainstream. The new objects of mass desire promised both inclusion in the very winds of circulation and the nested still life of a home or identity resting securely in the eye of the storm.

As previously public spaces and forms of expression were privatized, previously privatized arenas of dreams, anxieties, agencies, and morals were writ large on public stages as scenes of impact. Yet the world had become weirdly mysterious just when it started to seem like a private life writ large or some kind of collective psyche institutionalized and exported in a global mutation. It was like a net had grown around a gelatinous mutating substance, creating a strange and loose integration of planes of existence and sensibilities. Things had become both highly abstract and intensely concrete, and people had begun to try to track emergent forces and flows on these variegated registers without really knowing what they were doing. Somehow it was all personal, but it was also something huge flowing through things.

The feminist slogan, "the personal is political," took on a new charge of intensity and swirled in spinning and floating contexts far beyond any simple ideological clarity or political program.

## ◪ ORDINARY LIFE

We were busy. Homes were filled with the grounding details of getting the rent money together, getting or keeping jobs, getting sick, getting well, looking for love, trying to get out of things we had gotten ourselves into, eating in, working out, raising kids, walking dogs, remodeling homes, and shopping. There were distractions, denials, shape-shifting forms of violence, practical solutions, and real despair. For some, one wrong move was all it took. Worries swirled around the bodies in the dark. People bottomed out watching daytime television. Credit cards were maxed out. There was downsizing and unemployment. There was competition to get kids into decent schools and for them to keep their grades up. Schedules had to be constantly juggled to keep up with dance classes or layoffs. Dizzying layers of tasks filled in the space of a day.

People took walks in their neighborhoods, peering into windows by night and murmuring over beautiful flowerbeds by day. Or, we scrambled to find ways to get to work and back on unreliable buses that quit running at night. We baked birthday cakes or ordered them from the supermarket decorated with Tigger or a golf course. We "flipped off" other drivers, read the luscious novels and sobering memoirs, disappeared into the Internet, and shopped at Wal-Mart and the other megastores because they were cheap, convenient, or new and had slogans such as "Getting It Together" and "Go Home a Hero."

Positions were taken, habits were loved and hated, dreams were launched and wounded. There was pleasure in a clever or funny image. Or in being able to see right through things. Some people claimed that they could rise above the flow and walk on water. Others wore their irony like an accessory that gave them room to maneuver. There were all the dreams of purity, martyrdom, a return to nature, getting real, having an edge, and beating the system.

Just about everyone was part of the secret conspiracy of ordinary life to get what he or she could out of it. There were the dirty pleasures of holing up to watch one's secret bad TV show, taking a trip to the mall, working out in spinning classes at the gym, spending nights on the Internet, or playing music loud in the car on the way to the supermarket.

## ▣ GAMES

There were games you could play. One was the driving game of trying to predict when the car up ahead was going to try to change lanes. Some people developed a sixth sense about it. They discovered that if they concentrated on the car they could sense when it was considering a move, even when the driver was not signaling a lane change and when the car itself was not surreptitiously leaning to the edge of the lane or acting "nervous." The game of the sixth sense became a pleasure and a compulsion in itself. It spread fast, even without the usual help of expert commentary.

You could try out this game in supermarket checkout lines too. There the game was to try to size up the flow of a checkout line in a glance. How fast is that cashier? Does that woman have coupons? That one looks like a check writer. That one looks like a talker. But the checkout line game was harder than the driving game. Even a brilliant choice could be instantly defeated by a dreaded price check or the cash register running out of tape. And once you made your choice, you were stuck with it. Already impatient, you might then start to feel a little desperate. You could switch to multitasking—make a phone call, make lists in your head, or get to work on your palm pilot. Or, you could scan the surrounding bodies and tabloid headlines for a quick thrill or an ironic inner smirk at signs of other people's eccentricity or gullibility. Or, you could just check *yourself* out by opening and paging through *Home and Garden* or *Glamour* or *Esquire*. You could relax into the aura of tactile bodies, living rooms, and gardens that staged the jump from fantasy to flesh and back again right before your eyes. The glossy images offered not so much a blueprint of how to look and live as the much more profound experience of watching images touch matter.

## ▣ ODD MOMENTS

At odd moments in the course of the day, you might raise your head in surprise or alarm at the uncanny sensation of a half-known influence. Private lives and the public world had gotten their wires crossed. Any hint of private movement would be sniffed out and thrown up on public stages, and people now took their cues so directly from circulating sensibilities that the term "hardwired" became shorthand for the state of things.

Public specters had grown intimate. The imaginary had grown concrete on public stages. All of those bodies lined up on the talk shows, outing their loved ones for this or that monstrous act. Or the reality TV shows, with the camera busting in on intimate dramas of whole families addicted to sniffing paint right out of the can. We would zoom in to linger, almost lovingly, on the gallon-sized lids scattered around on the living room carpet and then pan out to focus on the faces of the parents, and even the little kids, with big rings of white paint encircling their cheeks and chins like some kind of self-inflicted stigmata.

The labor of looking had been retooled and upgraded so that we could cut back and forth between the images popping up in the living room and some kind of real world out there.

*America's Most Wanted* aired photos of bank robbers with and without beards so that you could scan the faces at the local convenience store looking for a match.

The streets were littered with cryptic, half-written signs of personal/public disasters. The daily sightings of homeless men and women holding up signs while puppies played at their feet could haunt the solidity of things with the shock of something unspeakable. *Hungry. Will work for food. God bless you.*

The sign hits the senses with a mesmerizing and repellent force. Too sad. The graphic lettering that pleads for the attention of the passing cars glances off the eye as something to avoid like the plague. Moving on. But it also holds the fascination of catastrophe, the sense that something is happening, the surge of affect toward a profound scene.

The handmade, handheld sign of the homeless on the side of the road pleads to be recognized, if only in passing. In its desperation, the sign makes a gesture toward an ideological center that claims the value of willpower ("will work for food") and voices the dream of redemption ("God bless you"). But it is abject; it offers no affect to mime, no scene of a common desire, no line of vitality to follow, no intimate secret to plumb, no tips to imbibe for safety or good health. Instead, it sticks out of the side of vision. The shock of something unreal because it is too real, too far outside the recognized world, unspeakable. There is no social recipe for what you can do about homelessness or even what you can do with your eyes when confronted with homelessness face to face. We live in a profound social fear of encounters like this.

Even to glance out of the corner of the eye at the sign on the side of the road is a dizzying sidestep. What the glance finds in the scene it glances at, half panicked, is the excluded other's abject surge to be included in the wind of circulation—the mainstream. Its message is too stark; it begs. It mimes the discourse of the mainstream to the letter, pushing it to the point of imitation or parody or fraud. It makes the mainstream seem unreal and heartless—dead.

A dollar bill stuck out of a car window gets a quick surge forward from the one with the sign and the heightened, yet unassimilated, affect of a raw contact. "God bless you."

Now we are trudging the rough terrain of bodies and the sensuous accumulation of impacts.

## ▣ WHATEVER

Jokes had started to circulate about how we might as well wire ourselves directly to sensation buttons and just skip the step of content altogether. One day an e-mail came her way from Penny, a friend in the neighborhood who liked to keep up a running commentary on quirky characters and scenes spied from her studio windows or fabricated on drowsy afternoon walks. Penny would stop by to report tidbits and then move on. A light touch. When she used the e-mail, it was to forward funny tales filled with delicious descriptive details sent to her from like-minded others building a corpus of matters to chew on. This one told the tale of something that happened shortly after the attacks of September 11, 2001, in a medical clinic where a friend of a friend of Penny's apparently worked:

> Of course, it's not the big money area and the building is very rinky-dink. Not a big target for anthrax, let's just put it that way. She works with mothers who have drug abuse problems and the office downstairs treats juvies [juveniles]. Apparently one of the women who works downstairs turned on the a/c [air conditioner] (window unit) and a white dust sprayed out all over her. Yikes. They called the CDC [Centers for Disease Control and Prevention] and men in white suits and gas masks invaded. My friend who works upstairs was dubious— and so the people in her office just stayed and worked while the downstairs was cordoned off and investigated. They rushed the substance off to the lab and put everyone who was in the office on Cipro. Then the test results came back. Low and behold, the substance tested positive for cocaine! So good, isn't it? They think one of the juvies hid his stash in the a/c when he was afraid of being searched. I think it's a brilliant idea to start pumping cocaine into the workplace. No need for caffeine anymore. Let's just move right on up to the next level of productivity inspiration. Whadya say?

## ▣ A LITTLE ACCIDENT, LIKE ANY OTHER

She was in a café in a small town in west Texas. A place where ranchers hang out talking seed prices, fertilizer, and machines and where strangers passing through town are welcome entertainment. The sun had gone down, and she was half-way through her fresh-killed steak and baked potato when the biker couple came in limping. All eyes rotated to watch them move to a table and sit down. The couple talked intently, as if something was up, and from time to time they exchanged startled looks. When she walked past the couple's table on her way out, they raised their heads and asked whether she was heading out on the west road and whether she could look for bike parts. They had hit a deer coming into town and dumped their bike. The deer, they said, had fared much worse.

The room came to a dead stop as all ears tuned in to the sentience of the crash, still resonating in the bikers' bodies. Slowly, taking their sweet time, people began to offer questions from their tables, drawing out the details. Then other stories began to surface of other deer collisions and strange events at that place on the west road.

As she left, she pictured how, during the days to come, people would keep their eyes open for deer parts and bike parts when they traveled the west road out of town. She imagined that there would be more talk. Conversations would gather around the event and spin off into other questions such as the overpopulation of deer, hunting regulations, and the new law that legalized riding without a helmet. There might be discussions of how to fix bikes (and especially this particular make of bike), what parts might break or twist when the bike is dumped, and who was a good bike mechanic. Or, people might talk about the condition of the roads. The image of hitting the wide open road or surviving the desert injured might come up. The talk might call up anything from the image of sheer speed encountering a deer caught in one's headlights to the abstracted principles of freedom, fate, and recklessness.

But one way or another, the little accident would compel a response. It would shift people's life trajectories in some small way, change them by literally changing their course for a minute or a day. The chance event might add a layer of story, daydream, and memory to things. It might unearth old resentments or suddenly bring a new conflict to a head. It might even compel a search for lessons learned. Resonating levels of body and mind might begin to rearrange themselves into simpler choices—good luck and bad luck, animal lives lost and threats to machine-propelled humans, risk-taking wild rides and good old common sense.

But for now at least, and in some small way in the future too, the talk would secretly draw its force from the resonance of the event itself. Its simple and irreducible singularity. And the habit of watching for something to happen would grow.

## Scanning

Everyday life was now infused with the effort to track and assimilate the possibilities and threats lodged in things. Newly charged forms of the desire to know, to see, and to record what was behind surfaces and inside systems formed a network of ordinary practices.

She was no different from anyone else. All of her life, she had been yelling "pay attention!" but now she was not sure whether that was such a good idea. Hypervigilance had taken root as people watched and waited for the next thing to happen. Like the guy she heard about on the radio who spends his whole life recording everything he does: "Got up at 6:30 am, still dark, splashed cold water on my face, brushed my teeth, 6:40 went to the bathroom, 6:45 made tea, birds started in at 6:53. . . . "

Or, there was the neighbor on a little lake in Michigan whose hobby was recording his every move on video—his walks in the neighborhood and in the woods, his rides in his Ford Model T, his forays into Polish folk dances where old women went round and round the dance floor together, the monthly spaghetti suppers at the Catholic church in town. He gave one of his videos to her and her friends to watch. They played it one night—three anthropologists peering at whatever came their way from the weird world out there. It was a video of him walking around the lake in the winter snow and ice. They heard his every breath and footstep. There were some deer droppings on the path and some snow piles with suspicious shapes. Then he was walking up to Bob and Alice's cabin (the couple were in Florida for the winter), and he was zooming in on a huge lump of something that was pushing out the black plastic wrapped around the base of the house. Uh oh. Could be ice from a broken water main. Maybe the whole house was full of ice. The neighbor guy wondered out loud, if in fact it was ice, what would happen when the ice thawed. Could be a real problem. He said that maybe he would send a copy of his video on to Bob and Alice down in Florida. Then he moved on. Back to his breathing and the icicles on trees and his footsteps in the snow. Tracking the banal, scanning for trauma.

The three anthropologists looked at each other. What was that? She was mesmerized by it, like it held a key to how the ordinary could crack open to reveal something big and hidden that it had swallowed long ago. The other two were not so easily swayed. It was some kind of weirdness that pushed banality to the point of idiocy and made no sense at all. A puzzle as to why anyone would want to record the droning sameness of things, looking for something worth noting to come his way. Some strange threat or promise that popped up just for a minute and then sank below the surface again as if nothing had ever happened. A shimmering—there one minute and gone the next. Or maybe some lyrical scene you would want to remember. Something with *meaning*.

All of this watching things was mostly a good-natured thing. Like happy campers, people would put up with a lot of nothing in hopes of a glimpse of something. The ordinary was the mother lode that they mined, hoping for a sighting of a half-known something coming up for air.

It could be that ordinary things were beginning to seem a little "off," and that was what drew people's attention to them. Or, maybe the ordinary things had always seemed a little off if you stopped to think about them.

There were the obsessive compulsives who kept track of things because they had to ("Got up at 6:30 a.m., still dark, splashed cold water on my face. . . ."). These people became sightings in themselves.

Or, there were those who gave shape to their everyday by inventing practices of mining it for something different or special. People like her friends, Joyce and Bob, who lived in the woods in New Hampshire. He was a lumberjack. She cleaned those little 1950s tourist cabins that were called things such as "Swiss Village" and "Shangrila." She had left her husband and four kids after years of living straight in a regime of beatings under the sign of Jesus. She went out the back window one day and never looked back. Then she met Bob when she was tending bar, and the two took a walk on the wild side together that lasted for a dozen happy years (although not without trouble and plenty of it). He had a drinking problem, and she let him have it because he worked hard. He would hit the bottle when he got home at night and all weekend long. She called him "Daddy" even though she was a good 10 years older and pushing 50.

Joyce and Bob moved from rental cabin to rental cabin in the north woods. They invited raccoons into their cabin as if the animals were pets. They got up at 5 a.m. to write in their diaries, and then when they got home at night they would read their daily entries out loud and look at the artsy photos of treetops and bees' nests that Bob took. Finally, they were able to get a "poor people's" loan to buy a little cabin they had found in some God-forsaken place on the north side of the lake and to fix it up. But then a card came from Joyce saying that Bob had left her for "that floozy" he met in a bar.

She wonders whether Joyce still keeps a diary, whether she still fancies the serendipitous discovery of happiness and looks for ways to deposit it in the ordinary, or whether something else has happened to her ordinary.

## ◫ THE ANTHROPOLOGISTS

The anthropologists kept doing the fun things they did together. Like knocking on the doors of the little fishermen's huts on the frozen lake. They would invite themselves in for a visit, but then they would sit down on the bench and the fishermen would not say anything. Not even "who are you?" or "what are you doing here?" So, they sat together in a wild and awkward silence, staring down into the hole in the ice and the deep dark waters below. The anthropologists could not think of a single question that made any sense at all.

When the anthropologists took walks in the woods, they would come across hunters. The hunters were more talkative than the ice fishermen. That is because they all wanted the friendly, nosy, overeducated strangers to know that they were not "Bambi killers." Maybe some other hunters were, but not them—the new breed. They were nice, and a lot of them had been to college and had things to say about politics and the environment and the state. Most of the time there was a woman in the group. The others were teaching her to hunt. Everyone—the anthropologists too—would cower when the mean-looking game wardens came around a bend looking for poachers. The wardens were the bad guys. They would drive slowly past in postapocalyptic cars with burned paint and giant guns and spotlights mounted on the hood. They would fix us with hard stares, and you could see the muscles jump under their camouflage hunting suits. These guys were jumpy.

## ▣  BEING JUMPY

Sometimes, the jumpy move would take over. Lingis (1994) saw that this had happened among miners at the Arctic Circle:

> The young miner who showed me the mine put out every cigarette he smoked on his hand, which was covered with scar tissue. Then I saw the other young miners all had the backs of their hands covered with scar tissue. . . . When my eye fell on them it flinched, seeing the burning cigarette being crushed and sensing the pain. . . . The eye does not read the meaning in a sign; it *jumps* from the mark to the pain and the burning cigarette, and then jumps to the fraternity signaled by the burning cigarettes. (p. 96)

## ▣  A SLASHING

On the river in Austin, Texas, in the early morning, joggers pass over the long high bridge and stop to stretch their hamstrings on its metal rails. Pairs of friends, about to part for the day, will stop to stare out at the expanse of watery sights laid out below—fishermen in flat-bottomed boats sit upright in straight-backed chairs, giant blue herons poise on drowned cottonwoods, new limestone mansions perched on the cliffs above throw reflections halfway across the river. Crew boats pass silently under the bridge like human-powered water bugs skimming the surface. Occasionally, a riverboat will thrust itself slowly up the river, dredging the hard mass of the water up and over its wheel. Here, the world-in-a-picture still vibrates, as if it was just at that very moment that the real world crossed paths with an imagined elsewhere and the two realms hung suspended together in a still life.

Sometimes there are scenes of quiet desperation.

Sometimes people leave memorials on the bridge.

One morning, a crude sign appeared, taped to the metal railing. Below it was a shrine—yellow ribbons and a Sacred Heart of Jesus votive candle with half-burned sticks of incense stuck in the wax. The names Angela and Jerry were written in bold letters at the top of the sign, like the names of young lovers repeated over and over in school notebooks or graffitied on train trestles. The star-crossed lovers' names were harshly crossed out and followed by the words "Relationship destroyed, with malice by Federal Agents & A.P.D. [Austin Police Department] for beliefs guaranteed under U.S. Constitutional Bill of Rights. I miss you Angela, Jessica, & Furry Dog Reef."

It was signed "Always, Jerry."

Below the signature were two graphics: the nickname "Yankee Girl" encircled by a pierced heart and a thick black box encasing the prayer "Please Come Back." Then a final howl and a promise:

Angela, Jessica and Furry Dog Reef. . . . I miss you.

May God have mercy on the souls of the hateful, evil, vindictive people who conspired to take you from me, and did so with success. Angela, I will love you always and forever.

I miss you babe,

Jerry

At the bottom, another pierced heart held Yankee Girl in its wounded arms.

The sign was both cryptic and as crystal clear as a scream. Bitter fury was its vitality and its end. Its drive to a sheer satisfaction quivered like flesh in its wavering letters. It heaved grief and longing at the world not as an outer expression of an inner state but more directly as an act of the senses making contact with pen and paper and matches. Its slashing was like the self-slashing of young women who cut themselves so that they can feel alive or literally come to their senses. It had the same self-sufficient fullness and did not ask for interpretation or dream of a meaning.

This is a sensibility as common as it is striking. It is the kind of thing you see everyday. In the elaborate poetics of graffiti—the signatures left so artfully, the politics of slashing through them, crossing them out, erasing them, replicating them all over town. Or in the signs of the homeless on the side of the road. Or in the countless verbal and visual signs that come to life on the charged border between things private and things public. It is the kind of sensibility that surges through the wild conversation of AM radio talk shows and Internet sites. It adds force to the railing of the enraged in everything from road rage, to letters to the editor, to the face-to-face raging resentments of workplaces and intimate spaces. It permeates politics from right wing to left wing.

Something in its roughened surface points to a residue in things, a something that refuses to disappear. It draws attention, holds the visual fascination of unspeakable things—transgressions, injustices, the depths of widespread hopelessness. What animates it is not a particular message but rather the more basic need to forcefully perform the unrecognized impact of things.

It flees the easy translation of pain and desire into abstract values or commonsense coping. Yet every day its dramas of surge and arrest are bathed in the glow of some kind of meaning or form of dismissal. Then there are these questions: Will the gesture of the slashing shimmer as a curiosity passed on an everyday walking path, and will you feel a little jolt as you pass? Or, will it just go in one eye and out the other?

Sometimes, it might have the vitality of a pure surge pushing back, gathering a counterforce to a point of intensity that both slashes at itself and spits at the world.

Other times, its very violence means that it will be erased, ignored, or drawn up, like blood in a syringe, to infuse new life into the enveloping categories of good sense, healthy protest, productive acts and lives, and mainstream moods by virtue of its bad example. It will be unwilling and unwitting nourishment for the more settled world of calculation, representation, value, and necessity that gave rise to its spitting fury to begin with. Yet even then, the sign, in its perverse singularity, will peep out of little cracks on barely public stages simultaneously defying and demanding witness. It will remain a partially visible affecting presence because what it registers is not only points of breakdown in "the system" but also lines of possible breakthrough beating unbidden in the blood of the mainstream.

A person walking by such signs might be touched by them or hardened to their obnoxious demands. But either way, a charge passes through the body and lodges in the person as an irritation, a confusion, an amusement, an ironic smirk, a thrill, a threat, or a source of musing. For better or worse, signs that erupt as events teach us something of their own jumpy attention to impacts by leaving visceral traces in their wake.

## ◙ STRESS

The lone body and the social body had become the lived symptoms of the contradictions, conflicts, possibilities, and haunted sensibilities of pervasive forces. Stress was the lingua franca of the day. If you had it, you were onto something, part of the speeding force of things-in-the-making. But it could puncture you too, leaving you alone during times of exhaustion, claustrophobia, resentment, and ambient fear.

The self became a thing filled with the intricate dramas of dreams launched, wounded, and finally satisfied or left behind. You could comfort it like a child. Or, you could look at the outlines of it against the relief of other people's missed opportunities. Or, you could inhabit it as a flood of events and relationships caught in a repetitive pattern that you recognized only when you got to the end of a cycle, and by then you were already onto the next one.

There were little shocks in the rhythms of splurging and purging and in the constant edgy corrections of the self-help regimes—take an aspirin a day (or not), drink a glass of red wine a day (or not), eat butter or low-fat margarine or canola oil, eat oatmeal to strip the bad cholesterol from your arteries, eat salmon to add the good cholesterol, try antioxidants or kava kava or melatonin.

The figure of a beefed-up agency became a breeding ground for all kinds of strategies of complaint, self-destruction, flight, reinvention, and experimentation as if the world rested on its shoulders. Straight talk about willpower and positive thinking claimed that agency was just a matter of getting on track, as if all the messy business of real selves affected by events and haunted by threats could be left behind in an out-of-this-world levitation act.

Against this tendency, a new kind of memoir began to work the lone self into a fictional sacrifice powerful enough to drag the world's impacts out onto secret stages. Self-help groups added density to the mix, offering both practical recipes for self-redeeming action and a hard-hitting, lived recognition of the twisted, all-pervasive ways in which compulsions permeated freedoms and were reborn in the very surge to get free of them once and for all.

## ▣ THE BODY SURGES

The body builds its substance out of layers of sensory impact laid down in the course of straining upstream against recalcitrant and alien forces or drifting downstream, with its eyes trained on the watery clouds and passing treetops overhead and its ears submerged in the flow that surrounds it, buoys it, and carries it along. The body surges forward, gets on track, gets sidetracked, falls down, pulls itself up to crawl on hands and knees, flies through the air, hits a wall, regroups, or beats a retreat. It knows itself as states of vitality, exhaustion, and renewal. It exerts itself out of necessity and for the love of movement and then it pulls a veil around itself to rest, building a nest of worn clothing redolent with smells of sweat or cheap perfume or smoky wood fires burrowed into wool.

The body cannot help itself. It is an extremist seeking thrills, a moderate sticking its toe in to test the waters, a paranoid delusion looking for a place to hide. It is a bouncing fool throwing itself at an object of round perfection in the dogged conviction that it is on the right track this time. What the body knows, it knows from the smell of something promising or rancid in the air or the look of a quickening or slackening of flesh. It grows ponderous, gazing on its own form with a Zen-like emptiness. As a new lover, it dotes on revealed scars and zones in on freckles and moles and earlobes. As one of the anxious aging, it is drawn to the sight of new jowls and mutant hairs and mottled skin in the bathroom mirror.

The body is both the persistent site of self-recognition and the thing that will always betray you. It dreams of its own redemption and knows better. It catches sight of a movement out of the corner of its eye and latches on to a borrowed intimacy or a plan that comes as a gift to sweep it into the flow of the world and free it of its lonely flesh.

The body consumes and is consumed. Like one big pressure point, it is the place where outside forces come to roost, condensing like thickened milk in the bottom of the stomach. It grows sluggish and calls for sweet and heavy things to match its inner weight. Or salty or caffeinated things to jolt it to attention.

Layers of invented life form around the body's dreamy surges like tendons or fat.

Lifestyles and industries pulse in a silent, unknown reckoning of what to make of all this.

The body builds itself out of layer on layer of sensory impact. It loves and dreads what makes it. At times, it is shocked and thrilled to find itself in the driver's seat. At other times, it holes up, bulks up, wraps itself in its layers. The world it lives in spins with the dancing poles of ups and downs and rests its laurels in a banality that hums a tune of its own.

## ▣ BODY FOR LIFE

She once took up *Body for Life* on the advice of a friend. Between them, it was a joke. They called it their cult. But they also knew that there was something *to* a little extreme self-transformation. Or at least the effort. *Body for Life* was a best-selling book with glossy "before-and-after" pictures of bodybuilders on the inside covers. It started as a bodybuilder's, movement-building, moneymaking challenge to the unwashed to put down the beer and chips and start loving life instead of just living it, to start thriving and not just surviving. It was "12 weeks to mental and physical strength."

She was not at all taken with the tanned, oiled, muscle man and muscle woman look on the inside covers, but the little game of moving her eyes back and forth between each pair of before-and-after shots caught her in a spell of momentary satisfaction. The eye jumped happily between the paired scenes. Now fat and pale, now muscled and oily and tan. Peek-a-boo. All of the bodies were white. They made her think of the body displays that she was always running into when she lived in Las Vegas. At the post office, or at the drive-in movie theater, or while waiting in line to get a new driver's license, there were always half-naked bodybuilders with wet-skinned snakes draped around their necks, or monkeys on leashes, or stars-and-stripes halter tops and permed blond hair.

Her friend called the people in the pictures "beefcakes." Class seemed to be somehow involved in all of this, but people would swear up and down that those who were into *Body for Life* came from all walks of life. That comfortable claim to plainness emerging out of some kind of mainstream. Some kind of mall culture. Ordinary Americans unmarked by anything but the will to change their bodies and by the real or imagined fruits of their success after those glorious 12 weeks. They were people who had been catapulted out of the back seat of life onto the magic carpet ride that turns flighty self-defeating dreams into vital generative flesh.

They had experienced their breakthroughs when they saw the inspiring photos on the inside covers, or when they took a good hard look at their own eye-opening "before" pictures, or when — while watching the inspirational video that they could get for a $15 donation to the Make-A-Wish Foundation—they were suddenly released from the feeling of being alone and felt hope instead. They began to crave the 12-week program even more than they craved a piece of key lime pie or a beer.

There is nothing weird about how this happens. It is laid out step by step like a 12-step program where the spiritual transformation flows directly through the flesh. You follow the steps in the book as if it were a recipe book, consuming each new exercise with relish. You create 12-week goals out of gossamer wishes. Done. You pull your dreams out of their shadow existence into the light of day. Okay then! You harness the force in your own faintly beating desire to change. Wow! Okay. You ask yourself hard questions. You write down the answers. You speak your goals out loud with mimicked confidence every morning and night until the confidence is real. You commit. You focus; forget the zoning out and drifting downstream. You create five daily habits. You imagine other people looking at your new body with gleaming eyes, and you hear their approving comments until the imagining is effortless and part of you. You surrender the negative emotions that hold everyone back, and you start looking forward. You realize that you will never again get sidetracked. Everyone who takes the 12-week challenge feels like a winner. You do not need a carrot on a stick anymore; you take your eyes off the prize (a blood red Lamborghini Diablo) and even consumer fetishism seems to fade into the background of a half-lived past. Now you are consuming your body, and your body is consuming you. It is more direct.

She was not really interested in the inspirational business, however, and she never actually read the book. She passed directly from the game of before-and-after photos to the charts near the end of the book that tell you exactly what you have to do and eat. She got organized. She made copies of the exercise charts so that she could fill one out each day like a daily diary. She memorized the acceptable foods in the three food groups and stocked up. She ritualized each meal and gleefully took off the 7th day each week, carefully following the instruction to eat exactly whatever she wanted that day and no less. She ordered boxes of the shakes and power bars and began to experiment with the recipes that made the chocolate shake taste like a banana split and turned the vanilla shake into that famous liquid key lime pie. She got the picture. She felt the surge. She let it become a new piece of her skeleton. Then there were the inevitable ups and downs, the sliding in and out of its partial cocoon.

A couple of years later, long after she had consumed the program enough to reduce it to a few new prejudices about how to exercise and how to eat, she drifted into Body for Life Community.com and the dozens of listservs and chat rooms in its nest. Some were modeled as Christian fellowships:

> The only requirement for membership is the desire to be healthy. This is not just a set of principles but a society for people in action. Carry the message or wither. . . . Those who haven't been given the truth may not know the abundant life we have found—a way out, into life, a real life with freedom.

Other listservs were just organized by state. In any of them, you could click on someone's name and up would pop a *Body for Life* photo, slipping you right into the culture of personal ads. In the chat rooms, things got really concrete. One woman confessed that she could smell the chocolate right through the wrappers in the bowl of Halloween candy by the door, and someone shouted support in capital letters: "HANG IN THERE! YOU CAN DO IT!!!" A man happily obsessed about how to prepare his shakes:

> My favorite is chocolate, and to prepare the shake I always use 3 cubes of ice from the Rubbermaid mold, put them (without water) in the jar, and then pour the water in. Use 12 and a half ounces and 1 centimeter, then blend for about 55 seconds. You [have] got to use

a stopwatch! I think this is why I love Myoplex, because I blend it for more seconds and I drink it cool without milk or bananas.

People exchanged stories of ongoing tragedies, seeking workout partners to help them get through the ordeals. Others just focused on keeping up the network connections:

> Good morning to everyone. Been off for a few days. Lizzy—sorry to hear about your migraine—scary! Jim—it's true—your pictures don't do you justice! Abs—I love your philosophy! It's true—we become what we think about. Deb—congratulations! Good luck with your photos—can't wait to see your progress! If you find something that covers bruises, let me know—I bruise just thinking about bumping into something. Can't wait to see you all at the upcoming events!

All of these self-expressions are excessive in their own way. They proclaim, confess, obsess, and gush. But that is not because the body really does just get on track and march forward armed with the drama of success and the minutia of disciplinary practices. It is because it slumps and gets sidetracked and rejoins its *Body for Life* self. It is because it wants and it does not want and because it might do one thing or another. It is because it smells its way along tracks, and new tracks intersect the old and carry it away. It is because it catches things out of the corner of its eye, and half-hidden things on the sidelines are always the most compelling.

*Body for Life* draws its own life from the force of a bodily surge enacting not the simple, deliberate, one-way embodiment of dreams but rather the pulsing impact of dream and matter on each other in a moment when the body is beside itself. Caught in a movement, floating, suspended between past and future, hesitation and forward thrust, pain and pleasure, knowledge and ignorance, the body vibrates or pulses. It is only when the body remains partly unactualized and unanchored that it seems intimate, familiar, and alive. This can be lived as an event—a moment of shock, climax, or awakening. But there is also something of it in the banal and quotidian—a continuous background radiation, a humming left unremarked like a secret battery kept charged.

*Body for Life* says that turning fleeting fantasies into the force of vitality is about making a decision, but making a decision is itself about playing games, looking at pictures, following recipes, mimicking desired states, inventing social imaginaries, and talking to yourself in the mirror. Getting on track and staying there is not the simple and sober choice of a lifetime but rather a thin line from which you can, and probably will, topple back to ordinary sloppiness or onto an "epidemic of the will" (Sedgwick, 1992) such as excessive dieting. Then the body might swing itself back to a state of moderation or exhaustion, stick its toe in to test the waters, and pull the blankets over itself to hide.

The proliferating cultures of the body spin madly around the palpable promise that fears and pleasures and forays into the world can be literally made vital all-consuming passions. But this promise (and threat) is already there in the body directly engaged by shifting public sensibilities, in the senses retooled and set in motion. Like an antenna, the body picks up pulses that are hard to hear, or hard to bear, in the normalizing universe of cultural codes. It stores the pulses in a neck muscle or a limb, or it follows them just to see where they are going. It dares them and registers their impacts. It wants to be part of their flow. It wants to be in touch. It wants to be touched. It hums along with them, flexing its muscles in a state of readiness.

### ▣ Sometimes When You Hear Someone Scream . . .

Laurie Anderson had a show at the Guggenheim Soho called "Your Fortune, $1." A spooky white plastic owl perched on a stool in a darkened corner spewed out a stream of two-bit advice, trenchant commentary, and stray advertising lingo plucked out of a realm of sheer circulation. The owl's mechanical yet sensuously grainy voice droned on and on, transfixing her in a flood of Hallmark greeting card schlock. She was fascinated to see how the flood's ordinary reality seemed to instantly deflate and become both laughable and alarming from the owl's simple mimicking.

Then it said something that she swore she had already been anxiously chanting to herself. *Sometimes when you hear someone scream, it goes in one ear and out the other. Sometimes it passes right into the middle of your brain and gets stuck there.*

It was one of those moments when the indiscriminate flow stops dead in its tracks. The supersaturated soup of sensory images and sounds gently prodding and massaging us like waves lapping a shore takes this opportunity to solidify into something momentarily clear or even shocking. Like a trauma we had forgotten or never quite registered that comes back in a flash. Or like a whiff of something hopeful or potentially exciting passing with the breeze. We perk up in a mix of recognition, pleasure, and alarm.

One minute you are afloat in the realm of sheer circulation. Then some random sound bite hits you with a force that seems to bring you to your senses. We sober up in the face of a cruel lucidity. But it is the hungry sense that has been awakened that drives the world back into the land of enchantment. The waves of desire lap at our feet, and we drift off again, held aloft by the sheer density of images, sensory signals, and objects drawn into play in the dreamworld.

When she heard the owl's line about screams that pass right into the middle of your brain and get stuck there, she went home and wrote down a story that had been lodged in her psyche ever since she heard it.

The story starts with a question lodged in a tactile sensate anxiety and then opens onto an aesthetic scene of the senses. The question: Do you ever wake up in the morning, or in the middle of the night, with a sense of sudden dread and start scanning your dreamy brain for the memory of what you have done or a premonition of what is coming? Some do this all of the time; for them, this is what morning has become.

The aesthetic scene: She has a big iron bed lodged against long wide windows looking onto the back deck. Tropical breezes waft over her in the night, carrying the sweet and fetid smells of kumquat trees and mimosa blossoms. At dawn, there are wild bird cries—mourning doves and grackles and parrots that once escaped their pet cages and now breed in the trees. At certain hours in the still of the night, the train cries in the near distance. The night pulses with the high lonesome sound of haunted machine dreams roaming the landscape.

When she has guests, she lets them use the iron bed, and they wake up talking about the bed and the wailing train as if they feel pleased to be set down in some kind of American Heartland. But she is only too happy to lay down a pallet on the living room floor and fall into a deep sleep with only the smell of old ashes from the fireplace because she knows why the train sings.

The train sings for Bobby, a homeless drunk who laid himself down on the tracks one night and passed out as if he too could lay down a pallet and escape from his ghosts. He and his old lady had been down at the free concert on the river where some of the street people party hard. The weekly concert was their moment to be at home in public, doing what everyone else was doing, only more. Some would laugh loud or make announcements or give people directions and advice. As the day went to full dark, the power of music would flow out from the stage, touch spellbound bodies, and spread out to the neon skyline reflecting in the dark glassy expanse of the river. There were always graceful moments—a dance gesture, a wide open smile, a sudden upsurge of generosity, the startled gratitude of pariahs who suddenly found themselves seamlessly rubbing shoulders with the housed. There were always crashes too—people falling down drunk in front of the stage; the vomiting; a man huddled and pale, too sick to party; flashes of hope and ease dashed on the rocks of familiar fury, frustration, humiliation, and grief; people making spectacles of themselves. Sometimes there were fights.

That night, Bobby had a fight with his old lady and stomped off alone. He followed the train tracks through the woods to the homeless camp, where he sat on the tracks alone, taking stock in a booze-soaked moment of reprieve. He loved the romance of the high lonesome sound in the distance and the train's promise of tactility and power—the rumbling weight of power incarnate rumbling past, the childhood memory of the penny laid on the tracks, the way the tracks carved out a "no man's land" where shadows could travel and live.

He laid himself down on the icy cold tracks and closed his eyes, as if tempting fate. As if that simple move held both the possibility of checking out and a dream of contact with a public world that might include him.

Somewhere in the middle of the long train passing over, he raised his head, awakening. They say that if he had not woken up, the train would have passed right over him.

Now the train screams out a warning when it draws close to that place on the tracks not far from her iron bed. It often wakes her. Or it lodges in her sleep and comes as an unknown shock of anxiety in the morning.

▣ ▣ ▣

## ▣ CODA

The stories that make up my story—disparate and arbitrary scenes of impact tracked through bodies, desires, or labors and traced out of the aftermath of a passing surge registered, somehow, in objects, acts, situations, and events—are meant to be taken not as representative examples of forces or conditions but rather as constitutive events and acts in themselves that animate and literally make sense of forces at the point of their affective and material emergence. More directly compelling than ideologies, and more fractious, multiplicitous, and unpredictable than symbolic representations of an abstract structure brought to bear on otherwise lifeless things, they are actual sites where forces have gathered to a point of impact, or flirtations along the outer edges of a phenomenon, or extreme cases that suggest where a trajectory might lead if it were to go unchecked. They are not the kinds of things you can get your hands on or wrap your mind around, but they are things that have to be literally tracked.

Rather than seek an explanation for things we presume to capture with carefully formulated concepts, my story proposes a form of cultural and political critique that tracks lived impacts and rogue vitalities through bodily agitations, modes of free-floating fascination, and moments of collective excitation or enervation. It attempts to describe how people are quite literally charged up by the sheer surge of things in the making.

My story, then, is not an exercise in representation or a critique of representation; rather it is a cabinet of curiosities designed to incite curiosity. Far from trying to present a final, or good enough, story of something we might call "U.S. culture," it tries to deflect attention away from the obsessive desire to characterize things once and for all long enough to register the myriad strands of shifting influence that remain uncaptured by representational thinking. It presumes a "we"—the impacted subjects of a wild assemblage of influences—but it also takes difference to be both far more fundamental and far more fluid than models of positioned subjects have been able to suggest. It is not normative. Its purpose is not to evaluate things as finally good or bad, and far from presuming that meanings or values run the world, it is drawn to the place where *meaning* per se collapses and we are left with acts and gestures and immanent possibilities. Rather than try to pinpoint the beating heart of its beast, it tracks the pulses of things as they cross each other, come together, fragment, and recombine in some new surge. It tries to cull attention to the affects that arise in the course of the perfectly ordinary life as the promise, or threat, that something is happening—something capable of impact. Whether such affects are feared or shamelessly romanticized, subdued or unleashed, they point to the generative immanence lodged in things. Far from the named "feelings" or "emotions" invented in discourses of morals, ideals, and known subjectivities (leave that to Hallmark and the Family Channel), they take us to the surge of intensity itself.

My story tries to follow lines of force as they emerge in moments of shock, or become resonant in everyday sensibilities, or come to roost in a stilled scene of recluse or hiding. It tries to begin the labor of knowing the effects of current restructurings not as a fixed body of elements and representations imposed on an innocent world but rather as a literally moving mix of things that engages desires, ways of being, and concrete places and objects.

▣ REFERENCES

Bakhtin, M. (1982). *The dialogic imagination* (K. Brostrom, Trans.). Austin: University of Texas Press.

Bakhtin, M. (1984). *Problems of Dostoevsky's poetics* (C. Emerson, Trans.). Minneapolis: University of Minnesota Press.

Barthes, R. (1975). *The pleasure of the text* (R. Miller, Trans.). New York: Hill & Wang.

Barthes, R. (1977). *Image–music–text* (S. Heath, Trans.). New York: Hill & Wang.

Barthes, R. (1981). *Camera Lucida: Reflections on photography* (R. Howard, Trans.). New York: Hill & Wang.

Barthes, R. (1985). *The responsibility of forms: Critical essays on music, art, and representation* (R. Howard, Trans.). New York: Hill & Wang.

Benjamin, W. (1999). *The Arcades Project* (H. Eiland & K. McLaughlin, Trans.). Cambridge, MA: Harvard University Press.

Benjamin, W. (2003). *The origin of German tragic drama* (J. Osborne, Trans.). New York: Verso.

Deleuze, G., & Guattari, F. (1987). *A thousand plateaus* (B. Massumi, Trans.). Minneapolis: University of Minnesota Press.

Foucault, M. (1990). *The history of sexuality: An introduction* (R. Hurley, Trans.). New York: Vintage.

Guattari, F. (1995). *Chaosmosis: An ethico-aesthetic paradigm.* Bloomington: Indiana University Press.

Haraway, D. (1997). *Modest witness, second millennium.* New York: Routledge.

Haraway, D. (2003). *The Companion Species Manifesto: Dogs, people, and significant otherness.* Chicago: Prickly Paradigm Press (University of Chicago).

Lingis, A. (1994). *Foreign bodies.* New York: Routledge.

Sedgwick, E. (1992). *Epistemology of the closet.* Berkeley: University of California Press.

Sedgwick, E. (1993). Epidemics of the will. In E. Sedgwick, *Tendencies* (pp. 130–145). Durham, NC: Duke University Press.

Sedgwick, E. (1997). *Novel gazing: Queer readings in fiction.* Durham, NC: Duke University Press.

Sedgwick, E. (2003). *Touching feeling: Affect, pedagogy, performativity.* Durham, NC: Duke University Press.

Stewart, K. (1996). *A space on the side of the road: Cultural poetics in an "other" America.* Princeton, NJ: Princeton University Press.

Stewart, K. (2000a). Real American dreams (can be nightmares). In J. Dean (Ed.), *Cultural studies and political theory* (pp. 243–258). Ithaca, NY: Cornell University Press.

Stewart, K. (2000b). Still life. In L. Berlant (Ed.), *Intimacy* (pp. 405–420). Chicago: University of Chicago Press.

Stewart, K. (2002a). Machine dreams. In J. Scanduri & M. Thurston (Eds.), *Modernism, Inc.: Body, memory, capital* (pp. 21–28). New York: New York University Press.

Stewart, K. (2002b). Scenes of life. *Public Culture, 14,* 2.

Stewart, K. (2003a). Arresting images. In P. Matthews & D. McWhirter (Eds.), *Aesthetic subjects: Pleasures, ideologies, and ethics* (pp. 431–438). Minneapolis: University of Minnesota Press.

Stewart, K. (2003b). The perfectly ordinary life. *Scholar and Feminist Online, 2,* 1.

Strathern, M. (1991). *Partial connections.* Savage, MD: Rowman & Littlefield.

Strathern, M. (1992a). *After nature.* New York: Cambridge University Press.

Strathern, M. (1992b). *Reproducing the future.* Manchester, UK: Manchester University Press.

Strathern, M. (1999). *Property, substance, and effect.* London: Athlone Press.

Taussig, M. (1986). *Shamanism, colonialism, and the wild man.* Chicago: University of Chicago Press.

Taussig, M. (1992). *The nervous system.* New York: Routledge.

Taussig, M. (1993). *Mimesis and alterity.* New York: Routledge.

Taussig, M. (1997). *The magic of the state.* New York: Routledge.

Taussig, M. (1999). *Defacement: Public secrecy and the labor of the negative.* Stanford, CA: Stanford University Press.

Williams, R. (1977). *Marxism and literature.* New York: Oxford University Press.

# 18

# "ARIA IN TIME OF WAR"

## Investigative Poetry and the Politics of Witnessing

### Stephen J. Hartnett and Jeremy D. Engels

ontemporary intellectual production in the humanities is haunted by two
scandalous hypocrisies. First, although *interdisciplinarity* and *excellence* are
the catchwords of the era, universities for the most part continue to teach,
hire, and tenure according to stultifying genre bound traditions rather than fresh
pedagogical, artistic, or intellectual ambitions. Second, although humanists can build
flashy careers using words such as *radical, intervention, transgression,* and *counter-hegemonic*—even while fitting snugly into safe discrete fields—the number of academics doing political work is embarrassingly small. In contrast to these two driving
hypocrisies, we invoke the spirit of Ralph Waldo Emerson, who demanded in a sermonic essay from 1844 that a poet should strive toward becoming "the Knower, the
Doer, and the Sayer." Emerson (1844/1982) told his readers that knowing, doing, and
saying "stand respectively for the love of truth, for the love of good, and for the love
of beauty" (p. 262). Filtered through a postmodern lens, we suggest that knowing

**Authors' Note.** An earlier version of the material in Section 4 of this essay originally appeared as part of
Hartnett (1999); that material appears courtesy of the National Communication Association. Parts of
Sections 2 and 4 of this essay appeared in a slightly different form in Hartnett (2003); that material
appears courtesy of Rowman & Littlefield Publishers. The authors are deeply grateful for the editorial
insights of Norman Denzin and Ivan Brady.

回 587

indicates the necessity of scholarship, that doing points toward activism and other forms of embodied knowledge, and that saying calls for an examination of and participation in the politics of representation. Read in this way—as calling for the combination of serious scholarship, passionate activism, and experimental representation—Emerson's transcendentalist dictum serves as a ringing indictment of the hypocrisies described previously and as a clarion call for what we describe in what follows as *investigative poetry.*

Although attempts to define a genre are doomed to failure and inevitably invite a cascade of counterarguments, refutations, and modifications, we nonetheless begin with the premise that investigative poetry exhibits these characteristics:

- An attempt to supplement poetic imagery with evidence won through scholarly research, with the hope that merging art and archive makes our poetry more worldly and our politics more personal
- An attempt to use reference matter not only to support political arguments but also as a tool to provide readers with additional information and empowerment
- An attempt to problematize the self by studying the complex interactions among individuals and their political contexts, hence witnessing both the fracturing of the self and the deep implication of the author in the very systems that he or she examines
- An attempt to problematize politics by witnessing the ways that social structures are embodied as lived experience, hence adding to political criticism ethnographic, phenomenological, and existential components
- An attempt to situate these questions about self and society within larger historical narratives, thereby offering poems that function as genealogical critiques of power
- An attempt to produce poems that take a multiperspectival approach, not by celebrating or criticizing one or two voices but rather by building a constellation of multiple voices in conversation
- A deep faith in the power of commitment, meaning that to write an investigative poetry of witness the poet must put himself or herself in harm's way and function not only as an observer of political crises but also as a participant in them

We elucidate these claims in what follows via a series of case studies. It is impossible to begin this essay, however, without noting that arguments over the possible relationships among poetry, politics, and social justice—to say nothing of the methodological criteria offered earlier—are as old as civilization itself. As Birkerts (1987) observes, "The poetry/politics debate began when Plato booted the poet from his ideal Republic, maybe even sooner; it will go on so long as there is language" (p. 55). But unlike Birkerts and the hundreds of other critics who have weighed in with weighty pronouncements on one aspect of this debate, often in tones that we can only describe as partisan at best and shrill at worst, we want to honor the epic and sometimes comic nature of that debate without descending into it. Instead, we offer readers a series of interlocking readings of some veins of work that we have found to be edifying. Our comments here may be taken, then, not so much as our levying an argument about how we think poets, activists, and scholars should proceed as our sharing some hopefully pedagogical thoughts on the literary and activist inspirations that have fed our fascination with and unbounded support for investigative poetry.[1]

Our essay unfolds in four movements. First, to frame our arguments about investigative poetry, we explore the poetic and political possibilities embodied in recent works by Carolyn Forché and Edward Sanders. Forché's (2003) *Blue Hour* is a haunting, elegiac, and spiritual meditation on the ever-piling wreckage of violence. Sparse and abstract, with words floating in the hushed glimmer of no-where and no-time, Forché's devastating poems feel like a dismal history lesson detached from history. Sanders's (2000) *America: A History in Verse* offers a different model. Packed with details organized chronologically, and reading like a catechism of lessons gleaned from the lost fragments of our national history, these celebratory poems offer readers an empowering investigation into the still great promises of the American experiment. By comparing these texts, we establish some of the benefits and consequences of pursuing these different modes of investigative poetry. Second, we review the literature regarding the recent turn across the humanities to a concern with social justice, hence grounding our thoughts about investigative poetry within the tradition of engaged scholars who use their positions as teachers and writers to try to help expand democratic rights, economic opportunities, and cultural aspirations for an ever larger circle of readers, students, and fellow activists. Third, to illustrate some of the promises and problems with one of the main intellectual traditions informing investigative poetry, we examine the literary, pedagogical, and anthropological ambitions of the movement known loosely as *ethnopoetics*. Although our reading of the various branches of ethnopoetics grants their important roles in initiating conversations about multiculturalism, bringing a literary consciousness to anthropology, breaking down positivism, and criticizing colonialism, our readings of specific ethnopoems finds them to be consistently removed from questions of power. Fourth, we celebrate the dense triumphs of John Dos Passos, the early Carolyn Forché, and Peter Dale Scott, all of whom merge concerns for social justice and a commitment to writing a political poetry of witness in texts that, although historical, political, personal, philosophical, and beautiful, consistently place a critique of power at the center of their work. Taken as a whole, these four sections offer readers a sweeping overview of the opportunities and obligations of both producing and consuming "Aria in Time of War"; that is, we celebrate those who honor the persistence of poetry in the face of horror, who commit their academic work to social justice, and who merge the two—scholarship and poetry—in the political work of witnessing.

▣ 1. Oscillating Between No-Time and the Blizzard of Facts: Forché, Sanders, and the Question of Historical Context

We begin with eight haunting lines from "On Earth," the central poem from Forché's (2003) unsettling *Blue Hour*:

a random life caught in the net of purpose (p. 26)

a search without hope for hope (p. 27)

America a warship on the horizon at morning (p. 29)

and it is certain someone will be at that very moment pouring milk (p. 30)

aria in time of war (p. 32)

black with burnt-up meaning (p. 35)

history decaying into images (p. 42)

inhabiting a body to be abolished (p. 45)

On and on it goes in relentless ethereal detail, working methodically through a 48-page alphabetically structured poem meant to approximate the feel of a Gnostic abecedarian hymn, ending with but one entry for the letter z: "zero" (p. 68).

These lines prompt readers to wonder about the mysterious relationships among agency and chance, personal volition and historical velocity ("a random life caught in the net of purpose"); to empathically walk a mile in the shoes of someone who bravely, yet apparently fruitlessly, pursues justice ("a search without hope for hope"); to ponder a world in which American power is feared by faraway peoples ("America a warship on the horizon at morning"); to know that despite such fears, someone somewhere is enjoying a quiet moment of sustenance and plenty ("and it is certain someone will be at that very moment pouring milk"); to listen closely to hear whether the explosions of war and the silent misery of poverty are graced with beauty ("aria in time of war"); to ask after all that has been lost in the ever-piling wreckage of history ("black with burnt-up meaning"); to ponder what it means to think historically in a world that appears with each day to possess meaning not from words and sounds and touches and smells but rather from the blinding whir of mass-produced pictures ("history decaying into images"); and to imagine for a moment what it must feel like to be one of the damned ("inhabiting a body to be abolished"), condemned perhaps to die on death row, or on skid row, or from the torturous spiral into hopelessness, where one inhabits a body that slowly loses meaning. Thus, Forché invites us on a terrifying voyage into the mysteries of life during an age of mass-produced misery.

Readers are left to fill in the blanks as they choose, to complete the jigsaw puzzle of horror by supplying details from their own warehouses of knowledge and memory and even fantasy, for who can hold such sweeping imagery together without moving from the realm of expertise and experience to imagination and projection? The danger of enabling such projection is that it invites readers to move from thinking about the specific causes and consequences of historical *loss* to nostalgically longing for some abstract *absence*. As LaCapra (2001) argues in *Writing History, Writing Trauma*, this shift from loss to absence is potentially dangerous because "when loss is converted into (or encrypted in an indiscriminately generalized rhetoric of) absence, one faces the impasse of endless melancholy" (p. 46). Moving from the healthy mourning of specific historical loss to the endless web of melancholy is fueled, LaCapra claims, by a tendency "to shroud, perhaps even to etherealize, them [historical losses] in a generalized discourse of absence" that relies on figures that are "abstract, evacuated, disembodied" (pp. 48–49). Forché's dilemma in *Blue Hour*, then, as in all works that strive to merge hard-hitting politics and joyous poetic reverie while roaming across a wide swath of time, revolves around the question of how to provide a cosmopolitan, truly globalizing perspective on the tragedy of life without falling into the trap of morose and politically paralyzing longing for immaterial absence.[2]

In her introduction to the magisterial anthology of poems, *Against Forgetting*, Forché (1993) argues, "The poetry of witness frequently resorts to paradox and difficult equivocation, to the invocation of what is *not* there as if it *were*. . . . That it must defy common sense to speak of the common indicates that traditional modes of thought, the purview of common sense, no longer *make* sense" (p. 40). We imagine that most readers will grant the wisdom of this claim, for who has not thrilled at the truth conveyed in an oblique poem or song or dance, bringing a rush of sensemaking greater than anything ever found in dry tomes of history or sociology or political science? And who has not found himself or herself walking through historical wreckage or working through a novel with the eerie sense that he or she were conversing with the dead (Gordon, 1997)? But at what point does defying common sense and invoking the dead fade into helpless abstraction, into the infinitely repeatable layering of random projections against one another (O'Rourke, 2003)? Like flipping distractedly through 100 channels of late-night television, or watching billboards tick by on some anonymous stretch of highway, don't such invocations of the dead and such refusals of common sense ultimately leave readers awash in confusion? Where are we? What is the date? What are the stakes? Who are the players? *Why does this matter?*

Sanders's (2000) *America: A History in Verse* answers these questions on every page. "I love the way my nation seethes/I love its creativity/& the flow of its wild needs," Sanders proclaims in his introduction (p. 9). Channeling the epic and synthesizing sweep of Whitman, Sanders thus offers readers a love poem qualified by the knowledge that "I know of course/that I have to trace the/violence of my nation" (p. 8). These poems matter, then, because they aspire to rewrite the history of America circa 1900–1939 and, by investigating specific historical losses, to provide readers with the factual knowledge, rhetorical resources, and political encouragement to try to reclaim the nation's better half from its lingering—and recently ascendant—demons. Sanders pursues this goal by studying the nation's players, institutions, struggles, and sounds, which he offers up in newspaper-like snippets organized by years. Thus, whereas Forché's melancholy *Blue Hour* offers a chillingly beautiful yet ultimately disempowering meditation on absence, Sanders's *America* offers a compelling, if didactic, tribute to the winners and losers of specific historical battles.

As one of the founders of the 1950s micropublishing culture that freed artists from corporate constraints, as a seminal New York hipster during the beat generation, as an accomplished pre-punk musician, as witness to the travesty of the Democratic Convention in Chicago in 1968, and on and on—in short, as one of those miraculous figures who seem to always be at the center of what is *happening*—Sanders has for the past 50 years or so been a tireless and good-natured gadfly watching America struggle to achieve the glory of its promises. Given his personal experiences with some of the leading artists and activists who have prompted America's cultural and political changes over the past decades, it comes as no surprise that Sanders reminds readers that history hinges in large part on individual actors exercising agency. *America* accordingly offers a "who's who" catalogue of heroes and villains in action.

For example, here is one of Sanders's many loving tributes to Isadora Duncan, who first danced in America in 1908 and who

> based her revolution in Dance
>
> on the natural grace of bodies moving in Beauty
>
> It was ancient, she said, from the form-loving Greeks
>
> & so when she showed a nipple or knee
>
> she could claim those ancient roots
>
> She was an advocate of free love
>
> a political radical
>
> & a stunning emblem to the women
>
> who wanted to smoke, strut, paint
>
> write, dance, & fuck more freely. (p. 80)

Sanders (2000) shows us a brave woman dancing her and her sisters' way toward freedom. Close readers might want more poetic detail here. *Just how did she reveal that nipple or knee? What did it look like? How did crowds respond? Were lovers actually thinking of Duncan when they fucked more freely?* But in these poems Sanders is less interested in the micro-logical details than in the ways iconic figures and actions function synecdochically, as representative parts that reveal the majesty of the whole. Indeed, as Sanders (1976) declares in his manifesto *Investigative Poetry,* "the essence of investigative poetry" is to create "lines of lyric beauty [that] descend from data clusters," hence both seducing and empowering readers with "a melodic blizzard of data-fragments" (p. 9). Synecdoche is therefore the rhetorical trope that enables Sanders to weave individual lines of beauty into a collective swirl of data fragments and thus to write poetic history.[3]

Indeed, *America* is based largely on the trope of synecdoche, which hinges on the convertibility between parts and wholes, on the representational electricity assumed to link actors to their epochs. For example, whereas Duncan stands as a representative woman, as the individual embodiment (part) of the period's struggle for women's freedom of mind and movement (whole), so Sanders reverses the equation and offers institutions (wholes) as symbolic aggregates of individual hope (part). Put differently, because even exceptional individuals are only as strong as their larger community bonds, Sanders is obliged to represent not only radical individuals but also the hope-sustaining and change-making institutions that support their visionary work. For example, Sanders's investigations into the struggle against racial violence lead him to celebrate the 1909 founding of the National Association for the Advancement of Colored People (NAACP):

> & there comes a time in the time-track
>
> when you work for good, no matter the danger
>
> . . .
>
> There comes a time—
>
> You can look in photo archives
>
> at the shiny-eyed trash
>
> gathered about a lynching tree
>
> as if it were the homecoming parade
>
> —therefore the NAACP. (pp. 83–84)

Although Sanders is a relentless critic of the "shiny-eyed trash" who choose violence over understanding, readers may wish for more details regarding the pleasures of crowds at lynchings. That is, instead of 4 lines describing the energies of white supremacists, why not 30 lines showing us in more detail what the alluded to—but not cited— "photo archives" teach attentive viewers? More than just a quibble about the focus or length of the poem, such questions carry for investigative poets a heavy methodological burden, for we proceed with the understanding that just as melancholia stands as the paralyzing result of failed mourning, so simply rebuking one's enemies—even lynch mobs—begins the process of moving from understanding specific historical loss to projecting terms of generalized absence and otherness. In this case, the complexities of white supremacy are glossed within a heroic tribute to the NAACP, but one cannot fathom the gravity of the task faced by the NAACP without a more nuanced understanding of what its members were fighting against. We are thus asking for the poem to accept the admittedly heavy burden of playing a more clearly pedagogical function.[4]

Moreover, without showing us the complexities of the players involved in a given struggle in a clearly pedagogical fashion, much of Sanders's *America* might feel to some readers like an exercise in nostalgia. For example, here is one of his many tributes to the International Workers of the World:

In Fresno in '11

another protest for the right of free speech

again the jails were packed

and Wobblies were singing and giving speeches

to supporters and the curious

gathered outside the jail

. . .

When it was obvious that

more and more Wobblies were coming to Fresno

to commit civil disobedience

the power structure relented

and rescinded the ban on speaking in the streets. (pp. 87–88)

In 1911, the Wobblies were fighting for workers' rights, yet they rocketed into national consciousness a few years later because of their brave stand against America entering World War I. But as Sanders notes in his poems from the years 1917 and 1918, it would not be long before the Espionage Act was crushing dissent, sending thousands of protesters to jail and shipping boatloads of socialists back to Europe. At the same time, the draft scooped up additional thousands of young men to be marched to their deaths in Europe's lice-infested trenches. Although many readers will thrill at the image of brave Wobblies fighting for justice in Fresno in 1911, the longer view is ultimately one of defeat: the Wobblies were crushed, free speech was curtailed, and America sloughed off to a disastrously bloody war. Regardless of what readers think of this narrative, the pedagogical function of investigative poetry suggests that Sanders should have offered extensive referencing so that readers could make up their own minds about this version of the Wobblies and America during the World War I era, yet no such reference matter is provided.[5]

Nonetheless, despite the sense that it is infused with nostalgia, that it lacks the referencing matter required to help readers take the pedagogical step of beginning their own research, and that it sometimes skims too quickly across the surface of events, Sanders's *America* accumulates into a majestic—even awe-inspiring—narrative, for by moving from the exuberance and genius of individuals (Duncan and her revolutionary dancing) to the strength and dignity of organizations (the NAACP and its fight against racism) to the brave triumph of struggles for freedom (the Wobblies' free speech victory in Fresno in 1911) and back again, zigzagging all the while through a kaleidoscopic montage of historical fragments, the poem offers a model of engaged citizenship, literally a handbook of democracy in action. Indeed, whereas Forché's *Blue Hour* can feel oppressively bleak—"collective memory a dread of things to come" (p. 30), "scoop of earth: slivers of femurs, metacarpals" (p. 51), "your mother waving goodbye in the flames" (p. 68)— Sanders's *America* reminds readers of the bravery of our forebears and thus of our obligations to continue their fights for justice.

In addition to this empowering and activating function, Sanders's *America* relishes the more traditionally poetic slices of joy that slither through daily experience. Indeed, by juxtaposing horror against the frivolous, joyous, and sometimes brilliant aspects of daily life, *America* provides a startlingly honest glimpse into the lived sensation of watching history crash all around you. Sanders is particularly interested in the relationship between sound and politics, as in this passage about 1925:

George Gershwin's *Piano Concerto*

Prokoviev's *Symphony #2*

Aaron Copeland's *Symphony #1*

and in Chicago Louis Armstrong began the Hot Five recordings

while December 10

the Grand Old Opry began radio broadcasts

Henry Ford, hating jazz

set up a series of folk dances. (p. 245)

One could obviously write hundreds of pages on each of these figures, but Sanders appears to be more interested in letting readers figure out the implications of such juxtapositions. Like Whitman's famous catalogue poems, then, Sanders makes no attempt to dive into the complexity of these figures, instead positioning them as icons loaded with apparently self-evident meaning, as synecdoches meant to suggest the larger forces at play. For example, it is assumed that one reads the line about Armstrong and understands the importance of the Hot Five moving away from big band formats toward what would eventually become hard swinging bebop; it is assumed that one reads the line about the Grand Old Opry and understands the significance of the mass production (via radio, press, and eventually television) of a nostalgia-based, quietly racist, down home country aesthetic; it is assumed that one reads the line about Copeland and understands how he sought to merge the nation's many musical vernaculars into a majestic symphony-of-the-whole; and so on, with readers left to surround each line with their own comprehension. In this sense, then, Sanders appears to be practicing less what we are calling investigative poetry than a Whitman-like catalogue poetry, for what we have here are not so much investigations into the complexity of specific moments as suggestive shards, fleeting images, and passing glimpses that are meant to be self-evidently and transparently significant (Buell, 1968; Chari, 1972; Mason, 1973; Reed, 1977).

The fact that these terms—self-evident and transparent—stand in absolute contrast to the allusive and impenetrably dense verse in Forché's *Blue Hour* demonstrates how even though both Sanders and Forché strive to write a political and historical poetry of witness, they practice dramatically different forms of investigative poetry. Indeed, the vast aesthetic differences between *Blue Hour* and *America* raise a host of questions about the possible relationships among different forms of poetry, politics, witnessing, and historical scholarship. In fact, the poems addressed here throw the terms listed earlier into question, forcing us to reappraise not only how they speak to each other but also what they stand for in their own right. Before addressing how investigative poetry speaks to these issues, it is necessary to review the ways that contemporary scholars have tried to reconsider and to merge historical, political, and artistic works to produce engaged scholarship that is both witness to and participant in struggles for social justice.

## ▣ 2. SOCIAL JUSTICE AND THE OBLIGATIONS AND OPPORTUNITIES OF ENGAGED SCHOLARS

Although Forché and Sanders both clearly see their poems as fulfilling political roles, their divergent aesthetic strategies might leave readers wondering about how the fight for social justice figures into such work. One way of answering that question is to shift genres and to address the flood of materials calling on scholars to become more active in their communities' various struggles for social justice. Although it is not difficult to piece together a loose genealogy of intellectuals concerned with issues of social justice over the past centuries, we are glad to see that during recent years scholars across a variety of disciplines have begun arguing in a systematic manner that those teacher-activists committed to the ends of social justice, while still cherishing the wondrously messy means of democratic life, need to approach issues of social justice not only as sites of research but also as sites of engagement with disadvantaged communities (Crabtree, 1998; Frey, 1998; Hartnett, 1998). Located loosely between Forché's melancholic absence and Sanders's exuberant lists, this social justice literature calls for scholarship that speaks to sweeping ideas by paying deft attention to local needs.

Our thinking here is deeply indebted to Dwight Conquergood, a performance studies professor at Northwestern University who spent years doing research on, and advocating on behalf of, the gangs with whom he lived as a neighbor, teacher, and substitute father figure in the decimated Cabrini Green public housing of Chicago. Conquergood lectured widely about his experiences and wrote about them and their implications for academics and activists in two brilliant book chapters (Conquergood, 1994, 1995). Inspired by Conquergood's bravery, Larry Frey, Barnett Pearce, Mark Pollock, Lee Artz, and Bren Murphy, colleagues at Loyola University in Chicago, implored their fellow speech communication scholars in 1996 to conduct research "not only *about* but *for* and *in the interests of* the people with whom" their research was conducted (Frey, Pearce, Pollock, Artz, & Murphy, 1996, p. 117). This means that scholars can no longer assume they are objective outsiders analyzing static objects of inquiry; instead, in this new model of engaged scholarship, researchers become subjects mutually enmeshed in the processes they are studying. Following Conquergood's lead, then, Frey and his colleagues asked engaged scholars to channel their academic work toward pressing community needs and thus to produce works that "foreground ethical concerns," "commit to structural analyses of ethical problems," "adopt an activist orientation," and "seek identification with others" (p. 111; see also Adelman & Frey, 1997).

For specific ways of thinking about the prospects of teaching on, researching about, and fighting for social justice, we have been influenced by Pierre Bourdieu's "For a Scholarship With Commitment," an essay adapted from a presentation he gave as part of a panel organized by Edward Said for the 1999 meeting of the Modern Language Association (MLA). Bourdieu (2000) recommends that scholars hoping to make a difference pursue four goals: (a) "produce and disseminate instruments of defense against symbolic domination"; (b) engage in "discursive critique," meaning analyses of the "sociological determinants that bear on the producers of dominant discourse"; (c) "counter the pseudoscientific authority of authorized experts"; and (d) "help to create social conditions for the collective production of realist utopias" (p. 42). We may conceptualize these imperatives as pointing to four modes of critical activity. First is helping to teach and popularize the critical thinking skills necessary for citizens to become more conscientious consumers of mass media; we may think of this as *debunking cultural symbolism*. Second is demonstrating through rigorous case studies how dominant discourse reflects the economic imperatives of elites; we may think of this as *analyzing class privilege*. Third is revealing and helping others to reveal the political assumptions and biases of experts within specific fields of inquiry; we may think of this as *becoming rhetorical critics*. And fourth is both imagining and advocating alternative ways of being; we may think of this as *inventing new possibilities*. In that same panel, Elaine Scarry put this fourth imperative in lovely terms— terms that would make Emerson and Whitman proud—arguing that teachers of literature and the arts share a special burden to cultivate in both their students and their communities "a reverence for the work of the imagination" (Scarry, 2000, p. 21; see also Becker, 1994). The task, then, is to fulfill Bourdieu's four critical criteria in forms that meet Scarry's aesthetic criteria, hence our fascination with the possibilities of investigative poetry.

The one obvious shortcoming of the suggestions of Bourdieu, Scarry, and their fellow MLA participants is that even while asking us to pursue scholarship with commitment, they tend to privilege certain traditional forms of textual production, hence excluding (perhaps unwittingly) many genres of human communication. This explains Conquergood's insistence that engaged scholarship and activism must take into account "the embodied dynamics that constitute meaningful human interaction" by striving for "a hermeneutics of experience, copresence, humility, and vulnerability." Recent literature on ethnography and performance studies has demonstrated the many ways these imperatives may be pursued, often with stunning results, yet as we detail in what follows, we fear that much of this work has tended to fall into a troubling pattern of sensationalism and narcissism, celebrating the raw immediacy of personal experience over any attempt to make structural sense of the larger historical, political, and cultural conditions surrounding daily life.

For both would-be investigative poets in particular and engaged scholars in general, then, the methodological conundrum is striving to balance self with society, text with context, the existential delirium of the now with the scholarly rigor of analysis— all the while honoring the obligations to social justice discussed here. Among the many subgenres and submovements within contemporary arts and letters, ethnopoetics stands as a significant attempt to tackle these conundrums; therefore, we turn to the problems and possibilities of ethnopoetics as a case study of how poets have sought to weave historical, political, and personal materials into a poetry of witness.

## ▣ 3. THE LESSONS AND LEGACIES OF ETHNOPOETICS

Ethnopoetics could be labeled investigative poetry's immediate predecessor, for it was a seminal attempt to make poetry political by merging a critique of colonialism, soft anthropology, and a poetics of witnessing. The term *ethnopoetics* was coined in 1967 by Jerome Rothenberg, Dennis Tedlock, and their colleagues. As Rothenberg (1990) argues, the project of ethnopoetics peaked during the late 1970s before *Alcheringa,* the magazine that Rothenberg and Tedlock founded in 1970 as an exhibition of ethnopoetic practices, finally sputtered out in 1980 (p. 8). Like defining any advanced cultural and/or academic practice, defining ethnopoetics is difficult (p. 8). As Friedrich (in press) argues, the term is "protean" and has adopted many connotations during the past three decades. For example, foregrounding its role in practicing what has since come to be known as multiculturalism, Tedlock (1992) defines ethnopoetics as the "study of the verbal arts in a worldwide range of languages and cultures" (p. 81). Likewise, Rothenberg (1990) argues that ethnopoetics "refers to an attempt to investigate on a transcultural scale the range of possible poetries that had not only been imagined but put into practice by other human beings" (p. 5). For Tedlock and Rothenberg, then, ethnopoetics is an attempt to think about poetry in a global context and thus to consider the roles of poets as witnesses to, critics of, and activists committed to healing the damage wrought by colonialism and violent modernity. Indeed, Rothenberg argues that one of the chief goals of ethnopoetics is to engage in "the struggle with imperialism, racism, chauvinism, etc." (p. 5). That quotation-ending "etc." is significant, for it indicates the off-hand, sloppy way in which much of Rothenberg's work on ethnopoetics collapses specific political crises into one catch-all basket of wrongs—*you know, modernity, colonialism, racism, chauvinism, etc.*

In contrast to that sweeping "etc.", we have argued here that investigative poetry is committed to a version of synecdoche in which grand claims can be supported only through micro-logical analyses based on deep historical scholarship. We return to this critique of the sloppy uses of "etc." that seem to plague the Rothenberg school of ethnopoetics later, but for now we turn to Friedrich, who argues that the genre falls into two categories: analytic and synthetic. Whereas analytic ethnopoetics operates on a "meta" level by inspecting other ethnopoetic works, synthetic ethnopoetics either creates an anthropological poem that bridges a gap between two cultures or translates a poem from one culture to another; in both synthetic cases, the goal is to make one culture familiar to another. For example, Friedrich (in press) praises Gary Snyder's "Anasazi" for "converting a foreign culture and poetry into poems that speak to Western, specifically American, sensitivities." Snyder's poem is a fine example of synthetic ethnopoetics, then, because it does the work of anthropology in the form of poetry, both enticing and enabling readers to transcend their provincialism.

Here is how Snyder (1974) brings the Anasazi to his readers:

Anasazi,

Anasazi,

tucked up in clefts in the cliffs

growing strict fields of corn

sinking deeper and deeper in earth

up to your hips in Gods

  your head all turned to eagle-down

  & lightning for knees and elbows

your eyes full of pollen

  the smell of bats.

  the flavor of sandstone

  grit on the tongue.

women

birthing

at the foot of ladders in the dark.

trickling streams in hidden canyons

under the cold rolling desert

corn-basked     wide-eyed

red baby

rock lip home,

Anasazi. (p. 3)

The poem offers a beginner's loving guide to some basic facts about the Anasazi, namely that they live on cliffs in the desert, corn is a major part of their culture, and they live in close proximity with their gods—in short, they are human. Snyder (1974) takes us to a different time and place, to a world he describes in "Control Burn" as one "more/like,/when it belonged to the Indians/Before" (p. 19). Like Rothenberg's "etc.", that poem-closing "Before" indicates the loose way in which this branch of ethnopoetics envisions itself as searching for a premodern, prehistoric, pre-Western world of innocence and virtue. But by conveying his sense of this lost civilization in verse that reads like a series of textbook stereotypes, Snyder teaches us little about the culture of the Anasazi. Indeed, the romanticization of Anasazi life makes the "Before" of "Control Burn" sound like a naïve plea to return to a world that is long gone and to do so while ignoring the fact that even when it existed it was—like our own world—wracked with political, economic, and cultural dilemmas.

Therefore, it is difficult to imagine anthropologists or historians taking such poems seriously. However, for Snyder and some ethnopoets, the function of such poems is not so much to stand as rigorous scholarship as to stand as rhetorical platforms from which to launch scathing critiques of Western modernity. For example, Snyder's (1974) "The Call of the Wild" leaps forward from the Anasazi to offer a blistering critique of "All these Americans up in special cities in the sky/Dumping poisons and explosives" (p. 23). Published amid the war in Vietnam, this clear reference to the saturation bombings sanctioned by President Richard Nixon invites readers to think about the deep historical connections among Indian genocide, environmental destruction, and the butchery under way in the name of defeating communism. By thinking in this multitemporal manner, by holding the Anasazi and the Vietnamese in one's mind at the same time, Snyder gains historical and political leverage for his claim in "Tomorrow's Song" that

The USA slowly lost its mandate

in the middle and later twentieth century

it never gave the mountains and rivers,

   trees and animals,

  a vote.

all the people turned away from it. (p. 77)

Reading these lines in the midst of another set of U.S.-triggered wars, raging now in Afghanistan and Iraq, one is struck by the commonsensical—yet so often overlooked—argument that there is an intimate relation between the violence used to demolish nature and the violence used to murder our fellow humans. Indeed, in the face of the well-oiled machinery of death that slaughtered the Indians, that murdered millions of Vietnamese, that is currently leveling Afghanistan and Iraq, and that has left a worldwide trail of ecological destruction in its path, we are struck by how relevant—how powerful—this poem feels 30 years after its first publication (Thomas, 1995).

Whereas Snyder thus uses loosely anthropological poems about the deep past to gain historical leverage for a political critique of the violence of colonialism and ecological destruction, other proponents of ethnopoetics see the genre as more directly concerned with producing a form of cultural criticism that points toward multiculturalism. For example, in his review of ethnopoetics in *Symposium of the Whole: A Range of Discourse Toward an Ethnopoetics,* Turner (1983) argues that ethnopoetics is committed to "making visible." "The more we are aware of the multiplicity of Others," he argues, "the more we become aware of the multiple 'selves' we contain, the social roles we have 'internalized'" (pp. 340–341). For Turner, then, ethnopoetics explores the polyglot multiplicity of the social self, thus leading to a self-reflexive humility that opens the door to multiculturalism: "Once they [our tired versions of 'self'] are 'made visible' they are revealed as faintly comic figures. . . . It may be that the recognition of diversity in cultural voices has the therapeutic function of confronting us with the problem of the One and the Many—a new reflexivity in itself" (p. 341). This version of ethnopoetics thus functions as verbal therapy, aspiring to help its readers question their taken-for-granted cultural assumptions, and includes the assumption that deconstructing tired versions of a unified Western self will help to bridge the distance between these now problematized selves and the multiple Others who linger outside the comfortable living rooms of the West. From this perspective, ethnopoetics aspires to produce cultural criticism capable of functioning both as political engagement and as personal therapy.

Given this framework, let us return to another piece of ethnopoetics, "The New (Colonial) Ball Game" by Robert C. Williamson. A professor of anthropology at the University of Saskatchewan, Williamson specializes in fieldwork on the Inuit Indians. Attempting both to make the humiliations of colonialism clearer for the colonizer and to vent his own frustrations at the difficulty of the process of making the invisible visible, Williamson (1985) offers the following scene:

Then the little man

Who'd just arrived

And felt important

And, of course, responsible

Said nicely, pompously

With British vowels

As tight and round

As his big ass

How everybody should be grateful

For the Christly whites

Who came, of course, to help

And not to satisfy themselves

And here in their own country

For their sakes

We all should

(As it surely must inevitably

Come to be

And the sooner, don't you see

The better for us all)—

Talk White

    For once their words will fit

    The words we hear the most

OK

Do this

Right now

And hurry, see?

Fuck off. (pp. 189–190)

Brady (2000) claims that "by varying their forms of expression to include poetry, anthropologists attempt to say things that might not be said as effectively or at all any other way" (p. 956). Williamson's (1985) poem-ending and resounding "Fuck off" surely fits this model, for it is hard to imagine this line finding its way into his professional academic work. So the poem gives Williamson the linguistic latitude to say what he cannot say elsewhere. But does this expressive latitude enable the poet to write a powerful poem? Does the poem show us anything that is not already the subject of hundreds, if not thousands, of stereotypical images? We do not even know where this colonial ballgame takes place, what the date is, who the players are, or what game is being played, so we are in the realm of abstraction, the generic, the ahistorical no-place of generalized anticolonial anger. The same concerns have been raised about Forché's *Blue Hour*, but at least that poem's stunning beauty leaves readers awash in reverberating images that (hopefully) provoke further critical reflection. In traditional poetry criticism, such abstract verse might be taken as allegorical, as aspiring to offer a transhistorical moral lesson, yet Williamson's "Fuck off" hardly counts as an allegory. So even though the poem succeeds as therapy for its author, who must have been carrying that "Fuck off" around with him for quite a while just waiting to launch it into space, the poem fails as a poem and fails as anthropology, amounting ultimately to little more than a self-serving rant. Moreover, given the professed pedagogical function of ethnopoetics to transcend racism and cultural chauvinism by making the faraway and the strange more human and thus more familiar to Western readers, we would have to say that the poem is a pedagogical failure as well, for it teaches us little about the people being oppressed by the "little man" who speaks with "British vowels."

We have seen how Snyder merges anthropology, history, and political criticism to produce blistering and beautiful poems that speak directly to the carnage of the war in Vietnam, and we have watched as Williamson uses a poem about colonialism as verbal therapy. To further complicate our treatment of ethnopoetics, let us inquire as well about its practices as a form of cultural translation. *Alcheringa* was among the primary sources of ethnopoetics. Its "Statement of Intention" (1970) claims that "ALCHERINGA will not be a scholarly 'journal of ethnopoetics' so much as a place where tribal poetry can appear in English translation & can act (in the oldest & newest of poetic translations) to change men's minds & lives" (p. 1). For example, consider this version of "What Harm Has She Dreamt?" (1970), a Quechua tribal poem translated in the first issue of *Alcheringa:*

Her long hair is her pillow

the girl is sleeping on her hair.

She cries blood

she does not cry tears

she cries blood.

What is she dreaming?

what harm is she dreaming?

Who hurt her?

who hurt her heart like this?

Whistle to her, whistle, whistle,

little bird

so she wakes

so she wakes now

whistle whistle

little bird. (p. 50)

The poem presumably enables a Western audience to hear a Quechua orator implicate the violence of colonialism, a force so powerful and insipid that it has seeped into the dreams of its victims. The effort is clearly heartfelt, yet without massive prefatory information, we suspect that most readers will learn little from this poem about the tribal culture in question. Where do the tribe members live? Who is causing the tribe's young women to cry tears of blood? These may seem like unfair burdens to place on any individual translation, yet without answering these historically specific questions, the poem/translation cannot help but produce a vague and characterless sense of some premodern other, some far-off culture about which we know little if not nothing. Rather than bridging the gap between smug Western assumptions of privilege and the lived experiences of cultures on the fringes of modernity, those that have been shattered by colonialism, such poems leave readers uninformed, clueless, feeling vaguely touched yet not empowered to take any specific action.

One of the many goals of ethnopoetics was to offer such translations as a corrective to what has been widely criticized as the creeping biases leading to sloppy, if not downright exploitative, translations of the works and cultures of non-Western peoples. As Basso (1988) argues, there is "a growing conviction among linguistic anthropologists that the oral literatures of Native American people have been inaccurately characterized, wrongly represented, and improperly translated" (p. 809). Such translating inaccuracies pose a significant problem for cultural critics from a variety of fields, for as Clifford (1988/1999) demonstrates in *The Predicament of Culture,* anthropologists such as Bronislaw Malinowski allowed their colonial biases to shape their fieldwork on other cultures, hence leading to supposedly scientific reporting that in fact mirrors Western prejudices (pp. 92–113). In response to this anthropological dilemma, ethnopoets sought to produce translations that were closer to the spirit of their originals, hence trying to bring to Western readers a more authentic sense of the foreign cultures under consideration. Although this is an admirable goal, the fact is that there can be no direct and unclouded transcribing of a tribal poem into forms accessible to Western readers. *All translations are interpretations.*

This fact is demonstrated nicely in *Nineteen Ways of Looking at Wang Wei,* a fascinating study by Weinberger and Paz (1987) of 19 translations of an eighth-century Buddhist poem by Wang Wei. Weinberger and Paz conclude, "In its way a spiritual exercise, translation is dependent on the dissolution of the translator's ego: an absolute humility toward the text. A bad translation is the insistent voice of the translator—that is, when one sees no poet and hears only the translator speaking" (p. 17). But as *Nineteen Ways of Looking* suggests, one always hears the translator speaking—often in rhythms and voices that bring new depth and meaning to the poem. Indeed, because all translations are interpretive acts that, at their best, aspire to fulfill pedagogical and artistic functions, ethnopoets have come to realize that translation is a form of cultural criticism and artistic production in its own right (Alfred, 1999, pp. 55–65; Rosaldo, 1989/1993, pp. 25–87; Smith, 1999). From this perspective, then, translating poems from cultures on the fringes of modernity amounts not so much to a doomed attempt to reclaim a lost past or an unsullied Other as to an attempt to multiply—and hence add diversity to—the voices mingling in our conversations about the norms, obligations, and hopes of modernity.

Given the sweeping nature of that last claim, it is important before closing our discussion of ethnopoetics to add yet another layer of complicating theoretical factors and one more set of readings of ethnopoems. We accomplish both tasks by turning to the work of Ivan Brady, who for many years has been among the leading theorists and artists of this vein of work. Brady is particularly instructive, for whereas we have referred previously to various strains of ethnopoetics, Brady prefers the term "anthropological poetics." For Brady (2004), anthropological poetics consists of three interrelated yet distinct categories: "*ethnopoetics,* 'the emics of native poetries that are midwifed by Western poets'; *native poetry,* the poetry of traditional native poets; and *ethnographic poetics,* the poetic productions of ethnographers" (p. 639). We have already addressed examples of native poetry (the Quechua poem "What Harm Has She

Dreamt?") and "ethnographic poetics" (Snyder's "Anasazi" and Williamson's "The New [Colonial] Ball Game"), and so we now focus on Brady's version of ethnopoetics. In anthropology, "emic" entails using the normative values and symbolic categories of those studied rather than imposing one's own cultural biases, and a "midwife" is someone who helps in the process of birth in particular and creation more generally (and who may, as in the case of the midwife who birthed the first author's first child, be a man); thus, for Brady, ethnopoetics relies on the local idioms of groups studied by anthropologists and the flexible forms of Western poetry, translation, and storytelling to aid in the process of creating new forms of expression.

To watch how this process unfolds, we turn to Brady's (2003) masterful *The Time at Darwin's Reef: Poetic Explorations in Anthropology and History.* We should note that Brady is an accomplished anthropologist who specializes in Pacific Island cultures, so whereas the ethnopoems and translations discussed previously felt slender on anthropological details, Brady's poems bristle with a lifetime of research and personal experience; this expertise is reflected in helpful sets of references and introductions to clusters of poems. As evidence of the book's (and Brady's) remarkably broad sense of time and place, *Darwin's Reef* closes with an alphabetical "Place List" and a chronological "Date List," both of which include information relevant to the other. For example, the Place List begins with "Abaiang Island, February 14, 1840," closes with "USMCRD, San Diego, California, August 27, 1958," and includes 60 other place/time entries sandwiched in between (pp. 128–129). Thus, before reading a single poem, readers recognize from glancing through the Place List and Date List that *Darwin's Reef* addresses the long history of naval conquest, beginning for the purposes of this book in the South Pacific during the 1840s, culminating in the world's largest floating arms depot, San Diego, during the late 1950s, and wreaking havoc on all the places in between. The Place List and Date List thus function as semiotic machines of imaginative yet historically grounded suggestions, producing juxtapositions, layerings, and clues meant to lead the reader on geographic and temporal journeys through the wreckage of colonialism.

"Time" at Darwin's Reef is therefore, as in Snyder's (1974) *Turtle Island,* less linear than in traditional historical writings and more like the twisting, reverberating, ecological, and even spiritual forms it often takes in folklore. For example, in the poem that names the book, "The Time at Darwin's Reef"—located with the place and date listings that preface each poem as "Playa de la Muerte, South Pacific, July 4, 1969"—Brady conveys time as "High Time, 1:05 p.m., Fiji time" (local clock time, p. 69), as "Time to Get Down" (from the Cessna flying overhead, p. 69), as "Island Time" (the deep ecological time of natural change, p. 70), as "Copy time in the coral" (the movements of coral reproduction as seen in "ejaculating rocks," pp. 71–72), as "Magic Time" (p. 73), and so on in a dizzying multiplication of possible times, most of them rooted not in Western notions of clocks but rather in the natural temporal forms of tides, seasons, and life cycles. Taken together, these layered "times" indicate a spiritual sense of completeness, of multiplicities woven into an organic whole, of ecological centeredness.

Lest readers assume that Brady's gorgeous experiments in temporal confusions lapse into political complacency, "Proem for the Queen of Spain" layers such temporal dislocations against spatial and political fragments, hence creating a sense of bitter poetic judgment. The bulk of the piece is a letter (fictional but true to its historical moment) from Fernando Junipero Dominguez, written in "New Spain" (Mexico) in 1539, in which the writer thanks the queen for bringing to his people "the Embrace of the Mission and the Love of God, Amen" (p. 51). This is a letter, then, that demonstrates how colonized peoples internalized oppression, in this case in the form of bowing to a foreign god brought to the New World by a foreign empire. Tucked within the letter, however, Brady offers expletive-laced commands from U.S. troops in Vietnam, who shout at the locals "Nam fuckin' xuong dat! Lie the fuck down! Or y'all gonna fuckin' die!" (p. 51). The end matter following the poem provides multiple historical references on the history of Dominguez, so the poem fulfills the pedagogical function of both seducing readers to think historically and then leading them to the necessary information to pursue their own further readings. Much like Snyder's juxtaposing the Anasazi against Nixon's saturation bombing of Vietnamese peasants, then, Brady's inserting dialogue from U.S. soldiers within a 1539 letter to the queen of Spain illustrates a sense of continuity linking the Spanish invasion of Mexico to the U.S. invasion of Vietnam. Against the deeply satisfying ecological times of "Time at Darwin's Reef," then, "Proem for the Queen of Spain" offers a chilling sense of *imperial time*, of the looping repetitive horrors of conquest.

Despite this numbing sense of the ways that imperial powers have savaged weaker peoples for centuries, the bulk of Brady's poems are committed to loving and often gorgeous tributes to the ways that even the strangest Others are in fact not only human but also human in ways that are deeply familiar to Western readers, for as Brady (1991) argues elsewhere, ethnopoems function by "defining the humanity of humankind and positing it as something to be achieved in practice" (p. 6). As demonstrated in *Darwin's Reef*, those practices will be so multifarious, so convoluted, and even so magical that it takes remarkable kindness and patience to appreciate their significance. As Brady (2004) argues, "Ethnographic poets meditate on the ethnographic experience or focus on particulars arranged to elicit themes of general humanity that might apply cross-culturally" (p. 630). Brady's *Darwin's Reef* offers us a glimpse of what such cross-cultural, anthropological, and poetic consciousness might look like, hence expanding our notion of who counts as our brothers and sisters while envisioning a new, better, and more generous way of being in the world. Thus, although Brady flags these works as "poetic explorations in anthropology and history" in the subtitle to *Darwin's Reef*, our readings of them would add that they are, like Snyder's poems, both politically progressive and deeply spiritual meditations, self-reflexive opportunities for postmoderns to move past irony and cynicism toward something like multicultural commitment.

As demonstrated in the preceding paragraphs, we are deeply moved by Brady's contributions. The only problem—and it is a problem not so much with Brady as with most works of art—is that regimes of truth often obscure the ability or the desire to see another as human. Stereotypes and prejudices cloud judgment, making the generosity demonstrated in Brady's texts a difficult enterprise. Brady (2004) sees the overarching problem of anthropological poetics as one of "plural 'knowables' and the frustrations of choosing among them. (Or having someone choose for you, someone or some institution with the power to enforce the choice, say, society, for example. Or the Taliban. Or your department head)" (p. 632). This is a crucial passage, for we suspect that this parenthetical aside regarding the powers that filter through all life, the powers that allow others to "choose for you," may be the most important blockage preventing the fulfillment of Brady's vision. Indeed, the investigative poetry to which we turn in our closing section begins from the understanding that someone or some structure is always trying to choose for us, meaning that our plural knowables are often the products of oppressive regimes, stultifying cultural norms, or bureaucratic deadweight. Whereas the ethnographic poetry studied here offers us a compelling set of models for thinking critically about and engaging politically in the world—with Brady's *Darwin's Reef* standing as our best exemplar of the rich possibilities of this work—we still want to ask more from investigative poetry, for without a nuanced and pedagogically rich articulation of how multiple forms of power filter through, and sometimes even structure, our contexts of action, we can never know how to rhetorically build consensus and common humanity. In short, in the final section, we propose—not so much as a critique of ethnographic poetry as a supplement to it—that society's power to choose for us is not an aside but rather the focal point of poetic criticism. The works we address in what follows thus move away from a sense of anthropological wonder toward hard-hitting political and poetic critiques of specific regimes of power.

## ▣ 4. Three Models of Investigative Poetry: Dos Passos, Forché, and Scott

The works considered here are immersed completely in, and are fully aware of their complicity with, the contradictions of U.S. power; they accordingly focus on case studies of economic, military, political, and cultural oppression. Indeed, the poems considered in this section work imminently, constructing their investigative poetry from within the very social systems they hope to examine. Whereas the ethnographic poetry considered previously works in an alluring sideways manner, thinking about U.S. power by working along its edges and using anthropology to teach us about the peoples affected by U.S. power, the works considered in what follows take a more direct approach. In fact, Peter Dale Scott, in particular, has been attacked by those who find his poems too political and not poetic enough. Our comments in this section therefore are not meant to stand as normative judgments about what is a better or more powerful form of poetry; rather, we offer them as the final piece of our puzzle, as a closing set of options and models of how our best poets have struggled to merge historical and political criticism in a form of investigative poetry.

First among these models is John Dos Passos's *U.S.A.* trilogy, consisting of *The 42nd Parallel* (1930/1969c), *Nineteen Nineteen* (1932/1969a), and *The Big Money* (1936/1969b). The bulk of these sprawling novels consists of traditional narratives following the misadventures of characters confronted with the various economic, cultural, and political complications following from the manic boom-and-bust cycles of unregulated capitalism and America's entry into World War I. Each story is followed, however, by short sections titled Newsreels and the Camera Eye and by poetic biographies of the period's key players. The Newsreels consist of newspaper headlines, snippets of newspaper stories, and snatched refrains from popular songs—*Oh say can you see . . . , Where do we go from here, boys?* Arrayed on the page as a string of disconnected shards of evidence, these Newsreels provide both a clear forerunner to the form of Sanders's *America* and an eerie glimpse into the world of popular culture, mass-produced misinformation, and the vast majority of events that have simply fallen into historical oblivion.

The Newsreels are followed by Camera Eye sections in which Dos Passos offers disjointed observations, literally camera shots of turmoil. In this case, we watch the angry response of socialists in Paris to the Treaty of Versailles: "at the République à bass la guerre MORT AUX VACHES à bas le Paix de Assassins they've torn up the gratings from around the trees and are throwing stones and bits of castirons at the fancydressed Republican Guards hissing whistling poking at the horses with umbrellas scraps of the *International*" (Dos Passos, 1932/1969a, pp. 396–397). As indicated by the random gaps in the passages just quoted, the confusion as to who is speaking, and the bristling sense of confused immediacy, these sections fade into the stream of consciousness, thus offering readers glimpses into the fractured experience of living daily life amid epochal historical transformations. Dos Passos follows these blasts of existential confusion with poetic biographies, from which we have taken this verse on Randolph S. Bourne:

> This little sparrow like man
>
> tiny twisted bit of flesh in a black cape,
>
> always in pain and ailing,
>
> put a pebble in his sling
>
> and hit Goliath in the forehead with it
>
> *War,* he wrote, *is the health of the state.* (p. 120)

Made popular in Zinn's (1980) magnificent *A People's History of the United States,* Bourne's phrase has stood for generations as an indictment of U.S. militarism (pp. 350–367). By chronicling the struggles of this largely forgotten figure, Dos Passos's biographical poem enriches our sense of American history, making it more somber and personal. The combination of the explanatory narratives, the evidence-offering Newsreels, the existentially rich Camera Eye sections, and the poetic biographies offers readers four perspectives from which to approach history. Dos Passos thus strives to merge these four modes of writing to form a collective whole capable of thinking simultaneously about the deep structural integrity of history and the baffling, awestruck wonder and confusion that fills each small moment of time.

A second important model of textual production influencing our arguement here is provided by Forché's *The Country Between Us* (1981) and *The Angel of History* (1994), her two books prior to *Blue Hour*. Based on her journalistic work in El Salvador during the height of that country's civil war, *The Country Between Us* offers a model for a poetry of witness in which the poet is not only a chronicler of hope and terror but also a participant in the processes she examines. The poems in this remarkable book thus veer from scalding political critiques of Salvadoran tyrants to self-implicating ruminations on how even the most mundane pleasures in the United States bear the stain of the violence our government funds in the Third World. Like so many of us who find that our grassroots political work changes the ways that we think about freedom (Hartnett, 2003; Tannenbaum, 2000), Forché finds that living in close proximity to barbarism in El Salvador casts shadows across daily space. Forché (1981) is thus unnerved by the sense of decadence and ease signaled by "the iced drinks and paper umbrellas, clean/toilets and Los Angeles palm trees moving/like lean women" (p. 17). Like so many of us, she finds the happy ignorance of many Americans regarding the brutality that their country foists on the world to be unbearable. Speaking to a friend, she laments,

> you were born to an island of greed
>
> and grace where you have the sense
>
> of yourself as apart from others. It is
>
> not your right to feel powerless. Better
>
> people than you were powerless. (p. 20)

Many of these better people appear in the pages of *The Angel of History,* where Forché (1994) expands her poetry of witness to encompass the European Holocaust and the impact of the United States dropping nuclear bombs on Japan. Taking her title from the well-known story told in Benjamin's (1940/1969) "Theses on the Philosophy of History," where an angel is blown backward into the future while watching the present produce an ever-growing pile of wreckage (pp. 257–258), Forché tackles the horrors of World War II in personal poems full of stories of her lost relatives and friends. While leading readers on this personally inflected historical journey into barbarism, Forché speculates—frequently through the voices of other writers and philosophers—on the possibilities of forgiveness. Much like Brady's *Darwin's Reef*, then, *The Angel of History* is less an investigative attempt to name names and pinpoint causes than a philosophical attempt to make sense of the persistence of hope in the face of unspeakable suffering. Aphoristic and enigmatic—and thus nearly impossible to quote without including pages of supporting material—the poems accumulate power from their many references to other texts, hence offering readers less a definitive statement than a series of beautiful theses, each equipped with what amounts to a list of suggested readings. Thus, while embodying the wonder and openness of elegant poetry, *The Angel of History* stands ultimately as a pedagogical tool for wondering what it means to cherish art during an age of destruction.

The third, and by far the most important, model of investigative poetry is Peter Dale Scott's *Seculum* trilogy. The first part of the trilogy, *Coming to Jakarta: A Poem about Terror* (1988), has been lauded in *The Boston Review* as "remarkable and unnerving" (Weiner, 1995, p. 31), in London's *Times Literary Supplement* as "a work of great richness and complexity" (Gunn, 1991, p. 19), in *Parnassus* as "revolutionary" (Campbell, 1993, p. 395), and in a special issue of *AGNI*—by no less a national hero than the Poet Laureate Robert Hass—as "the most important political poem to appear in the English language in a very long time" (Hass, 1990, p. 333). Like these enthusiastic reviewers, we have been deeply impressed by the sophistication and depth of Scott's political analysis, the epic sweep of his historical knowledge, the revelatory honesty of his self-implicating poems, and the sheer beauty of his verse. By interweaving these four qualities—political acumen, historical grounding, self-reflexivity, and poetic beauty—Scott produces what we call *an interdisciplinary aesthetics of provisional eloquence*. That is, by merging the four qualities just noted, and by doing so while confronting a political calamity, Scott provides us with an empowering and elegant example of the search for grace amid terror.

*Coming to Jakarta* was triggered by Scott's (1988) need to write "about the 1965 massacre/of Indonesians by Indonesians" (p. 24) while simultaneously questioning his own complicity—as poet, professor, one-time diplomat, father, husband, and activist—in the events that led to the Central Intelligence Agency (CIA)–sponsored butchery of more than 500,000 Indonesian "communists" following the coup that replaced Sukarno with Suharto.[6] For example, in the second poem of *Coming to Jakarta*, we find Scott suffering from

the uprising in my stomach

   against so much good food and

wine America or was it

giving one last broadcast too many

    about the Letelier assassins

  the heroin traffic

a subject I no longer hope

    to get a handle on. (p. 10)7

These lines depict Scott as an activist/intellectual speaking publicly about the sub-terranean links between assassination politics and the drug war, as a typical overcon-sumer gorged on too much decadence, and as a consummate researcher who, suffering from the nausea brought on by too much familiarity with evil, wishes that the facts would mysteriously vanish into the comforting oblivion of ignorance—but of course they do not.[8] Instead, history forces itself mercilessly onto Scott (1988), prodding him to engage in a relentless pursuit of *evidence,* dragging him deeper and deeper into both the psychology and the political economy of terror:

Already we are descending

  into these shadows which

hang about as if there

  were something much more urgent

left wholly unsaid. (p. 13)

Readers interested in the facts of the Indonesian massacre will find more than 100 sources listed in Scott's notes, which situate Suharto's coup and the ensuing anticommu-nist genocide within the overlapping politico-economic framework of post–World War II international finance; the transition from modern, empire-driven, and ideologically dri-ven colonialism into the postmodern neocolonialism of multinational corporations, underground think tanks, and globetrotting mercenaries; and the continuing subversion of democratic politics at the behest of the global caste-bound thugs who run secret gov-ernments as if they were their own private shooting galleries. The research used to doc-ument these charges is breathtaking, thus offering readers a tutorial in how to pursue interdisciplinary political criticism. In this sense, then, Scott is perhaps the most impres-sive cobbler of what we saw Sanders (1976) refer to earlier as "a melodic blizzard of data-fragments" (p. 9).

But whereas such melodic blizzards might leave many readers baffled, or at least searching for personal relevance in such waves of "data-fragments," Scott weaves his remarkable research around and through moments of daily life, hence showing us how power courses through even the most mundane activities. For example, watch here as Scott (1988) links the disparate strands of the international political economy of terror, U.S. weapons manufacturers, Indonesian and Saudi tycoons, the refuse of Nixon's henchmen, and the friendly neighborhood bank:

and I thought of Adnan Khashoggi

　the Indonesian shipping magnate

　Saudi friend of Pak

Chung Hee and Roy Furmak

　*$106 million*

　in Lockheed commissions

to Khashoggi alone

　and twice that

　amount withdrawn by Khashoggi

from Rebozo's bank in Key Biscayne

　in May and November '72

　and of Lim Suharto's *cukong*

who has bought the Hibernian bank

　with a branch on the Berkeley campus

from profits on arms deals. (pp. 127–128)[9]

　　Scott's awesome courage in exposing the shadowy operatives and offshore bankers and behind-the-scenes boardroom connections that fuel imperialism, in conjunction with his sweeping grasp of history and his uncanny ability to render such topics in recognizable terms—*a branch on the Berkeley campus*—render *Coming to Jakarta* a world-class example of the detailed historical and political analysis needed to render investigative poetry persuasive.

　　In fact, it took nearly 15 years following the publication of *Coming to Jakarta* for the mainstream media to begin to address the underworld U.S.–Indonesia connections first exposed in Scott's poem. For example, it is now known that Freeport MacMoRan, Texaco, Mobil, Raytheon, Hughes Aircraft, and Merrill Lynch (among others) are major financial sponsors of the U.S.–Indonesia Society, a lobbying group cochaired by President Ronald Reagan's Secretary of State, George Schultz, and featuring James Riady as a trustee and John Huang as a consultant. Thus, two of the central figures (Riady and Huang) in one of the Democratic party campaign finance scandals that rocked the Clinton presidency turned out to be significant U.S.–Indonesia Society figures. Press (1997) observed at the time that the society was "a public relations organ for the Suharto regime" (p. 19). Thus, beneath the surface scandal of the Democratic party accepting illegal foreign campaign contributions, journalists found the much deeper scandal of continuing links among Suharto's brutal regime, U.S.-based transnationals, and the U.S. government. That Scott's *Coming to Jakarta* exposed these connections 15 years before the mainstream press would even consider them demonstrates the remarkable depth and courage of the poem's political and historical analysis. Using Scott's *Coming to Jakarta* as a model, then, we argue that investigative poetry uses rigorous research to name names, to show who owns what and whom, and thus to lay bare the institutional and economic structures supporting specific modes of oppression.

Scott's work is just as impressive, however, as an experiment in reconstructing a new and problematic sense of an endlessly compromised self in the face of terror, hence Scott's revelation that

> To have learnt from terror
>
> > to see oneself
>
> > as part of the enemy
>
> can be a reassurance
>
> > whatever it is
>
> > arises within us. (p. 62)

Like the poems of Dos Passos and Forché, then, Scott's poems perform a dialectical interweaving of perspectives. Each well-documented scene of political barbarism segues into personal observations on the nature of complicity, each personal rumination on complicity fades into questions of commitment and the historical obligation of engaged citizens to at least attempt to speak truth to power, and each engagement with the numbing expanse of global power politics, in turn, leads back to the suspicion that perhaps grace can only be found, after all, amid those moments when daily life is lived as an aesthetic experience. Hence the prevalence in *Listening to the Candle* (Scott, 1992), the second part of the *Seculum* trilogy, of simple pleasures

> focused on the mysteries
>
> > of dailiness
>
> baking bread on Saturdays
>
> > smelling the freshness
>
> > of sun-dried laundry

while you fold the sheet

   against yourself

from the garden line. (p. 94)

Later in the poem, after chronicling the December 1980 murder of American evangelicals working with peasants in El Salvador, Scott (1992) suggests that

in such a time it is still good

having danced until midnight

   to Mika's and John's new band

after the family lasagna

all generations

   our children and their friends

dancing together singly. (p. 106)

Terror and grace thus jostle each other within the infinitely textured particulars of the day:

From the Bay Bridge

   on the way home from the opera

you could look down on the searchlights

of the Oakland Army Terminal

   where they loaded the containers

of pellet-bombs and napalm. (Scott, 1988, p. 103)

Like Forché's line about "aria in time of war," then, Scott shows us how even the drive home from the opera, that quintessential marker of high art, leads one past places of mass-produced violence. *If you look around,* Scott tells us, *you will find yourself implicated in things you have previously spent a great deal of time and energy pretending not to recognize.*

These epiphanic moments of realization need not be paralyzing, however, as Scott shows us again and again how to channel them into a renewed commitment to work not only politically for peace and justice but also personally for something approaching kindness. In fact, in *Minding the Darkness,* the third volume of the *Seculum* trilogy, Scott (2000) turns increasingly to Buddhism as a way of practicing what he calls mindfulness. Much like Snyder's ecological consciousness in *Turtle Island*, or Brady's spiritual sense of time in *Darwin's Reef*, Scott's Buddhism is woven throughout the book as a counterthread to his political criticism. Scott demonstrates its challenges and opportunities most explicitly in four poems chronicling Buddhist retreats (pp. 72–80, 140–148, 221–229, 244). In contrast to the scathing investigative poetry of *Coming to Jakarta* and the meditative work in *Listening to the Candle*, then, *Minding the Darkness* demonstrates a middle way of mindful politics, of both critique and contemplation. This turn to Buddhism clearly illustrates Scott's hankering less for the smoking gun that will rip away the lies of any given regime than for the *wisdom* that will help him to live amid so much waste and cruelty. Indeed, by tracking down his footnotes; by rambling through his childhood traumas and parental pleasures; by forcing ourselves to confront both his and our complicity with the global carnage of low-intensity anticommunism, unabashed designer capitalism, and the pleasures of high culture; by making paratactical leaps from fragmentary images and quotations toward our own approximate understanding of the text; and by enthusiastically embodying a turn toward Buddhist values, Scott teaches attentive readers to treat the poem as a heuristic—even therapeutic—device. The mysterious "something much more urgent/left wholly unsaid" (Scott, 1988, p. 13) appears here to be the realization that poetry—as a trigger for research, as a source of grace, as a means of confronting terror, as a process of self-critique and reconstruction—amounts to a self-regenerating process in which, as Scott says in an interview, "one works through personal resistance and disempowerment to re-empowerment" (Scott, 1990, p. 303).

We are reminded here of Terrence Des Pres's comment in a roundtable discussion on the possibilities of political poetry that

> we turn where we can for sustenance, and some of us take poetry seriously in exactly this way. . . . When it comes to the Bomb, or just to the prospect of empires in endless conflict, it seems clear we cannot do very much very fast. So the immediate question isn't what to do but *how to live,* and some of us, at least, turn for help to poetry. (Des Pres, 1986, p. 21)

The sustenance of *Coming to Jakarta, Listening to the Candle,* and *Minding the Darkness* derives from the pleasures of sharing one's burden as an informed and engaged citizen in a rapidly unraveling democracy while not devolving into solipsism, cynicism, or madness. Hence Scott's (1988) prudent advice about how to live in the closing section of *Coming to Jakarta:*

as for those of us

who are lucky enough

not to sit hypnotized

our hands on the steering wheel

   which seems to have detached itself

  from the speeding vehicle

it is our job to say

  *relax trust*

  spend more time with your children

things can only go

  a little better

  if you do not hang on so hard. (p. 129)

## □  5. Conclusion

We began our essay with the claim that despite the prevalence of buzzwords indicating the rise of *interdisciplinarity* and intellectual *border crossing,* the vast majority of scholarly production falls under the aegis of time-worn departmental and disciplinary norms. We offered ethnographic and investigative poetry as ways of moving past this hypocrisy. Likewise, we argued that despite the cultural cache of terms such as *radical, intervention,* and *transgression,* we know of only an embarrassingly small number of academics whose work engages in social justice concerns. The second section of this essay accordingly offered some guidelines for thinking about how to make social justice more central to what humanists do. The third and fourth sections then offered case studies examining how different poets have produced politically driven and interdisciplinary investigative poems. Taken together, the four sections of the essay offer concrete examples of how scholars, artists, and activists might begin tackling the seven methodological proposals with which we opened the essay. We therefore hope to have offered readers a series of working models, conceptual prompts, and historical examples of how to merge scholarship and poetry, social justice and self-reflection, hence producing texts that may serve the role of "aria in time of war." Indeed, given the remarkable proliferation of cultural offerings swimming in an apparently ever more specialized world of niche consumerism—a trend as problematic in poetry as in the general culture at large—the combination of detailed case studies and sweeping historical claims that marks the best investigative poetry offers a powerful model of engaged, artful, and cosmopolitan citizenship. At their best, these models of aria in time of war might well provide us, to borrow a phrase from an interview with Sanders (1997), "pathways through the chaos."

## ▣ Notes

1. Birkerts (1987) proceeds to make a formalist argument demonstrating his allegiance to a traditional version of poetry and an emaciated version of politics. For more empowering responses to this question, see the essays collected in Jones (1985). For more experimental responses, see the remarkable works in Bernstein (1990) and Monroe (1996). For more programmatic responses, see "The Art of the Manifesto" (1998).

2. For a case study of the difference between healthy mourning and paralyzing melancholia, see Kaplan (2001). See also Freud (1963, pp. 164–179) for his diagnosis of the problem.

3. The passages quoted here are offered in praise of Ezra Pound, whose use of such "data clusters" was poetically dubious at best and politically dangerous at worst (Hartnett, 1993). On the rhetorical complexities of synecdoche, see Hartnett (2002, pp. 155–172).

4. Although long a subject of scholarly analysis, the pleasures of lynch mobs came to popular attention via *Without Sanctuary: Lynching Photography in America*, a show that opened at the New York Historical Society on March 14, 2000, and that has subsequently toured the nation, searing into the minds of its many viewers images of lynch mobs laughing, drinking, barbecuing, and otherwise enjoying the spectacle of death. Some of the images from the exhibit may be seen online at the homepage of the New York Historical Society or in Allen (2000). See also the comments on the pleasures of racial violence in Hartman (1997).

5. To study the legislation alluded to here, see "An Act to Punish Acts of Interference . . . " (June 15, 1917) and "An Act to Amend . . . " (April 16, 1918)—the so-called Espionage Acts—from *Statutes at Large of the United States of America* (U.S. Congress, 1919, pp. 217–231, 531). See also "Chapter 75," the May 16, 1918, amendment to the Espionage Act, in *Statutes of the United States of America* (U.S. Congress, 1918, pp. 553–554). For Eugene Victor Debs's heroic response to these acts, see his June 16, 1918, "Canton Speech" in *The Debs White Book* (n.d., pp. 3–64). For the U.S. Supreme Court's upholding these laws, see *Schenck v. U.S., Frohwerk v. U.S.,* and *Debs v. U.S.* (all May 1919) in *The Supreme Court Reporter* (West Publishing, 1920, pp. 247–254). This case is cited by lawyers as 39 S. Ct. 247 (1919).

6. For analyses of Suharto's domination of Indonesia, his brutal 1975 invasion of East Timor, and Jakarta's place in the new global economy, see Anderson (1995), Curtis (1995–1996), and Fabrikant (1996). U.S. complicity with Suharto's occupation of East Timor and his bloody repression of oppositional groups in Indonesia continues. In fact, since Suharto's December 1975 invasion of East Timor, in which more than 200,000 people—more than 25% of the population—were slaughtered, the United States has sold Indonesia more than $1.1 billion worth of advanced weaponry. The Clinton administration alone sold close to $270 million worth of arms to Suharto (see Klare, 1994, and Washburn, 1997). Suharto was finally forced from power in the spring of 1998. For coverage of his departure, see Mydans (1998) and any major newspaper during the latter half of April and all of May 1998.

7. Orlando Letelier, the Chilean ambassador to the United States, was killed by a car bomb in Washington, D.C., in September 1976. Right-wing Cuban expatriates, trained by DINA (the Chilean Secret Service) and funded through illegal CIA connections, claimed responsibility for the blast. See Scott and Marshall (1991, pp. 30–34).

8. The impulse here is reminiscent of the lament that "There are times/I wish my ignorance were/more complete" in Hass (1973, p. 61). In fact, Scott (1990) later wrote of his "growing self-hatred for carrying around a head full of horrors which most people were less and less willing to hear about" (p. 300).

9. Khashoggi's perpetual role as banker to terrorists and thugs has been reprised in his post-9/11 acting as well, in this case working with Richard Perle, the recently disgraced member of President George W. Bush's Defense Policy Board. See Hersh (2004, pp. 189–201).

## ▣ REFERENCES

Adelman, M., & Frey, L. (1997). *The fragile community: Living together with AIDS.* Mahwah, NJ: Lawrence Erlbaum.

Alfred, T. (1999). *Peace, power, righteousness: An indigenous manifesto.* New York: Oxford University Press.

Allen, J. (Ed.). (2000). *Without sanctuary: Lynching photography in America.* Santa Fe, NM: Twin Palms.

Anderson, B. (1995, November 2). Gravel in Jakarta's shoes. *London Review of Books,* pp. 2–5.

Basso, K. (1988). A review of Native American discourse: Poetics and rhetoric. *American Ethnologist, 15,* 805–810.

Becker, C. (Ed.). (1994). *The subversive imagination: Artists, society, and social responsibility.* New York: Routledge.

Benjamin, W. (1969). Theses on the philosophy of history. In W. Benjamin, *Illuminations* (H. Arendt, Ed. and Trans., pp. 253–264). New York: Schocken Books. (Original work published 1940)

Bernstein, C. (Ed.). (1990). *The politics of poetic form: Poetry and public policy.* New York: Roof.

Birkerts, S. (1987). "Poetry" and "politics." *Margin, 4,* 55–62.

Bourdieu, P. (2000). For a scholarship with commitment. In P. Franklin (Ed.), *Profession: An annual publication of the MLA* (pp. 40–45). New York: Modern Language Association.

Brady, I. (1991). Harmony and argument: Bringing forth the artful science. In I. Brady (Ed.), *Anthropological poetics* (pp. 3–30). Savage, MD: Rowman & Littlefield.

Brady, I. (2000). Anthropological poetics. In N. K. Denzin & Y. S. Lincoln (Eds.), *Handbook of qualitative research* (2nd ed., pp. 949–979). Thousand Oaks, CA: Sage.

Brady, I. (2003). *The time at Darwin's Reef: Poetic explorations in anthropology and history.* Walnut Creek, CA: AltaMira.

Brady, I. (2004). In defense of the sensual: Meaning construction in ethnography and poetics. *Qualitative Inquiry, 10,* 622–644.

Buell, L. (1968). Transcendentalist catalogue rhetoric: Vision versus form. *American Literature, 40*(1), 325–339.

Campbell, M. (1993). Disaster, or the scream of Juno's peacock. *Parnassus, 17/18,* 380–403.

Chari, V. K. (1972). Structure of Whitman's catalogue poems. *Walt Whitman Review, 18*(1), 3–17.

Clifford, J. (1999). *The predicament of culture: Twentieth-century ethnography, literature, and art.* Cambridge, MA: Harvard University Press. (Original work published 1988)

Conquergood, D. (1994). Homeboys and hoods: Gang communication and cultural spaces. In L. Frey (Ed.), *Group communication in context: Studies of natural groups* (pp. 23–55). Hillsdale, NJ: Lawrence Erlbaum.

Conquergood, D. (1995). Between rigor and relevance: Rethinking applied communication. In K. Cissna (Ed.), *Applied communication in the 21st century* (pp. 79–96). Mahwah, NJ: Lawrence Erlbaum.

Crabtree, R. (1998). Mutual empowerment in cross-cultural participatory development and service learning: Lessons in communication and social justice from projects in El Salvador and Nicaragua. *Journal of Applied Communication Research, 26,* 182–209.

Curtis, M. (1995–1996). Hawks over East Timor: Britain arms Indonesia. *Covert Action Quarterly, 55,* 52–56.

Debs, E. (n.d.). *The Debs white book.* Girard, KS: Appeal to Reason.

Des Pres, T. (1986). Poetry and politics. *TriQuarterly, 65,* 17–29.

Dos Passos, J. (1969a). *Nineteen nineteen.* New York: Signet. (Original work published 1932)

Dos Passos, J. (1969b). *The big money.* New York: Signet. (Original work published 1936)

Dos Passos, J. (1969c). *The 42nd parallel.* New York: Signet. (Original work published 1930)

Emerson, R. W. (1982). The poet. In L. Ziff (Ed.), *Ralph Waldo Emerson: Selected essays* (pp. 259–284). New York: Penguin. (Original work published 1844)

Fabrikant, G. (1996, April 9). Family ties that bind growth: Corrupt leaders in Indonesia threaten its future. *The New York Times,* pp. C1–C2.

Forché, C. (1981). *The country between us.* New York: Perennial.

Forché, C. (1993). *Against forgetting: Twentieth-century poetry of witness.* New York: Norton.

Forché, C. (1994). *The angel of history.* New York: Harper Perennial.

Forché, C. (2003). *Blue hour.* New York: HarperCollins.

Freud, S. (1963). *General psychological theory.* New York: Macmillan.

Frey, L. (1998). Communication and social justice research. *Journal of Applied Communication Research, 26,* 155–164.

Frey, L., Pearce, B., Pollock, M., Artz, L., & Murphy, B. (1996). Looking for justice in all the wrong places: On a communication approach to social justice. *Communication Studies, 47,* 110–127.

Friedrich, P. (in press). Maximizing ethnopoetics: Toward fine-tuning (anthropological) experience. In C. Jordain & K. Tuite (Eds.), *Ethnolinguistics: The state of the art.* Montreal: Fides.

Gordon, A. (1997). *Ghostly matters: Haunting and the sociological imagination.* Minneapolis: University of Minnesota Press.

Gunn, T. (1991, February 1). Appetite for power. *Times Literary Supplement,* p. 19.

Hartman, S. (1997). *Scenes of subjection: Terror, slavery, and self-making in nineteenth-century America.* New York: Oxford University Press.

Hartnett, S. J. (1993). The ideologies and semiotics of fascism: Analyzing Ezra Pound's *Cantos* 12–15. *Boundary 2, 20*(1), 65–93.

Hartnett, S. J. (1998). Lincoln and Douglas meet the abolitionist David Walker as prisoners debate slavery: Empowering education, applied communication, and social justice. *Journal of Applied Communication Research, 26,* 232–253.

Hartnett, S. J. (1999). Four meditations on the search for grace amidst terror. *Text and Performance Quarterly, 19,* 196–216.

Hartnett, S. J. (2002). *Democratic dissent and the cultural fictions of antebellum America.* Urbana: University of Illinois Press.

Hartnett, S. J. (2003). *Incarceration nation: Investigative prison poems of hope and terror.* Walnut Creek, CA: AltaMira.

Hass, R. (1973). *Field guide.* New Haven, CT: Yale University Press.

Hass, R. (1990). Some notes on coming to Jakarta. *AGNI, 31/32,* 334–361.

Hersh, S. (2004). *Chain of command: The road from 9/11 to Abu Ghraib.* New York: HarperCollins.

Jones, R. (Ed.). (1985). *Poetry and politics: An anthology of essays.* New York: Quill.

Kaplan, B. (2001). Pleasure, memory, and time suspension in Holocaust literature: Celan and Delbo. *Comparative Literature Studies, 38,* 310–329.

Klare, M. (1994, January 10). License to kill: How the U.S. is building up military–industrial complexes in the Third World. *In These Times,* pp. 14–19.

LaCapra, D. (2001). *Writing history, writing trauma.* Baltimore, MD: Johns Hopkins University Press.

Mason, J. (1973). Walt Whitman's catalogues: Rhetorical means for two journeys in "song of myself." *American Literature, 45*(1), 34–49.

Monroe, J. (Ed.). (1996). Poetry, community, movement [special issue]. *Diacritics, 26*(3/4).

Mydans, S. (1998, May 21). Suharto steps down after 32 years in power. *The New York Times,* pp. A1, A8.

O'Rourke, M. (2003, June 9). She's so heavy: Review of *Blue Hour. The Nation,* pp. 36–43.

Press, E. (1997). The Suharto lobby. *The Progressive, 61*(5), 19–21.

Reed, M. (1977). First person persona and the catalogue in "song of myself." *Walt Whitman Review, 23*(4), 147–155.

Rosaldo, R. (1993). *Culture and truth: The remaking of social analysis.* Boston: Beacon. (Original work published 1989)

Rothenberg, J. (1990). Ethnopoetics and politics/The politics of ethnopoetics. In C. Bernstein (Ed.), *The politics of poetic form: Poetry and public policy* (pp. 1–22). New York: Roof.

Sanders, E. (1976). *Investigative poetry.* San Francisco: City Lights.

Sanders, E. (1997, November 18). Interview with Brooke Horvath. *Review of Contemporary Fiction, 19*(1). Available: www.centerforbookculture.org

Sanders, E. (2000). *America: A history in verse,* Vol. 1: *1900–1939.* Santa Rosa, CA: Black Sparrow.

Scarry, E. (2000). Beauty and the scholar's duty to justice. In *Profession: An annual publication of the MLA* (pp. 21–31). New York: Modern Language Association.

Scott, P. D. (1988). *Coming to Jakarta: A poem about terror.* New York: New Directions.

Scott, P. D. (1990). How I came to Jakarta. *AGNI, 31/32,* 297–304

Scott, P. D. (1992). *Listening to the candle: A poem on impulse.* New York: New Directions.

Scott, P. D. (2000). *Minding the darkness: A poem for the year 2000.* New York: New Directions.

Scott, P. D., & Marshall, J. (1991). *Cocaine politics: Drugs, armies, and the CIA in Central America.* Berkeley: University of California Press.

Smith, L. T. (1999). *Decolonizing methodologies: Research and indigenous peoples.* London: Zed Books.

Snyder, G. (1974). *Turtle Island.* New York: New Directions.

Statement of intention. (1970). *Alcheringa/Ethnopoetics, 1*(1), 1.

Tannenbaum, J. (2000). *Disguised as a poem: My years teaching poetry at San Quentin Prison.* Boston: Northeastern University Press.

Tedlock, D. (1992). Ethnopoetics. In R. Bauman (Ed.), *Folklore, cultural performances, and popular entertainments* (pp. 81–85). New York: Oxford University Press.

The art of the manifesto [24 contributors]. (1998). In J. Rothenberg & P. Joris (Eds.), *Poems for the millennium,* Vol. 2: *From postwar to millennium* (pp. 403–453). Berkeley: University of California Press.

Thomas, W. (1995). *Scorched earth: The military's assault on the environment.* Philadelphia: New Society.

Turner, V. (1983). A review of "ethnopoetics." In J. Rothenberg & D. Rothenberg (Eds.), *Symposium of the whole: A range of discourse toward an ethnopoetics* (pp. 337–342). Berkeley: University of California Press.

U.S. Congress. (1918). *Statutes of the United States of America, passed at the second session of the sixty-fifth Congress, 1917–1918* (Part 1: Public Acts and Resolutions, pp. 553–554). Washington, DC: Government Printing Office.

U.S. Congress. (1919). *Statutes at large of the United States of America, April 1917–March 1919* (pp. 217–231). Washington, DC: Government Printing Office.

Washburn, J. (1997). Twisting arms: The U.S. weapons industry gets its way. *The Progressive, 61*(5), 26–27.

Weinberger, E., & Paz, O. (1987). *Nineteen ways of looking at Wang Wei: How a Chinese poem is translated.* Wakefield, RI: Moyer Bell.

Weiner, J. (1995, February). [Review of Peter Dale Scott's *Crossing Borders: Selected Shorter Poems*]. *Boston Review,* pp. 31–33.

West Publishing. (1920). *The Supreme Court reporter* (Vol. 39, pp. 247–254). St. Paul, MN: Author.

What harm has she dreamt? (R. Jodorowsky, Trans.). (1970). *Alcheringa/Ethnopoetics, 1*(1), 50.

Williamson, R. (1985). The new (colonial) ballgame. In J. I. Prattis (Ed.), *Reflections: The anthropological muse* (pp. 189–190). Washington, DC: American Anthropological Association.

Zinn, H. (1980). *A people's history of the United States.* New York: Perennial.

# 19

## QUALITATIVE
## EVALUATION
## AND CHANGING
## SOCIAL POLICY

Ernest R. House

I n 1965, the U.S. Congress passed the Elementary and Secondary Education Act. At the insistence of Senator Robert Kennedy, this bill included an evaluation rider that became the stimulus for program evaluation. That same year, President Lyndon Johnson introduced the Program Planning and Budgeting System (PPBS), developed by the Pentagon, to the U.S. Department of Health, Education, and Welfare. The goal of the PPBS was to develop government programs that could be stated, measured, and evaluated in cost–benefit terms. Economists William Gorham and Alice Rivlin headed the evaluation office (McLaughlin, 1975).

Federal policy stipulated that key decisions for social services would be made at the higher levels of the federal government. The only true knowledge about social services was a production function specifying stable relationships between inputs and outputs. The only way of obtaining such knowledge was through experimental and statistical methods. "Information necessary to improve the effectiveness of social services is impossible to obtain any other way" (Rivlin, 1971, p. 108). To that end, several large-scale experiments were funded.

**Author's Note.** I thank Bob Stake, Yvonna Lincoln, and Norm Denzin for providing useful feedback in the drafting of this chapter.

Campbell and Stanley's (1963) classic work became the methodological guide. Experimental studies became the new fad, with Campbell and Stanley describing experiments

> as the only means of settling disputes regarding educational practice, as the only way of verifying educational improvements, and as the only way of establishing a cumulative tradition in which improvements can be introduced without the danger of a faddish discard of old wisdom in favor of inferior novelties. (p. 2)

During the early days of professional evaluation, both policymakers and evaluators put their faith in large-scale quantitative studies such as Follow Through, Head Start, and the Income Maintenance experiment. Policymakers and many evaluators thought that these large national studies would yield definitive findings that would demonstrate which programs worked best. The findings could serve as the basis for mandates by the central government to reform inefficient social services.

In time, these large studies proved to be extremely disappointing. One problem was their scale. The Follow Through experiment cost $500 million, and during one data collection Follow Through evaluators collected 12 tons of data. They were overwhelmed by the logistics to the point where they could not produce timely reports. Eventually, the government sponsors reduced the study to a fraction of its original size by reducing the number of sites and variables.

A more serious problem was that the findings of these studies proved to be equivocal. The studies did not produce the anticipated clear-cut results that could be generalized. For example, when the Follow Through data were analyzed, the variance in test score outcomes across the dozen early childhood programs being compared was about as great as the variance within these programs. In other words, if a given early childhood program had been implemented at six sites, two sites might have good results, two might have mediocre results, and two might have poor results. This was not the kind of conclusive evaluative finding on which the government could base national recommendations. After years of frustration and hundreds of millions of dollars spent, policymakers and most evaluators became disenchanted with large-scale studies because of their cost, time scale, and lack of definitive results.

Meanwhile, evaluators were developing alternative approaches, including qualitative studies, meta-analysis, and program theory. Small qualitative studies were practical. For example, if a school district wanted an evaluation of its early childhood education program, interviewing administrators, teachers, and students was a simple and cheap method, and the findings were easy to understand even if they could not be published in scholarly journals. Furthermore, generalizability was not the problem that it was for large national studies. The demand on the local study was that the results be true for this place at this time; they did not need to be true for sites all over the country for all time.

However, some evaluators did not consider qualitative studies to be scientific. Evaluators engaged in intense internecine debates about the scientific legitimacy of qualitative methods. This dispute preoccupied the profession for 20 years, even as qualitative studies became increasingly popular. After many words and much rancor, the field finally accepted the idea that evaluation studies could be conducted in a number of different ways (Reichardt & Rallis, 1994). Evaluation became methodologically ecumenical, although personal sensitivities lingered. By 2000, the quantitative–qualitative dispute seemed to be history.

Another alternative to large-scale quantitative studies was meta-analysis (Glass, 1976). Meta-analysis was more acceptable to quantitative methodologists, although not without controversy. In some ways, meta-analysis was a natural successor to large-scale quantitative studies. Meta-analysis assembles the results of many experimental studies—studies that have control groups—and combines the findings of these studies quantitatively by focusing on the differences between performances of the experimental and control groups. The technique is more radical than it sounds given that researchers might combine outcomes that are quite different in kind into summary scores. Meta-analysis became overwhelmingly popular in social and medical research to the point where today it is difficult to pick up a major research journal without finding meta-analytic studies.

A third alternative to large-scale experimental studies was program theory (Chen & Rossi, 1987). Program theory consists of constructing a model of the program that can be used to guide the evaluation. Earlier, some researchers had advocated basing evaluations on grand social theories, but those attempts failed. First, there were no social theories that had much explanatory power. Second, if such theories existed, there was still the question of whether they could be used to evaluate social programs. For example, given the task of evaluating automobiles, could evaluators use theories of physics to do the job? It seems unlikely.

Evaluators reduced the grand theory concept to theories for individual programs. This worked better. The program formulation is concrete enough to guide evaluations, and it communicates directly with program participants. Program theory delineates points where evaluators might confirm whether the program is working and enables evaluators to eliminate rival hypotheses and make causal attributions more easily (Lipsey, 1993). Underlying qualitative studies, meta-analysis, and program theory have been changes in our conception of causation. These changes suggest why these alternatives worked better than large experimental studies.

▣ CHANGING CONCEPTIONS OF CAUSATION

The conception of causation that we inherited is called the regularity or Humean theory of causation, named after David Hume's influential analysis of cause (House,

1991). Regularity describes the conception. Put simply, the reason why we know one event caused another event is that the first event took place regularly before the other event—regularity of succession. If one event occurred and another event occurred after it repeatedly, we would have reason to believe that the events would occur together again. We look for succession of events. In fact, Hume said that regularity, along with contiguity of events, is all there is to causation. The research task is to determine the succession of events. Put succinctly: If *p*, then *q*; *p*, therefore *q*.

This notion of cause is the underlying basis for most discussions of experimental design, and it is manifest in early evaluation books: "One may formulate an evaluation project in terms of a series of hypotheses which state that 'Activities A, B, C will produce [R]esults X, Y, Z'" (Suchman, 1967, p. 93). In other words, if we have a Program A under Circumstances B and C, it will produce Results X, Y, and Z. Furthermore, the perfect design for determining whether the result has occurred is the classic randomized control group design. No error could result from employing this design, according to Suchman.

Although this assertion sounds reasonable, it falls apart on closer inspection. If we return to the Follow Through studies, the same early childhood program at six different sites produced different outcomes. Why? Because social causation is more complex than the regularity theory suggests. Even with the same program, there are different teachers at different sites who produce different results. We might try to control for the teachers, but there are so many variables that might influence the outcomes, the researchers cannot control for all of them. Put another way, the program is not in and of itself an integrated causal mechanism. Parts of the program might interact with elements in the environment to produce quite different effects.

Such considerations led Cronbach to abandon treatment–interaction research altogether. He tried to determine how student characteristics and outcomes interacted. There were so many possibilities that could not be controlled, he gave up trying. Put more technically, the effects of the secondary interactions of the variables were consistently as strong as the main effects. Cronbach (1982) rethought causation and devised a more complex formulation: In S, all (ABC or DEF or JKL) are followed by P. In other words, in this particular setting, P, the outcome, may be determined by ABC or DEF or JKL. The problem for evaluators is that if A is the program, we get P only if Conditions B and C are also present. So we could have A (the program) and not have the outcome P. More confounding, because P is caused by DEF and JKL combinations as well, we might not have the Program A but still get P. Neither the presence nor the absence of the Program A determines P. Succession of events is not a definitive test of cause and effect. The classic control group design will not produce definitive conclusions if causation is this complex.

Even so, we could devise a determinate research design using Cronbach's formulation, albeit a very expensive and complex one. However, social causation is more complex than even Cronbach's formulation indicates. Cronbach based his analysis on

Mackie (1974), a seminal work on causation. Mackie's original formulation was this: All F (A . . . B . . . or D . . . H . . . or ) are P (the dots represent missing causal factors we do not know about). We have huge gaps in our knowledge of social events—not only gaps we do not know about) but also gaps we do not even know we do not know about. Because we can never fill those gaps, we can never be certain of all that is involved. This does not mean that experiments are hopeless, only that they have to be interpreted carefully. They are not as foolproof as advocates may claim. There are always things we cannot account for.

Qualitative studies, meta-analysis, and program theory work better than large-scale studies because each approach takes account of a more complex social reality by framing the study more precisely, albeit in different ways. Qualitative studies show the interaction of people and events with other causal factors in context, thereby limiting causal possibilities and alternatives (Maxwell, 1996). Meta-analysis uses individual studies, each of which occurred in separate circumstances of rich variation, thereby making generalization possible (Cook, 1993). Program theory delineates the domain investigated, thereby allowing the posing of more precise questions (Lipsey, 1993).

## ▣ CHANGING CONCEPTIONS OF VALUES

A second issue that shaped development in qualitative studies is the changing conception of values, often phrased as the fact–value dichotomy. This dichotomy is the belief that facts refer to one thing and values refer to something totally different. The fact–value dichotomy is a particularly embarrassing problem given that values lie at the heart of evaluation. I doubt that anything in the history of the field of evaluation has caused more trouble than this belief.

The distinction between facts and values has been around for decades, but the evaluation community inherited it through the positivists and their influence on social science. The logical positivists thought that facts could be ascertained and that only facts were the fit subject of science, along with analytic statements that were true by definition such as "1 plus 1 equals 2." Facts were empirical and could be based on pristine observations, a position called "foundationalism."

Values were something else. Values might be feelings, emotions—possibly useless metaphysical entities. Whatever they were, they were not subject to scientific analysis. People simply believed in certain values or they did not. Values were chosen. Rational discussion had little to do with them. The role of scientists was to determine facts. Others—politicians perhaps—could worry about values.

Donald Campbell, one of the great founders of the evaluation field, accepted the fact–value dichotomy explicitly (Campbell, 1982). However, he did not accept foundationalism about facts. Counter to the positivists, he contended that there were no pristine observations on which factual claims could be based because all observations are influenced by preconceptions that people hold. Knowledge is still possible because although one cannot compare a fact to a pristine observation to determine whether the fact is true (as positivists thought), one can compare a fact to the body of knowledge to which it relates. The fact should fit the whole body of beliefs. Occasionally, the body of knowledge has to change to accommodate the fact. In any case, one is comparing a belief to a body of beliefs, not comparing a belief to pure observation. This "nonfoundationalism" was counter to the positivist view.

Unfortunately, Campbell accepted the positivist conception of values. Values could not be determined rationally; they had to be chosen. It was not the evaluator's job to choose values. Once politicians, sponsors, or program developers determined values, evaluators could examine the outcomes of programs with criteria based on those values. Practically speaking, this meant that evaluators could not evaluate the program goals because the goals were closely connected to the values. Evaluators had little choice but to accept program and policy goals as they were.

Campbell had the correct idea about facts but not about values. Evaluators can deal with both facts and values rationally. Facts and values are not separate kinds of entities altogether, although they sometimes appear to be that way (House & Howe, 1999). Facts and values (factual claims and value claims) blend together in the conclusions of evaluation studies and, indeed, blend together throughout evaluation studies. We might conceive of facts and values schematically as lying on a continuum like this:

**Brute Facts**  **Bare Values**

What we call facts and values are fact and value claims, which are expressed as fact and value statements. They are beliefs about the world. Sometimes these beliefs look as if they are strictly factual without any value built in. For example, the statement "Diamonds are harder than steel" may be true or false, and it fits at the left end of the continuum. There is little individual preference built into it.

A statement such as "Cabernet is better than chardonnay" fits better at the right end of the continuum. It is suffused with personal taste. What about a statement such as "Follow Through is a good educational program"? This statement contains both fact and value aspects. The evaluative claim is based on criteria from which the conclusion is drawn and is based on factual claims as well. The statement fits the middle of the continuum—a blend of factual and value claims. Most evaluative conclusions fall toward the center of the continuum as blends of facts and values.

Context makes a huge difference in how a statement functions. A statement such as "George Washington was the first president of the United States" looks like a factual (historical) claim. But if this statement is made at a meeting of feminists who are excoriating the racist and patriarchal origins of the United States, the statement becomes evaluative in this context. The statement can be factual and evaluative simultaneously. It does not cease to be a factual claim. Similarly, claims that might seem factual in another context might be evaluative in an evaluation.

Evaluative claims are subject to rational analysis in the way we ordinarily understand rational analysis. First, the claims can be true or false. For example, Follow Through may or may not be a good educational program. Second, we can collect evidence for and against the truth or falsity of the claim, as we do in evaluation studies. Third, the evidence can be biased or unbiased, and it can be good or bad. Finally, the procedures for evidential assessment are determined by the evaluation discipline.

Of course, some claims are not easy to determine. In some situations, it might not be possible to determine truth or falsity. Also, we might need new procedures to help us collect, determine, and process fact–value claims. Just as we have developed procedures for testing factual claims, we might develop procedures for collecting and processing claims that contain strong value aspects so that our evaluative conclusions are unbiased regarding these claims as well. The claims blend together in evaluation studies. In the old view of values, to the extent that evaluative conclusions were value based, they were outside the purview of the evaluator. In the revised view, values are subject to rational analysis by the evaluator and others. Values are evaluations.

In a sense, this analysis of values helps to legitimize qualitative research. Qualitative researchers have been criticized for collecting information that merely reflects the opinions of those in and around the program when instead they should be collecting data not distorted by human judgment. Qualitative information is viewed as too subjective. In fact, the views, perspectives, and values of participants are vital pieces of information about the success of the program—if processed properly. Indeed, there is no information in evaluations that does not contain value elements. And qualitative methods are the best way in which to approach value claims, although they are not the only way

## ▣ Changing Conceptions of Social Justice

The saga of value-free research and the reluctance to do qualitative research and evaluation was not simply a philosophical position. The story must be understood within the historical, political, and social context in which the value-free ideas developed. There are political reasons why qualitative studies were viewed as too subjective and illegitimate. Ultimately, it has to do with social justice.

Principles of social justice are used to assess whether the distribution of benefits and burdens among members of a society are appropriate, fair, and moral. The substance of such assessments usually consists of arguments about the concepts of rights, deserts, or needs. When applied to society as a whole, social justice pertains to whether the institutions of a society are arranged to produce appropriate, fair, and moral distributions of benefits and burdens among societal members. As such, social justice is linked directly to the evaluation of social and educational programs because these entities, and their evaluations, affect directly the distribution of benefits and burdens.

In spite of the direct conceptual link between social justice and evaluation, social justice concerns are routinely omitted from evaluation discussions. There are two reasons for this. First, evaluators are not well versed in philosophy or political science and feel unprepared to discuss such concepts. Many evaluators have had methodological training that does not deal with social justice. Second, and more important, social justice concerns have long been excluded from social science research for political reasons.

In her history of the origins of American social science, Ross (1991) documented how social justice concerns were indeed topics of discussion in the social sciences during the early 20th century. However, several "Red Scare" episodes, stemming from fears of Marxism, swept the United States and intimidated social researchers. Some prominent economists and sociologists were dismissed from their university positions for supporting labor unions, child labor laws, and other social policies opposed by university boards of trustees, whose members came mostly from business.

The upshot was that many social scientists retreated from issues that might be seen as politically risky into concerns about research methodology. If social researchers could be persecuted for taking stands on political and "value" issues, they might be safe by focusing on which tests of statistical significance to employ or what sampling procedures to use—issues of no interest to politicians or boards of trustees. Those social researchers who remained concerned about social justice were relegated to the fringes of their disciplines as being too political. Certainly, given the history of American social science, the Marxists were considered out of bounds. Social science in other countries had different origins, and these differences were reflected in different discourses in other countries where critical theory and neo-Marxist approaches were acceptable. For example, qualitative evaluation in Britain was based on political control considerations from the beginning (MacDonald, 1977). In the United States, case studies were promoted as a means of illuminating the values of teaching and learning (Stake, 1978).

On the other hand, if social scientists with liberal positions were silenced or ignored (the fate of critical ethnographers), scholars on the political right continued to promote policies such as sterilization of the poor and elimination of social programs. A long history of biological racism stretching back to Galton, Burt, Spearman, Terman, Jensen, and others (Gould, 1981) continued unabated, reflecting the political temperament of the times. During the 1990s, this long tradition was manifested in *The Bell Curve* (Herrnstein & Murray, 1994). Scholars in this tradition claim that they are value neutral; they are merely following scientific evidence where it leads them, unfortunate though that may be.

This shift into safer political waters by many social scientists was bolstered intellectually by a convenient philosophy of science—logical positivism—that endorsed "value-free" research. Value-free social science became accepted research dogma. In the view of logical positivists and those influenced by them, values were not researchable. Only entities that could be confirmed by direct reference to "facts" were appropriate for scientific research.

Eventually, historical, philosophical, and sociological investigations into the nature of inquiry in the hard sciences demonstrated that the positivist view of science was incorrect. Nonetheless, the positivist interpretation of values continued, even among those who had grasped the nature of nonfoundationalism about factual claims. This attitude toward values was reinforced by the political climate during the cold war, the period when professional evaluation began. The origins of American social science were forgotten, and research methodology remained the primary focus of American social scientists. For many evaluators, social justice issues in evaluation retain nuances of illegitimacy and "politics."

The dominance of value-free social research meant that the conception of social justice embraced by politicians would be accepted without challenge in the evaluation of social programs and policies (except for those at the fringe e.g., neo-Marxists). For much of the 20th century, the liberal utilitarian conception of justice prevailed. This was identified with one of its main formulators, John Stuart Mill. Utilitarianism is captured in the phrase "the greatest good for the greatest number," although it is more sophisticated than the slogan implies. The way in which this theory played out in social policy was that overall benefits should be increased to the maximum. Society should be organized to maximize overall benefits. Hence, everyone could have more.

How those benefits were distributed was not a major issue. When applied to social programs, the nuances of utilitarian theory disappeared. The politics of more for everyone was more acceptable than the politics of distribution. As implemented in research practices, utilitarianism focused attention on outcomes. If the gross domestic product increases, that is good regardless of how it is distributed. The presumption is that there is more to distribute, even if not everyone gets more. Distribution is not an issue. If an educational program increases overall test scores, the amount of the increase is the focus regardless of the distribution of scores or resources—and sometimes regardless of the personal costs of obtaining the gains. Quantitative outcome measures fit well into such a framework; qualitative methods do not. Furthermore, the goals of social programs and policies, being value laden, were not subject to rational or empirical analysis by evaluators. The goals had to be accepted.

In the major reformulation of moral thinking during the 20th century, John Rawls challenged utilitarian theory with his "theory of justice," which was more egalitarian than utilitarianism. With sophisticated philosophical argument, Rawls (1971) proposed two major principles of justice by which to assess social arrangements. The first principle was that every citizen should have basic civil liberties and rights and that these rights were inviolate. These individual rights and liberties closely resembled those in the American Bill of Rights. There was little controversy about this principle of justice.

The second principle of justice, called the "difference" principle, was controversial. Rawls argued for the *distribution* of benefits—not only the overall level of benefits—to count as significant. Inequalities of economic fortune were permitted in the Rawlsian framework only if those inequalities helped the "least advantaged" people in society, defined as those with the fewest resources. For example, it was permissible to have medical doctors earn high fees if such financial inducements to study medicine helped poor people.

Hence, Rawls's theory was not strictly egalitarian because it did allow for significant inequalities in society. The Rawlsian theory did shift the focus to how the disadvantaged were treated and, in that sense, was more egalitarian than utilitarianism, which allowed trading off the benefits of the least advantaged (e.g., the unemployed) if such a move increased the level of benefits for societal members as a whole (e.g., a lower rate of inflation).

Both utilitarian and Rawlsian justice required manipulating social arrangements to maximize benefits. Unlike utilitarianism, Rawlsian justice placed constraints on the shape that the distribution of benefits could take. Social arrangements should be designed to tend toward equality in the distribution of benefits. The effects of circumstances that are arbitrary from a moral point of view (e.g., who one's parents happen to be) should be mitigated to this end and, if necessary, at the expense of maximizing benefits. Distributions resulting from the operation of markets must be held in check if those distributions are unjust, according to the second principle. (Yet a third theory of justice regards any distribution that results from free markets as socially just, no matter what that distribution looks like or what effects it has. The interplay of free markets determines social outcomes [Nozick, 1974]. This is called libertarianism. To this point, it has not been reflected in the evaluation discourse in any overt way, although many evaluators may hold this view implicitly.)

Following Rawls, some evaluators applied his theory to evaluation, arguing that evaluators should be concerned not only with overall test score gains but also, for example, with how test score gains were distributed among groups (House, 1980). How social benefits were distributed was important for evaluation. In addition, evaluators might have to solicit the views of stakeholders to determine which social benefits were at issue. Qualitative studies soliciting stakeholder views were necessary.

Of course, concerns about the distribution of benefits and calls for qualitative studies moved evaluators away from the value-free, quantitative methodology that the social sciences had been nurturing. Eventually, concern about stakeholders permeated the evaluation literature, even seeping into quantitative studies, and an acceptance of multiple methods, multiple stakeholders, and multiple outcomes in evaluation studies emerged, even among those not accepting egalitarian social justice.

During the 1980s and 1990s, Rawls's theory of justice came under criticism. One criticism was that the theory of liberal egalitarianism was insensitive to diverse group identities. In that sense, it could be oppressive and undemocratic. The theory focused on economic inequalities with little regard for other benefits that people might want. The criticism was that liberal egalitarianism identified the disadvantaged solely in terms of the relatively low economic benefits they possessed and proposed eliminating these disadvantages by implementing compensatory social programs.

Typically, this planning and evaluation process was conceived as requiring little input from those most affected. Liberal egalitarianism assumed that the benefits to be distributed, and the procedures by which the distribution would occur, were uncontroversial. In fact, the defined benefits might reflect only the interests of those in dominant positions. For example, consider a highly sexist curriculum with which girls, but not boys, have great difficulty. Providing girls with help in mastering this curriculum so as to remove their disadvantage is not a solution. The problem lies with the sexist curriculum. The distributive paradigm implied a top-down, expert-driven view. Critics saw such an approach as too paternalistic.

In response, philosophers revised the egalitarian theory of justice to take diverse identities into account, that is, to change the theory away from equality as a principle of distribution toward equality as a principle of democratic participation. In what might be called the "participatory shift," the requirements of distributive justice and those of democracy were intertwined. Justice required giving stakeholders, particularly members of groups that had been excluded historically, an effective voice in defining their own needs and negotiating benefits.

This shifting conception of social justice had implications for evaluation. The participatory paradigm fit views of evaluation in which equality was sought not solely in the distribution of predetermined benefits but also in the status and voice of the participants themselves. Benefits were to be examined and negotiated along with needs, policies, and practices. Democratic functioning became an overarching ideal. Some evaluators now advocate giving stakeholders roles to play in the evaluation itself, although evaluators differ on what roles participants should play (Greene, Lincoln, Mathison, Mertens, & Ryan, 1998). (Many who endorse participatory evaluation do so because they believe that stakeholders are more likely to use the findings for pragmatic reasons than because of social justice considerations.) In general, social justice continues to be controversial for historical and political reasons.

## ▣ BUSH'S NEOFUNDAMENTALIST POLICIES

As evaluation gradually moved away from quantitative methods and value-free studies toward multiple methodologies and qualitative studies focused on stakeholders, social justice issues, and participatory techniques, these trends did not go unnoticed by those in power. Not only did neoconservatives view such studies as too permissive, they did not like the direction in which the entire society was headed. Pointing to what they saw as postmodern excesses, they railed against modern trends, mostly to little avail.

However, the events of September 11, 2001, changed government policies regarding qualitative evaluation. The federal government is now promulgating what I call methodological fundamentalism—a manifestation of the neofundamentalism of President George W. Bush's regime. The Bush administration has embraced a new fundamentalism that permeates many aspects of American life. Before the September 11 terrorist attack, the Bush administration struggled to find traction. Bush emerged from a contested presidential election with fewer votes than the Democratic contender. Only through the peculiarities of the American electoral system and the notorious handling of ballots in Florida did Bush emerge the victor. As he assumed office in January 2001, his legitimacy was in question, his personal abilities were the butt of jokes, and his popularity was in decline.

On September 11, terrorists attacked the World Trade Center and the Pentagon, and Bush assumed the mantle of wartime president. The moral fervor with which he embraced this transformation fit his personal, born-again, religious fundamentalism. During his younger days, he had been a heavy drinker and drug user who converted to religion, saving himself from personal ruin, in his view. He embraced the new role that had been thrust on him with religious intensity, and he projected this moral certainty onto his administration and the country—a country traumatized by the attacks. This simple mission suited him. As observed by Condoleezza Rice, his then national security adviser, the worst thing she could say to Bush was that an issue was complex.

Previously, he had balanced the politics of his administration with people from different factions in the Republican party. He placed neoconservatives, such as Dick Cheney, Donald Rumsfeld, and Paul Wolfowitz, in key posts and balanced them with moderates such as Colin Powell. In foreign policy, the neoconservative vision of preemptively using American power to transform the world was checked by the realist view of maintaining multilateral international relationships. However, September 11 provided neoconservatives with the license they needed to pursue the hawkish policies they had long advocated, including the invasion of Iraq, an obsession of Wolfowitz, deputy secretary of defense. His plan called for preemptive military strikes on countries threatening American interests. He had prepared this policy during the first Bush administration, but the preemptive position had been dismissed as being too radical at that time. After September 11, it became official American doctrine. Bush's neofundamentalism emerged in full force.

Fundamentalism has several characteristics. First, there is one source of truth, be it the Bible, the Koran, the Talmud, or whatever. Second, this source of authority is located in the past, often in a Golden Age, and is associated with particular individuals. Believers hark back to that time. Third, true believers have access to this fundamental truth, but others do not. Applying the truth leads to a radical transformation of the world for the better. Fundamentalists have a prophetic vision of the future, that is, revelatory insight. Fourth, having access to the source of truth means that believers are certain they are correct. They have moral certitude, a defining attribute. They are "elected." Fifth, fundamentalists are not open to counterarguments. Indeed, they are not open to other ideas generally. They do not assimilate evidence that contradicts their views. They dismiss contrary information or ignore it. Sixth, they are persuaded by arguments consistent with their beliefs even when outsiders find these arguments to be incomplete, illogical, or bizarre. Seventh, people who do not agree with them do not have this insight, and fundamentalists do not need to listen to them. In fact, sometimes it is all right to muscle nonbelievers aside because they do not understand and only impede progress. Eighth, believers associate with other true believers and avoid nonbelievers, thereby closing the circle of belief and increasing certainty. Ninth, they find ways of promulgating their beliefs by means other than rational persuasion—by decree, policy, or laws—through forcing others to conform rather than persuading them—in short, through coercion. Finally, fundamentalists try to curtail the propagation of other viewpoints by restricting the flow of contrary ideas and those who espouse them.

The Bush administration has exercised this new fundamentalism in foreign affairs, domestic affairs, and even evaluation. In foreign policy, the fundamentalism is evident in the invasion of Iraq. The Golden Age for neoconservatives was the Reagan administration, and Reagan was the sacred figure. Many neoconservatives prefer to call themselves Reaganites and hope to restore the age during which the United States brought down the Soviet Union and won the cold war, in their view of history.

Bush's speeches have taken on a quasi-religious, liturgical tone, including phrases such as "axis of evil" as compared with Reagan's "the evil empire." Bush believes that he is a great leader like Reagan, Churchill, or even Lincoln. By his own admission, he talks to God every night. He has surrounded himself with fellow evangelicals who see him as "chosen" since his peculiar election, for which they prayed. And their prayers were answered. No matter what evidence was presented against his position on Iraq, it had no effect. If the Iraqis had no weapons of mass destruction, they were hiding them. If the Iraqis admitted to having weapons, they had violated the UN mandate. If the war might be disastrous for the region, if most nations in the world were opposed to it, and if world public opinion was overwhelmingly opposed to it, no matter. Others did not understand. They were "old Europe," unwilling to take risks.

The Bush team was closed to counterevidence. Bush team members presented arguments seen by others as inconclusive and at times strange. They concocted a revelatory vision of democratic transformation for Iraq that Middle East experts viewed as incredible. The more criticism that was encountered from outside, the more they banded together, like President Johnson and his advisers did during the war in Vietnam. Coercion was the tool of choice for compliance, whether it was used against enemies or allies. They either had little sense of how others might react to their actions or did not care. The fundamentalism of the Muslim terrorists was countered with the new fundamentalism of the American president.

## Methodological Fundamentalism in Evaluation

Bush's neofundamentalism has influenced other parts of the federal government, including evaluation. In evaluation, this takes the form of methodological fundamentalism. Government agencies that sponsor evaluations have aggressively pushed the concept of "evidence-based" progress, policies, and programs. The core of the evidence-based idea is that research and evaluation must be "scientific." In this definition, scientific means that research and evaluation findings must be based on experiments, with randomized experiments being given strong preference. Other ways of producing evidence are not scientific and not acceptable. There is one method for discovering the truth and one method only—the randomized experiment. This is a fundamentalist position.

This doctrine is embedded in Bush's education legislation, No Child Left Behind. In this legislation (www.ed.gov), the term "scientific" is repeated more than 100 times. The method of inquiry is written into the legislation itself, an unusual event. Imagine an allocation for research in physics specifying the methods by which physicists are to conduct studies. In addition, the U.S. Department of Education has established a What Works Clearinghouse to screen evidence-based projects and has encouraged the construction of lists of researchers who comply with the new methodological strictures— a white list as opposed to a black list.

An explicit rationale for evidence-based progress is provided in a report prepared for the U.S. Department of Education by the Council for Evidence-Based Policies (2002). The council consists mostly of Washington insiders, bureaucrats, and think tank fellows plus some social researchers. In accepting the report, Secretary of Education Rod Paige remarked that Bush's education policy was based on four concepts: accountability, options for parents, local control, and evidence-based instruction. The first two policies have been mainstays of the neoconservative educational platform for some time. As for evidence-based instruction, "for the first time we are applying the same rigorous standards to education research as are applied to medical research" (Paige, 2002). Standards will save the day once again. The disdain for the opinions of professional educators manifested in national and statewide testing systems was now carried into disdain for professional evaluators, disdain for professionals being a hallmark of neoconservative policy.

The basic argument of the Council for Evidence-Based Policies (2002) report is that education is a field of fads in which there has been no progress—progress measured by national tests—for the past 30 years. In contrast, there has been great progress in medicine: "Our extraordinary inability to raise educational achievement stands in stark contrast to our remarkable progress in improving human health over the same period—progress which . . . is largely the result of evidence-based government policies" (p. i). The claim is that progress in medicine has resulted primarily from randomized field trials.

Hence, the Department of Education should build a "knowledge base" of educational interventions proved effective by randomized trials and should provide strong incentives for the use of such interventions. "This strategy holds a key to reversing decades of stagnation in American education and sparking rapid, evidence-driven progress" (Council for Evidence-Based Policies, 2002, p. i). Such is the revelatory vision for the transformation of American education. The report recommends that all discretionary funds for research and evaluation be focused on randomized trials. After all, other research designs produce erroneous findings.

These arguments are weak, to say the least. They may be sufficient to persuade those who already believe in randomized experiments or those who lack knowledge of evaluation. They could hardly withstand the scrutiny of scholars in evaluation. It is the case that education is riddled with fads that have no research backing. Indeed, the neoconservatives have promoted many of these such as charter schools, vouchers, and accountability through test scores. One might also agree that the schools have not improved much over the past 30 years and that medicine has shown progress.

However, medical progress has not been primarily due to randomized field trials. Medicine is the beneficiary of decades of breakthrough research in the physical sciences, notably biophysics, biochemistry, biology, and molecular biology, that has resulted in elaborate theories about human disease. To my knowledge, no one in medicine has received a Nobel Prize for promoting randomized studies. Field trials only test ideas—a valuable service for sure, but hardly the primary source of progress.

It is true that education has no corresponding theory on which to base its practices. The social sciences that might have produced the underlying theory, primarily psychology, have failed to do so. Actually, psychology is a field that relies heavily on randomized trials. Not only has psychology failed to produce viable theory for education, it has failed to produce cures for mental illness comparable to medical advances. Similarly, criminology, which also uses randomized trials, has failed to produce solutions to crime. Otherwise, the United States would not have 2 million people in prison.

As Noam Chomsky noted, psychology is a methodology without a substance. Members of the Council for Evidence-Based Policies, several of whom are psychologists, would have been more honest to argue that because randomized methods have produced little of substance in psychology, maybe they will produce something useful in education. Actually, randomized trials are neither the problem nor the cure. I believe that we could use more randomized field trials in evaluation, but the evangelical arguments advanced by these proponents are embarrassing.

## Attributes of Methodological Fundamentalism

In addition to a revelatory vision that promises transformation, methodological fundamentalism has other features of neofundamentalism. It has a simple credo: Only randomized experiments produce the truth. There is one source of truth—the randomized experiment. If we but follow, it will lead us to a Golden Age. Methodological fundamentalism even has a storied past. The key figure is Campbell, who championed the concept of social experiments as the *only* way in which to evaluate social programs early in the history of evaluation. Although Campbell later relented, admitting that there were other valid ways of acquiring knowledge about social programs, many followers did not. Apparently, they have been biding their time and have found their opportunity in Bush's neofundamentalism as the neoconservatives have done with war policy.

The prescription for randomized trials has been written into legislation without extensive discussion in the relevant professional communities, whose members would oppose such a narrow prescription of how to conduct research and evaluation. But avoiding contrary ideas is part of the orientation. And of course, the prescription is enforced by government decree and incentives. One significant outcome of choosing randomized experiments as the only method for conducting studies is that it eliminates stakeholder views in studies. Most evaluations now incorporate the perspectives of stakeholder groups. This experimental approach precludes the views of stakeholders. Such exclusion must have appeal for those who do not want to be confused by contrary ideas and complex issues.

From a philosophy of science perspective, the difficulty is that the prescription is based on an overly simplistic view of social causation, namely the regularity theory of causation, as noted earlier. Social programs are not closed to outside influences in the same way as experiments in the physical world can be. Hence, definitive experiments to test theories are not possible because they sometimes are in the physical world. This is not to say that experiments cannot be useful. They can be valuable if they are used in the right circumstances and are supported by other evidence that provides the context for interpreting findings. Theory is not available for this purpose in social research, and findings are often interpreted ideologically or politically. There is a need for collecting and assessing various stakeholder views to aid interpretation.

The appropriate situation for randomized field trials is one similar to evaluating physical entities. For example, evaluating drugs by way of randomized experiments is extremely useful because the drugs themselves can be reproduced in identical form. Drug treatment does not vary nearly as much as social programs, although even in drug trials people react to drugs differently. When the treatment focuses on entities that are difficult to control, experiments become less useful. When educational programs are placed in different settings, there are dozens—if not hundreds—of influences that are impossible to control even in randomized experiments. This means that the results vary even when the treatment appears to be the same. Randomized experiments are one way of providing evidence, but they are not the only way. Field experiments are not appropriate in all situations, neither are they foolproof.

The utility of randomized experiments was discussed extensively in the evaluation community long ago and was abandoned as the sole way in which to conduct studies. The experiments-only advocates lost the debate, but now the same doctrine has been resurrected. This time advocates have appealed to government officials, who are easier to persuade given that they have limited expertise in research and evaluation. Government officials often yearn for certitude in evaluation findings as a way of bolstering their authority. It would make the task of mandating new programs much easier and less controversial. Evaluators have not been able to deliver such unequivocal findings. It is not difficult to understand why a method that promises certainty has appeal for them. However, the certainty that fundamentalism provides is false.

So, after 40 years, evaluation policy has come full circle. What is different this time around is that there is a sizable evaluation community that has considered, discussed, and dismissed the narrow focus on experimental method that is being promoted by the government. For those interested in how such differences will play out, they might look to history. Since its founding, the United States has been swept repeatedly by strong evangelical movements that claim to have absolute truth and attempt to restrict ideas. During the 20th century, these movements took the form of anticommunism crusades, and they had a profound effect on the shape of American social science. It appears to be time for the mettle of the current generation in evaluation to be tested.

## ▣ REFERENCES

Campbell, D. (1982). Experiments as arguments. In E. R. House, S. Mathison, J. A. Pearsol, & H. Preskill (Eds.), *Evaluation studies review annual* (No. 7, pp. 117–128). Beverly Hills, CA: Sage.

Campbell, D. T., & Stanley, J. C. (1963). *Experimental and quasi-experimental designs for research.* Chicago: Rand McNally.

Chen, H., & Rossi, P. H. (1987). Evaluating with sense: The theory-driven approach to validity. *Evaluation Review, 7,* 283–302.

Cook, T. D. (1993). A quasi-sampling theory of the generalization of causal relationships. In L. B. Sechrest & A. G. Scott (Eds.), *Understanding causes and generalizing about them* (New Directions in Evaluation, No. 57, pp. 39–82). San Francisco: Jossey–Bass.

Council for Evidence-Based Policies. (2002). *Bringing evidence-driven progress to education: A recommended strategy for the U.S. Department of Education.* New York: William T. Grant Foundation.

Cronbach, L. J. (1982). *Designing evaluations of educational and social programs.* San Francisco: Jossey–Bass.

Glass, G. V. (1976). Primary, secondary, and meta-analysis of research. *Educational Researcher, 5*(9), 3–8.

Gould, S. J. (1981). *The mismeasure of man.* New York: Norton.

Greene, J., Lincoln, Y. S., Mathison, S., Mertens, D. M., & Ryan, K. (1998). Advantages and challenges of using inclusive evaluation approaches in evaluation practice. *American Journal of Evaluation, 19,* 101–122.

Herrnstein, R. J., & Murray, C. (1994). *The bell curve.* New York: Free Press.

House, E. R. (1980). *Evaluating with validity.* Beverly Hills, CA: Sage.

House, E. R. (1991). Realism in research. *Educational Researcher, 20*(6), 2–9.

House, E. R., & Howe, K. R. (1999). *Values in evaluation and social research.* Thousand Oaks, CA: Sage.

Lipsey, M. W. (1993). Theory as method: Small theories of treatments. In L. B. Sechrest & A. G. Scott (Eds.), *Understanding causes and generalizing about them* (New Directions in Evaluation, No. 57, pp. 5–38). San Francisco: Jossey–Bass.

MacDonald, B. (1977). A political classification of evaluation studies. In D. Hamilton (Ed.), *Beyond the numbers game* (pp. 224–227). London: Macmillan.

Mackie, J. L. (1974). *The cement of the universe.* Oxford, UK: Clarendon.

Maxwell, J. A. (1996). *Using qualitative research to develop causal explanations.* Working paper, Harvard Project on Schooling and Children, Harvard University.

McLaughlin, M. W. (1975). *Evaluation and reform.* Cambridge, MA: Ballinger.

Nozick, R. (1974). *Anarchy, state, and utopia.* New York: Basic Books.

Paige, R. (2002, November 18). [Remarks at Consolidation Conference], Washington, DC.

Rawls, J. (1971). *A theory of justice.* Cambridge, MA: Belknap.

Reichardt, C. S., & Rallis, S. F. (Eds.). (1994). *The qualitative–quantitative debate: New perspectives* (New Directions in Program Evaluation, No. 61). San Francisco: Jossey–Bass.

Rivlin, A. (1971). *Systematic thinking for social action.* Washington, DC: Brookings Institution.

Ross, D. (1991). *The origins of American social science.* Cambridge, UK: Cambridge University Press.

Stake, R. E. (1978). The case study method in social inquiry. *Educational Researcher, 7*(2), 5–8.

Suchman, E. A. (1967). *Evaluative research.* New York: Russell Sage.

# READER'S GUIDE

| CHAPTER | SUMMARY | PRIMARY TOPICS | THEMATIC TOPICS |
| --- | --- | --- | --- |
| 1. | Overview of Collection | Epistemology, Methodology | Paradigms, Resistances, Moments |
| 2. | Forms of Narrative Inquiry | Disciplinary Models | Voice, Performance Analysis, Testimonio |
| 3. | Forms of Arts-Based Inquiry | History of This Methodology | Activist Art, Critical Performance Pedagogy |
| 4. | Major Interview Formats | Interview Society, Feminist Ethics | Interview as Negotiated Text |
| 5. | Recontextualizing Observational Methodologies | Observation as Interaction IRBs | Observational Ethics, Demystifying Observation |
| 6. | Visual Methods, Presenting Visual Materials | IRBs, Use of Photographs | Observing Public Life, Critical Visual Sensibility |
| 7. | History of Autoethnography | Personal Experience, Personal Narratives | Reflexivity, Personal History, Performance |
| 8. | On-Line Ethnogaphy | Intenet, Textuality, Self | The Other, Disembodied Relations, Ethics |
| 9. | Analytic Perspectives | Indigenous Modes of Organization | Modes of Analysis |
| 10. | Foucault's Methodologies | Archaeology, Genealogy, Care of the Self | Discourse, Disciplines, Interpretive Rules |
| 11. | Talk and Text | Reading Narrative | Membership Category, and Conversation Analysis |
| 12. | Focus Groups | Multiple Uses and Forms | Pedagogy and Politics |
| 13. | Criteria for Evaluating Inquiry | Relativism, Crude Empiricism | Forms of Resistance |
| 14. | Emancipatory Discourses | Indigenous Pedagogies | Critical Personal Narratives |
| 15. | Writing as Inquiry | Creative Analytic Procedures | Ethical Selves |
| 16. | Anthropological Poetics | Re-Grounding Method | Moral Aesthetics |
| 17. | Cultural Poesis | The Politics of the Ordinary | Forms of Fragmentation |
| 18. | Intestigative Poetics | Witnessing, Activism | Critiques of Power |
| 19. | Qualitative Evaluation | Social Policy | Neo-Conservativism |

# GLOSSARY

**Action ethnography:**  Critical ethnography involving the ethnographer in collaborative, social justice projects. See also *Critical ethnography.*

**Action research:**  Critical research dealing with real-life problems, involving collaboration, dialogue, mutual learning, and producing tangible results.

**Advocacy:**  Arguing for action research projects that resist traditional forms of privilege, knowledge, and practice.

**African American performance-based aesthetic:**  Using the tools of critical race consciousness to manipulate and criticize the tropes of minstrelsy that represent specific colonial racist practices.

**Antifoundationalism:**  The refusal to adopt any permanent, unvarying, or foundational standards by which truth can be universally known.

**Archaeology/genealogy:**  Textual and historical methods of interpretation, involving a complex set of concepts (savoir, connaissance, positivity, enunciation, discursive practice) associated with the work of Foucault; interpretive procedures showing how local practices and their subjected knowledges are brought into play, as in the history of sexuality.

**Authenticity, validity as:**  Hallmarks of trustworthy, rigorous, valid constructivist inquiry; *Types:* fairness, ontological, educative, catalytic, tactical.

**Autoethnography:**  Engaging ethnographical practice through personal, lived experience; writing the self into the ethnographic narrative.

**Autohistory:**  Use of the autobiographical form to write life history or personal life stories and narratives.

**Autopoiesis:** A self (auto)-creation (poiesis) using the poetic and the historical to understand the current moment.

## ▣ B

**Belmont Report:** Report issued in 1978 by the U.S. Commission for the Protection of Human Subjects. This report established three principles, or moral standards (respect, beneficence, justice), for human subject research.

**Biographical memory:** A social process of looking back, as we find ourselves remembering our lives in terms of our experiences with others. Sociological introspection (C. Ellis) is a method for reconstructing biographical memory.

**Black feminist thought:** Critical race- and gender-based discourse linked to revolutionary black feminism; includes the work of June Jordan, Toni Morrison, and bell hooks.

**Bricolage, bricoleur:** A bricoleur is a person who uses bits and pieces and anything else to make do, to assemble a quilt, a montage, a performance, an interpretation, a bricolage, a new formation, like a jazz improvisation. The postmodern qualitative researcher is a bricoleur.

## ▣ C

**Care, ethic of:** Carol Gilligan characterizes the female moral voice as an ethic of care, involving compassion and nurturance.

**Catalytic authenticity:** The ability of a given inquiry to prompt action on the part of research participants and the involvement of the researcher/evaluator in training participants in specific forms of social and political action if such training is desired by those participants.

**Civic journalism:** Journalism that shapes calls for a public ethnography and cultural criticism.

**Cochrane Collaboration:** An international group of clinicians, methodologists, and consumers formed to facilitate the collection, implementation, and dissemination of systematic reviews of multiple randomized clinical trials (RTCs).

**Collaborative storytelling:** An approach very similar to *testimonio*, in that it is the intention of the direct narrator (research participant) to use an interlocutor (the researcher) to bring his or her situation to the attention of an audience to which he or she would normally not have access because of his or her very condition of subalternity, which the *testimonio* bears witness.

**Communitarian model of ethics:** A model of ethics calling for collaborative, trusting, nonoppressive relationships between researchers and those studied. It presumes a community that is ontologically and axiologically prior to the person. This community has common moral values, and research is rooted in concepts of care, shared governance, neighborliness, love, kindness, and the moral good.

**Compassionate consciousness:** An embodied way of being and knowing that is a nonaccountable, nondescribable way of knowing.

**Compositional studies:** Contextual, relational studies that are sensitive to the fluidity of social identities and that analyze public and private institutions, groups, and lives lodged in relation to key social and economic structures.

**Constructivist grounded theory:** Associated with the work of Charmaz, emphasizing constructionist, not objectivist, leanings; criteria include credibility, resonance, and usefulness.

**Conversational interviewing:** A style of interviewing focused on encouraging subject participation. Interviews can be conducted in an informal manner, and interviewers may share more personal information about themselves than conventional interviewers.

**Creative analytic practices (CAP):** Writers interpret as they write, so writing is a form of inquiry, a way of making sense of the world. Laurel Richardson and Elizabeth Adams St. Pierre (Chapter 15, this volume) explore new writing and interpretive styles that follow from the narrative literary turn in the social sciences. They call these different forms of writing CAP (creative analytical processes) ethnography.

**Critical ethnography:** Critical ethnographers, drawing from critical theory and the Frankfurt school, emphasize a reflexive focus on praxis, action, experience, subjectivity, reflexivity, and dialogical understanding. See also *Action research*.

**Critical humanism:** An approach to inquiry that focuses on the structure of experience and its daily lived nature and that acknowledges the political and social role of all inquiry.

**Critical pedagogy:** The critical reflexive ways in which cultural agents resist and undermine particular hegemonic ways of understanding.

**Critical Race Theory (CRT):** Patricia Hill Collins (1991), Mari Matsuda (1995), Gloria Ladson-Billings (2000), and Patricia Williams (1992) have crafted Critical Race Theory to speak explicitly back to the webbed relations of history, the political economy, and everyday lives of women and men of color.

## ▣ D

**Decolonization:** Contesting colonial models of inquiry and domination, resisting hegemonic research protocols, and inventing new ways of knowing.

**Diaspora identity:** The identities of persons of color in the developing world who have been forced to move, to travel because of politics, economics, and other cultural forces.

**Discourse analysis:** The collection and analysis of spoken or written materials.

## ▣ E

**Ethnodrama:** Popular theater consisting of ethnographically derived plays located within the tradition of epic theater.

**Ethnographic gaze:** The classic look of the white male ethnographer and the "other."

**Ethnopoetics:** Ethnopoetics could be labeled investigative poetry's immediate predecessor. It is an attempt to make poetry political by merging a critique of colonialism, soft anthropology, and a poetics of witnessing. The term *ethnopoetics* was coined in 1967 by Jerome Rothenberg, Dennis Tedlock, and their colleagues.

**Evidence-based research:** A new methodological conservatism stressing scientifically based educational research, research using the biomedical, random, clinical trial model.

## ▣ F

**Focus group as strategic articulation:** Reconceptualizing focus groups as instruments for implementing critical pedagogy.

**Freirian pedagogy:** Pedagogy influenced by Paulo Freire in which the goal of education is to begin to name the world and to recognize that we are all "subjects" of our own lives and narratives, not "objects" in the stories of others.

## ▣ G

**Gaze:** Poststructuralists and postmodernists have contributed to the understanding that there is no clear window into the life of an individual. Any gaze is always filtered through the lenses of language, gender, social class, race, and ethnicity. There are no objective observations, only observations that are socially situated in the worlds of the observer and observed.

**Grounded theory:**   A largely inductive method of developing theory through close-up contact with the empirical world.

▣   H

**Habitus:**   Bourdieu used the concept of habitus to refer to a system of meanings and structures that generate and organize practices and representations that can be objectively adapted to their outcomes without presupposing a conscious aiming at ends or an express mastery of the operations necessary in order to attain them. Using a musical metaphor, they can be collectively orchestrated without being the product of the organizing action of a conductor.

**Hip-hop movement:**   A gendered political, literary, and performance movement involving, in some instances, liberation work and a revolutionary call to resistance for African American and other marginalized communities. Some scholars and performers have made connections with the hip-hop generation and revolutionary black feminism.

**Hybridity:**   Term that is characterized by literature and theory that focuses on the effects of mixture upon identity and culture.

▣   I

**Indigenous pedagogy:**   A pedagogy that privileges the language, meanings, stories, and personal identities of indigenous persons.

**Indigenous theater:**   Indigenous theater nurtures a critical transnational yet historically specific critical race consciousness. It uses indigenous performance as means of political representation through the reflexive use of historical restagings and masquerade. This subversive theater undermines colonial racial ideologies.

**Institutional ethnography:**   A form of ethnography, focusing on power relations, systems of discourse, and ethnographic realities connected with the work of Dorothy Smith.

**Interpretive sufficiency paradigm:**   Within a feminist communitarian model, paradigm seeks to open up the social world in all its dynamic dimensions. Ethnographic accounts should process sufficient depth, detail, emotionality, and nuance that will permit a critical consciousness to be formed. A discourse is authentically sufficient when it is multivocal, enhances moral discernment, and promotes social transformation.

## ▣ J

**Justice and investigative poetics:** Fight for social justice through poems calling on scholars to become more active in their communities.

## ▣ K

**Kaupapa Māori research:** In New Zealand, Māori scholars have coined a research approach as Kaupapa Māori or Dori research rather than employing the term *indigenist*. The struggle has been over the ability by Māoris as Māoris to name the world, to theorize the world. It is a particular approach that sets out to make a positive difference for Māoris, that incorporates a model of social change or transformation, and that privileges Māori knowledge and ways of being.

**Knowledge economy:** A term used by businesspeople to define the ways in which changes in technology such as the Internet, the removal of barriers to travel and trade, and the shift to a postindustrial economy have created conditions in which the knowledge content of all goods and services will underpin wealth creation and determine competitive advantage.

## ▣ L

**Layered texts:** A textual strategy for putting oneself into one's text and putting one's text into the literatures and traditions of social science.

**Liberation theology:** A school of theology, especially prevalent in the Roman Catholic Church in Latin America, that finds in the Gospel a call to free people from political, social, and material oppression, which uses *testimonio* as a way of expression.

**Local understandings:** Ethnographic studies tend to focus on locally crafted meanings and the settings where social interaction takes place. Such studies consider the situated content of talk in relation to local meaning-making practices.

**Ludic postmodernism:** Postmodernist currents associated with Derrida, Foucault, Lyotard, Ebert, and others.

## ▣ M

**Method of instances:** A method taking each instance of a phenomenon as an occurrence that evidences the operation of a set of cultural understandings currently available for use by cultural members.

**Methodological fundamentalism:** A return to a much discredited model of empirical inquiry wherein the "gold standard" for producing knowledge that is worthwhile is based on quantitative, experimental design studies.

**Mixed-genre text:** A text that crosses writing and interpretive formats (genres), including ethnography, history, fiction, poetry, prose, photography, and performance.

**Moral/ethical epistemology:** Epistemology that scholars of color have produced out of which critical theories emerged, where groups such as African Americans, Native Americans, Latinos, and Asian Americans have the experience of a racialized and postcolonial identity.

**Mystory performance:** Personal cultural texts that contextualize important personal experiences and problems within the institutional settings and historical moments in which the author finds himself or herself.

## ▣ N

**Narrative inquiry:** A form of inquiry that analyzes narrative, in its many forms, and uses a narrative approach for interpretive purposes.

**Naturalistic generalization:** Generalizations made entirely from personal or vicarious experience.

**Nonfiction, creative:** A term suggesting no distinction between fiction and nonfiction because both are narrative. Thus, the difference between narrative writing and science writing is not one of fiction or nonfiction but the claim that the author makes for the text and how one's "truth claims" are evaluated.

## ▣ O

**Online ethnography:** A form of ethnography acknowledging that computer-mediated construction of self, other, and social structure constitutes a unique phenomenon of study.

**Ontological authenticity:** A criterion for determining a raised level of awareness by individual research participants.

**Organic intellectual:** Educated citizenry to participate actively in democracy, knowing enough to "read the word and the world" (Freire, 1970); helping credentialed intellectuals do the reconstructive work.

**Other, as research subject:** It refers to those who are studied by action-oriented and clinically oriented qualitative researchers that create spaces for those "Others" to speak and making such voices heard.

◨ P

**Participatory action research:** A movement in which researchers work with subordinated populations around the world to solve unique local problems with local funds of knowledge.

**Patriarchal positivism:** Control through rationality and separation that forms the dominant biomedical paradigm.

**Performance ethnography:** A critical and emancipatory discourse connecting critical pedagogy with new ways of writing and performing cultural politics in order to catalyze social change.

**Performance methodology:** A collectivized ensemble of precepts used by those committed to the communicative and pedagogical potential that knowledge—the process of attaining, sharing, and projecting knowing—can be accomplished through doing.

**Performance of possibilities:** A set of tenets offering both validity and direction for performance ethnography.

**Performativity:** The stylized repetition of communicative acts, linguistic and corporeal, that are socially validated and discursively established in the moment of the performance.

**Poetics of place:** Form of poetics in which, through the conveyance forms and content of language and story, we enter an analysis of places and the events that unfold in them.

**Polyphonic interviewing:** A method of interviewing in which the voices of the respondents are recorded with minimal influence from the researcher and are not collapsed together and reported as one through the interpretation of the researcher.

**Postcolonial feminist thought:** A mode of thought arguing that feminism takes many different forms depending on the context of contemporary nationalism. With attention to the invidious effects of "othering," it argues that Western feminist models are inappropriate for thinking of research with women in postcolonial sites.

**Postmodern ethnography:** Ethnography acknowledging that ethnographic practice is not apolitical or removed from ideology. Ethnographic practice hence has the capacity to be affected by or to affect social formations.

**Poststructural feminism:** Theory that emphasizes problems with the social text, its logic, and its inability ever to represent the world of lived experience fully. Poststructural feminists see the "communitarian dream" as politically disabling because of the suppression of gender differences and the exclusion of subaltern voices and marginalized groups whom community members are loath to engage.

▣ Q

**Quality, emerging criteria:** Set of understandings in which the ethical intersects both the interpersonal and the epistemological.

**Queer theory:** The postmodernization of sexual and gender studies bringing a radical deconstruction of all conventional categories of sexuality and gender.

**Quilt maker, qualitative researcher as:** Texts where many different things are going on at the same time, different voices, different perspectives, points of views, and angles of vision.

▣ R

**Race, as social construction:** A social constructionist conception of race refuses the notions of an essentialist or a biological ground for race, asserting, rather, that race is a linguistically and historically determined construct.

**Racialized identity:** Essentialized concepts of race imposed on specific individuals or groups.

**Randomized clinical trial (RCT):** Clinical methodology that offers a compelling critical analysis of the biomedical paradigms and currently is considered to be the best external evidence when considering medical interventions.

**Reality, hyper:** It is a way of characterizing the way the consciousness interacts with "reality," when a consciousness loses its ability to distinguish reality from fantasy, and when the nature of the hyperreal world is characterized by "enhancement" of reality.

**Reflexivity, performative:** A condition in which sociocultural groups, or their most perceptive members acting representatively, turn, bend, or reflect back on themselves (Turner, 1988).

**Representation, crisis of:** A moment of rupture in scholarship when texts began to become more reflexive, calling into question issues of gender, class, and race and seeking new models of trough, method, and representation.

**Rhizomatic validity:** A form of behaving via relay, circuit, and multiple openings that counters authority with multiple sites.

▣ S

**Sacred epistemology:** This epistemology places us in a noncompetitive, nonhierarchical relationship to the Earth, to nature, and to the larger world.

**Safe spaces:**  Progressive social scientists have gained a foothold in the academy and have created safe spaces for themselves.

**Scholars of color, moral epistemologies as activists:**  Seeking racial justice, scholars of color, using Critical Race Theory (CRT), enact critical and moral epistemologies (double consciousness, sovereignty, hybridity, postcolonialism).

**Self-reflexive validity:**  A form of critical validity involving paying attention to one's place in the discourses and practices that are being analyzed.

**Silences:**  Silences can reveal invisible social structures, as well as point to moral and ethical dilemmas and lack of awareness.

**Social justice:**  A form of justice involving a moral commitment to social and economic reform and assistance to the poor; being an advocate for fairness and what is just.

**Solidarity research:**  Research that empowers and promotes critical consciousness and acts of resistance.

**Spirituality:**  A sense of the sacred, a sensuous and embodied form of being, including being in harmony with the universe.

**Standpoint theory:**  Speaking and theorizing from a historically specific standpoint or position.

**Subaltern:**  Colonized persons, made to feel inferior by virtue of class, color, gender, race, and ethnicity.

**Subversive theater:**  A theater that unsettles official versions of reality and challenges racism and white privilege.

## ▣  T

*Testimonio:*  A first-person text with political content, often reporting on torture, imprisonment, and other struggles for survival.

**Textualism:**  The study of documents and social texts as the site for the representation of lived experience. The media and popular culture are sites where history and lived experience come together. Nothing, Derrida reminds us, stands outside the text.

**Transformative action:**  Creative, political action that changes the world.

**Truth:**  A contested term, given different meaning within positivist, postpositivist and postmodern, and other narrative epistemologies.

## ▣ U

**Uncertainty:** The understanding that while social life is interdependent and displays regularities, the outcome of any given social event is uncertain and not fully predictable.

**Unstructured interviewing:** Open-ended interviewing involving an unstructured format, often used in oral history, participant observation, and PAR forms of inquiry.

**Utopian performative:** Performances that enact a politics of hope, liberation, and justice.

## ▣ V

**Validity, authenticity criteria:** The hallmarks of authentic, trustworthy, rigorous constructivist inquiry include fairness and four types of authenticity: ontological, educative, catalytic, and tactical.

**Validity, catalytic:** The extent to which research moves those it studies to understand the world and then act to change the world.

**Validity, transgressive:** A subversive approach to validity, connected with deconstructionism and the work of Patti Lather. There are four subtypes: ironic, paralogical, rhizomatic, and voluptuous.

**Verbatim theater:** A form of realistic theater or ethnodrama that uses oral history, news accounts, and verbatim reports, thereby quoting history back to itself, bringing the immediate past into the present.

**Virtue ethics of care model:** An ethics that goes beyond utilitarianism, to include feminist notions of care, love, and communitarianism.

**Voice, paradigmatic issues:** Hearing the other (and the author) speak in the text, presenting the other's self in the text.

## ▣ W

**Warranted assertion:** A conclusion or assertion that is justified by a set of socially shaped reasons or judgments.

**Wild places:** Sacred places where meaning, self, and being dwell.

**Women of color, as researcher:** Women of color are urged to address, from within white patriarchy, culturally sensitive issues surrounding race, class, and gender.

**Writing, as inquiry:**   Writing is a method of inquiry, writing is thinking, writing is analysis, and writing is a method of discovery.

**Writing, performative:**   The kind of writing where the body and the spoken word come together. Performance writing shows and does not tell. It is writing that does what it says it is doing by doing it.

## ▣   X, Y, Z

**Zombie research:**   According to Ken Plummer, a postgay humanist sociologist, in the postmodern moment, certain terms, such as *family*, and much of our research methodology language are obsolete. He calls them zombie categories. They are no longer needed. They are dead terms.

# SUGGESTED READINGS

▣ CHAPTER 2

Atkinson, P., & Delamont, S. (Eds.). (2006). *Narrative methods.* Thousand Oaks, CA: Sage.

Bell, S. E. (2006). Living with breast cancer in text and image: Making art to make sense. *Qualitative Research in Psychology, 3,* 31–44.

Bruner, J. (2004). Life as narrative. *Social Research, 71,* 691–710.

Clandinin, D. J. (Ed.). (2007). *Handbook of narrative inquiry: Mapping a methodology.* Thousand Oaks, CA: Sage.

Clandinin, D. J., & Connely, F. M. (Eds.). (2004). *Narrative inquiry: Experience and story in qualitative research.* San Francisco: Jossey-Bass.

Daiute, C., & Lightfoot, C. (Eds.). (2004). *Narrative analysis: Studying the development of individuals in society.* Thousand Oaks, CA: Sage.

Dollard, J. (1935). *Criteria for the life history, with analyses of six notable documents.* New Haven, CT: Yale University Press. (Reprinted in 1948, New York: Peter Smith)

Goffman, E. (1981). *Forms of talk.* Philadelphia: University of Pennsylvania Press.

Gottschalk, L., Kluckhohn, C., & Angell, R. (1947). *The use of personal documents in history, anthropology, and sociology.* New York: Social Science Research Council.

Gubrium, J., & Holstein, J. (2008). Narrative ethnography. In S. Hess-Biber & P. Leavy (Eds.), *Handbook of emergent methods.* New York: Guilford.

Lieblich, A., McAdams, D. P., & Josselson, R. (Eds.). (2004). *Healing plots: The narrative basis of psychotherapy.* Washington, DC: American Psychological Association.

Linden, R. R. (1993). *Making stories, making selves: Feminist reflections on the Holocaust.* Columbus: Ohio State University Press.

Myerhoff, B. (1992). *Remembered lives: The work of ritual, storytelling, and growing older* (Edited and with an Introduction by Mark Kaminsky). Ann Arbor: University of Michigan Press.

Plummer, K. (1983). *Documents of life: An introduction to the problems and literature of a humanistic method.* London: Allen & Unwin.

Riessman, C. K. (2007). *Narrative methods for the human sciences.* Thousand Oaks, CA: Sage.

## ▣ CHAPTER 9

Atkinson, P., Delamont, S., & Housley, W. (2007). *Contours of culture.* Walnut Creek, CA: Alta Mira.

Atkinson, P. A., Coffey, A., & Delamont, S. (2003). *Key themes in qualitative research.* Walnut Creek, CA: Alta Mira.

Atkinson, P. A., & Delamont, S. (2004). Qualitative research and the postmodern turn. In M. Hardy & A. Bryman (Eds.), *Handbook of data analysis.* London: Sage.

Charmaz, K., & Mitchell, R. (2001). Grounded theory in ethnography. In P. Atkinson, A. Coffey, S. Delamont, J. Lofland, & L. Lofland (Eds.), *Handbook of ethnography.* London: Sage.

Clarke, A. (2005). *Situational analysis: Grounded theory after the postmodern turn.* Thousand Oaks, CA: Sage.

Coffey, A., & Atkinson, P. (1996). *Making sense of qualitative data.* Thousand Oaks, CA: Sage.

Cortazzi, M. (1993). *Narrative analysis.* London: Falmer.

Cortazzi, M. (2001). Narrative analysis in ethnography. In P. Atkinson, A. Coffey, S. Delamont, J. Lofland, & L. Lofland (Eds.), *Handbook of ethnography.* London: Sage.

Dicks, B., Mason, M., Coffey A., & Atkinson, P. (2005). *Hypermedia ethnography.* London: Sage.

Mixed methods research [Special issue]. (2006). *Qualitative Research, 6*(1).

Narrative—state of the art [Special issue]. (2006). *Narrative Inquiry, 16*(1).

Riessman, C. K. (2002). Analysis of personal narratives. In J. F. Gubrium & J. A. Holstein (Eds.), *Handbook of interview research.* Thousand Oaks, CA: Sage.

## ▣ CHAPTER 10

Paras, E. (2006). *Foucault 2.0: Beyond power and knowledge.* New York: Other Press.

## ▣ CHAPTER 15

Ellis, C. (2004). *The ethnographic I: A methodological novel about autoethnography.* Lanham, MD: Alta Mira Press.

Lather, P. (2007). *Getting lost: Feminist efforts toward a double(d) science.* Albany, NY: SUNY Press.

Richardson, L. (1997). *Fields of play: Constructing an academic life.* New Brunswick, NJ: Rutgers University Press.

Richardson, L. (in press). *Last writes: A daybook for a dying friend.* Walnut Creek, CA: Left Coast Press.

Richardson, L., & Lockridge, E. (2004). *Travels with Ernest: Crossing literary/sociological divide.* Walnut Creek, CA: Alta Mira Press.

Sparkes, A. (2002). *Telling tales in sport and physical activity: A qualitative journey.* Champaign, IL: Human Kinetics Press.

▣ CHAPTER 16

Brady, I. (2007). Poetics, social science. In G. Ritzer (Ed.), *Encyclopedia of sociology* (pp. 3424–3426). New York: Blackwell.

Hartnett, S. J. (2007). Investigative poetry. In G. Ritzer (Ed.), *Encyclopedia of sociology* (pp. 2420–2424). New York: Blackwell.

Hartnett, S. J., & Engels, J. D. (2005). "Aria in time of war": Investigative poetry and the politics of witnessing. In N. K. Denzin & Y. S. Lincoln (Eds.), *Handbook of qualitative research* (3rd ed., pp. 1043–1067). Thousand Oaks, CA: Sage.

Hymes, D. (2003). *Now I know only so far: Essays in ethnopoetics.* Lincoln: University of Nebraska Press.

Hymes, D. (2004). *"In vain I tried to tell you": Essays on Native American ethnopoetics.* Lincoln: University of Nebraska Press.

Sammons, K., & Sherzer, J. (Eds.). (2000). *Translating Native Latin American verbal art.* Washington, DC: Smithsonian Institution Press.

Snyder, G. (1968). *The back country.* New York: New Directions.

Snyder, G. (1996). *Mountains and rivers without end.* New York: Counterpoint.

Solnit, R. A. (1994). *Savage dreams: A journey into the landscape wars of the American west.* Berkeley: University of California Press.

Solnit, R. A. (2005). *A field guide to getting lost.* New York: Viking.

# AUTHOR INDEX

# SUBJECT INDEX

# ABOUT THE EDITORS

**Norman K. Denzin** is Distinguished Professor of Communications, College of Communications Scholar, and Research Professor of Communications, Sociology, and Humanities at the University of Illinois at Urbana-Champaign. He is the author of numerous books, including *Interpretive Ethnography: Ethnographic Practices for the 21st Century; The Cinematic Society: The Voyeur's Gaze; Images of Postmodern Society; The Research Act: A Theoretical Introduction to Sociological Methods; Interpretive Interactionism; Hollywood Shot by Shot; The Recovering Alcoholic;* and *The Alcoholic Self,* which won the Charles Cooley Award from the Society for the Study of Symbolic Interaction in 1988. In 1997, the Society for the Study of Symbolic Interaction presented him the George Herbert Award. He is the editor of *Sociological Quarterly,* coeditor of *Qualitative Inquiry,* and editor of the book series *Cultural Studies: A Research Annual and Studies in Symbolic Interaction.*

**Yvonna S. Lincoln** is Ruth Harrington Chair of Educational Leadership and Distinguished Professor of Higher Education at Texas A&M University. In addition to this volume, she is coeditor of the first and second editions of the *Handbook of Qualitative Research,* the journal *Qualitative Inquiry* (with Norman K. Denzin), and the Teaching and Learning section of the *American Educational Research Journal* (with Bruce Thompson and Stephanie Knight). She is the coauthor, with Egon Guba, of *Naturalistic Inquiry, Effective Evaluation, and Fourth Generation Evaluation,* the editor of *Organizational Theory and Inquiry,* and the coeditor of several other books with William G. Tierney and with Norman Denzin. She is the recipient of numerous awards for research and has published journal articles, chapters, and conference papers on higher education, research university libraries, and alternative paradigm inquiry.

# ABOUT THE CONTRIBUTORS

**Michael V. Angrosino** is Professor of Anthropology at the University of South Florida, where his research and teaching specializations include mental health policy analysis, the influence of organized religion on contemporary social policy, and the methodology of oral history. He has served as editor of *Human Organization*, the journal of the Society for Applied Anthropology, and as general editor of the Southern Anthropological Society's Proceedings Series for the University of Georgia Press. Among his most recent books are *Opportunity House: Ethnographic Stories of Mental Retardation* (1998), an experiment in alternative ethnographic writing, and *The Culture of the Sacred*, an overview of the anthropology of religion.

**Paul Atkinson** is Distinguished Research Professor in Sociology at Cardiff University, United Kingdom. He is Associate Director of the ESRC Research Centre on Social and Economic Aspects of Genomics. His main research interests are the sociology of medical knowledge and the development of qualitative research methods. His publications include *Ethnography: Principles in Practice* (with Martyn Hammersley, 1983 and 1995), *The Clinical Experience* (1981 and 1997), *The Ethnographic Imagination* (1990), *Understanding Ethnographic Texts* (1992), *Medical Talk and Medical Work* (1995), *Fighting Familiarity* (with Sara Delamont, 1995), *M*

*aking Sense of Qualitative Data* (with Amanda Coffey, 1996), *Sociological Readings and Re-Readings* (1996), and *Interactionism* (with William Housley, 2003). Together with Sara Delamont, he edits the journal *Qualitative Research*. He was coeditor of *The Handbook of Ethnography* (2002). His ethnographic study of an international opera company is published as *Everyday Arias: Making Opera Work* (2005). He is an Academician of the Academy for the Learned Societies in the Social Sciences.

**Ivan Brady** is Distinguished Teaching Professor and Chair of Anthropology at the State University of New York at Oswego. A former President of the Society for Humanistic Anthropology and Chair of the Association for Social Anthropology in Oceania, he also served as Book Review Editor of the *American Anthropologist* for seven years. He is the editor or coeditor of several books and dozens of chapters, articles, and reviews. His poetry has appeared in various books and journals, including *Reflections: The Anthropological Muse* (1985); *The American Tradition in Qualitative Research* (2001); *The Qualitative Inquiry Reader* (2002); the *Neuroanthropology Network Newsletter; Anthropology and Humanism; drunken boat: online journal of the arts; Pendulum; Cultural Studies ↔ Critical Methodologies;* and *Qualitative Inquiry.* His latest book is *The Time at Darwin's Reef: Poetic Explorations in Anthropology and History.*

**Susan E. Chase** is Chair and Associate Professor of Sociology and a cofounder of the Women's Studies Program at the University of Tulsa. She is the author of *Ambiguous Empowerment: The Work Narratives of Women School Superintendents,* which analyzes how women educational leaders narrate their competence and accomplishments on one hand and their experiences of gender and racial discrimination on the other. She also coauthored *Mothers and Children: Feminist Analyses and Personal Narratives* (with Mary Rogers), a synthesis of feminist social science theory and research on mothers, mothering, and motherhood over the last 30 years.

**Sara Delamont** is Reader in Sociology at Cardiff University, United Kingdom, and an Academician of the Academy for the Learned Societies in the Social Sciences. She was the first woman to be President of the British Education Research Association, and the first woman to be Dean of Social Sciences at Cardiff. Her research interests are educational ethnography, the anthropology of the Mediterranean and Brazil, and gender. Of her twelve published books, the best known is *Interaction in the Classroom* (1976 and 1983), and her favorites are *Knowledgeable Women* (1989) and *Appetities and Identities* (1995). Her most recent books are *Fieldwork in Educational Settings* (2002), *Feminist Sociology* (2003), and *Key Themes in Qualitative Research* (2003), written with Paul Atkinson and Amanda Coffey. She is coeditor of the journal *Qualitative Research* with Paul Atkinson. She is currently doing an ethnography of *capoeira* teaching in the United Kingdom.

**Greg Dimitriadis** is Associate Professor in the Department of Educational Leadership and Policy at the University at Buffalo, the State University of New York. He is the author of *Performing Identity/Performing Culture: Hip Hop as Text, Pedagogy, and Lived Practice; Friendship, Cliques, and Gangs: Young Black Men Coming of Age in Urban America.* He is first co-author, with Cameron McCarthy, of *Reading and Teaching the Postcolonial: From Baldwin to Basquiat and Beyond* and second co-author, with George Kamberelis, of *On Qualitative Inquiry.* Dimitriadis is first coeditor, with Dennis Carlson, of *Promises to Keep: Cultural Studies, Democratic Education, and Public Life,* and second coeditor, with Nadine Dolby and Paul Willis, of *Learning to Labor in New Times.*

He has also authored *Urban Youth Culture.* His next edited collection is the second edition of *Race, Identity, and Representation in Education,* coedited with Cameron McCarthy, Warren Crichlow, and Nadine Dolby.

**Jeremy D. Engels** is a Ph.D. candidate in the Department of Speech Communication at the University of Illinois, Urbana-Champaign. His research focuses primarily on the construction of national identity in the early American republic, and his political writings have been featured in Urbana-Champaign's independent newspaper, *The Public-I,* and also in the University of Illinois's student newspaper, *The Daily Illini.*

**Susan Finley** is Associate Professor of Educational Foundations, Literacy, and Research Methodology at Washington State University, Vancouver. She bases her pedagogy and inquiry in arts-based approaches to understanding social and cultural issues in educational contexts. She is an activist who has implemented educational efforts with street youths and economically poor children, youths, and adults, housed and unhoused.

**Andrea Fontana** (Ph.D., University of California, San Diego) is Professor of Sociology at the University of Nevada, Las Vegas. He has published articles on aging, leisure, theory, and postmodernism. He is the author of the *Last Frontier: the Social Meaning of Growing Old,* coauthor of *Social Problems and Sociologies of Everyday Life,* and coeditor of *The Existential Self in Society* and *Postmodernism and Social Inquiry.* He is former president of the Society for the Study of Symbolic Interaction and former editor of the journal *Symbolic Interaction.* Among Fontana's most recent published essays are a deconstruction of the work of the painter Hieronymus Bosch; a performance/play about Farinelli, the castrato; an ethnographic narrative about land speed records at the Bonneville Salt Flats; and a performance based on the television series *Six Feet Under.*

**James H. Frey** is retired Dean of the College of Liberal Arts and Emeritus Professor of Sociology at the University of Nevada, Las Vegas (UNLV). He is the founder and past Director of the Center for Survey Research at UNLV. He is the author of *Survey Research by Telephone* and *How to Conduct Interviews by Telephone and in Person* (with S. Oishi). He has published papers on survey research, group interviewing, sport sociology, deviance, and work in the leisure industry.

**Douglas Harper** is Professor and Chair of the Department of Sociology at Duquesne University in Pittsburgh. He has written three ethnographies that rely heavily on photography, the most recent being *Changing Works: Visions of a Lost Agriculture* (2001). He is founding editor of *Visual Sociology,* now published as *Visual Studies.* His current research is on the social life of Italian food (coauthored by Patrizia Faccioli) and on expatriate communities in Hong Kong (coauthored by Caroline Knowles). He continues to refine and develop his use of still photography in sociological studies.

**Stephen J. Hartnett** is Associate Professor of Speech Communication at the University of Illinois. He is author of *Democratic Dissent & The Cultural Fictions of Antebellum*

*America*, which won the National Communication Association's 2002 Winans and Wichelns Memorial Award for Distinguished Scholarship in Rhetoric and Public Address. He is coauthor, with the late Robert James Branham, of *Sweet Freedom's Song: "My Country 'Tis of Thee"* and *Democracy in America.* Based on 12 years of teaching in, writing about, and protesting at prisons across America, in 2003, he published *Incarceration Nation: Investigative Prison Poems of Hope and Terror.* His current projects include *Executing Democracy: Arguing About the Death Penalty in America, 1683–1850* and *The Rhetorics of Globalization and Empire in an Age of Terror.*

**Phil Hodkinson** is Professor of Lifelong Learning in the Lifelong Learning Institute of the University of Leeds, England. He has an ongoing interest in research methodology from a broadly hermeneutical and interpretative perspective. He is currently researching learning in workplaces and college settings and learning lives and biographies.

**Stacy Holman Jones** is Assistant Professor in the Department of Communication at the University of South Florida. Her work focuses on socially resistive performance practices. She is the author of *Kaleidoscope Notes: Writing Women's Music and Organizational Culture* (1998) and the forthcoming *Music for Torching.*

**Ernest R. House** (Ed.D., University of Illinois) is Professor Emeritus of Education at the University of Colorado at Boulder and one of the world's leading evaluation experts. From 1969 to 1985, he was a professor of education at the University of Illinois in Urbana. He has been a visiting scholar at UCLA, Harvard, and New Mexico, as well as in England, Australia, Spain, Sweden, Austria, and Chile. His primary interests are evaluation and educational policy analysis. Books include *The Politics of Educational Innovation* (1974), *Survival in the Classroom* (with S. Lapan, 1978), *Evaluating with Validity* (1980), *Jesse Jackson and the Politics of Charisma* (1988), *Professional Evaluation: Social Impact and Political Consequences* (1993), *Schools for Sale* (1998), and *Values in Evaluation and Social Research* (with K. Howe, 1999). His evaluation novel, *Where the Truth Lies,* was published in 1992. He is the 1989 recipient (with W. Madura) of the Harold E. Lasswell Prize in the policy sciences and the 1990 recipient of the Paul F. Lazarsfeld Award for Evaluation Theory, presented by the American Evaluation Association. He has been editor (with R. Wooldridge) of *New Directions in Program Evaluation* (1982–1985), a featured columnist for *Evaluation Practice* (1984–1989), and a Fellow at the Center for Advanced Study in the Behavioral Sciences, Stanford (1999–2000). He currently serves as federal court monitor in the bilingual education legal settlement in Denver.

**George Kamberelis** is Associate Professor in the School of Education at the University at Albany–SUNY. He teaches and conducts research on the history and philosophy of science and social science, qualitative inquiry, social theory, and literacy studies. Professor Kamberelis has published in the areas of qualitative inquiry (especially researcher–research participant relationships), discourse and identity, and genre studies. Some of his recent publications include "Ingestion, Elimination, Sex, and

Song: Trickster as Premodern Avatar of Postmodern Research Practice" in *Qualitative Inquiry* and "The Rhizome and the Pack: Liminal Literacy Formations with Political Teeth" in *Space Matters: Assertions of Space in Literacy Practice and Research* (Kevin Leander and Margi Sheehy, editors). With Greg Dimitriadis, Kamberelis has just completed a book titled *On Qualitative Inquiry.*

**Annette N. Markham** is Associate Professor of Communication and Founding Coordinator of the Center for Technology and Learning at the University of the Virgin Islands. Her research focuses on sensemaking practices in technologically mediated environments, ethical practices in qualitative Internet research, interpretive methodology, and organizational communication. Her book *Life Online: Researching Real Experience in Virtual Space* (1998) has been regarded as one of the first in-depth sociological studies of the Net. She has published several chapters and articles related to interpretive qualitative methods in Internet Studies. Her forthcoming edited collection *Qualitative Internet Research: Dialogue Among Scholars* (Sage) focuses on practical and philosophical challenges of conducting research in computer-mediated environments. Since moving to the Caribbean and realizing electricity is not ubiquitous, her research focus is shifting from the ethnographic inquiry of life online to the study of privilege and identity politics offline. Markham received her Ph.D. from Purdue University.

**Kathryn Bell McKenzie** is Assistant Professor in the Department of Educational Administration and Human Resources at Texas A&M University in College Station. Dr. McKenzie received her Ph.D. in Educational Administration from the University of Texas in Austin. Her research foci include equity and social justice in schools, school leadership, qualitative methodology, and critical white studies. During her more than 20 years in public education, She was a classroom teacher, curriculum specialist, assistant principal, principal, and Deputy Director of the University of Texas at Austin Independent School District Leadership Academy. Her most recent publications include a chapter titled, "The Unintended Consequences of the Texas Accountability System" in *Equity and Accountability* (Linda Skrla and James Joseph Scheurich, editors); with James Joseph Scheurich, the article "Equity Traps: A Useful Construct for Preparing Principals to Lead Schools That Are Successful With Racially Diverse Students" in *Educational Administration Quarterly*; an article in *Educational Theory* coauthored with James Joseph Scheurich titled "Corporatizing and Privatizing of Schooling: Critique, Research, and a Call for a Grounded Critical Praxis." She is regional editor for North America for the *International Journal of Qualitative Studies in Education.*

**Anssi Peräkylä** is Professor of Sociology at the University of Helsinki. His research interests include medical communication, psychotherapy, emotional communication, and conversation analysis. He has publishded *AIDS Counselling* (1995) and articles on interaction in institutional settings in journals such as *Sociology, Social Psychology Quarterly, British Journal of Social Psychology*, and *Research on Language and Social Interaction.*

**Laurel Richardson** is Professor Emeritus of Sociology and Visiting Professor of Cultural Studies in Education at the Ohio State University. She is the author of more than one hundred articles. She has pioneered work on gender, poststructuralist theory, and alternative representations in qualitative research. Her book, *Fields of Play: Constructing an Academic Life* (1997) was honored with the Society for the Study of Symbolic Interaction's Cooley Award. Her most recent book, *Travels With Ernest: Crossing the Literary/Sociological Divide* (2004) is an experimental writing project coauthored with her husband, the novelist Ernest Lockridge.

**James Joseph Scheurich** received his Ph.D. from Ohio State University, spent 12 years as an assistant and associate professor at the University of Texas at Austin, and is now Professor and Head of the Department of Educational Administration and Human Resource Development at Texas A&M University. He has published five books, including *Anti-Racist Scholarship: An Advocacy, Research Methods in the Postmodern,* and *Leadership for Equity and Excellence* (the latter with Linda Skria as coauthor), as well as numerous peer-reviewed articles, monographs, chapters, book reviews, and newspaper editorials. He is the coauthor, with Miguel Guajardo, Patricia Sanchez, and Elissa Fineman, of a video documentary called The Labors of Life/Labores de la Vida. He currently serves on the American Educational Research Association's (AERA) Publications Committee. He is currently coeditor, with Carolyn Clark, of the *International Journal of Qualitative Studies in Education* and serves on the editorial board for several other journals. He has successfully chaired nearly 25 dissertations and has had 18 of his students become university professors. Finally, he has authored or coauthored over $3 million in grants and contracts.

**John K. Smith** is Professor of Education at the University of Northern Iowa. For the past 20 years, his interests have centered on the philosophy of social and educational inquiry, with a special emphasis on the issue of criteria. His work has appeared in such journals as the *Educational Researcher, Journal of Educational Administration,* and *Educational Analysis and Policy Analysis.* He also has authored two books: *The Nature of Social and Educational Inquiry* and *After the Demise of Empiricism.*

**Elizabeth Adams St. Pierre** is Associate Professor of Language Education and Affiliated Professor of both the Qualitative Research Program and the Women's Studies Institute at the University of Georgia. Her research interests focus on the work of language in the construction of subjectivity, on a critique of conventional qualitative inquiry, and on language and literacy studies. Recent published works include articles in *Qualitative Inquiry* and *Educational Researcher,* as well as chapters in *Dangerous Coagulations* (B. Baker and K. Heyning, editors, 2004) and *Feminist Engagements* (K. Weiler, editor, 2001). She is coeditor with W. S. Pillow of *Working the Ruins: Feminist Poststructural Theory and Methods in Education* (2000).

**Kathleen Stewart** teaches anthropology and is Director of the Center for Cultural Studies at the University of Texas, Austin. She has done ethnographic fieldwork in West Virginia, Las Vegas, Orange County, California, New England, and Texas. Her first book, *A Space on the Side of the Road: Cultural Poetics in an "Other" America* (1996), was recognized by both the Victor Turner Prize and the Chicago Folklore Prize. Her second book is forthcoming and titled *Ordinary Impacts: the Affective Life of U.S. Public Culture.* She has also written about nostalgia, conspiracy theory, apocalyptic thinking, daydreams, country music, trauma, and the pitfalls of the American dream. Her work has been performed in plays and has been supported by the Rockefeller Foundation, the National Endowment for the Humanities, the School of American Research, and the Institute for the Humanities, University of California, Irvine as well as by the University of Texas.